ld 'Binki

C000277273

Going, going gone—'Binkie'

ES 23 MAY 74

Londo home

Beaumont's 'art'

THEATRICAL memorabilia goes under the hammer next month when the large art collection of the late "Binkie" Beaumont, leading London theatre manager for 20 years, is sold at Sotheby's.

and five drawings by Stanley Spencer, the property of his late wife

Stars honour 'Bink

the "H. M. nia familiar, from the programmes, to thousands of theatregoers in Britain.

two payin

HUGH BEAUMONT

Although an outstanding figure in the theatric firmament, Mr. Beaumont is little known to pl

BY KENNETH TYNAN

BINKIE BEAUMONT

Eminence Grise
of the West End Theatre
1933-1973

BINKIE BEAUMONT

Eminence Grise
of the West End Theatre
1933-1973

Richard Huggett

Hodder & Stoughton
LONDON SYDNEY AUCKLAND TORONTO

To Ion Trewin

The Bernard Shaw letters, © 1989, are reproduced
by kind permission of the Trustees of the British Museum,
the Governors and Guardians of the National Gallery of
Ireland and the Royal Academy of Dramatic Art.

British Library Cataloguing in Publication Data

Huggett, Richard, *1929–*
    Binkie Beaumont: éminence grise of the
    West End theatre 1933–1973.
    1. Great Britain, Theatre.
    Beaumont, Hugh, 1908–1973
    I. Title
    792'.092'4

    ISBN 0-340-41269-0

First published in Great Britain 1989

Published by Hodder and Stoughton,
a division of Hodder and Stoughton Ltd,
Mill Road, Dunton Green, Sevenoaks, Kent TN13 2YE
Editorial Office: 47 Bedford Square, London WC1B 3DP

Photoset by Rowland Phototypesetting Ltd,
Bury St Edmunds, Suffolk

Printed in Great Britain by St Edmundsbury Press Ltd,
Bury St Edmunds, Suffolk

CONTENTS

Contents

ILLUSTRATIONS

Suite in Three Keys[4]
John Perry and Arthur Cantor[11]
With Mary Martin and David Merrick[1]
Passport photographs[4]

Acknowledgments

1   BBC Hulton Picture Library
2   *Illustrated London News*
3   Cecil Beaton Photograph, Sotheby's
4   Author's collection
5   The Theatre Museum, Victoria and Albert Museum
6   The Imperial War Museum
7   Mrs Otto Karminski
8   Vivienne Byerley
9   Desmond O'Neill
10 Angus McBean
11 *New York Times*
12 Solo Syndication
13 Marius Goring
14 John Turner

ILLUSTRATIONS IN TEXT

INTRODUCTION

Binkie Beaumont left to posterity something which was not mentioned in his will. It was a time bomb with a long fuse calculated to explode in his future biographer's face, which it did just four years after his death. The bomb was his firm instruction to all his close friends that he did not want a biography written and that on no account were they to give any help to anybody sufficiently foolhardy or importunate to attempt it. It is a familiar situation with famous men whose lives have been fraught with controversy and who have contrived to make a number of enemies, though Binkie might have learned from the example of Somerset Maugham the futility of such an embargo. There is, happily, no law against writing a biography. In his lifetime a number of publishers had also approached Binkie, trying to persuade him to write his memoirs, but he had refused them all. He was not a writer.

It was in the summer of 1977 that the idea started to take root. Binkie was a man of mystery and what better contribution could I make to theatrical history than to solve it? Naturally, I began with John Perry, his lifelong friend, fellow-director and heir. He began by being very helpful, and gave me a piece of information so essential that without it I could not have started: he told me Binkie's real name – which was not Beaumont. Thus I was able to look up his birth certificate and discover the facts of his childhood and adolescence which would otherwise have been a closed book. Perry also read and approved of a five thousand word synopsis which I wrote, but after that his initial show of friendly co-operation came to an abrupt end. "It's all too painful," he wrote apologetically, "and at my age my memory is going. I really can't remember a thing. I'm afraid that I can't help you any further." This non-help went to the extent of denying me permission to quote Binkie's letters whose copyright he had inherited. There are many hundreds, possibly thousands, scattered all over the world in museums, libraries and private collections, and some of them are of great interest. A lot of time and trouble were spent gathering them up but in the end it was all wasted. This explains their conspicuous absence from the book.

I have been lucky in that very few of his friends have refused to speak to me and those who did refuse did so for a number of reasons.

Sometimes it was sheer boredom at the thought of reliving the past, sometimes loss of memory: "I'm sorry, I really can't remember a *thing* about those years . . .", and sometimes for reasons of morality. "He was a close friend and it would be disloyal of me to betray that friendship." It became speedily evident that the sort of book which they thought I was writing and which Binkie was anxious to suppress was something written in short, sharp sentences and short, sharp paragraphs ('writing with a *punch*', as the sporting papers put it), concentrating on the sexual irregularities and consisting largely of press-cuttings, extracts from taped interviews, and illustrated with a few flashlight photographs, the whole ghastly conflation to be titled *The Secret Sex Life of Binkie Beaumont*.

When it became evident from a carefully selected chapter that this was not the sort of book I was writing, some of the Doubting Thomases (Keith Baxter, for example) changed their minds and spoke to me at length and great effect. Some of them, of course, continued to remain adamant; but my experience has been that if one person refuses to talk, you can usually get what they would have said from somebody else. It's all a matter of hard work and trouble.

John Gielgud was one whose initial doubts were soon quietened. One Sunday evening at the Garrick Club I told him of my plan and asked if he'd like to talk to me. "Oh, no," he said, shaking his Roman emperor's head, "I think it's a *terrible* idea. There are far too many modern biographies as it is and I don't approve of that sort of thing," he added, sounding rather like Lady Bracknell. "Also, my memory is going. I can't help you at all. I remember one evening when I wasn't working just after the war, he said, 'Let's go and see all our plays,' and off we went . . ." Thirty minutes later, after a torrent of witty and sparkling anecdote, he turned to me triumphantly. "You see, I can't remember anything." But he did consent to answer all my questions by letter and for months the sight of that tiny, neat, meticulous handwriting brought joy to my heart and richness to the book.

But what is a book without a publisher? I have to offer grateful and heartfelt thanks to Ion Trewin who, after some years of careful thought, finally overcame his initial doubts about its commercial future ("Ion is very, *very* tough," his mother, Wendy Trewin, smilingly warned me, and how right she was), and commissioned me to finish it with a generous advance. It is an immeasurable asset for an author to have an editor who brings not only enthusiasm for the subject but specialist knowledge, though in the light of his parentage you would expect this. It is also an asset to have an editor who, like the author, has very definite ideas on how good English should be written. The fact that these ideas were noticeably different resulted in

many weeks of delightful argument while we sorted out split infini-
tives (his *bête-noire*) and hanging prepositions (mine), whether 'recall'
or 'remember' was right for a particular context and whether 'the
Rebecca film' or 'the film of *Rebecca*' was stylistically purer.

I have to thank the Garrick Club Library, the libraries of the Savage,
Green Room and Savile Clubs, the New York Players, the London
Library, the Westminster Central, the Lincoln Drama Collection in
New York, the British Library, the *Sunday Times* photographic
collections, the Hulton picture library, the Cardiff reference library,
the British Museum library in Colindale, and the Mander and Mitch-
enson collection, and, above all, Sheila Fermoy in the offices of H. M.
Tennent Ltd for her invaluable help in supplying photographs and
giving me access to press-cuttings and documents.

PROLOGUE

The day, Thursday, March 22nd 1973, began as it had done for thirty years, with Anna Tuberti, his Italian maid, bringing him his coffee at six in the morning. Elvira, another and older Italian woman, was Binkie's residential, all-purpose housekeeper and he boasted that she made the finest coffee in all Westminster. Freshly brewed, it was the best way to clear the brain and start the day. He liked the early morning – it was free from interruption, from people, and from the telephone, and he could look at the playscripts which gathered on his bedside table having been brought over from the slush pile in the office. He could concentrate his mind as at no other time. He read quickly. After forty years of handling plays, he could finish a script in forty-five minutes. Sometimes less.

That morning there was one by Terence Rattigan called *In Praise of Love*. Binkie read it with enormous interest. Like all dear Terry's plays, it was beautifully constructed, written with great sensitivity and skilful stagecraft. Binkie remembered a conversation he had once had with Terry years ago when he had suggested that he write a play about death. He had written about virtually everything else but not that. Here, many years later, was the result.

In Praise of Love was clearly inspired by the real-life tragedy of Rex Harrison and his wife, Kay Kendall, close friends of Binkie for years. Kay had contracted leukaemia which was painless but incurable and the doctors had given her two years to live. Rex had been anxious that she should not learn the truth. It had been an unusually painful period of his life for he had loved her dearly, but he had succeeded. Her weakness and occasional fainting fits could be plausibly put down to low blood pressure: the secret was kept from everybody – family, friends and the press – with Binkie, Noël Coward and Terry alone knowing the truth. Kay had finally died without ever learning of her condition. It was a death which could be described as romantic since it took place on the balcony overlooking the bay at Rex's little house in Portofino in the evening sun and in his arms.

Binkie started to cast it. Rex was an obvious choice if he was willing. It was seventeen years since Kay had died. Was the memory still too painful or would he be able, after this time, to relive the exquisite pain of those tortured years? And the dying wife . . . ? Rex was now married to Rachel Roberts who had appeared in Binkie's *Globe Revue* of 1952, a tough, down-to-earth, no-nonsense, vigorous Welsh woman. She was a good actress but there was nothing remotely vulnerable about her. Celia Johnson, darling Celia, the epitome of English upper-class womanhood, who had spent a lifetime playing brave, persecuted, suffering heroines, she would be perfect. Except for the little matter of accent. Binkie referred to the text. The wife wasn't English, but Finnish and she had a good, horrifying scene in which she describes how she managed to escape a brutal death at the hands of the Nazis. Oh well, perhaps Celia could manage a Finnish accent, whatever that was. She'd managed a passably good Scottish accent in the film *The Prime of Miss Jean Brodie.* Would the audiences accept it? Within her limitations she had achieved an exquisite perfection, unknown since Marie Tempest, but her occasional excursions outside the Home Counties had not been happy. Her Saint Joan had gone no nearer the battlefields of France than a Bond Street beauty parlour, and her Cockney-Jewish East-End Mum in the film *A Kid for Two Farthings* had been, frankly, rather embarrassing though he had leant over backwards to avoid saying so when he met her. But was it necessary? Perhaps Terry would do some re-writing and make her English. Terry was always so obliging, never refusing any of Binkie's suggestions.

He re-read the play. Now he realised that it had one disadvantage: it was short and would play for only seventy minutes. With it was another one-act play, an amusing trifle called *Before the Dawn* about Tosca and Baron Scarpia, showing what would have happened if he had got his wicked way with her. Binkie disliked one-act plays, regarding them as hopelessly uncommercial whatever their merits, just as publishers view volumes of short stories. He continued to believe that the public didn't want to see one-act plays in a double-bill in a West End theatre even when events had proved him to be terribly wrong. *Playbill* and *Separate Tables* had both been enormously successful, as had Coward's marathon collection of twenty short plays which made up *Tonight at Eight Thirty* before the war. Maybe he was wrong about one-act plays. If Terry insisted on writing them, maybe he should take a risk. It was a difficult decision.

There was only one thing to do and that was to telephone Rattigan and discuss these pressing matters. Unlike many others, Rattigan was prepared to tolerate Binkie's habit of jerking him into an unwelcome and premature wakefulness with an early-morning call. There wasn't much to discuss on the subject of changes and re-writing, because on this occasion Rattigan refused to make any. He didn't wish to lengthen a seventy-minute play to a two-hour play with interval, for that would involve diluting the flavour and reducing its effectiveness. No, he didn't wish to make the wife English: the play depended on her having been a survivor of the German occupation. He agreed that Celia Johnson was not the right actress for the part and suggested Joan Greenwood who ultimately played it. "What about the husband?" asked Rattigan. Binkie suggested John Gielgud. This was not well received: Gielgud had once insulted and offended Rattigan most grievously: it was a quarter of a century ago but the memory still rankled. "Have you got any plans for him?" asked Rattigan. Yes, Binkie had, he was going to direct Maugham's *The Constant Wife*. As for acting, well, asked Binkie, "Do you think he could play Bernard Shaw *and* Beerbohm Tree? I mean in the same play. I've just had a comedy sent to me by a young actor I know slightly. Would you believe it, he's said no to having Johnny in the play. And Peggy. Can you *believe* it? But I think I can persuade him."

Called *The First Night of Pygmalion* and described on the title page as '*A Comedy of Bad Manners*', it gave a colourful account of the tempestuous love affair between Bernard Shaw and Mrs Patrick Campbell, and the story of rehearsals between these two and Sir Herbert Beerbohm Tree, the first Higgins, when these three were at permanent loggerheads. It was well constructed and devastatingly witty, Binkie thought. The author was an actor who had played a number of small parts in *The Visit*. His name was Richard Huggett, now aged forty-two. Apparently, he had presented it at the Edinburgh Festival acting all the male parts himself, followed by a tour of American university theatres. Now, it seemed, he wished to play it in the West End. Binkie had sent a message to him via his agent only last week that he would be delighted to accept it if he would be willing to allow John Gielgud and Peggy Ashcroft to play in it.

Greatly to his surprise, he received a letter from the author, politely but firmly turning down the suggestion.

25B Lisle Street
London W. 1.

March 20th 1973
Dear Mr. Beaumont,
The actor in my play shares no less than forty parts with the actress. She plays Mrs Pat and twelve others, he plays Shaw, Tree and about twenty-five others. This involves many changes of voice ranging from Shaw's Dublin brogue to Tree's Dutch-Jewish accent taking in on the way a varied assortment of American, Italian, Yorkshire, Welsh, Belfast and Cockney accents. I have the greatest respect for Sir John Gielgud's acting talents but, by his own admission,

mimicry is not one of them. "*I'm hopeless at accents and funny voices*", to quote his own words. He would not be happy to go through a long evening which would make such demands on his powers. Neither would you, nor your colleagues at H. M. Tennent and neither would I. In fact, the agony for me would be particularly punishing. I'm sure you understand this.

I did not write this play to add to Sir John's fame and fortune. He is already an international superstar and enjoys all the success and acclaim he could possibly want. None of this could be said of me. This play will be, I sincerely hope, my passport to the West End and I'm quite prepared to wait until I find a management willing to give a decent chance to a relatively unknown actor.★

May I please without disrespect point out one of the eternal truths of our Profession? A big star, miscast and acting badly, will do far more harm to a play than an unknown actor suitably cast and acting well.

> With all good wishes,
> Richard Huggett

Binkie had been rather amused by this delicately phrased impertinence and had privately admitted its good sense. It wasn't every day that an unknown author/actor turned down an offer from him and he couldn't help feeling a measure of respect and interest. A meeting was clearly called for and an appointment had been made for the following week.

By now Anna had run his bath. He climbed wearily out of bed and into it, putting an immediate telephone call through to the Mayfair flat occupied by his agent, Laurence Evans, and his wife, Mary. Evans, the most eminent agent in the West End, handling many of the big stars – Gielgud, Olivier, Richardson, Harrison – had been a friend and professional colleague for many years. Mary Evans was one of Binkie's closest friends. She was tall, slim and elegant. Every morning Binkie, lying in *his* bath, would speak to her in *her* bath and the two of them would spend a happy hour – and sometimes longer – gossiping and giggling about everything and everybody: there would be character assassinations of their friends and enemies (always a delightful occupation), plans for future parties and holidays, jokes to be told and re-told, new plays to be discussed and cast. Sometimes Laurence

---

★ *The First Night of Pygmalion* did get a West End showing in a tiny fringe theatre, the Act Inn in Brewer Street, coincidentally just behind the Globe Theatre, and went on to tour America, South Africa, Australia and Europe with the author and a variety of female partners of whom Maxine Audley was unquestionably the finest. The script was published, rewritten as a book, broadcast and televised by the BBC.

Evans in his separate bath would join in on his telephone extension and thus convert a duet into a trio, *allegro con brio scherzando*. It was the perfect way to start the day.

Today would be busy. *No, No, Nanette* was in rehearsal for an April opening at Drury Lane, but casting was a problem. Where were all the soubrettes, where had they gone? In his early days in the twenties and thirties, there was no shortage of attractive young girls who could sing, dance and act a bit, and look as pretty as a Corot or a Lely. Happily he had Tony Britton and Anna Neagle, two pillars of strength. But where was his Nanette?

Now the pains returned, those hideous back pains which had troubled and overshadowed his last few years. At times he could not get out of the bath or dress without support. Jack Osborn, his chauffeur and general handyman, assisted him downstairs and into the car – it was a ten minute journey to the Globe if the streets were clear of traffic – then out of the car, into the lift and thence to his office. He was in a bad state, shivering and sweating: his hands were shaking and his face had turned yellow. Members of the staff, Vivienne Byerley, Ian Dow, Joe Davis, Bernard Gordon, Lily Taylor and June Collin forgathered there for what was to be his final production conference. Vivienne Byerley recalls that Binkie spoke in short, sharp, staccato bursts, catching an aggressive bullying note which was entirely unlike him, yet he could still pull himself together and, hoping this would take away the sting of his abrupt manner, end a sentence with a smile and his usual endearment, 'dear'.

The meeting lasted for thirty minutes. Jack Osborn helped him out of his chair, down the corridor, into the lift, across the foyer and into the car. Vivienne Byerley came down with him and her final un-forgettable memory of Binkie was of him sitting up in the back of the car, hunched and quivering with pain, the very picture of misery.

He went to a meeting at the Connaught with Roger Stevens, the latest in the long line of American producers on whom the cross-fertilisation between Binkie and Broadway depended. Stevens was a bulky, balding man in his seventies, built like a Suma wrestler, and a comparative newcomer to the theatre which he had entered in 1950. Previously, he had been in real estate, retiring when his company bought the Empire State Building for a reputed fifty-seven million dollars. A few years earlier he had been appointed chairman of the Kennedy Center in Washington. He and Binkie had presented a number of plays in the West End and they had become good friends. On his trips to Washington Binkie had lunched with him at the Center. Now it was Binkie's turn to return the compliment with lunch at the Connaught. Later, over tea in the lounge, they discussed plans for 1973 which included the Royal Shakespeare Company with Peter Brook's legendary production of *A Midsummer Night's Dream* and Donald Sinden's even-more legendary performance of Sir Harcourt Courtly in *London Assurance*. Stevens remembers that Binkie chattered away in the most cheerful manner, his vitality restored and clearly free from pain. Obviously, there had been a brief remission as there usually is with painful diseases towards the end. He drank a great many cups of China tea and smoked innumerable cigarettes. After his departure, Stevens looked sadly at the smoking pyramid of cigarette ends in the ashtray. "Binkie's going to have to cut down on all that," he said to his wife, "or there'll be real trouble."

Binkie returned home, slept for a further hour and then at seven in the evening enjoyed an unexpected visit from John Gielgud and Ingrid Bergman. She was to play in *The Constant Wife* and was here in London to discuss the production with Gielgud, whom she loved and respected. Maugham was the most astute businessman Binkie had ever met and he watched over his theatrical empire with a jealous and possessive vigilance, granting remission for revivals only on special occasions when he thought the casting and the timing were right. Always scrupulously polite and affable, he was nevertheless rather intimidating and one of the few people of whom Binkie stood in awe. He had been present at a party which Noël Coward had given in the early fifties when Maugham had been coldly unreceptive to Coward's idea that he might adapt *Home and Beauty* into a musical. Maugham's wrinkled, tortoise face hunched miserably behind the horn-rimmed spectacles seemed to be a hundred years old instead of merely eighty and it was after that meeting that Coward had taken Binkie aside. "I have decided," he said, "that the only nickname we can give to poor old Willie is 'the Lizard of Oz'."

Binkie had always had a special affection for *The Constant Wife* which he considered to be the wittiest of all Maugham's comedies. He well remembered the first night in 1926 when the audience at the Strand had audibly shuddered over the more savage shafts of cynical wit.

During the first week of her 1971 appearance in *Captain Brassbound's Conversion*, Binkie had given a copy to Ingrid. She read it overnight and then called on Binkie who took her out to lunch at Scotts. "Binkie darling," she drawled in her soft husky Swedish accent, "I think it's a splendid part but the play is a little . . . old-fashioned." Fortunately he had an answer. "What is old-fashioned about this play, Ingrid, is its charm."

"But who is going to direct it? I need somebody I know, somebody I can trust. You know I am not altogether happy in English comedy."

"Don't worry, Ingrid dear," Binkie said cheerfully, "John Gielgud will direct it. He'll be perfect. It's very much his style and period. He knew Maugham. They were good friends. In fact, he directed Maugham's last play, *Sheppey*."

None of this was true. Maugham and Gielgud were not good friends, but Binkie had no hesitation in telling the occasional lie in the interests of business. Maugham had few close friends. He and Gielgud had met only twice before and there had been little rapport between them, Maugham taciturn and shy, Gielgud chattering compulsively. Although *Sheppey* had been highly admired by some it had failed, which had distinctly soured the aged author who announced rather grandly that after thirty years of theatrical triumphs he had clearly lost touch with public taste and would therefore write no more plays. Nor had Gielgud agreed to direct *The Constant Wife* for he had not yet been asked. But Binkie knew that he would never turn down a chance of directing the much-loved, greatly-admired Ingrid Bergman and it only remained for him to read it. Gielgud later related how he walked one day into a second-hand bookshop in New York and as he was browsing a book fell from a top shelf on to the floor. He stooped to pick it up. It was *The Constant Wife*. This was clearly a good omen. Touched by the coincidence, he read it quickly and agreed.

Darling Ingrid. She had done two plays for him, *A Month in the Country* and *Captain Brassbound's Conversion*. Both had been very successful. That the public adored her and flocked to see her irrespective of what play she was in was Binkie's definition of a star. Sadly – and Binkie was honest enough to face it although he never breathed a word outside the sacred enclosure of the Globe Theatre or his house in Lord North Street – Ingrid was not a particularly good actress. It was, quite simply, the language barrier. In films and in private conversation it was fluent enough but on the stage it was very hesitant. In dramatic or romantic parts she could get away with it but in high comedy where absolute accuracy of text was essential, the effect was appalling. She had a irritating habit of turning her head towards the audience and flashing her radiant regal smile whenever she made a mistake as if to plead for their sympathy and forgiveness. Naturally, all this fluffing, drying and stumbling, and all that garden-party radiance had a disastrous effect on the comedy, and in *Captain Brassbound's Conversion* it frequently made nonsense out of Shaw's exquisitely constructed sentences.

But the public didn't care about such petty details. All they wanted was to see her on the stage, the scandalous and adored star of *Casablanca* and *Escape to Happiness*, to listen to that throaty, sex-drenched Swedish accent, to hear the little giggle, and to gaze at the homely, clean-cut face breathing milk and Mother Earth. As a further bonus, Binkie would take care to surround her with the best available talent. The men's parts in *The Constant Wife* were not very interesting but John McCallum had accepted the best of them, the lover.

Ingrid and Gielgud were now in London to discuss the set, costumes and details of the pre-London tour, and here they were in his bedroom with designs and back numbers of the *Tatler* and *Sketch*. Rehearsals were due to start in July for a September opening, perhaps in Manchester? But Binkie had other ideas. "Let's *not* open the tour in Brighton or Manchester," he said cheerfully, "let's do something different. Let's open it on the Continent, Amsterdam, or Rome."

"Darling Binkie, that's a good idea. Or Stockholm, my home town. What could be more suitable?"

"Or Vienna," said Binkie. "There is an English-speaking theatre there which is, I hear, highly successful. Everybody in Vienna speaks perfect English."

"So does everybody in Sweden," said Ingrid. "My public would be so surprised to hear me speaking English on the stage."

"I think Paris will be very amusing," said Gielgud, "except that the French have never really understood English theatre." They discussed various continental cities and finally Amsterdam, Vienna, Stockholm and Paris were pencilled in. But what should she wear? Ingrid had brought with her special sketches by Cecil Beaton of some delicious mid-twenties gowns and frocks. Binkie looked at them without much enthusiasm. Dear Cecil seemed to have lost his touch: the décor for the recent revival of *Lady Windermere's Fan* had been disastrous, and these designs for Ingrid were uninspiring. Perhaps Oliver Messel would be interested or that clever young man who had done such good work at Covent Garden, Carl Toms. Oh, if *only* Rex Whistler were still alive. This last was a prayer he had breathed many times since the war.

Once again the pains returned. Seeing his drawn and lined face and noticing the sharp, tortured breathing, Gielgud and Ingrid tactfully withdrew. Binkie lay in bed for a couple of hours and then, as if by a miracle, the pains vanished. Another period of remission, but for how long? He felt much better. Strong and active. Quite well enough to go to a party and have some fun.

The party was a lively and cheerful affair with many old friends and some new ones. Binkie drank and smoked a lot. All this was strictly against Dr Janvrine's orders, but who cared? Doctors could be terribly wrong about a lot of things. They didn't know everything, did they? There was lots to eat and Binkie did so with renewed appetite. He felt well and happy. He even took a rare turn in entertaining the company by putting on a top hat, sitting on the piano and giving his impersonation of Marlene Dietrich singing 'Falling in Love Again'. At midnight he left and returned home exhausted. He collapsed into bed, made one final phone call to Arthur Cantor, his newly-appointed partner, and then fell into a deep sleep.

It seemed that the doctors were not such fools after all, because he never woke up.

ACT ONE

CHAPTER ONE

1908–22

The Early Years

1908 was a vintage year and March 27th a vintage day in the London theatre. Herbert Beerbohm Tree was playing Gaston de Nerac (Paragot) in *The Beloved Vagabond* in his beautiful *beautiful* theatre, His Majesty's. Gerald du Maurier, in *The Admirable Crichton*, was returning to his original part, the Hon. Ernest Woolley. Lewis Waller in jodhpurs and solar topee was being killed nightly to the screaming anguish of the young females who formed the 'Keen On Waller Society'. They filled the first five rows of the stalls and were heard to shriek "How *dare* he?" when the fatal shot rang out. Somerset Maugham had two plays, *Lady Frederick* in which Ethel Irving appeared without any make-up and proceeded to make herself attractive in front of her young admirer in order to disillusion him, and *Jack Straw* in which Charles Hawtrey displayed the comic gifts which showed clearly just why London flocked to any theatre in which he was due to appear. At the St James's, George Alexander was playing twins in *The Thief* using an actor whose close physical resemblance to him did not altogether disguise the ineptness of the play, and that exquisite little singing comedienne, Marie Tempest, was displaying her incomparable gifts in a vehicle specially designed for her at the Comedy Theatre, *Lady Barbarity*. She was the only star of the Edwardian theatre who survived her period and lived to work with Binkie some thirty years later.

Harry Lauder was showing the kilt and sporran to thousands of excited kilties at the Tivoli, and somebody who rejoiced in the name of Topsy Sinden was appearing in *Belle of the Band* in a Grand Military Finale.

The *Morning Post* reported that the King had a cold and didn't leave his house at Biarritz though by the evening he had recovered sufficiently to be host at a dinner party. In *The Times* Bradfield College offered three classical scholarships at ninety guineas per annum and the P and O lines a Mediterranean pleasure cruise lasting twenty days for the extortionate sum of twenty guineas.

33

And something else happened on that day which was not announced in *The Times* or *Morning Post* or any newspaper. Mary Frances Morgan gave birth to a baby in North London. It was Good Friday and by a curious coincidence she herself had been born on Good Friday some twenty-nine years earlier. The baby, a boy, was named Hughes Griffiths. Hughes Griffiths Morgan.

Of all his reputations, the Man of Mystery was the one which Binkie enjoyed the most, the one he sought most earnestly to cultivate and maintain. He achieved this partly by silence and concealment, partly by deceit. He kept very silent on the subject of his birth, parentage and upbringing. But sometimes, when he had been drinking and found himself in the company of either a close friend or a sympathetic stranger, he would tell the most preposterous lies. He had a childish love of secrecy and the most adolescent relish in spinning out his fantasies. To some he would say he was Jewish, though this could be modified to being *half*-Jewish. To others he would hint at illegitimacy and a tough, working-class background: he would paint a horrifying picture of drunken parents, a prostitute mother, midnight beatings, ragged clothes, selling newspapers in the rain, walking barefoot to school and all the other accessories of a wretched Dickensian poverty. Innocent, harmless little lies perhaps, but they indicated a fertile imagination, one which had been enriched and nourished by the novels of Dickens, Zola, Balzac and Dostoievsky. Not that he had read them, for he had no interest in books, though he would certainly have seen adaptations in the silent cinema and the theatre. What was so attractive about being poor, Jewish and illegitimate was something he could never have explained. The dismal and horrifying truth he wished to conceal was being born into a prosperous middle-class family, that his parents had been respectably married in the church of St John the Baptist, Cardiff, on November 11th 1899, that they were solidly Welsh and even more solidly Baptist, that his father was a barrister-at-law named Morgan Morgan, his mother the daughter of John Brewer, a wealthy civil engineer, and that the family lived in Cathedral Road, Cardiff's most exclusive and expensive residential district.

In its obituary, *The Times*, acting on misinformation, stated that Morgan Morgan had come from a mining family, that he went down the mines at the age of ten and, being a boy of outstanding intelligence, raised himself up by his bootstraps into the mining company office at the age of eighteen. None of this is true. Morgan left school and went into a lawyer's office as a clerk and from there to local government. At twenty-nine he became Cardiff's Deputy Mayor and in the same year he met and married Mary Frances Brewer whose family had supplied not only engineers but an impressive array of ministers and other dignitaries of the Baptist Church. Their first child was a boy, John Brewer Morgan. The family moved to London with its greater prospects for an ambitious young man. He continued his legal studies, was called to the Bar in the Middle Temple, and practised with intermittent success on the London circuit. He bought a house at 97 West End Lane, Hampstead, where Binkie was born, but soon returned to Cardiff to practise on the Welsh circuit. In 1910 Mary Morgan met and fell in love with a wealthy timber merchant called William Sugden Beaumont. In those gallant times it was the custom for husbands to allow themselves to be named as the guilty party when their wives committed adultery, and to allow the wife to divorce the husband. Morgan Morgan refused to have anything to do with this charming if illogical custom. He divorced Mary, naming her as the guilty party and Beaumont as the co-respondent. The Brewer family were united in considering this sort of conduct to be despicable and vulgar and most definitely *not* that of a gentleman.

Morgan Morgan played a shadowy, fleeting part in Binkie's life. A short, stocky, fun-loving little man with thick black hair and a large black moustache, he liked his beer, he liked a good laugh, he enjoyed his social life with a large circle of convivial friends. He had a marked resemblance to Lloyd George and there are stories of policemen saluting him and holding up the traffic for him when he was crossing the road. Little else is known about him. When the divorce was made absolute he moved out of his family's life and never returned to it. He continued to practise as a barrister on the South Wales and London circuits. In the next decade he entered politics and contested without success the Conservative seat at Ebbw Vale in 1922 and at West Ham in 1929. He also found time to start the Institute of Patentees and to become its president.

Binkie was two years old when his father left Cathedral Road. He never met him again, never knew him, never talked of him. It was as if he never existed. The divorce was not one of those civilised affairs where the two parties continue to meet. Binkie's mother never saw him again and never allowed his name to be mentioned in the house or in her company. She allowed Binkie to grow up thinking that Beaumont was his true father and it was years before he discovered the truth. Then he changed his name by deed poll and in later years he never discussed his true father and showed no curiosity whatever in his life and circumstances. We can only speculate on why Mary Beaumont cut off her husband with such malignancy even to the point of concealing his very existence from her younger son. What broke up the marriage? What soured what had once been a happy and fruitful relationship? It could be that he was not able to give her the wealth and security she clearly wanted, for the law has always been, to all but a few, a risky and insecure profession. Possibly she considered that she had married beneath her, for his father was in trade while her father was in a profession and in those snobbish Edwardian times there was a virtually unbridgeable social gulf between the two. It was possible that being branded publicly as an adulteress – albeit with truth and justification – filled her with the sort of ungovernable fury which hath no like outside the gates of hell.

Morgan Morgan died in 1935, just about the time when Binkie was becoming a power in the land. He never remarried and only an elderly spinster sister and a handful of legal colleagues were present at the funeral in Gravesend. And so the Morgan family, Mary, John and Hughes Griffiths, started a new life under the greatly more elegant name of Beaumont. Both boys were to be known under their step-father's name and in Binkie's case 'Griffiths' was firmly dropped as if it had never been. There was always to be a great deal of interested speculation about the origins of his famous nickname and it started when he was a baby in his pram. It was a Sunday afternoon when all good Cardiff families overcame the lethargic effects of a massive lunch by taking the air in the Castle gardens. The Beaumonts were there with Nanny. They sat down on a park bench and a couple of women from one of the lower depths of Cardiff passed by, gazed into the pram and shrieked with laughter. "Oh, he's a proper little binkie, isn't he?" they said and passed on. Binkie was the local slang word for black or negro, and by extension it could mean anybody who was dirty or unwashed. Young Hugh had blond baby hair, a pink and white baby face and was spotlessly clean and radiant as befits the son of a prosperous circuit lawyer living in Cathedral Road. To describe such an infant as 'a binkie' was a joke, a piece of heavy-handed sarcasm provoked by some weird, class-ridden jealousy. Mary and William Beaumont were more amused than irritated. They reported it to their various families when they all met for Sunday tea. There was a lot of laughter and the nickname was fixed. 'Binkie' Beaumont he became and remained.

If you have to be brought up in the provinces you could do worse than Cardiff. It is an attractive, well-planned city surrounded by some of the most beautiful countryside in Wales. Binkie's childhood took place in circumstances which were not particularly smart but which were undeniably comfortable. The house at 12 Cathedral Road was large: three storeys high with a billiard-room and a library, large drawing-room and dining-room, second-floor bedrooms for the parents and guests, and third-floor rooms for the children (with nursery) and the servants. There was a housekeeper, Mrs Williams, a parlour maid, Gwynnie, a cook, Ethel, and a nanny, but no butler, footmen or gardener, for the Beaumonts didn't live on that scale. Outside, the back garden was separated only by a low brick wall from the splendid gardens surrounding the Castle.

Binkie's upbringing was middle-class, conventional. He went to a local nursery school at six years old dressed in a white sailor suit still in favour with the haute-bourgeoisie of Cardiff unaware that sailor suits were going out of fashion in London. The school, housed at the far end of Cathedral Road, was run by a Mrs Jones. Binkie learned to read, write, sing to piano accompaniment, paint pictures in what Mrs Jones called the Free Development Class, and listened spellbound while she read aloud from E. Nesbit and the Bible in that thrilling voice which made the Crucifixion seem as dramatic and exciting as any rugby or boxing match reported in the *South Wales Echo*. Binkie's neighbour at the next desk was a dazzlingly pretty girl with black ringlets and blue eyes called Myfanwy Williams. The attraction was mutual. Myfanwy's dark colouring and Binkie's blond curly hair provided a charming contrast. Binkie gave her sweets, played games with her, took her home to tea where, under Nanny's affectionate supervision, they consumed large quantities of buttered muffins, dainty strawberry jam sandwiches and Fuller's walnut cake. Then as now this was a prized delicacy which conferred high prestige on any tea-table that it graced. One day Binkie asked her to marry him. Giggling, she accepted. It was his first recorded love affair and his only marriage proposal. Myfanwy was not slow to return hospitality and Binkie met her brother Tom, a year younger and soon to join them at Mrs Jones's school. Happily, their two nannies were friendly and social contact in the park was permitted. Miffy, as she was inevitably known to her family and friends, and Tom were Binkie's closest companions for many of those early years until Binkie left Mrs Jones and continued his education elsewhere. Geographical separation had its inevitable effect, and when Miffy's father emigrated to Australia in the post-war reshuffle to start his own engineering business and took the family with him, the breach was complete. Binkie and Miffy never met again.

Life in provincial Cardiff had much to offer a sensitive and intelligent boy. Tram rides into the town centre and happy browsing in the market by the railway station with Nanny and John, trips to the coast, picnics on the sand, excursions on the steamer to Weston-super-Mare, the local circus once a year, children's parties in those houses known and approved by one's parents, games in the park, tours of the Castle and occasionally, when Mother was feeling generous and Nanny was willing, a visit to the local cinema, where they could shake with laughter at Chaplin and Buster Keaton, sob with Mary Pickford and thrill to the escapades of William S. Hart.

The war finished and a year later, their cousins, the Gunns, returned from their wartime exile in Weston-super-Mare. Margaret Gunn was Mary Beaumont's sister and her daughter, Betty, was Binkie's great and inseparable friend. She was a lively, fun-loving girl with a remarkable family likeness to Binkie. Binkie, now ten years old, was a regular visitor to her house where they would play games, read, chatter, do jigsaw puzzles, go for long walks, enjoy endless self-searching conversations and organise charades and parties.

At twelve he was sent to Penarth Grammar, Cardiff's most expensive school, where his career was undistinguished, for he was no scholar and no sportsman. Rugby, cricket, boxing, swimming and athletics meant nothing, though he could take his place in a team if he absolutely had to, and do well. "Binkie was a handsome, well-built boy with golden, corn-coloured hair, amiable in disposition, polished in diction and impeccable in dress," recalls Iorwerth Howells, a school contemporary. "Even when playing in a football match, his clothing appeared to be as unruffled and as spotless at the end as it had been at the beginning, and this despite the grey, sticky mud that characterised the school playing field in those days." He had some interest in history and literature but none in Latin, Greek, maths and the Welsh language which the patriotically-inclined headmaster put high on the syllabus. Even French and German made no appeal. Neither then nor later was Binkie to show any talent for learning foreign languages.

During this period their friends and neighbours, the Davies family, moved from 92 Cowbridge Road round the corner to Cathedral Road and took up residence in the house right opposite the Beaumonts at number 12. Davies had a grown-up son better known to the world as Ivor Novello. He was twelve years older than Binkie so the generation gap effectively prevented a friendship from developing in those early years, and in any case Ivor was always away from home, either in the RFC during the war or carving his own career in the theatre in London. Only occasionally did he spend weekends at home to see his beloved Mam, this beautiful, sparkling bird of paradise glowing with wealth, success and glamour, illuminating the dull provincial society like a meteor, and vanishing. As a small boy Binkie could only watch from a respectful distance but Cathedral Road always seemed dull and pointless by comparison after Ivor had paid one of his infrequent visits. In a strange, indefinable way, Ivor Novello epitomised everything that Binkie wanted.

The one thing which seemed to have been in short supply at this time in his life was love. Domestic love. Ethel the cook would always give him advance samples of whatever cakes, tarts and puddings she had baked for tea and would let him scrape the left-overs from the baking tin, but like all children of similar social background he was not encouraged to spend too much time in the kitchen with the servants. There was Nanny who certainly loved him in her way but after he went to school there was no further need for her services. His brother Jack was seven years older, a beefy, strapping, active boy who had no interest in his younger brother. Jack was keen on sport and athletics: he excelled at rugby, cricket, squash, rowing, swimming and what those hearty Edwardians insisted on calling the *manly* sports which invariably went hand in hand with a searing contempt for those who did not share their tastes. Seven is an awkward age gap to bridge: too wide for Jack to be a contemporary and friend, and not wide enough for him to be a surrogate parent.

Their step-father, William Beaumont, was a small, chunky, muscular little man with a mane of red hair and a big red moustache. Like a Viking, it was said in admiration, but there was nothing romantic or adventurous in his life-style. Like all self-made men who have built up a small family business into a large one, he was totally obsessed with his work and had little time for his family. Believing most fervently in the Victorian view of hard work as inherently virtuous and ennobling, he put in a twelve-hour day at the timber yard from eight in the morning, summer and winter, returning home to dinner at 9 p.m. too tired and preoccupied to pay any but the most perfunctory attention to his wife and step-sons. He had no problems with Jack and his future. He was a likely lad and showed a marked interest in the timber yard, watching the sawing of the planks, and asking to be allowed to ride on the front of the wagon when old Dai, his driver, made his deliveries. But Binkie was different. "What's the lad going to do when he grows up?" he asked Mary one day when Binkie had turned twelve. Binkie had no idea. "Got to do something. You can come in with me if you like. You and Jack together. Start at the bottom and learn the whole business. One day he'll be partners with Jack." Binkie was taken to the yard for a preliminary visit and hated it on sight. He looked with dismay at the dark, chilly little office and the counting house with its high stools and desks, the dim gas lighting, the air of depression, discomfort and hardship, for however much money the firm made there was little to show for it in the salaries paid to the staff or the conditions in which they were forced to work. Beaumont, like so many self-made men of the nineteenth and early twentieth centuries, did not believe in mollycoddling his workers. The sound of the sawing and chopping upset Binkie and the smell of sawdust and glue and horse-droppings made him feel sick. To his step-father, Binkie was a strange boy: so lively, so mercurial, so impulsive and so feminine. Beaumont just did not understand him and made no attempt to do so.

Neither did his mother. Binkie was not a mother's boy and there was a distinct coolness between them. Mary Beaumont was not beautiful but like fashionable women down the centuries she was able to show that if you have elegance, dignity, charm, social poise and natural leadership, then mere beauty is superfluous. She was always charmingly dressed in the latest fashions and spent much of her time and a great deal of Beaumont's money at Madame Anthony's, the leading Cardiff fashion house. She could cut a real dash when she was dressed in her satins and silks and feathers and Cardiff society was pleased to pay tribute to one of its acknowledged leaders. It was a busy life: tea parties, dinner and luncheon parties, a car when these were still a rarity in Wales, the Women's Institute, charity balls and bridge. Playing bridge all afternoon and well into the evening, smoking and drinking were still considered rather 'fast' to use the current jargon, but she liked to think that she led the fashions, not followed them. Mary Beaumont had style and that was what she bequeathed to Binkie. He received nothing else, but he certainly inherited her style.

To describe Mary Beaumont as a heartless social butterfly callously pursuing her selfish pleasures and ignoring the demands of her family would be an over-simplification, but the Beaumonts' was a loveless house and it cannot be denied that Binkie was neglected as a child. Loneliness was something he would get used to and learn to live with, something he could one day turn to his advantage.

In 1920 when Binkie had just turned twelve, William Beaumont died of a heart attack. He had been in bad health for some time and the doctors had diagnosed a strained heart valve. "Nothing to worry about," they had said reassuringly to Mary, "keep him comfortable and quiet, see that he gets three meals a day, don't let him worry, and above all, don't let him work too hard." Forty years later he could have been given another thirty years with a heart transplant or a pacemaker. But Beaumont refused to take life easy and continued to work twelve hours a day and to neglect his meals. The result was not only inevitable but speedy. One evening in November as he settled down for his supper in the empty dining-room, he slumped forward, his head on the table, his hands hanging limply over the side. The doctor was called, but he was already dead.

The marriage had lasted for eight years. It had not been a success, though for respectability's sake they continued to live together and to play their separate matrimonial parts with a brave face. There had been little love lost between the pleasure-seeking, flirtatious, fashionable woman and the dull, serious-minded hard-working man old enough to be her father. However, it is unlikely that she had love in mind when she married him. After the uncertainties of life with her wayward, brilliant but intermittently successful barrister, the wealth and security offered by the timber merchant were welcome. Beaumont left his entire estate to her: the business and the considerable income it provided.

With specific talent and special ambition, Binkie had no definite ideas about what he wanted to do with his life. But he did, however, know what he *didn't* want: that bloody timber yard which was to him what the blacking factory was to Dickens a century earlier, the irreversible gateway to a living hell. Like Dickens again, he might be forced by parental pressure into working there, and who knows if he would have had the courage and the sheer strength of character to resist?

But one thing was abundantly clear to everybody and which in later years he would describe in amazement and incredulity: at this time he had absolutely no thought of the theatre as a career. It played no part in his life or dreams, for dreams need substance on which to feed. When London stars and actor managers with their companies paid a brief visit to Cardiff on an annual provincial tour, Mary Beaumont with some wealthy friends would put on their best gowns and jewels and fill the stage boxes as much to be seen as to see, but this was yet another fashionable activity like church parade or a New Year charity dance. She certainly did not consider the theatre a suitable activity for an adolescent boy (though paradoxically she accepted the cinema even though she seldom went herself) and had never even taken Binkie to the pantomime at Christmas. Up to 1922 Binkie had never seen a play or set one foot inside a theatre nor had he any clear idea of what happened there.

The abiding memory of these unsatisfactory years which he was to take through his life was *boredom*. School was boring and homework even more boring since he was temperamentally incapable of working at anything which did not interest him. Home and family were boring; Sunday church-going with its interminable sermons was boring, and so were the endlessly drawn-out family gatherings with his Brewer relatives, all of whom seemed to be in Holy Orders of some sort and could talk of nothing except religion, politics and the future of Welsh nationalism. Cathedral Road was boring and so were the neighbours. Most boring of all were the music lessons which his mother had insisted he take with Madame Novello Davies. She had made a considerable reputation for herself as a singing and piano teacher and much of Cardiff's musical life centred on her and her house. She and Mary Beaumont were friendly and it was inevitable that Mrs Novello should take a fancy to Binkie's angelic face and blond curly hair. "Proper little angel he is, make a good choirboy he would, send him along to me and I'll give him lessons." Binkie went there three times a week but he had no music in him, not a scrap, neither ear nor voice. Neither then nor later was he ever to take the slightest interest in music. After a month of trying to get that harsh little squeak on the note, even Mrs Novello had to admit defeat.

When he moved to London a few years later and while still under twenty-one, his friends would note his confidence and assurance, his worldly knowledge and sophistication, and would wonder how one so young could have learned so much. Where did he learn all this and from whom? They would speculate about the formative influences in his life: had he ever enjoyed a Pygmalion-style relationship with an older man who had played Higgins to his Eliza Doolittle, and who had taught him how to be a gentleman, the highest and most complex form of artifice? They were to discover that there had been two such people in Binkie's life who first entered the story shortly after Beaumont died. By his death he unknowingly did his step-son a great service. Shortly after the funeral, Mary Beaumont went to a dinner party given by the Novello Davies family. One of the guests was a former Army Entertainments and Welfare Officer, a Major Harry Woodcock. He had just arrived in Cardiff and was to start work next week as the manager of the Playhouse.

CHAPTER TWO

1922

Cardiff – His First Visit to the Theatre

The Victorian actors toured incessantly and indefatigably. Their sense of professional dedication required them to scatter the fruits of their talents over as wide an area of the nation as was physically possible. A London public is fine, but what about the public in Manchester, Birmingham, Edinburgh, Dublin, Liverpool, Bristol, Newcastle and Cardiff? They are every bit as hungry, demanding and enthusiastic. As the century gathered momentum the touring circuits increased and by the time Irving had taken possession of his kingdom at the Lyceum in 1871, there were enough provincial theatres for the same play, albeit with different actors, to have four companies touring it simultaneously without ever seeing each other except at Crewe station on a Sunday, the inevitable meeting point and clearing house. The theatres were graded according to their quality: there were the Number Ones, the Number Twos, the Number Threes and – God help the mark – the Number Fours. Consequently there were enough theatres to keep a touring actor busy without ever once touching London. There was also the money: rich pickings were to be had in the provinces which were considerably more loyal than the sophisticated audiences in the West End. Barry Sullivan, as Bernard Shaw never tired of pointing out, toured his Shakespeare company for forty years, never once played in London after his rise to stardom and died in 1891 with a fortune of one hundred thousand pounds.

Cardiff did very well out of all this. There had long been theatres of one sort or another there, and if some of them were not the grandest or most luxurious, at least the London actors did not refuse to come. But it was largely under Irving's influence, who had made frequent appearances in the old Corn Exchange there, that the City Fathers put their hands into their pockets and built one which was really worthy of the illustrious names they wished to attract. It opened under the name of the Theatre Royal, and it had its official unveiling on October 7th 1878 with Irving and his Lyceum company in *The Bells* – what else? It was an exceedingly handsome building. One façade was Victorian gothic with stuccoed exterior and pointed windows presenting the appearance of a mini-cathedral, very suitable for the religious suscepti-bilities of Wales where anything remotely ecclesiastical carried a built-in seal of respectability. The other façade which stood in St Mary's Road was classical in design with a pediment and double columns. Both façades had niches with the sculpted heads of Shakespeare, Ben Jonson and Garrick and various assorted tragic muses with laurel wreaths and expressions which were both saintly and stern.

This Theatre Royal was very well situated: round the corner was the Great Western Railway station making it easy of access to the weekly touring company. Opposite was the Great Western Hotel and behind it was the Royal Hotel: transport and accommodation and work all within fifty yards of each other. What more could those London actors possibly want? Prices were attractively low, from the stalls at five shillings to the gallery at sixpence. The Theatre Royal flourished. Every actor and actress of note paid regular visits. Bernhardt, Duse, Mrs Patrick Campbell, Ellen Terry, Irving, Martin-Harvey, Tree, Forbes-Robertson, Benson, the list is endless. But when the war came in 1914 it closed, to re-open in 1920 with a fanfare of trumpets and much civic ceremony as The Playhouse, the expenses for such a development being subscribed by a party of local businessmen to the tune of sixty-five thousand pounds. Yes, this was a theatre of which Cardiff could be well and truly proud.

And so it was – for a time. When the post of general manager fell vacant – to be discreetly advertised in the columns of *The Stage* and *The Era* – it finally went to ex-Major Harry Woodcock (Royal Fusiliers, retired), for his considerable experience of arranging enter-tainment in the Army during the war had given him not only a wide knowledge of the day-to-day administrative problems of theatrical management, but had also provided him with a host of good theatrical contacts which could always be useful. He had served the recent years since the Armistice in Germany and had arranged, amongst many other attractions, for Mrs Patrick Campbell with full West End company in support to tour the military outposts and civilian theatres in a revival of the play she had made famous, *Pygmalion*. Fat, forgetful and fifty-six, she was a source of sadness and unkind laughter to those who remembered her in the days of her beauty and glory, and mystery and fascination to those who didn't. The majority of those soldiers and officers in the audiences on this German tour had never seen her before: many of them had not previously set foot in a theatre, and as Eliza Doolittle's age is never actually mentioned they could remain blissfully unaware that she is supposed to be a young girl of seventeen.

Thus they could relax happily under the impact of Mrs Pat's superb comedy timing, majestic voice and grande-dame personality. Major Harry Woodcock saw to it that she was made much of and that she was entertained, feasted and accommodated like a queen-in-exile – a service which was to be useful to him and to Binkie in years to come.

On his arrival in Cardiff, he had the problem of finding suitable accommodation. It was unseemly that a man of managerial status and authority should live in a house where the lesser actors of the travelling companies were also staying. The two principal hotels were suitable but very expensive: after the rigours of barrack life he wanted something a little more domestic. Mrs Novello, ever generous, offered him her spare bed in the attic next to the music room, but after being woken up daily at six in the morning by her voice exercises, plus the loud piano thumpings of her early-morning pupils, he decided to look elsewhere. Mrs Beaumont then offered him a spare bedroom, which was now free following the death of her husband.

He was single and unattached: aged forty-two, six feet tall, well-built with reddish hair and a neatly trimmed moustache, a type to which, as has already been seen, she was greatly attracted. Harry Woodcock was another Viking though smoother, more elegant, more civilised than the others. He was also a gentleman, which was more than could be said of his predecessors. She was a Merry Widow, passionate, unfulfilled and rich. The attraction was therefore mutual. He accepted the invitation, moved in, and within a week it was clear to both of them that he was there to stay.

In those days it was fashionable to define a gentleman as one who was honest over money, gallant with women and unfailingly courteous to the lower orders. Harry Woodcock qualified on all three and particularly with the last. He knew how to make himself popular where it is most important. He was charming and considerate to the servants: he was always very appreciative of Mrs Fairfax's cooking, showing particular liking for her Welsh maidens, an iced cake with raisins and currants on top which appeared unfailingly for Sunday tea; he was very thoughtful of Mrs Williams, the housekeeper, and little Gwynnie, the maid, and went out of his way to be deferential to Mary's boring family when the routine Sunday lunches brought them together. Most sensibly of all, he made friends with the boys. He escorted Jack to the sporting events which have always played a vital part in Cardiff's life, the rugby matches and the boxing, and when the Welsh played England at Twickenham, a trip to London with an overnight stay just for the two of them was a regular annual event. He squired Mary round Cardiff when his duties permitted, being the most dashing and thoughtful of escorts and causing many an eyebrow to be raised in enquiry and envy.

With Binkie his success was immediate and lasting. Not only was he the most attractive and exciting grown-up in his life, but he was directly responsible for pushing Binkie into his chosen profession. It was Harry Woodcock who opened the doors to the magical world which Binkie did not even know existed and thus revealed his true and inevitable destiny. It happened in 1922 when Binkie was thirteen. On a sunny Saturday afternoon in early January Harry took him into the town centre to the Royal Hotel. They lunched in the big restaurant, Binkie's first experience of eating out. Then he took him to the theatre, gave him a ticket, which was handed over by a dignified and respectful man in the box office, and deposited him in the front row of the stalls, where the trio was playing tunes from *The Mikado*. Anxious to make this a gala treat, Harry gave Binkie a programme and a box of chocolates, and left him so that he could attend to his managerial duties. The play was *Bulldog Drummond*, starring Sir Gerald du Maurier and his full West End company straight from Wyndham's Theatre, London, and one of his greatest successes. It had run a year and was now, with its provincial tour, reaping the rewards with full houses and long queues everywhere.

From 1920 when he first appeared in a novel, Bulldog Drummond became a household word. Like James Bond, some forty years later, he satisfied the public's demand for a superhero with slightly super-human luck and powers to protect the world against those who seek to injure it. The words may have differed but the formula was the same . . . an ex-service officer waging war against the Master Criminals who seek World Domination the better to satisfy their evil lusts, and doing so in backgrounds which were elegant and locales which were colourful: snobbery, sadism, sex, violence galore, and the crudest racialism whereby all foreigners are potentially criminal and Jews doubly so, the original book and its sequels made an enormous and instant appeal. The bright yellow dust-jacket was a stroke of genius from somebody in Hodder and Stoughton's design department and a bookshop window filled with them could guarantee to create a crowd on the pavement. There he was, Drummond, roped to a sturdy chair, snarling impotently, while the unspeakably horrible Doctor Henry Lakington grappled with a wilting and terrified Phyllis, with intentions so loathsome that the author could never bring himself to tell his readers exactly what they were.

Gerald du Maurier was well-endowed with those qualities which were necessary for a successful career in the theatre. He had a tough-looking ugliness which, combined with great charm and humour, made him ten times more attractive than the regular features of conventionally handsome actors. Women found him irresistible; men admired him; his companies adored him. Bulldog Drummond was a part which Lt-Col. H. C. McNeile, better known to the world as 'Sapper', might have written specially for him, and it was the centre-piece of a very well-constructed play. For nearly 500 perform-ances, du Maurier had bullied, shouted and fought his way through two and a half hours of riotous action, smashing up Carl Peterson and his gang of kidnappers, spies and evil scientists in the most hair-raising and bloody manner possible. The big climax was a fight in the laboratory, arranged by du Maurier himself, and nothing was faked. On the first night in London it startled the audience into an unpre-cedented display of hysteria. They stood up and screamed their pleasure and excitement at the end. Not even the National Anthem could compete with that.

After this Saturday matinée had finished, Harry took Binkie through the pass door, showed him the stage and the army of brawny stage hands and stage managers changing the scenery, and then up to Number One dressing-room. Harry and du Maurier were old friends, having made useful contact during the war in connection with per-formances arranged by various service charities. By a coincidence, it was in this week that du Maurier's knighthood had been announced, so it was to Sir Gerald and not Mr du Maurier that Binkie, chattering with nervous eagerness, addressed his stammering compliments.

Sir Gerald was in a very good mood and was rather touched by the obviously sincere enthusiasm of this young schoolboy. He did some-thing which he had never done before: he took Binkie round all the dressing-rooms introducing him to the occupants, and thus obtained a complete set of autographs on his programme. And not content with that, he invited Binkie and Harry to tea which took place in the majestic aspidistral lounge of the Royal Hotel. The party included Ronald Squire and Sir Gerald's wife, Muriel. She had long since abandoned a promising career on the stage – they met in the original production of *The Admirable Crichton* – to devote herself exclusively to her husband, cosseting and cushioning him with a single-minded intensity which some people cynically hinted was worthy of a better cause. "She spoils him so, it's not good for him," they whispered. "Beaumont?" she asked when Binkie was introduced, "my maiden name was Beaumont, what a coincidence. I wonder if we're related?" They discussed the matter in some detail but, alas, there was no discernible family connection between the Hampstead-born London actress and the Welsh timber merchant.

The tea-time conversation sparkled most intriguingly as Ronald

Squire was to remember with what seems like total recall: there were gossip and witty anecdotes about Sir Henry Irving, Sir Herbert Beerbohm Tree and Mrs Patrick Campbell, some amusing and slightly malicious comments on the absent members of the company who were at that very moment consuming welsh rarebit and baked beans on toast in a nearby teashop, which made Binkie shake and collapse with tearful laughter – very much to Sir Gerald's approval for he loved a good audience for his jokes; and there was talk of Sir Gerald's future plans. Apparently, he and his great friend, Viola Tree, had decided to pool their talents and write a play. With her culture and literary knowledge and his theatrical flair the project promised success. The true authorship was not to be made public and it was to be presented under the pseudonym of Hubert Parsons. This device was not quite so clever as the two collaborators imagined; those who knew the two families might have guessed instantly; for Hubert was close to the Christian name of Viola's father and Parsons the surname of her husband, Alan, later drama critic of the *Daily Sketch*. All this was supposed to be a secret but Sir Gerald was a born gossip, as was Binkie, and no secret was safe with him. Binkie couldn't resist the temptation to tell everybody he knew what Sir Gerald had told him and as a result Cardiff knew the truth about Hubert Parsons long before London. The play, titled *The Dancers*, brought Tallulah Bankhead to England for her London debut, and it was an enormous success, running nearly a year.

"How old are you?" enquired Sir Gerald, deciding to be very friendly to this young local boy.

"Thirteen, sir."

"Any ideas about what you want to do with your life?"

"Yes, sir. I want to go into the theatre. I want that more than anything else in the world." He had come to this momentous decision within ten minutes of the start of the play.

"As an actor?"

"No, sir. I don't think I could do that."

"Well, that's a change," he said and everybody laughed. "When you come to London old man, come and see me. Maybe I can help."

Binkie wriggled with uncontrollable joy at being addressed as 'old man'. Being treated as a grown-up and an equal by a man of such distinction is every boy's dream. "Thank you, sir. *Thank you!*" He was pink-cheeked with excitement.

"I'm not making any promises. But I might be able to suggest something."

Finally the tea-party broke up. The du Mauriers and company and Harry Woodcock returned to the theatre for the evening performance and Binkie made his solitary way by tram to Cathedral Road, clutching his multi-autographed programme and his half-empty box of chocolates, and quivering with happiness and excitement. He had discovered theatre. He'd seen Sir Gerald du Maurier on the stage from the front row of the stalls, he'd met him in his dressing-room and obtained a complete set of autographs. Sir Gerald had given him tea and muffins and had treated him as an equal and, if all that wasn't enough, he'd offered to help him when he came to London. It had been a unique and unforgettable experience. What a way to start the New Year. And what a story to tell his mother and the other boys at school.

This meeting pinpointed two essential aspects of Binkie's character. The first was his social poise, remarkable for a schoolboy of only thirteen, whereby he could chatter away, if not in a relaxed manner – for how could anybody relax in such august company? – but without noticeable tension or inhibition: neither then nor later was he ever handicapped by shyness. The second was his ability to get on with important people. By projecting a personality which was likeable, amusing and bursting with boyish charm, he could win them over and persuade them, without apparent effort, to do what he wanted. Like all ambitious and successful people, he knew by instinct where the power lay and how best to deal with those who held it.

Now that the magic gates had been opened there was no keeping him back. This first visit had made an insatiable Oliver Twist out of him: having tasted the joys of the live theatre he wanted more and more. He went to the Playhouse every Saturday. When the house seats were available, Harry Woodcock sat him in the front row of the stalls. When the play was a big success and they were not, then he took his place in the gallery queue and paid his sixpence like the rest. His constant companion on these occasions was his cousin, Betty Gunn. Together they would rush up the steep, chilly concrete staircase as soon as the doors were opened, rush down to the front bench if they'd been in the queue early enough and a bit further back if they hadn't, pay a penny for a bag of sweets, another penny for a programme, and press their heads against the brass railings as galleryites have done for centuries to watch the theatre slowly fill up. At two-fifteen Mr Jack Davies and his trio of musicians would appear in the pit to loud cheers and play a selection of popular and easy pieces, artfully selected to reflect the mood and content of the play. For *The Lie* performed by Miss Sybil Thorndike's Principal Company (though not, alas, by Miss Thorndike herself, though you'd never guess this by looking at the posters, so artfully dissimulative was the punctuation and layout), the selection included the Overture 'Le Roi d'Yvetot', 'Wayside Sketches' by Minchin, and, as a concession to popular taste, gems from *Cavalleria Rusticana*. Not that Binkie cared about music. It helped to pass the time but he had no interest in it. He was waiting eagerly for the curtain to go up.

"From that day onwards, I was *mad* about the theatre," he said in a newspaper interview some forty years later. "My family and relatives were all *appalled*. They thought it was the *end*. They wanted me to be *respectable*." To those religious, puritanical, middle-class, suburban Welsh worthies, the theatre was the Gateway to Hell, the Temple of Vice, and the Ante-room to Moral and Spiritual Disintegration. Not that any of them had ever been inside one, but the minister on Sunday would preach a hell-fire sermon on the subject and who were they to question his judgement? If only Binkie could have been born into a working-class, mining community as had been Emlyn Williams' happy fate in 1905 in Flintshire, the story would have been different. The miners have always loved and encouraged the arts and although there would have been no Harry Woodcock providing free seats at the Playhouse, there would have been no parental opposition or dis-approval either.

Alas, there was plenty of both in Cathedral Road. The Brewer relatives combined in blaming Harry Woodcock for putting such silly ideas into the boy's head and Mary for allowing Harry into the family circle. Bad enough that he should be actually living in the house and she with no husband, grown-up relative or protector to save her good name. Tongues wagged, lips pursed, eyes glowered and the scandal spread round suburban Cardiff and beyond like wildfire over the Sunday joints and the tea-time muffins. But there was nothing they could do about it. Mary Beaumont may have been Harry Woodcock's mistress, though this was never proved, but she was also her own, and it was up to her to decide who should live in her house. Harry's influence was strong and became stronger as time passed. If Binkie wanted to visit the theatre, let him. And if he wished to make it his profession, then let him. And if Mary herself wished to pay occasional visits to the theatre in the evening as Harry's guest, then let her. It was her business. The Brewer relatives could gossip and complain and malign and talk endlessly but mere talk never moved mountains.

"I used to write to all the big stars for photos," said Binkie nostalgically years later when those same stars were working for him. *Female* stars, it must be pointed out, not the men. It was Sybil Thorndike and Marie Tempest and Mrs Patrick Campbell and Meggie Albanesi and Marie Löhr who fascinated him rather than Henry Ainley, Martin-Harvey, Owen Nares or Aubrey Smith. When the goddess of his choice arrived at Cardiff, Binkie would drop her a letter at the stage door. By Wednesday, or Thursday at the latest, the photo would arrive at Cathedral Road, usually with a signature. If by chance she had forgotten it, then after the Saturday matinée he would go round for a visit. By now he was well known to the theatre staff and the stage-door keeper would let him in without question. Sometimes the dresser would be a little reluctant to allow him into Number One dressing-room but he could usually charm his way in. The goddess would usually be rather touched by this podgy little schoolboy in his short trousers, three buttoned jacket and cap, and be happy to oblige. Sometimes he would get a cup of tea and a chat. Sometimes not.

He quickly became a regular reader of the stage columns of the local papers, the *Western Mail* and the *South Wales Echo*. There was never much to be gleaned apart from the news of next week's attraction, for neither paper believed its readers had any interest in the performing arts. But sometimes there would be an interview or some gossip about the star in this week's attraction, with her husband, her children, her future plans or her recent trip to and appearance in New York. Harry Woodcock subscribed to *The Stage*, *Play Pictorial*, *Playgoer* and other trade papers. Binkie read through them eagerly, devouring and remembering everything of their contents. Consequently he knew all about the plays long before they came to Cardiff. And what a wide variety it was: Constance Collier and Basil Gill in *The Red Lamp*, a drama of the Russian Revolution, all murdering Bolsheviks and beautiful spies. Comedy was not neglected: Seymour Hicks in *Sleeping Partners*, then *Up in Mabel's Room* which sounded saucy but was strangely innocent, and a familiar comedy, *Nothing but the Truth*. It wasn't all straight plays: musical comedy was represented by Jack Hulbert and Cicely Courtneidge in *Pot Luck* and Donald Calthrop in *My Nieces*. And there were entertainments which didn't seem to fit into any known category: 'Rex London presents a Production of Personalities called *Pantaloonacy*, not a Review but something New'. It didn't matter what it was, Binkie was there, loving it, for it was all grist to his future mill. He did, later, admit to a special fondness for the evening with Grand Guignol. It was billed as *Adults Only* but the doorman at the gallery entrance, knowing that he was the manager's protégé, slipped him in. Wide-eyed, open-mouthed, breathless, he took it all in without reservation or criticism. 'Stage-struck' was a phrase which might have been coined specially for him.

In the summer of 1922, the theatre closed for its two-month annual holiday, re-opening in mid-September with Mrs Patrick and full London company in *Hedda Gabler*. But Binkie wasn't there. He was in hospital having his tonsils out. He had been looking forward to this special treat, for Harry, who knew her well, had told him of the legendary queen and had promised him a unique experience. On the

Friday he felt headachy and dizzy but he was determined to be in the Playhouse gallery on Saturday come hell or high water. But Mary Beaumont was adamant. "I can go in next week, Mother," he shouted. "I'm all right. I don't feel as ill as all that, honestly I don't." For once he didn't get his own way and his rage and distress was pitiful to behold. He went in on the Friday afternoon and came out a week later but Mrs Pat had gone, leaving behind only the memory of eight packed performances, bouquets and standing ovations. It is likely that Binkie never quite forgave his mother for this.

Their relationship had left much to be desired but from now on it deteriorated rapidly. They were always quarrelling about something, it seemed, but these were the outward symptoms of a deeper resentment. Both were passing through a difficult time of life; Mary at forty-three was getting possessive and nagged him incessantly, Binkie at fourteen was a source of constant irritation. It seemed he could do nothing right. His clothes were too scruffy, "Why can't you keep them tidy, they cost enough"; his hair was too long, "Get it cut, you look like a pitboy"; the long hours he spent with Betty Gunn at her family's house where his beloved Aunt Margaret always treated him with charming kindness and never criticised him, "You have a home and family here, you know, I don't want you treating it as a hotel." "I wish it was a hotel," shouted Binkie provoked into impertinence by this, "at least the service would be better and the staff a little more polite", for which insolence he was sent to bed without any supper.

His education was a source of argument and discord. Binkie wanted to leave school at fourteen, the earliest age at which this was permitted legally, and start work without delay. School held no charms for him. He was bored, restless and irritated by everything and everybody and, like every ambitious schoolboy in history, he was convinced he was wasting valuable time there. Why couldn't he leave then and start as a callboy or scene shifter or office junior? "Finish your education first and then we'll see," was his mother's parrot cry. "But this *is* my education," he would retort. But for once Harry Woodcock came down firmly on his mother's side, privately asking him to be patient. That final year at school would not be a waste of time, he said, and his usefulness at the Playhouse would be that much greater. "You can start the day you're fifteen. No need to stay on till July and finish the school year. Leave in March when you're legally entitled," and Binkie had to be content with that. Harry Woodcock put all this to Mary Beaumont who had enough sense to see and accept the inevitable. She shrugged her exquisite shoulders and reluctantly agreed.

And so it was. March 27th 1923 fell on a Tuesday. The day was triply celebrated. Binkie's fifteenth birthday, his leaving school and his starting work the next morning as a box-office assistant. In the evening Harry and the family watched the current attraction from the stage box, an entertainment highly suitable for a family celebration. It was Jack Buchanan in *A–Z*. Binkie adored every minute of it.

Afterwards, Harry took them to the Royal Hotel for a celebration supper. With characteristic generosity he provided tomato soup, roast pork with all the trimmings and a meringue ice-cream, all accompanied by a magnum of pink champagne. Binkie was trembling with happiness. The frustration and boredom of the last years had vanished in a flash. It seemed that he had been a condemned prisoner who had been miraculously reprieved and even more miraculously set free.

CHAPTER THREE

1923

His First Job at the Playhouse, Cardiff

The Playhouse was not Cardiff's only theatre, although neither of the others could be seriously regarded as a rival for the carriage-trade. The Empire, a music-hall, was that week running a twice-nightly Charles Cochran revue, a magic name which, more than any other in the twenties, carried a guarantee of quality. The New Theatre, which housed the local repertory company and the cheaper touring plays, this week had *Charley's Aunt.* The City already had three cinemas which were just beginning to cream away the Playhouse public, though it was not until the coming of the talkies that they became a serious threat.

Many other things were happening in Cardiff quite apart from the dramatic start to Binkie's new life, as the *South Wales Echo* was happy to report. Father Dobson, a Catholic priest, pleaded guilty to an act of discreetly unspecified indecent behaviour with a girl while riding his motorbicycle and was imprisoned for three months, though popular imaginations speculated with wild curiosity about what he could possibly have done; two boys were birched for stealing and killing a lamb, and Ossie Male, a Welsh rugby fullback and a popular hero in Cardiff's sporting circles, was sent off ignominiously in an international match in Paris for professional misconduct.

Outside Wales a man called Edward Summer, a patriarchal figure with a long flowing white beard who was the last surviving member of Dotheboys Hall in Yorkshire, died of a heart attack in Whitby and Charlie Chaplin married Lita Grey in Los Angeles, his second marriage and her first. A little closer to home, Sybil Thorndike announced that she would be playing Joan of Arc in a new play specially written for her by Bernard Shaw, while Shaw himself declared that he had lost all interest in the theatre and would be writing no more plays. He had been saying this for the last twenty years so nobody believed him, quite rightly as it turned out, for he was to write a dozen or so more plays before his death in 1950.

Apart from that final item, none of this concerned Binkie who neither then nor ever took the slightest interest in anything which did not concern the theatre. His world had now shrunk to the four walls of the Playhouse; his dedication was total and exclusive.

No full-length portrait or photograph exists of Binkie at this first milestone and turning-point in his life so a description of him will not go amiss. He stands at five feet and six inches, his brown hair is still flecked with blond highlights; it is cut short at the back and the sides and he has the traditional schoolboy side parting. His figure is podgy and there are still traces of puppyfat in the face with the usual adolescent spots and pimples on the chin and cheeks, though this situation is not to last long: both face and figure will be slimming down shortly. His teeth are firm, regular and white, for the family has always been proud of his good teeth: his eyes are grey-blue and sparkle and dance with life. His fingers are thin: he waves them through the air and gesticulates constantly as he talks, which he does continuously, rapidly and with enormous enthusiasm for everything, it seems, and everybody. His movements are swift and he walks quickly and eagerly.

And the clothes? Gone are the ready-made schoolboy clothes, those horrible tweed jackets and short trousers, those scratching grey flannel shirts, heavy shoes and woollen stockings. Now he is wearing a three-piece suit of light brown worsted which Harry Woodcock has bought for him for thirty shillings, at Potter Gillmore's, the leading gentleman's outfitters in Cardiff. There is a white cotton shirt, brown shoes, brown socks and a light brown handkerchief peeping out of the breast pocket. Harry is a generous and thoughtful employer and as Binkie is visible to the public and working at managerial level he must be properly dressed for the job. There is also a double-breasted dinner-jacket for the evenings and a stiff white shirt-front with studs and cuff-links. Both ensembles are smart and appropriate.

On that first Wednesday morning, March 28th 1923, Binkie and Harry set off at eight-thirty for the theatre. Binkie wore a dark brown overcoat, scarf, Derby hat, leather gloves and carried a walking-stick, all paid for by Harry. He looked and felt proud and grown-up, not a bad experience at fifteen. Scorning the bus, tram, train, taxi or Harry's car, they walked the two miles to the theatre. It took only thirty minutes, and it was a refreshing and invigorating start to the day which was inevitably going to be sedentary and stuffy. Being an old army man, Harry had learned the value and virtue of regular exercise in the fresh air, and the daily routine was one into which Binkie happily fitted. They would go down Cathedral Road, past Ivor Novello's birthplace in Cowbridge Road East, past the Sophia Gardens, over the Taff river bridge on whose walls the famous stone animals had been carved, past the Angel Hotel from whose first-floor balcony victorious Welsh Rugby Union teams would acknowledge the acclaim of their followers, down Westgate Street, past the fire station and central post office and thus to the theatre. Harry would go to the suite of rooms in the dressing-room corridor and Binkie to the box office. Although small and poky, there was enough room for two and here he worked with Mr Sawin, the box-office manager.

He quickly picked up the routine. First there would be the post, a large pile of letters containing advance bookings accompanied by cheques and, sometimes, stamped addressed envelopes. These would be dealt with immediately, the tickets torn out of the book, placed with a compliment slip in the envelope and the number and ticket rows marked off on the plan. By this time the box office opened to the public at 10 a.m. and people would be there already queuing up. Binkie learned his way around the box-office plan, he learned the tidy disposition of the cash with silver and notes in their separate compartments, he learned how to give change speedily and accurately. He also learned, as all box-office staff in history have done, that there is no limit to the stupidity, the ignorance, the sheer wanton blindness of the public who seem congenitally incapable of reading and taking in anything they see in front of them, however big the letters or bold the display. "Two and two halves, dearie," says the burly collier's wife with husband and children, "and what time does the picture begin?" Binkie's smile was never more radiant than when confronted by working-class confusion. "This is a *theatre*, madam, and the *cinema* you want is round the corner in St Mary's Street. The main film starts at two-thirty so if you wish to rush you might just be able to catch it. Goodbye and enjoy yourself," and off they would shuffle, reassured by his friendliness. He always had a list of the theatre's past productions so if somebody wanted to book tickets for *The Devil's Disciple* for Tuesday next he could tell them this had been showing two months ago when the Macdona Players had the theatre for a fortnight but it would probably be returning next year.

"What's the play about? Who's in it? Will my sister like it?" became familiar questions. It was his pride that he knew all about the play and could chat about it in the most amusing and seductive way. By the time he had finished, the customer would buy six tickets for the family instead of the two he had planned for himself and his wife. He became very skilled in the art of persuading people to buy slightly more expensive seats than they had planned: "For an extra shilling, sir, you can move six seats further down and have a splendid view of Mrs Campbell's low-cut evening gown which will be a treat, I *do* assure you."

Normally, the box office closed for lunch when Mr Sawin would go to the bar at the Royal Hotel for a drink and a sandwich but Binkie pointed out that this was the time when many people who worked office hours wanted to buy their tickets, indeed, it was the only convenient time, and that, by closing, the theatre was turning away custom. Binkie offered to work through the lunch-hour. Mr Sawin was not particularly concerned one way or another. He had no intrinsic love for his work and nothing to gain from the theatre's prosperity since he was on a straight salary, but he had no objection to his eager-beaver young assistant working for an extra hour if he so wished. Harry Woodcock, however, noted his enthusiasm and his selfless capacity for work.

He and Mr Sawin shared the work between them. At five Mr Sawin would go home for ninety minutes leaving Binkie alone. At six-thirty he would return and Binkie was thus able to go out for his only snack meal of the day in a nearby tea-shop where eggs and toast and a pot of tea cost only sixpence, returning at seven to change into his dinner-jacket for the evening traffic. At eight-thirty they would close. The money would be counted and stacked into a bag, the returns would be prepared and Binkie was now free, usually at nine o'clock, to go home. Not that he ever did. For now came the most exciting part of the evening. He would go and stand behind the dress circle and watch the play. In the interval he would join Harry in his office and drink a glass of orange juice. At ten he would go home, usually by tram, and be in bed by eleven. This was his routine for six days a week and he was paid the princely sum of one pound. For a boy living at home with no responsibilities, it was enough.

"I always wanted to be in a box office," he said nostalgically decades later, "I *loved* it because box office means money and that's how theatres survive. The box office was the real centre of power and I loved that. I was a businessman not an artist. I like to be anonymous, to serve and work *behind* the scenes."

But it did not last long, only two months. Without his knowledge, Harry Woodcock had been keeping a watchful eye on his protégé and what he saw he liked very much. Binkie, he realised, had a passionate love for the theatre and burning enthusiasm for the job; he was happy and eager to work long, punishing hours and to do the work of two men without complaint; he had a good head for figures; he knew how to organise the work; he had picked up with astonishing speed everything which Mr Sawin had taught him; he could talk to the customers in a charming and ingratiating manner, and he had shown enterprise and initiative in suggesting that the box office should open during the lunch-hour with a notable increase in ticket sales and

goodwill. Quite obviously, promotion was indicated to a place where these inestimable qualities could be used to his and the theatre's best advantage. Harry made him his assistant, and installed a second desk with telephone in his office so that Binkie could see and hear for himself how the provincial theatre worked. Binkie's desk was opposite Harry's and next to the big window so they could share the second-floor view of the teeming, bustling life of Cardiff. Time would show, Harry reflected, if he had the brains for management.

What a fascinating world it was, Binkie decided, and how even the intriguing world of the box office paled by comparison. He and Harry would be at their desks by nine o'clock, the day's work would start with the letters, and what a pile it was: letters from London managements asking for bookings, letters confirming bookings, cheques for deposit on bookings, cheques in advance payment for bookings, contracts, photographs, programme and poster material, it never stopped, for in those halcyon days there were five posts a day. The telephone never seemed to stop. Binkie, on his extension, would listen enthralled as Harry dealt with all the conflicting claims and requests like a circus juggler keeping a dozen highly coloured balls in the air and never letting them drop. The Playhouse was a Number One theatre with high prestige and there was always a queue of managers wanting to send their companies there. Sometimes it would be a new play glistening with stars on its way to, or just from, the West End; sometimes an established London success with lesser luminaries after its long run; sometimes a repertory company with three or four plays and a single big name at the top; sometimes a company of hardworking unknowns touring with hope but no definite destination. Whatever it was, Harry knew just how to speak to them.

But it wasn't all booking the play and sending out contracts: there was the internal running of the theatre and dealing with the staff. Cleaners, bartenders, programme sellers, ticket ushers, and the orchestra had to be engaged, sometimes dismissed and replaced, and paid. Their uniforms had to be supplied and maintained. The heating and electricity and gas and telephone bills had to be paid and the bars stocked with food and drink: photographs for each play had to be placed in the cabinets, posters had to be displayed outside the theatre and at key points round the town. Programme material had to be assembled and delivered to the printer in good time, advertisements had to be inserted in the local papers and information given to the editor.

Sometime during all this hectic activity a short lunch interval might be taken, but Binkie had an impatience with lunch-hours unless taken for important business reasons – a trait he was to display throughout his life – and usually he and Harry preferred to have sandwiches and a pot of coffee at their desks. In the evening he would put on his dinner-jacket and stand in the foyer with Harry, smiling at the audience, making polite conversation and always quick to answer a question, to deal with a complaint, to sort out a crisis like a double-booking for which house seats were always kept in reserve. This was an especially enjoyable part of the evening. He and Harry made a striking pair, Harry six feet with broad shoulders, red beard and reddish, healthy complexion, and Binkie thin, fair-haired and still only five feet six – "Like a Viking sea captain and his cabin boy," somebody once remarked but not unkindly. Backstage to see if everything was in readiness, curtain up, a glass of orange juice in the bar and then to the best part of the day, the end product of all this managerial activity, watching the play from the stage box.

Binkie did something which probably no provincial theatre mana-ger has ever done: he watched the play every night, never once taking time off, and showing a dedication to his work which far exceeded the claims of duty. This was not only for the enormous pleasure it gave him – for then, as well as now, Cardiff had little else to offer – but because he learned so much. Only by nightly attendance could he see for himself how one performance differed from another, see those tiny details in an actor's speech and movement which vary from night to night, note with what resource, or lack of it, they cope with the minor crisis of a dry, a fluff, a late entrance, a missing prop, a wrong sound cue, or the familiar but nonetheless dreaded disasters of a door which refuses to open or a revolver which doesn't go off. This is how he could learn some of the mysteries of the actor's craft, one which he passionately loved but knew was not for him. Even more important, he could, from the vantage point in the stage box, watch the audiences and see how they differed from night to night. Why did one laugh a lot and another hardly at all? Why was one quietly attentive and another noisy and restless? These are the great imponderables of the theatre and though there is no easy solution, a man who is even aware of the question is half-way to finding the answer. In the two years he worked at the Playhouse he was to see nearly a hundred plays, good, bad, indifferent, everything from finely polished starry productions down to the wretched thrown-quickly-together rubbish which even the best organised regional theatres are sometimes obliged to accept in the slack summer season rather than close down. Even these last were to serve a useful purpose, for how could he appreciate the best if he were never to see the worst? These years in Cardiff were immensely valuable to somebody who aspired to management and there can be few who enjoyed such a fine, full apprenticeship.

Then to the bar for a drink with the company where he could radiate his own particular brand of enthusiasm, chattering compulsively, giggling and gossiping, listening to the theatre slang and the backstage chat, ". . . Went very well tonight, darling, didn't it? They just *loved* it and that second act love scene has never gone better . . . Yes, old man, I did see what you had to do and say to cover her late entrance and I thought you did it *terribly* well . . . He was here last week, and strictly between ourselves I don't mind telling you that I really can't decide if he's more boring off the stage or on it, but not a *word* . . ." Yes, this was his world and he wanted, oh so desperately, to be part of it.

No sooner had he found his feet and learned the essentials of the job than his natural enterprise and initiative surfaced. He started to suggest changes. The programmes had always been a drab four-page leaflet giving the essential information about the play and little else; Binkie persuaded restaurants, hotels and department stores to take advertising space. He turned out to be an exceptionally good, plausible salesman and within a few weeks there was so much advertising that it was economically possible to increase the programme to twelve pages. He also included the times of the last trains, buses and trams to the suburbs and outlying villages. This information did much to reassure nervous patrons and there was a noticeable increase in ticket sales. He persuaded the owners of the theatre to repaint the outside and redecorate the interior, bringing it away from the Victorian heaviness and gloom into the lightness and cheerful charm of the twenties.

A conscientious theatre manager makes actors feel happy and Binkie was a master at the art. He arranged for the theatre to open on Sundays so that the visiting company for the week could get in their scenery, furniture, the huge wicker baskets containing the costumes, properties and personal possessions, and if necessary, to have a technical rehearsal on the evening instead of the Monday morning as had always been the custom. This innovation was not popular with the local stage-hands even though they were paid extra for Sunday work, but it was welcomed by the actors who now had the whole of Monday free until curtain time. Binkie was always at the station to greet the company, to escort the stars in a taxi to the theatre and to hover in attendance while they settled in to their dressing-rooms. On Monday nights each actor would receive a complimentary copy of the programme with a greetings card from Binkie, the management and staff. He would visit each dressing-room before the performance wishing good luck and telling the good news that the house was sold out, that a queue waited hopefully for possible returns and that the crush of patrons in the foyer might necessitate holding the curtain for a few moments.

Another of his achievements was to improve relations with the local press. These had always been bad. Welsh newspaper editors had shown the most pitiful lack of interest in the theatre and until Binkie arrived there was little except a paid block advertisement announcing the next week's play. Binkie paid a visit to the editors of the two local newspapers, the *South Wales Echo* and the *Western Mail*, took them both out to lunch at the Royal Hotel, gave them a pair of tickets each for the current play, dined them and their wives lavishly, introduced them to the two stars, and suggested that it might be a good idea to publish a little more theatrical news. Why not have a weekly column about the forthcoming play and any titbits of gossip about the stars? Why not a drama critic and why not space for a photograph of the play? "We haven't any space, Mr Beaumont," was the predictable reply, but Binkie managed to charm them into trying it out just once "and then we'll see". Once became twice and then three times and before the season had finished the review, the column and the photograph were being run as regular features and a journalist in the features department had become theatre reporter and critic. Nowadays, theatre-goers tend to take this press coverage for granted but in those days every inch of publicity had to be fought for. Binkie never stopped fighting and he usually won.

Another innovation which he suggested to Harry was the Saturday night dinner. "We've got to send them away from Cardiff feeling *very* happy, and even if it costs a bit, it'll be worth it." Every Saturday night after the last performance he would be host to a private supper for the stars and a couple of leading actors from the company. The Royal Hotel had a splendid and beautiful panelled room where Captain Scott had been given his farewell banquet in 1911 before departing for the South Pole. It was much in demand for private parties, but Binkie managed to charm the manager into allowing him a regular booking on Saturday nights throughout the year. Binkie realised that a knowledge of food and wine was an essential part of his worldly education: he was also too sensible to pretend to know things which he didn't. Every Friday he would confer with the head waiter and the chef, humbly ask their advice and take it. The chef was delighted to be thus consulted and even more pleased that his professional skills were to be used to their fullest. "How about a nice little bit of vichyssoise to start off with, Mister Beaumont? Really nice when it is chilled, you'll see, and they'll love it . . . Or perhaps an avocado with prawns in a rich creamy sauce and you could serve the champagne with it – always makes a good start for a meal. The Bollinger 1918 is a good year and we've got some of that left . . . And then a trout with my special wine sauce and little button mushrooms and sprouts . . . *truites Jurassienne*, which is with a rosé wine sauce and cream with chopped onions and parsley . . . and then *boeuf en croûte*, that is a nice tender rump steak in a flaky pastry case, and we can have *pommes de terre duchesse* with it, that's little round balls of mashed potatoes with almonds stuck on the outside. The ladies will love that, Mister Beaumont, and we've a nice Beaujolais '21 to go with it. And to finish, how about a *bombe surprise* which is an ice-cream inside a meringue. You see, the meringue is hot but the ice-cream isn't melted, the heat doesn't get inside, and that always pleases the ladies a lot. And then some cheese to finish, how about a nice piece of Caerphilly; you want something local, don't you . . .?''

Binkie planned these little supper-parties with the same meticulous care as he was later to lavish on his productions. It was not only the food and wine which aroused his care and concern: he arranged that the best wine glasses should be brought out, the most beautiful dinner-service, the most elegant crystal decorations and flower arrangements. He even went to the trouble of persuading the custodians of the Cardiff Central Library to lend him the original menu of the Captain Scott dinner scrawled with the signatures of the guests so that he could get it duplicated. The printer ran off a hundred copies and in the months to come he presented each guest with one as a souvenir. Those little details impressed the guests. Binkie would be in his element on Saturday nights, chatting and laughing with the gods and goddesses of the theatre whom he had previously known as photographs in the glossy magazines but were now here in flesh and blood as his guests and treating him with respect and affection. Wisely, he did not confine this hospitality to the established stars but extended it to the unknowns, realising that nobodies can become stars just as surely as stars can become nobodies. With these supper-parties he was laying a bank balance of goodwill on which he would later be able to draw. One day he would need them and – who knows? – one day *they* might need *him*. The stars were delighted and flattered and took back to London some very pleasant memories of that charming young man who made their week in Cardiff so comfortable and amusing. It is doubtful if any of them realised that he was only sixteen.

On one unforgettable evening at the Royal Hotel, Mrs Patrick Campbell was the guest of honour touring with a repertoire which included *The Thirteenth Chair*. Here was a living legend, at fifty-nine still a strikingly handsome woman who had lost none of her acting skills nor her devastating wit. She enthralled Binkie with her memories of Bernard Shaw and *Pygmalion*, Pinero and *The Second Mrs Tanqueray* and Ibsen and *Ghosts*.

Bobbie Andrews, lifelong partner of Ivor Novello, and later a friend of Binkie, remembered the dinner vividly: "He looked so confident, so assured, and talked with such authority, you'd never guess how young he really was. And he knew so much, or he seemed to. I think Binkie was like a sponge, soaking everything up which could possibly be of the slightest use to him and never forgetting it. He had learned somewhere how to flatter. Stella took a great liking to him but she had always had a weakness for beautiful young men and Binkie was *very* attractive." But his eyes were always firmly fixed on the future. Although he was learning his trade in Cardiff and enjoying himself hugely, London was the theatrical Mecca. He laid plans for his entry with considerable care, writing to every manager in the West End, telling them about himself and asking what openings they could suggest when he finally arrived in London. Only one had the decency to reply, a Mr H. M. Tennent who was the head of the bookings department for Moss Empires. There was no position he could offer at the moment, but he would like Mr Beaumont to keep in touch and, in the meantime, write to him about all the new plays which passed through Cardiff, giving his candid opinion and his estimate of their probable success in London. Binkie was delighted to do so and at regular intervals sent reports on all new plays: *The Sixth Man* with Martin Lewis and Olwen Pearce was a well-constructed thriller which needed some re-casting and a much tighter production if it was to succeed; *The Man Who Came Home* with Henry Edwards and Chrissie White was a charming light comedy and nicely acted, which would probably do well; *Six Cylinder Love* was a love story, which Binkie found a bit winsome and sentimental but with Edna Best it would certainly attract the right sized audience; *The Bad Man* was total rubbish and the performance of its star, Matheson Lang, brought back to mind Mrs Pat's comment, "He *spits* all the time, you'll need an *umbrella*." Not for London but the touring prospects were healthy. Mr Tennent thanked him for his reports and hoped that one day they would meet.

CHAPTER FOUR

1925

Tallulah Bankhead and *The Man in the Wheelchair* – Philip Ridgeway and the Barnes Theatre

Ironically it was a bad play which took Binkie away from Cardiff and into London. *The Man in the Wheelchair*, as it was originally known, was every bit as terrible as its title, a play of staggering ineptitude. Adapted by Roland Pertwee from a novel by Mrs Allene Tupper Wilkes, it had an invalid in a wheelchair who may or possibly may not have been a murderer, stolen jewels, oriental servants, revolver shots every five minutes and screams in the night. It had ghostly visitations from Pharaoh's tomb, twittering maids, a dour Scots manservant and that indispensable feature of all pre-war detective fiction, the clod-hopping police inspector. It was an anthology of all those 1920s thriller clichés which made the period so attractive to theatre historians. It had all that and Tallulah Bankhead too.

You watched it in despair and disbelief that so many distinguished actors – Nigel Bruce, Sam Livesey, Eric Maturin, C. Aubrey Smith and others – could have been persuaded to entrust their time and talents to it, or that it was written and presented in the first place. But these were all middle-aged actors with successful careers in the theatre and who were now going through those uncomfortable middle years when work is difficult to find and they take what is offered: doubtless they needed the money. And Tallulah Bankhead was a woman without intelligence or judgement: she actually preferred rubbish to plays of quality because they gave her a greater freedom to indulge in her particular brand of theatrical nonsense.

TALLULAH!!! In those three syllables and accompanying ex-clamation marks are enshrined one of the theatre's most flamboyant and treasured legends. She whirlwinded into Sir Gerald du Maurier's dressing-room at Wyndham's and demanded to play the leading part opposite him in his forthcoming production, *The Dancers*.

"I'm sorry, my dear, but it's already been cast. I've promised it to . . ."

"Never mind who you've promised it to, daahling, you can go and

65

Eric Maturin and Sam Livesey in *The Creaking Chair*, as portrayed by Nerman in the *Tatler*.

unpromise it and quickly. In the meantime you're going to have supper with me, *now*."

She whirlwinded him into the Savoy Grill, bought him a four-course supper which included the rare beef and cos lettuce which she had discovered was his favourite food, because, like all clever and ambitious climbers, she knew the value of homework. She paid for this meal with money which had been loaned to her by Charles Cochran himself and succeeded in convincing Sir Gerald that although he may have made a verbal contract, there was nothing written and that this was a Tallulah part, hers by divine right. Sir Gerald was not accustomed to having his suppers paid for by strange actresses, nor to being hustled and bullied in this typically brash American style but he found the experiences not altogether disagreeable.

She got the part and after three weeks' rehearsal she opened. Overnight she had the London public in the palm of her hand. The success of Tallulah Bankhead was a phenomenon which belonged to the twenties. In the first place, the American accent, later to lose its novelty, was almost unknown in Britain and she had an exceptionally attractive one, steeped as low in sex as any human voice can go without being submerged. And even if she had little or no acting ability at that time, her appearance and personality would have taken the West End by storm involving as it did a mane of Titian-golden hair, a provocatively feminine figure, sensual lips and the biggest eyes since Mrs Patrick Campbell. "It was a face like an exquisite poisoned flower," wrote Emlyn Williams. "It was empowered not only to make strong husbands in the stalls moisten their lips behind a pro-gramme, but also to cause girls hanging from the gallery to writhe and intone her first name like a voodoo incantation." Various rubbishy plays followed in quick succession. Neither Tallulah nor her besotted fans had any taste or discrimination and it didn't matter because all they wanted was for her to be there, to play the fool gloriously and to project her particular brand of manic womanhood.

All this was known to Binkie before she arrived, and it was with a delicious sense of excitement and anticipation that he waited for her at Cardiff station. "She's not on the train, do you mind? She's far too grand now ever to go on such a commonplace thing as a train call," said Alfred White, the company manager, as he made himself known to Binkie on the crowded platform as the 11.17 from Birmingham disgorged its passengers. "She'll be driving up from town tomorrow morning – *if* you're lucky – and in the afternoon if you're not. She's got herself a very rich gentleman and it's Rolls-Royces all the way now . . . Oh, you wouldn't *believe* what I've been through trying to get her on the stage on time. She's heaven, of course, but hell to work with, my dear. You'll need an anaesthetic to get through the week without going stark raving mad."

The green and gold Rolls-Royce turned up at the stage door on the Monday afternoon at 5.45, just two and a quarter hours before the play was due to begin. Tallulah wore a green Molyneux dress, a cloche hat and a huge rope of pearls which she playfully twirled round her neck. She walked out of the car and, after Binkie had introduced himself, she kissed him lazily on both cheeks. "Daahling, you're *far* too young to be the manager, I mean you aren't really, are you, or are you . . . isn't he too young, daahlings?" she said to her retinue. "Does your mother know that you're here, is this wicked terrible play suitable for schoolboys?" All this was accompanied by shrieks from the retinue which, in typical Hollywood style, included a coloured dresser, a black chauffeur, a white secretary, a titled lover named Lord Napier Alington whose sizeable fortune was temporarily at her disposal, and two chinless Guards officers who were introduced amidst further screams of laughter as "my financial advisor and my father confessor". "Tell me, daahling," she said in a loud voice as they moved into the theatre, "do you fuck?"

The glittering phalanx passed across the stage, through the creaking set, up the staircase and into Number One dressing-room. "Daahling, you're an angel," she breathed with total sincerity as she gazed ecstatically at the six-foot refrigerator, on hire for the week, and its contents. It was filled with bottles of her favourite champagne, Perrier-Jouet, smoked salmon, garlic pâté, lobster mousse, southern barbecued chicken legs, large black grapes, all supplied from London by Fortnum and Mason. "How *did* you know, daahling?" The answer to this question was that Binkie had done his homework. He had made some discreet enquiries and had learned that Tallulah liked a few little delicacies to be in regular supply in her dressing-room "just in case I get a little hungry in the interval, daahling," and the way to her heart was to see that they were. "Sit down, daahling, and have a drink," was her royal command and so the party started. The champagne corks were popped and all was as bright as a Fabergé Easter egg with Tallulah reclining on the chaise-longue and drinking the champagne as if it were lemonade. "Miss Bankhead, do you really think this is wise just now?" stammered Binkie, showing doubt and alarm for the first time in his career, "I mean . . . the play starts in ninety minutes . . . and . . ."

"Daahling, don't worry. I've never been plastered on the stage yet, have I, daahlings?" she appealed to the retinue who all agreed firmly that this was quite true, and even if she had the effect on her performance could only be beneficial.

Binkie had never met anybody remotely like Tallulah. Neither had Cardiff. The house on that Monday was not only sold out with a long queue of hopefuls waiting for returns, but the audience stayed to cheer at the end for all of fifteen minutes. "Daahling, you must join us for supper," she breathed afterwards, and so it was she who whisked Binkie off to join the party at the Great Western Hotel whose manager had once known her father. It went on till three in the morning. Binkie drank a lot of champagne and for the first time in his life he became very drunk. He was taken home by Tallulah in the Rolls-Royce and put to bed by Harry Woodcock.

But it wasn't all Tallulah and champagne that week. There was C. Aubrey Smith, her co-star and employer, for he had gone into management to present the play. He had the tiresome habit of cornering Binkie in the theatre and while he sipped his beer and puffed at his pipe he gave Binkie an account of all the cricket matches in which he'd played, the centuries, the runs, the maiden overs, and the names of long-since forgotten players. Binkie listened patiently; he could never decide if Aubrey was more boring off stage or on it. Certainly, he was always reminded of Mrs Pat's famous dismissal of him when he was proposed as her Higgins for the first production of *Pygmalion*. "Nonsense, I could never act with a cricket bat." Smith, Nigel Bruce, Sam Livesey and Eric Maturin would forgather in pipe-smoking, beer-swilling conclaves in the bar of the Royal Hotel and rehash their schooldays and wartime experiences. It was all very different from the Tallulah set. Binkie tactfully kept his boredom to himself and even organised a local cricket team so that they would have something to do with their long empty days until the performance, but diplomatically begged to be excused from participation. "I'm an absolute duffer at all games, Aubrey, and I do have to be in the office in the afternoon, so if you'll forgive me . . ."

Tallulah held court nightly at the Royal Hotel restaurant and every night the party became bigger. She was a great collector of people and there were always new faces of those who had caught her attention in the day and whom she wished to enjoy for a little longer. Binkie tried to invite her to be his guest for the usual Saturday night farewell dinner but she refused. "Daahling, I can't ask you to pay the bill for all these . . ." and she indicated her retinue, now swollen with half London's peerage. They had made the pilgrimage to Cardiff on her account which for a week became the fashionable sort of slumming for the smart set, "*Frightfully* amusing, doncherknow, Cardiff, so *quaint*, natives awfully jolly, what? . . ." Seeing his disappointment, she kissed him. "But when we get to London, daahling, you can take me anywhere and do anything."

"London?"

"Yes, daahling, you're coming with me to London."

"Am I?"

"Yes, daahling, Alfred wants to leave, says his nerves are in shreds and he'll have to have a rest or he'll die and I don't mind telling you, daahling, that he'll be no loss. I made a great mistake giving him the job in the first place, didn't I, daahling, but there's no hard feelings on my side and none on his, is there, daahling?"

Alfred nodded. "None at all, darling, you'll do very nicely with Binkie, I can see that."

Nigel Bruce in *The Creaking Chair*. Nerman, the *Tatler*.

"I'll be paying you ten pounds a week and we'll have a lot of fun, daahling, so fill up my glass with some of that delicious bubbly and we'll all get stinko."

A career in the theatre is a strange and unpredictable growth, difficult to cultivate and subject to no precise law. Talent alone is not enough, neither is ambition, nor even a combination of the two. What is also needed is the luck to get the big chance, the vision to recognise it when it comes, and the ruthlessness to grab it even when it hurts others, for it is occasionally necessary for an ambitious man to be thoroughly selfish. Tallulah's offer had come just before the matinée, which gave him the whole day to consider it. He had been at the Playhouse for fifteen months. He'd been a big success in the job, his salary had recently been raised to five pounds a week and he now had four people working under him as administrative assistants. But he did not want to stay in Cardiff all his life. The Playhouse and Harry Woodcock had done all they could for him and the time had clearly arrived to move on. Here was this splendid offer to continue working with Tallulah and to make his triumphal entry into the West End on her shoulders and to earn the staggering sum of ten pounds a week. What more could you ask?

The only slight disadvantage was that it was such short notice. He had to leave Cardiff immediately. The next date on the tour was Torquay, the train call was midday on the next day, Sunday, which gave him just the rest of the day and the following morning to say his farewells and make his arrangements. He went to Tallulah after the matinée and told her that he accepted her offer. She kissed him warmly. "Daahling, that'll be marvellous, thank you." She liked Binkie very much indeed. He was so beautiful, so young and so good at his job. Since her own sexuality was a little confused she did not hold this against others and some of her greatest friends, then as well as later, were those whose gender was also uncertain. She liked androgynous men: they were so elegant and civilised, so courteous, so charming, so amusing. They made perfect friends and escorts because, amongst other qualities, they were *safe*, and that in itself was a greater asset than many women were willing to admit.

Binkie broke the news to Harry Woodcock between the performances. To his relief Harry was delighted and generously gave Binkie permission to end his engagement at the Playhouse as from that night. Not that formal permission was needed. There was no written contract and the tradition of giving a fortnight's notice on either side had not started. But there was the gentleman's agreement that permission should at least be requested. Harry was certainly a gentleman and Binkie was learning to be one, so the formal courtesies were faithfully observed. In fact, Harry was privately delighted for the pupil's success could only reflect well on the master.

The Playhouse did not long survive. From the middle of 1924 business steadily declined: both money and public support were lost. And with its closure Harry Woodcock left the Playhouse, left Cardiff, left Cathedral Road, left Mrs Beaumont. He and Binkie never met again.

It was his first visit to London. Nobody loves London more passionately than a boy coming to it from the provinces to discover it for himself and at an age when he can appreciate it. Like Dr Johnson, like Boswell, like the youthful Bernard Shaw, Binkie experienced a revelation of triumphant joy. After a month at the Regent Palace Hotel at five shillings a day which included a bathroom and breakfast, he moved to Pitt's Head Mews, just behind Curzon Street, and a tiny flat obtained through Lord Lathom, one of Tallulah's aristocratic friends who knew everybody and enjoyed some useful contacts in the property world. It had two rooms, kitchen, bathroom and a little roof garden and was thus the perfect London base for a young and unattached bachelor. Another of Tallulah's friends decorated it for him: Binkie had been influenced by Syrie Maugham, whose marriage to Willie had just started to break up and who had embarked on her successful career as an interior decorator. Under this influence he pickled the furniture, put down white carpets and rugs, painted the walls white, put framed Bakst designs on the wall and gold taps in the bathroom. Well, they *looked* like gold.

"Very *bijou*, my dear," Binkie would say to enquiring friends, a word he got from Tallulah and Lord Lathom who had created a new, smart, high-camp language of their own. It became Binkie's favourite word of approbation. "Oh, it's *terribly* bijou," "I think she's frightfully bijou," or "It's a nicely bijou little play/dress/meal/book/day." Like all new slang words it found many different meanings and applications. It is more than likely that Coward himself had been influenced by Binkie when he applied it, many years later, to the residence occupied by the immortal Mrs Wentworth-Brewster.

In the summer of 1924 the West End was prospering. Gladys Cooper and Owen Nares were starring in a revival of that popular Victorian melodrama, *Diplomacy*, and Evelyn Laye was half-way through the run of an exciting musical, *Madame Pompadour*. In *Our Betters*, Willie Maugham's savage exposure of the social ambitions of the American was attracting thousands to the Globe, and Sybil Thorndike, at the New, was showing quite clearly that being a mere forty-two was no handicap to playing Joan of Arc aged seventeen.

George Arliss was giving his usual polished performance, as the evil Rajah in *The Green Goddess*, one which was soon to take him to Hollywood and fame beyond all present imaginings.

At the Strand, the legendary Astaires, Fred and Adèle, were tapping their way through two hours of energetic nonsense, *Stop Flirting*. But once again, wherever Tallulah was appearing turned out to be the centre of attention. The title had now been changed to *The Creaking Chair* and it started to creak on July 22nd, opening to the now familiar demonstrations of ecstasy.

It would seem that Aubrey Smith had spoken to her rather severely about her performance, had begged her to curb her high spirits and not to indulge in those little extravagances like suddenly breaking into a song and dance when the play became dull or the action too complicated. His words would seem to have had the desired effect: her performance was, by comparison, a trifle subdued and even *The Times* commented, "She has a part so enigmatic as to be almost non-existent". But even without the hoydenish behaviour, Tallulah's personality, sexual magnetism and vocal cadenzas made an irresistible appeal and the customary displays of hysteria saw her through twenty-two curtain calls, into the Ivy for the obligatory first-night dinner-party and the notices carried by messengers from Fleet Street.

These were predictable and routine: terrible for the play and unqualified enthusiasm for Tallulah. One did not criticise her because there was nothing to criticise, just to acknowledge the existence of an irreplaceable life-force, knowing that whatever was said to its detriment was irrelevant to the future success of the play. Tallulah was simply *there* and London made its pilgrimage. There were hundreds of scruffy shopgirls in the gallery, the upper circle was filled with dark-suited middle-class families from the suburbs and in the stalls and dress circle, Tallulah's friends. She knew everybody and everybody wanted to know her. It was a nightly parade of the peerage with everybody else who made up *Burke*, *Debrett*, the *Almanach de Gotha* and the gossip columns of the *Tatler* and the *Sketch*, all in their white ties, tails, stiff shirt-fronts, long Worth and Molyneux evening gowns, and diamond tiaras whose formality was an obligatory feature of theatre-going when half the audience were more interested in themselves than in the play.

And there was Binkie in the middle of it all, standing in the little foyer in his single-breasted dinner-jacket and wing collar watching the glittering parade. Sometimes a member of the royal family would appear, like the Duke of Kent who came every week and was supposed to be deeply in love with Tallulah. Binkie would show him to the stage box and look after him in the interval with a backstage visit to Number

"The Creaking Chair," at the Comedy Theatre.

Tallulah Bankhead and C. Aubrey Smith.

One dressing-room whose occupant would treat him just like everybody else which was, of course, the secret of her success: "Lovely to see you, daahling, have some bubbly and let's get stinko." Sometimes the second act would be delayed while they proceeded to do just that and then C. Aubrey Smith who disapproved of interval-visits, let alone drinking during the performance, would send messages of increasing urgency and would finally make a visit to the dressing-room. Not that the audience minded. If Kent was in the theatre they naturally expected it and if Tallulah had been drinking with him, the performance would naturally benefit. Who knows *what* she might do in the second act?

Life with Tallulah, Binkie soon discovered, was hectic and feverish. She had an inexhaustible supply of wealthy friends and lovers and an endless amount of good ideas about how that wealth should be spent as amusingly as possible. Her parties quickly created their own legend: nude midnight bathing parties in the Serpentine were incompatible with the law but Binkie was amazed how quickly she could calm and suborn even the most aggressively dutiful policemen: bus parties for the races with a fleet of them commissioned to transport the company and partners. There were fancy-dress parties at the Tower of London cleverly arranged by Ned Lathom who seemed to know everybody, "come-as-the-person-you'd-most-like-to-sleep-with" parties in Cliveden and nursery parties in Ned's flat in Mount Street where the guests dressed up as babies and were wheeled there in prams. There were more formal parties at the Embassy Club which the Prince of Wales occasionally visited and where Tallulah might catch his eye. The Prince was young, handsome, charming and surrounded by the pomp and circumstance of his royal position. Not unexpectedly, Tallulah did catch the Prince's eye and he too paid regular visits to the Comedy Theatre. Never had that damned chair creaked more entertainingly.

Tallulah wasn't snobbish. She would as happily sleep with a policeman or a taxi-driver as a royal duke. "Daahling, you're as good as the future King of England," she once shouted from her bedroom window after a long and active night. "No wonder they say the English policemen are so waaahnderful, daahling," after a similar experience with a Metropolitan sergeant. Binkie was part of all this and included in many, if not all, of the parties. She liked him very much and responded to his youthful charm. Whether he ever slept with her is a matter of speculation: it is quite possible that he did: after all, youth is a time for experiment and Tallulah would have considered it something of a diplomatic triumph to have attracted to her bed somebody who rather noticeably had little sexual interest in women. Who knows, she might cure him and place him on the path of conventional normality for the rest of his life, for such is the self-appointed mission of many women with a strong sexual impulse and a devouring mother instinct. Binkie was not slow to respond. He gave a party for Tallulah and Ned Lathom in the flat. He ordered from Fortnums a light dainty meal of champagne, smoked salmon, chicken mousse and an ice-cream gâteau shaped like the Sphinx. "Just a few bijou items, simple peasant food, my dear, I don't want to embarrass her," he explained to Bobbie Andrews who raised a pair of enquiring eyebrows at the money he had obviously spent.

Enthralled as he was by Tallulah and her set, Binkie was sensible enough not to neglect the other members of the company or his employer. One day he decided to give a luncheon party for Aubrey Smith, Nigel Bruce, Eric Maturin and Sam Livesey. Lest they might think that the flat was a trifle too feminine and fluttery for their masculine tastes, he arranged to have the white furnishings, the pickled chairs and the Bakst designs removed for the day and to be replaced by brown leather club armchairs, a darker, more durable carpet and sporting prints by Stubbs on the walls. To add to the illusion he placed a blown-up framed photo of W. G. Grace on the mantelpiece and a rack of pipes. The meal consisted of brown Windsor soup, mutton chops and trifle, served with beer and claret. Throughout the meal he talked of cricket and showed rather an extensive knowledge of its history, greatly to his guests' surprise. After the meal he smoked a pipe with the ease of one who has been doing it all his life and even managed to produce Smith's favourite brand of tobacco from a silver jar. Once again, Binkie had done his homework well. The four men were delighted with his hospitality and were forced to admit that they had misjudged him. "I thought the boy was one of *those*," confided Smith to Willie Bruce later in the Army and Navy Club, "but he's a dam' good scout. There's hope for the feller yet." Binkie's diplomatic success can be judged by an invitation from Smith and Willie to lunch at Lord's and see a Test Match. To Binkie it was a day of staggering boredom but, like the royal family in similar circumstances, he succeeded in putting a happy, smiling face on it. Binkie was a good offstage actor. He could be all things to all men.

Once the press had been and done their worst, "it is reminiscent of something which has been fished from under the East India docks in Limehouse," was one of the kinder comments, Tallulah started to behave like a naughty child whose parents have gone out for the night and thus converted a possible failure into a glorious success, not for the first time in theatrical history. She reverted to her former extravagances and overacted and fooled around with shameless zest. But the others in the cast refused to follow her example and in this they showed admirable professionalism, for Tallulah's nonsense would only seem funny if the others were playing it straight. The public adored it all and queues down Panton Street and into the Haymarket were a daily spectacle. Smith raised the prices and also raised her salary from £50 to £75 a week. Binkie, knowing full well her wasteful extravagance, persuaded her to allow him to keep ten pounds a week in trust: "Let me be your banker, my dear." It was the first of his services to her and letting him do this was the first intelligent decision she ever made.

In the 1920s, all theatres had their matinées at two-thirty on Wednesdays and Saturdays. This was doubly tiresome; it restricted the public and made it impossible for those working in the West End to see other plays. But Binkie was able to arrange for one evening off each week and on the first he went to the Prince of Wales to see Ivor Novello in his new play, *The Rat*, and to enjoy the pleasure of a long-delayed reunion. It was years since they'd met at his mother's house on one of Ivor's occasional weekends at home.

Nature had been very generous to Ivor, giving him a famous and soon-to-be-legendary profile, an elegantly slim figure, a modesty and sweetness which no success was to spoil, a charm which remained unforced and uncalculated by adulation and that indefinable magnetism which guaranteed that its possessor should be the centre of attention in whatever gathering he found himself. Three silent films had shown the Profile to its best advantage, giving him millions of fans who quivered with ecstasy every time he appeared on the screen. His fame also rested on a song he had written at the beginning of the war, 'Keep the Home Fires Burning', which Dame Clara Butt had sung at the Albert Hall in the presence of the King and Queen. It was published with the Profile, now wearing Air Force uniform, on the front cover.

What he lacked was acting talent, training and experience. He had appeared in only four plays, none of which had run for more than a few weeks. He was dull and wooden, not knowing what to do with his hands; he walked stiffly; his voice was only just audible and lacked variety. But it did not matter. As long as he was there in his Profilic glory, trailing clouds of Hollywood and Air Force fame, the public was happy. This, Binkie was quick to realise, was what being a star is all about.

The Rat was credited as written by David L'Estrange, but it was an open secret, carefully leaked by Ivor himself who was a born gossip and could not keep quiet about anything for long, that it was written by Ivor in collaboration with Constance Collier, she providing the plot and he the dialogue. It concerned a wealthy, well-born young Parisian gripped by an irresistible *nostalgie de la boue* who decides to dive into the *boue* in no uncertain way. He puts on a striped turtle-necked pullover, a peaked cap, rough black trousers, places a half-smoked Gauloise in the corner of his mouth, goes into a low-grade bar in Montmartre and calls himself an Apache. He has a terrific time associating with the underworld of thieves, whores, blackmailers and murderers who accept him without being too curious about his true background. The play was weak and feebly melodramatic, banal in its emotions and Ivor's own performance failed to kindle any real life, but it did not matter. Ivor was there.

The Rat was not the only product of the Novello–Collier talents. They also started a little supper club, the Fifty-Fifty, just round the corner in Wardour Street. The Savoy Grill and the Ivy were fine for post-performance meals but you had to dress up in white tie and tails, or at the very least in a dinner-jacket, and be stared at by the public as you threaded your way through the tables and then be fussed and flurried and minced over by an army of waiters, all of which was fine if you were feeling energetic and did not mind giving an extra perform-ance (unpaid) of The Actor Eating His Way Through A Very Expens-ive Gourmet Meal, but if you were feeling tired and wanted to relax then it was a bore. The Fifty-Fifty, though a little grander than the already popular and famous Gargoyle Club in Dean Street, satisfied an important need in the life of any theatrical community, a place where you could relax, wear any clothes you pleased, talk shop with your colleagues and actors from other plays, and discuss how the play went that night. It was a basement with subdued lighting, a bar, a small dais for a piano and a dozen tables with red-check cloths where one could drink cheap Italian wine, eat spaghetti or bacon and eggs. Ivor would often be there, playing his latest song on the piano and Constance enjoyed reminiscing eagerly about her years with Sir Herbert Beerbohm Tree whose leading lady she had been at His Majesty's and in Hollywood during the filming of the ill-fated *Macbeth*.★ Binkie was made a member shortly after his reunion with Ivor and quickly became a regular visitor. In many ways, he discovered, it was more fun to be eating bacon sandwiches and drinking Chianti with Constance than sipping champagne and gorging himself on smoked salmon with Tallulah: he never quite knew what was expected of him when he was with Tallulah but all dear Constance required was that he should be a good listener. She loved an audience. Binkie liked her and spent many happy hours through the night listening to her scurrilous gossip and anecdotes.

Just before Christmas, the regular clientele was augmented by an unknown young actor. Not totally unknown, perhaps, for he had appeared in two West End plays and a revue which he had written himself but, in spite of good notices, none had run for more than a few weeks. Now he had written a third play about a dope-fiend whose mother is having a scandalous affair with a young man, no older than her son. Drugs, sex, adultery, vice and depravity, then as now, was a formula greatly to the taste of the public. It was presented for a preliminary two weeks in a draughty little drill hall in Hampstead Village (to become the Everyman Cinema), but had been full every night and now it had progressed down the hill to the Royalty Theatre in Dean Street. The presenting management had not wanted the virtually unknown young actor to play the leading part, but he refused to listen to the suggestion that a really big star was needed and insisted on playing it himself. In this he showed great sense as well as courage. The play was *The Vortex* and the actor was Noël Coward who was to become one of Binkie's closest friends and allies. With that play and that actor, the twenties, theatrically speaking, can be officially said to have started.

★ The Curse of Macbeth was particularly active after the film had been completed. Few feature films started with such high hopes or were so devastated by bad luck. The notices were so terrible that the Broadway run was cut short after a week: in London it lasted only three days. It is one of the famous lost films of the silent era and apart from a couple of film stills, has vanished without a trace.

The Creaking Chair gasped its last in February 1925. It had run for thirty weeks. Tallulah's savings had been lodged in the safe in Binkie's office throughout and it was typical of his newly acquired style that he presented the money to her in the form of three hundred newly-minted gold sovereigns in a large glass bowl in a beribboned, plush-lined presentation box specially created by Fortnum and Mason. "Daahling, you're an angel, let's have some champagne and get double-stinko . . . Oh, daahling, isn't it sheer and utter blissikins," an expression she had picked up from Syrie Maugham, "to do what you like and what comes naturally, *and to be paid for it.*"

He was out of work, out of pocket and he urgently needed to find a job without delay. It was the first time in his seventeen-year-old life that he had been unemployed and it was not an experience he enjoyed or wished to repeat. When in later life he boasted that he had never been out of work, that one job had led straight to another, this was not entirely true. There was this gap of three full weeks when he actually had to economise. The bijou life-style was difficult to maintain and through his friendship with Tallulah and her circle he had acquired some very expensive tastes. Now Tallulah had gone to New York to see *Rain* to try to cajole that elusive and misogynist author, Somerset Maugham, into letting her play Sadie Thompson in London, and her circle had scattered far and wide. There was nobody amongst them who could help Binkie. He made a few tentative enquiries but without success. The manager of the Comedy Theatre suggested that he might like to enrol with an agency who specialised in obtaining managerial and administrative positions for its clients, and generously offered to give him an introduction, but Binkie demurred with real alarm. "*Agency?!* Certainly not," he said with horror. "Nothing so *common.*" In his view there was something irredeemably vulgar about getting work through an agency as if you were a kitchen porter or an office junior, and who wanted to pay ten per cent? – an attitude well in keeping with the delicate snobberies and prejudices of the day. Accordingly he did something which theatre people had been doing for the last half-century: he answered an advertisement in *The Stage*. The following morning he received a telephone call and an hour later he found himself making an unfashionable pilgrimage into darkest Hammersmith and even darker Barnes on the top of a 73 bus to meet Mr Philip Ridgeway.

He was a strange, multi-faceted individual, who had been born and brought up in Blackpool. His father, a wealthy businessman, had made a sizeable fortune in tobacco; his mother, an operatic soprano was known mostly in the North and the Midlands. He had carved the

sort of career which always looks impressive in programme biographies: as an actor, he had started as a boy in Blackpool, progressing
into Miss Horniman's company in Manchester. He tried his hand at
designing scenery; he dabbled in music, attempting to compose light
songs for musical comedies; he trained as a lawyer at the Inner Temple;
he served as a cavalry sergeant in the Duke of Lancaster's Light
Infantry: after the war he entered politics and narrowly failed to be
returned as a Labour MP for Blackpool. But he had always yearned to
go into management and in 1925, backed by his father's money, he did
so.

His appearance and personality were unimpressive. He was short,
bull-necked, red-faced with a strong Lancashire accent. "Really rather
uncouth," was John Gielgud's description: he was the last person you
would expect to cherish a profound love for the English and Russian
classics. But he was shrewd enough to realise that the programme he
had in mind would attract little attention in the West End where the
competition was so keen, but in the suburbs there would be much
public interest and press publicity. West London, he rightly decided,
was a cultural desert so, fired by a strange evangelical zeal, he bought a
tiny disused cinema in Barnes opposite the Ranelagh Sporting Club
and converted it into a 250-seat theatre from which he spearheaded,
alone and single-handed, the English revival of Chekhov. From many
points of view he could be truthfully described as Putney's answer to
Lilian Baylis.

"How much d'yer want?" he boomed when Binkie was shown into
his tiny office.

"Well, sir, I was getting ten pounds a week from Miss Bankhead."

"Ten bloody pounds? You'll get five pounds here and you'll like it.
I've got a first-class company and they're mostly getting three pounds.
It's enough to live on. With five pounds, you'll be laughin'."

The position on offer was business manager. In a small organisation
such as the Barnes Theatre it was always difficult to define with any
precision just what the work entailed because everybody did a little of
everything. Binkie helped in the box office, he looked after the
company accounts, he paid the actors, making his weekly appearance
in the dressing-rooms with little pay-packets which he asked them to
open and then to return in order to economise on the cost of brown
envelopes (an economy which, in years to come, he was to encourage
in his own business managers), he banked the nightly takings, he
sometimes helped out on the stage-management when a production
was unusually complex, he did the publicity and press relations and
put on his dinner-jacket to be the host and company manager on first
nights. The position was noticeably different and fuller than either of

his first two jobs and it gave him a much wider range of valuable experiences. The plays were changed every month and each day was busy with a hundred different things to do and oversee.

The season started with an adaptation by Hardy himself of *Tess of the D'Urbervilles*, starring Ion Swinley and Gwen Ffrangcon-Davies. Ridgeway invited Thomas Hardy to come to see it. Hardy was an old man and had long been in retirement. He protested that his health was unequal to the journey so Ridgeway arranged to take the production to him. Ten actors and a couple of costume baskets made the journey to Dorset and the play was performed in the sitting-room in front of a blazing log fire in the presence of the author, his family and a gentleman from *The Times*. It was a brilliant stroke of promotion and the result was a success so great that the play ran for three months at Barnes. (Four years later it was in the West End.) But he discovered, as did Lilian Baylis and Joan Littlewood, that the locals were not interested in the theatre; they preferred to play croquet, tennis, bowls and archery at Ranelagh. The people who filled the theatre, as they did at the Old Vic and were later to do at Stratford East, were the regular dedicated theatre-goers of the West End, many of whom made the pilgrimage across Hammersmith Bridge in their Daimlers and Rolls-Royces.

Ridgeway prided himself on being a good judge of talent and the company he had assembled showed he was right. Robert Farquharson, his Uncle Vanya, was a big fleshy man who was supposed to have black-magic powers enabling him to put a curse on a play or actor who had displeased him. He exuded an aura of evil and decadence which made him a little difficult to cast but if the part suited him, the result was unforgettable. There was Charles Laughton, fresh from the Royal Academy of Dramatic Art where he had left in a blaze of triumph: he was fat, moody, morose, neurotic as hell, living in a state of despair at the gulf which separated his actual performance from his vision of it, and with a mind so twisted that he automatically despised anything which received good notices and public acclaim, and could only love and cherish what had failed. But although he was difficult to work with and did not fit easily into company life, he possessed the sort of talent which was to make him one of the most admired young actors within two years and an international star within six. There was young Lewis Shaw, aged sixteen, who had toured Australia in *Young Woodley* and was later to give up acting to become a director of *Spotlight* – from which position he became a godfather and father confessor to many generations of unemployed actors and actresses. And there was John Gielgud, aged twenty-one, already much talked about, who had played Romeo with Gwen Ffrangcon-Davies and understudied Noël Coward in *The Vortex*. Gielgud had many assets inherited from his Terry ancestors: a beautiful voice, a splendidly romantic profile, and all the charm in the world. He and Binkie became very friendly: they had so much in common and both enjoyed the giggling and gossiping in the Green Room. Little did Binkie realise that this was to be the most intimate and lasting friendship of his life, that he was to be Gielgud's employer, colleague and co-director, and that their careers were to be linked by the closest professional ties.

Ridgeway showed excellent judgement when he engaged Komisarjevsky to direct the Russian plays. Now that Chekhov is accepted unquestioningly as a great classical playwright, now that his plays enjoy an unassailable position in the repertoire of just about every theatre in the land, it is hard to conceive that it was not always thus. In the early 1920s Chekhov's work was usually regarded as dreary and pointless, rejected by the public, barely tolerated by the actors (only a tiny handful recognised his quality from the start) and performed at thinly attended matinées in obscure theatres to audiences of hospital nurses and off-duty policemen in an atmosphere of wet mackintoshes and chipped teacups. It was Komisarjevsky who pointed out that these plays were comedies, rather than tragedies, and that in Russian eyes they were very funny. This was a revolutionary concept but one which the company and the public found acceptable. The plays were soon performing to full houses. *Uncle Vanya*, *The Seagull*, *The Cherry Orchard*, *The Three Sisters*, *Ivanov*, *Katerina* and *Abraham Lincoln* formed a season which in its way made history.

"We had to construct our own scenery and make our own costumes. We had to make or borrow our own furniture. I had to find the materials and the workers as cheaply as possible. I had to find photographers and printers. I had to find ways of doing everything cheaply, to keep running expenses down to the minimum which was a valuable lesson to somebody who hoped to go into management," as Binkie later revealed to a reporter from the *Observer*. He worked the usual long punishing hours, being in the theatre at eight with the cleaners, and staying till after the performance. And he was always capable of putting in those three extra hours' work which, in the theatre, can make all the difference between success and failure.

Not everybody thought well of him. To be occupying a position of authority when he was so young – he was eighteen but looked fifteen – did not inspire confidence in most of the company and there were some who were strangely resentful. "I'm not going to be managed by a schoolboy, all pimples and puberty," said Robert Farquharson, in a much-quoted phrase, "he's only a bloody teaboy, dammit." Some found him cold, calculating and aloof. "He can read the whole of *The*

Times in five minutes including the advertisements," said another. "Those cold grey eyes seemed to bore right through you even when he was smiling," said a third. "He seemed to be as old as the hills. There seemed to be nothing he couldn't do if he wanted it."

Binkie's own memories of the Barnes Theatre were noticeably more joyful. "I loved the company and we all worked together well. It was the most interesting and enjoyable job I'd had. I had so much responsibility, so many important decisions to make. I learned so much that was to be very useful to me."

It was as much due to him as to the actors and the director that five of the plays transferred with Binkie as business manager. Between 1926 and 1929, he occupied that position in no less than five West End theatres.

CHAPTER FIVE

1929–33

Harry Tennent and Moss Empires

He had to wait three years before the next important milestone and this was the turning-point which completely transformed his life. With a fine sense of dramatic timing, Fate arranged for this to take place on his twenty-first birthday, March 27th 1929. The phone call came shortly after breakfast. The conversation, as Binkie was to remember years later, went as follows:

"Mr Beaumont?"

"Yes. Speaking."

"Mr *Hugh* Beaumont? Currently employed by Philip Ridgeway at Barnes?"

"Yes, that's right."

"Are you free to lunch with me today?"

"Well . . . er . . . yes, I think so."

"Verrey's. Do you know it?"

"Well, no, I don't."

"Top of Regent Street on the left just before Oxford Circus. It's downstairs in the basement. Shall we say 12.30?"

"Thank you. By the way, who is this speaking?"

"I was wondering when you would show the requisite curiosity to ask that question. My name is Tennent. Harry Tennent. We corresponded a few years ago when you were working in Cardiff but we haven't actually met. So, I'll see you at 12.30."

Harry Tennent was a shadowy figure not only in Binkie's life story but in the history of the theatrical twenties and thirties. He was unique amongst London theatre managers in that he was endowed with an impressive number of artistic and sporting talents. He not only employed people who could do things, he could do them himself as well, and in some cases a lot better. He had been born Henry Moncrieff Tennent, a selection of names with a decidedly Wildean ring, and it is tempting to speculate if the author of *The Importance of Being Earnest* had met him and noted his middle name for future reference. In 1896, when just eighteen, he went up to Oxford, which offered a delightfully wide range of activities without the pressures to work. Harry became President of the OUDS and played, amongst other parts, Hamlet, Romeo and Benedick with a girl who later became Nigel Playfair's wife. He was tall, handsome, smiling, with those large-boned sculptured features which always look good on the stage and which have always been attractive to women. He played the piano well, he sang with a strong baritone, he wrote songs. He achieved distinction as a scholar, winning the Newdigate Prize and taking a first in Greats. He played cricket, rugby and tennis. He swam, boxed and rowed. In short, he was the compleat Renaissance Man, as the late Victorians saw him: one who could translate Euripides in the morning, win three sets in the afternoon, play Charles Surface in the evening and entertain the party with songs to his own piano accompaniment at night.

With all those talents a number of brilliant careers were open to him. He rejected them all, for this was the age of the Gentleman Amateur. The old snobbery dies hard that if you were a gentleman you could not earn money at the arts and if you did then you were not a gentleman. Harry Tennent belonged to that class in which background was all-important: wealth and success were vulgar. Alas, though the family had breeding and pride, they had no money. He had to live. He joined the firm of Broadwood, the piano manufacturer, as head of their printed music department, and thus suffered a notable demotion of prestige in the eyes of his family. To earn in the arts was bad enough but to earn in *trade* was worse.

After the war he moved to Moss Empires as head of their provincial bookings department and assistant to the managing director. This was the position he held when he first made contact with Binkie. He had been rather amused by the reports he received while Binkie was at Cardiff and impressed by the accounts he later received about his success with Tallulah and at Barnes. Obviously the boy had intelligence, organising ability and an unquenchable love for the theatre. He needed some experience on the management side and time alone would show if he had the necessary entrepreneurial flair.

The meeting between Binkie and Harry Tennent was, in its way, as historic and as fruitful as those between Gilbert and Sullivan, Boswell and Johnson, Sherlock Holmes and Dr Watson. There were some interesting parallels in their two lives: both were men of exceptional talent, but both suffered from a slight uncertainty of purpose; both had enormous potential and both were marking time in unsatisfactory jobs; and, although neither realised it at the time and it was to be a couple of years before they did, each needed the other to act as catalyst.

Tennent was touching fifty, old enough to be Binkie's father, but this was one generation gap where the bridge was already in existence and was thus easy to cross.

Regrettably, there is no photograph of Binkie at twenty-one but a portrait can be painted from the memories of those who knew him at this time. He has now grown to his full height of five feet and nine inches. The skin has cleared up nicely and is now as smooth and silky as even the most fashion-conscious young woman could desire. The puppyfat on the face has gone and the structure is neatly outlined with well-shaped cheekbones, a strong jawline and a broad sweep of the forehead. The eyes are now a little more prominent and the eyelids just a touch heavier. His hair is still blond but slowly turning to brown: he sports the then fashionable side parting on the left. His smile is radiant, revealing perfectly formed white teeth. His eyes sparkle with a curious blue-grey light. 'Dazzling' was inescapably the word which summed him up. As most of his contemporaries were forced to admit, even when it hurt them, Binkie really was rather beautiful.

Looking so ridiculously young, like a glorified schoolboy on holiday, was something of a disadvantage when you are on show in the foyer of a theatre or trying to do business with people who are usually old enough to be your grandparents. Binkie's choice of clothes for this occasion indicated not only his urgent desire to look older and more important, but also his wish to reflect his artistic tastes. There was also the necessity of impressing his host. Choosing exactly the right ensemble had caused him hours of anxiety. He knew that this was the most important meeting of his life so far but even Binkie, with all his instinctive prescience, did not know just *how* important. He wore a black single-breasted suit, a scarlet and gold brocade waistcoat with golden buttons, a red silk tie, red silk handkerchief peeping out of the breast pocket, red socks, black highly polished pointed shoes. There was a grey trilby hat, grey kid gloves and he carried a silver-topped walking stick, all indispensable accessories for the man-about-town in the late twenties.

Verrey's had the distinction of being London's oldest restaurant. It was founded in 1826 by a Swiss confectioner, Albert Verrey, and his daughter, occupying a three-storey building at the corner of Regent Street and Hanover Street. Like all successful restaurateurs, Verrey understood that it is not enough merely to supply good food in pleasant surroundings: you must also appeal to the public's snobbery. He saw to it that the right people – the rich, the talented, the beautiful and the merely famous – came regularly to his establishment, that the papers would carry gossip paragraphs and that they were talked about in all the right places.

His success was immediate and lasting: throughout the nineteenth and well into the twentieth century Verrey's was both popular and fashionable. Regency bucks with their quizzing glasses drank their morning chocolate and consumed in quantity those cheese and ham tartlets whose special blend and lightness of pastry was Verrey's own secret. Their leader, Prinny himself, now George IV, sipped champagne with Mrs Fitzherbert at a table and chair which – according to popular rumour – had been specially designed and strengthened to accommodate his Majesty's excessive weight and girth. John Murray the First flattered and haggled with his authors over luncheon: Disraeli, Dickens and Bulwer Lytton dined there with their wives. The Prince of Wales enjoyed discreet late-night suppers with that ravishing Mrs Patrick Campbell one week and with the considerably less ravishing Sarah Bernhardt during another. In the Gay Nineties the mashers with their monocles consumed oyster pudding and champagne, while Oscar Wilde and his disciples eating Bombe Surprise Chartreuse specially prepared by Mr Verrey's grandson, showed that the decade was well named. The Edwardian bloods and nuts with their ladies filled the rooftop restaurant during those long hot summers, and while Mr Thomas Beecham and Miss Ethel Smyth, as they then were, toyed with Lobster Newburg, the little orchestra behind the potted palms fumbled its way through selections from *The Wreckers*.

In 1926 the lease ran out and the restaurant moved round the corner to the basement of 233 Regent Street. The guest list for the party given to celebrate the official re-opening with Bill Connors,* the journalist, making the speech of welcome, shows that Verrey's had lost none of its fashionable appeal. Throughout the twenties and thirties it continued to attract the leading figures of the theatre, cinema, music, literature, fashion and – the only profession new to the century – advertising. Harry Tennent had been a regular patron since the end of the war and was always given special treatment by the staff.

Binkie arrived punctually, left his hat, stick and gloves in the cloakroom and walked into the bar which adjoined and led into the restaurant. Never having seen a photograph of his host, he did not know what he looked like. He stood there uncertainly looking round the lunch-time drinkers. A man rose from a chair and strode over to him. He was handsome, distinguished, very tall, with a fresh open-air face, thinning dark hair and horn-rimmed spectacles. His handshake was firm, his smile attractive and his voice deep and musical.

"Mr Beaumont? I am Harry Tennent. Let us sit down. Now, what would you like to drink? How about some champagne?"

*Later to be known as the *Daily Mirror* columnist, Cassandra. The man who was single-handedly responsible for P. G. Wodehouse's wartime disgrace.

"Yes, please. I picked up a taste for that from Miss Bankhead."

"But she likes it sweet and my taste is for the very dry. And if yours isn't yet, then it soon will be."

And thus Dorian Gray met his Lord Henry.

They shared a bottle of Bollinger and then went into the restaurant. They ordered tomato soup, roast beef and Yorkshire pudding off the silver-plated trolley, followed by apple tart with Devonshire clotted cream. It was all good, solid, English food, the sort you would expect in the nursery of a prosperous well-organised country house where everything is made from the finest natural ingredients, everything most beautifully cooked and served. Traditional English food was Verrey's speciality and the reason for its success. You knew where you were and what you were getting. There were no surprises. It took the second world war to coax the public, feebly protesting, out of its gastronomic insularity, but in 1929 the public did not need any coaxing to Buy British. It just never occurred to them to buy anything else.

During the meal they talked of general things: the incredible success of R. C. Sherriff's *Journey's End*, still playing to capacity at the Savoy – "I just can't understand it," said Binkie, "not a woman in sight and who wants to remember the war?" – grief that the Cardiff Playhouse should have fallen on evil times, and how very interesting that Charles Laughton should have failed so completely as Mr Pickwick in Basil Dean's production. "It's not enough to be fat, you have to have *charm* and *sweetness* and Charles hasn't got it; and without it Mr Pickwick comes over as rather sinister."

In obedience to the ancient tradition of courtesy, all talk of business was kept until the meal was over. Harry continued to make general conversation encouraging Binkie to retell some of his favourite Tallulah stories and laughing heartily as if he'd never heard them before. When the table had been cleared, the coffee, port and brandies served, he lit up a large cigar and puffed it luxuriously.

"I'm going to offer you a job," said Harry. "How would you like to work for Moss Empires?" He briefly sketched in the history and activities of the firm. An Edinburgh businessman and property owner called Edward Moss had been a great follower of the music hall. The only theatre in the city was inaccessible, ugly and uncomfortable. Disgusted, he decided to build his own theatre whose beauty, comfort and central position would attract the big stars of music hall who had previously shown a marked reluctance to visit Edinburgh. The King's Theatre was such a success that he built another in Glasgow. And then another in Liverpool. Before the end of the century he had a whole chain of music-hall theatres up and down the north and the Midlands.

By the war he had built or taken over more theatres in the south and in London. All these became collectively known as Moss Empires. Harry Tennent's job was to fill these theatres year in and year out, to find suitable attractions not only in the music hall bills but also musical entertainments of every sort, together with the indispensable Christmas pantomimes.

All this was fine, but Harry had been getting rather bored with the routine of booking George Robey as Widow Twankey for the Palace, Manchester, and George Formby Senior with banjo for the summer season at Torquay. What he wanted was to extend the activities of the firm into the legitimate theatre, to present musicals, intimate revues and *plays*. This was his aim and having persuaded the firm to go along with it, it was now his new job. A special department had been created and he was the head. But he needed a suitable assistant, who would work in the firm's London office at a starting salary of ten pounds a week. If the new department showed a profit, then his salary and his powers would be increased. Was Binkie interested?

Binkie was.

With a dramatic sense of timing, Harry Tennent took him back to Cranbourn Street, through the brass-plated double-doors of Cranbourn Mansions and to the third floor where he had his office. It was a medium-sized room with two desks facing each other and a bow window which commanded a good view of Cranbourn Street below. Leicester Square was on the right and the façade of Wyndham's Theatre on the left. The office was a delightful clutter with posters and blown-up signed photos on the wall, contracts, letters, more photos and scripts on the desks and all the right sounds coming from the adjoining offices – telephones ringing, typewriters clattering and the high-heeled shoes of the secretaries clicking on the parquet floor of the corridors. Binkie sniffed an atmosphere which was already familiar and well-beloved. He turned to Harry, his eyes shining with anticipation. "When do I start?"

"When would you like to start?"

"How about now?"

"Yes, why not?"

"I'll telephone Philip Ridgeway *immediately*, and tell him that he has just lost his business manager."

Philip Ridgeway took the news with surprising calm. He knew that Binkie's rise in the theatre was going to be meteoric, that his administrative and diplomatic skills had aroused a rather acquisitive interest from other managements. In truth, he was just a little surprised that Binkie had stayed with him for so long.

It was not just a business partnership which started on that sunny March day at Verrey's: it was also a close friendship. An immediate rapport, a strong bond of sympathetic understanding, was struck as soon as they met. "We just clicked," said Binkie years later, "and we became the best possible friends from then on." Many of their mutual friends just could not understand this: apart from the difference in ages, they did not seem to have anything in common. Harry Tennent was a man's man in the Victorian use of the term. He wore plain, dark, well-cut suits, smoked a pipe, watched the Test Matches at Lords and the Oval, played the odd game for his old school, cheered the English rugby team at Twickenham, walked his labradors through the park, drank his beer and relaxed either in the bar of the United University Club over a pork pie and salad with a handful of pipe-smoking cronies, or in the deep armchair of his bachelor flat with the dog-eared, well-thumbed books he had loved as a boy – Talbot Baines Reed, Conan Doyle, Jules Verne and G. A. Henty of which he had the true bibliophile's passion and knowledge. His flat at Parkside, Knights-bridge, had big bay windows overlooking Hyde Park, deep comfort-able leather armchairs and sofa, an open log fire, pipe-rack and tobacco jar on the mantelpiece, framed prints of Marie Lloyd, W. G. Grace and Edward VII, group photos of his cricketing and rugby teams at school, a couple of crossed oars above the fireplace (souvenirs of his Oxford rowing days) and a stuffed lion's head, a gift from a hunting friend, on the wall – in short the sort of flat in which C. Aubrey Smith and Nigel Bruce would have felt at home. It was looked after by his resident manservant, Jennings, formerly his army batman, who com-bined the duties of valet, chef and butler. Harry Tennent was a confirmed bachelor.

He disliked the camera and only one photograph is thought to have survived. It shows a heavy, severe, judicial face which might have belonged to a hanging judge, a hell-fire preaching bishop or a flagel-latory headmaster. It gives no indication of the humour, the charm and the sweetness which could dissolve the severity into helpless schoolboy laughter. In his more relaxed moods, Harry was a great giggler and lover of private jokes.

He and Binkie were temperamentally poles apart and the friendship between them was the classic case of the attraction of opposites. In Harry's strength, wisdom and experience, Binkie found peace and comfort. In Binkie's radiant, garrulous vitality and eager enjoyment of life, Harry found a new stimulus and at fifty this was the age at which a man especially needs it. Harry gave Binkie a new life. Binkie gave Harry a new lease on the old life which had begun to go stale at the edges. Binkie was anxious to learn, Harry was happy to teach.

It wasn't long before Harry's influence began to be seen. Binkie's clothes were a case in point. Harry had looked with gentle amusement at the peacock dandyism which Binkie had sported on that first day in Verrey's, though he was far too kind to say so or to allow any hint of his true feelings to appear. Binkie was, after all, very young and good taste took time to mature. Let him have his fling but let him learn, and soon, how a gentleman dresses. He persuaded him to put aside the gaudy suits, the brocade waistcoats and garish ties. Playing Beau Brummell to Binkie's Prinny, he started to preach the doctrine of purity: a gentleman is known not by the colour of his clothes but by their *cut* and *style*, the first to be perfection, the second to be unobtrusive. Under Harry's influence, Binkie started to go to Savile Row whose ancient establishments brought their own brand of elegance to town suits of light grey flannel, brown and navy-blue worsted. Binkie had the slim, bony, perfectly proportioned figure which is a tailor's dream. He had no idea just how beautiful a really good Savile Row suit could be, and thereafter he never bought his clothes anywhere else. Although until then he had bought his clothes off the peg and the results had always been satisfactory, he had to admit that it was astonishing what a difference it made when you spent a few extra pounds to have them made to measure by a team of master craftsmen.

The only touch of dandyism which Harry approved was the carnation. He wore white in the day and red at night and so it was with Binkie. Once, when he was wearing a light brown suit, he carelessly suggested that a green carnation, specially dyed by a little man he knew, would be rather fetching. "That could be misunderstood, old man," laughed Harry kindly. "Some of your friends may suspect, but there's no need to advertise it."

Harry's influence extended beyond clothes and personal adornment. He took Binkie to art galleries, antique shops and auctions and helped him to know and enjoy the visual arts. Under his guidance, Binkie acquired some more expensive tastes: he bought Dresden china and rejoiced in the roguish charm of those famous shepherdesses. He bought Max Beerbohm's famous cartoon of Oscar Wilde and a Sickert painting of Venice. This was while Sickert still lived and before his paintings became fashionable, so were consequently of a reasonable price. "They're not only fun to have around," said Harry, "but they're a damned good investment. Everything you buy now will be worth double in ten years' time, you'll see."

Harry took his duties as a theatrical godfather very seriously. Now that Binkie had been made presentable, he must be presented. He started to introduce him into the highest summits of theatrical society as a good godfather should. This meant, more specifically, to Sir

Gerald du Maurier and Miss Marie Tempest; they were theatrical royalty, the acknowledged King and Queen of the West End. The first port of call was the du Maurier house in Hampstead, Cannon Hall, in whose spacious gardens tea-tennis-and-bathing parties were held every Sunday afternoon. It was open house for the friends and the company of whichever play Gerald was leading at the time. If you belonged to that charmed circle you could play tennis with Gladys Cooper, have a giggle and gossip with Ronnie Ward, eat a rather more serious cucumber sandwich with Owen Nares and his charming but possessive wife, Marie, and perhaps – if you were lucky – have your cup of tea spilled in your lap by Viola Tree, pitifully accident-prone, but great fun and always good for a laugh.

Binkie wore white flannels and a sporting blazer of unspecified pedigree though the gold crest and scarlet edgings provided an acceptable flash of colour. "Binkie looked like the schoolboy who had just scored a hundred runs at Lords in the Eton and Harrow match," remembered Ronnie Ward years later, "and Harry Tennent looked like the headmaster who had arranged it," whereas Dame May Whitty, the senior *Grande Dame* of the du Maurier set and the only other one with a title, saw them rather differently. She thought they looked just like Diaghilev and Nijinsky and idly speculated whether they enjoyed a similar relationship.

The du Mauriers greeted him and made him welcome so charmingly that within a few minutes he felt that he had known them all his life. They invited him to call them Gerald and Mo, remembered without prompting their first meeting at Cardiff six years earlier, took him round the party introducing him as "the young man who took charge of Tallulah single-handed and lives to tell the tale," and saw to it that he was made much of. He finally found himself sitting next to Gladys Cooper and her daughter, Joan (later to marry Robert Morley). Gladys Cooper had always liked attractive young men: under the impact of the most beautiful eyes of her generation, and fortified by Earl Grey tea, thinly sliced cucumber sandwiches and Fuller's Walnut Cake, Binkie chattered away in his usual artless manner. The child-hood fantasies which had lain dormant since he parted from Tallulah now surfaced again and had clearly gained by the hibernation. "My name isn't really Beaumont . . . you see, I'm illegitimate, what do you think of *that*? . . . I had the most *gruesome* childhood, my mother was a woman of easy virtue who used to bring strange men home in the afternoon . . . I'd be given sixpence to go to the flicks and buy some sweets . . . We lived in a basement in the town centre, just a single room with an outside toilet . . . If she hadn't earned enough to give my father his drinking money, he'd get terribly angry and beat her and then he'd beat me . . ." It is unlikely that either Gladys or Joan believed a word of all this nonsense but they were too polite to show any hint of scepticism. Gladys invited him to join the mixed doubles on the tennis court, but Binkie, knowing his limitations and hating all sports, politely declined. He preferred tea, sandwiches and gossip with the mercurial Edna Best and her rather stolidly charming husband, Herbert Marshall.

It was all very different when Harry took him to lunch with Marie Tempest and her actor husband, W. Graham Browne, in their house at 55 Avenue Road near Regent's Park. Before they arrived he gave Binkie some advice. "Don't praise any other actress in her presence however much you admire them. Don't mention Mrs Patrick Campbell in any context, they hate each other and don't even acknowledge each other's existence. Don't speak glowingly or praise any of her performances: she's been deluged with gush and flattery all her life and she isn't interested. She's totally unsentimental about the past so don't speak of anything but the present and future. In fact, it would be better if you didn't talk of the theatre at all unless she brings it up. Talk of things outside the theatre: foreign travel, she's done plenty, pictures, she's got plenty. The only flattery to which she will respond is a request after the meal that she should sing something. She's very proud of her voice and always privately regrets that she gave up a promising career in opera to go into musical comedy. She insists that she was a terrific Carmen but I have grave doubts about that." All of this was good advice and could be usefully applied to any actress of international repute.

The house, more bijou than Binkie believed possible, was filled from floor to ceiling with *objets d'art*, paintings, embroidery, glassware, silver, eighteenth-century furniture, brocade cushion-covers, Wedgwood china in illuminated cabinets. It was all in relentlessly good taste. As Binkie had just started to acquire some of this, he was able to show intelligent appreciation of her Fabergé Easter egg, her ivory miniatures, her Royal Doulton dinner-service and, in particular, the exquisite food which she served: avocado and egg mousse in aspic, smoked mackerel with lemon mayonnaise, chicken à la Kiev, and finally an orange and brandy sorbet. The good impression Binkie made on his host and hostess was sealed when he joined them in a round of bridge with Harry, a keen card player, filling the fourth place. Binkie took care to play well but not too well. His hostess liked that. He was also diplomatic enough to allow his hostess to win and paid over a modest sum of money with smiling good humour. She liked that even more.

Binkie worked as Harry Tennent's assistant at Moss Empires for four years. When his friends and family asked him what he did, it was always a little difficult to give them a satisfactory answer. It was a little of everything. He helped to negotiate contracts for the *artistes* – as they were then called – he engaged and sometimes had to dismiss the stage-management and backstage staff, he organised photo sittings and train calls, he discussed programme material with the producer and printer, talked about costumes with the stars and scenery with the painter. Sometimes he would put on his dinner-jacket and stand in the foyer of the Hippodrome when the company manager was ill. When a play was a big success and the pressure of business resulted in the box-office staff being grossly overworked, he would help out and take great pleasure in using the old skills which he feared might have vanished. "I was really a glorified office-boy," he would say modestly, and sometimes this would appear to be true. Certainly, this is how Peter Cotes recalls him. Cotes was working as a stage manager for *Bow Bells* at the Hippodrome. He and Binkie were about the same age and had reached roughly the same level in their chosen branch of the theatre. There was no rapport between the two young men but on the other hand there was no clash of personality and nothing to suggest that twenty years later there would be.

When they first met in the stage-door foyer of the Hippodrome Theatre Binkie was carrying a sealed envelope which contained various messages and the week's returns to be delivered to Murray Anderson, the expensively imported American director. Binkie was wearing a pin-stripe black suit, an off-white shirt, light yellow Sulka tie, semi-patent leather shoes, an Anthony Eden homburg hat and a black overcoat, the whole outfit very smart and the height of fashion for young executives-to-be. "He was smooth, very smooth, relentlessly charming," said Cotes many years later. "This was fine if you liked a diet of undiluted syrup."

But there was one who responded to his fluttering charm with open pleasure. Ginette Spanier, a beautiful dark-eyed girl who had spent most of her life in England and spoke English perfectly with only the slightest trace of a French accent, had just started her first adult job on the gift counter of Fortnum and Mason. One Saturday afternoon, just before closing time, Binkie dashed down on an urgent errand: Binnie Hale was due to open that same night at the Hippodrome in *Bow Bells*, and she needed a throat spray to use on the stage in one of her sketches, so that it had to look both beautiful and expensive. Could Mlle Spanier produce one like that? Mlle Spanier could and did. In gratitude, Binkie gave her a couple of tickets for the opening performance. This started at eight o'clock, in three hours' time, just long enough to get home, change and return with a friend. In the interval Binkie entertained them both to drinks in the management office and thus started a loving and fruitful friendship which lasted till his death, forty-one years later.

By 1932 he passed another little milestone – the first time his name was mentioned in a popular daily newspaper. It was a mark of rising status in the profession that the *Daily Mail* printed the following piece on June 25th:

FOYER LOUNGE SUIT
'FANFARE' MANAGER'S DRESS SHIRTS STOLEN.

Theatrical traditions were shattered in the West End last night when Mr Hugh Beaumont, the manager of the 'Fanfare' company at the Prince Edward Theatre, appeared in the foyer in a lounge suit instead of the customary evening dress.

This unconventional costume, all the more remarkable on the second night of a successful production, had a simple explanation.

Mr Beaumont's flat in Pitt's Head Mews, near Park Lane, W., had been broken into just before the evening performance. He told the *Daily Mail* reporter:

"A friend who called round to see me found the front door smashed open and at once telephoned me at the theatre. I went to the flat and found that all my cuff links, pins, waistcoat buttons and all my personal jewellery, my dress shirts and waistcoats, had been taken. The jewel cases and some of my letters have been found in Hyde Park."

That evening he had a quiet supper with Ivor and Bobbie. "My dear, I was absolutely *shattered*. I mean to say, you feel so *naked* and *exposed* when you find that some stranger has been reading your letters and going through your underwear. Of course, in a twisted horrible way it's a sort of compliment if burglars start taking an interest in you. It looks as if I'm *really* getting on."

Fortunately, he was covered by insurance. The police at Vine Street speculated as to the identity of the woman burglar. It was a crime in which remarkably few women indulged and if this represented a new wave of feminine liberalism then the police had cause to be worried. The following week a woman was arrested climbing out of a window in a house in Curzon Street. She was carrying a bag of stolen silver-plate. It turned out that she was a prostitute's maid working from a flat in Shepherd Market. In it, the police found a sizeable collection of stolen property including Binkie's shirts, waistcoats and a set of gold shirt-studs. She later made a confession. She had seen Binkie standing in the doorway of the Hippodrome Theatre as the audience was assembling and had been greatly attracted to his youthful beauty as well as his shirt-studs. She had made a point of passing by the theatre every night at the same time in order to catch a glimpse of him and after two weeks she decided that she was in love. She was too shy to approach him but one evening she followed him when he walked home, which was his custom in the hot summer weather. Her father was a retired burglar who had taught her some of the tricks of the trade and she managed to smash open the door with a crowbar. "I dint want ter steal from 'im, not *reelly*," she said in a tearful Cockney accent, "I just wanted somefing of 'is ter *keep*. If I 'ave a son, I 'ope it would be a bloke like 'im. 'E's *luvley*. I dint mean any 'arm, *honest*." Binkie had to give evidence at the magistrate's court and made a point of asking that the girl's previous good record be taken into account and that she should be treated with mercy. The magistrate generously agreed to do this and the girl was bound over for three months.

"I was glad to get the shirt-studs back," said Binkie to Bobbie and Ivor when they met outside the court, "but she would have been welcome to the shirts and waistcoats. But, my dears, what a *compliment*. You never *know* who's going to fall in love with you!"

CHAPTER SIX

1933

Howard and Wyndham – *When Ladies Meet*

The firm of Howard and Wyndham had no connection with the beautiful, intimate theatre which bore its name, nor with Sir Charles Wyndham, who started the famous theatrical family, and his son Howard Wyndham, a situation which has caused considerable confusion in the century during which both the family and the firm have been in existence. Howard and Wyndham was to the legitimate theatre (as it was then rather charmingly called), what Moss Empires was to the music-hall and variety. Once again it was in Scotland that the right element of enterprise had been found. The original Mr Howard and Mr Wyndham had both been Edinburgh businessmen who regretted the absence of good theatres in Scotland and were anxious to drag their country into a theatrical millennium and out of the dark ages in which John Knox and his supporters had imprisoned it. They succeeded. By the turn of the century they had a chain of theatres all over Scotland and in England as well. Consequently, they were the biggest theatre-owning, play-presenting and touring management in Britain.

Alas, the provinces had suffered a noticeable decline in the twenties when the increasing popularity of the movies forced a great many theatres to close and re-open as cinemas. When, in the thirties, the movies were transformed into talkies, their encroachment became serious. With decline came devaluation. There was a time when London stars toured the provinces regularly, basked happily in the warmth of the acclaim and earned a fortune to compensate them for the occasional losses of their London seasons. They loved the provinces dearly and came to regard them as a vital part of their lives. But no longer. Now the stars rejected the provinces and became increasingly reluctant to leave the capital. "*Vere* eez Bumm-eeng-ham," asked Elisabeth Bergner, "unt *vot* eez Bumm-eeng-ham?" which innocent enquiry seemed to sum up what many of the London stars thought of the capital of the Midlands. Contrariwise, there have always been actors of no little distinction who have spent their careers touring the provinces. Barry Sullivan, in the mid-nineteenth century, was probably the first, and Bransby Williams, a hundred years later, was probably the last.

By the early thirties, Howard and Wyndham's business was declining rapidly. It was difficult to get the right attraction, difficult to coax the public into the theatre, particularly in the face of such competition from the cinema. The brief offered to Harry and Binkie was to revitalise the organisation of Howard and Wyndham as they had done with Moss Empires. They had to find new stars, new playwrights, get good new plays out of old authors. They had to persuade established stars to tour and, if this failed, to get the best possible replacement. By 1933, Harry Tennent's ambitions were realised. He persuaded Moss Empires and Howard and Wyndham to amalgamate for the promotion of legitimate theatre and to appoint him and Binkie as their executive chiefs.

The newly created department was officially known as Howard and Wyndham Tours Ltd. Binkie's first task was to persuade the overlords at Moss Empires that the office they shared in Cranbourn Mansions was too small and that they must have a new one. Approval having been obtained, he found a suite of tiny offices at 142 Piccadilly. Three in all, one which Binkie and Harry shared with large desks facing each other next to the window overlooking Hyde Park Corner, one for the secretary and a waiting-room. There was also a minute kitchen. When friends raised enquiring eyebrows at the general air of pokiness, Binkie laughed. "There's simply *no* point in being grand, my dear," he said casually. "I'm all for keeping management costs down to a minimum even if we're not actually paying them. If people are to be impressed then it must be by the plays and productions and not by the miles of carpet they have to cross before they get to your desk. I mean, my dear, that's just *too silly*." In all this he outlined a principle to which he adhered all his life. Neither then nor later were the offices of H. M. Tennent Ltd anything but small and functional. Like 10 Downing Street, the unimpressive façade concealed far more power and influence than the outsider could ever suspect.

Now he had to find a new play for the inaugural production and it was not enough that it should be good; it had to be superb. All eyes were on them to see what they proposed to do and how they were going to do it. Naturally, they had many friends and supporters. But there would be some enemies, for how could any ambitious and talented person fail to make them, people who were jealous and spiteful and wishing him to fail? This was the darker side of the power-game and he took it philosophically, refusing to be upset, deriving great comfort from the old saying, 'A man who never makes enemies never makes anything'.

First, he had to decide what sort of play he wished to present, for there were so many. Binkie wasn't interested in the classics which could be safely left to that crazy old woman at the Old Vic, nor in costumed historical plays which now seemed to be Bronson Albery's special province, nor in plays with huge casts, many changes of scene and spectacular effects, which Basil Dean was doing at His Majesty's and losing a fortune in the process. He had no wish to compete with the cinema, and he didn't wish to tackle anything tragic, depressing or philosophical – the public wanted entertainment and to enjoy life, in Binkie's view, not to be reminded of death or disease. As for musicals, revues and pantomimes . . . he never wanted to see another comedian, however funny, or a line of chorus girls and boys, however beautiful; four years of that was quite enough. He would never be a pioneer or trail-blazer: the experimental should be left to those draughty cellars in Notting Hill Gate.

What attracted Binkie was the good, pleasant commercial play, preferably a comedy which he could cast easily, which would attract one or two stars and which would appeal to the middlebrow and middle-class audiences in the home counties who kept the theatre alive.

But how was he to get such a play? How does any new management find plays? There are some traditional methods. You contact the leading play agencies and tell them what you want. At the beginning they will not send you their best from leading authors, because there are older managements who have first call, but they will send you some if nobody else is interested and a steady trickle of playscripts arrived at the Piccadilly offices. You keep a watchful eye on the leading repertory companies and you stand prepared to make a journey if your spies tell you that something interesting is coming up. You see what is being done abroad, though successes in New York, Paris and Vienna are liable to be snapped up by rival managements, and Binkie faced considerable competition from Charles B. Cochran who seemed to have first call on everything and everybody. If you draw a blank with all these sources then you contact your play-writing friends. Noël Coward was in New York playing *Design for Living* with his dear friends, Alfred Lunt and Lynn Fontanne, but he sent Binkie a reassuring message and promised to remember him for the future. He had dinner with Ivor and Bobbie and told them of his problem. Would Ivor care to write something especially for Binkie and his new management? Ivor was in the throes of casting for his new play, *Fresh Fields*, and was having a great deal of trouble in finding a star actress for the leading part. He had written it for his great idol, Marie Tempest, who had agreed to play it but was now embarking on her favourite indoor game: being difficult. This game, which is sanctified by over three centuries of colourful tradition, is never more entertaining than when it is being played on a young and inexperienced author who adores you and will do anything you ask. The ground rules are simple. You object to all the other actresses who have been engaged to support you: you make impossible demands about the theatre where you will perform and those where the play will tour. You want it to be entirely re-written and when this is done you decide that you like the first version better. When the author writes frantic and lengthy letters you ignore them. If he calls on you at your home you are away in the country. At the height of the negotiations, when they are at their most complex, you go to Paris for a week so nothing can be said or done and the author is reduced to grinding his teeth in unbearable frustration. When he gets sulky and petulant and obstinate, you invite him to lunch and are so charming that all the ugly thoughts and bad temper melt away and he will forgive you everything. Now the final episode had been played out: she had turned it down. "I wrote it specially for her," said Ivor sadly, "and she would have been marvellous in it. Oh, it's *too* much." He had now offered it to Irene Vanbrugh and was waiting for her reply. As for writing a new play, he couldn't think of anything new at the moment but he did have some ideas and when he found time to put them on paper, then he would certainly remember Binkie.

When you have drawn a blank with your play-writing friends then you contact authors you don't know and who are not represented by agents and invite them to lunch. The first of these was J. B. Priestley who had always refused to employ an agent, who was not committed by contract to any existing management and who was thus approachable. But he had just enjoyed a huge success with his first play, *Dangerous Corner*, still running after seven months: everybody was after him and he was playing hard to get. Binkie took him to Verrey's and over the roast beef and Yorkshire pudding suggested that Priestley write something with perhaps a particular star in mind. This suggestion was very coldly received. "I don't write vehicles, I write plays," said Priestley aggressively. "And I've no time for bloody stars or the star system. If I had my way, we wouldn't have them. Just a lot of good actors. Look at Russia." Binkie did not wish to look at Russia nor, if the truth could be told, did he wish to look at J. B. Priestley. The meeting had clearly been a great mistake. No two men could have been more irreconcilable in outlook or personality. The boy from Cardiff chattered away nervously and compulsively while the man from Bradford, dour and monosyllabic, sucked his empty pipe and ate little. It seemed entirely characteristic of Priestley that he should have neglected to shake hands on leaving Binkie outside in the street and walked away without a word of thanks for the meal. They were never to meet or have any communication again.

A few days later Binkie went to a party and talked to a friendly and sympathetic stranger about the problems of getting good new plays. There was no shortage of *new* plays, he said, for they arrived by every post, but *good* new plays are very scarce and the few that he had read were totally unsuitable for the commercial theatre. What was happening to the English playwright? Where was he? Or she? . . . For authorship was one talent with which women could claim total equality with men and sometimes supremacy. Two days later these remarks were published, for it seemed that the friendly and sympathetic stranger was a journalist.

The predictable result was an avalanche of plays which descended on the Piccadilly office, from which it seemed that there were thousands of good and new English playwrights and every one of them a genius. Amateur writers of every sort, every vicar, housewife, maiden aunt, schoolgirl, every retired judge, admiral and general was a budding Shakespeare or Shaw or Molière with the exception of those who were embryo Cowards or Lonsdales. Plays, long since forgotten, were being taken out of every bottom drawer, dusted and sent off to the enterprising Mr Beaumont. There were plays about Joan of Arc and Jane Austen, about Jesus Christ and Queen Victoria, about George Washington and Beethoven. There were plays about the Indian Mutiny and the Crimea, about the American War of Independence and the Assassination of William Terriss. There were plays in rhyming couplets and plays in blank verse. "We've *got* to read them all," said Binkie despairingly, "you never know *what* you'll miss if you don't."

Every evening he and Harry took home a case full of scripts: they spent days and nights reading them but the slush pile never seemed to grow any smaller. They were like the Dragon's Teeth of legend: the more you disposed of them the more they proliferated. It was a thoroughly dispiriting experience, for what it cruelly revealed was not so much a lack of talent as a lack of originality. Nearly all of them were imitations of present or recent successes. Since *Beau Geste* everybody was writing plays about the Foreign Legion. Since *Richard of Bordeaux* all the kings of history were fair game, provided they were civilised and elegant and offered a suitable opportunity for that beautiful young John Gielgud. Since *Autumn Crocus* lovable Tyrolean inn-keepers were in vogue.

A month later he was still no closer to finding his first play. And then the situation was suddenly resolved in a manner and from a source which he least expected.

One afternoon in late January 1933 he received a telephone call from Willie Graham Browne, Marie Tempest's husband and manager, speaking from their house in St John's Wood. A manuscript had arrived from a New York agent of a new play by the American author, Rachel Crothers, who had long been an admirer of Marie Tempest and had asked that it be sent to her. It was called *When Ladies Meet*. Mary – she was born Mary Susan Etherington and this is how she was always known to her friends – had read it and liked it. They both wondered if Binkie would care to see it and come to lunch for further discussions if he felt like taking the matter any further. Marie Tempest sending him a new play caused the most rapturous wedding bells to sound but remembering Ivor Novello's experiences there were also warning bells tolling ominously in the background. An hour later the script arrived by special messenger. He told his secretary that he was not to be disturbed, sat down and read it without stopping. He was and had always been a quick reader. Thirty minutes later he phoned Willie and confirmed the luncheon meeting for the next day.

Rachel Crothers at fifty-five was the only woman playwright to enjoy continuous success on Broadway. Her first play had appeared in 1904 and had run for a year, a rare achievement at that early stage of theatrical development. The overlords of Broadway had been none-too-politely amazed that a mere woman could do anything creative and successful but she had confounded all the male chauvinists still further by writing and producing twenty-five smash-hits at the rate, roughly, of one a year. It was said that no season was quite complete without a new Rachel Crothers play. It is not difficult to see the reasons for her success. She knew that women form the great majority of the theatre-going public and it was the women who thus kept the theatre alive. Rachel Crothers wrote plays *for* women and *about* women. She specialised in dramatising women's problems, particularly those of a woman who, like herself, followed a career and competed with men in a man's world. But apart from their social content and their propaganda value the plays were well constructed and written with elegance and insight. In short, they were serious *and* commercial and whoever achieves that rare combination will please both the intellectuals and the public. She invariably produced* her

---

* Before and during the war the term 'producer' meant the person who took charge of rehearsals and told the actors where to move and what to do. Nowadays, and since the early 1950s, the term has been replaced by 'director'. The word 'producer' is still used but now it means the person who raises the money to present the play and who employs all those concerned.

plays and by insisting on this she was instrumental in getting an author greater control over the production, always a sore point and subject of much acrimony. She thus helped to start what was to become a cherished Broadway tradition and such names as George Cohan, Marc Connelly, Moss Hart, George Kaufman and Elmer Rice were pleased to follow it. It was this fertility and professional practicality which led the press to call her 'a female Noël Coward'.

Unhappily, her plays were not easy to export, and to date only one, *Let Us be Gay*, a vehicle for one of Tallulah Bankhead's more sober performances, had been seen in London. It had had a short run at the Lyric in 1930.

When Ladies Meet was in its second year on Broadway and starred Frieda Inescort and Walter Abel, both highly acclaimed Broadway luminaries. The plot dealt with a young best-selling female novelist who falls in love with her publisher. They decide to live together for a period and then, if the relationship is a success, they will inform his wife and between them they will amicably decide with whom the publisher will live. At a trial weekend in a country cottage, the young novelist meets a woman who is visiting. She confides her marital plan to this charming and sympathetic woman who later turns out to be the publisher's wife . . .

The circumstances in which the play had arrived at Avenue Road were unusual and dramatic. Mary was very fond of cards. She was a first-class bridge player and adored patience, specialising in those games which are truly bizarre. Her latest was so difficult and complicated that for five years it had never come out and she had managed to convince herself – being very superstitious – that if it did it was good luck and something splendid would immediately happen. This is exactly what occurred. Shortly after Christmas she was playing the game and to her astonishment it did come out. The following day the package containing *When Ladies Meet* arrived from New York.

Marie Tempest had been a star of Broadway and the West End for as long as anybody could remember. She had started in 1885 in a comic opera by Suppé, *Boccaccio*, at the Comedy Theatre in which her sweet soprano voice, her plump girlish prettiness and delicious sense of comedy had made her an overnight success. For fifteen years she toured all over America and England in a series of opera and musical-comedy successes, but following a disagreement with George Edwardes at Daly's, she left the musical world and entered the legitimate stage as an actress. She was thirty-five. It was better to cultivate her acting talents which would surely increase and multiply as she grew older and see her to the grave, rather than cling to a voice which wouldn't last for ever and would inevitably result in an early retirement. She was lucky both with her authors and her producers, seeing to it that she had only the best masters. By 1914 she was generally regarded as the most brilliant comedienne of her day.

She was a fascinating little woman. Like Queen Victoria she was short and dumpy, endowed with enormous dignity and the sort of personality which could intimidate an army of marauding desert bandits, but unlike Queen Victoria she had charm and style and was always beautifully dressed in the height of fashion. "She had such chic, she was so exquisitely elegant, her clothes were such a joy to the eye with those little feathered hats perched roguishly on the side of her head," said Gertrude Lawrence. Her acting was as beautifully polished and contrived as her life-style. Nobody could time a comedy line as she could, nobody could sweep down a staircase or enter through French windows as she could, nobody else could pour out a cup of tea or eat a cucumber sandwich with such grace. Nobody could scintillate with greater charm or radiance and over the years she acquired a considerable repertoire of twinkles, chuckles, gurgles, squeaks, tinkling laughs, pouts, moues and facial by-play which could put sparkle into even the dullest play. These technical tricks were usually on display in the character of a middle-aged woman who chatters endlessly, organises other people's lives and gives sympathy and good advice to her children and husband, all of which amounted to what the press had for years been describing as 'a Marie Tempest part'. She had tenacity and determination and a capacity for hard work. She knew that her talent was limited, for she was no fool. Her dramatic range was pitifully narrow but within these limitations she achieved a dazzling perfection. A Marie Tempest performance was like a Mozart allegro or a jewelled Fabergé watch: it glittered and sparkled. You could see the wheels move but, my God, *what* wheels!

By 1933 she was the acknowledged Dowager Empress of the London theatre. She had, naturally, a splendidly imperturbable sense of her own importance and expected others to share it. She accepted no equal amongst the other *grandes dames* of the time though she did extend grudging acknowledgment to the talent and status of Irene Vanbrugh, the detested Mrs Patrick Campbell and Dame Sybil Thorndike, the only actress of her generation to be thus honoured. "That's what comes of playing saints," was her waspish comment when she read the news in *The Times*. "Nobody asks *me* to play a saint." She didn't accept Dame May Whitty who, as far as she was concerned, didn't exist, wasn't a good actress, was never in England, and had sold out to Hollywood, which Mary considered, as did many stage stars at the time, to be a terrible betrayal of her profession; in any case, everybody knew that her title had been given for her war work in 1917 and *not* for her services to the theatre.

"But why has she sent the play to me? To us?" asked Binkie. "Why not one of the others?"

"Who are the others? Not Albery, it's not really his sort of play, he likes costume pieces, and they've never got on. Basil Dean? She can't stand the sight or sound of him and neither can anybody else. Cochran? Not for him, he's interested only in the big musicals and revues. No, she's come to us because we're new. She's thinking of the future and it's a smart move."

She was. She was coming up to seventy, painfully conscious that her memory was starting to decline and that it was becoming increasingly difficult to learn new parts. And, in addition, there were ominous signs that her besotted public was starting to discriminate. Her last big success, *The First Mrs Fraser*, had finished in 1931 a run of nearly two years, and since then the plays had shown a marked decline in quality and the audiences in numbers. None had run longer than three months and some had barely survived two. It seemed that the public wanted something more than yet another Marie Tempest vehicle; they demanded a good play as well. *When Ladies Meet* was nothing to get excited about but it was noticeably better than her previous five plays.

The next few years promised to be increasingly bleak unless she could find a new management willing to do what the old ones would not. This was, quite simply, to love and cherish and flatter her, to support her through thick and thin, to be both employer and acolyte, to find good new plays for her and present them in the style to which she was accustomed. Binkie was a dear, sweet boy, as clever as a cathedral full of cardinals, and her instinct, seldom wrong, told her that he was going to be a considerable power in the land. Binkie would look after her. He needed her as much as she needed him. And he was very young and inexperienced, he'd look to her for advice and guidance so she'd be able to handle him and get what she wanted. In this last consideration she was, as events were shortly to show, greatly mistaken. Nevertheless, her decision to send him *When Ladies Meet* was arguably the most sensible of her life and it was largely due to her good judgement in this matter that her final seven years were spent in work rather than idleness and in triumph rather than obscurity.

But she couldn't resist the temptation to play The Game but now it was teasing the manager rather than the author; that would come later. Over an exquisite lunch she made her demands. First, the part of Mrs Bridget Drake, the chattering foolish old woman, would have to be severely cut: she did go on and on and it would all be so much more effective if it were about half as long. Second, she must not be discovered at the beginning because her public liked to see her make an entrance, in fact they *expected* it and not less than fifteen minutes after the beginning of the first act. Third, a piano must be included in the country-house set in the second act so she could play and sing, which was another thing her adoring public expected. Fourth, they must open at the Haymarket which was her favourite theatre and one with which her greatest successes had been associated. Fifth, the pre-London provincial tour must begin at Brighton and stay on the south coast because she didn't like all that tiresome travelling and preferred to be near London. Sixth, darling Willie must produce and also play one of the men's parts, perhaps Roger Woodruff, the glamorous publisher; she didn't think she could cope without her husband constantly at her side. As for the other parts, the publisher's mature wife would be well cast with Everley Gregg or Martita Hunt or Cicely Oates, all good hard-working women, and the young novelist . . . what about that nice clever little thing, Ursula Jeans . . . or Clare Greet or the Thorndike gel, Ann Casson, about whom she had heard so much? As for the other men, well, Bobbie Andrews is a darling and so is Cyril Raymond.

It was his first experience of the extraordinary way in which star actresses behave when they have been too powerful for too long. Of course he knew he was being tested, knew that she was seeing how far she could push him, but darling Mary must *not* get the idea that because he was so young and inexperienced he could be pushed into submission. During that lunch, Binkie privately made a decision which was to be of incalculable importance and save him untold ravages of worry and aggravation – that he would *never* be bullied by his stars. 'Let them know who's boss' was an excellent principle and one on which his entire future success was to be based. Binkie played his part of the game most excellently. He did not show alarm or indignation at Mary's demands, nor argue, nor refuse her terms but then he did not agree to them and gave her no indication at that early stage of his feelings. "You've given me a lot to think about, Mary dear," he said, "and I'll discuss everything with the author when we meet next week." He then adroitly changed the subject and the meal passed in a scherzando of laughter, anecdote and bubbling goodwill.

The first act when he returned to the office was to telephone Rachel Crothers' agent and make an offer. Incredibly, no other management had been approached or had shown any interest. If Marie Tempest wanted Binkie to present it then that was perfectly acceptable to the agent. Terms were discussed and agreed. Binkie bought a year's option for this, his first play, for fifty pounds and proposed that instead of the standard royalty of five per cent escalating through seven and a half, then ten to a ceiling of twelve and a half per cent, that he pay ten per cent of the gross throughout the run. It was a calculated risk for both parties: if the figures were high, Binkie would lose. If they were not then he would gain. The agent agreed and what was then an innovation soon became standard practice.

Rachel Crothers arrived at Southampton the following week. Since this was his first production and he wanted to impress everybody with his generosity and lavish style, he paid for her passage on the *Majestic*, met her at the dockside with a hired Rolls-Royce and chauffeur. She was impressed by this and also by the champagne which he and Harry produced from a tiny refrigerator inside the car. She was impressed by the suite on the south side of the Savoy which commanded a spectacular view of the river, the Houses of Parliament and Big Ben and one which, alas, the average Londoner never sees, and by the press reception he had organised in which more champagne was drunk and imaginatively designed canapés were consumed. The press did not always get this sort of hospitality and they too were impressed. Both then and later they gave the play, its author and its stars excellent coverage. The fact that all this hospitality was being paid for by Howard and Wyndham added to Binkie's pleasure. Rachel Crothers was a big, ungainly woman, a Plain Jane with no pretensions to chic, whose clothes looked as if they'd been bought in a village jumble sale. But she was homely and charming and Binkie and Harry liked her very much. She was also no fool. She took the news of Mary's demands philosophically; she'd been in the theatre for thirty years and was accustomed to the ways of star actresses. "But why does she want the part cut?" she enquired with surprise not unmixed with amusement. "I've never heard of a star asking for *that*. It's a new one on me."

"Because her memory is starting to go," explained Binkie. "So she wants to make things easy for herself. But not a *word* to anybody about that."

Binkie explained to Rachel that Mary's version of the Power Game included surrounding herself with nobodies, so that she would look all the better by comparison and thus get the lion's share of the applause, the attention and, of course, the notices. There was nothing very surprising or shocking about this: stars had been doing it for centuries. If you looked at the cast lists of all her plays, you would see the names of people who were very young and inexperienced, noticeably lacking in talent or, if neither of these applied, wildly miscast. The people she had suggested had all worked with her before and could be trusted to know their place. Ursula Jeans, for example, was young, pretty and talented but she didn't carry anything like the necessary weight for the part of the novelist, which was long and difficult and required an actress of great experience and authority; all this was true of Clare Greet and Ann Casson. Everley Gregg, Martita Hunt and Cicely Oates were all excellent character actresses but all were strikingly ugly and for the part of Claire, the publisher's wife, you needed somebody glamorous and attractive. Cyril Raymond★ and Bobbie Andrews were all paid-up members of what could be loosely described as the Marie Tempest Repertory Company but Bobbie was a really terrible actor and would never work at all if it wasn't for Ivor Novello who wrote a part for him in all his plays and musicals, while Cyril was a crashing bore both on and off the stage. Binkie would never employ either of them if he could possibly help it. What Marie Tempest needed was to be surrounded by stars. As the part was going to be severely cut and she would thus spend more time in her dressing-room than on the stage the public needed something good to look at in her long absences. This would be a new experience for her and it would do her a lot of good to be forced to act with equals rather than inferiors. It would also be very good for the play.

The part of the Power Game which Binkie enjoyed most, and at which he was later to excel, was the bargaining, the exchange of favours for concessions or, as Rachel laconically put it, a little bit of good, old-fashioned horse-trading. "I'll cut the part and give her a late entrance if she's really keen on it. I'll put in a piano and she can play and sing as much as she likes. They're unimportant and she's welcome to them. But the one thing which *is* important is the fact that I will produce the play myself. And Willie is far too old to play Roger Woodruff. We need somebody younger and more attractive. Roger is only forty, not seventy."

A week later Binkie wrote to Marie Tempest enclosing a revised version of the play which would show that the author had agreed to all her requests. But he deeply regretted that it would not be possible for dear Willie to produce the play as the author insisted on doing this herself and as she had done this some twenty-five times in her long and highly acclaimed career, Binkie was sure that she would be pleased with the situation. As for the London theatre where the play would open, he sincerely regretted that the Haymarket was not available. *Ten Minute Alibi* had just opened, was playing to full houses and would

---

★Cyril Raymond was one of Kenneth Tynan's least favourite actors and became from 1951 onwards a constant target for his particular brand of mockery and disapproval. Raymond embodied all that Tynan disliked and disapproved about the theatrical establishment and the dreary, pompous, self-important, Home Counties acting style it inspired. Since mockery is always more damaging when it is disguised as praise, he invariably referred to him as "that-very-good-actor-Cyril-Raymond".

doubtless run for at least a year and probably longer. Unhappily, neither Brighton nor any of the theatres on the south coast were available and in any case the theatres which he could book for the tour would have to be amongst those owned by Howard and Wyndham who were presenting the play. Therefore the cities on the pre-London tour would include Liverpool, Manchester, Sheffield and Edinburgh.

Binkie also enclosed a contract which offered her ten per cent of the gross receipts. When she asked for a guarantee Binkie declined for reasons which combined the avarice of Shylock and the gross flattery of Mephistopheles. "Mary dear, I am not giving you a guarantee because I wouldn't dream of insulting you by implying that you weren't capable of filling every seat at every performance." She saw his point and withdrew the request. In time, this deal would become standard practice but in 1933 it was unheard of and in initiating this custom Binkie was making a small footnote in theatrical history. "It makes good economical sense," he later said. "After all, the star contributes just as much as the author, so why shouldn't she get a percentage?" People thought he was being generous, which is what he hoped they would think: the word spread quickly round the West End, which again is what he had hoped. But generosity and kindness of heart played little part in this contract: Binkie had his own Machiavellian reason for this as with so many other decisions.

"Giving a star a financial interest in a play's success does *wonders*," he later said happily. "You get hard work and co-operation and performances out of them which you never *dreamed* about." Ten per cent of the gross was an offer Marie Tempest could not refuse. Her signed copy of the contract came by return of post.

But the question of the casting had not yet been decided and once she had committed herself to doing the play she couldn't very well object to the others who were to act with her. She realised that Binkie had delicately outmanoeuvred her, and she respected him all the more. Also, it is part of the Power Game to know when it is over and to call a halt. She did just that. She had gained a few face-saving concessions so honour was satisfied. Besides, she liked the new version and she really did want to do the play.

In those days the West End actor led a life which was artistically restricted and geographically circumscribed. Radio drama was still in its infancy. The new and magnificent Broadcasting House in Langham Place had been ceremoniously opened by John Reith, and Val Gielgud had found that he now had the most modern and best-equipped studios in the world, but he was still unable to extend the drama output beyond one play a week. Television did not exist. The cinema had only started to talk six years earlier but it offered very little competition for the actor's services. The few studios were all in or near London, Islington, Ealing, Lime Grove, Twickenham and Walton, and there was very little in what they produced to inspire the theatrical fraternity's confidence. The working conditions were not attractive and there was also a terrible snobbery about working in the cinema – as there was to be some twenty years later about television. The West End actor was just not interested in getting up at six in the morning, having his face smeared with a heavy, yellowing make-up, spending hours under those bright arc-lamps which hurt the eyes so badly, repeating the same few lines of dialogue for hours on end in a draughty studio, and for what end? A few yards of celluloid whose flickering images would be shown on a thousand screens to unthinking, indifferent audiences and then forgotten.

The West End actor was a member of a small and highly privileged circle. He went from one play to another frequently without a break. Sometimes there would be a tour of the Number One theatres in the provinces after the London run had finished: sometimes he would go to New York with his London success for a few luxurious months, but for the most part his working life was in London. In those halcyon days – and Binkie would one day look back on them with genuine nostalgia as a Golden Age – actors were *available*. You could get anybody you wanted and you seldom had to wait more than a few months if they had other commitments. The appalling situation, whereby it took two years and sometimes more to cast a play because the people you wanted were either committed to a long television series or were filming in some far-flung corner of the Empire, was decades ahead.

As a result, he cast *When Ladies Meet* in three days, assembling a dream company for the period: Owen Nares, Mary Newcombe, Ann Todd and Robert Donat. Owen Nares was not the original matinée idol, for that honour belonged to Lewis Waller, but he fitted inescapably into that category. From the time he played the grown-up David Copperfield with Beerbohm Tree at His Majesty's in 1914 and triumphantly survived the experience of sharing the stage with Tree's holocaust of overacting in the double roles of Micawber and Peggotty, his popularity with the women who made up the bulk of the matinée public was assured. He was tall, slim, good-looking, charming, manly and a fine actor. Women saw him as a father figure, a category of actor which was to go sharply out of fashion after the war but in 1933 he was as big a star in his own way as Marie Tempest was in hers. It would, Binkie decided, be a very good thing to put these two exceptional talents together on the same stage. Mary Newcombe, an expatriate American, had become a star on the strength of her magical performance as a reformed prostitute in a play with the curious title of *The Infinite Shoeblack* in which she had co-starred with Leslie Banks in 1929. In private life she was married to a Lt-Col. Higginson, Master of Hounds in Dorchester, and thus cut a distinguished figure in society. Binkie, the compleat snob, was delighted to include in his company a lady who figured regularly in the glossy magazines at hunt balls, Ascot and Cowes Week. Ann Todd was young, pretty and intelligent, all qualities which were vital to make the young novelist of the play both interesting and plausible. Marie Tempest was notorious for tyrannising the young actresses in her company and turning them into slaves and she would certainly try her various tricks of doing this, but Ann was no beginner: she had ten West End plays behind her and would be able to take care of herself. One of the men's parts was to be played by Robert Donat, a strikingly handsome young actor who was rapidly making a name for himself. Alexander Korda had put him under a three-year contract to London Films, starting him off in two modest low-budget films, *Men of Tomorrow* and *That Night in London*. But their reception had been lukewarm, thus Korda had no immediate plans for him and when Binkie approached Korda to ask for Donat's services for the term of one year Korda was happy to agree. The company was completed by the pleasantly anonymous Ivan Samson, later to become a pillar of the BBC Radio Repertory Company, and a tall, thin, expatriate Russian actor called Boris Ranevsky who played the French butler, Pierre.

Rachel liked them all and happily agreed to their engagement. Binkie wrote to Marie Tempest putting their names to her for approval. It was no more than a gesture of courtesy and they both knew it. Binkie had no intention of changing anybody, but she did not object and rehearsals began at the beginning of February.

There was so much to do, so many decisions to make, so many mistakes to avoid, so many things to learn. There were some surprising gaps in his knowledge. Because of his inexperience he did not realise that scenery required a designer. Because there were only three simple sets required – a balcony in front of French windows, a country-cottage lounge and a small bedroom inset – he assumed that the firm of John Brunskill, who had been building sets for over a century, would use pieces of scenery out of stock and fit them together. And that the Harker brothers would paint them according to verbal instructions from the author. This is exactly what happened. Then he and Rachel Crothers paid a visit to Peter Jones and chose the carpets, curtains, and furniture. All this produced three perfectly satisfactory sets which were very cheap, but it was an odd initiation for one who was later to acquire such a splendid visual sense and to employ some of the greatest, and most expensive, designers in the world. If nobody commented favourably on the sets at least nobody complained and they did not offer any competition or distraction from the acting which was taking place in front of them.

As for the costumes, the three ladies all had their own dressmakers who were happy to supply them with what was required in exchange for a credit in the programme. Binkie did not have to pay for them since it was the custom for a modern play in those far-off days for the company to supply their own clothes. They also received extensive publicity, for this was the era when the public was passionately interested not only in what the star actresses were doing off the stage but in what they were wearing on it. Through the publicity firm of S. T. Hale, he leaked the sort of sartorial gossip which the press lapped up and which also sold the seats:

> Marie Tempest enhances her reputation for chic in her first appearance at a cocktail party. For this she has a two-piece of dress and coatee in yellow and white chiffon, the coatee's cape-sleeves weighted with broad bands of white fox fur. White loose gauntlet gloves, a smart white pochette out of which appears a black lacquered flapjack, and a draped hat of yellow to match the dress, make up a cool and charming ensemble for an elderly lady who has kept both looks and figure . . .
>
> The country clothes for the second act include a trim long tunic of white crêpe for Miss Tempest, the skirt knife-pleated in front. Her large garden hat of white chip straw with its garland of green leaves is becoming and practical. Miss Tempest's negligée in the last act is of the palest blush pink with a silvered leaf design, her sweeping angel sleeves being of silver lace.

Marie Tempest continued to be a figure of extraordinary fascination and glamour to Binkie, and her life-style in work was as uninhibitedly grand and regal as it was out of it. She refused to have anything to do with those bleak, comfortless rehearsal rooms which are the bane of the actor's life. At her request, Binkie booked the Vaudeville Theatre for the month. She would rehearse only in the mornings for two hours and in the evenings for a further two hours. The afternoons were spent at home in Avenue Road resting and gardening. At seven she would return to the theatre with Willie in discreet attendance, wearing one of her most glorious evening gowns and dripping with jewels. She would imperiously require the others to do the same: the gentlemen were expected to rehearse in their white ties and tails though a

By 1933 Binkie had overcome his camera-shyness to the point of visiting Sasha, a well-known society photographer of the period. This is positively the first studio portrait of Binkie. He looks like a fifteen-year-old schoolboy, but is in fact all of twenty-five.

His cousin Betty Gunn, the only surviving member of the family. The likeness is remarkable.

This exquisitely-posed profile is Cecil Beaton's only portrait of Binkie and was taken shortly after the Second World War.

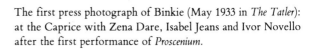
The first press photograph of Binkie (May 1933 in *The Tatler*): at the Caprice with Zena Dare, Isabel Jeans and Ivor Novello after the first performance of *Proscenium*.

Binkie's mother Mary Morgan, whose beauty and style has been elegantly captured in this Cardiff studio portrait.

Binkie's father Morgan Morgan, whose likeness to Lloyd George was the subject of much comment.

Harry Tennent, a rare photograph of a man who was even more retiring than Binkie.

BELOW: An ENSA touring company during the Second World War somewhere in North Africa. On Binkie's right are Beatrice Lillie and Vivien Leigh with an unknown dancer.

dinner-jacket and black tie were *just* acceptable. At nine she would put down her script, put away her spectacles, climb into the Rolls-Royce parked outside the theatre with those members of the company who were in favour, and drive the fifty yards across the Strand to the Savoy Grill for dinner. She had a round table on permanent reservation in the centre. "It's where people can see me," she explained to Binkie who naïvely thought that she might enjoy a little peace and privacy after a hard day's work. "I mean, there's no point in dining out in public if you can't be seen, is there, Binkie dear?"

During the rehearsal month, Owen Nares was appearing at the Apollo in a domestic drama called *Double Harness*. As he was thus unable to rehearse in the evenings his hours were largely restricted to the mornings though he and the others were happy on occasions to rehearse in the afternoon in Marie Tempest's absence. This meant that some of them were working morning, afternoon and evening. In later years, Equity would place strict limitations on rehearsal, but in 1933 actors still worked unlimited hours in the interests of the play and without payment.

Two things were happening to Marie Tempest for the first time: she had never before appeared in a play written by a woman nor had she ever been produced by a woman, let alone the same woman. Neither experience was altogether agreeable to her and with her notorious dislike of women and her total absence of women friends, Binkie did wonder rather nervously if she was going to make trouble. It turned out that he had no cause for alarm. Her version of the Power Game did not include antagonising this new, young manager who was, she was sure, going to be so useful to her in the years to come, and it is quite possible that apart from all thoughts of self-interest, Binkie had succeeded in arousing what little maternal instinct she possessed. He was a dear, sweet boy and she really did want the play to be a success for all their sakes. So she decided to play another part – that of the Star Actress being Gracious and Charming to the Unwelcome Outsider.

"How very nice to meet you, dear Miss Crothers, and may I say what a lovely play this is and how much I am looking forward to playing it. You don't mind if I call you Rachel, do you . . . and you will call me Mary, won't you?" She accepted all instructions and notes without question, treating her with unfailing courtesy. "You wish me to sit on that line, well, of course I will, what a good idea . . . You'd like me to say that line a little quicker and with an upward inflection? Nothing could be easier, my dear."

It was all an act and Binkie knew: sometimes Mary would turn and give him a conspiratorial wink as if to say, "You see how beautifully I can behave when I want to? What they say about me being a

trouble-making old cow is just not true. Aren't you pleased with me?"
Binkie was. Happily, her performance included being very nice and
friendly to the photographers and journalists whom Binkie invited to
the rehearsals.

His first crisis took place at the beginning of March, the final week of
rehearsal. It had nothing to do with Marie Tempest. Robert Donat's
agent telephoned: with discernible and justified embarrassment he
asked whether, even at this late stage, it would be possible to release
him from his contract. Alexander Korda was due to start his new film,
The Private Life of Henry VIII, starring Charles Laughton, and he
badly wanted Robert back for the part of Thomas Culpeper, an
important romantic part in the film.

    Binkie's first instinct was to refuse. If he started making this sort of
concession then all the company would want it and if he did it for one
then he would have to do it for all or undergo charges of favouritism.
Actors must really learn to honour their contracts regardless of the
consequences. Otherwise chaos would rapidly take charge and neither
this nor any other play he presented would ever get to its first night.
But diplomacy told him not to make an immediate decision. A refusal
now would make him unpopular. Better by far to find a scapegoat and
thus deflect whatever anger and disappointment resulted. "I'll have to
consult my partner, Harry Tennent," he said. "And the author. After
all, she is producing the play." Rachel would soon be back in America
and it was one of Binkie's most sensible business principles that the
absent can always be safely blamed.

    An hour later he received another telephone call and this time it was
from Korda himself. Binkie knew all about him just as everybody did
in the profession. A penniless but talented Hungarian who had
suffered ignominious failures in Berlin, Hollywood and Paris to set up
his own film company, he had now gatecrashed the sacred precincts of
the English cinema and had succeeded where everybody else had failed
– in getting money from the City which had previously shown no
interest whatever in the film world and had conceived, with good
reason, a profound distrust of the people who ruled it. Korda had
raised enough money to start London Films and to set up his first film,
The Private Life of Henry VIII. Now he was inviting Binkie to dine
with him that evening. "Just for the pleasure of your company,
Meeztair Beaumont, and to discuss a few liddle unimportant madders
which I zeenk will be of mutual interest, okay . . . ?"

    Binkie was intrigued by the honeyed Hungarian accent (which
Korda knew how to use to his advantage) and flattered by this
approach. He accepted. A Rolls-Royce collected Binkie from his flat

and drove him to Claridge's. The chauffeur took him inside the foyer and presented him to Korda's butler who whisked him up in a private lift to the Penthouse Suite.

This was the Power Game in the Hungarian style and Binkie was greatly amused to see how they played it on the Continent. Dinner included vintage champagne, Beluga caviare, fresh *foie gras* and various Hungarian delicacies unobtainable, so Korda swore, in England – goose-liver pâté and a special goulash with soured cream invented by his mother. The other guests included Korda's brother, Vincent, a painter who was to design the splendid sets for *Henry VIII* and many other Korda films. Binkie never discovered till years later that Korda was completely penniless and that all this splendour was obtained on credit.

No two men could have had so much in common or have been temperamentally so different. Both came from small towns, both had an insatiable ambition, both lusted after power, both were supreme diplomats and accustomed to getting what they wanted. Both enjoyed playing the Power Game and were expert at manipulating other people and their careers. On this occasion Binkie had the advantage because he possessed something Korda wanted and wanted badly enough to lay on this extravagant hospitality. Now *he*, Binkie, was to be manipulated and cajoled; now the charmer from Cardiff was himself to be seduced by the charmer from Turkève. Korda had done his homework well and knew enough of Binkie's background and the steps by which he had climbed to his present position to decide on the right approach. "Zis Donat he eez a pootiful young actor, and ver' talented. *Henry* will be great success, ever'body in it will be beeg star . . . [later events showed this prophecy to be accurate] . . . eet would be great pity to stand in his way . . ." Seeing the doubtful look on Binkie's face he changed gears. "And when he eez beeg star, Mister Beaumont, zen he weel be more useful to you."

"But it will establish a dangerous precedent, Mr Korda, and I don't *really* want to do that . . ."

"Call me Alex."

"Alex, then. I don't want my actors to get the idea that I will release them *merely* because something more attractive has come up. It just *wouldn't* do."

"But Beenkee, I veel make it worth while. You veel not lose. Indeed, I see to it that you gain."

This was Binkie's cue to discuss money. Korda would have to buy Donat's contract and pay a lump sum of a thousand pounds, representing his salary for the run of the play, which Binkie estimated at being one year. If it ran longer he would lose, if it ran for a shorter period then he would have gained. It was a gamble he was willing to take. This was a bargain so hard that even Korda opened his eyes in surprise but he had to agree because he really did want Donat not only for *Henry* but for other films. In addition, Binkie succeeded in extracting a verbal promise that Korda would put money into future productions. Cleverly appealing to the Hungarian's self-interest, he convinced him that if he liked to regard the West End as a nursery and breeding ground for stars who would one day enrich London Films then he should do all in his power to make it as healthy and fruitful as possible. Korda smilingly agreed and was as good as his word, another Hungarian trait.★ He thus became one of Binkie's backers and until the beginning of the war, he put small sums of money into Binkie's plays, enough to qualify for a ticket on the first night – which he never used – and a statement of the weekly returns.†

So it was a coincidence when Donat himself also approached Binkie and nervously asked if he could be released from his contract. He didn't care for the part or the play and had agreed to do it only because he would be working with his much adored Marie Tempest; he was becoming increasingly dissatisfied and discouraged by her, as she believed he was too young and altogether the wrong type, so he was now asking Binkie for the supreme managerial favour.

Binkie, with a convincing show of careful thought and reluctance, agreed. Donat rushed to tell his wife, Ella, and thus a lifelong friendship between Binkie and Donat was sealed. Binkie made Korda and Donat's agent promise never to reveal the truth about the secret negotiations and they never did. For the rest of his life, Donat assumed that it was yet another example of Binkie's famous generosity. He left at the end of the Manchester week and was replaced by Cecil Ramage, a dark-eyed, saturnine, sinister character who later cornered a tiny

---

★ Another trait was a diplomatic indecisiveness. The Hungarians have always found it difficult to make up their minds about anything and to keep their business colleagues and rivals fretting with impatience gives them a distinct advantage. Either Binkie had some Hungarian blood mixed with the Welsh, or the Korda influence was stronger than was thought. By his mastery of indecision he transformed it into an art form. He had his own method of dealing with an agent who was pestering him about a play or an actor under consideration. He would fasten his famous sphinx smile on him. "Well, I won't say *yes* and I won't say *no*," he would purr. "I'll say mmmmmmmmmmmmmmmmm . . ."

† Korda was totally obsessed with the cinema and had no interest in any of the other arts except as source material for more films. Books, music, opera, ballet, even the drama, meant nothing to him. He never went to the theatre to see a play and even when he was given tickets for Vivien Leigh's début at the Ambassadors, in *The Mask of Virtue*, he delayed his arrival until the end, getting there in time for the curtain calls which told him all he needed to know about her.

place in posterity by playing the counsel for the prosecution in the film, *Kind Hearts and Coronets*.

When Ladies Meet opened in Manchester in the middle of March. It was Marie Tempest's first appearance there for ten years. She was a little shaky on her lines but the play went smoothly, the reception at the end was enthusiastic, the notices on Tuesday were uniformly excellent and as it had been sold out long in advance, they played to capacity and grossed £2,000 in the week. It was a good start and an excellent omen for the future.

Binkie's attitude towards publicity was simple. It was all good and he took care to cultivate amicable relations with the press. It was publicity for the play and the company which he wanted, and not for himself. It wasn't that he was shy or timid or diffident, quite the contrary. He just felt that Hugh Beaumont was not a name which meant anything to the public: he did not, unlike Cochran, Bronson Albery or that horribly egocentric Basil Dean, hanker to see his name and photos in the newspapers, and considered that any space given to this would be wasted.

Marie Tempest did not really care for newspaper interviews: she gave them with reluctance and rather bad grace but Binkie persuaded her that it was in the play's and her own interests to be co-operative and thus she was given considerably more press coverage than she had ever had before, much of it being surprisingly candid and revealing. "It is my misfortune to be a *fashionable* actress rather than a *good* one," she said to the *Manchester Guardian*, "and I'm blamed for taking fluffy, empty parts. But I have to take what is offered. Oh, if only I had the chance to play the classics. Lady Macbeth, Gertrude, Beatrice, Volumnia, Lady Bracknell, Mrs Candour."

Binkie had always been amused by the pretence held by fashionable actresses that they were innocent victims of Fate, frustrated at every turn by adverse circumstances, whereas with the power and influence they had they were in a position to do anything they wanted. He had once asked Mary if she would like to go to the Old Vic for a season and play all the parts she claimed to love. She shuddered. "In *Waterloo*?" she asked in tones of unmitigated horror, and he never brought up the subject again. Clearly, though the *idea* of playing the classics was attractive, the *reality* was not.

"Mary dear, try and say something nice about Manchester," he asked her after the play had opened and the reporters were queuing outside the hotel. "People don't often do this and it will make you and the play very popular." Then as now this was not easy but Binkie was full of good ideas, one of which she accepted, doubtless with a cynical smile. "I cannot speak too highly of the *water* in Manchester," she said effusively at the press conference, "It's so good for washing and so good for the complexion. If I had my way, I would take *barrels* of it to London. Oh yes, it is so soft and tastes delicious. I wish all the provincial cities had such beautiful water."

In those days the big Cochran musicals and spectacular revues invariably opened in Manchester for a fortnight and sometimes a month, before making their triumphal entry into the West End. But the straight play, with only a few exceptions, tended to open cold in London after one or maybe two dress-rehearsals. They would tour extensively after the London season had finished but seldom before. To Binkie, this situation seemed absurd. Even though *When Ladies Meet* had only seven in the cast and only three simple sets with barely a dozen light and sound cues, a hundred things could still go wrong, and even if they didn't the company needed time to play themselves in to a smooth running of the play. It is an ancient theatrical truth that however much rehearsal actors have, there is no substitute for performances, and plenty of them, given in front of a paying audience. To Binkie, this seemed to be the most unarguable common sense. From the start of his management career he toured his plays before the London opening and under his influence all other managements did likewise. What started as an intriguing innovation soon became a rule and long before the end of the decade, a cold West End opening of any play of importance was unthinkable.

The company had its followers. Owen Nares was accompanied on the tour by his wife, Marie, a former actress of little talent and no achievement who looked after her husband's financial, domestic and professional interests with a jealousy worthy of a better cause. She stood in the wings watching him closely when he was on the stage and sat with him in the dressing-room when he was not. She had little interest in the play and little love for her husband, but she was obsessively anxious that the girls in the company should not make a nuisance of themselves. Ann Todd was very pretty and attractive, Owen was notoriously susceptible and they shared some charming love scenes . . .

As it happened, Marie Nares had no cause for alarm: Ann Todd was in love with and engaged to the racing driver, Victor Malcolm, grandson of Lillie Langtry; her interest in Owen Nares never went beyond a purely professional regard and friendliness. But the girls in the audience and mostly from the gallery, who had formed various Owen Nares Fan Clubs, had to be kept at a distance. They would queue up outside the stage door with their autograph books held out, they would accost him in the street, they would attempt to gatecrash his hotel bedroom and dressing-room. In Marie Nares' absence

Owen, who was a genuinely kind-hearted man, would have made himself accessible and would have enjoyed his tour all the more. But with his wife watching every movement there was no chance of that. Binkie did not like seeing his leading man hag-ridden: he considered exercising his managerial authority and banning her from the theatre, which he was fully entitled to do, but in the interests of diplomacy he decided that the fewer waves he made the better. Owen did not seem to mind that much and there had been no complaints from the company. So he let the matter stand.

Marie Tempest did not care for Owen's wife, indeed she did not care for any of the wives though she was always scrupulously polite, and as she had her own darling Willie with her she could hardly object to Marie Nares. Willie watched the play from the front every night, sometimes standing at the back with Binkie, sometimes sitting in an empty box. In the interval he would go and sit with his wife in her dressing-room. He was useful because he could keep a lovingly critical eye on her performance and tell her when she was over-acting, the sort of criticism which she would not take from anybody else. "Nobody seems to realise how difficult it is to act comedy," she once said to Binkie, "I need all the help I can get."

The play started to take shape in Manchester, improved in Liverpool and Glasgow, achieving real polish in Edinburgh. Binkie watched the performance every night, usually with Rachel, and spent many evenings over supper with her in the hotel discussing it in minute detail. The scene change in act two was too long and must be cut by a minute; the offstage piano in act one was too loud and must be softened; the cocktail glasses were ugly and distracting, a new set must be found; the sofa in act two blocked the entrance and must be moved to the right to leave the doorway clear . . .

Binkie was greatly amused by the tribalism of the Scottish hoteliers. "So ye're off tae Edinburgh tomorrow mornin'?" said the hall porter at the St Enoch's Hotel, "och awa' they're a load o' bluidy snobs, ye'll wish ye were back here in Glasgie where folk really appreciate what's guid." And in Edinburgh the housekeeper said with great contempt, "So, ye've just come fra' Glasgie, och they're terrible rough and common, them folk, it's only here in Edinburgh that ye get treated like gentlemen an' ladies." Glasgow and Edinburgh are traditionally difficult cities to please: the cultured few have always held a strange love-hatred for English culture and even big names and highly acclaimed plays can be greeted with empty houses. In fact, both cities showed themselves well capable of appreciating the play and its stars and Binkie was pleased to see capacity houses for both weeks.

Everything was now set for the big West End opening and at the

Lyric Theatre at eight-fifteen on April 26th 1933 *When Ladies Meet* got
precisely that. Outwardly, it was no different from the hundreds of
other big opening nights which Binkie had attended. The same queue
of taxis, gleaming Daimlers and shining Rolls-Royces, the extra police
called in to manage the traffic overload, the same queue of titled,
ennobled and society celebrities entering the theatre, the same masses
of fans waiting on the pavement to watch them, the same parade of the
then obligatory white ties, tails, evening gowns and tiaras, the same
marked reluctance of the audience to leave the bar, to stop screaming
and gushing at each other, and take their seats. But this time there was
one big difference for Binkie. Now it was *his* play. And even though
he was officially only a salaried employee of Howard and Wyndham,
the responsibility was all his: he must take whatever blame or credit
resulted from the evening. His future in the theatre depended on
tonight's reception. "I was absolutely *terrified*," he later admitted and
with good reason. "I've never been so frightened in my life." But
nobody could have suspected this from his behaviour that evening.
Standing in the foyer, looking exquisitely elegant in his white tie
and tails, smiling and chattering with those he did not know, shaking
hands and kissing those he did – which seemed to be nearly everybody
– he looked superbly confident.

In the manager's office there was a mountain of greetings telegrams,
good-luck messages, letters, and presents, for it seemed that just about
everybody in London wished him well and wanted the play to be a
success. They came from friends, casual acquaintances, people he had
not seen for years and – most touchingly – from total strangers. But
what Binkie received he also gave. He was anxious that his reputation
for generosity should not be limited to the occasional party and to the
good salaries he paid, so his presents to the company reflected this.
There was a Dresden shepherdess for Marie Tempest, a tobacco jar
and set of pipes for Owen, a leatherbound, gilt-edged book of
Victorian sporting prints for Mary Newcombe. For the rest there
were cuff-links for the men and earrings for the women. "And one of
each for the others?" was Lilian Braithwaite's acid comment. But
there were no others. Binkie's first company of actors was as straight
as a billiard cue. In this ecstasy of goodwill he also gave a bottle of
Bollinger to all the stage-hands and theatre staff, oblivious of the fact
that most of them would have preferred beer. But the gesture was
remembered and appreciated even if the champagne was not.

Stardom has a number of attractive fringe benefits: you occupy the
number one dressing-room which is larger and better appointed than
the others and usually, though by no means always, closer to the stage.
You get star billing on the posters and outside the theatre which means

not only your name above the title but on the left-hand side which, by an inexplicable tradition, carries marginally more status than the right. And if all that wasn't enough, you have a full-page photograph in the front of the programme. The star's photo appears first and then others follow in descending order of importance so it can be seen that the position of your photo in the programme reflects your status in the company. In normal circumstances Marie Tempest's photograph would have appeared first, Owen Nares' second and Mary Newcombe's third but these were not normal circumstances at all, for when the audience settled in their seats and opened their programmes they discovered a truly astonishing break with tradition. The first photograph was Owen Nares, the second Mary Newcombe and Marie Tempest came third. Mary Newcombe taking precedence over Marie Tempest, and Owen Nares taking precedence over them both, when it was usual for the male star gallantly to defer to the ladies, was a situation which caused the gossips of the West End to buzz with excited speculation. Obviously, Binkie had decided to present them in alphabetical order but it could only have been done with Marie Tempest's knowledge and permission, and how in heaven's name had he persuaded her to co-operate in this? "He's got the old woman eating out of his hand; obviously she'll take anything from him," they said. "He's showing her who's boss. Clever, *clever* Binkie. But *how* did he do it?"

He sat with Rachel and Harry in the stage box and suffered further agonies of fear and embarrassment wondering if the audience was watching him instead of the play. They were not. But it was something he never did again. The play went very smoothly, Owen Nares received a loud and long ovation when he was discovered with Ann Todd at the rise of the curtain, and Mary received one which was louder and longer when she made her entrance.

At the end, the curtain calls followed the traditional formula. The company walked on separately in reverse order of status, starting with Boris Ranevsky, then Ivan Samson, then Cecil Ramage followed by Ann Todd and Mary Newcombe. Loud cheers for Owen and finally the long long pause which precedes the star's solo call while the audience lashes itself into a frenzy of expectation. Very slowly she came on, very slowly she walked down to the footlights, very slowly and gracefully she curtsied and extended both hands to the audience as if echoing Irving's declaration, "Your humble, obedient, grateful servant". She rises, turns and joins the line behind her, allowing Owen Nares to kiss her right hand and extending a loving cheek for Mary Newcombe to kiss. Then the company goes off leaving her to take another solo call. Suddenly her little dog rushes on to the stage barking furiously. She tries to push him off but he will not go. She tries again, making stern gestures but still he refuses. With a look of despairing resignation as if to say to the audience, "Well, what *can* I do, he does love me so," she picks him up, making much of him, wagging her finger, "you *naughty* little dog," and smiling lovingly. The audience goes into further raptures. What a wonderful person Marie Tempest was, a great actress and an animal lover and, as well as all that, an irresistibly delightful woman. The whole matter looked like a charming accident but of course it wasn't. The dresser had the dog waiting in the wings. At a sign from his mistress she pushed him on and the dog proceeded, like the born actor he was, to play his part. The whole routine had been as carefully rehearsed as the play itself.

The audience roared and screamed its enthusiasm and there were cries for the author. A speech from the author, or at the very least an appearance on the stage, was a traditional part of the first-night performance and history had been made by those who could, or lamentably couldn't, live up to expectation. Rachel belonged to the latter category. She was no actress and she firmly believed that her place was in front of the footlights and not behind them. Ignoring the applause and Binkie's urging, she stayed firmly in the stage box. The National Anthem was played but the audience was determined that she should do something. There was a tornado of applause and further cries of "Author, author" directed at the stage box and finally she consented to stand up and wave and smile. The National Anthem was played again. Twice in all. Nobody in the Lyric Theatre that night could complain at not getting their money's worth. Then through the pass door with Harry and Rachel and it was around the dressing-rooms where the superlatives fell like golden confetti. The tails and tiaras were lined three deep down the staircase and in the corridors outside the dressing-rooms to pay their respects and drink the champagne.

A first night without a party afterwards was unthinkable; Binkie had taken over the whole of Quaglino's for the company and family, their friends and half theatrical London as well as all the white ties and tiaras who could cadge an invitation and some who did not bother, but Binkie had already learned that you must never be upset by gate-crashers because they are a good-luck omen, indicating that your party is worth their attention. Once again, Binkie was the proud host, chattering and giggling with apparent happiness and confidence to everybody who passed his table. "But I was literally *throbbing* with anxiety," he later confessed, "it was worse, *much* worse than the performance because I couldn't think of anything but those notices which were due out any moment." Waiting up for the notices was, on both sides of the Atlantic, an ancient and positively ghoulish custom which could in a few seconds turn a party into a Coronation if they were good, or a Requiem Mass if they were not. The newspapers were on the street by two in the morning. A messenger on a motorbicycle waited in readiness for a complete set, before whirling them back to Quaglino's to be devoured by those who could get their hands on them first. Binkie's hands were trembling as never before as he turned over their huge, unwieldy pages. Happily, they were all good.

The advance booking took them up to the end of May; there was a long queue outside the theatre when the box office opened and by lunch time Binkie had finalised a ten thousand pound deal with the ticket agencies.

Binkie noted with interest and approval that once the play had opened Marie Tempest displayed a life-style which was almost regal in its regularity and meticulous care. She never went anywhere, did anything or met anybody. Not for her the busy social life, the endless round of luncheon parties, tea parties, cocktail parties and late-night supper parties, the art galleries, the visits to the cinema in the afternoons, the shopping at Harrods with which other fashionable actresses filled those long, empty hours before the evening perform-ance. She stayed at home all day, pottering around in the garden, receiving no visitors, resting in her bed all afternoon and arriving at the theatre two hours in advance for the long, leisurely preparations. It was a regime calculated to preserve her naturally diminishing energies and to keep her fresh for the performance which was, she never stopped insisting, her first priority. She had a lofty and deadly disapproval of anybody who had spent the day in the film studios and kept a watchful eye for any signs of fatigue from other members of the company.

On her arrival, she would strip to the waist and then proceed to powder her breasts. But if Binkie or Harry or Owen wanted to talk to her, she would invite them in. She was not modest or prudish about appearing half-naked in male company and after the first shock, Binkie would enjoy sitting down next to the dressing-table and chatting away while those strong, large breasts danced around in front of his eyes. When she was called on to the stage, the assistant stage-manager led the way with a torch and when she left the stage to return to the dressing-room, he would have to stand ready and available for the same simple service. She always had a little card-table and chair set up behind a screen in the wings so that she could pass the time between entrances in the most pleasurable way she knew.

During that long, hot summer a number of interesting things

happened. Binkie managed to leak them to the press and thus get the fullest publicity out of them. On May 30th Mary celebrated the forty-eighth anniversary of her first appearance on the stage. Photographs of her as a plump-faced soubrette filled the glossy papers, contrasting rather charmingly with the plump-faced dowager she had now become. Binkie gave a party for her and the company at the Ivy. The following month she celebrated her seventieth birthday. Another party, but a small private one for her and Willie at the centre table in the Savoy. In July, Mary Newcombe asked Binkie if she could appear in a one-act play to be presented as part of a double bill at the Ambassadors. "It's a monologue about a woman pleading with her lover, it takes only twenty-three minutes and it's gorgeous and it'll give me plenty of time to get to the Lyric, and I'm not on the stage till nine-thirty . . ." Binkie agreed. The press made a lot of this simple item, for it is not every day that a star appears in two West End plays simultaneously. She received excellent notices and it was observed that the audiences at each play, having seen her in the one, made a pilgrimage the following evening to see her in the other, so both theatres did rather well out of it. "The trouble with being in two plays at the same time," she later said, "is that when you revert to being in only one you do feel terribly out of work."

On July 13th, Binkie had his first royal visit. Queen Mary came to a matinée accompanied by Lady Mary Cambridge, and wearing – as the press was anxious to inform its readers – a mauve and silver brocade dress and a cloak of white velvet. King George V hated books, music, and all the visual and performing arts; the only tune, he frequently asserted, that he could recognise was the Indian Love Call from *Rose Marie*. His wife found it extremely difficult to coax him into a theatre, but when she persuaded him into seeing *Cavalcade* a couple of years earlier, he had reluctantly admitted that he quite enjoyed it. Queen Mary, however, loved the theatre and had always been a great admirer of Marie Tempest, never missing one of her plays for she recognised quite clearly that she was as much royalty in the theatre as Queen Mary was at the Court of St James's. The visit was to be private and unofficial but the necessary arrangements had to be made. Binkie and Harry received her in the foyer, made their bows and escorted her to the stage box while the audience turned and applauded and the orchestra burst into the National Anthem. Afterwards, the two Queens, with Lady Mary Cambridge and Willie in discreet attendance, had tea in the dressing-room and chatted about their domestic affairs. As a result, yet another signed photo of Queen Mary in its obligatory silver frame was to decorate the piano at Avenue Road.

The play did capacity business for the first six weeks. This, Binkie was to learn, is when you get the cream of the theatre-goers, those who love it so much that they will see everything of interest without waiting to hear what their friends have to say. These are the connoisseurs. But if the general public fails to respond then the business will slowly tail off and those ominous pockets of empty seats will appear on the side of the stalls and circle. *When Ladies Meet* was just not good enough a play to attract the general public, who are not primarily interested in a star vehicle, and they stayed away. Binkie had already paid off the production costs and had been in profit since the opening. He had everything to lose and nothing to gain by keeping it on. Three months in 1933 was considered a good, respectable run, not the huge success he would have liked but by no means the failure he hoped to avoid. He put up the obligatory fortnight's notice and the play was withdrawn at the end of July, going on tour for eight lucrative weeks in those provincial towns where the public is more interested in seeing its divinities on the stage, never minding the quality of the play.

The day after it closed, the film version – made in Hollywood the previous year, starring Myrna Loy, Ann Harding, Alice Brady and Frank Morgan – opened at the Empire cinema. Binkie had been warned that the release was imminent and he came to a special understanding with Warner Brothers to hold it back till the West End run had finished, a situation which was to recur endlessly in the future. Obligingly, and not a little surprisingly, they agreed and though Korda always denied it, Binkie suspected that he might have had a hand in this, his first experience of cinema politics. Not that it would have mattered if they had refused. The film was so bad that it would have offered no competition to the company at the Lyric. It was quickly withdrawn, and has since vanished without a trace.

CHAPTER SEVEN

1933

Proscenium

In promising his next play to Binkie, Ivor Novello was as good as his word. This, Binkie noted with great approval, was one of the more attractive aspects of Ivor's character. Even at the height of his fame as actor, writer and composer, he could find the time to extend a friendly hand to somebody at the bottom of the ladder who needed all the help he could get. As soon as he had cast *Fresh Fields* and seen it open at the Criterion in January 1933, for what turned out to be a very successful run of over a year, Novello sat down and wrote the play which had been beating a tattoo in his brain for some months. It was a drama about a beautiful young actor who is playing Romeo in a long-running production of *Romeo and Juliet* in a West End theatre. The young actress who is playing Juliet is in love with him and so is the middle-aged woman who is the manageress of the company and consequently his employer. To complicate matters, this woman some fifteen years earlier had been in love with his father during the last year of the war when he was briefly on leave from the army. Can a man love two women equally and at the same time? This was the burning question raised by the play. It also put forward the not strikingly original idea that theatre people are rather different from ordinary people, and that it is the proscenium arch of a theatre which separates the emotional, false, highly-coloured dramas of the first from the commonplace humdrum life of the second. Ivor had always yearned to write a backstage drama and this was clearly a wish fulfilment in more ways than one.

The cleanly typed script with the stage directions underlined in red ink arrived at Binkie's office at the beginning of April, just as *When Ladies Meet* was starting its tour. It was sent up to Manchester by special messenger and in his suite at the Midlands Hotel Binkie settled down to read it at a single sitting. This had been and would continue to be his sensible custom. He phoned Ivor to thank him, congratulate him and to buy it on behalf of Howard and Wyndham and Moss Empires. Successful management, Binkie quickly realised, was not only quality but also quantity. Continuity was important. Each new production must follow the last with the minimum delay and if plays can overlap each other so much the better. He now had his second play all ready for preparation before the first had finished its pre-London tour. This was a good apprenticeship for the days when he would have a dozen plays in London and on tour simultaneously. "The art of management is to be able to do twenty things at once," he said in an interview and he responded eagerly to the challenge. Titled *Proscenium*, here was a superior woman's magazine story, helped by Ivor's writing which had improved enormously since *The Truth Game*. It was well constructed and whenever the content threatened to become banal and cliché-ridden, the author saved the day with a good joke or a line of witty dialogue. Clearly it promised to be a big success. Binkie, however, noticed with a sinking of the heart that Ivor had included a lengthy scene from *Romeo and Juliet* to form a subplot to the main theme.

Ivor, a frustrated classical actor, had always wanted to play the romantic Shakespearean parts; he intended to do so, somehow, somewhere, sometime. A number of his more sycophantic friends and associates had encouraged him to believe that he could, but Binkie had attended Ivor's private play-readings in his flat and he knew that Shakespeare lay outside his range: to demonstrate this in public could do nothing but harm. It could be argued that his public would support him regardless, but the public can also be horribly fickle and cruel where their idols are concerned. Of course, he would look splendid in the costume and his natural dark looks had a definitely Italian flavour but he could not speak the verse. Nor did it help his cause that John Gielgud had demonstrated at the Old Vic two years earlier how romantic classical acting should look and sound. The *Romeo and Juliet* scene was abandoned.

It wasn't just Ivor's problem; it was one which affected the whole of the profession. Shakespeare just was not popular in the commercial theatre. It was the great actor-managers who had kept Shakespeare alive in the late nineteenth century and up to the war. They lived on him and drew at least eighty per cent of their repertoire from his more popular plays. By 1918 they were either dead or in retirement. Shakespeare became unfashionable for the first time in 300 years and was banished to the provinces, the schools and to a converted Temperance Hall in the Waterloo Road where Lilian Baylis tried, with only partial success, to sell him to her local costermongers and charladies. The fashionable actors and authors of the 1920s and 1930s had no interest in him. Coward, Lonsdale, Maugham, Galsworthy and Novello were the gods of the new realism, and du Maurier, Ronald

Squire, and Coward himself were the apostles of the new, delicate and apparently effortless high comedy. This was the new religion and there was no room for blank verse, heavy make-up and ham acting.

Thanks to Ivor's popularity it was an easy play to cast. "Everybody wants to be in it," said Binkie, when he and Harry met Ivor and Bobbie for a protracted business lunch at the Ivy. "They're just queuing up to play your mother." Zena Dare, a lifelong favourite of both Binkie and Ivor, was finally selected. Ivor's still youthful appearance helped. Although he had just turned forty, he still had that dewy, boyish twenty-one-year-old look and in fact had, only a few years earlier in the 1928 film *Downhill*, played with conviction the part of an eighteen-year-old rugby-playing schoolboy. Binkie cast *Proscenium* in one morning. Fay Compton for the father's former mistress who might or might not have been the boy's real mother (though Ivor cunningly left this point unresolved), pretty, fluffy-haired Joan Barry, leading West End ingenue – as they were then charmingly known – for the actress playing Juliet and a fine collection of character actors and actresses who were, and had always been, the English theatre's pride and joy.

One part remained to be cast. "Who is to play your father?" asked Binkie. "Who is there who is the right age and looks like you and is willing to appear in one short scene of little more than fifteen minutes?" "No problem," said Ivor firmly, "I'll do it myself." Ivor had always wanted to be a character actor and although nobody could have been more narcissistically in love with his own beauty, there were times when he could not wait to get away from it. Putting lines and wrinkles and eyebags on his face, a white wig and a shaggy moustache was not only fun, it showed the world that he was not merely a pretty boy, the idol of every shop-girl in the Home Counties, but also an *actor*.

Proscenium opened on June 14th 1933 at the Globe Theatre in front of an audience which, the press calculated, was eighty per cent female. On this occasion, Binkie watched it all from a gangway seat half-way up the side of the stalls, easy of access and egress. The party afterwards at the Monsignor was given and paid for by Ivor: the *Tatler* published what was probably the first-ever photograph of Binkie to appear in the press. He is at a table with Zena Dare on his right, Isabel Jeans and Ivor on his left. He looks incredibly young and pink-cheeked. He is, in fact, all of twenty-five, but he looks little older than a teenage schoolboy on a parents-day party, wearing his father's dress clothes and keeping rather nervous company with the head prefect, the matron and the headmaster's glamorous wife.

A week later, Ivor suggested to Binkie that if he couldn't have an excerpt from *Romeo and Juliet*, could he at least have a short scene in mime? He and Joan Barry, exquisitely costumed, would go through the motions of the balcony scene with no words but with suitably romantic music. Ivor really had no need to ask permission: as star, author and principal backer he could easily have done what he wanted, but strictly speaking, Binkie was still the manager of the play and his employer, so it was yet another mark of Ivor's courtesy and professionalism that he deferred to Binkie's judgement and was willing to abide by the decision. In fact, he had no cause for alarm. Binkie took the sensible attitude that as he had earlier won a considerable victory the time had now come to be generous. A few days later the mime scene went into the play. Ivor looked gloriously beautiful in his silken tights, jerkin and red Romeo cap which set off his dark, Italianate features to perfection. Some of the press returned to have another look and agreed that it was a good idea, adding a delightful interlude to what was already a well-graced and charming play.

Proscenium was not easy or inexpensive to stage. It had a cast of sixteen and seven changes of set which whirled round smoothly and comfortably on a specially installed revolving platform on the stage floor. But in those halcyon days when actors were cheap, labour plentiful and theatre rents low, a play with these requirements did not alarm theatrical managements. The public enjoyed seeing a well-populated stage and an ever-changing scene, and thus playwrights were positively encouraged to spread themselves and not confine their inspiration to what in a later age became the obligatory one set and a cast of four.

Proscenium was budgeted at £1,625 which in 1933 was regarded as a very high figure (the equivalent in today's money would be two hundred thousand pounds). Ivor put a thousand pounds of his own money, leaving Binkie and Harry to find the other six hundred and twenty-five. In contrast to other authors, Ivor regarded it as positively good luck to back his own plays. He drew a hundred and fifty pounds a week in salary and contented himself with a mere five per cent author's royalty. The rest of the salaries for seventeen actors amounted to three hundred and eighteen pounds a week: fifty each for Zena Dare and Fay Compton, twenty-five for Joan Barry, and salaries of fifteen, ten, six and down to three pounds which was then the agreed Equity minimum for the West End. A glance at the surviving balance sheets indicate that for the week ending July 23rd 1933 the gross receipts were one thousand four hundred and ten, the running costs were twelve hundred and forty-eight and thus it was making a profit of a hundred and sixty-one pounds. In all, during the seven-month run, its profit amounted to over four thousand pounds, enough to pay for four more medium-sized productions. Binkie could reflect that from every point of view it was all very worthwhile.

In the years to come Binkie either presented – or was associated with – a number of Ivor's plays and musicals but *Proscenium* – as he was to say nostalgically at Ivor's death in 1951 – was his favourite. It did, after all, embody and celebrate the one supreme grand passion of his life, his profound and emotional love of the theatre which overwhelmed and eclipsed any love he ever felt for a human being. People died, they departed from your life for one reason or another, they betrayed you or somehow turned out to be a disappointment. The theatre might change colour or shape or structure or style, but it was always there. The theatre never let you down.

For Ivor, love of the theatre went along parallel lines with a deep suspicion and resentment of the cinema, the only popular art form which in his book could be considered a serious rival. He had, admittedly, appeared in a number of films, had quite enjoyed making them and appreciated that much of his fame and popularity was due to them, but he could never take them seriously as an art form. In this ambivalent attitude he showed that, like everybody else, he was not entirely consistent. "I've saved Joan Barry from the cinema," was a rather waspish remark he made to the press shortly before the play opened and in a speech given to the theatre magnate, played with great relish by Keneth Kent, he said: "I believe in the Theatre. I believe that in the Theatre lies a long road back to sanity. I want to give the people a chance to dream again and I want to show them that there is an art beyond the reach of mechanical devices of black and white shadows chasing each other round a white screen." These could have been Binkie's words and in this simple, heartfelt declaration his whole life, work and philosophy are neatly summarised.

Nevertheless when Ivor's recent film, *I Lived with You*, based on his successful play of the same name, had a royal premiere at the late hour of 11 p.m. to allow him to attend, he did so taking the entire company and Binkie with him. And when Norma Shearer and her husband, Irving Thalberg, newly promoted studio head of MGM in Hollywood, arrived in London, saw *Proscenium*, took Binkie and Ivor out to dinner to discuss a possible film to be made with Ivor, and Norma Shearer in the Joan Barry part, Ivor listened attentively and gave his agreement if the right time, money and circumstances could be arranged. Binkie wasn't at all happy at the prospect. As we have seen, he disliked losing his actors to the cinema, particularly a star like Novello, already, he had decided, one of 'his' actors. Ivor's place, he felt strongly, was in the West End, with excursions as far, perhaps, as

Glasgow or Edinburgh, but certainly no further. He had no business wasting his time in Hollywood. He talked to Ivor. Ivor listened. Thalberg's offer was gently but firmly refused and the film of *Proscenium* was never made. Indeed Ivor appeared again in only one other film, *Autumn Crocus,* released in 1935.

The run was not without incident: two members of the cast, Fay Compton and Joan Barry, went to hospital with minor ailments, to be replaced by Madge Titheradge and Ursula Jeans, a favourite of Ivor; then an epidemic of hay fever suddenly swept through the company in the summer causing missed performances and understudy rehearsals.

To celebrate the two hundredth performance on December 7th Ivor gave another party at the Monsignor. Thanks to the handsome profits, Binkie gave the company a week's holiday over Christmas. Never in the memory of the oldest actor in the company had this been done before. "With pay, I suppose?" asked Ivor. "*Without* pay, Ivor dear," replied Binkie. "I'm always pleased to be generous and heaven knows everybody's earned it, but we don't want to go too far, do we?" And so it was. It cost Binkie a week's receipts plus the hire of the theatre and staff salaries amounting to over £1,500, but the return was an immense amount of goodwill which, as Binkie never tired of pointing out, was worth more than rubies and diamonds.

This was the first time that Binkie had worked with Ivor and it marked a subtle change in their relationship. He had started as a young neighbour in Cardiff, became a casual friend in London and now he was Ivor's employer, a situation which never ceased to thrill him. Binkie always looked at him with hero-worshipping eyes as the glamorous and richly talented elder brother (fourteen years older) who could do no wrong. Well, *almost* no wrong. Even at his most wide-eyed Binkie never lost his good sense or his critical capacity. He tried to dissuade Ivor's Shakespearean ambitions and if Ivor sent him a play he disliked, he had no hesitation in refusing it. This is exactly what happened. Ivor was never more fertile and creative than when working full blast, giving eight performances a week, enjoying luncheon, supper and cocktail parties, and all the fringe activities which seemed to be an inseparable part of his stardom. He wrote another comedy with a theatrical theme, *Sunshine Sisters*: an elderly actress and her actress daughter get a job as cook and housemaid in a stately home whose owners are to be kept in ignorance of their former occupation. Binkie gently gave it back. "Sorry, Ivor dear, not this time, I really think not."

One of the good things about Ivor was his total lack of resentment. He decided to present it himself and thus for a brief period he had three plays running simultaneously, *Fresh Fields* still playing to full houses at the Criterion with Lilian Braithwaite, *Proscenium* at the Globe and now *Sunshine Sisters* at the Queens. Two of these were next-door neighbours in Shaftesbury Avenue which led Binkie to say regretfully, "If only *Fresh Fields* were at the Apollo, that would be three theatres in a row showing your plays, then we could rename the street as Novello Avenue." A hat-trick was a very rare occurrence in the West End. Binkie organised a rather elegant little presentation, a large Wedgwood plate with the three titles in letters of gold round the rim and enough space in the centre for the signatures of all in the three companies, also in gold. This was given to Ivor at a midnight party at the Ivy organised and paid for by Binkie.

Sunshine Sisters received poor notices, played to lukewarm houses for a couple of months, surviving Christmas, and was withdrawn just after the New Year 1934. Once again Binkie had been proved right, not that Ivor minded. He was totally without professional jealousy. It merely confirmed Binkie's good sense and judgement, and the wisdom of Ivor's own decision in sending him *Proscenium*. Ivor had an enormous affection and respect for Binkie but this too was not uncritical. Binkie had to prove himself before there could be any serious professional association. Ivor watched Binkie's progress with great care, but after *When Ladies Meet*, it was abundantly clear that Binkie assuredly possessed the impresario's gift.

Proscenium finished at the end of January 1934. Ivor took Bobbie Andrews and Binkie on a Mediterranean cruise. It was Binkie's first foreign holiday. He lazed and laughed in the sun: he swam, speared an octopus at midnight, wandered in the bazaar in Jerusalem, being grossly overcharged by the traders, consumed large quantities of local wine in Cairo, made the routine trips to the Pyramids and the Sphinx which he declared 'madly disappointing', and went, slightly under protest, with Ivor and the party to the Cairo Opera House to see *La Traviata*. But nothing could stop Ivor from working. He spent all one week on the yacht scribbling away furiously. As there was no typewriter on board, Binkie was allowed to read the new play in manuscript. It was a thriller called *Murder in Mayfair* and it was so good that Binkie immediately agreed to buy it and present it in the autumn.

On April 26th 1934, Harry and Binkie had another cause for celebration – the first anniversary of their joint partnership under the Howard and Wyndham banner. It was exactly a year to the day since *When Ladies Meet* had opened at the Lyric, a good year with no less than five productions to their credit, which everybody said was surely a record for a new and young management. There had been *The Wind and the Rain*, a comedy drama by Merton Hodge about medical students in lodgings, their loves and hates, dreams and disappointments and their exams. It had received a Sunday night try-out from the Repertory Players, and Binkie had liked it so much that he bought it on the spot. In common with his usual custom, he recast it entirely, bringing in Celia Johnson whose big beautiful eyes and delicate tinkling voice were neatly counterbalanced by Robert Harris's handsome profile and smoothly modulated baritone. It was largely due to them that the play ran for two years. There was *The Old Folks at Home*, a domestic comedy by H. M. Harwood which again gave Marie Tempest an opportunity to organise other people's lives, this time in a retirement hospital for the elderly, and had a solid five-month run, and in March 1934, a gruesome macabre thriller, *Double Door*, with Sybil Thorndike making commercial capital from her undoubted talent to frighten the public as shown in her famous season of Grand Guignol plays. Although lasting only a month, Binkie and Harry could boast that they had three plays running simultaneously. It was another hat-trick and this time it was Ivor who organised a presentation plate with a gathering of all three companies at the Ivy.

For the first time in his life, Harry opened up his parkside flat for a party. Food was provided by Harrods and champagne by Berry Brothers in St James's. His servant Jennings, wearing his number one army uniform with white gloves, combined the duties of butler, waiter and barman. It was a convivial evening. Marie Tempest sang songs by Schubert and Fauré: Sybil Thorndike, a fine pianist, played Chopin and Scarlatti, Ivor tinkled his way through a couple of waltzes he had written on his Mediterranean holiday, Binkie sat on the piano with a top hat and did a Marlene Dietrich imitation, 'Falling in Love Again', Lewis Casson, with a splendid disregard of what was suitable, recited some Welsh poetry in Welsh and was immediately followed by Owen Nares imitating him reciting Welsh poetry in Welsh and thus revealing a talent for comedy which, alas, the public never saw. Harry was coaxed, with considerable difficulty, to the piano where he sang to his own accompaniment a selection of his smoking-room songs composed for a late-night cabaret while at Oxford, and even Jennings was persuaded to leave the bar and recite one of Kipling's more stirring Barrack-Room Ballads; this, Harry later told Binkie, was a triumph as he had *never* done that before in the presence of glamorous strangers. It was that sort of evening.

Later in the year, Harry Tennent was offered – and took – the post of general manager at Drury Lane; it was one of supreme importance in the West End. The Lane, as it was affectionately known, was in the doldrums and not for the first time in its chequered history. But these doldrums were the worst. Two disasters had followed in quick succession. *The Land of Smiles* started well, as anything by Lehár always did, but the persistent absenteeism of its genial, overweight, popular star, Richard Tauber, cut short its run. This was bad but a musical called *The Three Sisters* was infinitely worse, one of those mistakes which should never have been allowed to happen. It had nothing to do with Chekhov, but the public could well be forgiven for thinking otherwise. The theatre was now closed, eating up money in essential heating, electricity, and staff wages. The future was bleak.

Harry Tennent's brief was to find successful shows, plays or musicals, and restore the Lane to its former glory. But where was he to find them and who was to write and compose them? He was a first-class administrator but he was not an impresario in the good, old-fashioned sense of the word. Left to himself, he would have approached any of those who had written successful musicals – Noël Coward, the team of Vivian Ellis and A. P. Herbert, Herbert Farjeon, versions of Lehár or Straus, but Noël Coward was in New York, the Ellis–Herbert partnership was already contracted to Cochran and all the worthwhile operettas by Lehàr and Straus had been done to death. He lacked the ability to discover new talent or to recognise it, or to arrange for it to work in the right surroundings. Fortunately, he had Binkie to advise him. "Try Ivor Novello," was Binkie's suggestion. Even though Ivor had never written a large-scale musical, Binkie had an instinct about his boyhood friend and idol. His plays showed that he had vision and the playwright's gift and surely anything was possible from the man who had composed 'Keep the Home Fires Burning'. Over lunch at the Ivy, Harry and Ivor came to their agreement: Ivor would write, compose and star in a musical suitable for the wide-open spaces of Drury Lane and the sky was the limit. It is now a matter of history that he did this not merely once but three times. *Glamorous Night*, *Careless Rapture* and *Crest of the Wave* were all spectacularly successful. The Lane's fortunes were restored and Ivor thus carved a new and exciting career for himself which was to last until his death in 1951.

CHAPTER EIGHT

1934

The Winding Journey – Moonlight is Silver

Binkie's reputation was increasing rapidly.★ The word was rapidly spreading around the West End that not only was Binkie the youngest of the London managers but also the cleverest, the most resourceful and the most delightful. And if all that wasn't enough, he had a special interest in women, particularly if they were beautiful and glamorous. Everybody knew that the theatre is basically a man's world with all the best parts written for men and that suitable modern parts for women are difficult to find, particularly if they happen to be middle-aged or elderly. Binkie was the one person who was both willing and capable of redressing the balance; he had a remarkable talent for finding the right parts in the right plays. Marie Tempest, Sybil Thorndike, Zena Dare, Fay Compton and Celia Johnson, to name only five, already had good reason to be grateful to him. 'A ladies' man' was not quite the phrase which came readily to mind when Binkie was the subject of conversation, though in another sense it was an accurate description. So it seemed only natural, when Gertrude Lawrence found herself temporarily unemployed after her six-month run in the Cole Porter musical, *Nymph Errant*, at the Adelphi, that she should approach Binkie.

They had known each other since the original *Private Lives* at the Phoenix in 1930. Gertie, as she liked to be called, had taken a great liking to him and had included him in many of her parties. Needless to say, Binkie adored her in return. "Nobody realised until they met her that she was just as fascinating off the stage as she was on it," he said. "She had a radiance which lit up like a lighthouse whenever she appeared. You couldn't take your eyes off her, she glittered and sparkled like a Christmas tree. She never gave the same performance twice and sometimes she could be very naughty and irresponsible, but at her best she was sheer magic and there was nobody – not even darling Tallulah – who could give you the same thrill."

★ "Who is this Bunkie, or Bonkie, or Bankie?" Robert Atkins was heard to snarl in the Green Room Club one day.

The analogy with Tallulah Bankhead was apt: the two ladies had much in common and there were some interesting parallels in their lives and careers. Both were possessed of a unique comic talent which they failed to take seriously and which they could destroy by unprofessional behaviour: both were capable of giving a superb performance on one night and a terrible one on the next. Both failed lamentably to transfer their quality to the screen, for the few films made give only tantalisingly brief glimpses of their enchantment. Both collected aristocratic Englishmen as some people collect penny blacks or first editions and both had a marked liking for beautiful, androgynous young men. Gertie had the advantage in that she could sing and dance – after a fashion but it was a fashion which was very much to the public's taste – whereas Tallulah could be an impressive dramatic actress when the right part and right director were simultaneously available as they were in Lillian Hellman's *The Little Foxes*.

Nymph Errant, with its twenty costume changes, eight numbers, four dance routines and its endless running around, plus the responsibility of carrying a show whose failure would plunge a great many people into unemployment, had been exhausting. What she now wanted was a nice little comedy with one set and a small cast, something simple and easy which she could do without killing herself every night. By a coincidence, Binkie had received only that week a new play which offered Gertie just such an opportunity. The author, Philip Leaver, a podgy-faced character actor, had carved a useful apprenticeship in the provinces and the fringe of the West End playing fast-talking, shifty-eyed, over-ebullient foreigners. His career had taken a fresh turn in 1932 when he started writing plays and had two presented in the West End in consecutive weeks. Neither had run for more than a few weeks. But he had made his mark and Binkie had lost no time in contacting him and commissioning a new play. This latest was a light marital comedy about a bride and groom discovering on their wedding morning that each had been involved in a pre-marital affair. Binkie liked it very much.

Gertie also offered the services of a leading actor with whom she wished to co-star. This was Douglas Fairbanks Junior, her latest in a long line of lovers. Most of them had possessed either a title or wealth but Doug – as he liked to be known – had neither: thirteen years later he achieved both, an honorary knighthood for services to England during the war, and a million of money by shrewdly placed TV and property investments. But in 1934 he was merely famous and very attractive. He was tall, slim and good-looking with much of his father's charm and vitality as well as his famous name. He had made a dozen little-known, undistinguished films, which had laid the foundations for what he was the first to admit was only a moderately successful film career.

Binkie took Gertie and Doug to lunch at the Savoy Grill and enjoyed the flurry of attention which they caused. The Savoy regulars were used to having celebrities in their midst but it wasn't every day that two such beautiful people were seen together. It was an idyllic meal. They were clearly head over heels in love with each other and it was quite obvious from her conversation that she wanted a theatrical as well as a domestic partnership. What she had in mind was a man-and-wife acting team which could rival Alfred Lunt and Lynn Fontanne whose superlative talents and shrewd choice of material had given them a huge and adoring public on both sides of the Atlantic. The Lunts were, at that very moment, playing to capacity houses at the Lyric with *Reunion in Vienna* which Gertie and Doug had seen on the first night.*

The possibility of a long-term partnership between Gertie and Doug was exciting and full of possibilities, but Binkie knew that to succeed it was necessary not only to have the right plays which gave good parts of equal value to both, but plenty of them. This new play by Philip Leaver which had no title as yet could comfortably inaugurate a new era. But who was to produce? It needed somebody rather special, for Gertie had a marked tendency to overact and spoil her best effects, while Doug, like so many film actors then as now, had enjoyed limited stage experience: a little summer stock in America and two tours, *Young Woodley*, when he had been a schoolboy, and the Leslie Banks part in *The Man in Possession* the previous year.

It was Sybil Thorndike who suggested Lewis Casson. "Darling Binkie, Lewis is *marvellous* at dealing with temperamental actresses, he'll take care of Gertie, don't you worry. And he is better than anybody I know at getting performances out of students and beginners which, bless him, is what Doug really is." Lewis read the play and had grave reservations but Binkie urged him to accept, promising that the author would do any rewriting necessary on the tour and that with Doug and Gertie the play – indeed, any play – could hardly fail.

It went into rehearsal in April. The preliminary press announcements merely stated that Gertrude Lawrence and Douglas Fairbanks Junior would be co-starring in a new play as yet untitled by an author who wished to remain anonymous which caused – as Binkie shrewdly

---

* Years later, Binkie asked Alfred Lunt how he and Lynn had coped with the Great Depression when theatres were going bankrupt, closing overnight, and thousands of good actors were out of work and on the breadline. "We played *The Guardsman* for a year on Broadway and two years on tour," he said. "We had full houses everywhere and made ourselves a fucking fortune."

intended – a great deal of excited speculation. "You'll find that Gertie can be a real handful," Binkie warned his fellow-Welshman, "but don't stand any nonsense from her." But the real difficulty came with Doug and many times in the early weeks Lewis Casson would drop into Binkie's office to report progress. "He hasn't got any technique," he said, "he hasn't got any voice, it's weak and inaudible, he can't move, he doesn't know what to do with his hands; one moment they're behind his back, the next they're clasped in front of his flies. Then he folds them across his chest and a minute later they're in his pockets. He's just like a drama student. He looks marvellous, heaven knows, but he sounds so boring."

Binkie would always listen sympathetically. "Do what you can, Lewis dear. I want you to look on this as a *challenge.*"

The author finally decided on a title and *The Winding Journey* by Philip Leaver opened its provincial tour at the Theatre Royal, Bradford, still in 1934 a Number One touring date. Houses were full and the notices were, predictably, raves for Doug and Gertie and indifferent for the play. But a nagging suspicion that it was not good enough was fully confirmed by the time they arrived in Manchester. Gertie's initial enthusiasm for the play came to be severely tested when she started to work on it and now she was overacting most horribly, pulling out every trick from her repertoire and grimacing like a gargoyle. Lewis had been able to smooth some of the rougher edges of Doug's technique but the performance was still flat and dull. Trainloads of their fans, including half *Burke* and *Debrett*, travelled up to Manchester for the opening at the Opera House, filled the Midlands Hotel afterwards and tried to convince them that they had a success on their hands. Binkie knew better. As it stood – and the notices the next day confirmed it – it was not nearly good enough to come into the West End.

There was only one thing to be done and he did it. He sent an SOS to Clemence Dane.

Born Winifred Ashton and known as Winnie to her many friends, Clemence Dane was a leading figure in London's literary and theatrical community. She had written many popular novels including one best-seller, *Broome Stages*, a saga of epic dimensions about a Victorian theatrical family: her plays had always aroused great interest and one, *A Bill for Divorcement*, which had made a star out of the exquisite but tragically short-lived Meggie Albanesi, had enjoyed a spectacular success all over the world and had ended up in Hollywood being filmed with John Barrymore. She was also a painter and a sculptor. But her greatest talent was for friendship. In her crumbling little house in Tavistock Street, Covent Garden, she held court to a colourful circle of authors, poets, playwrights, musicians, painters and film producers, thus giving London in the thirties and forties its only real artistic salon. In her cheerfully cluttered spacious drawing-room overlooking the market there were musical evenings, poetry recitals, play-readings, film conferences, and endless fascinating talk augmented by quantities of delicious food prepared by Olwen, her devoted secretary and companion with whom Winnie shared her house and her life. It was so much more fun than the Bloomsbury Set, they said, those wealthy, titled charlatans who took themselves so seriously but never actually achieved anything. Winifred's circle laughed at everybody and everything and actually got things done. Plays were written, novels completed, poems published, paintings finished and production deals finalised. Winifred's friends were real artists. They didn't just talk about doing it, they *did* it.

Winnie was the most lovable woman Binkie had ever met. She was large with no pretensions to beauty or chic but she had enormous charm, unquenchable vitality, shining eyes and a radiant smile, so who cared? She was warm-hearted, extravagantly generous and always happy to help and advise him, introducing him to an actor or actress he wished to meet, recommending a new play, advising him on his productions or offering consolation when a love affair was not running smoothly. She was, and continued to be, the mother he had never had and it was not until their friendship started that he realised what he had been missing. He was introduced to her by Val Gielgud, then the recently appointed head of radio drama at the BBC, and it was in her house that he first met Alfred Lunt and Lynn Fontanne, heard Constant Lambert thunder out his new ballet score, *Rio Grande*, listened to Gabriel Pascal boast just how he had persuaded the reluctant Bernard Shaw to part with the film rights of *Pygmalion* and witnessed a splendid row between Hannen Swaffer and Lord Berners who had taken passionate objection to remarks made by the journalist in a recent notice of his latest ballet, *Wedding Bouquet*.

"You are the Lady Blessington and Madame de Sevigné of Covent Garden," Binkie said to her. She was delighted by this shrewd and flattering comment and quoted it widely in the circle. Later, Binkie was honest enough to admit to Val Gielgud that it represented not his own original ideas but those of Michael Sadleir whom he'd met at a party and whose book about the Blessingtons had just been published to great acclaim. "I had no idea who either of them were," he giggled, "so I had to go to the library and enquire. But I think it's very true." A reputation for wit did Binkie no harm, but, as he discovered, it is rather difficult to live up to.

Winifred responded to the urgent message with commendable

speed, immediately travelling up to Manchester and seeing the Tuesday night performance, followed by a summit conference at the Midlands Hotel over supper with Gertie, Doug and Harry Tennent. "Winnie dear, the author has rather lost interest in the play," explained Binkie. "He says he doesn't like rewriting; when he's finished a play, that's it. So he's given me *carte blanche* to do what I think best. Can you do anything for it?"

"As it stands, Binkie darling, it just isn't good enough for the West End and to make it so would involve rewriting it completely. If I'm going to devote time and trouble to it I might as well write a new one specially for Gertie and Doug. I have got an idea which might suit."

And so it was. Binkie accepted the situation, put up the notice and after its fortnight in Manchester, *The Winding Journey* was quietly forgotten. It has never been published or performed since and the only copy of the original typescript lies in the vaults of the British Library.

Winifred did not let him down. Always good in a crisis or an emergency, she was a quick worker and the new play was ready a month later, tentatively titled *The Ring of Truth*, and then, *Here Lies Truth*. It was a charming light comedy of marital misunderstanding about an engineer who returns home after a business trip in America to be told that his glamorous wife has been having an affair with their wealthy neighbour, to the glee of his play-writing brother who regards the matter as excellent material for a new play. The wife mischievously decides to give the husband cause for jealousy even though she is totally innocent. After a series of splendid family rows, everything ends happily. Binkie rose early and read it in his bath, a habit which was to last all his life.

Once again he had to find a producer to cope with Gertie and Doug. Definitely not Lewis Casson whom he privately blamed for the failure of *The Winding Journey*. Binkie had not wanted him in the first place: he did not really like him, and had engaged him only because he wanted to oblige Sybil. Lewis had hinted that he was available and interested, but Binkie would throughout his career rarely give second chances to those who had either offended or disappointed him. The matter was eventually decided for him when Winifred announced that she would like to produce the play herself. She was not without some practical experience of the theatre, having assisted Basil Dean in the production of her three earlier plays. Like Rachel Crothers with whom she had much in common, she believed that she knew best what was good for her plays. Binkie was a little worried that Gertie might object: Gertie had little time for her own sex and had never been produced by a woman, let alone acted in a play by one, but it was a false alarm. Gertie was an old friend of Winnie's, and declared herself delighted by the arrangement.

Happily, there were no casting problems. As with *Proscenium*, everybody wanted to be in it and enticing lists of those eager to appear with Gertie and Doug arrived daily from the agents. Gertie's mother in the play was clearly another Marie Tempest part, which Binkie offered to her as if by divine right, but she declared herself not entirely happy to be Gertie's mother, to share the stage with her for long periods of time and to take second place on the billing and the dressing-room allocation. She too had no great love for other women, privately or professionally, and although she would never have accepted Gertie as an equal she did acknowledge her as a possible rival.

In her absence he offered the part to Helen Haye who, alas, was quite accustomed to getting Mary's rejects, being generally regarded as a poor man's Tempest. Martita Hunt, Barry Jones and Cecil Parker comfortably filled the other principal parts. The rehearsals started at the Globe at the beginning of August and took place in an atmosphere of extreme cordiality and mutual esteem. "Miss Lawrence works much harder than I do," gushed Winifred to the *Daily Mail*. "The way she throws herself into a part and slaves at it is new to me. And her patience and brilliant good temper!"

"I spoke to Miss Lawrence as she emerged from the rehearsal with Mr Fairbanks," said the *Daily Express*. "'I adore working with Clemence Dane,' she told me, 'she is so thoughtful and considerate and she understands an actress's problems. Unlike some producers she doesn't expect you to know every word by the end of the first week,' and off she went with Mr Fairbanks for a cosy lunch at the Ivy."

Here Lies Truth opened its pre-London tour in Bournemouth at the end of August. It was a thoroughly dispiriting evening for Binkie. Admittedly, the house was full with a queue of hopefuls waiting for returns, the applause at the end was enthusiastic with seven curtain calls and the audience managed to give the distinct impression that it had enjoyed itself, but he knew that it wasn't good enough. Production and performances were all terrible. It was quite evident to him that the company had taken shameless advantage of his apparent youth and Winifred's directorial inexperience to give a lot less than their best: Gertie was obviously exploiting their friendship in the belief that she could get away with anything. He sat in the bar during the second interval chatting away to the theatre manager and the local press, presenting a plausible façade of smiling confidence and ease but inwardly he was furious. They would never *dare* behave like that if he had been Basil Dean or Komisarjevsky or Bronson Albery or Charles Cochran; but because he was only twenty-six and looked much younger, because he had only a year and a half of practical managerial experience, they had decided to treat him like an office-boy. Binkie was inflexible in his resolve that nobody should patronise him. Something had to be done – and quickly.

As he was to show many times in the years to come, Binkie was at his best in a crisis. He took the company and Winnie out to supper at the local sea-front restaurant. Champagne encouraged laughter and reminiscence and Binkie listened, smilingly courteous, while the company chattered with more than a touch of complacency about the performance and how successful it had been. "Went rather well, I thought," said Gertie. "Not bad at all," said Barry Jones. "They loved it," from Doug and "I think we're on to a winner," from Martita Hunt. Binkie's smile was never more radiant, his eyes never more shining than when he was angry. Here was a time bomb waiting to explode. To an outsider it seemed as cheerful and bright as a hundredth performance party, but when they reached the coffee and liqueurs, Binkie started to talk about the play and very gently to pull them all to pieces . . . Gertie had fluffed and stumbled a few times, she had taken a number of rather audible prompts and the whole performance had a certain . . . er . . . er . . . *hesitancy*: it might not be a bad idea to have another look at the script tonight before she went to sleep . . . Doug, he thought, seemed a bit awkward on the stage, he still had a tendency to keep his hands in his pockets, could he possibly try to relax a bit? It might help if he had his pockets sewn up . . . Helen's voice was just the *teensiest* bit difficult to hear, she tended to drop the voice at the end of the line and it was just on the brink of being inaudible . . . Martita had a slight tendency to rush her speeches and to tread on other people's lines which made things a bit untidy, almost *ragged* . . . Dear Cecil had missed some good laughs by mistiming and the business with the telephone wire wasn't going to work unless it was properly synchronised with the dialogue . . . Darling Winnie's production was just a bit static; it seemed to Binkie that a lot of people were standing around an awful lot of the time and it was all rather *conventional*. Perhaps she could devise some patterns of movement which would brighten it up . . . The third act needed tightening and the second sagged a bit in the middle; Binkie noticed that the audience seemed to be losing interest, perhaps darling Winnie could do some rewriting. All these criticisms were accurate and perceptive.

"I'll do some rewriting with pleasure, Binkie dear," said Winnie. "I'll have them by the end of the week."

"By *tomorrow morning*, Winnie dear, even if it means staying up all night. That is what pre-London tours are for. But I'll stay up with you with pleasure, if you like."

"Anything you say, darling."

A suitably chastened company returned to their hotel in a couple of taxis paid for by Binkie. "The boy's quite right," said Cecil Parker. "I don't think you should call him a boy any more," said Helen Haye, "he's no fool. It's the classic case of the old head on young shoulders." Barry Jones snorted impatiently, "He gives me the bloody creeps."

"Now, my darlings, I'm calling a rehearsal for ten o'clock tomorrow morning and we'll work on it right through till five and I'm sure you will all be astonished by the improvement." Binkie had just rejoined them after a word with the stage manager. "Good night and sleep well."

It wasn't every day that a young impresario could take seven people of high theatrical distinction, many old enough to be his father or mother, admonish them severely and send them all to bed but it was all done with such tact and exquisite humour that nobody was offended. To quote Tyrone Guthrie's famous comment, the iron fist was wrapped in many layers of velvet glove but nobody who was present could doubt for a second that the iron fist was there. It was a formidable display of authority combined with diplomacy and Winnie was deeply impressed. Nothing of the affair appeared in the papers but Winnie was a born gossip and lost no chance of spreading the word so that by the time the play reached London all the West End knew about it. It did Binkie's reputation no harm whatsoever.

Binkie's remedial work and Winnie's extensive rewriting had the desired effect. She managed to find an alternative title, even slushier than the first, and *Moonlight is Silver* opened at the Queen's Theatre on September 13th 1934. The notices were ecstatic and it seemed to be set for a good long run. The promotional and publicity opportunities were better than usual with those two stars and Binkie took them all with enthusiasm and a skilful awareness of how to manage the press.

It did no harm at all that the public knew that Gertie and Doug were lovers and hardly a day passed without a photo of them together, opening bazaars, attending charity balls and first-night parties, punting on the Thames, recording a four-minute scene from the play at the HMV studios, feeding the swans in St James's Park or serving teas at the annual theatrical garden party. When news was slack, Binkie used the classic method of artificially creating it – inventing a rumour and then denying it. "Douglas Fairbanks to seek English citizenship" announced the press one day to be followed on the next by "'Not true,' said Douglas Fairbanks as he came to the theatre, 'I am an American and I intend to stay that way.'"

It also did no harm that they should occasionally have a full-blooded row. Inspired by the most generous of motives, Doug arranged for the diamond bracelet, ear-rings and necklace worn by Gertie in the second act to be sneaked out of her dressing-room, taken to a Bond Street jewellers and real diamonds substituted. Gertie wore them for a whole week, unsuspecting, before Doug told her the truth. Instead of being pleased she was furious. She took them up, threw them at him with a scream of anger and ordered him out of her dressing-room. It is doubtful if he had ever been so astonished and flabbergasted in his life by this unpredictable feminine reaction.

"What's the matter, Binkie, what have I done?"

"She's very superstitious, Doug dear. Didn't you know that it is considered very unlucky to wear real jewels on the stage? My advice is to go to Gertie and apologise. Take a set of false diamonds for the play and give her the real ones for offstage. I think you'll find that this will please her mightily."

It did.

Moonlight is Silver looked set for a long run, but fate and Gertie's doctor had other ideas. In November she started to complain of giddiness and dizzy fits, probably due to the malnutrition caused by the excessive dieting in the interests of beauty. Armed with a certificate from her doctor she went into a nursing home. Her understudy was a young actress, Elizabeth Corcorane. Normally, managements keep very quiet when the star is temporarily absent: apart from a typed notice outside the box-office window or a small printed slip in the programme, nothing is said in order not to discourage the public from buying tickets. Binkie did the opposite. He arranged for a big splash of headline and pictorial publicity. "Miss Corcorane is beautiful, lustrous, and with a stately carriage," as the *Daily Express* rather quaintly put it. "Last night she gave a superb performance at short notice and had the audience cheering loudly at the end." STANDING OVATION FOR ELIZABETH CORCORANE . . . STAR OVERNIGHT . . . FAIRYTALE DREAM COMES TRUE FOR DORSET UNKNOWN. Once again, Binkie's motives were misunderstood: it was widely assumed that he was being generous to the girl, but the truth was rather different. He was not altogether convinced that Gertie was as ill as she said. If that was so, then nothing would more speedily bring her rushing back to the theatre than the knowledge that her understudy was enjoying a big success in her absence. Binkie's devious handling of the situation paid rich dividends. Gertie missed only three performances. But the following month, something considerably more serious cropped up. Gertie began to suffer from an abscess in her right ear. Binkie arranged for his own doctor to examine her, and he confirmed the original diagnosis. Gertie returned to the nursing home, the abscess was cured and she also put on weight to the general improvement of her health. GERTRUDE LAWRENCE GAINS SIX POUNDS made an intriguing headline.

At this period in her career Gertie was literally irreplaceable and without her the play had little appeal to the public, even with the stately and lustrous Miss Corcorane ready and willing to fill the gap. With great reluctance Binkie was compelled to withdraw it after a run of only ten weeks.

Shortly afterwards, three things happened, all of far-reaching importance. Binkie introduced Winifred to Irving Thalberg, who looked in to see the play and immediately invited her to Hollywood to adapt *Anna Karenina* for Greta Garbo. This did her career a lot of good. Gertie and Doug played Mimi and Rodolpho in a rather pedestrian film version of *La Bohème* without music, which was indifferently received, and did their careers no good at all. It was probably in the long run the cause of their affair coming to a premature end.

And Binkie met Tyrone Guthrie.

CHAPTER NINE

1934–5

Sweet Aloes – Hervey House

At six feet and five inches, Tyrone Guthrie, both literally as well as figuratively towered above his contemporaries. He was a true virtuoso, a pioneer filled with missionary zeal, just as happy directing unknowns in a tent in Canada as big stars at the Haymarket, just as skilled and resourceful with three actors in a small set as with 500 on a vast open stage. His visible assets included passionate enthusiasm, unlimited imagination and a wide assortment of technical skills. He could act,★ he could write plays, he could design sets and costumes, he understood the financial and contractual complexities of play presentation and theatre ownership. And if all that wasn't enough he was a superb diplomat. Not only did he coax Charles Laughton into abandoning Hollywood at a thousand dollars a week to return to the Old Vic at twenty pounds, he also succeeded in the considerably more difficult task of persuading a suspicious and resentful Lilian Baylis that employing a star of international fame was a Good Thing. The financial and artistic success of the season seemed to justify his advice.

Guthrie was the Compleat Theatre Man and if he had gone into management he would assuredly have rivalled, if not overshadowed, Binkie. But he had no such ambitions: the day-to-day administration of a successful play and the running of an office would have bored him to distraction. He preferred to travel the world, directing a play here, a pageant there, opening a new theatre somewhere else, always on the go and never staying in one place for long. More than most of his rivals, he could be truthfully described as one of Nature's gipsies. Yet

---

★ He appeared briefly in the film *St Martin's Lane* (1938), a colourful slice of London life written by Clemence Dane and produced by Charles Laughton while they were still great friends, not a situation which lasted long, alas. Despite the combination of three major talents, Laughton in his prime, Rex Harrison and Vivien Leigh in, admittedly, embryo, it was Guthrie's show-stealing cameo as a very camp busker dancing to his own harmonica – an exquisite gem, wildly funny and tinged with sadness – which is the best reason for seeing it. It is the only surviving record of a uniquely eccentric comic talent.

the two men had much in common. Both rose above their origins – Guthrie, who was brought up in Belfast, had nearly got rid of his Ulster accent though a touch remained all his life lending extra colour and charm even to his least utterances. Both chain-smoked furiously, both were compulsive talkers and good listeners. Guthrie, a wit and fine raconteur, had a wicked sense of humour and, like Binkie, enjoyed giggling and gossiping for hours on end. He could make Binkie laugh. In short, he was *fun*, and in his company Binkie could relax and enjoy himself as he could with no other person, with the possible exception of his beloved John Gielgud.

"In 1934 he called me to his office," wrote Guthrie in his memoirs. "At that time I had heard his name but knew very little about him. What I met was a very slight, fair young man with a glib line of fashionable expressions and a pair of very shrewd, watchful grey eyes. His talk of the forthcoming project was amusing, human, unpretentious and extremely commercial. I liked him very much."

By 'extremely commercial' Guthrie meant a cosy little drawing-room play with two simple sets and a cast of thirteen. ("My lucky number, Tony dear," purred Binkie.) *Sweet Aloes* was a woman's play in the best, most complete sense of that much-abused phrase, written by a woman, about women and dealing with specifically women's problems. Linda, a nice, respectable young girl, living with her aunt in the Home Counties, has an affair with the son of the local baronet. The son is heir to his father's title and fortune and married to an invalid who cannot have children. Linda finds herself pregnant and agrees to sell the baby to her lover in return for a substantial financial settlement and a new life in New York where she finds true love with a nice, unsuspecting American businessman. Five years later both couples meet again, but the truth about the baby is effectively concealed (shades of *Lady Windermere's Fan*?) and everybody lives happily ever after. With adultery, illegitimacy and a form of surrogate motherhood as its themes it was a play considerably in advance of its time and it might have been censored by the all-powerful Lord Chamberlain, but its charm, humour and delicate pathos, its skilful stagecraft and well-drawn characters robbed it of all offence.

The author was Jay Mallory, described by the press as "a wealthy, elderly English lady currently living alone in New York", but it was an open secret in the West End that it had been written by Joyce Carey, the actress daughter of Dame Lilian Braithwaite. It was her first play.

Binkie took Guthrie to Verrey's, the first of many business lunches they were to enjoy. Verrey's continued to be his office extension during the early thirties: he was such a familiar figure that a table was always kept reserved for him. Lilian Braithwaite, in a passing taxi, just happened to catch sight of them as they walked down Piccadilly: Guthrie taking his usual giant strides and Binkie trotting quickly behind him, only just able to keep up. "It was," she remarked, "like seeing a pekinese rushing to pee against a mobile lamp-post."

"Who's going to play Linda?" was Guthrie's first question as they settled happily into their tomato soup and roast beef.

"Diana Wynyard. She's the only one and she's *gorgeous*."

She was already one of Binkie's favourite actresses. She had a delicate beauty which, however hard the press tried to avoid the cliché, they invariably likened to an English rose. She had a quiet dignity and elegance, qualities which admirably qualified her for the long portrait gallery of Englishwomen under stress. Like Flora Robson, she could suffer with exquisite poignancy, but unlike her it was not nervous, frustrated spinsters but long-suffering and persecuted wives. She had come to Binkie's attention in *Lean Harvest* where she had been cruelly neglected by Leslie Banks' power-crazy millionaire, and made a much greater impression with her unhappy Charlotte Brontë in *Wild Decembers*. She had done a year's hard labour in Hollywood, as Clive Brook's wife in a very good film version of *Cavalcade*, Mrs Patrick Campbell's niece in a passable film, *One More River*, from the Galsworthy novel, *Over the River*, and Ethel Barrymore's daughter in *Rasputin and the Empress*, which to everyone's surprise turned out to be indescribably terrible. Now she was back in London, firmly refusing all film offers,★ anxious to return to the comparative sanity of the theatre and all set to be a big star.

Guthrie wrote of meeting her at another lunch in Verrey's. "She was even more beautiful than her photographs and with a sensible, straightforward manner delightfully at odds with all the glamorous publicity she was getting." She also had another quality known only to her friends: she was a superb comedienne. It is not given to every English rose to imitate Ethel, John and Lionel Barrymore, concurrently and consecutively, having a blazing row on the set, and to throw in Mrs Patrick Campbell as well, but she did, and she had Binkie and Guthrie roaring with delight.

Years later, Guthrie recalled only one point on which he and Binkie were not in total agreement: Joyce Carey's desire to appear in her own play as Lady Farrington, the invalid wife who becomes the mother of the adopted child. Although a comparatively small part (appearing only in the last act), it was full of wit and sympathy and Joyce had

★ She had dozens, the most attractive being to co-star with George Arliss in *Wellington*. The part was offered around and was finally taken by Gladys Cooper who gave a very tense and chilly performance in what was her screen début. The film was not a success.

written it especially for herself. Binkie wasn't at all keen on having the author in the company. "It creates embarrassment, Tony dear. The company will find that they can't speak candidly about the play and they'll all be nervously watching her, wondering what she's thinking. An author makes trouble, and if she's in the company she can make it better than one who isn't. Take my advice and keep the author out of the theatre."

But Guthrie would not tolerate such nonsense. "You wouldn't say that if it were Noël Coward, would you, Binkie, my dear? Authors don't make trouble if they are genuine theatre people. Joyce has been in the profession for many years, she is a fine actress and popular with her colleagues. Also, I'll need to consult her about changes and cuts and rewrites: she might well accept another offer, so the only way to guarantee that she's there when I need her is for her to be in it."

These were powerful arguments. Binkie knew well that the final word on casting should lie with the producer who, after all, did have to work with the company. Binkie could be very firm but Guthrie could be very persuasive. Binkie finally relented and Joyce Carey was formally invited to play Lady Farrington.

Even after eight productions in two years, Binkie still had plenty to learn about management. Once again, he did not think to engage a designer and the sets had to be sketched out by Guthrie on the backs of envelopes and delivered to the carpenters. They both went to Selfridges to choose the furniture and fittings and watched while a little woman whom Guthrie knew stitched on slip covers and made cushions. This rather haphazard system seemed to work because none of the critics complained and audiences were not as design conscious in the thirties as they were later to become. But now Binkie made a curious error of judgement. As ever, he was hypnotised by fame and the famous: thus it seemed logical that if you are presenting a star actress in a star play then you should engage a star designer to provide the costumes. He approached Captain Edward Molyneux, the leading couturier of the early thirties. Alas, Molyneux knew nothing of the theatre and did not ask to read the play first. Nor did Binkie, strangely innocent of the fashion world, think to send him a copy. Consequently, Molyneux prepared his designs without any idea of what was required. All he knew was that the play was contemporary, that day frocks and evening gowns were required for that beautiful, elegant Diana Wynyard plus three other ladies, and that Binkie was prepared to pay a lot of money. When the dresses and gowns arrived at the final rehearsal they were splendid and gorgeous beyond belief, the sort worn at a royal garden party or a gala night at the opera, but totally unsuited for nice, middle-class, moderately well-off ladies living a quiet life in a Home Counties village. Diana collapsed with laughter. "Darling Edward, I couldn't possibly wear them," she said. "Can you see me walking down the High Street and doing my daily shopping at the butcher's in *this*?" and she held up a long dress in pink tulle whose puffed sleeves were covered with silver roses.

"Edward, my dear, it's all my fault," apologised Binkie. "I should have told you . . . they're far too grand. We need something simple and commonplace."

Molyneux took back the dresses and a substantial cheque from Binkie to cover the costs and his trouble. As he was able to resell them to his regular customers he did rather well out of it. Binkie, meanwhile, took Diana and Joyce and the others in a taxi to Bourne and Hollingsworth where they bought simple, ordinary dresses off the peg for a fraction of what he had paid Molyneux. Binkie had made a big and expensive mistake and admitted as much to Howard and Wyndham, but it was characteristic of him that there were no rows, no retributions, no scapegoats. He blamed nobody but himself. It was a mistake he never repeated.

The tour opened at the Manchester Opera House on June 13th. "Did you arrange this date deliberately?" asked Guthrie curiously. "No, Tony dear, it just happened that way. But isn't it a *lucky* thing?"

Manchester has always loved the theatre, and its acclaim, though reluctantly given and always hard earned, has long been regarded as an accolade, but this love is possessive and jealous. When a play embarks on its tour, Manchester wants to get it first. The fact that the production, after only four weeks of rehearsal, might have many rough edges and be seen at considerably less than its best, did not bother the Manchester critics and public. All they wanted was that they should have first bite of the cherry.

The tour lasted three months, very much the Howard and Wyndham policy, keeping the provincial theatres open and audiences happy, giving the company every chance of settling down and paying off the production costs. *Sweet Aloes* was thus in profit long before its London opening. Throughout the tour Guthrie and Binkie would watch the play, Guthrie prowling round the back of the stalls or circle, Binkie from whichever stage box was free. In the intervals they would meet in the bar and compare notes. It was Binkie's method to watch three separate members of the audience in different parts of the house, one in each of the three acts, and note their reactions. "There was a man with pince-nez in the front row of the stalls who consulted his programme just as Joyce was saying that line about the boy being like a burglar . . . perhaps she could point it a little more sharply . . . A woman in Row K looked down to select a chocolate just as Jack came on, perhaps we could move the sofa elsewhere because it seems to be blocking the entrance . . . They seemed rather restless in act two, perhaps it ought to be tightened . . . I'm not happy about the ending . . ."

Sweet Aloes finally reached Wyndham's on October 31st, the reverse of his lucky number. The first-night reception was wildly enthusiastic with thirteen curtain calls, no more and no less, carefully arranged and orchestrated by Binkie from the prompt corner. Afterwards, he gave yet another of his enormous parties. But the nervous strain of wondering if this mob of friends, strangers and miscellaneous well-wishers (not to mention those who wished otherwise) would find themselves, when those damned notices finally appeared, at a wake rather than a wedding, finally convinced him that large first-night parties were a great mistake, even if somebody else paid the bill. In this case he could hardly cancel it or refuse to attend since the nominal hosts were Howard and Wyndham and Moss Empires. When the papers finally arrived at 1 a.m. precisely – "thirteen hundred hours, Tony dear, once again my lucky number reappears as if by magic" – they were all good. More precisely, they were cautious and cool about the play: ". . . It is reminiscent of *Hay Fever* without the wit and *The First Mrs Fraser* without the meaning" (*Daily Telegraph*), but vibrating with unqualified enthusiasm for Diana Wynyard. *Sweet Aloes* ran for over a year.

The year was not uneventful. In the spring of 1935, Binkie received an urgent message from the Theatre Guild in New York. It seemed that Joyce Carey had played Elizabeth in a revival of *The Barretts of Wimpole Street* in 1933 and they were planning to revive it for a limited season. Could Mr Beaumont possibly see his way to releasing her for six weeks, no more, so that once again she could ravish Broadway with her performance which charmingly combined pathos with radiance? Leave of absence when still under contract was not something which Binkie liked granting: if he did it for one he would be pressured into doing it for all and that way chaos lay. But Joyce was a dear sweet girl who had written him a very successful play which was bringing in fourteen hundred pounds a week, so he owed her a favour. Also, the Theatre Guild was becoming increasingly powerful and rapidly cornering the market in good new plays and good new actors. He did not wish to antagonise them. Once again, expediency triumphed. He gave his consent and Mercia Swinburne took over the part for eight weeks with no noticeable decline in business.

Later in the year, Diana Wynyard, suffering from appendicitis, had to leave the company to go into hospital for an operation. The doctors

said that she would be away for a month. She had made the part of
Linda so much her own that no replacement would have been acceptable to the public or to Bronson Albery who owned Wyndham's
Theatre. Binkie persuaded Howard and Wyndham to close the theatre
during her absence and to pay the company during the closure – half
salary to those earning sixteen pounds or over and full salary to those
earning less. This was virtually unheard of – though Charles Cochran
had paid a similar compliment to Elisabeth Bergner with a three-
week closure during the run of *Escape Me Never* – and once again
Binkie managed to get the credit for exceptional generosity. *Sweet
Aloes* finally ran for fourteen months, finishing on February 8th 1936
after a run of 477 performances.

Diana Wynyard had acquired a large and devoted following. Something about her cool, poised graciousness, her rather asexual beauty,
made an irresistible appeal to the female section of the public. Her fans,
mostly schoolgirls and young women, stood patiently outside the
stage door of Wyndham's every night waiting for her arrival and
departure, begging for autographs if they saw her in the street and
writing impassioned letters seeking urgent advice on their clothes,
their make-up and their love affairs. She took all this as she took her
fame and wealth – philosophically. But in November 1934 John
Gielgud made his second appearance at the New Theatre as Hamlet in
his own much-acclaimed production. Gielgud too had his devoted
following and they too were mostly schoolgirls and young women.
Overnight loyalties changed. When Diana Wynyard emerged from
the stage door of Wyndham's,* she saw all her fans but now they had
their backs to her, for they were waiting for the beautiful and romantic
Mr Gielgud. The essential fickleness of the public can hardly have been
demonstrated so emphatically and memorably. It was typical of Diana
Wynyard's sensible approach to life that she saw it as a huge joke:
when Binkie called to take her to the *Hamlet* first night party at John
Gielgud's flat, she told him, and Gielgud and all those present about
the treacherous behaviour of her fans as if it was the funniest thing
which had ever happened to her.

Not everybody liked her. Junior members of the company found
her less than friendly. Jack Allen, who played the small part of Lord
Farrington, the father of the illegitimate baby, had one disagreeable
experience with her: "She was aloof and chilly, she didn't have
anything to do with the company and was very unwelcoming when
she did. Throughout the run I had one understudy rehearsal a week.

---

*The stage doors of the New and Wyndham's Theatres face each other across a
narrow alley way, St Martin's Court.

One day I had to go on at short notice. I received a summons, via her dresser, to go down to Miss Wynyard. She didn't invite me to sit down, she merely looked at me coldly and said, 'Do you know it?' I said that I did. She merely nodded and continued making up. She didn't even wish me good luck. Forty minutes later I was in the wings waiting. In the play she and I had to enter together, me slightly behind her. Well, she wasn't there. Suddenly the pass door flew open and Diana sprinted across and ran through the door on to the stage. I was so confused and upset by this that I could hardly blurt out my first line and it emerged in a strangled croak. She looked daggers at me, but I managed to get through the scene without any further mishaps. But when the act finished and she was able to speak to me all she said was, 'There, I *thought* you didn't know it.'"

The great success of *Sweet Aloes* did not please Marie Tempest, who disliked Diana Wynyard and disapproved of any play being a big success unless she was in it. She attended the special matinée which Binkie arranged for the profession and then went all over London saying that the play was no good, that Diana Wynyard was terrible, and that the only good performance was given by Jack Allen.

Between the wars actors of the highest eminence forgathered in the Ivy, the acknowledged social centre of the West End, to bitch each other non-stop. No harm or malice was intended: this was all part of The Game, one of endless variations and great complexity, bewildering to the outsider but enormously entertaining to those involved. Marie Tempest had her regular table just inside the entrance on the left, and Lilian Braithwaite had hers on the right. Between the two was a no-man's-land which was seldom if ever crossed. On this occasion, Lilian was giving lunch to Joyce Carey, her daughter, and Diana Wynyard, a great favourite and close friend. Marie Tempest and Willie had specially invited Jack Allen to lunch so he could, albeit unknowingly, be a participant in this variation on The Game. "Dear Jack, I *must* tell you how good you are," she gushed. "You're so *talented* and you have such a splendid future. You're the *only* good thing in that depressing and boring play and in your next I hope you'll have some worthwhile people to work with." All this was delivered in that low thrilling voice which was her speciality, quiet enough to be mistaken for intimacy but projected with sufficient clarity to be audible at all the nearby tables. Diana and Joyce, the intended targets of this delicate onslaught, played their part in The Game by pretending not to hear and continuing their conversation. Finally Lilian decided to take action. She rose, crossed the dividing line and hovered above Marie Tempest's table. "Daaaaaaarling Mary, I'm *sorry* to hear that your play isn't doing very well,"* she cooed with poisoned sweetness, "so saaaaad, so sa-a-a-a-ad. But I do hear that you are really very good in it even though you are a bit old for the part. You mustn't over do it, darling, we don't want to lose you. Why don't you let your understudy do the matinées? Eight performances a week are such a strain at your time of life."

Crossing swords with Lilian Braithwaite was a hazardous occupation; Lilian was a wit which Mary was not: Lilian had an acid tongue and a wicked sense of humour, and even though they were not quite up to Mrs Pat's standard, some of her witticisms have become part of theatrical legend. Mary couldn't cope with all this. "Oh . . . oh . . . *go away*, your hat's on crooked," was the best she could manage. Lilian returned to her table with the smile of victory on her elegant bony features.

Unknown to Mary, Binkie was lunching with Noël Coward on his table. He saw and heard everything. Coward rather expected Binkie to show signs of resentment but Binkie merely chuckled appreciatively. "Dear Mary is up to her usual tricks, I see," was all he said. Binkie understood how to play The Game as well as anybody and there was no room for hard feelings. *Sweet Aloes* was playing to full houses every night with a long queue of people being turned away, and all Mary's delicate trouble-making couldn't hurt it.

Guthrie was good luck. Guthrie was good news. Dear Tony, such a valuable addition to his professional life, and a man he wished to employ again as soon as possible. King George V's jubilee was coming up in May 1935 and Binkie, in common with all the West End managers, looked on this as a heaven-sent opportunity to make a spectacular financial killing. "After all," said Binkie to Guthrie in Verrey's one day, "millions of extra visitors and tourists will be *flooding* into the country and they'll want some sort of entertainment." But they agreed that it had to be something special and suitable. Something patriotic, something with pageantry and spectacle.

Victoria Regina, Laurence Housman's sequence of thirty short plays covering Queen Victoria's entire reign, had been published though nobody had presented them. This seemed suitable, even though rumours abounded that the royal family was not amused and that the Lord Chamberlain might feel bound to censor or even ban them. The last thing Binkie wanted at this early stage in his career was to antagonise the Establishment. Also, what about the casting? "It's the

---

* *Theatre Royal* at the Lyric, a comedy based on the life and scandals of the Barrymore family. In fact, it was doing very well.

Juliet syndrome," explained Guthrie. "Where in hell do you find an actress who's young enough to look eighteen, looks like Victoria and yet is sufficiently old and experienced to play this supremely long and difficult part, *and* to age convincingly up to eighty-five?" They thought long and hard. "Oh, if *only* Meggie Albanesi was still alive," said Binkie sadly.*

Once again, the answer came from the most unlikely source. The Theatre Guild in New York sent over the script of a new play called *Hervey House* by C. R. Avery, somebody unknown to Binkie. A chronicle, a generation play covering thirty years in the life of an aristocratic family and set in a fictional house in Grosvenor Square, its cast included a duke, handsome and dignified, but rather dull; his duchess, beautiful, dignified and virtuous; the duke's mistress who was beautiful, not in the least bit virtuous but very amusing and charming, as well as a private secretary, an estate agent, lots of aunts, uncles and miscellaneous cousins, and an army of servants including a sternly authoritative butler, a twittering ladies' maid, footmen in livery, grooms, pantry boys and gamekeepers without livery. The plot was one of Dickensian richness and complexity. The Duke of Shires, a staunch Liberal and close friend of the Prince of Wales, is offered high office on condition that he puts his house in order, gives up his mistress and is seen to be living with his wife in rather greater connubial bliss than formerly. Reluctantly, he agrees and starts to play the happy husband. Twenty years pass; it is 1914 and everybody is getting ready for the trenches including his son, previously a boy of eleven now in his thirties and commissioned into the Guards. Another twenty years pass; everybody gets older and older ageing at the rate of, approximately, one year a minute. The son is now a staunch Socialist and has sold Hervey House to a redevelopment company. The duke is now very poor, reduced to his last million and his last castle. Hervey House stands ready for demolition and rebuilding as a hotel. In its empty, deserted, echoing drawing-room, the duke, duchess and mistress have a sentimental reunion. The moonlight shines through the dusty window pane, a jazz band is heard in the distance, and the three old people shuffle away. The curtain slowly falls.

Written with great skill, charm and vitality, it had woven into the fabric a wealth of accurate social comment. It also echoed a number of other plays: *Cavalcade* without the music, mixed with *Milestones*,

---

*Meggie Albanesi died at the tragically early age of twenty-four after a career of only six years, most of it under Basil Dean's management at the St Martin's. She was beautiful, charming and tender. Her style was one of exquisite delicacy, and virginal innocence, but her private life was anything but innocent. She had a very active sex-life and her death was said to be due to a clumsy abortion.

flavoured with a spoonful of *The Cherry Orchard* and a touch of *Heartbreak House* added for good measure. But familiar ingredients have never been a disadvantage with the public provided they are of good quality, mixed with skill and satisfactorily baked, as it were, in a good oven. Binkie and Guthrie liked it very much. There was a cast of forty, ten different sets and twenty-five changes of scene: it would be hideously expensive but Binkie was confident that the directors of Howard and Wyndham would give their approval and with the appropriate starry cast he had no doubt that it would run a year. After all, what could be more suitable for a royal jubilee?

But many changes would have to be made. The number of charac-ters and scene changes had to be drastically reduced and a lot of the dialogue rewritten. The slang of the 1890s was inaccurate, the sen-timental scenes were unconvincing and Avery's view of society seemed to owe a lot to the novelettes of Marie Corelli and Ouida. Who was C. R. Avery? Obviously he had read a great deal about London society before the war, but had clearly never been part of it. Then word came from New York that C. R. Avery was Jane Cowl, the actress, who had written that classic, that monument of melodramatic rubbish, *Smilin' Through*. "Well, that explains it," said Binkie. "Only an American would make all the young men say 'ripping' and 'topping' as if there had never been any other words of slang. Only an American would have the duchess refer to the Prince of Wales as 'Marlborough House' or to the old Queen as 'Osborne'."

Jane Cowl was a big star on both sides of the Atlantic. She was America's leading dramatic/romantic actress who had been a sen-sation in London in 1926 in Noël Coward's *Easy Virtue*. Binkie had been there on the first night at the Duke of York's. As with all intelligent Americans, she had not merely fallen passionately in love with England and the English, she was hopelessly besotted, totally infatuated, with the social life, the countryside and architecture and the literature. She had read every word of Dickens, knew him better than most Englishmen, quoted him at great length, and knew all the houses, pubs and streets with Dickensian connections. She had come to England for a holiday every year since she was a girl of sixteen; she hired a bicycle and toured the countryside, invariably wearing old-fashioned Edwardian knickerbockers. She had many society friends, and had been a guest in their homes, though never more than once, and could drop a titled or royal name like a dozen gossip columnists working all night in shifts. In short, she was suffering from an advanced case of rampant, and possibly terminal, anglophilia.

Binkie sent Guthrie to New York to discuss cuts and rewriting. Guthrie reported back to Binkie that it took him a long time to steer her away from countesses and royal princes, but when he finally succeeded he found her strangely uncooperative. Cuts and changes were out and she objected to His Majesty's Theatre, *Hervey House* being an intimate play that needed a small theatre. Guthrie had explained that a play as expensive as hers needed a large theatre to make the money necessary to keep it afloat. Also, it was the only theatre available.

"Tell her that unless she makes the changes to your satisfaction I will not present her play," said Binkie in a telegram. "But do it tactfully. I want to do it, but only on my terms."

Later in the week, Guthrie and Jane Cowl had a further meeting in Chicago in the second week of her tour. In the meantime, he had talked to Reg Lawrence, the co-author, who agreed to all Guthrie's suggestions. Confronted with Binkie's ultimatum, Jane Cowl suddenly gave in. She cut the characters from forty to thirty and the scene changes from twenty-five to nineteen. She also rewrote much of the dialogue and cut some of the more repetitive and outmoded slang. At the beginning of April, Guthrie made a triumphant return to London.

Guthrie and Binkie started casting immediately. Nicholas Hannen was a good choice for the Duke. He wasn't the most exciting actor in London, but he had an undeniably aristocratic appearance, bearing and voice, deep and booming as all good stage dukes should have. The Theatre Guild had him under contract, but now that they and Binkie were on such good terms they happily agreed to release him. He returned rather late, but one week's hectic rehearsal was enough. Fay Compton was an obvious choice for the long-suffering, saintly duchess: once again, Binkie had no great love for her on or off the stage, but since she played the shy school-mistress in *Autumn Crocus*, she had become a star. The part of the duke's mistress was short, but showy, ideal for Gertrude Lawrence. She was very much in demand at the beginning of 1935. Cochran wanted her for the Ethel Merman part in the London production of Cole Porter's *Anything Goes*, then a hit on Broadway, and Hollywood had offered her unheard-of money if she and Douglas Fairbanks would co-star in *It Happened One Night*, a comedy which had been offered around for years.* But neither Hollywood nor big musicals interested her. She was determined to

---

*If she had accepted she might have won the Academy Award and become a major Hollywood star, which is what happened to Claudette Colbert who eventually played the part (with Clark Gable). It is interesting to speculate how her career would have shaped out. There would have been fewer plays but a lot more films, and one of them might well have been a re-make of *Private Lives* with Noël Coward. And Margot Channing in *All About Eve*, originally offered to and turned down by Colbert.

prove herself as a good dramatic actress and this part was just what she wanted. Margaret Rutherford as a dotty, garrulous aunt, Desmond Tester aged eleven, England's most likeable and busiest child actor, making his first appearance in the West End, and Laurier Lister as a Socialist MP were the high spots of a large and distinguished gathering.

This was Binkie's first period play. Clearly, his usual method of designing sets on the backs of envelopes would not do. For the ten elaborate period constructions Molly McArthur was hired on condition that a huge turntable be installed so the nineteen changes could take place quickly and smoothly. The costumes were all faithfully copied from dresses in the Victoria and Albert Museum and made up by a woman in Jermyn Street who was known to Binkie. He and Guthrie spent a lot of time outside rehearsals buying furniture and properties. "It's so much cheaper to buy than hire," said Binkie shrewdly, voicing yet another piece of theatrical wisdom. "After all, when the play is over you can always sell them or hire them out to other companies."

The opening was set for the Manchester Opera House at the beginning of May but before the company travelled up north, Binkie found himself with a serious diplomatic problem, the perennial argument over star billing. Harry Tennent had warned him that having two star actresses of equal status in the play was dangerous and that they would make trouble. Binkie refused to believe him: and if they did make trouble he could cope with it. During rehearsals they behaved well. They posed for rehearsal photos with Guthrie, they were seen admiring the model of the set and walking down the Haymarket for lunch at the Carlton Grill. But when it came to the point, both demanded star billing; not simply their names above the title, but each demanded the name on the left side of the poster. The matter couldn't be resolved by putting both names in the middle, for one would have to be above the other, but which? Binkie, ever the diplomat, produced a solution. He had two sets of posters printed, one giving the star billing to Fay Compton the other to Gertrude Lawrence. Both agreed to this and Binkie was vastly amused that arriving at the Midlands Hotel in Manchester, they both separately hailed taxis and drove all over the city counting the posters to make quite sure that there were an equal number of each. There were. Binkie had seen to that.

Then there was the even trickier problem of dressing-room allocation. Theatres have only one star dressing-room. Who was to occupy it? And who was to get her photograph first in the programme? Binkie showed remarkable tact and cleverness when he persuaded them to toss for it and to abide by the result. To his joy, the winner was Gertie and for the whole of the tour and London run she occupied Number One dressing-room and had her photo first in the programme. In fact she had two to Fay Compton's one, for Edward Molyneux took a full page advertisement with a large photo announcing to the world that he and he alone designed her clothes outside the theatre. Fay Compton was not at all pleased by this but there was nothing she could do about it. It was widely believed that Binkie had somehow managed to mastermind this situation, but he neither confirmed nor denied it – another example of his increasing deviousness.

On the first night in Manchester, young Desmond Tester got hopelessly lost backstage and flew about in a frenzy through the over-furnished rooms all pre-set on the turntable, searching for the right entrance. Margaret Rutherford and Stafford Hilliard, looking out through the French windows into the offstage garden and pretending to see him, improvised page after page of dialogue with great skill and plausibility. The boy finally made a breathless entrance not by the door or the windows but through the fireplace, on hands and knees. The actors on stage were politely surprised to see him, but the audience thought it a perfectly natural and absolutely delightful thing for a small boy to do. There was a big laugh and a round of applause, and no suspicion that anything had gone wrong. Because of this Binkie suggested to Guthrie that it should be kept in as a permanent feature of the play. Every night young Tester made his recumbent entrance and received his round of applause.

The three stars and those junior members of the company who could afford it (including Laurier Lister) all stayed at the Midlands Hotel. Nicholas Hannen and Fay Compton both had modest rooms, but Gertrude Lawrence had to have the biggest, a suite of three rooms with bathroom and shower and a Bechstein grand piano which she needed, she explained, to keep her voice in trim. Throughout the week she gave lavish luncheon and supper parties for the company and her many friends who journeyed up from London to see the show and visit her. Champagne flowed; caviare, chicken and other choice delicacies were there in abundance. It was all very splendid and extravagant: the fact that she couldn't afford it merely added to her pleasure. It was just like Marie Antoinette entertaining the French court at Versailles.

The moment of truth came on Sunday morning when the company collectively descended to the reception desk. Nicholas Hannen and Fay Compton had bills of only thirty pounds for the week. But Gertie's came to over three hundred. She flashed her irresistible smile at the manager. "I don't have the cash on me, darling, but you will take my cheque, won't you, darling?" Unhappily, the manager turned out to be the one man in history able to resist Gertie's famous charm. "I'm very sorry, Miss Lawrence, but as you are an undischarged bankrupt I am unable to accept a personal cheque." Gertie burst into tears and gave a magnificent performance of grief and distress as if she was a toothless old-age pensioner being driven out of her chilly basement room. She couldn't cope with it all, she wailed, it was gross harassment, everybody was against her, life was not fair, she felt she ought to kill herself. Fay and Nicholas were horribly embarrassed and a crowd started to gather. Gertie's lamentations grew louder as the manager continued to shake his head. At this point Binkie appeared. He had arrived on Saturday to see the play and had stayed the night at the Midland. Clearly, it would be bad publicity for the play if the press got hold of the story – which is exactly what Gertie wanted him to think – so he paid the bill for her, having been assured by a grateful and relieved manager that his personal cheque was acceptable. "He handled the awkward situation with great charm and style," said Laurier Lister. "Whether Gertie repaid him, or whether he took it out of her salary, I don't know."

Jane Cowl, having obtained leave of absence from her play in New York, arrived in London for the first night. Binkie, Harry and Guthrie gave her lunch at Verrey's. "As soon as I checked into the Savoy I hired myself a bicycle and made a little trip round London to see that Buckingham Palace and Westminster Abbey were still there," she gushed to the press at a reception Binkie had arranged. "Tonight's opening will be the first time I've been back in His Majesty's Theatre for twenty years. I still think it's a bit large for the play but I'm inclined to believe that it's a good omen."

It opened on May 19th. The first-night audience included a number of well-known names who were regulars and never missed a first night . . . Dodie Smith, tiny and bird-like and always in the front row, Gordon Selfridge representing commerce and usually in the company of one or other of the Dolly sisters and sometimes both, Sibyl Colefax, self-appointed leader of London society, Schiaparelli, Molyneux's only serious rival in fashion, Sir Patrick Hastings, QC, and Golding Bright, Jane Cowl's literary agent, who had once had Bernard Shaw, no less, as a client. The play went without incident: the turntable turned smoothly, nobody got lost in the backstage pre-set, the opening scene, where the Prince of Wales attends a grand reception in his honour with the stage filled with a platoon of liveried footmen and beautifully costumed guests, gave Guthrie the chance to indulge in the spectacle and pageantry which was his speciality, and was loudly applauded.

Altogether a remarkably successful evening and the cheering at the end was a very good omen. One tiny incident, however, struck an ominous note, though Binkie was able to make a good joke out of it. Half-way through the second act he was watching the play from the side of the stalls and he noticed that James Agate, sitting in his usual gangway seat on the end, was fast asleep. He was about to go and wake him when the theatre manager stopped him. "I wouldn't do that if I were you, Mr Beaumont. Agate's notices are always very good when he's been asleep."

He was right. Agate's long review in the *Sunday Times* achieved the usual mixture of sardonic wit and waspish approval.

There are three things with which the theatre cannot compete: a heat wave, a general election and a big royal event. The first two require no explanation but the public (and also, alas, the profession) have never been able to understand why a coronation, a jubilee or a royal wedding should be bad for the theatre. Binkie's trust – which, it must be firmly stated, he shared with all the other London managements – that the extra millions who poured into London for the jubilee celebrations would fill His Majesty's Theatre, was sadly misplaced. The millions were visibly and aurally there, but they did not wish to spend their evenings, let alone their afternoons, inside a stuffy auditorium decades before air-conditioning had been invented. Houses at His Majesty's were good, though by no means full, for the first week but jubilee night took place in the second: fireworks on the Embankment, an illuminated pageant of boats on the Thames and dancing in all the parks. How could *Hervey House* compete with all that? It couldn't and didn't, playing to only a handful, little more than the size of the cast. Had the audience been smaller than the cast the performance could have been cancelled, for such is theatre tradition. But it wasn't and Gertie and Fay and Nicholas and the company had to sweat out the evening in their heavy uniforms and elaborate period dresses. Their reward for dedication to duty was a splendid dinner party given by Binkie and Harry in the Dome of the theatre. "This was Sir Herbert's private apartment," said Jane Cowl happily. "He used to do all his casting and play-reading here. Many's the time . . ."

The jubilee celebrations continued for a month and theatre audiences were alarmingly small. For already successful plays with a healthy advance, their production costs long-since paid and cheap to run, a few weeks of bad business wouldn't matter. But *Hervey House* was monumentally expensive: it had to play to full houses to show a modest profit. Binkie nursed it for a month, pouring in yet more capital from hopeful investors including a number of Jane Cowl's titled friends, but it was the classic case of throwing good money after bad. After six weeks, Binkie admitted defeat and withdrew it. But it wasn't only the money. There was another reason for the failure. Jane Cowl had been quite right in her early warning: His Majesty's *was* too big for the play whose gentle intimacies seldom got beyond the middle row of the stalls, and no amount of spectacle and production flourishes could turn this essentially delicate little piece into an epic.

Even in defeat, Binkie was calm and philosophical. He blamed nobody but himself for his errors of judgement. Once again there were no scapegoats and no whipping boys. He succeeded in convincing the directors of Howard and Wyndham that the money had been well lost, that *Hervey House* was a masterpiece of theatre and that it had been a great privilege for them and him to have been allowed to present it. One splendid masterpiece which fails is worth, in the long run, a dozen mediocrities which succeed. In fact, *Hervey House* was to be one of his favourite productions and in years to come he would talk about it with love and sadness.

Hervey House, however privately humiliating, had also been instructive. Binkie had learned never again to trust in a royal event – a decision which was to be greatly to his advantage during the 1953 coronation – never again to ignore an author's advice when it came from somebody as skilled and experienced as Jane Cowl and *never* to cast two star actresses of equal status in the same play and thus allow himself to get involved in their stupid and time-wasting squabbles.

By the time the interminable jubilee celebrations ended Binkie had other problems on his mind. One of these was an unknown young actor called Robert Morley. In the summer of 1935 he was distinctly fat, physically awkward, desperately shy and conspicuously unsuccessful. Nothing could be done about the first two liabilities and nothing ever was, but the third and fourth did not last long, for which metamorphosis Binkie can claim a generous measure of credit.

CHAPTER TEN

1935

Short Story

Robert Morley was twenty-seven and had done what unsuccessful young actors have been doing for centuries. He had written a play called *Short Story*. Not one which offered him a spectacular acting opportunity, for the shyness did not permit this gesture of egotism, but a good play designed with a star in mind, always a sensible ploy for a novice playwright. In his case the Adored One was Marie Tempest. He sent the play to her manager, Alban Limpus. Back it came by return of post. "I cannot in all fairness waste Miss Tempest's time with what I honestly believe is one of the worst plays I have ever read," was his blunt comment. But Morley had learned one of the facts of theatrical life while in his salad days of provincial touring and rep: that tenacity is just as important as talent. Saddened, but in no way deterred by this initial setback, he decided to send it direct to Marie Tempest.

Her response was equally swift. Two days later he found himself lunching with her and Willie in her bijou dining-room in Avenue Road listening enchanted to the only music which the novice play-wright wants to hear – how much she liked the play and how she couldn't wait to start rehearsals. In fact, she added, it would go into production immediately. Of course, it still needed a little work, in fact it would have to be rewritten completely. "Georgina Leigh is sup-posed to be a bad actress. Do you really expect my public to accept *me* as a bad actress? Me? No, you'll have to make her a star. A big star. That will make more sense."

Morley could have pointed out that it would make no sense at all, for it would effectively destroy the whole point of the comedy which depended entirely on the actress's extreme and demonstrable badness, but he did not. The novice playwright who defies his star and refuses to accede to her modest and reasonable demands has not yet been born. He realised that he had everything to lose and nothing to gain by being obstinate. Rewrite the play completely? Of course, nothing could be easier. He agreed.

"And I shall want Tyrone Guthrie to produce it," she added. She had seen *Hervey House*. Not only had he handled the large cast and multiple scene changes with panache, but he had contrived to get a respectable straight performance from that detestable Gertrude Lawrence. Guthrie was a rising young talent *and* a man; such a combination she had always liked.

At three o'clock the luncheon was over. She went upstairs to her bedroom to rest and Willie took Morley into his study. "I expect you'd like some money," he said kindly, and scribbled out a cheque for a hundred pounds which he placed into his trembling hands. A novice playwright might expect an advance of twenty pounds for his first play so this extravagant sum was an indication of how much Mary had liked the play and its author. "Despair gripped me," wrote Morley. "I became convinced that I was asleep; at the same time I was determined to stay asleep as long as possible. I glided along Avenue Road in what I was conscious was a somnambulistic trance. I crashed suddenly and painfully into a pillar box. I realised I was awake. I don't think I have ever felt such overmastering happiness."

However, overmastering happiness was not the principal emotion visible when Guthrie and Binkie forgathered at Verrey's. "There's going to be *trouble*," said Binkie gloomily. "I can feel it in my bones, Tony dear. She's behaved like an angel in the last two plays she's done for me, so the devil will have to break out some time. She'll take you into a corner, complain about the other performances and suggest replacements. She'll argue with *everything* you say. She'll try and upstage the others. She'll start moving the furniture. She's got a long catalogue of tricks, lovingly worked out over the years, and she'll try every one. Do you think you'll be able to cope?"

"It'll be a baptism of fire. But I'll try."

"I'll be behind you every *inch* of the way. And if you need me at the rehearsals I shall be there."

Morley's first meeting with Binkie took place a few days later in the Piccadilly office. After the initial courtesies had been exchanged, they sat down on opposite sides of the large desk which dominated the room. Morley's most lasting memory on this occasion was of Binkie's gloves. They were pearly-grey and close-fitting. An indispensable part of every young man-about-town's sartorial equipment. There was a long pause and Binkie started to take off the gloves. He did this not with a single sweep, as any lesser mortal would have done, but slowly, finger by finger, inch by inch, concentrating silently as if nothing else in the world existed. Morley watched in fascination: never before had a pair of gloves seemed so important. The long and oppressive silence was finally broken when Binkie laid them on the desk and turned his pale grey eyes on the hypnotised young author. Both men were the same age, twenty-seven, born within a month of each other, but no observer would have guessed it, for Binkie still looked like a schoolboy, whereas Morley with his Pickwickian face and figure, looked old enough to be his father.

"I might be able to get Sybil Thorndike," he said.

"I thought we had Marie Tempest," said Morley, startled.

"Not *instead* of. As *well* as. For Lady Bucktrout."

"That'll be very nice. But it's not much of a part. Do you think she will?"

"She will if I ask her," which was a superbly arrogant, splendidly confident remark from somebody who had been in management for little more than two years. In fact, he had already engaged her though Morley did not discover this until weeks later. This meeting was interrupted by the sudden arrival of A. E. Matthews.

"Sorry to bother you Binkie, old man, but I thought I ought to let you know that I've read the play. Candidly, I don't care for it. The plot's rather weak, none of the dialogue is funny, my part isn't interesting and the second act doesn't have a good curtain."

"Thank you for being so candid, Matty dear. May I introduce you to the author?"

"Glad to meet you, old man. Nothing personal, you understand, but I feel I ought to be truthful."

He left. Morley turned in distress to Binkie. "Well, we've lost him. Who else do you have in mind?"

"But we haven't lost him. He'll do it."

"But he . . . he . . . doesn't like the play. He's just said so."

Binkie smiled patiently. "Oh yes, he does. He likes it well enough to want to do it. You see, Robert, my dear, whenever actors come in and criticise the play this means they'll end up by doing it. They do this merely to keep face, to make you think you're not getting them cheaply, that they're doing you a favour. It's only when they breeze in and praise it in lavish terms that you know they'll end by saying that Cochran wants them for a new musical at the Adelphi or Korda has got a good part in a new film. That's when they say, 'Sorry, old man, can't do it.' But we've got Matty all right. You'll see."

When Binkie had doubts about a play – and in spite of Morley's extensive rewriting he had plenty – he filled it with stars. The galaxy for *Short Story* included A. E. Matthews playing yet another of his bumbling Home Counties colonels, Willie Graham Browne as another baronet, and Ursula Jeans, as the glamorous interloper, with the virtually unknown Margaret Rutherford and Rex Harrison filling in the show-stealing cameos. Margaret Rutherford in her only other

West End appearance, in *Hervey House*, had made a definite mark on press and public alike: as Miss Flower, a gossiping village spinster, she would make an even greater one. Rex Harrison, like Binkie and Morley aged twenty-seven, was a strikingly good-looking, smooth-as-silk young actor from Liverpool who had made brief appearances in six undistinguished West End plays and had made no mark in any of them. But Binkie, whose eye for talent, if not infallible, was certainly shrewd, saw a future for him – possibly his most spectacular piece of talent-spotting.

"Why do you want me to play a middle-aged American film producer?" asked Harrison.

"My partner and I have worked out the average age of this company and we find that it is slightly over seventy," replied Binkie, "and we thought that a younger actor would bring this average down a little."

Harrison was enormously amused by this remark and thus began a firm friendship.

Rehearsals took place at the Adelphi and were chaotic. Rex Harrison was then appearing in a play in Nottingham – called *The Wicked Flee*, it was every bit as terrible as the title suggested – and could rehearse only in the morning. Marie Tempest had interminable dress-fittings in the morning, rested in the afternoon and thus could only rehearse in the evening. But there were other complications. A. E. Matthews disliked driving and distrusted public transport. Every day he would cycle down from Hampstead wearing cavalry trousers and a belted Norfolk jacket. It was noted with amusement that the absent-mindedness which was a prominent feature of the parts he played now began to overlap into his private life. He could never remember in which theatre he was supposed to rehearse.

Margaret Rutherford was another cyclist. She would travel up from Wimbledon every day. For years Noël Coward retained a vivid memory of her pedalling vigorously across Waterloo Bridge against a strong wind, wearing tweeds and sensible shoes with her hand-knitted cloak streaming behind her. It is highly probable that both *Blithe Spirit* and Madame Arcati were born at that moment. Having trouble finding somewhere to chain her bicycle, she used to bring it inside the theatre and prop it up against the back wall of the stage. Marie Tempest did not approve of any of this, for she had no sympathy for eccentrics.

Rehearsals were exciting. At the beginning it was all sweetness and light. Mary had decided that Guthrie was the greatest producer in history and she flattered him outrageously. But the honeymoon did not last long, stopping rather abruptly towards the end of the first week when she discovered that she was not going to get her own way in everything and that this dear sweet boy – as she invariably referred to him – had a mind of his own and every intention of using it. Binkie had prophesied correctly. She *did* start to make trouble and it was arguments, criticism and headstrong obstinacy all the way. From her extensive catalogue of tricks, she had one which was cleverly calculated to sow seeds of doubt in the mind of the author and the management. She would suddenly pause before one of her lines came up and look rather worried. Everybody would wait for her to speak. The pause extended further and further, painfully. "I wonder . . . if . . . I really *should* say this line, Mr Guthrie," she would say doubtfully. "And why not, Miss Tempest?" A much longer pause. "Well . . . you see . . . I've said it so many times before in my other plays . . ." She would smile vaguely in the direction of the author in the stalls. "Perhaps you could change it, Mr . . . er . . . Mr . . . er . . ." for it was part of The Game that she should pretend not to remember his name.

Another of her whipping-boys was the prompter – always an easy target for the petty tyrant. If he failed to give the prompt not merely at the moment when it was wanted, and at seventy she wanted plenty of prompting in the early stages of rehearsal, but the moment before, then there was hell to pay with compound interest.

Rehearsals continued to be disturbing. Nothing was right for her. The grouping and moves were all wrong, nobody was capable of giving any sort of performance – were they all amateurs? – and the furniture was badly placed. One day Binkie paid a discreet visit to the theatre and sat in the stalls next to Guthrie. The rehearsal was stormy and the dispute centred on the furniture. Guthrie had arranged it in his way, she wanted it rearranged in hers. There was a pouffe in the centre near the footlights which particularly annoyed her. She wanted it taken off the stage and Guthrie insisted that it stay. She finally settled the matter by kicking it into the orchestra pit. "What a horribly common little woman, to be sure," whispered Guthrie. "Will you tell her, Binkie dear, or shall I?" Then he strode down to the footlights, all six feet five of him quivering with well-simulated rage, and shouted, "Miss Tempest, why are you being such a bitch?" The longest and tensest pause in theatrical history followed. The savage glare she directed at Guthrie slowly faded and she started to smile. "Very well, Mr Guthrie, shall we continue with the rehearsal?"

She was one of nature's bullies. If you allowed her to dominate you, then she would make your life a misery, but a modest show of resistance went a long way to making her docile and co-operative. This is what happened. The Pouffe Affair, as Guthrie and Binkie would always gigglingly refer to it, was the turning-point in the rehearsals and from then on it was all sweetness and light once more. "You've cut her down in public," whispered Binkie a little later, "now see if you can build her up. She's lost face. See if you can put some of it back."

The chance arrived rather sooner than he expected. Rex Harrison was on the stage with a phone call which wasn't getting the comedy it should. "Mary, dear," said Guthrie, "Mr Harrison is having trouble with his telephone scene. Would you show him how to do it?" She was indeed happy to demonstrate her own matchless comedy technique. "But I couldn't do it like that in a hundred years," gasped Harrison after she had finished, "it's marvellous." "Nonsense, dear boy," she said graciously. "Of course you can and of course you will."

Ursula Jeans was not so lucky. Mary disliked young actresses unless they were willing to become her slave which Ursula Jeans, a young woman of spirit and independence, refused to do. She had an important scene with Mary in which she had to sit on a chair with Mary sitting on the sofa. As Guthrie produced it, the chair was on the same level as the sofa and both ladies played the scene in equal profile. Mary didn't like this and one day Ursula found that her chair had been set a foot downstage and facing up it. Calmly replacing it in its original and correct position, she played the scene as it had been produced. The following evening the chair had once again been placed downstage, but on trying to replace it she found that it had been firmly screwed down, leaving her no alternative but to play this important scene with her back to the audience. Mary was expert at upstaging people but this was the first time she had stooped to rearranging the furniture, the incident adding yet another chapter to the Marie Tempest legend. Needless to say, when Binkie heard about it, which he did that same evening, he immediately gave instructions to the stage manager that it was not to be repeated. He also had a discreet word with his star. "I think it would be better, Mary dear, if you were to leave the furniture alone. The scene plays very nicely as Tony produced it and you have nothing to lose. Don't forget, Ursula is a clever, talented, sweet little thing, but she can't offer you any competition. You have nothing to fear from her or anybody."

Sybil Thorndike had some amusing things to do at a writing desk which raised loud laughter. Mary decided to put a stop to it. One evening the business was received in silence. Sybil looked downstage to see what was happening and saw Mary doing some even funnier things with a pocket handkerchief and thus killing the scene. But Sybil knew how to deal with this situation. The following night Mary discovered that her scene was being received in silence. She looked upstage and saw Sybil kneeling on the floor playing a game of patience and getting the rapt attention of the audience. As they left the stage they held a brief whispered conversation which was lovingly remembered by Sybil years later. "You're a very clever actress, aren't you?" from Mary, and Sybil's reply was, "Not especially, darling, but clever enough to act with you." Mary knew when she had met her equal and from then onwards the two *grandes dames* were the best of friends.

Another of her victims was Margaret Rutherford who was reducing the audience to near-hysterics in their scenes together. She didn't like this at all, for nobody else was supposed to get laughs in a Marie Tempest comedy and for a lesser actress to do so was *lèse-majesté* of the grossest sort. She had a number of interesting tricks for dealing with this situation but the one she now selected was distraction. While Rutherford was chattering away, Mary kept up a running commentary of abuse. "This is terrible . . . you're so obvious . . . you're too slow . . . can't you see that the audience is bored to distraction? . . . nobody's interested . . . hurry *up*, you silly old cow, hurry *up* . . ." All this was spoken in a whisper so quiet that nobody in the audience could hear it or had the least suspicion that anything was happening which shouldn't. But once again she had made a miscalculation. Rutherford may have been inexperienced, but she was nobody's fool and she had a generous measure of confidence. Although she had to fight to keep her concentration, keep it she did and her nightly reward as she made her rapid exit through the French windows was a round of applause. This was even less to Mary's liking for even she, with all her destructive skills, was unable to kill it or even to cut it short.

For two purgatorial weeks, Rutherford was compelled to endure this persecution. Then she received an imperial summons to the Number One dressing-room. "Miss Rutherford, your scene is too slow," snapped Mary, flashing baleful eyes, "it's killing the play. You must hurry it up. I can feel the audience is getting impatient and restless. You *must* take it quicker . . ." and a great deal more in similar vein. Rutherford, who hadn't been asked to sit down, listened patiently and then drew herself up to her full height. "Miss Tempest," she said quietly, "when people tell me I must act more quickly, it has the extraordinary effect of making me act even slower." With her dignity unimpaired, she left the dressing-room. Game, set and match.

It will be noted that all these victims were women. The men were immune from these petty tyrannies, amused spectators of this ancient blood sport, watching from the touchlines with cynical relish. She liked men as much as she disliked women. They were far too attractive and valuable to be antagonised by any sort of bad behaviour or unprofessionalism. She was particularly nice to Rex Harrison and managed to teach him a great deal about the art of acting light comedy. There was one trick which he watched with amazement and disbelief – the noble art of coaxing applause from an unresponsive audience. As she turned upstage to make her exit through the French windows, she started to clap her hands vigorously. The audience, thinking it came from some enthusiast in the stalls, took it up obediently and applauded loudly and lengthily. "I looked sidelong at her, thinking it was a joke," he recalled, "but not at all. She was deadly serious and it happened at every performance."

When it came to planning the first night, Binkie decided to try out another of his innovations. While he disliked the critics he did concede that theirs was a difficult job and full of hardship. Instead of being able to relax with friends over a late-night supper or hobnob with the stars at the first-night party – which, he learned to his amusement, most of them would very much like – they were sadly compelled to stand in draughty booths shouting their words of wisdom down a telephone. "But if we opened on a Saturday night, they could have dinner somewhere and then spend all of Sunday relaxing and thinking about it, and they'd all be so *grateful* that they'd all write lovely things," he confided to A. E. Matthews. Consequently, *Short Story*, after a week in Edinburgh, opened at the Queen's Theatre on Saturday, November 2nd 1935 with a modest little party on the stage afterwards for the cast, their families and a handful of friends from other West End plays. On Monday the wisdom of Binkie's new policy seemed justified, for the notices were all splendid. But word got back to Binkie with some speed that Saturday openings were not in favour with the critics because they interfered with the weekend.

In spite of Binkie's devious planning, the luck was against him. The pre-Christmas weeks are traditionally difficult. In addition, there was a great deal of illness around that year. Sybil Thorndike had to leave the cast for a week with a poisoned shoulder, and Mary for a fortnight when her rheumatism became too much for her. Binkie closed the theatre for two weeks, but the re-opening was delayed for a further week by the death of the King. The gloom cast by a royal funeral and three empty weeks effectively killed the public's interest in the play, already at a low ebb, so on February 14th, *Short Story* was withdrawn, leaving the last word on the subject with Sybil Thorndike. "I wouldn't go through all that again," she said to Binkie, "for all the money in Howard and Wyndham."

CHAPTER ELEVEN

1935

Call it a Day

When Dodie Smith entered Binkie's life she had enjoyed the sort of career which is every ambitious person's dream – instant fame, overnight success from poverty and obscurity to wealth and international renown in eight hours. SHOPGIRL WRITES HIT PLAY was the headline which summed it all up.* The play was *Autumn Crocus*, the year 1930, the stars were Francis Lederer, as the handsome Tyrolean innkeeper, and Fay Compton, as the shy schoolteacher who falls in love with him. Two more successes in the next three years showed that this was no flash in the pan, but a lasting talent. More than any other playwright of the time she epitomised the thirties. The plays were neither original in content nor style for she was no pioneer. Her favourite metier was family life: on holiday in the Tyrol (*Autumn Crocus*), in a Scottish seaside hotel (*Touch Wood*), working in a department store threatened with closure (*Service*), weekending in the country (*Bonnet Over the Windmill*), assembling for a golden wedding anniversary (*Dear Octopus*) or showing twenty-four hours in the family's homelife (*Call it a Day*). Just ordinary people leading ordinary lives, but observed with humour, occasional flashes of wit, and perception. She gave the public the cosy, undemanding realism which they wanted and delivered the results with such great theatrical skill as to guarantee their life after a half century. More than most plays of the thirties, these have survived their period.

The architect of this good fortune was Basil Dean who alone discerned her quality and produced her first three plays. Dean, one of the greatest single figures of the period and one of its most chillingly tenacious legends, had started as an actor, graduating to become Sir Herbert Beerbohm Tree's stage manager at His Majesty's. In 1919 he formed his own company, took over the St Martin's Theatre and

---

*In the interests of a better story, the press had rather exaggerated the lowliness of her position at Heals. She was not a shopgirl standing behind a counter and serving the customers. In fact, she was the head of the Buying Department with her own office, a secretary and a staff of three.

proceeded to astonish London with a series of dazzlingly inventive productions. He was a true pioneer, offering the public new ideas, new production techniques, new designs, new actors and above all, new plays. By the mid-1930s he was beginning to move into the cinema. When Dodie Smith's new play was ready he declared himself too busy to produce it but insisted on buying the year's option, which was his contractual right. The author's agent, Aubrey Blackburn, tried to persuade him to release it, but Dean, in true dog-in-the-manger spirit, refused. It was a frustrating and ludicrous situation but Blackburn managed to find a face-saving solution which seemed to satisfy all parties. Let Dean co-present it with Howard and Wyndham and Moss Empires. Binkie would thus take entire charge of the administration and leave Dean free to concern himself only with the production and all the artistic problems which might arise.

The new play showed a typical day in the life of the Hiltons, a nice, middle-class family living in a five-bedroom, three-bathroom house with front and back gardens in St John's Wood. It began with the parents waking up to early morning tea served by the housemaid and ended in the same bedroom at midnight with the parents going over the events of the day. The father is an accountant with a thriving practice in the City, the mother goes to Harrods for her shopping, the Gaiety for a matinée and to the Ritz for tea; the eager schoolgirl daughter who loves poetry, reveres the Kings of England, plays the piano brilliantly (her repertoire includes the devastatingly difficult "*Si Oiseau J'Etais*") and has one of the few genuinely witty lines in the play, "You can't shock a person whose favourite king is Charles II"; the teenage, school-leaving son is mad about motor cars and keen on the pretty girl next door; the nearly grown-up daughter of nineteen is in the throes of an unhappy love affair with an artist who is painting her portrait. There is a chattering housemaid, a solidly reliable cook and a grumbling melancholy charwoman. It was just an ordinary family of its period living an ordinary life in ordinary surroundings like the thousands of families who would come to see it. The nicely appropriate title was *Call it a Day*.

Binkie approved. With charm, humour and insight it was her best so far. It was also democratic in that the lives of the servants below stairs in the kitchen were shown with sympathy and without patronage. He knew that it would give extreme pleasure to a great many people and would run at the very least a year. How did she do it? By what mysterious alchemy did she take the commonplace and tedious small change of everyday life and transmute them into theatrical magic? Binkie thought it over at great length and finally came to the conclusion that it was because she made it all look so easy. He was prepared to bet a sizeable sum that every Home Counties matron, every retired colonel, every vicar and vicar's wife, every schoolgirl and teacher would walk out of the theatre convinced that they too could write a play as good if only they had the time. After all, if a mere shop girl could do it, surely they could too.

The only fly in all this was the tiresome necessity of working with Basil Dean. Dean was *le monstre plus sacré* of the London theatre. Every generation produces at least one supreme ogre, but Dean was vintage. The Dean atrocity stories are all well documented and testify to his cruelty, his power-mania and his tyranny. It all adds up to a legend which is as powerful now, half a century later, as it was at the time. Dean was a man who liked to rule by fear because he couldn't rule by anything else. He enjoyed making actresses cry and strong men shake and flinch. Those cold eyes, that glowering stare, that rasping, cutting voice, that devastating abuse and sarcasm could terrify anybody. *But* – and it was a big but – he was a genius. He could get performances out of his actors they didn't know they had in them. A Dean production was always a major and truly exciting event in the season and young actors and actresses fought to get into it. The experience was truly hellish but they emerged as real professionals and, in many cases, as stars.

It was also hellish for his authors, particularly if they were young and feminine. Dodie Smith was small, neatly-built, quick and bird-like, conspicuously successful and not in the least shy. On her first meeting with him she told him that she had not liked his production of *A Midsummer Night's Dream*, and revealed that his nickname in the profession was 'Bastard Basil'. She knew what she wanted, she would not tolerate any nonsense from Dean, and was not overawed by his talent or his position. She would frequently swear at him over the telephone calling him "bloody Basil, bloody fool", and when on the second night of *Autumn Crocus* she discovered that he had made extensive and damaging cuts without her permission, she lost her temper with him in the upper-circle bar and screamed that she would take out an injunction to get the play stopped if he did not restore the cuts immediately. No, Dodie Smith was not in the least bit shy.

But there was a problem with *Call it a Day* which had to be settled even before it was submitted for the Lord Chamberlain's licence. In a scene in the third act Martin, the son, is talking to Alistair, his best friend. Martin is seventeen, a nice, fresh, clean-limbed healthy youth in whose life the cricket bat and tennis racket and white flannels are never far away. Alistair is twenty, very smooth, polished and worldly. He knows about the arts and about life and Martin is impressed by his friend's superior intelligence and sophistication. Martin is due to start, reluctantly, in his father's accountancy practice. Alistair suggests he join his interior-decorating business. The scene ends with Alistair inviting Martin to see a new film at the very expensive Curzon cinema, with Alistair paying. The scene is short and written with delicacy, but the implications would be clear to any perceptive theatre-goer. What Alistair has in mind is something a lot closer than mere friendship. The subject of sexual deviation, however discreetly camouflaged, was abhorrent to the Lord Chamberlain and, by inference, to the public, and any play in which it was portrayed would either be denied a licence or censored beyond recognition. The author felt that the scene was essential to the overall view of the family and the lives they led. She would be very upset if it had to be cut or blandly and boringly rewritten. What was to be done?

Fortunately, Binkie knew the answer. There were two methods, he explained to her. The first was distraction. You wrote in an extra scene, something so shocking that the Lord Chamberlain would pounce on it in horror and demand that it be cut. You then defend it passionately. A lengthy correspondence results. You finally make a brave show of giving in and in the triumph of victory, the dangerous scene will be passed unnoticed. "But I think something a little simpler will be to our advantage, Dodie dear," he said one day in his office. "Retype the pages with a lot of long and boring stage directions. These will break up the dialogue and he'll be so bored with them that he probably won't even notice what the characters are actually saying to each other." Once again, his deviousness had the desired result. The play was returned to Binkie's office untouched. "It never fails," said Binkie when he and Harry had their next lunch.

If people complained the Lord Chamberlain could attend a performance and order changes, but as Binkie told Harry, "Get the right actor, somebody really attractive and *virile*, and you won't hear a squeak from *anybody*."

"Any ideas?"

"Yes," said Binkie happily, "he's coming to see me this afternoon and he's *gorgeous*."

He was an actor called Bryan Coleman. He was tall, blond, handsome, unmistakably heterosexual, and his vigorous, athletic presence effectively camouflaged the true significance of the scene. Binkie's judgement was once again proved sound, for in the whole of the long run there wasn't a single complaint or murmur.

Binkie was no less meticulous in the rest of the casting. Owen Nares and Fay Compton for the Hilton parents were an inspired choice: they achieved such sympathy and rapport that some of the press and many of the public thought they really were married. Engaging Owen

Nares' real-life son, Geoffrey, to play his stage son, Martin, was a delicate diplomatic gesture. Owen thought the world of his boy and it pleased him enormously to have his son in the same play. Geoffrey was not a particularly good actor but he was fresh, clean-limbed and nice-looking with a lot of coltish charm: his presence with his father would trigger off valuable publicity.

"I was terrified of Binkie," said Bryan Coleman years later. "He was so powerful and we all knew it. I was expecting him to make a pass at me but he didn't and it made me very nervous. He was much more interested in Geoffrey Nares with whom I shared a dressing-room. Binkie was in and out all the time fluttering over Geoffrey and it was so obvious that they wanted to be alone that I was virtually forced into leaving the dressing-room so they could be together. Geoffrey was a nice boy and we became friendly. He had quite a good stage career going for him, largely due to his father who didn't hesitate to pull strings on his behalf."

There were other casting problems. With a fine and characteristic disregard for convenience or cost, the author had written a play with a cast of sixteen and nine changes of scene. Only the five members of the Hilton family went through the play: the supporting parts were all important, extremely well written and required casting of a high order of status and experience. Binkie thus had the diplomatic problem of persuading Marie Löhr, Valerie Taylor, Muriel George and Austin Trevor to play characters who appeared only in one scene. Lest they might feel under-employed and wasted, he succeeded in convincing them that it was a bargain. "All that money for twenty minutes' work a night, Marie dear" – her West End salary was £50 a week – "it's money for jam. Think of all the reading you'll be able to catch up on, all the knitting you can do. *You* should be paying *me*."

There was further trouble over the casting of the schoolgirl daughter. Once again, it was the Juliet problem. "Oh, if only Owen had a schoolgirl daughter," said Binkie sadly one day, but nature had not been so generous. He found a young actress called Alexis France. She was in her early twenties but Dean did not like her. "She's too old," he snapped at the auditions but Dodie Smith persuaded her to return in a gym-slip and her hair in schoolgirl plaits. She looked every day of fifteen. Dean reluctantly gave her the part but became increasingly bored with her and Binkie noticed that he was giving her less and less direction as the rehearsals progressed. Dodie Smith was reduced to giving her private direction out of rehearsal time with the help of Fay Compton who ran her own acting school and was used to coaching young actresses.

Dean turned out to be every bit as difficult and unpleasant as Binkie had feared. Though there had been no outward hostility between him and Dodie Smith, the tensions were undoubtedly there and Binkie realised it was only a matter of time before there would be rows. He wanted to avoid this above all else: rows wasted time, and were bad for company morale. Dean was far more interested in upholding his authority than serving the play's best interests if they happened to conflict with his own: he hated criticism and the resentment he inspired in his companies was as much due to carelessness and inefficiency as to his tyrannical behaviour. Matters came to a head in Glasgow where the play had its out-of-town opening. The scene in the garden took place at sunset and Dean had bathed it in a deep golden glow which was not only wrong for the stated time of year – the author had made it abundantly clear that it was a pale spring twilight she wanted – but very unbecoming to Fay Compton's complexion. Of the two the latter was far more serious. More on her behalf than her own, Dodie protested to Dean who received the criticism impatiently, but finally agreed to relight it. But when they came to this scene at the dress rehearsal in London, nothing had been changed. It was still the detested and disfiguring amber glow.

In her book *Look Back with Astonishment*, Dodie Smith has given a detailed and richly entertaining account of the productions of her six principal plays, thus contributing a valuable chapter to the chronicle of the decade as well as an indispensable source book for future theatrical historians. She recalls that when the moment of crisis came they were all sitting in separate groups in the stalls. She complained to Binkie, seeing in him her best ally. He agreed: authors and star actresses had to be kept happy for in the long run, they are worth more than pro-ducers, however gifted. "Leave it to me, I'll speak to him. I'll sort it all out." He threaded his way to the stalls where Dean was sitting and spoke to him quietly. "Basil, dear, I really must talk to you about this lighting. Dodie isn't happy about it and neither is Fay and you did promise to change it." Dean, angry at being interrupted and furious that once again his authority was being challenged, turned on him. "Don't interfere, Beaumont, it's got nothing to do with you." Binkie smiled patiently and shook his head. "But, Basil, it's got *everything* to do with me and I must say I really don't like your attitude . . ." and before he could say another word Dean rose to his feet, grabbed his furled umbrella, raised it above his head and made what all witnesses agreed was a threatening gesture. There was nothing which Binkie disliked more than violence and unpleasant confrontation: he retreated hastily. "Dodie, he's gone *mad*, absolutely *mad*, I thought he was going to *hit* me. What's the *matter* with him?" Nothing like this had ever happened before or was to happen again. Dodie then went over to

Basil and asked him again to relight the garden scene according to her instructions in the play. Once again he refused. "I'm sick of being taught my business by you," and once again he brandished his umbrella and this time it really did look as if he was going to hit her: it was a question of Goliath getting his own back on David, for Dodie was tiny, little more than five feet high, whereas Dean was a heavyweight, all of six feet three inches and built on massively solid lines.

But this Strindbergian drama of jealousy, possessiveness and wounded pride now turned into farce. Seeing his wife at the point of receiving grievous bodily harm, Alec Beesley, her husband, rushed to protect her, though climbing over a series of stall seats in a theatre is not the easiest or quickest form of progression. He would have been quite prepared to wrest the umbrella from Dean and hit him with it, but this drastic action was forestalled and rendered unnecessary by the sudden appearance on the stage of Owen Nares in vest and underpants. He had been hastily summoned from his dressing-room by Fay Compton who told him excitedly that Dean and Alec Beesley were fighting and he must come at once or he would miss it. Other members of the company in varying degrees of undress appeared: the prospect of seeing Dean suffering a little bodily harm was too good to be missed. Alas, they were disappointed. The absurdity of the situation was obvious even to Dean in his volcanic fury. Still clutching his umbrella as if it was a rifle and he was going over the top at the Somme, he left the stalls, climbed on to the stage and stumped into the wings to the prompt corner, closely followed by Binkie. The conversation, as remembered by those of the company in earshot, went as follows:

"Basil, you must control yourself. This is *too* much. Calm down."

"Don't *you* tell *me* to calm down."

"You've got to do something about the lighting."

"Go away, Beaumont, you stupid little man. I'm the producer of this play. What do you know about lighting?"

"Of course you are, Basil dear, but Dodie knows what she wants and so does Fay. Now please calm down and let's talk reasonably."

"Everybody seems to think they can teach me my business."

"Nobody is trying to do that, Basil dear. You're a great producer. Give the play what it needs, it won't take a minute to relight the garden scene, you're so good at that sort of thing. Please, darling Basil, *please* . . ."

Binkie's particular brand of soothing oil stilled the troubled waters, and Dean eventually submitted. "All right, I'll relight it tomorrow morning: will that satisfy you?" and off he stumped still clutching his umbrella. "Don't worry, my darlings," said Binkie to the company, "he's going to do it and he's called a rehearsal for first thing tomorrow morning." And so it was. It is quite possible that Dean felt a touch of remorse for having made so much unnecessary trouble, for he made handsome amends by relighting the garden superbly. Neither Dodie nor Binkie had any further cause for complaint.

"There are many advantages to opening a play out of town, but I believe that God only comes to one first night and if he uses his ticket in the provinces the London opening may be smooth but lacking in electricity," was Dodie Smith's witty and perceptive comment in her book. The first-night performance was dull and lacking in sparkle: some of the company were deeply dissatisfied with their contributions, but this is a familiar situation at an opening when the actors are in such a state of high nervous tension that nothing is good enough. But none of this interfered with the audience's obvious enjoyment, which was considerable. The notices were excellent and the play ran at the Globe for fifteen months.

Binkie organised a short provincial tour after the London run. The company remained intact except for Geoffrey Nares who was replaced by Peter Osborn, one of the most strikingly beautiful young actors Binkie had ever seen, who had just achieved a well-deserved success playing Lord Alfred Douglas in Sewell Stokes' play about Oscar Wilde. The company morale was good, but in Edinburgh there was trouble. Binkie received an urgent summons from Fay, "Come at once, Owen has gone mad." He took the first train in the morning – the Flying Scotsman boasted that it could do the non-stop journey in seven hours – and went straight to Fay's dressing-room at the theatre. It seemed that Owen had suddenly and for no apparent reason gone on to the stage without his toupée revealing that, except for a little fringe on the sides, he was totally bald. "It makes him look so *ugly*," she complained, "and it's a pity because he is such a beautiful man. But the women in the audience obviously love it and they're looking at him *all the time*. I might as well not be in the play at all."

Binkie watched the performance and noted with great interest that every time Owen made an entrance there was an audible gasp of amazement, and that throughout his scenes the women clearly concentrated on him and not on the play. Clearly, the baldness was a matter of obsessive fascination. After the performance he took Owen out to a quiet supper. "Why have you done it?" he asked and Owen explained. "Well, you see, Binkie, I had lunch with Cedric Hardwicke a few weeks ago and he told me that he had been asked by a rather impertinent reporter if it was true that being bald gave you extra sexual potency, and he had replied that it *might* be true but it gave you fewer chances of proving it. Now, I thought that was rather an interesting thought so I decided to put it to the test. There's no doubt about it, my baldness does seem to be very attractive to all those women out there."

Over the meal, Binkie tried to persuade Owen to abandon the experiment and replace the toupée. "It's for the good of the play, Owen dear, you look so much better with it on and it is very distracting. The company isn't happy and neither is Fay. We don't want to upset her, do we, Owen dear?" he added, playing what he clearly thought was the trump card. Owen did not really mind upsetting Fay since relations had slightly cooled off in the last few weeks, but he had no desire to upset Binkie. The toupée was back the following night and once again the Hilton family was at peace.

ACT TWO

CHAPTER TWELVE

1936

H. M. Tennent – *The Old Maid* – *The Ante-Room*

January 1st 1936 was no ordinary New Year's Day. It was the second important milestone in Binkie's life, the year in which he persuaded Harry Tennent that the time had come to break away from Howard and Wyndham and start their own company. "Three years and twelve productions, most of them highly successful, it's enough for an apprenticeship, Harry dear, and I think we should cut the umbilical cord and be independent." The new firm was to be called H. M. Tennent Ltd, for Binkie was still a little shy about having his name appearing in public. "I can work so much better if I'm anonymous and tucked away in a back office," he said in explanation. "Eminence Grise is a role which I was destined to play."

A suite of offices high up above the Globe Theatre had been untenanted for some months: they were dimly lit, cramped and inaccessible. Nobody else wanted them and therefore Binkie got them cheap. Staff were engaged: Elsie Beyer, a small, plain woman, became Binkie's trusted secretary; a young South African, Kitty Black, for Harry in his penthouse office above Binkie's; a telephonist, Morrie, and an office-boy, the irrepressible Banks.

To reach them you could either climb an exhausting flight of concrete stairs from the street to the upper-circle entrance, or you could go by what rapidly became known in the West End as 'The Smallest Lift in the World'. It was tiny, big enough for one, though two could *just* squeeze in, which involved standing very close, knee to knee, stomach to stomach, chin to chin. It was an old lift which made its ascent very slowly and creakily. Visitors found this enforced proximity either very embarrassing or wildly funny, according to their taste and temperament. Legends abound.

"My name's Margaret Rutherford," said the young character actress making polite conversation to the tall slim actor who shared the lift with her. Owen Nares was not noted for his sense of humour and his reply was uncharacteristic: "What a coincidence, so's mine." Miss Rutherford was not amused. A very thin, young actor found himself sharing it with Dame Marie Tempest, short, podgy with a large bust which was pressing rather uncomfortably into his stomach. The young actor couldn't think of anything to say and the lift seemed to take a lifetime before they were finally released. "After all that, young man," said the Dame sternly, "we will just have to get married."

The office which Binkie had commandeered for himself was at the end of the short corridor. Although tiny, from its three small round windows with their splendid view of Shaftesbury Avenue and Piccadilly Circus, he could keep a watchful and lovingly possessive eye on his kingdom. This was his retreat, his eagle's nest, his power house, his Berchtesgaden, though there were those who thought this last analogy could be taken several stages further. The setting and furnishings were simple but, like the best simplicity, it wasn't cheap. The walls were panelled, there was a brocade settee seating two on which favoured visitors would be invited to sit, a very large desk, an ordinary chair on one side for less favoured visitors and Binkie's own chair, an elaborately carved affair with arms and head rest, reputedly bought in Germany and made of Bavarian pine. The office was uncluttered and decidedly ungrand. "Why should I waste my money as darling Alex Korda does with miles of carpet for people to cross before they come to the desk? It's a terrible waste and it doesn't impress anybody." However, there were different ways of playing the power game and Binkie wasn't above some of its ploys. Binkie's chair was on a rostrum, the visitor's chair was not, so the visitor, once he or she had sat down, found himself on a lower level, literally as well as figuratively looking up at Binkie. Not the greatest power ploy but psychologically actors always felt at a slight disadvantage when they were sitting down and attempting to talk about money.

But he had another ploy for putting actors at a disadvantage when money was being discussed. He would chat most amiably for a time, lulling you into a feeling of false security, and then he'd say, "Well, let's talk about money. What do you want?", and just as he said that he'd lean forward to offer you one of his special Du Maurier cigarettes and then his gold cigarette lighter, light it up and smile most charmingly as you took your first puff. After all that you didn't feel in such a good bargaining position and you'd probably accept what he offered even if it was less than you had in mind. Ralph Michael admitted that he had been caught by this little trick again and again until one day he refused the cigarette and thus put Binkie at a slight disadvantage. He forced Binkie to make an offer, asked for more – and got it.

Niagara was Binkie's nickname for the pile of unsolicited playscripts sent in by unknown but hopeful authors. Normally, it was a steady stream which rose to a positive waterfall after each first night when the accompanying publicity reminded the unseen army of playwrights that he was in management. This has been the lot of every theatre manager in history and it always will be. Now, in January 1936, the waterfall swelled into an avalanche once the announcements had appeared in the newspapers. But things had changed in three years: now the plays came in from all over the world: the Far East, Canada, South Africa, Australia and all the states in America. Now he didn't have to beg the big play agencies to send him something good: they arrived by every post with flattering letters.

His choice for the management's inaugural production was terribly important. All the West End was waiting to see what he was going to do and once again, as in 1933, there were many who wanted him to fail. The first play had not only to be good and successful, it had to be glitteringly so. No longer could he hide behind the Howard and Wyndham cloak if things went wrong. Now it was not only his reputation which was at stake but his money and that of his backers.

For weeks, with Harry Tennent and Elsie Beyer, he ploughed through hundreds of playscripts, all day and well into the night for weeks, but there was nothing which Binkie liked or felt he could cast properly or which struck a chord of interest and sympathy. "I go entirely by instinct," he said in one of his rare press interviews. "I can tell within ten pages if the play is going to appeal to me and although I like a famous name on the title page as well as anybody else, it is no guarantee of quality. I have to trust my instinct about what will work and what won't, for I have nothing else to judge by." Amongst the famous names who lamentably failed to rise to Binkie's standard were Bernard Shaw, St John Ervine, James Barrie, Eugene O'Neill, Frederick Lonsdale and Ivor Novello.

The search appeared to be over when his old friends, the Theatre Guild in New York, produced *The Old Maid*. The smash-hit of the 1934–5 Broadway season, it had been adapted by Zoe Akins from Edith Wharton's prize-winning novel, had won the Pulitzer Prize and the offer included Lillian Gish trailing shining clouds of her Hollywood glory. It was a seductively attractive package and when Binkie heard that every other West End manager was anxious to buy it for London and that he was being given first refusal, he did not hesitate.

The principal backer of the new firm was an old university friend of Harry's called Ted Cripps, with further contributions from Howard and Wyndham, Alexander Korda and Ivor Novello. The usual method of raising money, then as now, was to approach friends to contribute small amounts rather than try for the whole sum from a single backer. If this failed there were the professional backers known in theatrical parlance as 'angels'. Binkie always put a little of his own money into his plays. It was considered to be good luck, and if the play was a success it proved a lucrative investment.

The Old Maid was a novelettish story of a spinster who has an illegitimate child and manages to keep the secret from everybody except her best friend who, being childless, tries to win the child's love for herself. It was one of those plays which was doomed to be branded 'a woman's play' . . . by a woman, about women and for women. "It's pure tosh, Binkie," said Elsie Beyer laconically when she'd read the typescript, "but I don't see how it can fail." Binkie agreed with her: he didn't see how it could fail either. But they were both to find out with alarming speed.

The big mistake he made, and in later years he was to writhe in impotent fury at this stupidity, was to engage Leontine Sagan to produce the play. She was one of a group of women who had a talent for producing and were being given some enviable opportunities to display it. She had been born in Vienna, brought up in South Africa, trained by Max Reinhardt in Berlin and made a spectacular début in 1932 in London when she produced *Mädchen in Uniform*, a traumatic drama about schoolgirls under the tyranny of a cruel headmistress who drives one of them to suicide. Binkie liked the production and when they met at the first-night party, he liked her too and was therefore delighted to ask her to direct Ivor Novello's *Murder in Mayfair*. Her behaviour throughout rehearsals was pleasant and un-assuming; she got on famously with Novello who entrusted two of his best-known musicals to her. She was, however, a distinctly unattract-ive character: a ferocious bull-dyke, decades before the term had been invented, a sadistic lesbian who liked to rule by fear and tyranny; Binkie did not know the full extent of her character nor could he possibly have anticipated the circumstances which brought it to the surface, though he might have made an educated guess from her masculine clothes – dark suit, collar, shirt and tie – closely cropped grey hair and her desire to be addressed and referred to as Leo.

Lillian Gish arrived at Southampton on the *Queen Mary* and at Victoria Station on the boat train to the sort of reception from her many thousands of fans which might have been considered a little excessive for the Second Coming, but seemed entirely right and proper for the star of *Intolerance, Birth of a Nation, Way Down East* and *Broken Blossoms*. At forty she still looked like a young girl, as pretty as a picture by Corot or Titian with all the sweetness and vulnerability of her much persecuted screen heroines. She was unmarried, a fact which may well have planted unjustified hope in her producer's heart. It is not known precisely where, when or how the inevitable overtures were made but Lillian Gish was not interested. The love whose name

Leontine Sagan not only dared speak but was anxious to shout from the rooftops, thus turned to hatred. She gave Lillian a hard time and the company were forced to witness a particularly distressing display of cruelty and psychological sadism. Nothing that Lillian had suffered at the hands of Griffith or Stroheim, who had their own version of the cruelty game but always for the sake of a better film, could have prepared her for this holocaust of insults, abuse, sarcasm, offensive personal remarks, bullying and all bad things short of physical violence. It was all done with one object in mind: to shatter her confidence, reduce her to abject servility so she would come begging for help and, if possible, destroy the performance so Binkie would have to sack her and replace her with another whom Leo would select from the many pliant young actresses she had at her disposal.

Lillian was an easy victim: she had enjoyed little stage experience, only six plays in her life since she had given up the cinema, and little enough confidence. She had always been under the control of a strong and dominant master-brain, but she had never before experienced anything like this. Leo had learned a number of confidence-eroding ploys. When she addressed the others by their first names, she called Lillian simply "Gish", as if she, Leo, was the chief wardress of Holloway Jail – which most of the company thought was her spiritual home – and Lillian a new and rebellious life prisoner. "*Gish*," she bellowed in her harsh Teutonic accent through the loudspeaker from the back of the gallery, "I can't hear a bloody word you're saying, speak *up*," thus forcing the wretched woman to speak louder and louder till she ended up shrieking her precious vocal chords to shreds. "*Gish*, you don't know a single bloody word of this play," if she paused to take a prompt in a long and difficult speech. "*Gish*, you're the worst actress I've ever seen. Where did you learn how to act, *if* you ever did . . .?" The company protested, first mildly, and then with rising indignation. The last week of rehearsal took place in Glasgow where they were due to open at the King's Theatre in mid-March. Irene Vanbrugh called a company meeting: the situation was becoming intolerable and to avoid total disaster something must be done. A telegram was sent to Binkie, signed by all the company, putting the facts before him and inviting him to Glasgow to see for himself what was happening.

Binkie took the night train, sneaked into the theatre and watched the rehearsal from the stage box, unseen by producer or company. He saw that nothing had been exaggerated: Leo was behaving like a sadistic monster and Lillian was clearly terrified by this treatment. In the lunch-hour he called a company meeting in the dress-circle bar, telling them that the matter was very serious and clearly Leontine Sagan had to go, "but not until the end of the week, so please don't tell her or even let her know I'm in Glasgow". The company managed to struggle through the final week of rehearsals with lighter hearts, knowing that she would soon be gone.

When *The Old Maid* opened Lillian did her best but it was clear that the savage punishment she had suffered over the past month and the strain of it all had taken its toll of her energy and confidence. Her performance was competent, but little more. The local notices were respectful and in deference to her film-star fame the houses were good but not full. Obviously much work had to be done on the production and on Lillian before either were ready for London. In the meantime, the matter of a replacement producer was urgent. Guthrie McClintic who had directed the play in New York was in London. At Binkie's behest he travelled to Glasgow and saw the Tuesday night perform-ance, sitting with Binkie in the stage box. McClintic, however, did not care for anything he saw: he disliked the sets and costumes, thought Lillian Gish was very dull, the supporting cast inadequate and everything which Leo had done wrong. In addition, he had become bored with the play. "Sorry, Binkie, old man," he said as they travelled back to London, "if you'd asked me to produce it from the start I'd have been happy, but I really don't like taking in other people's dirty washing." Binkie tried to persuade other producers of note to come to the rescue – Guthrie, Irene Hentschel, Murray Macdonald – even Komisarjevsky – but all were either uninterested or unavailable. *The Old Maid* struggled on for three more dispiriting weeks and what was left of her was finally given a decent Christian burial in Manchester.

It had been a perfectly horrible experience. Apart from the humili-ation of defeat there was the financial blow, for the production had cost well in excess of three thousand pounds, every penny of which was lost. It was hard to decide which was the more insufferable: the sympathy of his friends who were politely surprised that there was to be no London opening, or the barely concealed gloating of his enemies. Some managers could take failure in their stride: Bronson Albery was always philosophical, but he owned his own theatres and the loss was correspondingly small: Basil Dean snarled a bit, but he was always too full of the future to be bothered about the past: Cochran's beaming smile was never more radiant and reassuring than in the face of defeat. But Binkie took it very hard. It was his first taste of real failure: *The Winding Journey* had been bad enough, but at least it had been given a rapturous first night, it was a very happy company and the solitary week had generated a lot of goodwill and glamour from its film stars. It was nothing like *The Old Maid* whose atmosphere of gloom and despondency had put the black mark on it from the start.

Binkie could not even bring himself to take a proper leave of it. He did not see the play after he had put up the notice, he did not say goodbye and thank you to the company after the final performance, there was no farewell drink and supper with Lillian Gish who, greatly to her surprise, was left to fend for herself. A more resilient manager would have done all these things, but for once Binkie's good social behaviour deserted him, and in so doing set a pattern which was to last for the rest of his life. He viewed failure as the medieval priests viewed the Black Death: not only to be shunned, but all memory to be exorcised. Nobody and nothing which had touched it would ever be used again lest they contaminate a healthy new play with the deadly infection. None of the actors was ever to act again in a Tennent's production and the sets, furniture and costumes, instead of being kept for a lucrative re-hire, were sold. Binkie's forty years of management were to be exceedingly well documented with every programme, press cutting and photograph meticulously preserved, but nothing survives of *The Old Maid*, not a solitary notice, programme or picture. Binkie never referred to it and the associates working in the office were firmly discouraged from doing so either. *The Old Maid* just did not exist. It had never existed. It was a play that never was.

This still left the problem of finding an alternative new play to inaugurate the H. M. Tennent management in London, all the more urgent since the West End was watching and waiting. But bad luck is not so easily exorcised. With one exception during the year which followed Binkie seemed to have lost his judgement. "What could possibly have attracted him to *The Ante-Room?*" enquired his friends in despair in months to come. It was likely that Binkie had been blinded by famous names. Kate O'Brien, the author of the original novel, was a famous, best-selling novelist, her book had won the Hawthornden Prize and the dramatisation had been made by Geoffrey Gomer, an actor-playwright with many original plays and adaptations to his credit. It was a study of a middle-class Irish family living in a dimly-lit draughty house in Tipperary. A spinster daughter, deeply in love with her sister's husband, finally commits suicide as a desperate remedy for the horrifying situation: a mother is dying of cancer. There are tears, lamentations and hysterics. It all takes place in a single dark, late-Victorian interior, as if Lady Gregory of the Abbey Theatre had rewritten Ibsen under the influence of Strindberg.

More famous names were enlisted. Guthrie McClinic declared himself delighted to accept the challenge of what he freely admitted was a difficult play: Diana Wynyard read it while listening to the gramophone in her newly-acquired Sussex cottage and admitted that the tears were streaming down her cheeks. Jessica Tandy and the ever-elegant Ronald Ward, one of Binkie's favourite actors, joined the company. The vital part of the chilly, sexually frustrated brother-in-law was not easy to cast and when Bill Linnit, a friend of Binkie and one of the few London agents he really liked and trusted, told him that there was a young actor in Liverpool who was worth considering, Binkie did not hesitate. He drove there in Bill's car.

The young actor was Michael Redgrave who had been at the Playhouse for over a year. He had been a schoolmaster at Cranleigh and was now married to the actress, Rachel Kempson. He was playing Richard of Bordeaux on the night Binkie and Bill made their trip to Liverpool, but owing to a mechanical breakdown they were delayed and did not get to the theatre until the end of the evening, time enough to see the last two scenes. "I *am* sorry, I am truly sorry," said Binkie with fervour when he finally met Redgrave in his dressing-room. "What a shame, what a terrible thing. But I thought you were *splendid*." It was evidence of the low profile which Binkie had managed to keep during the last three years that neither Michael Redgrave nor Rachel Kempson had ever heard of him though they gathered from some long-distance phone calls which Binkie proceeded to make on the backstage telephone that he was something to do with the theatre. "Rachel and I decided that rather than take them to supper at the Adelphi Hotel, it would be more chic for us to give them white wine and smoked salmon in our rooms," wrote Redgrave. "Mr Beaumont, we learned, was a new and powerful producer. He asked me if I knew *The Ante-Room*. I didn't, I replied. 'Pity,' he said, 'I was thinking of offering you the leading male part in a dramatisation of it.' At nine the next morning, Rachel and I were up and out searching every bookshop in Liverpool for Kate O'Brien's novel. My part, if the novel could be trusted, was a good one and the prospect of landing such a leading role in the West End was immensely pleasing. Meanwhile, Binkie said arrangements could be made and a script sent to me as soon as possible."

But the theatre has one thing in common with politics – a week is a long time. Within seven days of this conversation with Binkie, Michael Redgrave met Tyrone Guthrie who offered him and Rachel a full season at the Old Vic under his direction, with an interesting selection of parts in the company of Laurence Olivier and Edith Evans. It was an offer he could not think of refusing. Binkie had talked about fifty pounds a week, whereas Guthrie could offer only twenty, but the professional advancement was worth infinitely more than the financial gain. It was a good, sensible decision and one which he never regretted. Replacing Redgrave was not easy but one evening at Clemence Dane's flat, the subject was brought up by Eddie Marsh. He was one of those people that every artistic community needs: a man who knows everything and everybody, a man of extensive knowledge and inspired judgement, a man of ideas, a man who can advise and guide without thought of self-interest or advancement. He was a regular first-nighter and party-goer, a close friend of everybody who mattered (he had been Winston Churchill's right hand for twenty-three years) and when he mentioned the name of Marius Goring, Binkie listened and remembered. Goring had recently attracted a great deal of critical attention in *The Happy Hypocrite* which Clemence Dane had adapted from the Max Beerbohm story for the particular talents of her other close friend, Ivor Novello, and he was clearly an actor marked out for special attention and treatment.

Binkie approached him and made the offer, which was instantly accepted. The play went into rehearsal and opened in Edinburgh a month later at the end of July. It was a difficult part to play convincingly. The young doctor was supposed to be irresistibly charming but he was also thoroughly evil. How does an actor reconcile these two opposites? "It required an actor of far greater age and experience than I," Goring later remembered, and he received his first hint that all was not well in Manchester when he saw Laurence Olivier in the stalls. Months later at the Old Vic, they discussed it. "Binkie asked me to take over," he said, "but I couldn't. This part was not for me. And I didn't see any actor playing that part successfully. It could only be done by emphasising the charm and letting the brutalities speak for themselves. You have to work against the text. I think Michael Redgrave might just have got away with it." At the end of the Manchester week, Binkie spoke to Marius in his dressing-room. "I'm going to have to say something rather *nasty* and the last time I said anything like this was to Robert Donat. I'm terribly sorry, Marius dear, but I don't think it's going to work," which verdict came as no surprise to the unhappy actor. "Let's talk about money. Call at my office sometime next week." It was all done very charmingly.

On Monday, Goring presented himself at Binkie's office.

"What do you want?" asked Binkie.

"I thought of two weeks' money," replied Goring.

"I was going to give you four weeks," said Binkie. "Let's split the difference and make it three." He gave him a cheque there and then for one hundred and fifty pounds – "A lot of money in those days," said Goring, "and Binkie did it with great delicacy." A week later Goring started rehearsals for a new play, where he met Lucie Mannheim, the actress, and eventually married her. Binkie always liked to take the credit for any matrimonial events in his companies. "You did rather well out of *The Ante-Room*," he later said to Goring. "If it hadn't been for me you would never have met your wife."

Clifford Evans was the final replacement and *The Ante-Room* had its London opening at the Queen's Theatre on August 14th to notices which veered between the respectful to the downright hostile. "Tennents claim they are presenting a Victorian comedy," said the *Daily Telegraph*. "What do they mean by comedy? It's one of my favourite novels but a story where a man shoots himself because he's fallen in love with his wife's sister is not in my view a comedy." The acting was praised and it was generally agreed that Diana Wynyard had never acted with greater poignancy, but the critics did not like the play and those dreaded words, 'gloomy', 'tragic', 'depressing' and – the most destructive word of all – '*intelligent*' had their inevitably discouraging effect on the box office. "Why does he call it *intelligent*?" exclaimed Binkie with unusual petulance the following day. "Intelligence has got nothing to do with it. Who wants intelligence when they go to the theatre? Are they trying to kill us?"

The Ante-Room closed after ten unhappy days. It was never published and quickly vanished into limbo. A few weeks later Michael Redgrave opened at the Old Vic as Mr Horner in a sumptuous new production of *The Country Wife*, designed by Oliver Messel and backed by American money, and thus started on the long road which was to lead to stardom and a knighthood.

Out of the debris of *The Ante-Room* did emerge the lighting engineer, Joe Davis. Already well known and highly respected, he had lit many of Cochran's productions, most notably *Helen!* with Oliver Messel's legendary décor, and was largely responsible for the visual beauty which was Cochran's speciality. The one kind thing which the critics had said about *The Ante-Room*, and on this point they were all in agreement, was to praise its lighting. It was beautiful, subtle and imaginative: the sombre flickering glow of the coal fire and the pools of darkness in the oppressively brown and blood-red drawing-room in which the play's most important scene was played, added immeasurably to the doomed atmosphere.

Guthrie McClintic had enjoyed working with Joe and had been greatly impressed by the results and the press reaction. He telephoned Binkie the day after the first night. "Is Joe Davis free? I've got a couple of plays I'd like him to light for me in New York."

What followed was a good example of Binkie's well-known deviousness and skill in manipulation. "Get back to Brown's Hotel, Guthrie dear, and I'll come back to you as soon as I can." He called in Elsie Beyer. "Elsie dear, what sort of arrangement do we have with Joe Davis?"

"No particular arrangement, Binkie. He is free to take work where he wants. We don't have him under contract."

"I wonder if we should? Good lighting men of Joe's calibre are terribly important and I'd never forgive myself if I let him get away." He put a call through to Joe at his home in Ilford, engaging him to work for Tennents on a permanent basis. Binkie then phoned Guthrie McClintic at Brown's. "I'm terribly sorry, Guthrie, terribly sorry to disappoint you but I've just learned that Joe Davis does have commitments in England which make it quite impossible for him to go with you to America. I'm very sorry. You'll have to approach the other Joe" (Jo Mielziner, the American lighting designer). He was careful not to reveal where and for whom those commitments had been made and it was years before Guthrie found out.

Binkie was one of the few managers who appreciated to the full the importance of a first-class lighting designer and the contribution he makes to the theatre. It was evidence of Binkie's rising fame in the West End – despite current failures – that Joe Davis accepted his offer without hesitation or conditions. H. M. Tennent was obviously going to be a very busy management: the work would be interesting and of the highest quality. There was no contract and there never would be. Like all the Tennent's staff, Joe trusted Binkie, Binkie trusted Joe and that trust would never be betrayed by either side. Joe Davis was not ambitious, or greedy for wealth or fame. He was a simple man who wanted only to be able to do his work under ideal conditions and with the secure knowledge that there would be plenty of it. Binkie did not believe in paying his staff more than necessary since he firmly believed that the honour of working for him would fully compensate for any slight financial loss: it was a measure of his success that he was able to persuade so many people for such a long period of time that this was so. He paid Joe £7 a week and kept him at that for ten years, increasing it to £10 a week in 1946 during the *Oklahoma!* rehearsals at Drury Lane.

Binkie did not believe in giving unnecessary publicity to his staff lest it might make them conceited and give them unwarranted ideas of their importance: also, he did not want rival managements to approach them with better offers with which he did not wish to compete. Throughout their thirty-seven years together Joe never once had his name or photograph in the press and not for the first ten years did his name appear in the programme. "Why should he?" argued Binkie when the subject came up. "Joe hasn't asked for it and doesn't want it. His professional status is not dependent on credit. He has a permanent job with me and that's all he wants, so we're all happy." Play followed play with no more than a week in between – for which he was not paid – and a fortnight's unpaid holiday every year. But he did receive good seats for all first nights and other performances as required, a card from Binkie on first nights, an invitation to the party, a bottle of wine from Fortnums at Christmas. "I don't want credit," Joe used to say. "After all, everybody knows that I do Binkie's lighting and they can see it's mine, they don't need to see it in the programme."

In America it was all very different. The lighting designers were treated like royalty: not only a huge initial fee, but a percentage of the profits. Jo Mielziner, with over three hundred productions to his credit, had an apartment in the Dakota overlooking Central Park, drove a white Rolls-Royce, received a number of awards and became one of the best-known figures in the New York theatre. If Joe Davis had known of Guthrie McClintic's offer and had accepted it, he would have enjoyed a similar career, and it was characteristic of his good, sweet nature that when he did eventually discover the truth, he accepted it without resentment.

The dismal saga of failure continued as disaster followed disaster. Had Binkie totally lost his judgement, the friends and the firm asked in alarm, even despair? What, for example, could possibly have attracted him to *Farewell Performance* by the Hungarian, Lajos Zilahy? A world-famous actress learns that she has terminal cancer, but instead of going into hospital, as any sensible woman would have done, she puts on a white wig, granny clothes, lines and shadows on her face and spends the next few months in a mountain holiday hotel to taste – as she naïvely puts it – the pleasures of being old without the uncomfortable realities. These pleasures consist of little more than being fussed over by the waiters, having doors opened for her by page-boys, and being pestered for details of her past life by the other old ladies. Not unreasonably, she gets very bored by all this and returns to the theatre. In the last act she makes a splendid and glamorous comeback, conveniently dying in the dressing-room in the arms of her lover, played with dash and charm by Griffith Jones, another of Binkie's discoveries (after some small parts elsewhere) and a fellow Welshman.

There were various reasons why this farrago of absurdities figured in the H. M. Tennent autumn schedule for 1936, hardly satisfactory when so much of other people's money was involved. Firstly, Harry Tennent liked it and Binkie had acquired a healthy respect for his judgement. Secondly, Mary Ellis adored it. On the crest of Coward and Novello successes, the public loved her. Thirdly, it had been a huge success in Budapest and elsewhere in Europe, and fourthly, Alexander Korda recommended it, placed a copy into Binkie's hands and managed to work himself into a state of great excitement, assuring Binkie over many extravagant suppers at Claridge's that the entire resources of the Austro-Hungarian Empire would be at his disposal: brother Vincent would design the three sets, brother Zoltan would produce it, Molnar, Hungary's most successful and esteemed playwright, would give it his seal of approval in the press announcements and he, Korda, would see to it that the Hungarian Ambassador would attend the first night and give a large party afterwards at the Embassy. Binkie was greatly amused by this demonstration of national solidarity. "Every Hungarian in London wants to have a finger in the goulash," he said to Harry, "and they're all so *loyal* to each other. We shall have to call them the Magyar Mafia." In addition to all these small services, Korda would put up two thousand pounds, representing half the required capital.

Alas for national solidarity: Vincent Korda declared himself too busy to design the sets for the theatre nor would he accept the modest fee he was offered: Zoltan had never produced plays in the theatre in England and Binkie was unwilling to risk such an expensive and delicate task on a novice. And although the Hungarian Ambassador occupied the royal box and the Diplomatic Corps turned up in force, adding several extra degrees of medalled and ribboned splendour to the occasion, nothing could save the play. The gallery came perilously near to booing, having been restless throughout the whole of the last act, as the press eagerly pointed out. It staggered through the weekend and second week but Binkie was finally forced to withdraw it after only eleven performances. This was one more than *The Ante-Room* but with the firm losing four thousand pounds, this was no cause for rejoicing. And plays translated from the Hungarian were overnight placed firmly at the top of Binkie's special black-list and remained there for the rest of his life.

What *did* the public want, asked Binkie despairingly? Maybe home-grown London favourites rather than expensively imported Americans. Edna Best had had a devoted public following ever since the mid-twenties when she had scored such a huge success as Tessa in *The Constant Nymph*. Basil Dean brought Lesley Storm's *Follow Your Saint* to Binkie and declared his intention of putting up half the money and producing it, another tribute to his favourite actress and the one with whom he was supposed to have been deeply in love. It was a four-handed marital drama and the kindest comments in the indifferent notices were 'wishy-washy' and 'tepid'. Edna Best had lost that youthful radiance and was now a matronly, middle-aged figure. The play lasted for ten performances.

Perhaps the public wanted historical spectacle with all the joys of period sets and costumes? *Charles the King* by Maurice Colbourne was placed in his hands with a strong recommendation by Tyrone Guthrie who had been asked to produce, but was not available even though here was very much his sort of play.

Maurice Colbourne belonged to that rare category of actor whom the theatre happily and fruitfully produces on occasions: the gifted amateur, the wealthy dilettante who can act a little, write a bit, and produce sometimes when the mood takes him. He had inherited a fortune from his father, an industrialist, so he could please himself about what he did and where and with whom. With his lifelong friend and partner, the actor Barry Jones, he formed a company to take the plays of Bernard Shaw across America and Canada: he took over the lease of the Ambassadors Theatre and presented a number of plays which failed to make money but were drenched in good, respectful critical comment. He found time to write a book, *The Real Bernard Shaw*, to teach students at RADA and to become a Governor at Stratford-upon-Avon. There have been very few men in the theatre endowed with so many talents who can practise each of them with distinction, but Maurice Colbourne, aided and abetted by Barry Jones, contributed much to that flavour which characterised the theatre between the two wars.

Binkie and Maurice had met on the first night of *Moonlight is Silver* – in which Barry Jones played Gertrude Lawrence's brother – and struck an instant rapport. Maurice was just the sort of man Binkie liked: handsome, charming, sophisticated, bursting with talent and one who loved the theatre above all else. Binkie and Harry were frequent visitors at the spacious house at 48 Campden Hill Square, which Maurice and Barry Jones shared throughout their lives, and weekend guests at the house in Jersey where Barry had been born.

Charles the King, with Barry Jones as Charles, Gwen Ffrangcon-Davies as the Queen, George Merritt as Oliver Cromwell and Colbourne himself as the Earl of Stafford, was a chronicle play in fourteen plodding scenes and three hours of turgidly pedestrian dialogue, not quite gadzookery, but bad enough to cause real problems for the actors. It opened on October 9th 1936 and it seemed at last that Binkie was right: the public did most definitely want history and spectacle. *Charles the King* ran for six months, but it lost an appalling amount of money in the process. With thirteen elaborate settings, including an accurate reconstruction of Westminster Hall for the trial, a cast of forty-seven and over a hundred period costumes and wigs, it could hardly do otherwise. With hindsight, this was one of those plays which could never have made money no matter how long it ran, for the expenses always exceeded receipts, even in a good week. Fortunately, the author backed the production out of his own pocket, so Binkie and the firm did not lose any money. But nor did it make any, apart from its management fee.

Diana Wynyard was surely the answer to all Tennent's problems. The public had lamentably failed to support her in *The Ante-Room* but fickleness does not last for ever and surely they would return. *Heart's Content* by W. Chetham Strode was a charming little piece about a girl who marries a boring banker – played by that-very-good-actor-Cyril-Raymond – the son of an aristocratic family, but leaves him to live with a foreign waiter. The play contained much witty writing and some amusing comments on social snobbery and the pre-war social scene: the author showed courage in placing his last act in 1941 and having his waiter-hero return as Austrian Ambassador, but it opened on December 23rd 1936, and Binkie should have realised that January and February are traditionally dead months. *Heart's Content* struggled for two months before dying of hypothermia in what was one of the coldest winters in memory. It deserved better.

"Surely we can't fail with Marie Tempest," said Binkie to Elsie Beyer one day with the air of a heavy gambler producing his Queen of Trumps. *Retreat from Folly* by Amy Kennedy Gould and Eileen Russell offered yet another, and entirely typical, Marie Tempest part. Once again she is a bustling, capable, efficient matron who organises other people's lives, in this case a husband and two grown-up children whom she hasn't seen for twenty years since the divorce and whose lives are in a terrible mess, the daughter living with a married man and the son involved with criminal activities.

Notices were good in the uncritical Tempest-worshipping provinces – her "performance is not so much a gem as a Koh-i-noor diamond," said the *Scotsman* sycophantically – but by February 1937 London press and public showed they were getting a little bored with Marie Tempest vehicles, mechanical and predictable in their plotting and development, and in which she spent all of two and a half hours on the stage, leaving it only briefly for her seven costume changes.

It might have struggled through a respectable three months but it was cut short when Willie Graham Browne, who had been enjoying good health in the Indian summer of his life, suddenly died of a heart attack in the afternoon of March 3rd 1937. Mary had spent all her life putting the theatre first before everything and everybody. "The show must go on" was one of her favourite and most oft-stated principles.

Now she had a unique chance of putting it into practice. Binkie offered to cancel the performance, but she refused. The rumour that she would not act in any play without her husband turned out to be untrue. The understudy, Jack Lambert, rehearsed all afternoon with the company. In front of a packed audience, tense, expectant, deeply sympathetic but bursting with curiosity to see how she would cope with the crisis, the show did indeed go on. At her entrance and for her solo call at the end she received what was generally regarded as the greatest ovation of her entire career.

"Take me home, Binkie darling," she said afterwards, and he did. They stayed up till the small hours unable to sleep but instead talking and weeping and talking. He helped her to her bed and stayed while she talked and cried, cried and talked some more and eventually fell asleep. The following day Queen Mary called to offer her condolences and the widow of little more than a year was able to mourn and advise the widow of twenty-four hours. Binkie diplomatically kept this meeting out of the papers, but saw to it that everybody in the West End knew about it nevertheless. *Retreat from Folly* was withdrawn after only six weeks.

CHAPTER THIRTEEN

1937

George and Margaret

The situation which had been serious was now desperate. The money had all gone, the backers were badly demoralised and already rumours were circulating that Binkie was bankrupt. If a winner could not be found the firm would have to cease trading and close down heavily in debt and that, after only a year, would be an unthinkable humiliation. Only a miracle could save Binkie and the firm which is precisely what he got, and it came from a totally unexpected source.

Gerald Savory, a young actor who, like Robert Morley, was unknown, unsuccessful and unemployed, had written a light domestic comedy called *George and Margaret*. He had sent it to the twelve principal West End managements and it had been rejected by all of them. By irony, the first to do so was Binkie himself in a routine rejection of which he sent dozens every week. When subsequent events made it inevitable that he should be confronted with this letter he laughed loudly and apologetically. "You can't seriously expect me to read every play which is sent to me," he said, "I do have to trust my readers." He had two outside the office: a young journalist, Richard Clowes, and a young actor, George Astley, a friend of Harry Tennent. It was Clowes who later remembered reading the play. "It didn't seem to have anything remotely funny. I struggled through two of the three acts and then gave up in despair. You see, it didn't read at all well." Some plays read well: their quality is immediately apparent, for the words seem to jump off the page. But other plays, even very good ones, read badly: it needs an X-ray eye and a stupendous feat of the imagination to see how they would act on the stage and an over-worked reader with twenty scripts to be reported on by Monday will frequently have neither.

Understandably, Savory was deeply discouraged. He put it away in a bottom drawer and *George and Margaret* might never have been presented, Savory might never have written another play, H. M. Tennent might have been driven into the hands of the Official Receiver, Binkie might have been forced into a humiliating return to the economic safety of Howard and Wyndham, and this book would never have been written, were it not for the sudden appearance on the scene of a middle-aged gentleman with grey hair, upright figure, aquiline face and a well-pressed three-piece tweed suit. His name was H. G. Stoker.

Harry Stoker had spent his early life in the Royal Navy. In the First World War he saw action at Jutland and Gallipoli and had retired at the age of thirty-five with the rank of commander. Drifting casually into the profession, he had become an actor entirely by accident,* something which, though not impossible, would be extremely difficult under present-day regulations but which was not uncommon in those carefree days before Equity started. His first appearance was in *A Grain of Mustard Seed* in 1920, but is better remembered for creating the part of playing the colonel in the Sunday night try-out and the subsequent two-year West End run of *Journey's End*. Harry Stoker was a close friend of Gerald Savory's mother and had known the family all his life. He was ideally suited to the role of godfather, for not only was he by now a good and experienced actor, he was also a playreader working in the drama department of the Curtis Brown literary agency, and if all that was not enough he was on the committee of the Repertory Players.

This was one of the many Sunday play-presenting societies which flourished between the wars and with good reason. Then as now, there was an urgent need to try out new plays and give showcase performances which might tempt the managements to buy options for the West End. The repertory theatres were a frequent and obvious choice and over the decades had been a fruitful breeding-ground for actors as well as plays. But provincial casting had its pitfalls: there was

---

*Harry was fond of describing just how it happened. He and an actor friend were strolling down Maiden Lane on their way to lunch at the Garrick Club and they passed the stage door of the Adelphi Theatre. "I've got to pop in for a moment, old man, to do an audition. Why don't you come down and watch? You might find it amusing." Harry had never witnessed a theatrical audition, and did not even know what it was but he followed his friend down to the stage and found himself in the wings surrounded by middle-aged actors who went on the stage, read the scene and came off. His friend in his turn did the audition. "It's your turn now," said the stage manager thinking that Harry was another actor, pushing him on to the brightly lit stage and giving him the script. Harry read the scene and then he and the friend walked to the Garrick, chuckling with delight over what they thought was a wonderfully funny joke. The laughter ceased abruptly when they arrived at the Garrick to find a message for Harry from the management. He'd got the job and could he start rehearsals tomorrow. History, alas, does not reveal the name of the actor friend nor any details of his subsequent career but it is safe to assume that he never again made the mistake of taking a civilian friend to an audition.

always the possibility of a couple of good performances at the top and mediocrity underneath. Also, the London managers were strangely reluctant to put themselves out in any way. Journeys, even to cities as close as Birmingham or Manchester were troublesome. "You'd think it was Siberia the way they go on," said one Hull playwright bitterly. A good showcase had to be accessible. The obvious solution was to present new plays in a London theatre and on a Sunday night. The advantages of this arrangement were that you could get actors currently working in West End plays, you could get the theatre without charge, and – if suitable – the set currently in use. Costumes, wigs, furniture and props could often be borrowed and the only unavoidable expenses would be the double-time demanded by the stage and front-of-house staff.

Gerald gave *George and Margaret* to Harry who read it immediately and liked it. At this distance of time it is difficult to explain just why this ex-sailor was able to see what so many experienced managers did not but maybe his eyes, after so many years of scanning the horizon for enemy ships, had acquired an extra sharpness. He put it into the hands of the Repertory Players' committee and gently steered it through the channels of procrastination and red tape. There was no great enthusiasm but they had not done a light comedy for some time and with nothing else remotely interesting they decided to do it. Theatrical casting is always difficult: the actors you want are not available and those who are you don't want, but casting for the Repertory Players tended to be more haphazard because you could only use actors who were members and were willing to work for nothing. Nevertheless, Richard Bird, the producer, managed to assemble a cast which varied between the inspired down to the merely competent and *George and Margaret* had its very first performance on January 15th 1937 at the Strand Theatre.

Binkie disliked Sunday night performances and usually refused to attend unless there was some special reason. It meant cutting into his country weekend and as he spent every weekday night in the theatre it was a pleasant change occasionally to get away from it. Also, he was slightly repelled by the faint smear of amateurishness which prevailed: the atmosphere of poverty, of high hopes and low budgets, of making do with second best, of emotional over-eagerness. He had noticed that the audiences for these occasions were deeply depressing, consisting mainly of second-string critics and friends and families of the actors and author eagerly applauding every entrance and laughing too loudly at every quasi-comedy line. The plays were rarely interesting – the last really big success rising out of a Sunday night had been *Journey's End* – but you could never be sure and it would be extremely painful to allow a rival, the dreaded Basil Dean or the ubiquitous Alberys or the all-embracing Charles Cochran to find something good merely because he didn't know it was there: thus Sunday night performances were always attended by somebody in the Firm.

On this particular Sunday Elsie Beyer deputised for him. In the second interval, she made a phone call to Binkie: "This play is absolutely marvellous," she said excitedly, "we've got to get it. I'd say it was the funniest thing I've seen for years." A lesser man would have insisted on seeing the script, would have taken his time thinking about it, by which time the play would have been snapped up by somebody else. But Binkie knew better. If Elsie Beyer thought it was as good as all that then it certainly was and no argument. She knew what he liked and what the Firm wanted. It was one of Binkie's great assets as a leader. It was not enough that he employed first-class people: he also trusted them.

George and Margaret was one of those light comedies with farcical trimmings whose content is difficult to describe and whose success is impossible to explain. Gerald Savory had cunningly taken every cliché character and situation from decades of comic tradition and had woven a richly entertaining soufflé: absent-minded father for ever puffing his pipe and doing *The Times* crossword (Noel Howlett), fluffy, foolish, endlessly chattering mother (Joyce Barbour), girl-chasing, car-driving younger son (Nigel Patrick), pompous bespectacled older son (John Boxer), flirtatious daughter (Patricia Hayes), pretty as a picture and wearing slacks, still considered rather daring in 1937. The plot, such as it was, dealt with preparations the family make for the imminent and dreaded arrival of boring friends from India – the George and Margaret of the title. The comedy springs from their continual failure to turn up. Eventually when they do appear, the curtain descends before they actually step on to the stage. *George and Margaret*, like *Rebecca*, was one of those rare plays whose title characters are never seen.

"When the play is almost over," said Savory, "I like to give them something unexpected to send them home feeling very happy." The bonus was a new maid whose first entrance is delayed until three pages before the end. She had only a few lines to say but owing to excessive shyness never managed to say anything audibly but just stood there mouthing in silence. The audience had laughed uncontrollably throughout the evening. "It was one of those plays where the audience laughs and laughs without really knowing why," said Nigel Patrick. "And it was bloody clever of Gerald to keep his trump card until just before the end." After the final curtain, Elsie Beyer made a beeline towards the author who was standing in the foyer with Harry Stoker and Spencer Curtis Brown himself. "We'd like to buy it," she said promptly. He smiled. "You and a few hundred others," he said quietly. "Ask Binkie to call me tomorrow."

All the West End managements telephoned Curtis Brown on Monday, except for those who decided to call in person, begging to be allowed to buy the rights. He chose Binkie because he liked him, he wanted to help him out in his hour of need, and he realised that to do a favour to one who was certain to occupy an exalted position in the West End could do the agency nothing but good; it was further evidence of Binkie's success that he could inspire such confidence even in bad times.

Spencer Curtis Brown had inherited the authors' and playwrights' agency from his father, the original Curtis Brown (not least among his playwrights was Somerset Maugham). Spencer was a big, clumsily-built, red-haired man who adored and pursued women, had kept his Henrietta Street offices in Covent Garden in their original Dickensian gloom rather than redecorate them in the brightly lit, Art-Deco style of the thirties. He and Binkie struck an immediate rapport. Spencer was an astute businessman and a hard bargainer, and as he was now in a position of considerable strength, the bargain was hard indeed. In the 1930s the normal play contract allowed the management to buy world rights, but as Binkie had originally turned down the play, he could have London and Broadway rights, but no amateur, touring, repertory, continental or commonwealth rights. No radio, film or television rights, and although television was barely two years old the television play was clearly going to be an increasingly important factor in the theatrical scene. These subsidiary rights would be withheld as the continued property of the author, to be sold separately. All the same, if the play was a success the London and Broadway rights alone represented a financial killing.

Binkie now had only to recast the play and find a suitable theatre. The first could be done easily since everybody in London wanted to be in it, every agency offered its choicest clients. Binkie, Richard Bird and Elsie Beyer forgathered in his office with the agency letters and three copies of *Spotlight* which in those halcyon days accommodated all the advertisers in a single volume. Most of the cast were so good that they could not possibly be replaced with advantage. But there were three replacements urgently needed. Alec Clunes was charming, strikingly handsome and possessed one of the most beautiful voices in the London theatre, even more beautiful than Gielgud's, it was whispered, all of which would lead him inexorably to a well-deserved fame as a romantic classical actor. But he had little sense of comedy, and was replaced by Ronald Ward, a popular light comedian with a good background in Lonsdale and Coward. Patricia Hayes was not considered pretty enough for the ingenue, and even though the author had written the role especially for her, she had to go. "We need a star for this part," said Binkie, "so how about Jane Baxter?" Enchantingly pretty in an English-rose style, she had made a name for herself in films. Although the two she had made in Hollywood had not caused more than a ripple, the mere fact of going to Hollywood counted enormously and this is what Binkie had wanted. Finally, the tiny show-stealing cameo of Beer, the late-arriving maid, presented a casting problem. Beatrix Fielden-Kaye had been good, no question, but Richard Bird had all along got the feeling that much more could be quarried from the role. What was needed was somebody much more grotesque, a character actress who was funny in herself rather than in what she did.

On February 2nd, Savory and Richard Bird travelled to Swiss Cottage in north London to see the début at the late age of thirty-six of a student who had spent a year of study at the Embassy School. The play was a social comedy called *Night Alone*. Billed in the Embassy's programme as The Stout Woman, she walked across the stage in a night-club scene wearing a tightly fitting evening gown. She had just the one line, "Oh come on, Bert", but the audience laughed and laughed. It seemed that there was something indescribably funny about that ugly, scowling little podge face and those twisted, tortured vowel sounds alternately posh and common. Here was exactly the sort of comic talent Binkie was looking for. Irene Handl was asked to audition at the Globe. "Miss Handl, it's a rather difficult part to audition because there is no dialogue," said Binkie. "We have to judge by appearance and personality. But if you will make up something and say it so quietly that we can't hear, just move your lips and open your mouth, then that'll give us some idea." She did just that and to her pleasure and surprise Binkie and Dickie Bird howled with uncontrollable laughter. "That's wonderful, Miss Handl, I don't think we need look any further, the part's yours if you want it." She did.

Night Alone transferred to Daly's and ran a month. It so happened that the last two weeks coincided with the first two weeks of *George and Margaret* at Wyndham's, so by kind permission of the Embassy, Irene Handl was allowed to play both parts simultaneously. With over an hour between her two brief appearances she had plenty of time to make an unhurried journey between the two theatres. "I was earning two salaries at three pounds a week each," she later remembered happily. "So at six pounds I was doing very nicely, thank you. But I never worked for Binkie again or even met him. He always saw me as a comic maid and parts like Beer come once in a lifetime."

As for the theatre, Binkie had set his heart on Wyndham's which was perfectly suited to the delicate intimacies of the play. *Mademoiselle* was still in occupation though struggling unhappily through its final week. Bronson Albery promised he could have it as soon as it was available, but that could not be at once as a new play, *Because We Must*, starring Vivien Leigh and Cecil Parker, was already booked. How long would it last? With a bad, boring title like that, not for long, surely? On the other hand Vivien Leigh was the actress everybody wanted to see since her sensational overnight stardom in *The Mask of Virtue* two years earlier. But the play was already in trouble, with one member of the cast forced out with appendicitis. There was a two-day postponement and *Because We Must* finally opened on February 6th. "Oh, I *do* hope it's going to be a failure," murmured Binkie as he took his seat in the stalls, "the sooner this gets out the sooner we get in." He felt guilty at harbouring these treacherous thoughts for he had great affection for Vivien Leigh and the cast included a number of actors who had worked for him before, but business was business and must at all times take priority over friendship and sentiment, as he never stopped pointing out. The first act was not good, his spirits rose: the second act was excellent, his spirits fell: the third act was terrible, the audience's response was muted and when he read the notices in the morning (lukewarm to hostile), he knew that it could not survive. Nor did it. Albery telephoned to say that the advance was poor and that if the Sunday notices were also bad Binkie could have the theatre at the end of the month.

By coincidence, Savory was working in the *Because We Must* company as stage manager, compelled by the formal custom of the time to wear dinner-jacket and stiff shirt front. "Every evening I would go into Vivien Leigh's dressing-room to say good evening. She was absolutely charming to me as she was to everybody, one of nature's aristocrats, whereas Laurence Olivier, who was naturally a frequent visitor to her dressing-room, struck me as being by comparison very dull. Vivien gave copies of *Gone with the Wind* to everybody in the company as a first-night present, begging us to read it. 'Don't you think I should play Scarlett O'Hara?' she would ask us anxiously. Naturally, we all thought she should but as the film was still two years away none of us had the slightest suspicion that she would.

"Every night during that first week she would say, 'The house is better, I think it's going to be a success,' and I felt so guilty because I knew that the notice would go up, but Binkie had put me under oath of secrecy so I wasn't able to say anything and when it was made public I had to pretend to be as surprised as anybody else."

George and Margaret finally opened on February 25th 1937, a first night when the accumulated enthusiasm and goodwill and word-of-mouth virtually guaranteed success. It was happy laughter all evening, rising to sheer hysteria when Irene Handl, making her West End début, gave her agonised silent mouthings as Beer, the new maid. It was unlikely if anybody, not even Margaret Rutherford in *Short Story*, had made an audience laugh so much by doing so little. The notices the next day and on Sunday were the sort which Binkie could have cheerfully written himself. *George and Margaret* would run for two years.

For the happy author, the immediate fruits of success were a cheque for a hundred pounds from Curtis Brown representing his advance on royalties. "I had never had a cheque in my life, and here was my first. It was a fortune. It shows how young and innocent I was that I didn't have a bank account and didn't know what to do with it. I remember going into the first bank I saw and asking, 'Is this a good bank?' and the clerk said, 'If you'll wait a moment, sir, I'll go and ask the manager!'" The further fruits were not slow to accumulate: Warner Brothers bought the film rights for ten thousand pounds and cheerfully accepted the proviso that the film be made in England. Royalties for the play came to approximately two hundred pounds a week so by the end of its two-year run he had earned twenty thousand pounds.

Good luck continued to play its part: a major royal event was precisely what was needed to put *George and Margaret* on the top of the list of plays which everybody wanted to see. If the abdication cast a gloom over London theatre-going, then the coronation in early June, contrary to Binkie's expectation, did exactly the opposite, and a frivolous domestic oh-so-*English* comedy was the first to benefit from the visitors flooding into the capital. It was also the first play the newly crowned King and Queen saw in their reign, the royal visit taking place on June 26th, less than a month after the coronation. George VI took little interest in the arts but *George and Margaret* was the sort of play which even a royal philistine could enjoy. Squashed uncomfortably into the tiny stage box at Wyndham's, members of the royal party, which included Queen Mary, were seen to be laughing. Binkie, Harry Tennent and Bronson Albery had welcomed them in the theatre foyer: Joyce Barbour and Noel Howlett were presented in the interval.

Had Binkie arranged this royal visit? He was, as ever, busy cultivating friends in high places and it is likely to have been Noël Coward having a word with the Duke of Kent, his greatest friend in the royal family, who in his turn had a word with the new Queen. Once again it was seen that what the Crown does the rest will follow, and during the summer all the royal family, in twos and threes, visited Wyndham's, sometimes more than once.

Coward loved the play and Binkie agreed that he could direct the New York production. This turned out to be a mistake. Coward had decided that the play was too slight for Broadway consumption. It needed to be tightened up. This, as Savory discovered, meant cutting out the delicately sentimental love scenes and replacing them with extra lashings of wit, but it was Coward rather than Savory wit and the two did not blend. It was not the happiest of collaborations and Coward was unexpectedly tetchy in directing the company. "Alan, you're no bloody good, you must either be a juvenile or a midshipman with piles," he shouted to Alan Webb, his then close friend. The production opened in Toronto where, to a public consisting largely of expatriate English, it did surprisingly well, but in New York it expired quickly. The American co-producer was John C. Wilson, Noël Coward's business manager, who put up the bulk of the money and who shouldered most of the losses. But the London production, playing to capacity houses, brought in two thousand pounds a week.

By the end of its London run it earned the Firm close on a quarter of a million pounds. Not only did it save Tennents from likely bankruptcy, but it laid down the financial foundations which enabled him to build his empire in all its strength and power. "And it was all due to dear Harry Stoker," he said later, and he was right. "There have been three Harrys in my life," he said, "Harry Woodcock, Harry Tennent and now Harry Stoker and they have all been milestones. It's quite a coincidence." Binkie had had, and was to have, many crises, but this was the first and only time that he had been rescued by the Royal Navy.

CHAPTER FOURTEEN

1936–7

Candida

In September 1936, back in the pre-*George and Margaret* days which Binkie throughout his life always referred to as his Doldrums, he and Harry had been spending the weekend with Ivor and Bobbie at the newly-acquired Novello country home, Redroofs, near Maidenhead, when Ivor ventured a suggestion. If Binkie's declared policy of modern commercial plays calculated to please the public and achieve instant popularity was failing, then he should abandon them and turn his attention to the classics. Binkie was not keen but Ivor could be very persuasive. He had recently met Ann Harding, the American film actress who was in London to co-star with Basil Rathbone in a film version of *Love from a Stranger*. Over supper in Ivor's flat, she had discussed her future plans. In common with so many Hollywood stars – then as well as now – she wanted to act in the West End and the part on which she had set her heart was Candida. Unlike many Hollywood stars she had had some stage experience: she had played the part in Chicago in 1924. "Of course, I was a little young but the experience was valuable. Now that I'm thirteen years older I'm the right age and I want to play her again." And under the author's supervision.

Binkie found Shaw's plays boring and in normal circumstances would have had no interest in reviving *Candida* which he had seen only once in Cardiff in a rather unexciting touring production by Sybil Thorndike's company. But Shaw was popular with the public and his plays accepted as modern classics and if a star wanted to appear in one of them, then that was different. Throughout Binkie's life, his occasional Shaw revivals were only as star vehicles. Ivor also advanced another good reason for a *Candida* revival. "It's prestige for you and the Firm and that's something you need just now. If you lose money, then this time it will be in a good cause."

Candida had one advantage over other Shaw plays: with only one interior set and a cast of six it would be cheap to present. Elsie Beyer discovered that although it was a staple of repertory and touring companies, it had never had a proper West End run: occasional matinées and brief seasons at the Royal Court in Sloane Square, but nothing in the West End. So this proposed revival would have all the advantages of a première.

Presenting *Candida*, however, meant business dealings with Bernard Shaw, a prospect which exhilarated and frightened Binkie. At eighty, Shaw's masterpieces were all written. Only a few more plays were to come, the final spluttering, grape skins and seeds, of what had once been a uniquely rich harvest. But if his creative genius had gone, his vitality and enthusiasm were undiminished. Shaw was that exceedingly rare creature, an author of genius who was also an astute businessman; he could not be cheated, beaten down or undervalued by a penny or an inch. He drove a hard bargain, but he always gave good value for money. It was an unusual experience for Binkie to deal with an author who would allow no negotiation, who knew precisely what his plays were worth and who presented a simple case of take it or leave it.

At the beginning of November 1936, Binkie wrote to Shaw asking formal permission to present *Candida* with Ann Harding at the Globe Theatre in the spring of 1937 after a short provincial tour. He mentioned that he proposed to present it in partnership with Howard and Wyndham and Bronson Albery working through his production company, New Theatres Limited. It so happened that Shaw disliked theatrical partnerships, regarding them as unbusiness-like and wasteful. A characteristic blast of Shavian grumbling and common sense roared back to the Globe Theatre.

November 1936

Dear Mr Beaumont,

I do not understand why you are dividing this adventure with two other firms. You say it increases my security and makes no other difference to me; but this is not so. One manager and one author make quite as much as a moderately successful play can bear. Now even the most successful play tails off into moderate success at the end of the run. If there is only one manager – and one is all that is necessary – it is worth his while to go on with a moderate profit unless he wants his theatre very badly for a promising new play. But if he has to divide with two superfluous partners, each with a rake-off, he will stop the run much sooner and leave the author destitute.

You have a theatre. You have capital enough to produce the cheapest play on earth. The author is quite satisfied with your proposal. Where, then, do H & W and N. T. Limited come in? What do they contribute? Do you feel lonely without them, like the Americans, who are never happy unless they are giving half a dozen rakes-off for nothing to the nearest deadheads? These questions have troubled me so much in drafting the agreement that I should like to have a word with you about them before I go any further.

Faithfully,
G. Bernard Shaw.

P.S. Probably the explanation is that the three firms are all the same men; but if so I would like to know which of you this multiform genius is.

Confronted by this unexpected impasse, Binkie had no choice but to tell Albery and Howard and Wyndham that he now wished to present the play on his own and find the backing he had expected from them elsewhere. A note to Shaw gave the quarrelsome author the reassurance he was expecting.

10th November 1936

Dear Mr Beaumont,

I enclose a draft agreement for your approval. You will see that it excludes any secondary or joint management. My plays will not bear more than one profit; and my rule is that there must be no sub-letting, and that no one who does not take the financial risk and do the work is to have any interest in the affair or receive any rake-off whatsoever. The manager has the author on his back and the landlord on his back and perhaps his banker or a money lender on his back too, all taking money out and putting none of it in. These he cannot do without; but if in addition he wants to admit other deadheads, I conclude that he is an idiot.

In this case Mr Bronson Albery could come in only if the play was to be produced on sharing terms at the New Theatre . . . He would have been very welcome to the play at any time as we have always been on the best of terms. I understand that he contemplated a Harding-Candida production at the New Theatre under his own management. That would have been quite in order. But now that he has dropped this scheme and left the play to be produced by you at your theatre, there is no ground for assuming that he has any interest in it.

I may add that unless you are to be the sole beneficiary manager, I shall require, in addition to my percentage of the gross receipts, 50 per cent of the profits, if any. If there is room for a sleeping partner, it may as well be occupied by the author.

Faithfully,
G. Bernard Shaw.

Binkie approved the draft and wrote to Shaw to express agreement on every point. A hand-written postcard followed without delay.

20th November 1936

Dear Mr Beaumont,

Herewith the agreement. Please fill in the date and execute and return the counterpart.

I have altered the production date to "on or before the 31st March" which we can change if anything turns up to alter the arrangements. Do not forget that 26th March will be Good Friday. *Candida* is perhaps pious enough nowadays for Passion week but it may be better to wait for Easter Monday.

Naturally, Shaw had full casting approval, for even at eighty he knew every likely actor, even if he seldom went to the theatre. Binkie took Ann Harding to meet him. Shaw liked her very much – even at eighty he was susceptible to a pretty face – remarking that she reminded him of Ellen Terry. Shaw suggested Nicholas Hannen for Morell. Sighing, Binkie agreed, indeed he had no choice, but brightened when Shaw suggested Hannen's wife, Athene Seyler, a brilliant comedy actress with slightly pop eyes and one of those gurgling voices, as Prossy. As to the producer, Shaw reluctantly agreed to Irene Hentschel, who was married to Ivor Brown, the drama critic of the *Observer*. Rehearsals were due to start in December. "He'll want to produce it himself," warned Hannen. "He'll try to take it all over, you see what happens at the first rehearsal." He had played Marchbanks in younger and slimmer days with the author in aggressive, if intermittent, attendance and knew whereof he spoke. After this first meeting, Shaw and Mrs Shaw were so charmed by Binkie that a new note of friendliness and cordiality entered the correspondence.

11th December 1936

Dear Hugh Beaumont,

I enclose copy for the programme note. It is for the instruction of the critics, and need not be used after the first night in London. It might therefore be printed on a fly sheet unless your programmes are several pages long, with portraits, when it will make good entr'acte padding.

Unless I am held up by fog I shall come up from the country on Monday in time to reach the Globe at 11 or very shortly after. I must stick to the rehearsals for a week so as to save waste of time and get the stage business firmly settled, book in hand. Then they can knock off for Christmas and to swallow the words.

I have had a talk with Irene H. who will be in the programme as producer. I hope to make the job as easy as possible for her.

> Faithfully,
> G. Bernard Shaw.

They all met again on December 14th 1936. As was his custom, Binkie turned up to introduce Shaw to the company and the company to Shaw and was thus privileged to witness what he had been told by everybody was characteristic Shavian behaviour. Shaw strode in, his eyes flashing and his beard quivering: he took great exception to an impromptu press conference which Ann Harding was giving in the wings and he shouted angrily to the army of photographers and journalists who had turned up to get out of the theatre.

> 14th December 1936

Dear Mr Beaumont,

Please give iron orders that no pressmen or cameramen are to be let into the theatre again until we are ready for them, not even your own press agent if you have such an incubus. I was appalled to see Miss Harding letting them take scores of flashlight shots at her in ugly surroundings and in rehearsal mufti looking like nothing on earth . . .

Shaw criticised Geoffrey Nares' setting. He changed the arrangement of the furniture and when he had made what he thought was enough trouble, invited the company to sit down and listen to him read the play. The company, on that day and the week following, found two things about Shaw which actors had been discovering for decades: that his readings were models of vocal splendour and dramatic insight – "He read all the parts far better than we could," said Hannen gloomily, "it was all very discouraging" – and that his visual sense hardly existed. He was interested only in the beautiful lines he had written and how the actors said them, not in what they were doing or where they were standing. He would spend hours coaching them in the exact rhythms and intonations, making them repeat the words until they were saying them exactly as he wanted.

As far as movement and stage business, Shaw's ideas were sometimes ludicrous. Athene Seyler was one of the victims of this: as Prossy, she had to make an exit through the door of the Morell sitting-room in a drunken state, having had too much to drink at the supper party. Shaw had instructed her to fall over and crawl on all fours out of the room. She had indignantly protested against the coarseness of this. It was clear that Shaw, being a teetotaller, had no experience of drunks. Athene insisted that a genteel spinster with ladylike pretensions would walk out slowly and carefully in a wide arc. Perhaps she would stagger just a little bit as she approached the door and grab at something to steady herself, the door handle, perhaps, but nothing more. "You'll find this not only more accurate, Mr Shaw," she said, "but a lot funnier. The audience will love it." Shaw invited her to demonstrate, watched her carefully, laughed loudly and agreed. Underneath his arrogance there was genuine humility: he was always willing to learn from others and admit that he had been wrong.

Shaw was relentless and indefatigable. Everything was grist to his own active creative instinct. Every afternoon Irene Hentschel would take the rehearsal, giving moves, groupings, advice about interpretation and helpful instructions generally, and every morning Shaw would sweep in and, with enormous enthusiasm, undo all the work she had achieved by taking it all to pieces and reassembling it to his own satisfaction. Nothing Irene could do pleased him. By the end of the first week, the company was in a badly demoralised state and Binkie had the unenviable task of having to go to Shaw and gently ask him to stay away. It would be so much better if he would allow Irene Hentschel, a producer of wide experience and great acclaim, to serve the play and the author in her own manner. Ann Harding was nervous and confused; she might choose to withdraw from the play and Binkie might thus be compelled to close it down. Shaw was no fool. He agreed to withdraw and to stay away until the dress-rehearsal.

. . . Miss Hentschel has just told me over the phone that she took the first act again after I left and altered all my arrangements with the general approval of the company. Now, it's impossible to have them rehearsing one way in the morning and differently in the afternoon: there must be one undivided stage direction; so as Miss I.H. doesn't like my production or my methods and has no superstitions about loyalty to the author, and as it will be an enormous relief to me (to say nothing of the money I shall gain) to get rid of this job, I shall just drop out and let her carry out a new production of her own. So you have seen the last of me at the rehearsals.

I do not think my retirement will hurt the enterprise. *Candida* is the sort of play that, if the story and the characters can get across, can be played in any sort of scene or no scene at all. No tricks that Miss I.H. can play with it will make twopennorth of difference if the cast is equal to the situation. And her plan may be quite a good one. Anyhow, it will be a novelty and as such will interest me as much as anyone else.

Don't build too much on a big success. The cast is not *quite* right and whether it is near enough depends on how Miss Harding develops.

Faithfully,
G. Bernard Shaw.

Shaw's inexhaustible energy found an outlet in letters which thundered into Binkie's office unceasingly: a torrent of criticism, advice and occasional shafts of good-humoured abuse questioning all Binkie's business arrangements and administrative decisions. It was a mark of how Binkie's confidence and assurance had been dented by the year of doldrums, putting him under a great strain, that he was being assailed by terrible doubts. Newspapers were full of the abdication crisis: would the public know that the play was in rehearsal, or that they intended to open in the New Year? "Beaumont, you're an idiot," said Shaw. "Publicity is no use except on the nail, everything is forgotten in a week. Who cares now about the Duke of Windsor?" Binkie wondered if the play was a little dated? "*Candida* is a work of genius though the Candidamaniacs have always over-praised it. I have no fear that it is in any way out of date, though some of the audience might well be in that condition. A play that will not last for forty years and be all the better for it, is not worth writing in the first place." Irene Hentschel wanted to make some cuts in the second act. "No cuts, Beaumont. Every word of *Candida* is written with my heart's blood."

> . . . as to the production, I should like to be assured that you and your partners have fully considered the situation, as otherwise you may consider later on that I have let you down by abandoning the work to Miss IH.
> The business of the producer is to carry out the author's design. Miss IH, says "Oh no: I am going to carry out a new design of my own" . . . In the normal course you would say "that is not what you are engaged for: so we must replace you by some producer who will give us Shaw and not IH." And I, in the normal course, should insist on this. But instead we both agree to take a sporting chance and let her try her plan, knowing that my plan is sure fire and hers untried and unknown to us. It may produce misfits between the business and the dialogue that may be awkward, especially as the new producer cannot, as I could, alter the dialogue to fit the new business; and heaven knows what would happen then.

Now I am taking this chance with my eyes open. But it will be more serious for you than for me if the play flops. Nothing can shake my reputation or that of the play; a flop will not ruin me and I can afford to indulge myself by letting Miss IH have her chance now that I am too old for the drudgery of rehearsals. But you stand to lose a lot of money if things go wrong; and I am not sure that your eyes are as wide open as mine; for I doubt if you have given much thought to the matter; and you might with some justice reproach me for not making the case clear to you if the results should prove disappointing.

However, as I have already said, the play if it gets its grip, will stand a much greater degree of inadequacy than we have any reason to fear from Irene. So let her rip by all means if you feel like it.

So now my conscience is no longer uneasy; and I must apologise to you for having eased it at such length.

As to pressmen, a little experience will convince you that you may as well shut up your theatre as throw the stage open to them. Treat them as I do. You need not be afraid of offending them: they must have legitimate news or perish; but you must control it.

Early in the New Year – before the out-of-town opening of *Candida* – came two events for which Binkie secured excellent press coverage: first the film of *Love from a Stranger*, which had brought Ann Harding to London, had its première at the Odeon, Leicester Square, attended by the entire company, all the Firm, but not, alas, by Shaw. "I'm too old for these junketings. Also I have no desire to steal Ann's thunder for it is her evening." A few days later, Ann Harding married Werner Jannsen, a Swedish conductor, at Caxton Hall. More photographs, more interviews, more valuable publicity. *Candida* opened in Brighton on January 11th in a snow-storm. Nevertheless, the house was full and the press reception enthusiastic, as Binkie informed Shaw in a telegram. Shaw replied:

16th January 1937

Dear Hugh Beaumont,
I will come to the Wednesday matinée at Brighton. Barry Jackson and my wife will be with me so they must hold three seats for me. As the Shaw family is now a little on the deaf side, don't put us further back than the fourth row if we are in the stalls. A box, if there is such a thing at the Hippodrome, would be better, provided it is not a stage box on stage level; for an author must not be shoved too close to the company: he gets on their nerves.

There is no Macdona Repertory now: Charles has had enough of it; and I can if necessary keep the local repertories off *Candida* at any moment. But it doesn't really matter, as the success is Ann's, not mine. Without her *Candida* would have drawn £18 instead of £181 at Blackpool in midwinter. I hope Athene piled up the drunken scene for Blackpool, but she mustn't do it for genteel Brighton.

In London *Candida* opened at the Globe Theatre to excellent notices (preceded by a one-act curtain raiser, *Love and How to Cure It* by Thornton Wilder) while *George and Margaret* was still in rehearsal. *Candida* ran for three months. It was clear that Tennent's luck had changed and that Binkie could now do no wrong, a feeling confirmed when the BBC wrote in to ask permission to broadcast an extract. Shaw replied:

> . . . I do not like the notion of cutting a pound of flesh out of *Candida*; but possibly a broadcast of the first act from the theatre might make people want to hear the sequel. That is all that can be done; and unfortunately the curtain raiser gets badly in the way, because it is very important that the broadcast shall not get across the news: it is 8.30 to 9 or nothing. So the curtain raiser would have to be cut out for that evening.
>
> I doubt if the broadcast would prove practicable in this form and in any other it will kill the play stone dead. Only an appetizer is permissible; and the first act is the only part that could be used for this.

Further confirmation that Binkie's luck had changed dramatically for the better came when he was invited to take *Candida* to Paris for five performances, with M. Blum, the President, who spoke little or no English, in bored and bewildered attendance at the first night. Shaw's programme note was translated into French; houses were full for the first two performances and thin for the remaining three.

CHAPTER FIFTEEN

1937–8

Bonnet Over the Windmill – Dear Octopus

It was something of a relief to get away from a bearded genius. But although *George and Margaret* and *Candida* suggested that the Firm's luck had changed for the better, Binkie still had to endure two successive failures at the Globe, a revival of Somerset Maugham's *The Constant Wife* with the American film star Ruth Chatterton (only 36 performances) and *They Came by Night* by Barré Lyndon, another crime thriller by the author of *The Amazing Doctor Clitterhouse*. This managed 76 performances.

Fortunately Dodie Smith (who wrote the sort of commercial theatre Binkie most liked) re-surfaced after a year with the exciting news that she had an idea for a new play. It would be about six students: three girls, all training for the stage, and three young men, one an aspiring playwright, one an actor and the third a musician, a would-be composer. There would be a gossiping landlady, a former chorus-girl, full of memories of the Good Old Days. There would be a rooftop between the two flats which could be used as a suitable spot for a picnic to which the young actor's father, himself a famous actor-manager, would be invited. He becomes interested in one of the drama students who in her turn starts to fall in love with the young playwright. The second act takes the party to the actor-manager's estate for Sunday lunch, and the last act to the young playwright's place in the country.

It turned out to be the most difficult of all her plays to write. Each time she finished an act she put it away in despair. The characters refused to come to life, the writing was stuffed with clichés. But just as Molière had his cook for advice and encouragement, so she had Binkie who suggested that she might find it useful to read it aloud. "Nothing better for seeing where you've gone wrong," he said cheerfully and she agreed. These readings took place in her flat to an audience of Binkie, her husband Alec, her secretary Jean Batters, Murray Macdonald, who was to direct it, and Harry Tennent. Binkie knew that enthusiasm must be tempered with critical insight. "The last act must have a big windmill on the stage," he said at one of the readings, and it was a suggestion like that which, according to her memoirs, made all the difference. Once finished everybody liked it. After a time, so did she. And so *Bonnet Over the Windmill* was announced for the early autumn of 1937.

Here was an example of the inspired casting which would become Binkie's hallmark: Cecil Parker and Mary Hinton for the actor-manager and wife, Ivy St Helier (of *Bitter Sweet* fame) for the ex-chorus-girl and Peter Coke, as the aspiring composer. He also cast two comparative newcomers who were each destined to make a considerable mark. William Douglas Home was invited to audition in Binkie's office. He arrived at the top of the Globe to find Binkie, Murray Macdonald, Cecil Parker and Dodie Smith waiting for him, a quartet of theatrical authority which even the boldest actor would have found intimidating. He was asked to read a scene with Cecil Parker and in his state of nerves did so very badly in an artificial upper-class accent. At the end, Murray Macdonald and Binkie whispered together. Murray shook his head and dismissed him. As he got to the door, Binkie stopped him. "Come back, Mr Home, I have a feeling that you could do better. Read it again and this time speak with your normal voice." Home did so and was immediately engaged. Once again, Binkie had shown that he could see through the façade of nerves and attitudinising to the real talent which lay underneath.

The same situation occurred with the next young actor, James Mason. His reading was so bad that Dodie Smith wondered if he could read at all. After he had been politely dismissed, Binkie took Murray and Cecil out to lunch. "I think he'll do. He's terribly good-looking: I adore that stern, dark, Byronic look. I'm sure you can get a performance out of him, Murray dear." And Murray did. Within a few rehearsal days his performance was beginning to take shape and when the play opened he came near to stealing the show. It seemed that Binkie was not the only person in Greater London who liked dark, sternly handsome, Byronic looks.

Dodie Smith's rising esteem ensured that she was besieged with offers of money to back her. Her new play was an all but guaranteed money-spinner. After all, her previous five plays had each run for a year or more so why should *Bonnets*, as it lovingly came to be known, be any different? For some time she and Alec had wanted to go into management and this seemed to be the opportunity. Binkie proposed a co-production deal, and it was not cheap: three elaborate sets and a cast of ten with three changes of costume each, two thousand pounds. Binkie and Harry Tennent put up half, and Dodie, supported by Alec, Murray Macdonald, Ambrose Heal and Cyril Hogg of Samuel French, who would later publish the text of the play, the rest. And if all that responsibility wasn't enough, Dodie decided that she would co-direct the play with Murray Macdonald. Basil Dean would have refused in the most offensive and bullying manner, but Murray Macdonald welcomed her and seemed pleased to have her special skills and knowledge at his disposal.

The rehearsals were unusually happy. Instead of Basil Dean's savage and sadistic tyranny reducing them to tears, Murray Macdonald was gentle and quietly authoritative, but he gave everybody freedom to make suggestions and to develop their interpretations as they pleased. They all loved him and their performances blossomed in this soothing atmosphere of goodwill.

All except one. Anne Firth, an inexperienced young actress, had been spotted by Dodie at the auditions for a part which was difficult to cast: the young drama student, unhappy and frustrated until she falls in love with the playwright, required a combination of qualities not easy to find in one person. Anne had an unusual style of beauty which could become quite commonplace and unattractive when she wanted: she could convey the loneliness of the girl's life without effort. Neither Binkie nor Murray was keen to have her. "We want Vivien Leigh," said Binkie at the auditions, "she'd be *perfect*." Dodie did not think so: Vivien Leigh was already so famous and beautiful that she would overbalance the delicate structure of the play because the audience would look at no one else while she was on stage. "And how could any audience believe that a girl who looked like that would be lonely and have trouble getting a man?" she said and that clinched it. No Vivien Leigh. Dodie was determined that Anne Firth should get the part and eventually convinced Binkie.

But Anne turned out to be as much of a liability as an asset. She was moody, over-emotional and egotistically anxious to be the centre of attention. She began to get on everybody's nerves: even the eternally patient John Gielgud, whose near neighbour she was in the country, began to show signs of petulance when she called without invitation and talked for hours about her unhappy childhood and many illnesses. In rehearsal her performance varied greatly in quality. In some scenes she was excellent, in others she was clumsy. In the final week she decided to throw a fit of rebellion and refused to continue with the part. Binkie had dealt with Gertrude Lawrence's and Marie Tempest's temperaments and he certainly was not going to allow a mere slip of a girl, only nineteen, who had been in the West End less than three years, to make trouble for the author and producers. With Dodie and Barney Gordon, the stage manager, he took her out to the Ivy for dinner, and spoke to her severely. "Anne, my dear, I don't allow young actresses to make scenes. If you are not at rehearsal tomorrow at ten I shall bring in another actress to play the part who is at this moment standing by waiting for my call. I can't stop you from breaking your contract but if you do you will be blacklisted by Equity and I can promise you that you will never work in the West End again," and his cold grey eyes flickered menacingly. "You have a distinguished career ahead of you and I would hate to see you throw it away. Please be *sensible*, my dear." His carefully chosen words had their desired effect. Anne recovered her senses, apologised, rehearsed well and ended by giving a performance which fully justified Dodie's touching faith in her and Binkie's harsh words. On the first night at the New Theatre in London, Binkie insisted that she take a solo call and stand in the final line between Cecil Parker and Mary Hinton in the centre. "If you want to make a new star, you must treat her like one. And she *will* become a star, I know it," he said happily. (Sadly Anne Firth died in the war before fulfilling Binkie's prophecy.)

The first-night audience chuckled at the large, colourful programme which Alec Beesley had designed with a windmill on the front. They applauded rapturously at the first sight of the windmill with its grassy mound and the blue sky behind in the third act and at the end there were cries of "Well done, Dodie" from the gallery. Binkie gave a private party for the older members of the cast and some friends at his Piccadilly flat but any forebodings they might have had were instantly dispelled when the notices were delivered by special messenger. Charles Morgan in *The Times* had reservations but the others were ecstatic.

The following morning she and Binkie discussed the notices in his office. Dodie believed that the play was still too long and needed to lose half an hour, not by wholesale cutting of scenes which had been Basil Dean's method, but by the subtle trimming of sentences and words. The future looked rosy until Barney Gordon came in with the news that there was no advance booking and tonight's house was going to be empty. "I'll have to paper it," said Binkie, "I don't often have to do this and some managements *never* do it which I think is silly. But the company must not have to play to empty seats and you never know what the word of mouth can do." Then as now there is a special art in papering an empty house. Out-of-work actors and drama students must be avoided. The first tend to be ungrateful and spread the rumour that the play can't be any good if they're having to give away seats so soon, and students tend to be hypercritical, nothing is ever good enough, and their bad report can be very damaging. The best categories are student nurses from the hospitals and the police.

Binkie's papering worked so well that by Saturday the play was getting full houses. After six weeks the production costs had been paid off and Dodie felt confident enough to take a short holiday in America. Binkie did not share her optimism about the play: he expected a respectable run but not a wild success. He was right. The play began to lose money as soon as Dodie left London and when she returned she had to make an agonising decision. As an author she naturally wanted to let it run but as co-producer with five hundred pounds of her own money at stake, she wanted to cut her losses. Binkie watched with cynical amusement the struggle between author and manager taking place in the same female breast. Inevitably, the manager won. Good notices were all very well but losing money was a catastrophe. After three months, she and Binkie decided to take it off. Her author's royalties compensated for the managerial losses, but nothing could alter the fact, or soothe the pain, that *Bonnet Over the Windmill* had failed.

There had been no financial loss but on the other hand no profit, for the production had broken even. Binkie was used to failure but Dodie was not and it was the humiliation which hurt. "Nothing like hard work to take your mind off your troubles, my dear," said Binkie helpfully, "start writing your next play now." Taking his advice, she produced her next with little delay and far less than her usual trouble. Once again, it was about a family. Everybody has a family of sorts and the bigger the family – the more people can identify with it. Obviously, it had to be a family reunion. Mr and Mrs Randolph, both in their seventies, are celebrating their golden wedding. The first act shows all the now grown-up children and grandchildren assembling at the big country house where they were brought up. The second has a nostalgic family tea in the nursery where various family tensions surface; there is a good, resounding quarrel, and a minor sexual scandal peeps coyly out of the closet. In the last act, a dinner takes place and the eldest son, Nicholas, makes a long and beautiful speech to the aged couple. Their health is drunk. The family scatters, the stage empties and old Mr and Mrs Randolph are left holding hands by the glow of the fire.

The actual writing was easier for Dodie Smith than with her earlier plays, but no less exhausting. She even felt sufficiently confident not to read it aloud act by act which had always been a symptom of insecurity. Typed copies were circulated. Binkie liked it enormously and told her that it was her best, and that he was certain it would be a huge success if he could get the right actress to play Mrs Randolph. "It's a Marie Tempest part without a doubt," he said to Barney Gordon, once again the stage manager.

"Do you think she'll do it?" asked Barney.

"Like a shot, Barney dear. She hasn't worked for a year and she's getting restless."

But there was one small diplomatic problem. Mrs Randolph in the play was seventy-two. Marie Tempest was seventy-five, but she did not look a day older than fifty, a source of considerable pride. Would she be willing to make up the extra twenty years? Would she forgo her habitual golden wig and wear a white one more suitable for an old woman? Yes, she would, she told Binkie. It would make her look very grand but she'd look that anyway and this pinpointed the root of what Binkie realised too late would be a gross piece of miscasting. She was too regal and awe-inspiring to play anyone remotely provincial. She resembled a Dowager Queen Mother in exile in Versailles. And what about Leon Quartermaine, cast as her husband, and John Gielgud, as their eldest son? Nobody watching them would have guessed that they were supposed to be a retired Colchester linen-draper with his wife and that their eldest son was an advertising copywriter. Had he made a terrible mistake?

Dodie Smith admired Marie Tempest, but told Binkie that she made nonsense of the play. "I want somebody like Mary Jerrold," she said sadly. "We need a star, my dear," said Binkie firmly. "Otherwise the public won't be interested and we won't be able to get anybody really good to support her." Dodie saw the point of these two good arguments but remained unhappy. But who else was there? Sybil Thorndike or Lilian Braithwaite? Irene Vanbrugh or Marion Terry? But they were all overpoweringly grand and none could be described as middle-class provincial. "There's always Mrs Patrick Campbell," said Barney Gordon one day. Binkie laughed loudly. "You must be joking, Barney dear," he said. "She'd be marvellous, but she'd ruin the play and we'd never get anybody to act with her, they're all afraid . . ." So Dame Marie Tempest – as she now was – was engaged. She had viewed the play with caution, commenting only that it seemed to lack comedy, but as there was nothing else suitable on offer she decided to go ahead. Binkie needed her and what Binkie wanted he got.

With Marie Tempest, Leon Quartermaine and John Gielgud there was no trouble getting others of distinction in support, including Angela Baddeley, Valerie Taylor, John Justin and the young Muriel Pavlow. But there was one casualty. Murray Macdonald said that he did not think he could direct a play in which the three principals were so terribly miscast. "Rehearsals will be a series of arguments and rows. None of them can be other than they are and it will be a waste of time to try and force them into an unnatural mould," he told Binkie and Barney Gordon in the office. Binkie knew better than to keep anybody against his will and accepted Dodie's suggestion that he should engage Glen Byam Shaw, the actor recently turned producer, as a replacement.

After John Gielgud's spectacular success in the early thirties, a new wave of actor became very fashionable. They were tall, beautiful, poetic, elegant in movement and highly mellifluous in voice. Glen Byam Shaw was one of these and although his talent was never in the same class he had understudied Gielgud in *Richard of Bordeaux*. In production, and later in administration, he found a talent which enriched the theatre for many decades and became one of the key men in the Tennent organisation.

Dodie had not worked with Marie Tempest and the experience proved a valuable lesson in the art of *grande-damerie*. She still demanded, and received, royal treatment. There was a definite etiquette, a protocol, enjoyed by no other actress: she was always called a couple of hours later than the rest of the company, the rehearsal stopped when she arrived while everybody drank coffee and made polite conversation, and when the rehearsal started again it was always with one of her scenes, regardless of what had been rehearsed before. All calculated to avoid waiting in the wings with nothing to do except watch others rehearse. "Oh, it's so *boring*," she would complain, "none of them know how to do it properly." Contrariwise, she would get very irritated if the company were not watching her when she was rehearsing: they had so much to learn from her and that failure to show proper respect was a form of *lèse-majesté*. It was Binkie who suggested that this routine was impractical, that an armchair be installed in the wings, that she be escorted to it on her arrival and allowed to sit there until needed, with her table and patience cards on hand if she found the rehearsal too irritating to watch. Binkie himself performed this little diplomatic gesture on the first day and then delegated it to Barney Gordon.

Her power was considerable. She insisted that any chair or sofa on which she sat had to have a hard base so she could get up easily. She disapproved of the tea-party scene where she had to pour out ten cups and staged a splendid temperament to persuade Dodie to cut the cups down to three. She wouldn't allow the company to smoke in rehearsals, she refused to take time off for lunch or allow anybody else to do so and insisted that everybody rehearse without a break until 3 p.m. She took a great hate to Kate Cutler, who played her sister-in-law, and begged Binkie to dismiss her. But while Binkie was willing to go along with her wishes in small matters, he was not going to give her casting approval. He knew that Mary would have liked to play it from the start: Binkie said no.

She was having great trouble learning her lines and stumbled so badly in one important scene that she told Dodie to leave the theatre, a curious piece of impertinence since Dodie was also the co-director. Dodie agreed to do so. "Would you like me to give up the part?" she asked Dodie. Dodie tried to reassure her even to the extent of promising not to attend the first performance if that was what she wanted.

Mary had always been an autocrat who liked to have everything her own way but in old age she became something more. She had the habit of sending for various members of the company to whom she had taken a liking and questioning them closely about their health, their love-affairs, their careers. To the older actresses she gave unasked-for advice about their clothes, hair, make-up and deportment. If anybody felt resentment at this they were sensible enough to keep it to themselves. Mary regarded herself as the mother of the company and her love was both jealous and possessive. There had probably never been an actress so self-centred.

Binkie warned Dodie about her egocentricity. "She never reads a whole play, only her own scenes. In rehearsals, she never watches or even listens to anything which doesn't concern her. Even when she's actually on the stage acting with others, she never listens to their speeches, she's only waiting for her cue. As a result you'll find that she has very little idea what's happening in the play." This last turned out to be only too true. Throughout rehearsals and the play's run she was under the impression that she was playing the title role. In fact, the 'Dear Octopus' referred not to the mother but to the whole family.

After a short tour, including Newcastle and Manchester, the play opened at the Queen's on September 14th 1938, the middle of the Munich crisis with the country more concerned with the imminent possibility of war. The audience was quietly attentive, and made no response to the comedy. But in the first interval, word spread that Chamberlain had flown to Germany to talk to Hitler and that there would be no war. The response of the thankful and relieved audience was like an author's dream. They loved everything and listened with ecstasy to John Gielgud's big speech at the end as if it had been the toast from *Cavalcade* itself.

That evening gave Dodie Smith her greatest triumph and also her greatest public humiliation. It had been arranged that she take an author's curtain call and make a speech from the centre of the cast line, standing between the two stars. To her horror, and the audience's bewilderment, Mary refused to shake her outstretched hand but rudely turned away. As a result Gielgud felt unable to take her hand

lest this might imply criticism of Marie Tempest. She was therefore left standing alone, feeling most horribly snubbed. Afterwards,
Binkie gave her the explanation. Mary had been in a bad temper: she
had been asked not to make a speech because both he and Harry
Tennent were bored with the charitable appeal which she always
managed to introduce. Mary was convinced that Dodie was behind
this, hence her display of bad manners. Binkie tried to convince her
that he and Harry alone were responsible, Mary did not believe him
and neither then nor later did she ever apologise to Dodie for her
appalling rudeness.

For John Justin it was a home-coming. The previous year he had
been at the Queen's carrying assorted spears in Gielgud's company in
Richard II, his first appearance in the West End. Now he had returned
for his first proper part in London, playing one of Marie Tempest's
grown-up sons. The engagement was nerve-racking in the extreme.
He was surrounded by stars, he was only twenty-two, pitifully
inexperienced and unsure of himself. Within eighteen months he
would be one of Alexander Korda's contract actors and would be
starring in *The Thief of Baghdad*, but in September 1938 he was an
unknown young actor, urgently needing help and affection. Fortunately, he found both within the company. Marie Tempest's liking for
beautiful young actors had grown with age and widowhood. John was
very handsome, he had so much to learn and he seemed to be happy
that she should teach it.

"I was very nervous of her for she was a real little tartar. She was
getting very old and doddery, she had great trouble remembering the
lines and was always in a panic before she made her first entrance.
Then, she would be clinging to my arm tightly as if afraid that she
might fall over but the minute the door opened she would loosen her
grip and rush forward to the footlights to get her inevitable round of
applause. From that moment onwards all would be well."

On the whole, it was a happy company which worked well together
but he remembers that there were always tensions.

"I was very shy. The trouble was that John Gielgud was as shy as
me, and we used to pace up and down behind the set waiting for our
entrance. He never said a word and I never dared speak to him. One
evening, after we'd been running for about three months, he tried to
say something which came out as if he was clearing his throat, 'errr
. . . errr . . . uhmmmm . . . mm . . . erhhhaaahhh . . .' I tried to say
something back but I couldn't get it out. However, it did break the ice.
A week later he managed to say 'Good evening' and so did I. A month
later this progressed to 'Good evening, how are you?' nearly a whole
sentence, and by the end of the run we were almost carrying on a

conversation. After a year we became rather friendly and later we did become very close."

His most worrying problem was dyslexia. The condition existed in 1938, but not the name nor the public's sympathetic awareness. Dyslexia is much more than just a jumble of words and letters which makes reading impossible. It also involves forgetfulness to a degree which can be deeply embarrassing. If Justin met somebody he knew, he did not recall his name or anything about him. This happened three months after *Dear Octopus* opened. He was sitting in the Dorchester Bar at lunchtime when a pale, elegant, exquisitely dressed young man appeared and stood above him. John knew the face very well, but not the name, nor the identity. Who was he? What did he do? In what part of John's life did he figure? Was he a fellow-student at RADA? Had he been carrying spears in the Gielgud company? Was he an executive in the Denham film studios? John had no idea. He would have to bluff it out and hope that the subsequent conversation would answer all the questions. He sprang to his feet, grasped the exquisite young man's hand and pumped it up and down enthusiastically. "My dear fellow, how frightfully good to see you again . . . what fun . . . you're looking terribly well. Tell me, what are you doing these days? Do sit down and let me buy you a drink. Remind me, when did we last meet?"

The exquisite young man had been looking very surprised during all this, as well he might, but now a gentle smile of sympathetic understanding appeared. He sipped his gin and tonic. "John," he said in measured tones, "I am Hugh Beaumont, though most people call me 'Binkie' which you are very welcome to do if you like. My company is presenting *Dear Octopus* which makes me your employer. We first met in my office when I was considering you for the part you are now playing. Later, I came to your audition, and spoke to you afterwards. On the first night I came to your dressing-room beforehand to wish you luck and afterwards to congratulate you on a very charming performance. The last time we met was last night at John Gielgud's party which he gave in his flat to commemorate the hundredth performance of the play, at which we talked for about half an hour about the theatre in general and your future in it in particular. Thank you for the drink and now, if you will excuse me, I have a luncheon engagement inside." All this was said with such charm and delicate humour that John did not feel embarrassed, and for decades to come he would tell and retell this story with increasing pleasure as an example of Binkie's tact and discretion.

Dear Octopus was the climax and the conclusion to two remarkable women's careers. It was Dodie Smith's greatest triumph and her last. Other plays were to be written and presented after the war, but the talent had faded. It was the thirties which provided her with inspiration and when the decade finished there was little left. It was Marie Tempest's final appearance. The shock of being a widow, for she missed her adored Willie every waking minute of the day and night, the strain of growing old and frail and the humiliation of her increasing forgetfulness, these all combined to drive her into a very unwelcome retirement. In 1942 Binkie was able to coax her back when he persuaded Jack Hylton to offer her the leading part in a light comedy, *The Grand Manner*. She accepted with touching enthusiasm, and rehearsed with the script for two weeks. But her memory had gone completely and she could not learn a single line. Binkie undertook the painful task of telling her that the management wished her to resign the part. "I quite understand," she said as the tears rolled slowly down her cheeks. He escorted her to a taxi, took her back to her flat, put her to bed and stayed talking until she fell into an uneasy sleep.

She had never before been compelled to suffer the indignity of dismissal and the shock was too much for her. Six weeks later she died.

Dear Octopus ran for three years, became a popular standby in the repertory companies, was filmed after the war, and had the distinction of being the only one of Dodie Smith's plays to enjoy a major West End revival, at the Haymarket in December 1967, with Cicely Courtneidge, Jack Hulbert and Richard Todd.

CHAPTER SIXTEEN

1937–9

Operette – Design for Living – Robert's Wife

1937 was the year in which John Perry entered Binkie's life. Son of wealthy Irish gentry, he had started as an actor, yet another to be cast in the Gielgud mould. He was tall, willowy, fair-haired, and exuded a radiant, feminine charm which most women – and many men – found difficult to resist. He became a close friend of John Gielgud, moved into his London flat in St Martin's Lane, and his country house near Henley. As partners – each putting in £5,000 – they went into management to present a season of classical drama in the West End. Binkie had no interest in Shakespeare, Sheridan or Chekhov, but he put in one thousand pounds and arranged for them to have a year's lease on the Queen's on very favourable terms. The two Johns, as they came to be known in Binkie's circle (though Gielgud was invariably referred to as 'Johnnie') presented *Richard II*, *The School for Scandal*, *The Merchant of Venice* and *The Three Sisters*; the season, a huge success, played to packed houses for a year. Gielgud gave three of his finest performances and added greatly to his stature as a classical actor, though his failure as Shylock was total and revealed that whatever his gifts in comic and romantic parts, he was as incapable of portraying evil as he was of understanding it. Binkie earned back his private investment with a profit and now viewed Gielgud's future plans for classical drama with considerable commercial interest.

John Perry had no great ability as an actor – imitation Gielguds were ten a penny in the late thirties – but revealed where his real talents lay late in 1937 when he walked into Binkie's office with John Gielgud carrying the typescript of a new play written with an old childhood friend, the novelist Molly Keane, who wrote under the pseudonym of M. J. Farrell. *Spring Meeting* was a charming, boisterous farcical comedy about a crazy Irish family who live for the racing. Binkie liked it very much and happily agreed to present it with John Gielgud directing. As Aunt Bijou, the eccentric old spinster who has a genius for spotting winners, Margaret Rutherford gave her greatest comedy performance to date and the play ran for over 300 performances.

John Perry and Binkie now became very close friends. Perry moved out of Gielgud's flat into Binkie's in Piccadilly and later to the house in Finchingfield, Essex, which Binkie borrowed for ten years from Dodie Smith. They had many tastes in common: both loved racing and never missed an important meeting; both loved gambling, visited card clubs and casinos and would happily spend the night playing bridge and poker with other kindred spirits. John Perry gave Binkie a very loving and professionally fruitful friendship: his importance in Binkie's life and career cannot be exaggerated. In return, Binkie later made him a director of H. M. Tennent. "He thus became Mason to Binkie's Fortnum as purveyor of quality goods to the carriage trade," to quote Bryan Forbes' elegant phrase. He gave him the Lyric, Hammersmith, to look after and left him everything in his will.

1937 was the year in which Binkie's social life began to extend out of the narrow world of the theatre into the equally narrow but no less intriguing worlds of politics and society. Thanks to Eddie Marsh, and partly due to Noël Coward, who knew everybody, he was invited by Mrs Churchill to lunch at Chartwell. Mrs Churchill collected celebrities with a connoisseur's eye and although Binkie was not a celebrity yet, he employed celebrities in large numbers, and his status had risen since he started working for himself instead of being a mere employee. Also, Mrs Churchill liked beautiful young men and Binkie certainly qualified for her table. At twenty-nine he was still very attractive. It was an exciting occasion, for it was not in every stately home that one could sit down to luncheon with Noël Coward, Anthony Eden, Sir Thomas Beecham, the Duke and Duchess of Kent, Lord and Lady Castlerosse and Lord Beaverbrook at one and the same time. He greatly endeared himself to both Churchills when he said "mixing guests at a luncheon party is like mixing a salad dressing: you must always find the right balance between vinegar and oil." This epigram greatly strengthened his reputation as a wit and, then after, Mrs Churchill always referred to him as "Eddie Marsh's clever young friend". It was lucky for him that nobody present recognised it as a quotation from one of Oscar Wilde's early plays.★

Both vinegar and oil were well represented on that day, Lady Castlerosse being a good example of the former. She and Noël Coward had been friends for years: Noël whispered to Binkie that she and her husband had been the models for Amanda and Elyot in *Private Lives* and that their well-publicised fights, both privately at home and publicly in the Savoy Grill, had inspired the second act of the play.

★ *Vera or the Nihilists.* Inexplicably it has never been professionally performed.

"Her wit when she's in the mood can be devastating," warned Coward, "but she doesn't give a tuppenny damn about people's feelings. So watch out." Binkie realised that this was no exaggeration when she described him, to others but in his hearing, as "a baby-faced butcher". This struck him as being not so much witty as extremely rude and a significant comment on his reputation outside the theatre.

The oil which offset this vinegar was the charm and courtesy of Anthony Eden. He was just the sort of man whom Binkie liked: tall, handsome, always beautifully dressed and, above all, *successful*. Eden, enjoying his career as England's most glamorous Foreign Secretary, was just as much a star in his world as Noël Coward was in his. Eden and Binkie became close friends. He attended Binkie's first nights and his parties. When late sittings in the House of Commons became too tedious, he would look in at the Piccadilly flat and chat happily to Binkie and his other guests over champagne, smoked salmon and caviare. The personalities of the theatre and the state would be wittily dissected, and Binkie found himself, greatly to everybody's surprise, becoming interested in politics, for were not all politicians actors at heart, and wasn't the House of Commons the greatest theatre in the country?

Eden was going through a difficult and critical time: Binkie liked to organise other people's lives outside the theatre as well as in it. He later insisted it was largely on his advice that Eden resigned over the Abyssinia crisis. This claim was viewed by his close friends with a degree of scepticism. It did not seem likely, but with Binkie you could never be certain whom he knew, or what he knew, or where his influence could be felt. He was good at keeping secrets, there was always an air of mystery about him and in spite of his apparent openness and naïvety, you never knew what subplots were lurking and weaving round his life. It was quite possibly true that his voice was heard and heeded in Westminster, but as both men are dead we shall never know for sure.

1937 was also the year in which Binkie's and Noël Coward's professional lives crossed for the first time. *Operette*, written at the suggestion of Binkie who was good at planting seeds in the minds of creative people, had as its catalyst Fritzi Massary, the popular star of the Vienna Opera House. For six months, Binkie paid regular visits to Coward's country retreat, Goldenhurst, listening to the progress of the music and the lyrics. He later saw to it that a star cast, including Irene Vanbrugh and Griffith Jones, supported Fritzi Massary, that the sets and costumes were magnificent and that a bevy of Royals (the Kents, the Gloucesters and the Princess Royal) attended the opening in Manchester where it played to full houses for a month. But Binkie knew that it was not quite right. Coward did as much remedial work as was possible, cutting, rearranging, rewriting, but the opening night at His Majesty's in March 1938 left Binkie in no doubt that Coward's theatrical flair had momentarily deserted him. Coward had made the great mistake of allowing the piece to go forward with a weak libretto and in the process had broken one of his cardinal rules. It was full of good things: 'The Stately Homes of England' was a first-night smash-hit and if the rest of *Operette* could have been as good it would have run for years, but the good things failed to add up to a satisfactory show, which lost a great deal of money.

But compensation was found in *Design for Living*, which Coward had written for the Lunts. They had appeared in it together in New York, but the idea of the three of them repeating their performances in London never materialised. When Coward was free the Lunts were busy, when they were free Coward was not, and he had no desire to appear in it without them. In fact, there was some doubt if he wished to appear in it at all. He had done five months in New York, two more than his much-stated maximum, and nothing bored him more than repetition: "Never boil your cabbage twice, Binkie," was his favourite piece of advice when he was being pestered for revivals.

Nor was the Lord Chamberlain happy about the play's sexual content. Was a *ménage à trois* entirely respectable? Could such domestic intimacy be shown without causing offence? Coward was well used to the ways of censorship and Binkie could be very persuasive. He pointed out that the New York theatrical public, whose standards of morality were as stringent as anybody's, had found the play acceptable, so why should the London public be treated like children? Binkie pulled strings, Coward pulled strings: between them they succeeded in getting a licence for the play which opened in January 1939 at the Haymarket. It was Coward's farewell to the thirties.

But the casting was far from ideal. Anton Walbrook, a refugee from Germany, was a strikingly handsome man in early middle age. He was a fine actor with distinction who exuded a warm Viennese-Jewish charm which guaranteed great success and popularity during the years to come, but he did not understand Coward's style. Even Rex Harrison, whose public comments on his colleagues have always been noted for generosity and absence of malice, described his personality as "heavy and Teutonic". Diana Wynyard had her attractive English-country-rose beauty, her charm, style and elegance, but neither she nor Anton Walbrook was in the least degree funny nor did they manage to raise a laugh in a play which was full of them. Also, she was prim, too proper, making it impossible for audiences to believe that she changed her lovers as some women change their hats. "Gilda needs to have a touch of the gipsy," said Coward. "She needs to be a bit common. Oh, if *only* Gertie were available." But Gertie was making a triumphal tour of America, earning a fortune in *Susan and God* by Rachel Crothers. This left only Rex Harrison whose unique gift for comedy enabled him, in part, to fill the gap, but he was not yet a star.

Design for Living was not one of Coward's best, as Binkie realised at the final dress-rehearsal. It was too long – a rare mistake for Coward – and repetitive. Harold French produced and with the combined reputations of the author and two of its three stars, however miscast, it ran comfortably for two hundred performances. It marked the photographic début of Angus McBean whose imaginative fantasy pictures decorated not only the front cover of the programme, but the front-of-house display and surely beckoned many a theatre-goer.

Every author has his favourite play and, perversely, it is frequently one the public has tended to shun. *Design for Living* was Coward's and it remains one of his least popular plays. He closed his eyes to its obvious defects and until the end of his life continued to pester Binkie to revive it, spending considerable time searching for the perfect cast, the trio whose talents and personalities would complement each other and thus enrich the play. Binkie always managed to find an excuse for postponing plans for a revival, his conversations and correspondence on the subject forming a curious *leitmotif* in the opera of his life. The perfect cast was like the Holy Grail and Binkie was no Parsifal. A good, if not ideal cast was eventually assembled in 1974 – Vanessa Redgrave, John Standing and Jeremy Brett – and the play enjoyed a respectable run at the Phoenix Theatre, but neither Coward nor Binkie lived to see it.

1937 also saw Edith Evans enter Binkie's life, not as a goddess to be worshipped from afar, but as an employee. Her career had followed a curious pattern. Never out of work or unappreciated by her followers, she had for years been admired only by the critics and by a small band of theatre-goers, which was part of the price she paid for working so much at the unfashionable Old Vic and in so many fringe theatres. But the change came in 1932 when she played Madame Irela, a malevolent, egocentric opera singer in a chronicle play, *Evensong*, written by Beverley Nichols. An open, unashamed portrait of Melba whose social secretary he had once been, Nichols showed wit, malice and theatrical flair. Here was a woman whom Edith understood and it gave her a chance to display the flamboyance, temperament and outsize personality which became her authentic style. From that moment onwards, she was a star.

A private person, she kept her personal life secret. Her husband, Guy Booth, a mining engineer with no interest in the theatre, had died two years before. But Mrs Booth was used to living alone even before his death as his job kept him travelling. Indeed few people knew she had been married. "Would you like me to give up the theatre?" she had once asked her husband. He knew well how important it was to her and shook his head. "I'd rather have ten per cent of you alive than a hundred per cent dead," was his kind and sensible reply. She was deeply religious and a Christian Scientist, but also puritanical and intolerant of other people's frailties. Nobody is entirely consistent and she could take people by surprise as she did Bryan Coleman, who was stage managing *Evensong*. One day during the first week of rehearsal, she appeared in his little office and put a piece of paper on his desk.

"These are my dates."

"Your dates?" he asked.

"Yes, young man, my dates."

"But there aren't dates for this play, Miss Evans. We open cold at the end of the month. There is to be no tour until after the London run."

"You silly, *silly* boy," she said with a peal of laughter, "I mean the dates of my periods. They're on the 2nd of every month and they last for three days."

Binkie had been present at the first performance of *Evensong* and had noted with excitement that she received an ovation at the end of the first act and that her every entrance from then on was loudly applauded, a special accolade. Like everybody else he succumbed totally to her magic, her wide range of acting abilities, the fascination of that uniquely beautiful voice, and the aura of eternal and universal womanhood. From then on he was looking for a suitable play for her, but whenever he found one which seemed possible she was not available. With the classical theatre taking priority, she enriched the London stage with her Rosalind, her Lady Fidget, her Millamant, her Madame Arkadina.

As her triumphs continued, as her fame and popularity increased, so her legend developed. She was always consulted about the casting of her plays and thus enjoyed considerable power. People tended to be very much in awe of her, adding to her isolation and loneliness, for she was basically shy and insecure and had few real friends. Binkie was secretly rather frightened of her which, for him, was a new and unwelcome situation. In her presence he had to be on his best behaviour as with royalty, no forceful or bad language, no risqué jokes, no relaxing, cosy, giggling chats over a cup of tea as he could have with Marie Tempest or Sybil Thorndike or Irene Vanbrugh or

Lilian Braithwaite. With her he was uncomfortably aware of his youth: never had the gap of twenty years loomed so large.

Amongst the many plays offered to her was Bernard Shaw's *The Millionairess*. Shaw admired her well the other side of idolatry and claimed to have written it specially for her. He spent many years pestering her to do it and she spent many years gently declining. When Binkie read it he thought it an exceedingly bad play but a superb vehicle for an actress who can impersonate a human whirlwind. If Edith should change her mind, he would present it. If not, there was nobody else.

The situation was resolved with the arrival at his office of an untitled play by St John Ervine. It was about an Anglican parish priest and his wife. She is a doctor and runs a local clinic which urgently needs five thousand pounds. Various local spinsters and her husband's curate disapprove of the clinic's instruction in birth control. Her son is a pacifist and is sent to prison for his anti-war activities. By sheer strength of character, womanly charm and diplomacy, she succeeds in organising everything to everybody's satisfaction. It was well written, deeply sentimental and it worked like a dream. The play had caused the author a lot of trouble but Edith went down to his house to hear him read it. St John Ervine always swore that her intelligent suggestions finally made the play what it was and Binkie put it into production with Edith and Owen Nares. The last thing to be written was the title.

"Shall I call it after the priest?" asked Ervine anxiously. "*Robert.*"

"I don't think Edith will like that," said Binkie.

"Well, shall I call it after the wife, *Sanchia.*"

"I don't think Owen will like that and we don't want to upset him. Also people might think it was set in Spain. I think the best thing is call it after the two of them, then they can both claim to have the title part." Ervine saw the wisdom of this and *Robert's Wife* it was. It opened at the Globe in November 1937 and ran for a healthy six hundred performances. After her parade of royals, aristocrats, kings' mistresses, and Restoration countesses, the public responded with extraordinary enthusiasm to Edith portraying a humble, ordinary, provincial vicar's wife. Humble ordinary provincial vicars' wives flocked in their hundreds to see her, and some, as the press reports excitedly testified, came three and even four times.

This was only a stepping stone to what was undoubtedly her greatest triumph: Lady Bracknell in *The Importance of Being Earnest*, which started as a series of charity performances at the Globe, early in 1939, masterminded by John Gielgud who had first played John Worthing at the Lyric, Hammersmith, in 1930 and had cherished a lifelong love for Wilde's masterpiece. Binkie did not care for charity performances: they were usually of low quality, everybody miscast and under-rehearsed, thrown on to the stage with tatty sets and costumes. But when Anthony Eden told him that Queen Mary would attend the first performance which would be given in aid of the Soho Hospital for Women, then Binkie, who liked royalty in his theatre almost more than anything else, reacted with enthusiasm. The company he built round Edith and John included Joyce Carey as Gwendolen, Margaret Rutherford as Miss Prism, George Howe as Canon Chasuble and Ronald Ward as Algy. As Edith was still in *Robert's Wife* and Joyce Carey and Margaret Rutherford were also playing in *Spring Meeting*, the performances had to be in the afternoon. The three sets and many costumes were designed by Motley and were superb. The first matinée was attended not only by Queen Mary in the stage box, but by three members of the original cast: Irene Vanbrugh (Gwendolen), Allan Aynesworth (Algy) and Franklyn Dyall (Merriman), who remarkably, after forty-four years, were alive and in good health. With the eight matinées rapturously received, Binkie immediately planned a full-scale run as soon as Edith finished in *Robert's Wife* which it followed into the Globe in August. The recording which HMV made of Edith and John Gielgud playing the handbag scene – and later of the whole play – brought these two performances into thousands of homes, thereby guaranteeing that for the rest of their lives people would be imitating them. Thus the legend was not only born, but cemented and fixed for ever.

Binkie loved the play, loved the production and adored Edith in the part. He never tired of watching it and it remained his favourite. The company offices above the Globe gave him easy access to the back of the upper circle, but he never announced his intention, which was probably just as well for the peace of mind of the cast. "You'd never believe that she comes from a working-class family in South London," he once said to Barney Gordon after they'd both stood at the back to watch the handbag scene, "or that she was born speaking broad Cockney, or that she worked as a dress-maker's assistant, would you? It must surely be the greatest transformation in theatrical history."

The summer of 1938 had been busy but not in the least lucrative. It was yet another of those tiresome periods when Binkie's good judgement seems to have temporarily deserted him. The plays he chose started out with the highest hopes but all failed: they could be likened to a diamond necklace, which on closer inspection turned out to be glass beads from Woolworth's.

Plan for a Hostess by Thomas Browne was a charming, witty and inventive light comedy and surely in this summer of anxiety the public would want to laugh. Binkie liked it and immediately assembled a cast which included Adrianne Allen, Ronald Squire and the inimitable Yvonne Arnaud. A shrewd lady, she discovered at the beginning of her career in London in the early twenties that the public adores a really strong French accent and if this involved a savage assault on the language then so much the better. In private life her English was perfect and she sensibly kept this a dark secret, but on stage and in public – and this included the company of her fellow-actors who never learned the truth in her lifetime – the Gallic linguistic massacre was complete. Ronald Squire was the most elegant, polished and witty of the elder comedy actors and he was one of Binkie's favourites. Between them they managed to keep the play alive at the St Martin's Theatre for six respectable months, but it should have been two years with that cast. The nagging suspicion that the public did not want to laugh seemed to be confirmed a year later when *Sugar Plum* by the Tennents in-house author, Arthur Macrae, who was as witty on stage as he was with his pen, didn't even make a single month at the Criterion.

Maybe an intimate, small cast, middle-class domestic drama was what that damnably fickle public wanted. Joyce Carey had now written her second play, and Binkie liked it very much. It was about an Ambassador who meets another woman on holiday, starts an affair and has to explain things to his eternally forgiving, endlessly sweet-natured wife at home. *A Thing Apart* attracted the goodwill of Harold French as director, and such good actors as Freda Jackson and Ralph Michael but after eight weeks on tour to good but not overly enthusiastic notices, the Manchester Opera House audiences made it clear that the author of *Sweet Aloes* had, alas, *not* done it again. The critics had another small complaint: the incidents of the second act took place several months before those of the first, and those of the third several months after. The critics found this confusing and made it clear that playing tricks with time was encroaching on what J. B. Priestley firmly claimed as *his* territory.

Another author who lamentably failed to do it again was St John Ervine. From the author of *Robert's Wife* much was expected but the theme of local and domestic snobbery and class hatred as shown in *People of Our Class* turned out to be a sad disappointment. The daughter of a wealthy, retired major-general living in a stately home wants to marry the son of the local butcher living above the shop. Is this a scandal which will overturn the social system or is it a healthy gesture of democracy? "Who cares?" was the unmistakable message of the empty houses at the New Theatre.

What about those which got away? The saddest casualty of the period was *The Corn is Green* by Emlyn Williams who had arrived in London in 1929 and had started his professional career with six lines in a charming play about Mr Pepys, *And So to Bed*. Within eight years he had written his famous murder play, *Night Must Fall*, and thus became a star actor and star playwright. This new play was an autobiographical drama about his close, loving relationship with the school teacher, Miss Cooke, who had discovered and encouraged his talent. It was sensitive, beautifully written and – like all his plays – splendidly theatrical. He and Binkie were friends, so the shock and disappointment when it was rejected were considerable.

Binkie never allowed friendship to come before a business decision; he admired the play but the theme did not appeal to him, nor would it appeal – so he thought – to the public. Education in whatever form was high on his private black-list of unattractive and uncommercial subjects. "Nobody wants to go to the theatre to see plays about people going to school," he said and it is difficult to see how he could have come to this conclusion in defiance of all the facts to the contrary as *Housemaster, Goodbye, Mr Chips* and *Mädchen in Uniform* had all been enormously successful. The play was finally bought by Stephen Mitchell, a young manager, who had presented only one play, but seemed to have a talent for raising money. This turned out to be a little easier once he was able to offer Sybil Thorndike and the author as co-stars to his backers. At thirty-five and with prematurely greying hair, the author was reluctant to portray an eighteen-year-old miner/schoolboy in public but with a little help from Mr Leichner he was able to dye it black and thus achieve a remarkably convincing impression of gangling adolescence. *The Corn is Green* which opened at the Duchess Theatre in October 1938, was an enormous success, one of the few modern classics, and ran for nearly two years.

Binkie never failed to experience a slight *frisson* of disappointment whenever he passed the Duchess Theatre to be confronted by huge blown-up photographs of Emlyn and Sybil smiling down at him, but he was neither jealous nor resentful and his friendship with Emlyn Williams lasted all his life. He'd made a silly mistake but it was good to see his friend – and a fellow-Welshman – doing so well.

Apart from *Design for Living*, 1939 was a disaster. What for instance could have attracted Binkie to *Rhondda Roundabout*, they asked at the

Tennent office? A grim, serious uncompromising drama about Welsh miners in a deeply depressed valley, it had poverty, hunger, unemployment, tyranny, religious bigotry and suffering, but under all that the courage and humanity of these oppressed people shone out and eventually triumphed. Not exactly West End material but John Gielgud who had been sent the script, fell in love with it, insisted on co-producing it with Tennents and provided most of the money, the rest coming from the author, the Welsh poet and journalist Jack Jones. All Binkie had to do was to present it from the Tennent offices and pocket the management fee. It opened at the Globe to splendid notices: it was clear that the critics had been deeply moved by the excellent acting and the simple, uplifting tale of heroism under adversity, but the public lamentably failed to respond. Bookings for the first week were thirty pounds a night which at pre-war prices of 12s 6d for a stall meant that about forty-five people were in the audience. A public appeal was made by the author and supported by a number of celebrities including Emlyn Williams, ever loyal to a fellow-Welshman, J. B. Priestley, Clemence Dane, Sybil Thorndike and Sir Stuart Malcolm, Commissioner for Special Areas.

Business picked up dramatically for a while with houses which were nearly half full, but this did not last and the play was withdrawn after six weeks. It is easy half a century later to find answers for the public's lack of interest. The title, as the press never stopped pointing out, was ridiculous, and more suggestive of a revue at the end of Llandudno pier than a serious play about the perils of mining. With a cast of eighteen, seven sets and eighteen changes of scene it was monumentally expensive to run and would have to play to full houses for months before the production costs had been paid off. And with not enough Welsh actors in London, amateurs had to be expensively imported from the Rhondda Valley to give support to the small professional nucleus who included Mervyn Johns, Hugh Griffith, George Devine, Julien Mitchell, Roddy Hughes and Raymond Huntley. Instead of keeping, this a dark secret, Binkie made the mistake of allowing W. Macqueen Pope, the Tennent press officer, to leak it. The papers took it up in a big way and thus gave the public the entirely wrong idea that the whole cast was amateur which did the play no good at all. Finally, it speedily became evident that too few Welsh were attending this much-acclaimed play about their lives, written by one of their fellow-countrymen. The obvious solution would have been to tour it in Wales either before or afterwards but obvious solutions are always liable to elude even the smartest men.

For Noël Coward, meanwhile, spring 1939 had been busy and fruitful, for he had written two full-length plays, and proposed that

Binkie should present them in repertoire. *Present Laughter* was about the domestic and professional turbulence of a conceited star actor whose successes included plays with titles like *Pity the Blind, Laughter in Heaven* and *The Lost Cavalier*. As a study in egocentricity it had all the hallmarks of truth and experience. Was it a picture of Noël Coward's private and public life? Undoubtedly. Was Garry Essendine a portrait of Coward himself? Certainly. The play was devastatingly witty and cynical and showed quite clearly that Coward had lost nothing of his humour and theatrical skills. Those few who had seen him in *Private Lives* would not be disappointed.

The other play could hardly have been more different. *This Happy Breed* was an account of twenty years in the life of a lower middle-class family living somewhere in south London. It was one of Noël's serious plays and while conceding its good structure, excellent characterisation and theatrical sense, Binkie did not like it. "Let's just do the comedy, Noël dear," he pleaded but Coward refused. The play was his tribute to the class which produced him, to which he was, and remained, steadfastly loyal. His suburban background was important. "You must never, never forget your roots," he once said to Binkie as if rebuking him for disloyalty. Binkie had no wish to remember his middle-class, Nonconformist Welsh background, in fact he could not forget it quickly enough, and if that made him a snob then so be it. Noël insisted that the two plays were a pair and that Binkie could either take them or leave them. Wisely, Binkie took them. He gathered together a company which included Coward's dear friend, Joyce Carey, Judy Campbell and Dennis Price. Coward was to play the leading roles in both plays but because he insisted on a holiday, which took in most points of the European compass, rehearsals were crammed into three confusing weeks for both plays. Binkie had booked a six-month tour to start on September 11th. In London he hoped they would follow *Design for Living* at the Haymarket. But with the outbreak of war the productions were cancelled.

Binkie's method of dealing with unpleasant things like failure, death or war, was to pretend that they did not exist. "This silly war just isn't going to happen," he announced defiantly in July 1939; "as far as I and this management are concerned, it's business as usual." While the storm clouds of impending war cast increasingly long shadows over the country, while more and more uniforms were appearing in the streets, theatres and restaurants, while volunteers were parading in Hyde Park, while trenches were being dug and sandbags filled, while gas masks were being compulsorily issued to everybody, while the news from the Continent became increasingly more threatening, and while Mr Chamberlain's references to *Herr* Hitler and *Signor*

Mussolini became sickeningly more sycophantic, Binkie was making massive plans for the autumn as if this uneasy peace would continue indefinitely.

The novel, *Rebecca*, had been written by Daphne du Maurier in 1938 but throughout 1939 its popularity increased. "You really must read it, it's quite the best novel I've read for years," said John Gielgud enthusiastically, but Binkie never read novels until they had been regurgitated into plays and not even the news that it was the declared favourite of both Winston Churchill and the Queen could persuade him. He was impressed nevertheless and approached Daphne du Maurier to ask if she would care to dramatise it. She at first declined, having never written a play, but Binkie was never more diplomatic and persuasive than when confronted by feminine diffidence and timidity. He took her out to lunch with John Gielgud at Scott's, and finally succeeded in breaking down her shyness. The result was a splendidly actable and stage-worthy play: she wasn't Gerald du Maurier's daughter for nothing. "Oh, what a pity he isn't alive," he said sadly; "he would have been *marvellous* as Maxim de Winter." Gielgud decided to play the part himself – and to direct – and it went into rehearsal in the last week of August with Jill Furse, a young actress of astounding beauty and delicacy, whom the press tipped as being another Meggie Albanesi.

Finally, there was to be a production of *The Cherry Orchard* directed by Michel Saint-Denis and with a cast to dream about – Edith Evans, Peggy Ashcroft, Gwen Ffrangcon-Davies, Ralph Richardson, Cyril Cusack and Alec Guinness. Several unknown young actors who later did rather well for themselves were engaged as understudies, James Cairncross, James Donald, Peter Ustinov and Noel Willman.

The approach of war has to be added to that list of things – which includes a general election, a heatwave and a coronation – with which the theatre cannot compete. In the last weeks of August attendances fell dramatically. The phony peace, as it came to be called, was clearly about to end and the public was far too worried about the future to have much interest in popular entertainment. Hitler invaded Poland on September 1st, a Friday. In her memoirs covering this period, *Upper Circle*, Kitty Black recalls that all the Tennent stars currently working, Marie Tempest, John Gielgud, Rex Harrison, Diana Wynyard, Anton Walbrook and Edith Evans, came up to Binkie's office at lunchtime to find out what plans he had made. Binkie said that as there was no advance booking and as passing trade had fallen to virtually nothing he had no option but to close the theatre on the Saturday evening. Binkie had never in his life cancelled a performance and this more than the barrage balloons visible above the Shaftesbury Avenue skyline, rubbed home to the horrified actors that the war was a shocking reality. Most of them were close to tears, though the only one who actually did cry was Anton Walbrook.

CHAPTER SEVENTEEN

1939–40

The War – *The Importance of Being Earnest – Rebecca*

On Sunday morning, September 3rd, at ten-thirty, the demoralised *Cherry Orchard* company assembled for what Binkie had told them on Saturday would be the final day of rehearsal. "The theatres will be closed, productions will be cancelled, the future is just too gloomy and uncertain. I'm very much afraid that we will have to call a halt." The company sat on the stage of the Queen's while Binkie, Bronson Albery, John Gielgud, John Perry and Michel Saint-Denis grouped themselves in the front stalls. A portable wireless set was brought on by one of the stage hands and at eleven o'clock exactly the shocked and appalled company listened in silence to the tinny, distant voice telling them that as Herr Hitler had made no response to his ultimatum, a state of war now existed between England and Germany. Then the air-raid sirens started their first wartime warning. For those who had never heard it, its wailing scream was a rather frightening sound. Edith Evans started to panic and Binkie had to calm her down. He knew that the systems were merely being tested and that although violent death by bomb and fire *might* be their fate, it was not going to happen before lunch. But Edith was inconsolable. "I'm an actress, I can't do anything else but *act*," she moaned. "What am I to do? What's to become of me?" Alec Guinness, who had become something of a friend and confidant, accompanied her on a tearful, self-pitying walk in Hyde Park. Binkie took the company to Scott's. A farewell lunch for Michel Saint-Denis was the least he could do before he departed for France and immediate enlistment in the Infanterie Coloniale. John Gielgud left early but he did shake hands solemnly with Michel Saint-Denis and wished him *bonne chance*. Saint-Denis returned to France the following day and was lost to the theatre until 1944 when he returned to direct Laurence Olivier in *Oedipus Rex*.

It was typical of the panic which characterised so many of the government's actions in those early war days that it was decided that all theatres should be closed till further notice on the grounds that large gatherings of people in one place would be very dangerous in the event of an air-raid, which was still expected to take place any day. This meant that *The Importance of Being Earnest*, *Design for Living* and *Dear Octopus* were forced to shut down. It was a horrible experience for Binkie to see his beloved Tennent empire suddenly collapse in ruins, but there was nothing he could do about it. After consulting Harry Tennent, he announced that full salaries for the three companies, actors and stage staff, would be paid till the end of September. "Darling Binkie, you're so generous," murmured Marie Tempest, as she allowed him to kiss her cheek.

She was right, but like so many of Binkie's generous acts there was a healthy basis of self-interest. Without any commitment in London there was nothing to stop the actors from enlisting in the armed forces, emigrating or just retiring. All these things were liable to happen anyway but not in the immediate future if they were contracted to him. Putting them on salary at least guaranteed that for a month his empire would remain intact. When he wanted them they would be there. It cost him only a few thousand pounds, a small price to pay for the distinct advantage over the rival managements in the West End. "I've worked terribly hard to build up H. M. Tennent," he said to Barney Gordon later on that first Monday of the war, "and it would really break my heart if it crumbled away merely because of that lunatic in Berlin."

Shaftesbury Avenue and all the surrounding streets were empty, the theatres were all closed, the whole of the West End had that hideously deserted look. That morning he found a solitary figure standing outside the Globe: it was Geoffrey Edwards who had played Lexy Mill, the curate, in *Candida*. They chatted for a few minutes. "Let's go and have a cup of coffee," said Edwards. They went to a nearby coffee bar in Denman Street. It was called the S & F, standing for 'Stage and Films' and was much frequented by the profession. They sat silently at the counter, gloomily sipping their coffee. Suddenly Binkie emitted a sound which was half-way between a sigh and a whimper. "I just don't know what I'm going to do," he whispered in a voice of despair. "He looked like a schoolboy who had just been expelled," said Edwards. "And I thought there can't be many people in the world who have seen Binkie Beaumont in this unguarded unhappy moment of truth."

And so Binkie prepared for war. The next time he arrived at the office he was beautifully dressed and exquisitely groomed, not a hair out of place, smiling radiantly, and carrying a gas mask. He had regained his confidence. Throughout the day he supervised the staff as they filled fire buckets, put up blackout curtains and stuck green netting over the windows to stop the glass from shattering should a bomb fall nearby. With Binkie organising and actually helping, what would otherwise have been a boring chore became great fun. It was a good omen for the future of the Firm.

The first official announcement after the declaration of war had been another to close all theatres, and cinemas, but this lunacy did not last long. Binkie organised a deputation from the Theatre Managers' Association: with Bronson Albery, Prince Littler and Basil Dean, he called at Number Ten and after a wait of two hours they were admitted to the Cabinet Room to present their case. Happily, wiser heads there realised that in times of national emergency, entertainment takes a high priority. Binkie made personal calls to Anthony Eden and Mrs Churchill; he even sent an official letter to the King and Queen, and to Queen Mary. By Thursday he had his result. The government made an official announcement that theatres and cinemas could be re-opened in what was diplomatically described as *safe* areas. This meant the provinces. "I really don't see the logic of this," said Binkie. "Why should the Opera House, Manchester, be considered safer than the dear old Haymarket? But I'm not complaining. Let's be thankful for small mercies and get the show on the road."

The show in question was *The Importance of Being Earnest* which re-opened in a blaze of publicity on September 14th at the Golders Green Hippodrome and, as Binkie never stopped boasting with glee, this was the first play to do so in the London area, Golders Green being considered, by the inscrutable logic of the government, to be *safe*. It is unlikely that any play Binkie presented during the next five years did so much for public morale or enhanced the gaiety of the nation to such a pitch of hysterical enthusiasm. It filled the Hippodrome to overflowing for eight performances a week with audiences who laughed as they had never laughed before at the exquisite nonsense which seemed to be even more delicious when a well-placed bomb scoring a direct hit could blow them all to eternity. In the fevered atmosphere of those early months, it was a matter of vital concern whether John Worthing should marry Gwendolen Fairfax, whether or not Algy was his brother and would there be any cucumber sandwiches left for Lady Bracknell? It was a mark of their success that the passionate intensity of John Gielgud's and Edith Evans' acting should convince their audiences that those same cucumber sandwiches were the most important things in the world.

Meanwhile *Design for Living* re-opened in Birmingham for a year's tour. Noël Coward took up an intelligence job for the government which involved living and working away from London, but he was so good at keeping his secrets that neither Binkie nor Harry Tennent nor anybody at the Globe knew what he was doing or where. *Present Laughter* and *This Happy Breed* would have to wait.

Gradually familiar faces reappeared in uniform. Glen Byam Shaw went into the Royal Scots, Murray Macdonald rejoined his former regiment from 1918, Henry Sherek, once they had found a uniform to fit his Falstaffian figure, was posted to a training camp in Sussex, and Stephen Mitchell, only two years in management but beginning to make his mark, was on the Reserve and stood by for the summons. Harry Tennent was too old to be called up. "I went through all that in 1914 on the Somme," he told Binkie, "and I don't expect to go through it again in 1939." But Binkie, at thirty-one, was quite young enough for the armed services. "Which branch will you choose?" asked Basil Dean at an ENSA meeting, exercising one of his rare flashes of grisly humour. "The Military Police? The Pay Corps? The Royal Household Cavalry?"

Binkie laughed nervously. "Oh really, Basil dear, can you imagine *me* as a soldier?" Basil had to admit that he could not: nor could anybody in the Firm. The mental picture of Binkie shivering in denims on a rain-swept parade-ground, peeling potatoes in a steamy kitchen, running over muddy trenches with a bayoneted rifle, queuing up in the canteen for chips and baked beans, buying a beer in the NAAFI, standing naked by his iron bed in the chilly, windswept barrack-room for a VD inspection, being charged by an uncouth sergeant-major for insubordination and being forced to scrub the guard-room floor with a toothbrush or scrambling with twenty others into the back of an army lorry for a secret destination in darkest Scotland, all these made the imagination boggle. One could more easily picture Oscar Wilde picking oakum in Reading Gaol.

On the advice of Llewellyn Rees, an actor and currently Equity secretary, he made a formal application for exemption and asked that his profession of theatrical manager should be listed as a reserved occupation. This received support from Marie Tempest who said, "It is grotesque that the government should even think of sending Binkie into the trenches. He can make a far better contribution to the war effort in the theatre." "If he continues in management," said Edith Evans in her best Lady Bracknell manner, "he will be creating, whereas if he has to go to the trenches, he will be destroying. As a Christian Scientist I do not approve of killing." "He would be the worst soldier in the world," said Sybil vehemently. "But his theatrical knowledge is beyond price."

The applications were heard by a committee from Equity and other trade unions at the offices of the Society of West End Managers (SWETM for short, ironically pronounced 'sweat 'em'). The committee's recommendations were sent to Ernest Bevin, then Minister of Labour, who accepted them without argument. Contrary to the uncouth image he presented, he was a man of culture, who loved the theatre, fully appreciated its importance in wartime, and did everything to see that it got top priority. Binkie was a very important figure in the theatre, he could be trusted to keep it thriving, he was far too important to be wasted as cannon fodder.* He was granted his exemption. John Gielgud was also granted exemption: his profession as a leading classical actor was likewise regarded as a reserved occupation.

Binkie, John Gielgud and Harry Tennent celebrated their good fortune with a lunch at Scott's, after which Binkie arranged for a press conference at Drury Lane where Gielgud announced that he was joining the Old Vic to play King Lear and Prospero in *The Tempest*. Furthermore, he said, with a missionary gleam in his eye, he would play nothing but Shakespeare and the classics for the duration of the war. And, if that was not enough, he made a solemn vow to join ENSA and take these productions anywhere in the world where there were troops awaiting entertainment.

In those early months of the war, the sight of a healthy young man who was not in uniform caused raised eyebrows. It was a far cry from the hostility of the white-feather brigade of 1914 but enquiring glances from the police could be embarrassing. Binkie decided to join the ARP as a warden. According to legend, he had his navy blue uniform specially made in Savile Row and appeared at the ARP post in Eaton Square exquisitely groomed and tailored, charming, smiling and eager to help. From the memories of those who worked with him, he was the worst ARP warden in history. "He did his best, but he just didn't have the knack," said Ted Matthews who served with him for a couple of weeks before being posted north. "He hadn't got a clue about what to do in an emergency and he was more trouble than he was worth. A nice bloke, we all liked him, but he couldn't even make a good cup of tea. He wanted to serve us with that Chinese muck. He couldn't type, he couldn't learn the morse code, though I spent hours trying to teach him, he hadn't a clue about first aid and couldn't even tie a simple bandage neatly, and worst of all he didn't know the area, and a sense of geography is very important for an ARP warden. So finally he had to go." The immediate consequence was a letter from the Ministry of Labour thanking him for his services and regretting

---

* By a curious coincidence Hitler had come to exactly the same conclusion about the two Wagner grandsons, who spent the war years working on a farm. It was uncomfortable and boring but at least it was safe.

that they would no longer be required. And that was the extent of Binkie's contribution to Hitler's downfall.

By October the preliminary war scare had started to fade and one by one, like children playing Grandmother's Footsteps, the West End theatres cautiously started to re-open. The public wanted entertainment badly, they *demanded* it in no uncertain terms and were quite prepared to risk their lives getting it, but was it really so dangerous? There was no sign of the bombers; maybe Hitler did not want war with Britain as everybody said. By December Shaftesbury Avenue was back to normal: normal, that is, if you overlooked the blackout, the sandbags piled high in the windows and doors, the hundreds of different uniforms of all services and every nationality filling the street and the posters sternly warning 'Careless Talk Costs Lives'.

"We want something light and undemanding," said Harold French who had become one of the Firm's most employed directors. "A revue. Girls, comics, legs, laughs, songs, dances, funny sketches." Binkie shuddered when the idea was put to him. He disliked the genre, having served his unwilling apprenticeship in those early years at Moss Empires. In peacetime he would never have soiled his exquisitely manicured fingers with anything so coarse and common but his good sense told him that in wartime the ordinary rules of civilised behaviour may have to be quietly set aside. Harry Tennent favoured the project: he had produced revues during the First World War and had written many charming songs for them. Binkie gave in. But he announced that he was having nothing to do with the setting up or administration. Since the two Harrys knew and understood the art of revue, he could safely leave it to them.

The only redeeming feature was Beatrice Lillie. She had become a good friend. She was the only one of his stars who could always make him laugh. Her marriage into the aristocracy, which made her Lady Peel, and her production of a charming and extremely good-looking son added richness to a relationship which was already very satisfactory. "Darling Binkie," she said when he took her to lunch at Scott's. "I want to go to France to entertain the troops and I want to go to New York and do a musical with Charlie Butterworth."

"And who is Charlie Butterworth?"

"He's a Hollywood comedian and he's *divinely* funny."

"Darling Bea, there are very few troops in France, most of them are still over here, so why don't you do a revue for them and for us? It starts rehearsing next month and opens in Brighton on the fifteenth. And while you're waiting do some troop concerts, I hear they're *screaming* for you in Scapa Flow."

All Clear opened at the Queen's on December 30th and the party which Binkie gave for the cast combined the twin celebrations of Binkie's first new production of the war and the New Year. The notices were excellent since Bea Lillie had her critics in her hand for whom she could do no wrong. But the public did not respond because it just was not good enough. There were some gems: she sang 'I Went to a Marvellous Party', thus giving it the London première. Noël Coward had written it especially for her in an ill-starred revue, *Set to Music*, which had a brief career in New York in 1938. She and Bobby Howes as two evil choirboys with angelic faces caused a lot of amusement and Fred Emney was Fred Emney, which was fine because neither the public nor the critics ever wanted him to be anything else. But there were too many longueurs. Bea Lillie appeared only seven times in a two-hour show; for the star of the show, this simply was not enough. It played to diminishing houses throughout January and February and on February 28th he took it off. But he had learned one good lesson: never *never* to put on anything he did not wholeheartedly believe in, no matter how much his colleagues and employees pestered him. There are some things you just cannot delegate.

By then he was already in rehearsal. In later years he enjoyed testing his friends' knowledge of theatre history by asking them two key questions which might well have been included in a *Times* Christmas quiz. "Which new play was the first to compete successfully with the film running at the same time?" and "Which West End play changed its leading lady more frequently during its London run and tour than any other?" In both cases the answer was *Rebecca*. Everybody in the Firm warned him against presenting *Rebecca* with the film announced for its London showing. "With all those stars and all the publicity it's going to get nobody will come anywhere near the theatre," but Binkie smiled like a sphinx. "Oh yes, they will, they'll come in droves, my dear, the film will not spoil the business at all, you'll see."

Gielgud was busy at the Old Vic playing and rehearsing *King Lear* and *The Tempest* so as he was not available either to direct *Rebecca* or play Maxim de Winter – not to mention his highly publicised commitment to a wartime diet of the classics – a substitute had to be found. Glen Byam Shaw was Binkie's first choice but he was on the Officers' Emergency Reserve and liable to call-up any day. George Devine had started to make his name as a skilful freelance director who could get good performances out of the most unlikely people and had a special skill in atmospheric lighting. With this play Binkie showed his rare talent for unexpected casting. Owen Nares was an actor in the du Maurier mould with a lean, bony face and a special talent for underplaying. The part of Maxim de Winter represented a complete break with the past. Here was an empty shell of a man disillusioned with life, tortured by guilt and fear. Delighted to get away from the routine romances and light comedies with which he had filled his career, he brought to the part all his considerable powers and technical skills – like Gerald du Maurier, he was a much better actor than anybody except Binkie realised – and gave what everybody agreed was the best performance of his life.

For the part of the sinister housekeeper, Mrs Danvers, there were many hatchet-faced actresses available, but Binkie would have none of them. "I don't like obvious casting," he said to George Devine. "I do like to *surprise* people." Only Binkie would have realised that under Margaret Rutherford's double chins and eccentric comedy talents there lurked a frustrated tragedienne. "How did you know I wanted to play something dramatic, Binkie darling?" she asked curiously. "I hear strange drums beating," he said, flashing his inscrutable smile, and that was the only answer she received. In the event she made the part so much her own that it became difficult to imagine that she had ever played anything different. Nobody who was present at the first night will ever forget her first entrance at the top of the curved staircase which dominated Roger Furse's gloomily atmospheric set or the brooding menace with which she slowly walked down to greet the new Mrs de Winter. At that moment all those gossiping spinsters and gambling maiden aunts of the last five years were swept away as if they had never been.

It opened on April 5th 1940 to unanimously good notices: even the tiresome, difficult-to-please James Agate splashed out superlatives on everybody. It seemed from the five minutes of applause at the end and the speed with which the theatre filled up the following night, that Daphne du Maurier's Gothic masterpiece – and there were many who considered that this praise was not too high – held just as strong an attraction on the stage of the Queen's Theatre as between the two covers of the Gollancz edition.

The film had been expected two weeks earlier, but Binkie had powerful friends in the film world. It took only a single phone call to Alexander Korda in Hollywood, where he was energetically trying to raise the money to finish *The Thief of Baghdad*, and another phone call from Korda to David O. Selznick, to arrange for the London showing of the *Rebecca* film to be delayed for three months. This, Binkie rightly calculated, was the minimum period which *Rebecca* needed to establish itself with the London public as a solid success. When the film opened the play had been playing to capacity for three months and with enough advance booking to keep it going happily until Christmas.

The film was eagerly awaited: it was Selznick's first since *Gone with the Wind* – how was he going to live up to *that*? By a miracle he did, for nobody was disappointed. Far from getting in the way, the film and the play were a great help to each other. Binkie encouraged the press to make comparisons: he arranged for centre-page picture spreads in the film magazines, showing stills from the film and photographs from the play side by side: in the cinema foyer big placards announced: 'If you have enjoyed seeing Laurence Olivier and Joan Fontaine and Judith Anderson in the film, go to the Queen's Theatre and see Owen Nares, Celia Johnson and Margaret Rutherford in the play.' In one respect, however, the play had the advantage in that it was more faithful to the book. Maxim de Winter murders Rebecca and gets away with it which the Lord Chamberlain was perfectly happy to pass. But in Hollywood, the restrictive morality of the Hays Office refused to allow it. Rebecca's death has to be by accident and Maxim is given a long speech to explain why.

Taking into account the endless tours and its return seasons in different West End theatres, *Rebecca* ran for three years and managed to get through seven leading ladies. Jill Furse had rehearsed it for two weeks before the war broke out, Celia Johnson played for three months, then Peggy Ashcroft took over, to be succeeded in turn by Barbara Mullen, Isolde Denham, Jill Balcon and finally a pretty unknown, Yvonne Owen, who had formerly understudied the part. Inevitably, Owen Nares, who played with all seven of them in turn, was asked which he liked the best. "They were all splendid," was his tactful reply. But there was no secret about Binkie's opinion. "If *only* Celia Johnson had appeared in the film."

In *Rebecca*'s last year Owen Nares' son Geoffrey died in North Africa from malaria. His father was devastated and it was this, rather than boredom with the part he had played for so long, which caused him to leave the *Rebecca* company. He was replaced by Stewart Granger, then virtually unknown. He had been born James Stewart in 1913 but on entering the theatre had changed it for one good, obvious reason, though he continued to be addressed as 'Jimmy'. At thirty, but looking a mere twenty, he was wildly miscast and far too young, but good actors were in short supply during the war and Binkie, like the other West End managers, had to take what he could get and like it. Jimmy was spectacularly good-looking in a dark, brooding, Byronic manner, he had charm and a very striking stage presence. He had a fine baritone voice and if all that was not enough, he could act. Hadn't Bernard Shaw allowed him to play King Magnus in *The Apple Cart* at the 1937 Malvern Festival? Hadn't he played Tybalt to Robert Donat's Romeo and given what many people, including James Agate, described as the definitive performance of this showy but difficult part?

"As soon as I signed the contract I went to see the play," said Granger years later. "I thought it was a perfectly terrible production and that Owen Nares was a very dull, ineffectual actor. I thought, well, I can do better than *that*. As you can see, I certainly did not lack self-confidence. The rest of the company were as boring as hell. They kept on telling me what Owen had done, how he'd said this line or that line and eventually I lost my temper and shouted that I didn't give a fuck what Owen had said or done and that this was *my* performance and I was going to do it *my* way. The young girl who played Mrs de Winter had been the understudy and she hadn't been in the business more than a couple of years yet she had the cheek to try and tell *me* how to act."

If the company were upset by Granger's admitted arrogance Binkie was not. He would pay regular visits to the rehearsals and chuckle happily. "You're going to be very good, Jimmy my dear, very good indeed."

Granger received good notices when he finally opened, *Rebecca* continued to play to good houses and amongst those who came to see him was film director Leslie Arliss. Two weeks later, Granger received an offer which was to have a decisive effect on his career, to play the romantic lead in a film, *The Man in Grey*. The part was good and he would co-star with James Mason, Phyllis Calvert and Margaret Lockwood. Binkie's permission was essential. Although unhappy at the thought of losing Jimmy Granger he was shrewd enough to realise that Granger the film star would be of greater value to the Firm than Granger the unknown actor. Binkie agreed, not only in allowing him to do the film, but he also gave him time off on matinée days. It was a huge success and Jimmy was now a star.

Binkie was always a little cool because he did not consider that Jimmy had shown sufficient gratitude to him for allowing him to make the film. He claimed that he had discovered Jimmy and that he alone was responsible for his later success but he always liked to get full mileage of credit for his acts of generosity. Jimmy always hotly disputed his debt to Binkie. He had been acting for ten years before he even met Binkie and the producers of *The Man in Grey* were so anxious to get him that, if necessary, they would have postponed the film until he was contractually available.

CHAPTER EIGHTEEN

1940–1

Cousin Muriel – The Devil's Disciple – Harry Tennent's Death – *Blithe Spirit*

Quite apart from the success of *Rebecca*, the spring of 1940 was an exceptionally busy period.

> Clemence Dane
> Has done it again

was Binkie's poetic reaction when the script of *Cousin Muriel* landed on his desk just after the New Year. Dearest Winnie had written something which, as ever, had an excellent idea and some passages of fine writing but unhappily these did not add up to a satisfactory play. Like so much of her writing, it just missed being good. "She's scored an outer ring but not a bull's eye," was his summary. His first instinct was to refuse but dearest Winnie, who could be devious in her own way, had cleverly anticipated that by sending it first to Edith Evans, who had now sent it to Binkie with her enthusiastic endorsement. Binkie could see why. Winnie had described Cousin Muriel as 'beautiful' and 'glamorous' and in so doing had brought a much-needed balm to one of Edith's sorest points.

Edith had this astonishing gift of looking lovely on the stage when the part called for it: after seeing her Rosalind, or her Madame Arkadina, you would have sworn that she was a blazing beauty. But off stage she was always painfully aware that she was plain to the point of ugliness. When she looked into her mirror she did not see the great actress who had enslaved millions, the possessor of the West End's most beautiful voice. All she could see was the heaviness of her features, the mouth which was too wide, the nose which was too prominent, the cast over one eye, the thickness of her ankles, the podginess of her legs. Every night she would sit in front of her dressing-room mirror shouting, "I AM beautiful, I AM beautiful, I *am*, I *am*." And now at last here was a playwright of distinction who believed her and had written a play not for an actress who *could* be beautiful but for one who *was*.

Cousin Muriel is a judge's housekeeper who lives in a luxurious flat in Knightsbridge. She has a son in advertising. She also has an unfortunate habit of forging cheques and stealing things from shops. Binkie assembled a highly prestigious company around her: Frederick Leister as the judge, the young Peggy Ashcroft as his daughter, the even younger Alec Guinness as Muriel's son. The smoothly discreet direction was by Norman Marshall, one of those reliable people on whom Binkie came to depend when there was a temperamental star to be coaxed and flattered.

The rehearsals were fraught with tensions and difficulties. Once Edith had got over the first shock of delight in having to be beautiful, she found that she had no sympathy at all for Muriel's criminal tendencies. "I don't understand crime," she said. "I just don't understand how such a fine woman like Muriel can do such terrible things. Of course, she doesn't actually *steal*, she merely *borrows* because she likes beautiful things. She is like a magpie. Winnie dear, why don't you call this play *The Magpie*. That would be *much* nicer." It was with such silliness as this that valuable time was wasted during rehearsals. "It's all that Christian Science nonsense," complained Binkie with justified peevishness, "she thinks that crime, like sin, doesn't exist. Why can't she be a Catholic like darling Sybil? Then we'd have no trouble."* (Sybil was a high Anglican.)

It took a couple of long and expensive lunches at Scott's for Binkie, supported by Norman Marshall and the author, to convince Edith that her fears of the public not accepting her as a forger and a thief were totally unfounded. "Not only will they accept it, Edith dear, they'll love it. After all, it's what many women would like to do if they thought they could get away with it."

Further trouble came from a totally unexpected source. It was a measure of Edith's unhappiness that she sent a copy of the script to Bernard Shaw to ask his advice about playing the part. Shaw was still pursuing her in the hope of persuading her to play *The Millionairess* and he declared himself only too happy to oblige. He advised her that a

---

*There was one aspect of her Christian Science which caused Binkie a great deal of trouble which was her belief that illness and disease were not physical facts but existed only in the mind and thus could be cured by prayer. During the run of *The Chalk Garden* her stomach began to swell, she had difficulty in walking and breathing, she was in considerable pain, but in spite of all Binkie's entreaties, she refused to see a doctor. Finally, she collapsed on the stage in the middle of a performance and had to be taken in an ambulance to the Middlesex Hospital where a successful operation was performed. She was back in the play within a fortnight.

criminal heroine would certainly antagonise the public, and it was a mistake he himself had never made, neatly forgetting that Medea and Lady Macbeth had been enthralling audiences for centuries. He had no high opinion of the play and did some uncalled-for rewriting, sending along several typed sheets containing a new ending. Edith liked it but nobody else did. Far from being flattered by this act of generosity, Binkie was politely surprised by his presumption though others had a less courteous word for it.

But it may have been Shaw's willingness to help her in a crisis which finally melted Edith's heart and caused her to change her mind. Or it may have been that after the pedestrian improbabilities of *Cousin Muriel*, *The Millionairess* seemed to be a much better play and Epifania a more exciting part. Whatever the reason, she finally agreed and *The Millionairess* was scheduled to follow *Cousin Muriel* with the least possible delay. By the time rehearsals for the latter started, letters of agreement and a contract for the former between Shaw and Binkie were being drawn up.

5th February 1940

Dear Hugh Beaumont,

THE MILLIONAIRESS.

The agreement for *The Millionairess* can be the same as the *Candida* one dated 23rd November 1936, except the following changes.

2. "31st March shall be" immediately following the London run of Miss Clemence Dane's play entitled   ?

3. The casting of the play shall be subject to the author's approval and in particular the part of Epifania shall be played by Miss Edith Evans until she voluntarily withdraws from the cast.

14. The licence granted by this agreement shall be extended for a year following the end of the London run to cover a provincial and suburban tour of (list) on the same terms.

If this is satisfactory I will have copies typed for execution.

Faithfully,
G. Bernard Shaw.

Cousin Muriel opened on March 7th. With a pale make-up, long ringlets of raven-black hair and a gown of shimmering white chiffon Edith looked lovelier than ever before and elicited gasps of astonishment and pleasure from the audience, for the contrast with her forbidding and dragonish Lady Bracknell only six months earlier made her present radiance all the more dramatic and satisfying. There were further gasps of astonishment when she sat down at the piano and played superbly. She had her back to the audience and the keyboard was visible so the audience were able to see for themselves that she really was playing Bach, Chopin and Beethoven. It was a mark of her dedicated professionalism that she had spent weeks practising on a dumb keyboard. The unseen performer was Kitty Black who, in addition to her secretarial and translating skills, was thus revealed as an expert pianist. Or rather, *unrevealed*, for the secret was well kept and Edith was to receive much praise for her musicianship.

The deluge of letters written by Shaw to Edith begging her to play his millionairess, extensively quoted by Bryan Forbes in his biography *Ned's Girl*, makes sad reading. In his love for his deeply unsatisfactory, inferior play, he could see no fault, whereas Edith could see nothing but fault. However, once she had given her reluctant consent and once Binkie had signed the contract, a further avalanche of letters descended on the Globe Theatre. At eighty-four his restless energy and passionate interest in all aspects of the production were undimmed by age. Months before the rehearsals started he pestered Binkie with casting suggestions, enquiries after touring dates and waspish comments on the current West End theatre:

If you can get Peggy Ashcroft for Patricia, you need look no further. My suggestion of Gabriel Toyne for Blenderbland is important because he understands the falls and an actor who didn't could sue you for damages. James Agate declared him the greatest undiscovered actor on the English stage. Sagamore must be an agreeable fellow like Roberts or Squire . . . Marie Ault would be all right for the woman in the sweater's den. Any good utility could manage the sweater. Any presentable juvenile will do for the hotel manager.

I have had to give up producing: I am too old for such games. Edith had a crazy notion that Leslie Henson ought to produce it. She probably thought her part was a funny one. It isn't; it's tragic all through . . . how did you get on with Irene Hentschel over *Candida*?

The scenery is all plain sailing. The designer can let himself go in the transmogrified inn at the end.

The casting of the Indian doctor is very important. What about Gielgud? Failing him, Stephen Murray? If you need to fall back on a remoter generation, Wontner could give a good show. You will have to secure Sarah Tapping. She is a Black Belt which is the highest judo dignity and a qualified actress from an old theatrical family. She is the only expert understudy for Edith . . .

. . . I have just had a talk with Sarah Tapping and I find that she must not give private lessons in Judo for money as she would thereby lose her amateur status. But she can take an engagement as a producer of a scene (or a whole play, she produces for Leon M. Lion) as that, and acting, is her profession. She says she can arrange an effective show that will impose on the audience as real Judo . . .

. . . The casting is getting very difficult. Both Toyne and Stephen Murray are called up.

Toyne's wife would be a success as Patricia and you could give them a joint if my earlier suggestion of Jean Cadell falls through. I am liable to be forty years out of date with my suggestions.

Binkie had no objections to being thus pestered. A selection of these letters, postcards and contracts were gathered together, taken home to Finchingfield, pasted into a gilt-edged album and became one of his most valuable treasures.

Apart from these casting suggestions, Shaw made many hypocritical expressions of goodwill towards *Cousin Muriel* whose failure would speed up the arrival of his millionairess. "I hope that *Cousin Muriel* is doing well . . . I trust that Clemence Dane will enjoy a long success . . . how is Miss Dane's play doing so far? . . . I hope the public is flocking to see Edith's kleptomaniac . . . there is no hurry about my play."

Edith's beauty and piano-playing kept *Cousin Muriel* running throughout the spring and summer of 1940 for a respectable four months. After a week's holiday, she started rehearsals for *The Millionairess* opening at the Manchester Opera House in August. After all his years of planning and cajoling, the result was a sad anti–climax. Edith was not happy, the production was lacklustre, the public apathetic in view of the deteriorating war situation and the houses thin. In Manchester and the following week in Edinburgh, the receipts were averaging eight hundred and forty pounds a week, indicating half-full houses. Lack of public response as well as the start of the blitz in late August gave Binkie a good excuse for cancelling the London opening at the Globe in September. Edith was convinced that Binkie's motive was a heartless avarice, "He wouldn't risk it in London because he was afraid it wouldn't make enough money for him." But this was only half true. "It's for your safety, Edith dear," he said smoothly. "We can't have you as a casualty of the war. You're far too valuable."

Two more contestants in this boisterous Shavian war game kept not only Kitty Black, Binkie's current secretary, busy at her typewriter but also Miss Patch who had performed single-handed a similar service for Shaw for over twenty underpaid and overworked years.

There was a small play and a big one. Binkie had sent John Gielgud on a tour of the army camps with a double bill comprising plays by Noël Coward and Gordon Daviot. They had given pleasure to a great many people and Binkie decided to send them out again on a further tour of ENSA dates. "There's only one thing better than two short plays," he said, "and that's three. Or four." Gielgud wanted to include *The Dark Lady of the Sonnets*, a gem of Shavian wit and imagination in which, for the first time in his life, he would play the part of Shakespeare. Binkie wrote to ask permission. Shaw returned Binkie's letter with a characteristically waspish reply written at the bottom of the sheet.

You don't say where this lunacy is taking place? Not that it matters. A fixed fee for one performance would be two guineas. For a week either, my ordinary terms divided equally among the three copyrighted plays if the authors will agree, or £5 plus 5% of the surplus if any.
Shakespeare blacklegging as usual.

G.B.S. 7.8.40

The big play was *The Devil's Disciple* starring Robert Donat. It was seven years since he had resigned a small part in *When Ladies Meet* to take up a Korda film contract. His performance of Mr Chips in the 1938 MGM film had not only won him an Oscar in the 1939 awards, it had elicited the highest praise from a number of other Hollywood actors, and had made him the best-known and best-loved male film star in England. The fates had been very good to him, giving him virility, charm, beauty and a wide assortment of acting skills. Binkie used to say that if you scratch a young and handsome romantic with a special talent for theatrical heroism you will find an antique character actor struggling to get out. Robert was naturally proud of his good looks but, like Ivor Novello, there were times when he was happy to escape from them. It is an interesting comment on his career, and a tribute to the intelligence and good taste of his public, that the handsome star of *The Citadel*, *The Count of Monte Cristo*, *The Thirty-Nine Steps* and *Knight Without Armour* should have enjoyed his greatest success when playing a frail and vulnerable old man, unrecognisable behind white wig and moustache, a hundred lines on his face and a sagging suit. To go from clean-cut heroes to doddery old men did induce a certain schizophrenia and Robert was never quite sure in his mind which he wished to be. But whichever it was, Binkie knew that he was one of the few actors who could fill a theatre single-handed.

Like so many of Shaw's best-known plays, *The Devil's Disciple* had earned its popularity in the repertory companies and the endless Charles Macdona tours. West End revivals had been few and short-lived. Donat's first appearance in the play was at the Buxton Festival, directed by Tyrone Guthrie. Binkie travelled up with Harry Tennent to see it. He disliked the production and was bored by the supporting cast, but he admired Donat this side of idolatry and longed to present him in a suitable play. This was clearly it. He wrote to Shaw asking permission to tour it and suggested Milton Rosmer as Burgoyne and director, together with the young Rosamund John as Judith. He also suggested that because of the destabilising effect of the war and the uncertain commercial future of the theatre, he might consider lowering his royalties.

By all means try a tour of *The Devil's Disciple*: there is more prestige to be gained on that particular road to ruin than on most of the others. But why do you want me to reduce my terms? I have not raised them for forty years, though all other prices in the theatre and out of it have sky-rocketed. And I cannot reduce them for you without reducing them for everyone else as well. How do you expect an author to live. Dash it, if business is under £50, you can afford a shilling in the pound. I get about five pence of it: the government takes the rest. Anyhow, what else do you propose?

I daresay Rosmer will give a good account of Burgoyne, but be careful about Anderson. Unless he is strong and sympathetic and can bring off the explosion at the end of the second act, he can weaken the play dangerously.

Judith is a leveller: there must be nothing of the strong woman about her.

Have a good record for the Dead March. I presume you can hire costumes from the Old Vic.

The tour opened on April 20th 1940 in Bristol to a handsome return of £1,920 followed by a record £2,263 at Glasgow. It was a spectacular start to an eight-week tour which grossed £13,432. It brought hundreds of thousands to the theatres during a summer which offered as counter-attractions a suffocating heatwave, the retreat from Dunkirk, the fall of France and nightmare rumours of the impending invasion by the Nazi hordes. But it was not a happy tour for Robert: his marriage was crumbling and would soon end in separation and then divorce: his health was troubling him and the asthma, which would one day kill him, would render him incapable of speech for hours on end, resulting in many cancelled performances. He was intensely irritated by the endless letters from Shaw of complaint and advice and worried by the publicity which Binkie had launched on his behalf. He protested that his name on the posters was bigger than the title and that Bernard Shaw's name was scarcely visible – surely the first time in theatrical history that a star has made this complaint, but Donat was nothing if not modest. Happily, both his health and his spirits improved. *The Devil's Disciple* opened at the Piccadilly on July 24th to excellent notices and full houses. Binkie did persuade Shaw to look in and see a matinée.

17th August 1940

Dear Hugh Beaumont,

I saw *The Devil's Disciple* on Wednesday. It is a success: but between ourselves – it is an Elephant and Castle success not a West End one. The stage management is hopelessly bad and the production in the final scene is very provincial. I am sorry that I did not see a rehearsal. I could have saved some of the worst blunders. However, a success is a success, so you must keep all this for future revivals.

Faithfully,
G. Bernard Shaw.

Binkie had taken good note of Shaw's advice. He offered the part of Anderson to Stewart Granger. It was a piece of inspired casting for he brought great passion and urgency to the part and thus provided the perfect companion piece to Donat's Dudgeon. Their big act two scene together made a great impact and it is unlikely that the two parts have ever been better played. The two men became great friends. Donat had a firm respect for Granger's talent and a strong belief in his future. When, two years later, he was asked to play the itinerant actor in *The Man in Grey* film, he turned it down being unavailable, suggested Granger and rejoiced mightily in his success.

Alas, Granger joined the Gordon Highlanders at the beginning of July and so was unable to repeat his success in London. He was replaced by the husky-voiced Roger Livesey. *The Devil's Disciple* opened at the Piccadilly on July 24th, but the plans for a long run, which it would certainly have enjoyed, were cut short. The blitz which all England had been most horribly anticipating finally arrived, just a year after the declaration of war. The phony war was over, and the Battle of Britain had begun. The sordid realities of war were now in the West End and began to chip off the gilt from Binkie's life-style with alarming speed.

The flat which the Johns, Gielgud and Perry, shared in St John's Wood had to be hurriedly evacuated when it was commandeered by the War Office. They moved into Binkie's flat at 142 Piccadilly and thus suffered their first experience of over-crowding. This did not last long, however, because the house next door at 145 received a direct hit. It shattered the skylight of 142 and made it uninhabitable. They were lucky to escape with their lives as glass, girders, wooden struts, floorboards and plaster rained down on Binkie's long wooden table while they were preparing their frugal wartime dinner in the kitchen. Kitty Black helped him to pack his belongings in a series of suitcases and tea chests and was vastly amused to see that he had collected dozens of little carved wooden animals to float in his bath.

The first night air-raids on London had started on September 6th, and were reported with many dramatic photographs the following day. On that evening there were twenty-two West End theatres open, among them three with Tennent productions, *Rebecca*, *The Devil's Disciple* and *Thunder Rock*. Over the weekend came a mass closure: on Monday only six theatres remained open and on the Thursday, September 12th, only two: *White Horse Inn* at the Coliseum and the appropriately named *The Infernal Machine* by Cocteau at the Arts. A week later there were still only two, Robert Atkins' company doing lunchtime Shakespeare, anticipating Wolfit, and the Windmill. The hardship of the war for the intelligent theatre-goer can be measured by this simple choice: either tatty, fourth-rate lunchtime Shakespeare or tatty, tenth-rate nude revue. This state of affairs continued for three months up to Christmas when eight theatres were open, including the Coliseum, which housed the inescapable English pantomime, *Aladdin*.

The bombs continued to rain on the West End. Popular legend has slightly exaggerated the damage to the London theatres: they were not all devastated, though Nazi propaganda insisted otherwise. But the damage was bad enough, though in this respect, Binkie was lucky. Only one of the theatres in his empire was destroyed, the Queen's which received two direct hits and remained an empty shell for nineteen years. Other casualties in the West End included the Saville, Little, Kingsway, Royalty and the Shaftesbury. There was severe damage to the Theatre Royal, Drury Lane, but not quite bad enough to interfere with performances. The offices occupied there by ENSA were untouched and it continued to operate from room number nine for the rest of the war.

As air-raids started as soon as it got dark so theatres were compelled to close earlier to allow the public to get home. This restricted the performances to the hours of daylight which shortened as the autumn slowly turned into winter. In September they started at two-thirty, by November they were taking place in the morning at ten o'clock and sometimes nine. Whatever the time and inconvenience, nothing was going to stop the public from enjoying the theatre. The actors took all this in their stride. Getting up for a nine o'clock performance in the West End was better than getting up even earlier for an eight o'clock film call. The work may not have been so well paid but it did not last as long and the journey was much shorter.

Sometimes the raids would start in the day. Anybody who wanted to leave during a performance was welcome to do so, but it became a matter of honour for the actors to continue and the audiences to stay regardless of the risk to their lives. There were some variations on this theme and *Thunder Rock* by Robert Ardrey was a typical example. This was an allegory about a lighthouse keeper who is haunted by the ghosts of those who were drowned in a shipwreck a hundred years earlier. Strongly anti-war, it occupied a theatrical niche half-way between *Mary Rose* and *Outward Bound*. Starring Michael Redgrave, it had been tried out at the Neighbourhood, a long-vanished fringe theatre in Kensington. "I must say that I don't normally like plays with a message," Binkie told Redgrave, "but the feeling of the play fits the current mood of 1940 perfectly. I found it terribly moving." He transferred it to the Globe.

Redgrave soon revealed a real flair for public relations and public speaking. When the air-raid warning sounded he would stop the play, advance to the footlights and tell the audience that the play would resume as soon as the all-clear was sounded, but in the meantime they would entertain the audience in a rather more basic manner. This meant music-hall and wartime songs. Kitty Black would leave the office and go down to the piano in the orchestra pit where she would play the accompaniment. The Tennent's office staff would stand at the back of the upper circle to swell the choruses. Nothing short of an air-raid would have persuaded the shy and inhibited English public to talk to and sing with strangers in public and on these occasions there was a real gala atmosphere. "There aren't many people who can claim to have seen Binkie singing 'Run, Rabbit Run', 'They're Going to Hang Out the Washing on the Siegfried Line' and 'Take Me Back to Dear Old Blighty' at the top of his voice and clearly loving it," said Cathleen Nesbitt, "but I did and it was a very reassuring sight." The word got round and soon audiences from other theatres would look in to join the fun. They were enjoying it so much that there was a real feeling of disappointment when the all-clear sounded and the performance of *Thunder Rock* was resumed.

Many of the London theatres may have been unavailable but those in the provinces were not. All over the country there were hundreds to be filled and millions of theatre-lovers to be made happy. Touring, endless touring was the answer and thus it was. If he could not present plays in the West End Binkie now organised tours of every play he had in London and revived many which had enjoyed West End runs but which he considered had considerable mileage left: *Dear Octopus* with Marie Tempest and as many of the original cast as were available, *Rebecca*, *The Devil's Disciple*, *On Approval*, Lonsdale's popular favourite which had by now become a modern classic, *The First Mrs Fraser*, a Marie Tempest vehicle from the late twenties, two plays by Ivor Novello, *Ladies into Action* and his evergreen *I Lived with You*.

Binkie's urgent problem now, and it was one which wouldn't go away and remained to torment him for many years, was what to do with John Gielgud? How was he to be kept busy and happy? Since he had publicly renounced everything except the classics there were not many options. Being accepted as England's leading actor with a devoted following all over the country, every new appearance would be not only eagerly awaited by the public demanding nothing but the best and confident that they would get it, but would be subjected to the fiercest critical scrutiny. Both he and Binkie had to be very careful. John Gielgud was the ace of trumps of the Tennent organisation and must be kept in reserve until he could sweep the board.

There was no shortage of suggestions: the public wrote in, dozens of letters a day, everybody in the Firm had ideas, all the friends and associates had a list of neglected classics which would repay study and revival: Tamburlaine the Great, the Jew of Malta, Mirabell in *The Way of the World*, Oedipus, Lord Ogleby in Garrick's *Clandestine Marriage*, all were considered and rejected: "Oh *no*, it's not exactly *me*, is it?" was to be a familiar *cri de cœur* in the Tennent office, and most were later to be played and with success by other actors. It was Binkie who finally suggested *Dear Brutus* by J. M. Barrie. Gielgud, as a schoolboy of thirteen, had seen the first performance at Wyndham's in October 1917 and had been enormously impressed not only by the play but particularly by Gerald du Maurier's superbly emotional performance. The plot is, and always was, difficult to summarise: an unsuccessful artist, John Dearth, lonely, middle-aged and tormented by a childless, loveless marriage, is given a second chance to have what he always wanted. In this case it is a child. On midsummer night a magic forest appears outside his house and in it he finds a ten-year-old girl, the daughter he never had. He sets up his easel in a clearing and they talk while he paints. Their conversation is tender, loving, teasing, full of in-jokes and affection. When dawn comes, both the forest and the girl vanish and he returns to the misery of the life he has always known. It was a vivid example of Barrie's whimsical imagination and it had enjoyed the most enormous success. The idea of a second chance had made a strong appeal to a public devastated by the war, the raids and the countless bereavements and it had run for a year.

There had been a post-war revival in 1922, which Binkie had seen, and although everybody said it was not to be compared with the original, Binkie loved it. *Dear Brutus* opened on January 21st 1941 to excellent notices, and Gielgud was acclaimed even by those who had vivid memories of Gerald du Maurier in the part. It ran for five months and then toured. Not all the Canadian and American servicemen who saw it showed the right level of appreciation and there were certain lines of Barriesque feyness where the thin ice started to crack, like, "Oh, Daddykins, I do love you so and I don't want to be a might-have-been . . ." Muriel Pavlow delivered this and others with charming sincerity but this did not stop the audience from guffawing and shouting, "Hey, youse guys, what fuckin' crap is this, hey?" But Binkie pointed out to the company that it was their wartime duty to play these modern almost-classics even to the ignorant and the uncouth.

The most important development in 1941 had nothing to do with the war. On June 10th Harry Tennent lunched at the United Universities Club, eating his favourite food: pork pie, green salad, jacket potato and a slice of apple tart, a menu strangely unaffected by wartime rations. It was a very hot day and as he left the Club to walk back to the Globe, he collapsed on the pavement. An ambulance took him to the Middlesex Hospital. All day he lay in bed and in the evening he died without regaining consciousness. It was a heart attack brought on by anxiety, over-work and age.

Binkie, and all those in his circle, naturally assumed that he would inherit everything – for who else was there? – and a curious legend has since risen that he inherited a thousand pounds and the Firm. It was mentioned in the press, it was mentioned in *Who's Who in the Theatre* and has since been quoted in various books of theatrical memoirs. The truth was otherwise: Binkie inherited nothing and was not even mentioned in the will, an omission which naturally astonished him. The will was made four days before Harry Tennent's death; there is no evidence of either suicide or murder so it must be regarded as premonition or a coincidence. It consists of a single typewritten sheet.

This is the last will of HENRY MONCRIEFF TENNENT of Parkside, Knightsbridge, London, S.W., Theatrical manager, which I make this sixth day of June 1941.

I appoint my friend, Captain George Astley of Melton Constable

Park in the county of Norfolk as my executor and leave to him absolutely all the property of whatsoever nature of which I die possessed.

George Astley had been an actor before the war and had first met Harry in 1935. "He was a shy, retiring man with a quirky sense of humour," Astley said later, "and over the years we became fast friends though not as intimate as many would suspect." He became a play-reader for Harry and was able to give him the common man's view of many scripts received in the Tennent office, though a streak of independence made him refuse all Harry's generous invitations to first nights. After Harry died, George Astley found himself lunching with Hermione Baddeley, an old and beloved friend. "Darling George," she said excitedly, "do you know that Harry Tennent has left everything to a totally unknown young man?" She clearly had no idea who this totally unknown young man could possibly be and she teased him about it mercilessly throughout the meal. Finally, he could stand this no longer. "Yes, Totie darling, I do know who the young man is. It's *me*", and he watched her with relish as she fell off her chair on to the floor laughing like a maniac.

It had always been assumed by Harry's friends and associates that he was a rich man. His salary at Moss Empires, Howard and Wyndham and at Drury Lane had always been big; the Firm, though it had had its fair share of failure, had enjoyed many lucrative successes and Harry's songs brought in a steady flow of royalties. But if Binkie felt hurt and rejected at being left nothing, there must have been some slight consolation when it was revealed that there was nothing to leave. Inexplicably, Harry died penniless and where all his wealth had gone was a mystery which Binkie never solved. The account was not only empty but overdrawn and there would be massive death duties and other debts to pay. But George Astley had always liked Binkie and he now showed himself to be a truly generous man when he gave Binkie the golden signet ring which Harry had always worn and his OBE, still in its presentation case. His reward was a pair of complimentary tickets for all the Tennent plays for the rest of his life: it could never be said that Binkie failed to show appreciation of kindnesses received. A further reward for Astley came with the royalties from Harry's songs, particularly 'My Time is Your Time', always a popular favourite. These flowed in regularly and still do; they enabled him to pay for his farm in Farnham, Surrey, and the education of his two children. They also paid off Harry's death duties and his debts.

Even though Harry Tennent had been the managing director there was no question of his leaving the firm to Binkie because it was not his to leave. The structure and organisation of big business is never as easy or as simple as that. The new managing director would have to be democratically elected by the board and there was no reason to assume that his fellow directors would automatically choose Binkie even though he had shown, on past achievements, that he had the qualities to keep the firm going with success. Binkie had no illusions about the board's true opinion of him. He knew that they liked him on a superficial personal level, but they had grave suspicions about his integrity. In their eyes he was too smooth, too fond of power, too much of a playboy and not enough of a businessman. Also, they were all married men and there was a faint smear of disapproval hovering in the air about the unorthodoxy of his private life. In short, they didn't trust him and would be much happier to have some dreary accountant or lawyer. Of course, he would still be the effective artistic head, but the figurehead and controlling influence over what the board considered to be his extravagance should be somebody from a more sober profession.

The meeting took place in the Howard and Wyndham offices a week after Harry's death. The other members of the board were Stuart Cruikshank, former chairman of Howard and Wyndham, Willie Gillespie, accountant, and George Gwatkin, lawyer. A unanimous vote was required if the new appointee came from outside, and two if one of the existing board was to be promoted. Binkie went in with the light of war in his eyes and the smoke of it in his nostrils.

Binkie pointed out that he had been the effective head of the firm since it started five years ago, that the plays, directors and actors had all been chosen by him, that it was his artistic judgement which had made H. M. Tennent the most important management in London, that he alone could attract the stars and find the plays which kept the firm in business. He told them that if he was not appointed he would resign and start up his own company elsewhere, that all the stars, tied by love and loyalty, would follow him wherever he went. "Can you imagine an H. M. Tennent Ltd in which John Gielgud, Edith Evans, Peggy Ashcroft, Vivien Leigh, Noël Coward, Terence Rattigan and Emlyn Williams, to name only seven, play no part?" He asked them if they would rather have him as a colleague or as a rival. As a final and telling argument, he told the board that all the Tennent staff would resign in sympathy if he went and that they would find they had nobody to work for them.

There was nothing the board could do, for Binkie had all the trump cards. He was unanimously elected as managing director. When he returned to the office, Kitty Black remembers that he tore up all the letters of resignation he had previously asked them to write and which he was keeping as a last resort. It was a happy moment and made even happier when he announced that, as a start to the new regime, everybody would get a twenty-five per cent raise in salary.

Binkie felt the same hatred and fear of death as he felt about failure. He did not want to talk about it. Death must never be discussed or even mentioned casually in passing. He never talked about Harry Tennent, did not wear any sort of mourning, refused to go to his funeral. Harry's desk was cleared of all his personal belongings and the office was given over to the secretaries. His name on the playbills and letter heading was unhappily a constant reminder and, for a time, he did think of changing it to Globe Theatre Productions ("How about H. G. Beaumont Ltd?" was Elsie Beyer's cynical suggestion) but he was finally persuaded that this would be unlucky.

But it was a bizarre coincidence that the first play he presented under the new regime should have been a light comedy about death. Noël Coward triumphantly gave him his latest piece, *Blithe Spirit*, and informed Binkie that he had written it within a week while on holiday in Port Meirion, Wales. "It's my best," he said. "It has 'smash-hit', 'long run' written on every page. Shakespeare never wrote anything so quickly. Not even *Twelfth Night* or *Macbeth*."

"But *Twelfth Night* and *Macbeth* have lasted for over 300 years," pointed out Binkie. "Do you think *Blithe Spirit* will still be acted in the twenty-second century?"

"We shall never know, but I don't see why not."

There were some interesting parallels between Shakespeare and Noël Coward. Both were very quick workers: *Blithe Spirit* was written in six days, *Private Lives* in four, whereas *Twelfth Night* and *Macbeth* according to tradition, were written and rehearsed and ready for their first performances in ten days. Both authors were also good actors who, with a few exceptions, appeared only in their own plays. Shakespeare had Richard Burbage, the head of his company, and the administrative machinery to present plays. Coward had Binkie and H. M. Tennent Ltd. Shakespeare had his Globe Theatre. Binkie had *his* Globe Theatre in Shaftesbury Avenue; he didn't actually own it but it was his whenever he wanted it, as were most of the desirable theatres in the West End. Shakespeare had a company of actors in permanent employment. Binkie didn't enjoy that luxury yet – though he did later – but he could get anybody he wanted since nobody would turn down the chance of appearing in a new Noël Coward comedy.

Except one: Margaret Rutherford, for whom Coward had written the part of Madame Arcati, one of the finest outpourings of his comic genius, returned the script with a polite note of apology only two days after receiving it. Coward was suitably bewildered and shocked. He was also alarmed, for although she was not irreplaceable – there were a number of comedy actresses in London who could give good performances in the part as subsequent events clearly showed – she was the only one whom he wanted to see playing it first. "But why, Binkie, in God's name, *why?*"

"I've no idea, Noël dear, but I'll take her out to lunch and find out."

It was better that he should speak to her privately. She had an unqualified admiration for Coward's writing and acting talents, but his sharp polished wit, his quick, sophisticated mind and the aura of glittering success all combined to make her feel uncomfortable. But with Binkie she could feel happy and relaxed. She loved and trusted him. "He's such a *cosy* man," she said warmly. Binkie had one talent in common with Disraeli: he knew how to flatter women to his own advantage, though this was inspired as much by genuine love for them as by self-interest. "Tell an ugly woman she is beautiful", could be the first instruction in the Beaumont Seduction Book and he did this to such good effect that in his company she forgot the double chins, the wide mouth, the big bottom, the thick ankles, the fat stomach and the shapeless legs. She had become very neurotic about her appearance, hated looking into a mirror and refused to have one in her flat. But when Binkie looked at her with those lovely blue-grey eyes, when he smiled at her with those nicely-formed white teeth, when he gently stroked her cheek with his right thumb, then she felt beautiful. As a little gesture of sincerity and love, Binkie invariably kissed her full on the lips, something which no other man had ever done.

Over a delicious lunch at Scott's, she explained why she did not wish to play Madame Arcati. She had a great respect for spiritualism, but this play made a mockery out of it all and she did not want any part of it. It was a matter of conscience. Binkie was an expert in persuading his actresses to do things against their will and better judgement, and he now used some very devious arguments. In his softest, silkiest voice he explained that the play was poking gentle fun at *fraudulent* mediums, not the genuine ones, that Madame Arcati was entirely bogus and therefore a little mockery was justified. But she was no fool. "Will you explain how she raises *two* ghosts if she is a fake?" Binkie was ready for this. "By chance, Margaret dear. Even fake mediums can sometimes have a stroke of luck and this doesn't stop them from being fakes, does it now?" Having planted a seed of doubt, he sent her home in a taxi. Next day she telephoned to say she would do it. "But it's got to be straight. I regard this as a very serious play, almost a tragedy. I don't see it as a comedy at all."

"Of course, she always wanted to do it," said Binkie when he reported his success to Coward. "She's far too sensible not to realise what a terribly good part it is. But she needed a face-saving way of saying 'yes', and that's exactly what I gave her."

It opened at the Piccadilly Theatre on July 2nd 1941. The surrounding streets were full of craters and bomb damage. The smartly dressed audience in black ties and uniforms had to pick its way daintily over the rubble to get to the blacked-out, unheated theatre where a comedy about multiple death and marital discontent awaited their pleasure. With Cecil Parker, Fay Compton, Kay Hammond and Joyce Carey, the four principals made music which sparkled and scintillated like a Mozart *divertimento*, as James Agate charmingly described it. But the evening's principal triumph was Margaret Rutherford's. It was this superlative performance which promoted her from being a much-admired supporting actress to a star in her own right. But there was a price which the other members of the quintet had to pay.

Margaret Rutherford was naïve, unworldly and innocent. "She was slightly dotty," said Joyce Carey who played Mrs Bradman in both the West End and in the film. "You see, she hadn't had that much theatre experience, only nine plays in the West End, and didn't have much technique, though she was so gloriously funny you'd never guess it. She never thought of herself as a comedienne, she didn't like people to laugh at her and she never understood why they did, which is why she was so good. But she was always treading on Fay and Cecil and Kay's laughs, not out of malice but because she genuinely didn't know how to time a laugh. She trod on her own too, as a matter of fact. The others would get rather irritated but they never got angry with her because she so obviously didn't know any better." Her performance tended to vary considerably from night to night, which doubtless explains the single cryptic reference to her in Noël Coward's diaries, written ten days after the play opened. "Saw part of *Blithe Spirit*. Audience good. Performance okay except for Margaret Rutherford." But imitation was still the sincerest form of flattery. It was a part which Coward always declared he would love to play. "I'd be marvellous in it," he said firmly. Foolishly, Binkie and Joyce Carey tried to dissuade him. Coward persisted, continuing to talk about it for years, always waiting for the special occasion. But it never came and a unique theatrical experience was thus lost.

Blithe Spirit ran for five years, seeing the war out and overlapping well into the peace, surviving several transfers and many cast changes. The film, excellent in spite of the author's reservations, immortalised the unique and irreplaceable performances of Margaret Rutherford and Kay Hammond and has guaranteed the play's survival all over the world. From all the repertory, touring and amateur performances money flowed unceasingly into the Tennent coffers. After half a century it is still as popular as ever.

If Binkie had doubts about that, he could have had no doubt whatever about one thing – those six days in Port Meirion had been exceedingly well spent.

CHAPTER NINETEEN

1941—2

The Doctor's Dilemma – *Spring Party* – ENSA Tour – Entertainment Tax – *Macbeth*

It is no exaggeration to say that during the war years after the colossal and empire-shaking★ success of *Gone with the Wind*, followed by the infinitely more modest but no less satisfying *Lady Hamilton*, Vivien Leigh became the most famous, admired and sought-after actress in the world. Alas, this fame brought her little satisfaction because the all-consuming impulse in her life was the passionate and obsessive love for Laurence Olivier, which devoured her so totally that it was a matter of the utmost anguish to spend any time apart. There were many such separations, as with the boring and commonplace *Waterloo Road* which David O. Selznick forced her to make as part of the contract that was to be a thorn in her side for the next seven years. Success turned out to be a double-edged sword: it could shut doors as well as open them, kill as effectively as it could cure, for she was now typecast as a ruthless bitch: producers, including the civilised and far-sighted Selznick, did not wish her to play anything else. She lost two splendid parts to lesser talents: the mousy, plain submissive Mrs de Winter in *Rebecca* and the radiantly charming Elizabeth Bennet in *Pride and Prejudice*. The fact that her co-star in both would have been her beloved Larry made it unusually painful.

It was her misfortune that her career coincided with two malignant snobberies which between them effectively prevented her from getting the true appreciation she deserved. There was the belief that if nature had endowed you with exceptional beauty then you couldn't possibly have any talent: nature is never that generous, sneer the critics. Gladys Cooper was a well-known victim of this silliness. The other snobbery was essentially a product of the twenties and thirties though it lasted well into the forties and fifties. It said that if you were a film star of international fame then you could not possibly be any good

★ Empire-shaking is a carefully chosen adjective. *Gone with the Wind* succeeded in destroying a number of legends: that the public wasn't interested in war films, particularly *Civil War* films, that they wouldn't accept an unsympathetic, ruthlessly unscrupulous woman as a heroine, and that they wouldn't sit through a film lasting four hours. After *Gone with the Wind* Hollywood was never the same.

in the theatre and that if you were foolish enough to have ambitions to be a *classical* actress, then these could not be taken seriously. This one was to be a real torment to her in the years to come, and was largely responsible for the twelve-night Juliet disaster in New York.

Naturally, Binkie was above all this nonsense. He had a great love for her as a person and a healthy respect for her talent. Very few knew how much she owed her fame and success to his secret manipulations on her behalf and she did not discover it herself until many years later. When the astonished and delighted Selznick had his first coruscating, traumatic glimpse of the exquisite, raven-haired beauty, in whose green eyes the fires of Atlanta were still dancing, and decided in ten seconds that she and only she could be his Scarlett (thus saving the world and posterity from the horrors of Tallulah Bankhead, Norma Shearer and many others), he was deeply unhappy to learn that she was already under contract to Alexander Korda, who did not wish to release her. By one of the supreme ironies of history, Korda had decided that four hours of ruthless malice was not a good part for his charming Vivien and that even if it was, she wouldn't be able to play an American. It was Binkie who persuaded him otherwise and obtained for her the necessary release, for he was never more persuasive than over the long-distance telephone. And it was Binkie who later suggested Lady Hamilton as a good and suitable part for her.

Two years after Scarlett O'Hara, she had divorced her nice, generous, boring husband, the lawyer Leigh Holman, and Olivier his nice hardworking actress wife Jill Esmond; their respective children, Suzanne and Tarquin, were safely evacuated to Canada and California, and they were finally married. And for fifteen years they created their own special legend in one of the great theatrical partnerships of all time.

In the summer of 1941, Olivier was an officer with the Fleet Air Arm in a camp near Winchester and Vivien was a service wife living in a bleakly furnished Victorian house in the village of Warsash, about fifty miles away. It was a deeply unhappy period of her life: he was able to drive over on occasional evenings and even more occasional weekends but she was alone most of the time, decorating the house, looking after the garden, playing with her cat and reading. She urgently needed company and she needed work and this is where Binkie showed himself to be a good and loyal friend, staying with her when Olivier was unable to get away and telephoning her every day.

"Tell a beautiful woman that she is intelligent", could be number two in the Beaumont Seduction Book, and Binkie did just that. There was no hardship in this ploy, for Vivien *was* intelligent. She was also well-educated and widely cultured with an interest in literature, music and the visual arts. And if that was not enough she had a quick mind and lively wit which made her company a real delight. Binkie talked to her of painting, took her to auctions, giving her a Max Beerbohm for her birthday and a Sickert for Christmas. He talked to her of poetry, giving her a rare edition of Elizabeth Browning's sonnets and suggesting that she should give a poetry recital with Larry, perhaps in the Fleet Air Arm training camp at Winchester to an audience of enthralled naval ratings, if the Admiralty were interested. He gave her books; the latest novel by Evelyn Waugh was supposed to be very funny and everybody was talking about this *History of England* by Arthur Bryant. He had not read them himself but like Korda, like the Duchess of Windsor, he did not need to. He could glean from friends and newspaper comment enough about them to make intelligent conversation.

The one thing he never did was to tell her she was beautiful. She knew it. The whole world had been saying it for years and it was not something she wanted to hear because it bored her. One compliment, which she detested, was being likened to a piece of Dresden china, something which made her green eyes sparkle with irritation. But beauty is never total: the greatest beauties will have flaws of which they, and perhaps they alone, are uncomfortably aware. She was self-conscious of her hands which she thought were clumsy and podgy, of her legs which she thought were insufficiently well-shaped, of her neck which was too long and which one critic had rudely compared to a giraffe. Because of those defects, she liked to wear gloves, long skirts and high collars. It is no coincidence that much of her best work was in period costume.

But the most urgent need was not first editions or recordings of the Pastoral Symphony even when conducted by her friend and admirer, Malcolm Sargent, it was work, and here even Binkie found his hands tied, for anything Vivien did had to have Selznick's approval. "It's that *fucking* seven-year contract," she shouted one day, using her favourite adjective at a time when it still carried considerable force and shock value. This was the one aspect of her character which he did not like: Binkie was strangely old fashioned in some ways and it really distressed him to hear obscene language from a woman, particularly a lady of Vivien's quality. He suggested *Rebecca* and arranged for her to see it one day. She liked the play very much and under normal circumstances she would have accepted it like a shot but she did not want a part which had already been played by four other actresses, her public would be disappointed not to see her either in a classic or in something new and in any case she did not wish to act with the elderly and now rapidly tiring Owen Nares playing a part which Larry had done so electrically in the film.

ABOVE LEFT: Elvira, his faithful and loving cook-housekeeper, and the dogs. They are standing outside the house in Lord North Street.

ABOVE RIGHT: The front door. Binkie's obsessive love of lions extended even to the door knocker. INSET: Anna, who worked as a maid.

With Clemence Dane.

One of the finest photographs of Binkie at work in his office. By Otto Karminski.

The Globe Theatre, Shaftesbury Avenue, the powerhouse and headquarters of the Tennent empire.

Vivienne 'no-news-is-good-news' Byerley: Binkie's hard-working and devoted press officer.

With Peter Glenville.

At rehearsal.

Another office photograph, some time in the 1950s.

Angus McBean has caught with great effect the cunning, devious look in the eyes.

In Moscow with the *Hamlet* company. In the background: Mary Ure and Richard Johnson; with Binkie an unnamed Russian interpreter.

With the British Council Director ill, Binkie was asked to step on to the stage as the official representative of the English company – the first and last time he appeared in front of an audience. Luckily he was not asked to speak, but he later described the experience as 'totally terrifying'. Also on stage: Peter Brook and his wife Natasha Parry.

He wrote to Lawrence Langner at the Theatre Guild in New York who suggested that Vivien should play Cleopatra to Cedric Hardwicke's Caesar in a national tour and Broadway season of the Shaw epic. But Vivien would not leave England. She had to be near Larry all the time: a year's absence would kill both of them. But a film version of the play and made in England was a very different matter. Binkie spoke to Gabriel Pascal who made a career out of film adaptations of Shaw's plays, and planted the seed of an idea. Pascal was interested. But a film was a major undertaking and could not be set up in a few weeks. Also, the author's permission and approval on all casting was still required. But as a long-term plan it interested him very much indeed and a headstrong Cleopatra would be a good and suitable part to follow a headstrong Scarlett O'Hara.

It was Olivier who suggested *The Doctor's Dilemma*. He and Vivien had been offered the two parts of Jennifer and Louis Dubedat for a radio production before the war. The offer had been changed to *Pygmalion* which they had accepted even in the face of Vivien's doubts if she could do the Cockney accent, but Olivier's departure to Hollywood to make *Wuthering Heights*, and Vivien's speedy pursuit of him, cancelled all broadcasting plans. Binkie read it and was most impressed. He'd never seen it before and there had not been a major West End revival since its original production at the Court in 1906.

Binkie had become great friends with the Shaws. An exchange of formal business letters was no longer necessary. All he had to do was to go down to Ayot St Lawrence and put his proposal over tea. Shaw was delighted to give his permission, but warned Binkie that he was too old and tired even to look in at the rehearsals let alone see a performance. "The part is unusually difficult to bring to life," he said. "Jennifer Dubedat is the sort of woman I really dislike. Perhaps you'll warn the young lady of this."

It was an expensive production: five acts, three big sets, a cast of thirteen and a great many period costumes were required to bring this fascinatingly labyrinthine plot to life. But with Vivien's name there was no trouble in raising the money and getting the finest actors in London to support her. Once the preliminary announcements had been made the provincial theatres queued up to book the play and within a week Binkie had a six-month tour contracted. Rehearsals started in London in August under Irene Hentschel, with Frank Allenby, Austin Trevor and Charles Goldner. The part of Dubedat required the most careful casting. He has to have the most irresistible charm to explain not only Jennifer's passionate love but the ease with which he was able to captivate the cynical and hard-headed doctors. Charm is a quality which must enchant an audience as well as the characters in a play and actors who have it are few. But in Oxford Binkie, Vivien and Larry, doing a bit of talent-spotting, saw Cyril Cusack, the young Irish actor, in a revival of *The Playboy of the Western World*. By the first interval they had decided unanimously that their search for the perfect Dubedat was at an end.

The tour opened in Manchester and in six months played to houses filled night after night, with playgoers curious to see Scarlett O'Hara on the stage. What they saw was worth what they spent. Elizabeth Harris of the designing firm Motley produced six ravishing Edwardian gowns and Vivien had never looked more enchanting. Her voice had developed and her acting had acquired a new dignity, grace and emotional power: the special coaching she had received for the ill-fated Juliet eighteen months earlier was now showing good results. The tour was extremely uncomfortable. The war meant interminable train journeys, late to start, late to arrive and endless unexplained stoppages in draughty underheated carriages: it meant chilly hotel bedrooms without service or hot water, it meant restaurants closing early with no meals available after the theatre, it meant discomfort, little sleep, living out of suitcases and a slowly accumulating exhaustion; it meant that every night it was a little bit more difficult to give a good performance.

A theatre company takes its morale from its star. With Vivien in the Number One dressing-room it was high. She was unfailingly polite and friendly to everybody from the elderly actors with many decades of seniority down to the humblest call-boy or wardrobe assistant. Vivien never complained about anything, whereas Frank Allenby, Charles Goldner and Austin Trevor never stopped, a fact which Frank Woolfe, the stage manager, dutifully reported back to Binkie in his daily report. "They are very lucky to be working," was his cool comment and he was right. But there was something which went a long way to compensating them and that was the money. To guard against loss in the uncertainty of wartime touring, Binkie had devised a new way of paying his actors. He paid everybody £10 a week plus a percentage of the profits on a points system, the amount to be assessed according to their status, the size of their parts and the bargaining power of their agents. In fact, business was so good in the wartime boom that everybody profited; Vivien's name outside the theatre and above the title guaranteed full houses everywhere. A call-boy on five pounds a week found himself with fifteen, and Austin Trevor who would normally command fifty pounds found that his first pay packet in Manchester contained eighty-five. "We were a very friendly company," recalls Cyril Cusack. "Vivien was absolutely sweet to me and we got on very well. Robert Helpmann, a great friend of hers, was in constant attendance and we played the game of catching autumn leaves. If you caught twelve then you had twelve good months ahead of you.

"We didn't see much of Larry though she managed to get home most weeks. One day we were travelling in a train near Winchester where he was stationed and a couple of air force cadets entered. Vivien was fast asleep in the corner of the compartment. One of them asked me, 'Is that Vivien Leigh?' and I said 'No.' 'Just as well,' he said truculently, 'that husband of hers, Larry Olivier, is our training officer and he couldn't fly his way out of a fucking paper bag.' I remember that in a later conversation she said that Larry was going through a religious phase, 'But I'll soon get him out of that.'"

They had a glorious opening at the Haymarket on March 4th 1942 with Olivier accompanied by Admiral of the Fleet, Sir Dudley Pound, in the front stalls and rows of heavily medalled, gold-braided admirals in support. The audience cheered itself hoarse and when Vivien took her solo call at the end she received what the staff at the Haymarket said was the greatest and most prolonged ovation in their memory. The notices were like love-letters and within a week there was six months advance booking. But before long there was trouble.

The dismissal of Cyril Cusack from the cast of *The Doctor's Dilemma* for scandalous misbehaviour in the second act and Binkie's subsequent revengeful treatment of him is one of the West End's most tenacious legends and, like dragon's teeth, has proliferated many different versions. It was believed that he had taken his understudy, Geoffrey Edwards, on a pub crawl to celebrate St Patrick's Day, that they had both become hopelessly drunk, that he had forced his way on to the stage, insulted and even assaulted Vivien Leigh, that he had vomited on the carpet, scandalised the audience, reduced the play to a shambles, had been forcibly carried off to his dressing-room, had been instantly sacked and compelled to leave the theatre to find himself boycotted from the West End not only by Binkie but by every management under his malign influence. This had been the legend for nearly half a century, but like all such stories it has gained mightily in the telling.

None of it is entirely true, most of it is fiction. It lies in that grey area, that limbo of half-truths which, in their total sum, are far more damaging and misleading than a complete lie.

The facts, when stripped of the sensational trimmings, are noticeably less dramatic. It was March 17th 1942 and the play had been running for two weeks. Cusack did go to a club in Shaftesbury Avenue to have a whiskey and then to another club to have another, two in all, but normally this would have had no bad effect. However, during the war, real whiskey was difficult to get: this was an inferior brand, illegally distilled, little better than poteen. It did not make him drunk, but it did make him feel ill and sick. It was now four o'clock so he went to the theatre. He went to his dressing-room, lay down on the couch and slept. The performance was due to start at six o'clock and at five-twenty-five the young assistant stage manager, Leslie Phillips, arrived at the theatre to be told that he must get some strong black coffee. "I went through the pass door and got it from the bar and received a terrific bollocking from Charles La Trobe, the stage director, because this was something I was not supposed to do." Strictly speaking, he should have left the theatre and walked up the Haymarket until he found a snack bar with a take-away service. It would have taken time but Dubedat does not appear in the first act which runs an hour and is followed by a fifteen-minute interval. "I took it up to his dressing-room and gave it to him. He wasn't drunk or anything like that or he would not have been allowed to go on at all. But he wasn't. He was just feeling a bit ill."

Cusack drank the coffee and it went a long way to restoring him to good, workable health, but when he made his first entrance in his white tie and tails in the Richmond Hotel dinner-party scene, he was still feeling groggy and frail. He got through it satisfactorily but in the next scene, the artist's studio, he showed further signs of strain; he fluffed and fumbled the lines, misquoted, improvised and finally, when his mind went a total blank and rather than bring the play to a halt or conduct one of those highly embarrassing duets with the prompter, he started to quote from the only play he could remember, *The Playboy of the Western World* of whose hero, Christy Mahon, he had given many hundreds of performances before the war. The audience did not know that there was anything wrong. Those who knew the play and were able to identify the extra lines as Synge, assumed that Shaw had done some discreet rewriting at Binkie's request, for one Irish author was surely entitled to quote another if he chose.

For Vivien Leigh it was a moment of horror and bewilderment. Nothing like this had ever happened in all her eleven plays and she had no idea how to cope with it. She tried to continue with the play but her concentration was disturbed and she too began to stumble and cast panic-stricken looks into the prompt corner. It was Frank Woolfe who, acting on his authority as the stage manager, brought down the curtain. Vivien walked off the stage and went straight to her dressing-room. Cusack sat down and buried his face in his hands until Phillips gently helped him up and led him upstairs to his dressing-room.

"My next job was to go to the understudy, Geoffrey Edwards," Leslie Phillips recalled. "He was getting ready to play the Newspaper

Man and I'll never forget the look of horror on his face when I told him that he had to go on for Dubedat and right *now*."[*] It is always difficult to find capable and experienced actors to understudy, a job which nobody wants and which they do under protest; Binkie was very lucky to find an actor as good as Geoffrey Edwards, well known in the profession for hard-working and conscientious professionalism. Throughout the tour he had been understudying Sir Colenso Ridgeon, a very long part, and at the end of the tour he was suddenly asked to understudy Dubedat as well, a part which was not so long but much more difficult and complex.

The West End managers, and this included Binkie, took a traditionally careless, casual attitude towards their understudies. They never employed enough, they were not always of good quality and they were seldom given adequate rehearsal. Edwards and the two other understudies, Courtney Bromet and William Murray, had to cover no less than eleven actors. On tour there had been one brief and unsatisfactory rehearsal but with three actors rushing about the stage saying one line as one character here, another line as another character there and a third line as yet another somewhere else, it was chaotic and entirely unfruitful. As soon as the play opened, Geoffrey Edwards asked the stage manager, Frank Woolfe, to arrange for immediate rehearsals. The request was firmly refused. "It's too early," he was told, "you'll have to wait until next month." This referred to a curious and insane tradition, officially approved by Equity, that understudy rehearsals need not be held until the play has been playing at least three weeks. However conscientiously an actor learns his lines, however many hours he spends reciting them in his home, the street or his dressing-room, he never really knows them until he has rehearsed them on the stage, with moves, business, furniture and props if possible, and the other actors. Understudy rehearsals were not an expensive luxury, as the managements thought, they were an absolute necessity, as the actors knew, and without them the management was just asking for trouble.

When the unsuspecting Edwards was told that Mr Cusack had suddenly been taken ill and that he would have to play in his absence,

---

[*] One part of the legend has him hiding behind the water tank in an empty attic on the top floor, weeping with fear and resisting all Leslie Phillips' attempts to get him down to his dressing-room. Not true. Edwards had suddenly been struck by a curious premonition of disaster and was in the Green Room – converted from what was normally the Number One dressing-room on the second floor – nervously going over Dubedat's lines. It is further evidence of Binkie's casual attitude towards understudies that a proper costume had not been provided. He couldn't get into Cyril Cusack's because he was too tall, so one had to be improvised out of his own casual grey trousers and a loosely fitting shirt looking rather like an artist's smock.

he was unrehearsed and therefore unprepared and it was entirely the management's fault. He knew that if he went on the stage it would be a shambles: he would dry, fluff, stumble and probably make a nonsense out of the text which would seriously inconvenience Vivien and the other actors. He decided that he would read it and announced this to the company.* They understood, accepted the situation and were all very sympathetic. A brief announcement was made and then the nightmare started. "The script was a small one," he remembers, "a paperback Constable acting edition. After a time the audience forgets that the script is there and they just listen and watch. I thought it all went very smoothly." So did the company and so did Vivien. At the end she insisted on Edwards taking a solo call with her. He had the satisfaction of hearing the audience applaud loudly.

The following morning the euphoria vanished quickly when he received a telephone call from the management office. Would he please come to the theatre at 10 a.m. as Mr Beaumont wished to see him? On his way to the stage door he passed Frank Allenby outside the front of the theatre. "You're a disgrace to the profession," he snarled angrily, "you ought to be expelled from Equity." When he went through the stage door he found Cyril Cusack already waiting, for he too had received a summons.

Binkie had decided to hold his court of enquiry in the little dressing-room on the ground floor. Others present included Vivien, Irene Hentschel and Frank Woolfe. Between them they made up a solemn and intimidating judicial body. "You do know that I'm terribly angry with you, don't you, Cyril dear?" was Binkie's opening remark and the rebuke which followed was couched in the mildest of terms and in the gentlest of voices. There was no need for him to be angry or harsh, which was not Binkie's style anyway. The unhappy actor knew what he'd done and even though Binkie accepted his explanation that he was not drunk so much as *ill*, the whole affair was terribly unfortunate and there were other people to think of: the company, the reputation of the management, the good name of the theatre and the public itself. "Well, do your best, keep trying and good luck for the future, Cyril dear," was Binkie's cordial valediction. When Edwards went into this Star Chamber, which was what it most resembled, he burst out unhappily, "Oh, Binkie, *never* be an actor . . ." Binkie smiled sympathetically. "I made that decision many years ago, Geoffrey dear," he said, "I was much *much* too shy."

* Another part of the legend has Cyril Cusack leaving his dressing-room, tottering to the stage, taking in the scene with a horrified glance and pointing an accusing finger at his understudy. "What the divil does he think he's doing, readin' it? *I* coulda done that just as well!!!" None of that is true either. He had already left the theatre.

Both actors were given the customary two weeks' notice: it was a melancholy and embarrassing fortnight. The attitude of the company had changed: now they were both treated like lepers. "They boycotted me, sent me to Coventry," remembers Cusack. "They didn't speak to me and neither did Vivien who was very cool and cold. I was made to feel an outcast and this may have been due to the fact that I was Irish and hadn't contributed to the Spitfire Fund." But on Saturday a fortnight later there was a surprise in store for him. Vivien decided to be forgiving and she took him out to dinner at the Carlton restaurant. The best food in London could be obtained there and it remained, with the Ivy, the theatrical centre during the war. It was a superb meal. She was charming, witty, and she sparkled as only she could when she was in a happy, relaxed mood. The events of St Patrick's Day were never mentioned. She took him to the station in a taxi, saw him off, kissed him and wished him good luck. They never met again.

It was obvious to everybody that Binkie had no wish to sack the two actors and equally obvious that there were pressures working on him which even he, with all his much-vaunted independence, could not resist. Nobody knows to this day who was responsible, though there was a good deal of gossip and speculation. It was probably Vivien herself who insisted that she couldn't act with either of them again and threatened to walk out if her wishes were ignored: confronted by that situation he would certainly have agreed to do as she asked. But would she have done that on her own initiative or was she under pressure from somebody else? It was known that she telephoned Olivier every night to give and receive a report on the day's events. On the night itself, she would certainly have told him all about it but not knowing the full facts her account would inevitably have put both actors in a bad light. It is quite possible that Olivier would have told her what to do and as she was, theatrically speaking, very much under his influence, she would have done it. It is also possible that he would have telephoned Binkie at home* and, again without knowing the full facts

---

*Though they were superficially on friendly terms there was, for a number of complex reasons, no love lost between them, as Irene Selznick perceptively comments in her memoirs. Olivier disliked and distrusted homosexuals though there were exceptions to this, as with Noël Coward and Robert Helpmann. He was jealous of Binkie's close friendship with Vivien Leigh from which even he was sometimes excluded when the marriage was going through its periods of tension, whereas Binkie was horrified by Olivier's admitted uncouth and violent behaviour towards her in moments of great stress. Thirdly, they were rivals in management, always looking out for good new plays and sometimes finding themselves in competition for the same one. They were able to work together smoothly enough but there were always tensions.

and speaking in good faith, have told him that his darling Puss – as he lovingly called her – should not be exposed to further trouble and harassment when she was herself under a great strain and needed all the help she could get. The truth will probably never be known.

It was entirely Cusack's decision to return to Ireland and build up a career which had started so promisingly under the tutelage of his father-in-law, the Irish actor Brefni O'Rorke (who made a gallant but unsuccessful attempt to persuade Binkie to reverse the dismissal). In the twenty years which followed he wrote, directed and acted in plays; he took over the management of the Gaiety Theatre and formed his own company, Cyril Cusack Productions. He toured Ireland with a repertoire of Shaw's plays, and took his company to festivals in Europe and America. In all this time he never had another offer from Binkie, but when he wrote to ask permission to present *A Man for All Seasons*, he received a personal letter from Binkie giving it. The tone was, admittedly, rather cool, "Dear Mr Cusack . . ." and signed, "Yours sincerely, Hugh Beaumont," but at least he did get a prompt reply. There was no question of his being boycotted in the West End, for many managements made him good offers but he turned them all down, preferring to be a star in Ireland rather than a supporting actor in London. Finally, in 1962, exactly twenty years later, the Royal Shakespeare Company at the Aldwych made him an offer he couldn't refuse – to appear in Dürrenmatt's superb play *The Physicists*. His co-stars were Irene Worth and Alan Webb.

Geoffrey Edwards' banishment lasted for twenty-eight years, but he was finally reinstated with full honours and no hard feelings when Binkie invited him to play Lane in another revival of *The Importance of Being Earnest*, and Nelson's vicar brother in *A Bequest to the Nation*. It was a homecoming in more ways than one, for both the plays were presented at the Haymarket.

On March 18th Peter Glenville was engaged to rehearse Dubedat and replace Cusack when the fortnight was over. At the age of twenty-nine he already had a distinguished classical career at Oxford and Stratford: he had played in *The Light of Heart* the year before. His good looks, charm and personality had made him one of Binkie's favourite actors and his talent for direction was to make him one of the pillars of H. M. Tennent. He played Dubedat for five months before an attack of jaundice compelled him to leave. He went into hospital on the Saturday and on the following Monday when the audience opened its programmes they found a little printed slip. To their amazement and delight it stated that the part of Louis Dubedat would be played at this performance, and at very short notice, by Mr John Gielgud.

Binkie, now sharing a rather luxurious furnished Park Lane flat with him, had made the suggestion over the weekend. Gielgud did not like Shaw's plays and had no desire to play in them but he did admit that there were two parts he rather fancied, Marchbanks in *Candida* and Dubedat. He had never before acted with Vivien Leigh and their professional contact had been limited to a performance of *Richard II* at Oxford before the war in which she had played the Queen and he had directed. He declared that the prospect of acting with her was "most frightfully amusing", and since the director in him was always bubbling just below the surface he was confident that he could add to and improve her performance. He learned the part over the weekend, rehearsed with the company throughout the Monday and opened that evening. The part was much more difficult than he anticipated and a little bit of history was repeated when he decided to take the script on to the stage with him and read sections of it. After a few days, when it settled down, his performance was judged poetic and noble. Perhaps it lacked the sharply astringent edge and satire which indicated the essential cruelty of the character, but it had a romantic beauty which was his speciality and what the public wanted from him. It was the first time in the play's history that Dubedat had been played by a major star and if anything was calculated to start another landslide to the box office, this was it. As Shaw never stopped pointing out to the cynically disbelieving Mrs Patrick Campbell, two stars are *always* better than one.

The days can hang heavily on your hands when you are in a West End play and living away from your husband. Vivien was restless to do some war work. She told Binkie that she wanted to drive an ambulance, do fire-watching on the roof of the Haymarket or enrol as an auxiliary policewoman as Celia Johnson had resourcefully done in her Oxfordshire village. But Binkie gently discouraged her: she was far too valuable to risk her life with such dangerous activities in the blitz. "Your war work is just what you are doing," he said. "You're giving pleasure to the public, cheering up the servicemen on leave, keeping people *happy*." But he did arrange for her to take a first-aid course and was very pleased when she enlisted enough local volunteers to roll up sufficient bandages to win an award.

For one charity performance, he asked her to do the screen scene from *The School for Scandal* with Cyril Maude, now eighty. He was one of the greatest Sir Peter Teazles of his age and she showed that she was just as much at home in the eighteenth century as in the twentieth. It was not quite her first contact with the play for she had played Lady Teazle on the radio which anticipated her celebrated performance with

Olivier on the Old Vic's post-war Australian tour and the season at the New Theatre after the war.

By the summer, plans for the *Caesar and Cleopatra* film were well advanced. As usual, Shaw had the final word on everything. Pascal reported to Binkie that he had tried very hard to sell Shaw the idea that Vivien would be perfect casting but Shaw refused to commit himself until he had met her. He had refused to attend either the rehearsals or performances of *The Doctor's Dilemma* and admitted to Pascal that he had never seen her either on stage or screen. "Do you mean to tell me, Mr Shaw," asked the incredulous Hungarian, "that you have not seen *Gone with the Wind*?" "Life is too short," he had replied. "I really can't afford to waste four hours of it watching a young woman winning the American Civil War single-handed." So Binkie arranged a tea-time meeting one Sunday afternoon in Shaw's flat in Whitehall Court.

In the taxi Binkie, dashing and elegant in a light grey suit, gave her some good advice. Now that he had become so friendly with Shaw he was in a position to do so. "Don't flatter him, darling. He's been swamped with that all his life and he is not interested. Don't talk about the play or the film, let him bring up the subject." Vivien had dressed very carefully for this meeting. She wore a trimly waisted, pleated dress of light green silk, no jewellery and no make-up apart from the lightest dusting of face powder. The total effect was one of the most exquisite simplicity. Binkie looked at her with amazement. It was not merely that she looked more beautiful than ever before but it was just the sort of beauty you would expect from an unsophisticated child-Queen. How could the Old Man resist?

He was pleased to see that Vivien took his advice. During the thirty-minute meeting, she chattered and rattled on about everything in the most charming and amusing manner, never once touching on the subject of the meeting. It was Lady Teazle mixed with Beatrice and a touch of Lady Blessington thrown in for good measure. Binkie watched her with fascination as she proceeded to put the Old Man into the palm of her hand. Shaw listened with a wicked Irish twinkle in his eye. He said very little because he knew the rules and his part in it. He was clearly enjoying every moment. Finally he broke the steadily rising tension when he enquired after her age. "Twenty-eight," she replied. He chuckled. "It's a curious thing, my dear, but every actress who has set her heart on playing my Cleopatra has been a fifty-year-old giantess. Gertrude Elliott, the first, was fat and forty and not at all good. What it needs is a tiny and delicious little Persian kitten. You know, I've suddenly had an idea. You ought to play my Cleopatra. Would you like to?"

It was a moment of triumph but even in victory she played it very cool. "Oh, do you think I'd be good enough, Mr Shaw?" she said in mock surprise. But even at his most magnanimous, Shaw had no time for false modesty. "You'd *look* wonderful," he said shortly. "You don't have to be a good actress. Just say the lines as I wrote them. The part is foolproof." He escorted them to the front door, and the meeting ended with one of his most enigmatic remarks. "You are the Mrs Patrick Campbell of the age." Vivien and Binkie were left to speculate just what he meant by this. It was Richard Clowes who explained that not only was she the great beauty of her day, she had given positively the first performance of his Cleopatra for a single evening in 1899 to establish copyright, *and* she had a unique talent for getting what she wanted. More than anybody else, as their published correspondence was later to show, she could twist Shaw round her little finger.

The Doctor's Dilemma had thirteen months at the Haymarket, and it contrived in the process to make Binkie a very healthy profit of £28,000. "I shall never speak disrespectfully of Shaw's plays again," he said gleefully. "There is as much money in him as in Shakespeare."

The Doctor's Dilemma was finally withdrawn at the beginning of April and once again she was free, day, evening and night, to be Mrs Laurence Olivier, a respectably married woman devoting her time exclusively to the requirements of her adored husband and the pleasure of his company. But it brought her little satisfaction for he was now filming *This Demi Paradise* at Denham Studios on special temporary leave from the Fleet Air Arm. It meant getting up at five in the morning for a two-hour drive, spending all day under the arc lights and returning late in the evening, exhausted and irritable with the maddening delays and stupidities of filming, fit only for sleep. There was little time for much married life in that schedule. By the middle of April she was bored, restless, impatient, still unemployed and deeply unhappy. Her services were very much in demand and every day her agent, John Gliddon, would telephone to give her news of the latest offers, most of them from Broadway or Hollywood. All were instantly rejected for under no circumstances would she leave England during the war, away from her beloved Larry.

This Demi Paradise was about a young, serious-minded Russian engineer who arrives in England to arrange an important government contract and stays with a ducal family where he learns all about the English Way of Life. He is without charm or humour or intelligence but the daughter takes a great liking to him and escorts him round the country giving him a vivid glimpse of English eccentricity at its most endearing, most of which was summed up in Joyce Grenfell cycling merrily along the village High Street, Margaret Rutherford queening it at the local pageant and Leslie Henson devastating Rachmaninov at the Palladium. It has been hopelessly overshadowed by Olivier's greater successes before and after and is little known, but it was witty, inventive and charming; an Ealing comedy before the genre was invented; it was considered to be excellent wartime propaganda at a time when Russia was a glorious ally, and it remained for Binkie one of his favourites of all Olivier's films. "How *frightfully* clever of darling Larry to invent an entirely new Russian accent," he said admiringly to Vivien one day, "and how *convincing* he makes it sound." He was quite right. Olivier, whose passion for accuracy was well known, had worked hard with a genuine Russian to perfect his accent and had finally rejected the result preferring, as he had done with the French Canadian accent in the film, *49th Parallel*, to concoct his own. It was greatly praised, which confirmed what every actor knows, that if you do something, however wrong, with total confidence it will seem triumphantly right. The part of the daughter would have well suited Vivien but Selznick refused permission. This was very disappointing for she would have had all her scenes with Olivier. It finally went to the tall, blonde and statuesque Penelope Dudley Ward, then married to Carol Reed.

It was an even greater disappointment when Selznick wouldn't allow her to play Princess Katherine in the *Henry V* film which Olivier was planning to make in the summer. She spoke excellent French, she would have looked exquisite in Roger Furse's costumes and the protracted love scene with Olivier at the end would have provided a delicious climax. It was clear from Selznick's telegraphed refusal – ABSOLUTELY UNDER NO CONDITIONS WILL YOU PERFORM MEDIOCRE PART IN HENRY V. YOU ARE STILL CONTRACTUALLY OBLIGATED TO SELZNICK. REMEMBER? SO STOP. DAVID – that he was still annoyed with Vivien for leaving Hollywood just when he most needed her and turning down all his offers which included a new version of *Jane Eyre*. "Why is he being such a dog in the manger?" she asked Binkie. "Can you do something?" Binkie tried to convince Selznick that far from being insignificant, Princess Katherine, though small, is the best of the supporting parts, that it needed a star of Vivien's status and that nothing but good would come from it. But his appeal fell on deaf ears. Selznick was well known to be a man of culture with a knowledge of European literature, but this apparently did not extend to Shakespeare. Like so many American film producers, he was obsessed by grandeur. Only big was beautiful, only size had status. It never occurred to him that a small part can also be a very good part.

This is where Binkie had a chance of exercising his well-known deviousness. Taking Vivien out to lunch he told her of his master plan. "What dear Larry ought to do is to film all the Katherine scenes with you after he's finished filming them with Renée Asherson. The scenes can be kept in a vault until your seven-year contract has finished and then they can be slotted in to the film."

"Rather hard on her," said Vivien. "I don't think she would like that."

"Not so hard. She'll get the première and she'll be in it for the first few years. Better than nothing. So there would be two versions of the film and they can both be shown. It's never happened before and it'll cause a *sensation*. The cinemas can show both versions on alternate days: just think of the publicity."

It was a splendid idea and characteristic of Binkie that he should have thought of it. He and Vivien giggled happily at the prospect while they speculated on Selznick's reaction. But the idea was aborted by the film company's legal department and was never heard of again. So Vivien never played Katherine to Olivier's Henry and Binkie never stopped regretting the loss.

Something had to be done to keep her happy and busy, and a tour with ENSA seemed an obvious solution. In any case, all actors and actresses who had not been called up were required to give up six weeks to play for ENSA. Binkie had organised a short tour the year before with Gielgud and Edith Evans doing scenes from *The Way of the World* and *The Importance of Being Earnest* in Gibraltar. It had been such a huge success that he was asked to arrange another. He took her to an ENSA meeting at Drury Lane to discuss what she should do. Like so many straight actresses she was under the disadvantage of not being able to sing or dance: what could she do to hold a stage by herself and keep a large, demanding and unsophisticated audience happy?

"How about the potion scene from *Romeo and Juliet*?" she suggested, to elicit from John Gielgud one of his famous dropped bricks:

"Oh no, Vivien, you have to be a really great actress to get away with that."

"You don't need to do anything," said Dean curtly. "Just stand around looking beautiful. That's what they want."

ENSA's reputation in the profession was very low. It was mostly concert parties which were considered very second-rate by those who saw them, quickly thrown-together rubbish on the grounds that anything goes for the troops. A popular joke of the time suggested that the initials 'ENSA' really stood for 'Every Night Something Awful'. This seemed to be Basil Dean's attitude but Binkie decided to improve the situation by assembling a party which would be considered an asset in any West End theatre. Vivien, Dorothy Dickson, Nicholas Phipps, Beatrice Lillie and Leslie Henson were to be the principals. It was finally decided that poetry was the answer. She would recite 'Plymouth Hoe' by Clemence Dane, 'You are Old, Father William' from *Alice in Wonderland*, and a satirical poem about *Gone with the Wind*, written by Sagittarius, a very witty lady who had contributed poems to the *New Statesman* since 1934.

It was Anthony Quayle, the ADC to General MacFarlane in Gibraltar, who had masterminded the previous year's tour and now this one, pulling strings right and left to make sure that they would be given adequate facilities and accommodation. But it was very nearly cancelled, as Kitty Black recalls:

Two days before they were due to leave, a message came from the Air Ministry to say that the special plane would not be available. Leander's efforts to swim the Hellespont to meet up with Hero were puny compared to energies which Binkie now devoted to sweeping aside all denials and forcing the Air Ministry to honour their promises. Finally, at five-thirty in the afternoon, he came back to the office after yet another session to say that the only hope would be for complete copies of all the correspondence relating to the visit to be in front of the members of the Council before nine o'clock next morning. There were about a dozen letters, some running to two pages, and about eighteen members of the council, so as there was no question of using carbons, each letter had to be typed out eighteen times. We decided that Binkie should type the short letters, Elsie Beyer would take the medium-length ones and I would embark on the two page ones.

The evidence was carried to High Wycombe, the Council agreed that the plan had gone too far to be cancelled and the party duly assembled at Paddington to catch their train to an Unknown Destination where the plane would be waiting.

Spring Party, as it was officially titled, toured the Middle East for three hot and exhausting months, taking in Tripoli, Cairo and Algiers as the major dates and as the smaller ones places with names like Bone, Bougie, Philippeville and Djidjelli, all of which seemed to have sizeable garrison theatres. At each, hundreds of sweating, exhausted soldiers watched Leslie Henson displaying how not to play Rachmaninov, learned from Beatrice Lillie how to buy double damask table napkins, heard all about the Nightingale which sang in Berkeley Square from Judy Campbell, and feasted their glamour-starved eyes on Vivien's red crinoline as she told them that she was not such a scarlet Scarlett O'Hara.

Binkie travelled with them. It was an experience he would not miss. He would, as all good leaders should, share his company's discomforts and sufferings as well as their triumphs. The daily routine of theatrical management turned out to be much the same as at the Globe Theatre, whether it was a mosquito-infested company office in Djidjelli or an air-conditioned room in Admiral Cunningham's villa in Tunis. He was in his element, like a small boy in a toyshop, chatting endlessly over the long-distance telephones, arranging transport, equipment, performances, programme schedules, parties and complimentary tickets for visiting VIPs. One day Alec Guinness and Peter Bull, both officers in the Royal Navy, turned up at the Garrison Theatre at Bougie, on the way to Algiers. They were late and were firmly refused admission to the performance even though they had received a telegram inviting them signed by Vivien Leigh and Beatrice Lillie. They were directed to the town centre and told that they needed a special pass from the major commanding the whole town. Alec Guinness recalls:

> We found it without difficulty but there was nobody there. The street door was wide open, as were the doors to the other rooms. There was a droning silence, flies buzzed and papers on the notice boards curled in the heat. Then we heard a voice down some distant passage clearly speaking on the telephone. I recognised the voice, with its gentle emphasis, immediately. "You can tell Basil Dean that, if that's his attitude, we are not going to play Cairo. Repeat *not*." There was a click of the receiver and we followed the sound. There, occupying the Town Major's swivel chair for the afternoon, was Binkie Beaumont, in navy-blue silk shirt and white cotton slacks.
>
> It was astonishing as well as delightful to find him in a small Algerian town conducting business on his usual lines. He accepted our sudden presence as perfectly normal, as if he had been expecting us and very possibly had been responsible for the signal we had received from Vivien and Bea. There was nothing he could do about getting us into the theatre so late in the afternoon but he took us backstage where we had a happy twenty minutes with our two hostesses.

The tour included ten days at Gibraltar, where they played to many thousands of servicemen and civilians. With Binkie and company resident in General Macfarlane's spacious villa, Anthony Quayle as his

ADC and John Perry posted there as his assistant, the Rock quickly became a further outpost of the Tennent empire. There was plenty of social life. One evening Quayle took Binkie over to Spain to dine with some friends who lived in a large and splendid house formerly occupied by the French Resistance. They missed the ferry and were forced to stay over. They were given two separate couches in a large sitting room and talked all through the night. They had been briefly acquainted before the war though they had never actually worked together but in this situation a special intimacy and friendliness suddenly developed. Binkie, enjoying the luxury of the warm Spanish night and the company of a good listener, opened up about his unsuccessful love affairs, and one in particular, while Quayle talked about the actress, Dorothy Hyson, whom he loved and was later to marry. "It was a sort of high spot in our lives," said Quayle, "and we were never again quite so friendly."

Celebrities always meet other celebrities and in military and political terms the tour was truly star-studded. There was General Eisenhower who had never moved in theatrical circles and was a little uncertain what to say, though he did his best to be charming: there was Montgomery, cold, calculating and charmless, whose little-known speech defect, similar to Churchill's, made him a good target for mockery. Binkie's imitation of him saying "the militawy twaditions of the Army are vewy dwaconian to say the least" was one of his favourite in-jokes, though only the closest friends were privileged to hear it. And there was the King himself who either brought a formidable royal memory into play or was prompted by an equerry when he reminded Binkie that they had met when he saw *George and Margaret* some five years ago. "I'd like to see it again, it was a very f-f-f-funny p-p-p-play," he stammered. "Perhaps you could b-b-b-b-bring it out here, the ch-ch-ch-chaps would love it, I think . . ."

The tour gave thousands of men their first glimpse of live theatre and was for Binkie and the company a unique experience. It is unlikely that any of them had had such fun in all their lives. It also supplied theatrical legend with one more vintage witticism. On the flight back to England, Vivien Leigh looked round the distinguished company and asked, "What would happen if this plane were to crash and we were all killed?" Binkie's reply is now part of history. "There would be a two-minute silence in the Ivy."

It was towards the end of 1941 that Hannen Swaffer, critic and theatrical journalist who had once enjoyed the distinction of having his face publicly slapped by Lilian Braithwaite in the Savoy Grill, met Binkie in the Ivy and asked him what was the greatest single threat to the commercial theatre. It was clear that he was expecting Binkie to say a heatwave, a cold spell, a newspaper strike, a coronation, the blitz or the shortage of good actors. Binkie said none of these things. Instead he took a deep breath and replied with – for him – great feeling, "It's that *bloody* entertainment tax." Swaffer was to remember this, for Binkie seldom swore or used strong language. "Do you realise, Hannen dear, that I have to pay twenty-five per cent of the gross receipts, not just the net? They tax not only profits but *every* penny which comes in."

Binkie spoke for everybody. The tax was a gangrenous thorn in the sensitive side of everybody in the West End and the biggest cause of complaint at a time when the wartime prosperity in the theatre, and all the arts, had produced the greatest financial boom since 1914.

The tax started a quarter of a century earlier during the First World War, the brainchild of the Chancellor of the Exchequer, Reginald McKenna. By 1916 the country had been at war for two years and Mr McKenna had become increasingly concerned by the vast sums of money being earned by such popular successes as *Chu Chin Chow*, *A Little Bit of Fluff*, *Romance* and *The Maid of the Mountains* which went straight into the pockets of Sir Herbert Beerbohm Tree, Mr Oscar Asche, and Sir George Alexander instead of the government account at Coutts Bank in the Strand. In addition to financial acquisitiveness there was a vein of puritanism in that much of the Establishment, and by extension many of the government ministers, considered it immoral for people to enjoy themselves in the theatre when the gallant boys in uniform were being shot to pieces in freezing trenches. The logical argument was that if theatres were taxed they would lose so much money that they might be forced to close down which, the puritan element considered, would be a good thing. It would be just a temporary wartime measure and convince the gallant boys in uniform that the country was solidly behind them. The fact that these same gallant boys in uniform depended on these same theatres for much-needed entertainment when they were on leave never occurred to them. Incredibly, some of the leaders of the profession who had been consulted thought the new tax was reasonable and that the theatre should be taxed just like any private individual.

This Olympian tolerance did not last long. By November 1917 a new and heavier rate of tax was imposed: business in the London theatres fell by forty per cent and restrictions on travel made it impossible to book tours in advance. As the tax was levied on every ticket whether or not it had been paid for by the customer, and as many of the theatres were giving a great many tickets away to those same gallant boys in uniform, the theatres were suffering even greater losses. A deputation to the Prime Minister to appeal against it was led by Ellen Terry and H. B. Irving. Nature had endowed Ellen Terry with a rare talent for twisting men round her little finger: Mr Asquith was unable to resist her charm and powers of flattery, in which respect he was in the good company of Bernard Shaw and Sir Henry Irving. The tax on complimentary tickets was abolished and once more the gallant boys in uniform tasted the joys of *Trilby*, *The Prisoner of Zenda* and *The Merry Wives of Windsor* free of charge. In 1917, as in the Second World War, it was the straight plays which were most popular with servicemen.

By the time the war ended in 1918 the puritanical distaste for the theatre had vanished but the Entertainment Tax remained. It crept up and up during the twenties and thirties and by the time of Binkie's outburst to Hannen Swaffer it was thirty per cent.

To appreciate how brilliantly Binkie manipulated the tax exemption laws to his own advantage it is necessary to go back and describe how these laws were first defined. From the start in 1916 the Finance Act laid down the special circumstances in which the tax would not be levied: if the entertainment on offer was wholly educational, and if it was either *partly* educational or partly scientific and offered by a society, institution or committee which was not established to make a profit. Incredible as it now seems, it was the Commissioners of Custom and Excise who were appointed to administer the Finance Act and decide the educational and cultural status of any particular entertainment. Since the men who administer the laws of Custom and Excise are traditionally drawn from the Royal Navy (with the Merchant Navy *perhaps* just getting a look in) their knowledge of artistic and theatrical matters was inevitably deficient. They granted exemption to the Royal Zoological Society but refused it to the Shakespearean repertory companies of William Poel and Ben Greet. They then took this lunacy further by announcing that nothing that had what they called an 'artistic representation' should be regarded as either educational or cultural. It was a triumph of philistinism and for eighteen years nothing that took place inside a theatre received exemption from the tax. It meant that the money which school children paid to see the chimpanzees' tea party at Regent's Park Zoo was exempt from tax whereas the money which those same children might have paid to see Lady Sneerwell's tea party in Regent's Park Open Air Theatre only a few hundred yards away was not. It was an insanity which might well have graced a new edition of *Alice in Wonderland* if Lewis Carroll had been alive to write it.

This is when Lilian Baylis entered the story. She was outraged by the suggestion that Shakespeare was not educational when the plays were studied in the schools and thousands of children filled her theatre for special matinées. She was a shrewd business woman. She was also an inspired and indefatigable campaigner. With the assistance and encouragement of Sir Reginald Rowe, the Vic's financial adviser and one of its governors, she arranged a meeting with the Prime Minister. Although she did not have Ellen Terry's beauty or powers of seduction, she did have her own special way of getting what she wanted. According to legend, she stormed into the Cabinet Room, fell on to her knees in the middle of the carpet and started to pray. Mr Baldwin gazed in astonishment at the famous, semi-recumbent figure muttering inaudibly in the much-imitated Cockney accent. "I've asked God if I should continue paying this silly Entertainment Tax," she finally said fixing him with a stern eye. "Sorry, dear, but God says no."

There was no argument against God's edict. Mr Baldwin knew when he was beaten. New legislation was pushed through both Houses, giving tax exemption provided the drama on offer was of a sufficiently high standard, though the government sensibly did not make too much of an issue out of this last proviso for even an indifferent performance of *Hamlet* can educate. So from 1934 onwards, Shakespeare and the classics were deemed educational and therefore tax-free. It was expected that there would be a stampede from the London managements and theatres all over the country to take advantage of the new laws, but strangely enough this did not happen. The West End seemed curiously indifferent to its possibilities: by the end of the decade only some of the better known provincial reps, Stratford-upon-Avon, Robert Atkins at Regent's Park and the ubiquitous Donald Wolfit had claimed and had been granted tax exemption.

Binkie was the first to realise that to get it a company was not forced to present only plays which were little known, intellectual and appealing to the minority. As long as the standard was high and the constitution of the company was correct according to the letter of the law it could present anything it chose. It was the *company* which had to be educational and not necessarily the *plays*. It was enough to announce that your company intended to present *King Lear*: once that was accepted it was welcome to present *Hay Fever* or *Ten Minute Alibi* and still get tax exemption. He was the first to see that once the company had been formed there was no limit to the number of plays it could present simultaneously and get a management fee from every one. This was an entirely legal payment taken by the manager and it covered simple running expenses such as heat, light, telephone, stationery, wages for office staff and part of the rent. At £25 a week per play it quickly added up to a sizeable sum.

"But if it was all so easy why didn't the other West End managers form non-profit distribution companies and thus escape the Entertainment Tax?" was the question which was frequently asked at the time and for years later. The answer was simple: under the Finance Act they were obliged to plough all the profits back into the company as further capital and not distribute it as dividends to the backers and directors as had been their lucrative practice. This meant no cash for those luxuries which company directors could once enjoy as a privilege of office: a country house, a swimming pool, a cellar of vintage wines, a yacht or a trip round the world on the *Queen Mary*. But Binkie did not need this extra money to line his pocket, for his income from H. M. Tennent plus his dividends from other theatrical investments were already substantial. He was happy to put the profits back into the company and thus make it bigger, richer and more powerful. Which is precisely what happened.

The new company was to be called Tennent Plays Ltd. It operated from the same office and with the same staff and same board of directors as H. M. Tennent Ltd. It was entirely legal for a commercial and a non-profit-distributing company to be so geographically and administratively close and it had the full blessing and approval of Lord Keynes, chairman of CEMA. This was a council formed in 1940 with American money from the Pilgrim Trust and a government grant of £50,000 to encourage the drama and music during the war when they needed all the encouragement they could get. Maynard Keynes was a passionate lover of the arts, he was married to the Russian ballerina, Lydia Lopokova, and was a fully-paid-up member of Binkie's inner circle of friends. His influence was prodigious and his enthusiasm unquenchable. Thanks to him, Binkie was able to present many plays in association with CEMA. It was not a financial contribution but one of advice, guidance and government contacts.

To inaugurate Tennent Plays Ltd the first production had to be not only a classic but a *popular* classic, and it was vitally important to get the right one. Gielgud was still the ace in Binkie's hand and the choice of play should be his. He took his position of England's leading classical actor very seriously – it was a couple of years before Laurence Olivier thundered into the field to challenge him with his Richard III – and he was aware that this carried responsibilities. To show that you were a serious Shakespearean actor you were compelled to climb the twin Mount Everest peaks, one of which was Macbeth.* Even if you

---

*The other was King Lear. Gielgud had an obsessive desire to succeed in this, the most inaccessible of all the Shakespearean summits, and he made four gallant attempts before he finally admitted defeat.

were unsuited to the part the public expected it and there was 300 years of tradition weighing down on him. Gielgud had done it once before, in 1930 at the Old Vic, directed by Harcourt Williams between mouthfuls of vegetarian pie and beer. Although too young (only twenty-six) and inexperienced, he was acclaimed by the Old Vic regulars in whose eyes he could do no wrong, and praised lavishly by the press, including the astringent James Agate who had displayed the most colossal impudence in paying a backstage visit in the interval to tell him that though he had done the first half well he did not think he could do the second. Gielgud had not been satisfied with his own performance and he was anxious to do it again.

In spite of its obvious faults of plot and construction, *Macbeth* has always been relentlessly popular with the public, the press and the profession. There can hardly be a single actor in history who has not yearned to roar "Lay on, Macduff, and damn'd be he who first cries, 'Hold, enough!'" or an actress who doesn't want to show that Mrs Sarah Siddons was not the only lady in history who could chill an audience with her sleepwalking scene. The ghosts, witches, headless children, and other supernatural happenings offer an irresistible challenge to the director and designer. The composer is anxious not to be tied to the bagpipe cliché and wants to produce music which suggests Caledonian intensity without being literally tied to it. And the public loves it. However bad the acting and production, the theatre is always full.

Gielgud had been working on it for months, throughout the *Dear Brutus* tour: those endless and boring train journeys and those long nights in lonely, remote hotels were a splendid chance to make his plans. Michael Ayrton and John Minton were to design the sets and costumes and William Walton, new to the theatre but Gielgud had heard and liked his *Belshazzar's Feast*, was to compose the music. There were only a handful of trumpet calls, sennets and tuckets, and some music for the witches' cauldron scene, but he did succeed in striking a suitably barbaric note and even the unmusical drama critics noticed it. But the chief trouble was the casting of Lady Macbeth. This has always been difficult, defeating the talents of some of the greatest actresses from Ellen Terry to Mrs Patrick Campbell, but when the right actress plays it then history is made. Gielgud approached Edith Evans but she turned it down. Once again it was her Christian Science which made the decision. She did not understand Lady Macbeth's ambition, her power drive, her evil or her ruthlessness. What she did not understand became a bore and so she couldn't portray it. And she added one more darkly gleaming brick to the Edith Evans legend when she said, "I could *never* impersonate a woman who had such a *peculiar* notion of hospitality." There were, of course, some other objections. The character does not change or develop; she does not do anything in the all-important banqueting scene but just sits there and allows Macbeth and the others to have all the fun and the action. And she dies offstage, a decision by the author which has annoyed and bewildered actresses for three centuries. And throughout she is overshadowed by Macbeth. It is *his* play.

So who else was there? *Grandes dames* were rather thin on the ground in 1942. Sybil Thorndike was too old and lacked sexuality: for her, this had not normally been a handicap but Lady Macbeth does have to be sufficiently attractive to explain the hold she has over her husband. Flora Robson? Gielgud had seen her play the part with Charles Laughton at the Old Vic and had considered her 'absolutely terrible'. Lady Macbeth is all rigidly controlled evil and determination, whereas Flora Robson's speciality was nervous hysteria: the two were not compatible. Peggy Ashcroft? Too young. Marie Löhr? Not a Shakespearean actress. Binkie suggested open auditions but nobody suitable appeared and there was a real possibility of cancellation when news came from South Africa that Gwen Ffrangcon-Davies was interested and was willing to cut short her current tour. She was well aware of her limitations and so was Binkie but at least she and Gielgud were old friends, they had worked together in two very successful plays, *Richard of Bordeaux* and *The Importance of Being Earnest*, and they knew each other's styles.

Much against Binkie's advice, Gielgud insisted on directing the play himself. He had so many ideas of how it should look and sound that it seemed a waste of time to be forced to explain them to somebody else. His method was to direct the play from the front, using his understudy, and then gradually to phase himself into the production in the last week of rehearsals. It was a method which he was to use with great success in future classical revivals where he directed and starred.

Casting the principals was not difficult, for everybody wanted to work for Binkie and with Gielgud. But assembling the rest of the company was very difficult indeed. All the good young actors were in the services and those who weren't hovered unhappily in that limbo between liberty and conscription. The only actors immediately available were either waiting to be called up, like Frank Thornton, Alan Badel and Terence Alexander, too old for fighting, or medically unfit. It was a very strange and unsatisfactory crowd who greeted Gielgud every day at rehearsal. They were also pitifully few in numbers and a great deal of ingenuity was required to make them seem remotely like an army or a coronation throng.

Binkie lived through the rehearsals, the tour and the West End run in a state of acute anxiety. Typical of a Welshman that he should be superstitious, typical of Binkie that he did not want anybody to know about it. It remained a dark secret, for how could a glittering sophisticate with a Savile Row suit and a golden cigarette holder admit to being superstitious like any old tenant farmer in Cardiganshire? He admitted his secret fears to one person only, not a close friend but an employee with whom he normally had little social contact – the lighting designer, Joe Davis. Davis had a good knowledge of theatrical history and was able to fill Binkie in on the horrifying, blood-stained legends of the play and how the Curse pervades everything and everybody.

The Curse wasted no time in making its presence felt. Beatrix Fielden-Kaye was cast as one of the witches but a slight heart spasm prevented her from rehearsing it. Binkie had always liked her and admired her courage so he kept her on full salary until such time as she was well enough to play the part. She watched rehearsals from the wings of the Scala Theatre and insisted on travelling up to Manchester and watching the first performance at the Opera House, wrapped in fur coats and blankets and sipping hot soup. She returned to the hotel in the interval and died in the middle of the night. Marcus Barron, an elderly actor playing Duncan, died of angina pectoris and another witch, Annie Esmond, collapsed from a heart attack on the stage while dancing round the cauldron. Binkie sent an urgent message to Ernest Thesiger who was at that period preoccupied with some vitally important war work – helping Queen Mary embroider an enormously long carpet which was to be sold in aid of American war charities. Hour after hour, day after day the two old Queens stitched away and thus forged the bond of a genuine friendship. It was with the greatest reluctance that Thesiger tore himself away from Marlborough House and made the journey to Manchester to rehearse and appear as Third Witch.

Further harassing activity from the Curse included school children for whom "Out, out damned spot" and Lady Macbeth's death scream as she plunges to her end are the greatest comic climaxes since *Charley's Aunt*. They made mayhem of all their school matinées in Edinburgh. One by one the thanes, soldiers and servants vanished into the services leaving a very thinly underpopulated Scotland behind them.★

After an exhausting tour of six months *Macbeth* finally opened at the

★ By coincidence, Margaret Webster directing the Maurice Evans/Judith Anderson *Macbeth* on Broadway, was having precisely the same problem. The Curse had caused an upset unique in theatrical history: a month after the production opened, the Japanese attacked Pearl Harbor and thus brought America headlong into the war.

Piccadilly on July 8th 1942 to mixed notices. While admiring the beauty of his verse-speaking the critics found it impossible to overlook the fact that Gielgud and Gwen Ffrangcon-Davies were irretrievably miscast. He had created a splendidly evil, wolfish make-up, but every time he opened his mouth all illusion vanished: this was definitely not a man who led armies and murdered his house-guests. It has never been essential for Lady Macbeth to be a big woman, though it helps, but to be as tiny as Gwen Ffrangcon-Davies does make it difficult for her to show how easily she can dominate her husband. Agate was not slow to point out in her defence that small women can still wield enormous power and nurture homicidal tendencies, but there is such a thing as *optique du théâtre*, a law which annoyingly states that if a thing does not *look* right then all arguments in support of it will not help while the audience is still in the theatre watching it. And thus it was. Both of them spoke the verse with real intelligence: neither was able to evoke the slightest shiver of evil.

But it did not matter. *Macbeth* played to full houses everywhere on tour and for three months in London. Binkie was able to sigh with relief when it was over. There had been three fatalities but *he* was still alive, so was dear John. It had made a great deal of money for Tennent Plays Ltd and he could happily reflect that his first voyage into those uncharted seas of tax exemption had been artistically successful and financially lucrative. Also, Gielgud had finally got Macbeth out of his system: nine months of being a Caledonian Primitive was enough and he would never play it again.

CHAPTER TWENTY

1943

Love for Love – Haymarket Repertory Season – *Hamlet* – *A Midsummer Night's Dream* – *The Duchess of Malfi* – *The Circle*

Binkie felt very keenly that it was necessary to get as far away as possible from the murk and gloom of Scotland, from evil and wickedness and all things horrible. The next play to be presented by the new company must be a comedy, but not necessarily by Shakespeare, for Gielgud had played *Much Ado About Nothing*, *As You Like It* and *Twelfth Night* and wanted to explore some of the less trodden paths. Then he remembered playing in *Love for Love* at the Oxford Playhouse in the twenties. Town had been deeply shocked by its scurrility, but Gown loved it and filled the tiny theatre for the month's run, the students enjoying with particular relish language which they would never have heard at home or in the lecture rooms. The production had been primitive, the sets and costumes makeshift, the supporting company as inexperienced as himself but he had enjoyed it enough to want to do it again in rather better circumstances.

Considering that it is the funniest and finest of the Restoration comedies, with the possible exception of *The Relapse*, and filled with splendid acting parts which actors will fight to play, it is odd that *Love for Love* has been so seldom performed. Starting in 1681 with Betterton playing Valentine, one of the two star parts, it had only two productions in the fifty years which followed. Admittedly, it is very bawdy, but it is odd that in spite of its supposed permissiveness, the eighteenth century should have rejected it. The last West End production had been at the Gaiety in 1871, except for an occasional Sunday night in a fringe theatre and Guthrie's production at Sadler's Wells before the war under the auspices of the Old Vic. Because of a curious snobbery of the period, this was not considered West End even though the company was headed by Charles Laughton, Elsa Lanchester, Roger Livesey, Ursula Jeans and Flora Robson.

The other star part is Tattle, played at Sadler's Wells by Charles

Laughton as an effeminate old queen, thus starting a tradition which survives to this day. Not too effeminate, of course, for Tattle was a ladies' man: he loves them, they love him and there is a particular flavour of feminine virility which very few actors can catch. This presented Binkie and Gielgud with a serious casting problem and they spent many hours looking through *Spotlight*, talking to agents and visiting the reps. Binkie even held open auditions but no one suitable turned up. One day Gielgud was in Broadcasting House listening to a playback of an eighteenth-century play, and one of the voices struck him as being entirely right. He made enquiries and to his and Binkie's astonishment it turned out that the voice belonged to an actor they both greatly admired but had never for a moment associated with period comedy – Leslie Banks.

Tall, handsome and dignified, his West End and film successes had given him a truly international reputation. He was the shining epitome of upper-class virility, specialising in generals (*Farewell Again*), barristers (*Twenty-One Days*), Royal Dukes (*Fire over England*) and colonial governors (*Sanders of the River*). He had been born in 1890 into a wealthy Liverpool shipping family, but an accident at birth, a careless delivery by an inexperienced nurse using the then-popular forceps method, cut a vital nerve in his neck. This resulted in the left side of his face being totally paralysed for the rest of his life. When he entered the profession in 1911 it was noticed that he had two quite different profiles: the right was clean-cut with regular features: the left was twisted and lop-sided. When the two were combined in full face the effect was intriguingly sinister. Throughout his life people assumed this had something to do with a war wound and it was a tribute to his charm, talent and tenacity that, even with this handicap, he was able to persuade the public to accept him as a handsome leading man. Having two profiles did his career no harm. Film directors favoured the right side if the part was heroic and the left during his occasional excursions into villainy. The former can be seen in *Red Ensign* in which he plays the shipping owner heroically sacrificing himself to save the yard and restore business to the dockers; the latter in *Jamaica Inn*, where he glowers and snarls most intimidatingly as the homicidal leader of the smugglers.

Not only had Binkie never employed him, they had not even met, which is odd when one considers what a small, enclosed place the West End was before the war. But now he had something definite to offer. Leslie responded with enthusiasm. Except for a brief and disastrous month in *The Taming of the Shrew* with Edith Evans in which both of them contrived to give very bad performances, misconceived and misdirected, he had never touched the classics. However, he wished to extend his range and get away from the three-piece suit and the cocktail cabinet. But his Scottish ancestry made him cautious: he wanted reassurance that he could play seventeenth-century comedy on the stage. Leslie invited Gielgud and Binkie to dinner in his house in Oxford.

Some actors are lucky to be blessed with wives who are not only loving and loyal but intelligently devoted to their husbands' interests. Alas, Leslie was not one of these. The marriage had been happy enough in its early years for Gwen had charm, youthful vitality and a pleasant line in social chitchat. She had also contrived to give him three totally delightful daughters, Daphne, Virginia and Evangeline. But there had been a passionate love affair with his co-star, Mary Newcombe, during the long run of the curiously titled play, *The Infinite Shoeblack* in 1929. The love of a woman who is beautiful, elegant, cultured and talented was something Leslie had never known and it nearly drove him mad with frustration to play long and erotic love scenes at the Comedy Theatre every night. Inevitably, drama and life began to overlap and merge. It never got to the point of divorce as they decided to stay together for the sake of the children. Now, thirteen years later, the ice was wearing very thin though they were still carefully keeping up appearances. Only close friends knew the truth.

Gwen Banks was not attractive. She was the most terrible snob. Her only interest in Leslie's career as a fashionable West End actor was the wealth and social position it gave her. The artistic side did not interest her in the least. She had no knowledge of what parts he should play, how he could extend his range and stretch his talent or which plays could give him the opportunities he needed. She was concerned only with the social round of Cowes, Henley Regatta, Wimbledon, charity balls, first nights, smart Mayfair dinners and country house weekends in the company of *soi-disant* friends who were mostly titled or royal. She insisted on a grand and extravagant life-style – something he didn't want and couldn't afford – which, during his heyday in the late thirties, included a large house in Chelsea, servants, an expensive car, three cottages in Dorset, expensive public schools for the girls and accounts in all the fashionable shops. "It's a fucking treadmill," Leslie once complained most bitterly to Binkie during a rehearsal lunch, "all she thinks of is money and how to spend it. I've had to do all these silly plays which bore me horribly and all those rubbishy films just to earn enough to keep going. But if something really good and unusual turns up she makes the devil of a fuss." It was the strain of all this which, amongst other causes, contributed to his early death in 1952.

When she met Leslie's friends she could not talk of their work, because she did not know anything about the theatre and was, in any case, bored by it. She was always polite to the stars whom she considered important, and coldly disdainful to the lesser actors who were not. All this made her very unpopular. "Leslie's a darling and I'm very fond of him," was the verdict of friends, "but she is trying to ruin him." "What she really wants is for dear Leslie to get a knighthood," said Binkie one day with his usual perception; "she would absolutely *adore* to be Lady Banks. But I don't think that he is *remotely* interested."

That dinner in Oxford, where to Tattle or not to Tattle was the subject of much discussion, was very tense. Gwen made little effort to conceal her dislike of the play and the part and finally, in a sudden moment of truth, she revealed why. "Surely, Mr Gielgud, you don't want my Leslie to play a silly old poof," she burst out, "I think it's a disgusting and ridiculous idea. What will people think?" "Thank you for being so honest, Gwen," he replied calmly, "I'm relieved that at last you have told me what you really feel. As to what people will think, they will think he is a very good and versatile actor and they will be impressed. Anyhow, Tattle isn't really a poof. After all, they did things rather differently in the seventeenth century."

The matter was still undecided when Gielgud and Binkie left to catch the train back to London. The next day she telephoned Binkie and in the conversation revealed further reasons for discontent. "I suppose you'll put Leslie into Number Two dressing-room," she said malevolently. "Don't forget, Mr Beaumont, that he has been a West End star for fifteen years and he has always had Number One. And who is going to get the star billing? I suppose you'll give it to John Gielgud?"

Binkie was accustomed to the stars fighting for billing and accommodation but it was an unusual experience to have the star's wife doing battle, which Gwen proceeded to do with a fury and tenacity worthy of a better cause. He knew what to do: invite her to lunch at the Ivy and talk some good sense into her. He understood very well that she could see nothing but the loss of status if Leslie joined the company and thus became one of a number of stars instead of the only one, but he hoped that she would understand that Yvonne Arnaud was to join them and she too had been a star for many years, but was willing to sacrifice a little of the status in exchange for the chance of acting in a play which carried such high prestige and culture. Leslie was a magnificent actor, he'd always thought this; he would enjoy extending his range from the Establishment types he'd portrayed with such success. Gwen listened, but for once Binkie's famous charm didn't seem to be working. Then he had an inspiration. "Don't forget, Gwen dear, that the royal family have recently acquired a taste for the drama and they will all come to see it once we've opened with good notices.

And don't forget that honours are usually given to actors who have distinguished themselves in the classics rather than to those who haven't. If Leslie joins the company to play Tattle, and other parts, who knows what might happen?"

At this point she started to look interested and by the end of the meal she was smiling radiantly. Binkie was quite right, she said, of *course* Leslie must play Tattle, it was silly of her to have thought otherwise. Gwen Banks did have one valuable asset: she knew when she was beaten. Her change of heart may have meant a happier domestic background for Leslie but, strictly speaking, it had not been necessary for he had already decided to take the part. At heart he was a crafty diplomat and he well knew that nothing but good would come of joining forces with England's greatest classical actor and the management which was presenting him.

As was revealed on April 9th 1943 at the Phoenix, Gwen's earlier fears were groundless. Leslie scored one of his greatest successes as Tattle and the audience roared and applauded with delight to see Sanders of the River camping it up in a full-bottomed wig and a beauty spot. Society and the royals flocked to the theatre, the bawdy made a strong appeal, as it always does, and the splendour of Rex Whistler's sets – the last, alas, before he was killed in France with his tank regiment – guaranteed that the eye would be as abundantly satisfied as the ear. It transferred to the Haymarket in August, ran for over a year and contrived to bring in a great deal of money to Tennent Plays Ltd. Overnight, Restoration comedy went to the top of Binkie's White List for he never realised that when a cast of characters glistening with titles indulges in lighthearted immorality in colourful, elegant surroundings, not only money flows in but also prestige.

But already the storm clouds were gathering and the largest and blackest was Lewis Casson. He was one of the original CEMA Committee and later appointed to be Director of Professional Theatre Activities. He became Binkie's declared enemy, appalled by what he saw as his unscrupulous exploitation of the legal loopholes of tax exemption and fought him tooth and nail on every occasion. Casson considered that CEMA's money was to support inexpensive tours of small-cast plays round the Welsh mining valleys and army camps, or to subsidise uncommercial or experimental plays in London, which would probably not make money or be produced at all without CEMA's generosity. It was *not*, he firmly insisted, to support all-star West End revivals of popular classics which could well look after themselves and pay their own way without any help. Nor was it there to support flagrantly anti-government Socialist propaganda like J. B.

Priestley's *They Came to a City*, his view of a Utopian state as seen through the eyes of a Merchant Navy seaman and a teashop waitress. Subterranean rumbles had been heard from the Prime Minister's office. In theory a new and better England was fine but in practice it must be a Churchillian view based solidly on upper-class values and culture. Churchill could not ban the play as he had succeeded in doing with Priestley's legendary Sunday night postscripts, but he could and did encourage Lewis Casson to raise a storm about the CEMA backing. With this tacit unofficial support Casson continued to attack Binkie's activities. *Macbeth* and the Priestley were bad enough, but *Love for Love* was the last straw. Surely it was a public scandal that a play as disgusting and as obscene should be presented at all, let alone with government money? It revolted him to see the public laughing uncontrollably – was there no morality and taste left? – and as for it being seen by parties of school children . . . What sort of example was that to set? What would happen if they grew up taking such a light-hearted view of sexual morality, would civilisation come to an end?

Lewis Casson's other great enemy was Lord Keynes who had no particular interest in the needs of Welsh miners and servicemen but a lot of interest in Binkie and his plans. In answer to Casson's criticisms, he replied that there had never been any guarantee that *Macbeth* would play to full houses even with Gielgud's presence, that the raids had taken place continuously during its run and it was quite possible that it might have been forced to close prematurely. That it was a tribute to the public's courage and good taste that it hadn't. He pointed out that Tennent Plays Ltd had not received a penny in cash from CEMA. There had been, he fully admitted, a £5,000 guarantee against loss, but this had not been taken up. Keynes had always been deeply impressed by Binkie's taste and achievements: he admired his high standards and noted that his nothing-but-the-best policy was reaping rich and well-deserved rewards. Casson could not deny any of this, much though he would have liked to do so, and the fact that many of his cut-price bargain-basement tours were not only drab, dreary and dismal but also played to empty houses did not help his case.

One memorable day during the *Macbeth* run, but before *Love for Love*, Casson and Binkie met face to face across the committee-room table in the CEMA offices in St James's Square. Casson may have been a fanatic and a missionary – always a tiresome and dangerous combination – but he was no diplomat. He foolishly decided to launch an angry and abusive attack. Binkie was very cool and played his cards with admirable discretion. To everything which Casson said, Binkie merely smiled and said, "Lord Keynes doesn't think so. We've discussed the matter and his ideas are different from yours, Lewis dear. After all, he *is* the chairman." Binkie kept his temper but inside he was seething at this stupid boring little Welshman's silliness. Charles Landstone, the Council's secretary, recalled that it was the only time that he had ever seen Binkie's eyes turn green with anger.

Lord Keynes took him to lunch at the Treasury to report the outcome. It was a decisive points victory for Binkie. "Tennent Plays Ltd can do any play you like," he said happily. "But Lewis insists on being consulted. After all, he is the drama director for the Council."

"Of *course* he must be consulted and of *course* he will always be free to give his opinion. Of course, we don't have to take any notice of it, do we, Maynard dear?"

When, some months after that conversation, *Love for Love* was being planned, Binkie dutifully wrote to Casson to invite his opinion. He got it. Casson said the play was an insult and must never be put on. Binkie thanked him and put it on. When Casson started to complain and write angry notes to the chairman, Binkie smiled and shrugged his exquisite shoulders. "He doesn't seem to have any knowledge of recent theatre history. When Guthrie wanted to do *The Country Wife* at the Old Vic in 1936 people complained for exactly the same reasons. Guthrie went ahead and it was a *huge* success."

And so it was at the Haymarket. *Love for Love* was so popular, with people coming twice and even three times, that it ran for sixteen months, the longest run in the play's three centuries of life. Now was Binkie's chance to realise a long-cherished dream: to stage another season of classical repertory built round Gielgud with the finest available talents in support, a season to rival and even surpass the glories of the 1937–1938 season at the Queen's. Binkie would have the Haymarket as a permanent base, it would show the Tennent flag on Broadway, it would tour America, tour England and tour the world. It was an exciting prospect. It would keep Gielgud happy and occupied, always a problem with the terrible shortage of suitable new plays, it would after the war give employment to the rising tide of good young actors with classical talents and ambitions, it would enable him to continue his prestigious association with CEMA and enjoy the financial rewards of tax exemption.

Binkie now encountered one totally unexpected obstacle: Gielgud did not like the idea. He'd done all the good classical parts before and the others did not interest him. Could Binkie or the press or the public see him as Cleopatra's Antony, or Richard III or Othello, or grotesquely padded as Falstaff? But Binkie could be very persuasive and Gielgud, always vacillating and uncertain, could be persuaded. He began to see possibilities. He'd done *Hamlet* three times but there was no reason why he shouldn't do it for a fourth. Some might say that at forty he was too old but there was consecrated theatrical tradition spreading over two centuries of actors no longer in the first flush of youth bringing their wisdom and maturity to the part – Garrick, Kemble, Kean, Fechter, Irving, Booth, Tree, Forbes-Robertson had all played the part in middle-age (and sometimes later). It would be difficult to spurn a part which had brought him so much satisfaction and acclaim, surely a farewell performance would be acceptable. He had many ideas he would like to try out. Also, an actor always looks ten years younger on the stage. He wouldn't look more than thirty and that is surely young enough for Hamlet. *A Midsummer Night's Dream* would provide a good contrast. He hadn't been at all satisfied with his performance of Oberon at the Old Vic and liked the chance of playing him again. Also, he had a lot of good ideas which he'd discussed with Rex Whistler at the beginning of the war for an aborted production which would have taken place in 1940 if Rex had not been killed.

The *Love for Love* company was a little on the old side, an inevitable situation during the war, but with a formidable variety of talents it was large enough for a repertory of classical plays. Admittedly, some of those who had given the 1937–1938 season its special lustre, Alec Guinness, Michael Redgrave, Glen Byam Shaw and Harry Andrews, were away in the services, but a company which included Leslie Banks, Leon Quartermaine, Cecil Trouncer, Miles Malleson, Angela Baddeley, Isabel Dean, Rosalie Crutchley, Yvonne Arnaud and Marian Spencer could cope with any play. Alas, for Binkie's carefully laid plans, the season was a disappointment. It is difficult to understand why John Gielgud decided to enlist non-professional talent to direct the two Shakespeare plays. George Rylands and Nevill Coghill, dons at King's College, Cambridge, and Exeter College, Oxford, respectively, were both scholars with an extensive knowledge of the Shakespearean texts. They had both done good work in university drama and Gielgud had admired some of their productions, but hardened professionals with the experience and skill of Leslie Banks and Leon Quartermaine did not take kindly to directors who had hitherto worked only with students. With his head buried in the prompt book and seldom looking at the stage, Rylands showed that he cared more for the verbal than the visual magic. He was very particular about inflections but was strangely indifferent to where the actors stood or what they did. The production was static and dull. Gielgud was feeling his age and found that he was unable to bring to Hamlet the vitality and freshness which had made his earlier performance so memorable. Leslie Banks should have been very good and effective as Claudius but, demoralised and depressed by the lack of useful direction which he, more than the others, urgently needed for this, his first tragic Shakespearean part, he was a disappointment. "I've come to the classics too late in life," he confided to Binkie. "I should have started thirty years ago."★

A Midsummer Night's Dream was also a disappointment. Hal Burton's designs were splendid but somehow the magic had fled and the whole production seemed dull and routine. Both Gielgud and Peggy Ashcroft failed to make much of Oberon and Titania. It was a brave piece of casting to have Leslie Banks as Bottom, but for once Binkie's enterprise was mistaken. Leslie was not by nature a *buffo farceur*, and he had the additional strain of following Ralph Richardson whose performance at the Old Vic only six years earlier was still fresh in public memory. At fifty-four an actor is liable to be very set in his ways and miscasting can be a cruel experience, revealing the narrow limitations of his talent. An actor can go against nature so far but no further. Whether he played homicidal Danish king, treacherous Venetian adulterer or simple-minded Athenian weaver, the polished English gentleman was always dimly lurking under the surface.

The Duchess of Malfi – "Marvellous part for Peggy," he said – was high on George Rylands' list of unjustly neglected minor classics. Occasional revivals had been scattered during the early years of the century but he, too, was a great persuader. Nobody liked it, not even Gielgud, but CEMA's prestige and lucrative tax exemption did occasionally involve a little collective theatrical masochism. A depressed and dispirited company worked hard and did their best to bring this difficult and inaccessible play to life, but the notices were no more than polite, the audiences no more than respectful and respectable. "At least Lewis liked it," said Binkie, when the season had finished. "He'll probably want us to take it round the Welsh mining villages. Can you *imagine*?"

It was Binkie's suggestion that the twentieth century should not be totally ignored and that as a fifth play, Somerset Maugham's *The Circle* – "Marvellous part for Yvonne," he said – would suit the company well and provide a strong, refreshing contrast with the plays which surrounded it. Since its original production in 1921 it had been twice filmed and done to death in rep, tours and productions round the world, including a very successful season on Broadway, but this was the first West End revival. It is undoubtedly Maugham's masterpiece and in giving it such a splendid production Binkie guaranteed that

---

★It was because of this that he did not get the part in the film. Laurence Olivier did give him serious consideration, but finally, and regretfully (for they were old friends), he decided against it. "Claudius is a hundred per cent shit," he later explained, "and Leslie wasn't."

from then on it would be regarded as a modern classic. The plot and construction are of noble simplicity. A prominent society hostess elopes with a cabinet minister. Her social life and his political career are both destroyed by the scandal which follows. Thirty years later, devoured by curiosity, she returns to her home to see her now grown-up son, his wife and her former husband, still unmarried after thirty happy, carefree, bachelor years, only to discover that her daughter-in-law is contemplating the same mistake she herself once made. The ex-husband comes up with a fine solution to stop her doing this, but will it work? The audience is left in no doubt that Maugham's cynical ending is a happy one – of sorts. Far from seeming in the least dated, it emerged as fresh and alive. It provided the company with parts which fitted them like Bond Street gloves. Yvonne Arnaud as Lady Kitty squeaked and sparkled deliciously, Leslie Banks as the ageing disillusioned lover glowered and snarled most intimidatingly, Cecil Trouncer as the deceived husband threw off some of Maugham's best epigrams with style and wit and Gielgud brought to the priggish son the right degree of nervous tension and a fine comedy technique. To everybody's astonishment and delight it was a huge success, the most popular play of the season. Maugham, who had been considered very *passé* for over a decade, was now back in fashion and public favour with a new lease of life which guaranteed further revivals of his better-known plays in and out of London. He wrote a short con-gratulatory note to Binkie saying he wasn't interested in seeing it yet again, and couldn't anyway as he was then living in America, but that the money, his ten per cent author's royalty, was very welcome. With that he showed, beyond argument or question, just where his priorities lay.

CHAPTER TWENTY-ONE

1943–5

Flare Path – While the Sun Shines – There Shall Be No Night – Love in Idleness

These war years were an exceptionally busy period for Binkie. His life was not a single line of production but a series of parallel lines, for many things were happening at the same time. While John Gielgud and Gwen Ffrangcon-Davies were touring *Macbeth* around northern cities, while Owen Nares in *Rebecca* was changing his wives at the rate of roughly one every six months, while Mrs Dubedat was enjoying a similar multiplicity of husbands in *The Doctor's Dilemma*, while Madame Arcati was nightly making her tumultuous entrance on an offstage bicycle with a slow puncture and while *Watch on the Rhine* was proving through its 673 performances that if the Nazis couldn't cross the English Channel, plays *about* the Nazis could comfortably cross the Atlantic Ocean, while all this concurrent and consecutive activity was taking place a new star had entered Binkie's orbit: playwright, Terence Rattigan. He had already written *French Without Tears* which enjoyed a two-year run at the Criterion before the war. Binkie had been present at the first performance on November 6th 1936. He remembered how the actors had nearly ruined everything by their nervousness, bad timing and loss of memory but had pulled themselves together and steered the play away from near-disaster into a blazing triumph. Although he was in the middle of a very bad period professionally, with H. M. Tennent just formed, three failures in the recent past and three more to come, he had managed to enjoy the evening and to exclaim with pleasure at the spectacle of such a superbly constructed and witty light comedy.

Rattigan had gone through the conventional educational mill for a slightly gilded upper-middle-class boy – Harrow, Oxford and the OUDS. His father was Consul-General at the Tangier legation: like so many fathers, he was anxious that his son should follow him into diplomacy but he chose a rather undiplomatic method of persuasion. He sent him to a school in France where the sons of other diplomats suffered the ordeal of having instant French crammed into them.

Rattigan stayed only three months; he was bored, restless and lonely but it did provide him with a splendid idea for a new play, thus confirming that of all the experiences which can be useful to a writer, it is the unpleasant ones which are the most fruitful.

He was a friend of the two Johns, Perry and Gielgud, and had been a regular weekend visitor. Here he met all the important theatrical people so he and Binkie enjoyed a slight, casual acquaintance. In the first interval of *French Without Tears*, Binkie and Rattigan had a drink in Bronson Albery's office.

"Terry, darling, your play is too *too* divine," said Binkie, slipping easily into the high-camp idiom of Syrie Maugham, though it was years since they'd last met. "But why didn't you send it to *me?*"

"My agent tells me that he did," replied Rattigan, "and he told me that you had turned it down."

"Story of my life, my dear, but I can't read everything which comes into my office."

During the war, Rattigan volunteered for the RAF. As Pilot Officer Rattigan and working as a rear-gunner wireless operator he saw plenty of action. Sometimes his life was dangerous, sometimes very boring. The first gave him material for a new play, the second gave him the chance of writing it. *Flare Path* was set in an hotel where the aircraft-men and officers and their wives were staying. The men go out on dangerous missions over Germany and the wives wait for them to come back. There was not much plot but plenty of incident, emotion, character and humour. This time only two managements were allowed to get a preliminary glimpse of it: Bronson Albery, who had the contractual right to see Rattigan's next play, and Bill Linnit, who had put money into *French Without Tears* and to whom the minimal courtesy was due. Both turned it down. Albery viewed with snobbish distaste the working-class characters in it while Linnit, who was an agent, decided that there was nothing suitable for his star client, Leslie Banks. Both men were in full agreement on one thing, that the public did not want plays about the war. Binkie was number three on the submission list. He thought *Flare Path* very well constructed, packed with sentiment, social comment and comedy. Most important of all, it caught the mood of the moment and many, many thousands of people would appreciate its authenticity.

Binkie had only one serious reservation and that was about the happy ending, in which a Polish pilot, reported to be missing after a raid on Germany, reappears ten minutes before the end and is shown to be very much alive to the carefully concealed pleasure of his wife. After the final dress-rehearsal he spoke to Rattigan telling him that the ending was false and sentimental and that something more brutally tragic would be right for this play. "I have an instinct about these things, Terry dear," he said, "and it's seldom wrong. The public will always know if you're not truthful with them." In this he had the full support of Noël Coward who also believed that unhappy endings are necessarily more truthful than happy ones. "But happy endings do sometimes happen in real life," Rattigan said, "and that's the sort of truth I'm after." For all his shyness and lack of confidence he was not so easily bullied. Throughout his life he was dominated by stronger personalities, but on this one occasion he knew he was right. He stuck to his guns and refused to change the ending. *Flare Path* opened at the Apollo on August 13th 1942 with Kathleen Harrison, Phyllis Calvert, Adrianne Allen, young George Cole (aged sixteen) and Leslie Dwyer. It was directed by Anthony Asquith, an old friend from Rattigan's Oxford days. An audience filled with aircraftmen, WAAFS and high-ranking officers from the Air Ministry, including the Air Chief Marshal, made it abundantly and noisily clear that they liked the play as he had written it. A few weeks later, Churchill paid one of his rare visits to the theatre and declared it a masterpiece, a view fully endorsed by the public who kept it alive for 600 performances. With that sort of success, Binkie forgot his reservations and made it clear to Rattigan that there was a permanent home for him at H. M. Tennent and looked forward to reading his next play as soon as possible.

Seeing what excellent propaganda he was making for the service, the overlords of the RAF decided to free him from active duty so he could write more and better plays. This meant that he was virtually demobbed and allowed to lead what was, in effect, a civilian life, writing film scripts, *The Way to the Stars, The Day will Dawn* and *Uncensored*. He moved into chambers in Albany, a far contrast from the officers' mess at the RAF station at Bathurst, and began to write another play. Nobody could accuse him of being slow to use life's experiences. His new play, *While the Sun Shines*, another light comedy, was set where he lived. The hero and owner of the chambers was the Earl of Harpenden and it was odd that Rattigan should have chosen a title like that for his young and attractive hero, for he always had a snobbish taste for aristocratic names. "Terry dear, have you ever *been* to Harpenden?" asked Binkie when he read the script. "Well, it's the most dreary place imaginable. Why don't you call him the Earl of Albany? Sounds *much* nicer." Rattigan defended his choice by stating that Bobby was a rather commonplace young man and therefore he should have an ordinary name.

Three servicemen are the triple heroes of the play and they rush in and out of the Albany chambers in traditional style. There are three services and three countries represented. Bobby Harpenden is Royal

Navy, Joe Mulvaney is US Air Force and Lt Colbert is Free French Army. The plot requires them to be in love with the same girl, Bobby's fiancée and the daughter of the Duke of Stirling. Once again Rattigan caught the mood of the moment. London in wartime was filled with foreign servicemen looking for sex, food, companionship, somewhere to stay, somewhere to sleep. It was a period of casual pick-ups, of the blackout, and of food rationing though, paradoxically, there was no shortage of drink; certainly, the whisky flowed freely in the Albany chambers whose guests never stop filling their glasses. The plot includes a butler with a nice line in imperturbable efficiency, who manages his young master's affairs with a skill which Jeeves might envy, an extra girl with the delicious name of Mabel Crum, and an impoverished duke with a taste for gambling, bad business ventures and chorus-girls. Mix all this together, stir well and you have a play which carefully observes the letter as well as the spirit of traditional English farce. "It's sheer Wodehouse mixed with Feydeau and Pinero," said Binkie happily when he read it, "and I love it. Your best yet, Terry dear." "Is it as good as *French Without Tears*?" enquired Rattigan anxiously. "Oh better, much, *much* better," replied Binkie.

Binkie never had such an easy time casting, for it was a play in which everybody wanted to appear. The Duke fell into Ronald Squire's lap, and it was amazing that Rattigan's father, Frank, never recognised himself. Michael Wilding had the right charm as the much-put-upon Bobby, Jane Baxter was everybody's idea of what a Duke's daughter should be and Brenda Bruce completed the cast as Mabel Crum. She was the youngest and least experienced of that distinguished company and she nearly lost the part during the first week of the tour. In later years she was to enjoy great success as an astringent light comedienne, but as Mabel Crum she revealed, most surprisingly, no talent for it whatever. She just was not funny. Binkie was very worried because so much of the comedy depended on her. "You're too sad and serious, my dear," he said sadly. "If it hasn't improved by the end of the month you'll have to go back to Birmingham. I'm sorry." Noël Coward, who had a lot of money in the play, agreed with him. Rattigan and the producer, Asquith, spent time working with her. Rattigan rewrote many of her lines, gave her extra laughs and rehearsed her in new bits of business. By the end of the tour their patience and hard work were paying rich dividends. "I can hardly believe that it's happened," said Binkie admiringly. "Is this the little mouse of a girl who made it all so melancholy?" he said to Asquith. On the first night she scored a great success in the part and became one of Binkie's favourite actresses.

He opened on Christmas Eve 1943 at the Globe, something which before the war he would never have done. Christmas was the week in which everybody wanted to go out rather than stay in. Binkie gave a first-night party which at the stroke of midnight became a Christmas party. "It's the best Christmas present anybody has ever given me, Terry dear," he said happily, kissing him on both cheeks, "thank you very much and I think it will run a year at least." The advance booking took the play well into the summer of 1944 and when the notices finally appeared, James Agate described it as a masterpiece. For once Binkie's estimate was totally wrong. It ran for all of three years, totalling 1,154 performances and becoming the popular standby of reps, tours, amateurs and fringe theatre for many decades after the war.

While all this was going on, the Lunts had re-entered Binkie's life. Their last appearance had been just before the war in *Amphitryon 38* under John C. Wilson's management though Binkie had put money into it and allowed Wilson to use the Tennent office and staff. Now they were working for him and very much part of his empire. They had brought their big Broadway success, *There Shall Be No Night* by Robert Sherwood, a searing drama set in wartime Finland, and showing a doctor and his family surviving gallantly under the horrors of Nazi occupation. This was only their fourth appearance in London but already they had started to create their own legend. They had done this craftily by severely limiting their London appearances, keeping the public begging for more. The Lunt legend was hot and strong in 1943: they represented the absolute perfection, the ultimate in light comedy acting; their partnership was one of such exquisite understanding, of such technical skill and bound by such sympathy that they seemed to be one rather than two. This style of acting produced a naturalism never before attempted whereby they could overlap speeches and sometimes even speak together as people do in real life when they are angry or loving. It was a rapport which no other acting couple achieved, neither the Oliviers, nor even Tracy and Hepburn. With this was their single-minded dedication to their work, which compelled them to think about the play and to rehearse it all the time not only in the theatre but going home in the car, on the train, in the restaurant after the performance, in the hotel, and sometimes in bed.

One evening during the run of *Amphitryon 38*, after it had been running for a few months, Binkie invited them to have dinner with him at home. Alfred had been rather silent and withdrawn while Lynn chatted and rattled away in her usual artless style. Suddenly Alfred came to life. "Lynnie," he said, "I know how that line in act two should be said, at last I've got it," and he said it. "Yes, darling," replied Lynn delightedly, "that's absolutely right," and she said the line which followed it. Alfred continued, and before Binkie realised what was happening, he found himself witnessing the run-through of the entire scene which he had just seen in the theatre done, as he wrongly thought, to perfection.

In 1944 during the run of Rattigan's *Love in Idleness* they were spending the weekend in Binkie's country home; on the Saturday night Binkie was woken up by the sound of laughter, crashes and voices raised loudly. He went to investigate and found the Lunts in their pyjamas rehearsing. It seemed that Lynn had woken up and said to Alfred, "Darling, I've had the most marvellous idea for some business you could do in the telephone scene in act two," and demonstrated it. Alfred watched sleepily but it was so funny that he was jerked into immediate and responsive wakefulness, "Yeah, yeah, Lynnie, it's good." "It's more than good, Alfred darling, it's *great*." Bright as two buttons, they leapt out of bed and before Binkie knew quite what was happening they were running the whole scene, adding little bits of funny business and greatly improving what Binkie had thought was a very fine piece of acting.

This endless passion for perfection continued up to the last performance. When Binkie paid his usual visit to their dressing-rooms in the second interval of the final performance of Coward's *Quadrille* in 1953 he found them busily rehearsing a bit of new business for the last act. Even when they had officially finished with a play they continued thinking about it. "Oh, Binkie, I wish you'd revive *Love in Idleness*," she said during the run of *The Visit*, in 1960. "Alfred has thought of some marvellous new ideas for the dinner-party scene in the last act."

There Shall Be No Night ran for two years on Broadway before touring during 1940–1, and was the most controversial play they had ever done. It was undeniably magnificent wartime propaganda and received hysterical endorsement from the President and Mrs Roosevelt. It successfully divided the country into two opposing camps: the Isolationists, who believed that the war in Europe was not America's business, and those who believed that it was, which finally oversimplified into warmongers versus peacelovers. There was talk of making a film of it but Lunt, over-pessimistic, decided that the Hollywood moguls would cut it to ribbons and thus deprive it of all point. The controversy was dramatically resolved when the Germans invaded France, Holland, Belgium and – capping it all with a monumental act of insanity – Russia which now joined the war on the side of the Allies. At the same time Finland surrendered to the Nazis who occupied it for the rest of the war. This neatly removed all the dramatic significance of the play which finished prematurely at the end of 1942.

It was Lynn who decided that they should spend the war years in London. It must be remembered that she was English-born and bred, never lost her English citizenship and retained a passionate love for her mother country all her life. The move was important because of her family. How could she and Alfred remain in the safety of New York when her sister was facing nightly raids from the Luftwaffe? With a little help from Binkie, whose special talents as a fixer were never seen to better advantage and whose influence seemed to penetrate everywhere, even the American State Department, special passports were obtained, travel permits were issued and a long and dangerous journey followed by ship to Lisbon and then by plane to London. They did not know till afterwards that it was this same route which was taken by the plane on which Leslie Howard met his death only two weeks earlier.

In view of the wartime shortage of hotel accommodation it was nothing short of a miracle that Binkie was able to arrange a suite at the Savoy. He obtained ration books, identity cards, torches for the blackout and gas masks, everything which a well-equipped Londoner needed for the years of austerity. Since they were both anxious to do something really active for the war effort, active apart from acting (a feeling he understood and knew full well), he arranged for them to become ARP wardens in the Strand district. Since Alfred's appetite for self-sacrifice wasn't satisfied by his nightly appearance in the shelter where – as Binkie had done three years earlier – he made tea, manned a telephone and took instruction in first-aid, he further arranged for him to become a porter and orderly at St George's Hospital at Hyde Park Corner, where he served meals on trolleys, arranged flowers, distributed books and medicine and even emptied bed-pans. He worked under a false name and throughout his time there nobody had the least idea of the true identity of this tall, handsome and very helpful man with the American accent and the charming manners. One day, in a fit of mischief, he persuaded Binkie to join him. For several hours Binkie worked away: rolling bandages, sweeping dust from under the beds, serving food and moving screens were all acceptable but chamber-pots and bed-pans were not. "I don't think this is really *quite* my sort of thing, Alfred dear," he said apologetically, as he put away his orderly's uniform. "It's not exactly *me*, is it?"

In the meantime, Binkie had persuaded Robert Sherwood, the author, to make some essential changes in the play. As the Peloponnese had been overrun by the Nazi hordes, and as the Greeks were now suffering all the agonies of enemy occupation, it was very topical and effective that the action should be taken away from Finland and set in

Greece. And so it was. From Dr and Mrs Valkonen living in Helsinki, the Lunts now became Dr and Mrs Vlachos living in Athens. The Lunts were not altogether happy that Equity and State Department regulations had made it impossible to bring over the original Broadway cast and Binkie did diplomatically agree that it was a pity that London could not see either Sydney Greenstreet, fresh from his Hollywood triumphs in *The Maltese Falcon* and *Casablanca*, or the nineteen-year-old Montgomery Clift as the doctor's son. Alfred, who was producing the play, and Binkie got down to the auditions without delay but the wartime shortage of good actors had now reached a crisis point. Casting turned out to be a very frustrating business, everybody was away fighting and it became necessary to use some who had never acted before, but Alfred had a special talent for getting performances out of inexperienced actors. Rehearsals went smoothly and by the time they opened in Liverpool he and Lynn were able to write home to Sherwood that the cast was even better than Broadway's, including Muriel Pavlow and Terence Morgan. The London opening at the Aldwych Theatre on December 15th 1943 played to an audience consisting largely of servicemen of all nationalities. Most of them were in tears and were seen to be crying quite unashamedly as they stumbled out of the theatre into the street. Even Binkie, who was not sentimental or easily moved to emotion, was red-eyed at the end. He staggered through the pass door, across the stage and into Lynn's dressing-room where he, and other close friends, sat down and openly wept. "It was the most amazing experience I have ever had," he later confessed. "I had never seen a dressing-room after a triumphal first night turned into a wake."

The success of *There Shall Be No Night* confirmed that the public liked the straight plays and tragedies just as much as the musicals and light comedies. The raids were at their worst in early 1944 but nothing, it seemed, would stop the public from filling the theatre at every performance. If there were no buses or trains, if there was a thick fog which blacked out even the dim light of the torches, if they had to walk to the theatre stumbling through the darkness a foot at a time, somehow they would get to the Aldwych and punctually. How they did it neither Alfred nor Lynn could guess, but they were enormously impressed by the courage of the audiences during the air-raids which continued to devastate London during those early winter months. When the warning went and bombs screamed terrifyingly as they fell, nobody left for the shelters. They just stayed there, determined to see the play. "I can't imagine a New York audience behaving like that," said Alfred. Binkie was present one night when a bomb fell very close. The blast swept through the theatre backstage, causing one of the canvas flats to buckle and sway alarmingly. Alfred, making his entrance, was just able to keep it upright with his right hand and, by a bizarre coincidence, his next line to Lynn was, "Are you all right, darling?" The hysterical laughter, applause and cheers which greeted this lasted for all of one minute by Binkie's watch. "Now you'll know how to say that line," he said gleefully to Alfred after the performance. "I knew that something good would come out of the war. We must all offer a little vote of thanks to Hermann Goering and the Luftwaffe."

It was the play which everybody had to see and Binkie was in his element arranging visits to the Aldwych by VIPs for whom the stage boxes were kept in permanent reservation. The King and Queen were first, and then all the lesser royals. Getting the Churchills was not easy as he had little spare time for the theatre, but Binkie eventually managed to get them both into front stalls where he smoked two of his famous cigars. The King of Greece was an obvious candidate and he arrived with his entourage. Afterwards he went round to Numbers One and Two dressing-rooms thanking the Lunts and Binkie on behalf of his unhappy country for the splendid propaganda. The result was a party he gave for the company in his suite at Brown's Hotel where he was spending a very comfortable wartime exile. It was a hilarious evening with Greek food and wine, Greek dancers and singers in national costume. Binkie drank a lot of ouzo and retsina, joined in the dancing, and drank a lot more retsina and ouzo.

At midnight he finally collapsed, had to be carried into the King's private car by two muscular black-moustached *evsones*, driven home and put to bed. It is not entirely surprising that from then on he became a fervent supporter of Greece and the Greeks, a true Phil-hellene of the sort only England produces. He also seriously considered buying a holiday villa in Corfu when the war was over.

Another person who passionately wished to see the play was the Dean of Windsor but old age and increasing infirmity had made the journey impossible. This wish was as good as a royal command so Binkie arranged for the company to travel down to Windsor and give a private performance to the Dean and fifty guests. They had lunch, moved into the drawing-room, and gave the entire play using the castle furniture and the few props they had brought with them. As it was a fine summer afternoon, there was enough daylight coming in through the tall bay windows to make artificial lights unnecessary. As anybody knows who has done it, this circumstance produces a special, concentrated sort of intimacy which made it, they all agreed, perhaps the finest performance they had ever given.

June 1944 produced the D-Day invasion and a general feeling that the war would soon be over. At the same time the Nazis were finally driven out of Greece by the Allies, but any euphoria which might have resulted was quickly destroyed by the arrival of the flying bombs, which came over in their thousands and did more damage than the previous blitzes put together. Life became very dangerous for the Lunts, but nothing would stop them walking from the Savoy to the Aldwych. Binkie pleaded with them to take a taxi or a car but they refused. They wanted to be treated like ordinary Londoners and not Broadway stars. This democratic gesture nearly resulted in their death on a couple of occasions when the bombs crashed only a street away, causing them to throw themselves down on to the ground. With the fortunes of war changing so quickly, the play began to lose its topicality and when a bomb knocked down a wall next to the theatre, putting it out of action, Binkie had no choice. He sent the production on tour round the theatre-starved provinces and military camps where the success they enjoyed was even greater. So was the pressure of work because the Lunts insisted on giving extra performances for all the service charities and audiences, tickets either free or half-price if in uniform. For many it was their first glimpse not only of the play and the Lunts but of live theatre. Binkie scrupulously paid the entire company for the extra performances and gave them a bonus out of the considerable profits when the play finally closed in Blackpool in July.

But the war was not over, not yet, and the Lunts had no intention of returning to Broadway to do yet another revival of *The Guardsman* in which the Theatre Guild nagged them to appear. They wanted to do another play immediately and it so happened that Binkie had one all ready for them.

Love in Idleness by Terence Rattigan had a curious pre-natal history. It was written for, and at the specific request of, Gertrude Lawrence whom Rattigan worshipped. She had been in London setting up an ENSA tour. Binkie had taken her to *While the Sun Shines* and afterwards invited them both out to supper. "Have you got a play for me?" she asked Rattigan. "Not yet, but I've got a good idea for one. I'll write it and send it to you." And he did. There weren't many wartime light comedies which could claim to have been inspired by *Hamlet* but this was one. The young hero was an eighteen-year-old who has spent his war in Canada and returns to his mother's flat in London to find that she is having an affair with an English cabinet minister, who is living with her in her flat. The boy is neurotic, passionately left-wing, loathes the Establishment and is very jealous of the lover's hold over his mother. It is the same situation as Hamlet, Gertrude and Claudius. He persuades his mother to leave her cabinet minister and live with him in a small and uncomfortable flat in Earls

Court. The cabinet minister by various devious means succeeds in arousing the boy's interest and affection and all ends happily.

By the time Rattigan had finished it, Gertrude Lawrence had returned to America and Binkie sent it to her with a covering note, "This is the play you asked Terry Rattigan to write for you." Binkie was surprised and rather shocked when she replied saying that she did not remember asking for a new play, that she did not even remember meeting Rattigan, that she was already committed to a tour of the Pacific naval bases in the Far East, and that, in any case, she did not like the play or the part. Binkie tried to persuade her to change her mind, asking her in the process just why she did not like it. He did not get much sense out of her for throughout history star actresses have always been wayward and illogical about their choice of material and will turn down the most splendid parts for no apparent good reason. She did say that the immorality of the play upset her, she did not wish to play the part of a woman openly and flagrantly living a life of sin, and that she was not altogether happy about playing the part of a middle-aged woman with a grown-up son. She was still playing women in their early thirties and that's how she wanted things to stay. She did not feel ready to become a matron just yet, though there seemed a conspiracy on the part of some managements to push her prematurely into old age.

All this was reported to Rattigan over another lunch at the Ivy. Binkie snorted contemptuously as he passed on the sad news. "She would never have said any of these things before the war but strange things happen to women when they reach their forties. She admits to being forty-three but I happen to know that she is all of forty-six. It's the menopause." He explained to Rattigan that it was vanity and working-class puritanism which had turned her against the part, that he was not to worry, that he had a much better place for it. Alfred and Lynn. Rattigan shrugged his handsome shoulders over Gertie's rejection. He resisted all suggestions that he should make the boy ten years younger and happily agreed that Binkie should show it to the Lunts.

They liked it but as the part of the cabinet minister was shorter and of less dramatic interest – the emphasis being on the son and the wife – they suggested that the play might be rewritten, just a little bit, to build up Alfred's part. Rattigan was not altogether happy about this, but agreed and later admitted that the result was a much better play. In the process it had changed from a strong and emotional marital, domestic drama into a feathery light comedy. One person who thought that he had spoiled it was Noël Coward who had money in the play, saw it in Liverpool, took a great hate against it and tried to persuade Binkie and Rattigan to withdraw it now as nothing but trouble and disappointment would come if they opened it in London. "It's just not *good* enough, Binkie," he said firmly, pacing up and down, "it's not *funny*." But nobody agreed with him. Binkie loved it, the Lunts loved it and nothing could stop them from opening in London at the Lyric Theatre, which they did on December 20th 1944 on a night of thick fog which, however, did not prevent the theatre from being sold out. "Nothing will keep the English from their theatre: come hell or high water, they'll be there," said Alfred Lunt admiringly.

Rattigan now had three plays running simultaneously all in adjacent theatres, *Love in Idleness* at the Lyric, *Flare Path* at the Apollo and *While the Sun Shines* at the Globe. If the Queen's Theatre had not been bombed, and therefore unavailable, that was where Rattigan's next play would undoubtedly go. "Then we could have renamed the street Rattigan Avenue," said Binkie gleefully. However, three plays in the West End was a notable achievement, even if the record had been held by Somerset Maugham with four and it was something only Ivor Novello had achieved.

Noël Coward's reservations were clearly not shared by the audience who laughed and applauded continuously throughout the evening, but the press tended to agree with him, although the Lunts got their usual rave notices. Most of the critics condemned the play as being trivial, unimportant and unworthy of its two shining talents. It is, and always has been, difficult to find good plays for outstanding talents and the greater the actors' success, the more keenly will the critics condemn the plays as being unworthy. It is one of the penalties of stardom and it was to trouble and worry the Lunts for years to come. From *Love in Idleness* onwards, their choice of new plays would always be savagely criticised.

Binkie did his public-relations act with even greater effect during the run of the play, most notably by getting Churchill once again. The audience started to cheer him as he entered the theatre and the play was delayed for ten minutes while he smiled, waved, puffed his cigar and took his place with Mrs Churchill and the entourage in the centre of the front stalls. There was one little incident which Binkie loved to describe whenever he was feeling in a nostalgic mood. In the play Alfred had a line, "I've just come back from Number Ten," Lynn then had to say, "Was he nice about it?" and Alfred had to reply, "Oh yes, very much so." Churchill had given Alfred one of his famous cigars as a present and at this point in the play, Alfred took it out of his pocket and lit it. The applause and cheering brought the play to a halt while the two great men, separated by only a couple of feet, solemnly smoked their two cigars. Only when Churchill stood up and bowed to the audience did the noise subside and the play proceed. Never before had the Lunts found themselves upstaged by a member of the audience.

Even more exciting – if that was possible – was a special performance which Binkie arranged in Westminster Hall for several hundred civilians who had been working on a highly secret project in the basement under the House of Commons, not totally unconnected with explosives and munitions, a decidedly Guy Fawkes situation, Binkie thought. There was not much light, though Binkie arranged for some spot bulbs to be brought along, and the vast, high-ceilinged echoing expanse of the hall could have killed the feathery lightness of the play, but the enthusiasm of the audience and the goodwill which they created made it into a very stimulating experience. It was, apparently, the first time in its history that actors had been invited to appear there.

After three months, the Lunts decided that they wanted to go home, for they had been absent for nearly two years, but Binkie persuaded them to stay on for a further three months so they could give performances to American hospitals, air bases and military camps in Britain, newly-liberated France and behind the Allied lines in Germany. While they were in Germany the Germans surrendered: the war in Europe was over. Acting in London during the blitz had been a unique and unrepeatable experience for both of them and it was a memory they treasured. "If you can keep your head and concentrate on your performance while bombs are crashing all around you," said Alfred, misquoting Kipling, "then you can call yourself an actor. We wouldn't have missed it for the world. You could say that we had a very good war."

ACT THREE

CHAPTER TWENTY-TWO

1945

The Heyday

He wasn't the only one. Binkie had also had a good war. "It may sound cynical," he said to Rattigan, "but the war has been the making of me. Can't complain about a thing. Look at me and look at the Firm. And to think that I owe it all to Hitler." In six years he had presented fifty-nine plays in the West End and of those only seven had failed: the others had all had good long runs, many of over a year and some record-breaking marathons of over a thousand performances each. He'd presented over a hundred plays on tour which included theatres up and down the UK, ENSA tours at home and abroad and the activities of the Tennent repertory companies. These toured endlessly around Scotland with companies that included Michael Denison and Dulcie Gray, newly wed, and on the threshold of their distinguished careers. No other manager in London had done so well, it was an achievement of which anybody could be proud. The wartime boom in the theatre which brought the millions rushing to the box office was an enormous asset and he was lucky that so many of his rivals were in the forces and conveniently out of the way.

The official ending of the war in Europe was on Tuesday, May 8th. On that day, of the thirty-six theatres open in the West End, eight of them housed Tennent companies presenting a total of twelve plays: there were two Cowards, *Private Lives* at the Apollo and *Blithe Spirit* at the Duchess; two Rattigans, *While the Sun Shines* at the Globe and *Love in Idleness* at the Lyric; the prolific and industrious Emlyn Williams had just opened at the St James's in *The Wind of Heaven*; a minor Lonsdale, *Another Love Story*, was still running at the Phoenix; Daphne du Maurier's second play, *The Years Between*, at Wyndham's, showed that she had lost none of her theatrical skill; and at the Haymarket the repertoire of five classical plays *Hamlet* was the one actually playing on VE night. No other London manager could compete with that list in quantity or quality. Within a year the figures would be doubled. Yes, Binkie had had a very good war. Would he have an equally good peace? He knew without doubt that it would be even better. On that historic day, May 8th 1945, it is unlikely that anybody in the West End had more confidence, assurance and happy insight into the future.

In the evening he made a triumphal and decidedly alcoholic tour of the eight Tennent theatres, "Just keeping a watchful eye on the empire," he said to Rattigan. He saw a little bit of all eight plays, had drinks with the cast of *While the Sun Shines* before the show, with the actors in *Blithe Spirit* in the first interval, with Alfred and Lynn in the second interval at the Lyric, and with John Clements and Kay Hammond after they had finished their performance of *Private Lives*. Then he walked down Whitehall and through Parliament Square mingling with the crowd. Six years ago the streets had been cold and empty. Now they were filled with hundreds and thousands of hysterical singing Londoners, dancing with strangers and policemen and getting ecstatically drunk. He dined with John Gielgud in his flat with Lady Cunard and the Granville-Barkers. He had hoped that Barker might be persuaded to return to active work, despite his wife's unconcealed hostility to the theatre: perhaps to direct Gielgud in yet another revival of his favourite part, Richard II, for the prestige would be enormous. As for Emerald Cunard, Binkie had been a frequent guest at her famous dinner-parties. She was a fool but a rich fool and she loved the arts. He might persuade her to divert some of her husband's millions away from the worthy cause of Sir Thomas Beecham and English opera and towards H. M. Tennent and the classical drama revival. He succeeded in the second but Harley Granville-Barker died before the first could be pursued.

Binkie was now thirty-seven though he still looked like a school-boy. "Not a *young* schoolboy because he'd lost that baby-faced look," said Chips Channon to Terence Rattigan about that time, "more like a prefect in his last year at Westminster. Perhaps the Head of the School Debating Society." He was now slightly more than half-way through his life with another twenty-eight years to go, but these were to be the peak years, the years of fulfilment and legend. In fact, the legend had already started because in the four years since he took over the management of the Firm, following Harry's death, he had made H. M. Tennent the most powerful, the most sought-after, talked-about and wealthiest management in London. And with many hundreds of actors and actresses being demobilised and returning to civilian life to pick up the threads of their careers – or maybe even to start a new one – what had been an embarrassing shortage of good actors had now turned to a plenty. Most of them made a swift approach to H. M. Tennent, either by letter or phone or by personal call at the Globe offices, hoping that Mr Beaumont might provide them with work. Now Binkie could pick and choose since he had plenty to choose from. Now he could return to the perfectionism of meticulous casting which had been his acknowledged hallmark before the war.

The heyday had begun.

His rise to the top had been greeted by the West End fraternity with the liveliest curiosity, astonishment and more than a touch of despairing envy. "*How* does he do it?" they asked. It was a good question and is still being asked when his name crops up in conversation. Just what did Binkie have which his rivals didn't? Where did he have the advantage over Bronson Albery, Charles Cochran, Firth Shephard, Stephen Mitchell, Jack Hylton, Prince and Emile Littler, Bernard Delfont, Peter Daubeny, Jack de Leon, Bill Linnit, Alec Rea, E. P. Clift, Tom Arnold, to name only fourteen? Like Diaghilev, like so many of the great impresarios of history, Binkie had no particular talent of his own. He couldn't act or sing or dance or play an instrument: he couldn't paint a foot of scenery or design a costume or write a single line of dialogue or direct actors and tell them what to do and where to stand. But then he didn't need to, for he had others to do all these things for him. However, he did have the talent to recognise talent even when it is not immediately visible to others, which in itself is a rare and valuable talent. He also had the diplomat's ability to persuade disparate talents to work together, plus the special mastery in organising a world where these talents could flourish. He had, too, a profound theatrical instinct, excellent taste in design, a flair for casting (which is generally admitted to be sixty per cent of successful play-producing), good judgement of new plays and – perhaps the most important of all – a tremendous love for everybody who worked in the theatre: well, *nearly* everybody; there were a few exceptions. Unlike some of his rivals, he did not secretly despise actors: he realised that of all the people who make up the theatre they are the only ones who are totally essential and that without them the theatre cannot exist.

In addition, he had a definite policy which he made evident from his first productions and thus gave the press, the profession and the public a clear guideline to what H. M. Tennent proposed to contribute. This was nothing less than the best of everything, commercial theatre at its most glittering. It was a policy of the greatest stars in gorgeous classical revivals amidst the most sumptuous settings which taste and money could devise. It meant Edith Evans in *The Importance of Being Earnest*, John Gielgud in *Love for Love*, Isabel Jeans in *Lady Winder-mere's Fan*, Leslie Banks in *The Second Mrs Tanqueray*, Eileen Herlie in *The Eagle has Two Heads*, Emlyn Williams in *The Winslow Boy* and Robert Morley in *The Little Hut*; it meant designs by Rex Whistler,

Cecil Beaton and Oliver Messel; it meant music specially composed by William Walton and Richard Addinsell. All these were perfect examples of the Tennent house style, unforgettable displays of the London theatre at its best.

Of course this is not the whole picture. Other managers had taste, judgement and dedication but the essential difference lay in Binkie's personal qualities. His stars liked to be flattered and cherished and employed. Binkie knew everybody. He could gossip with delicious indiscretion, he would take you out to lunch at the Ivy or the Savoy Grill or the Caprice, spend a fortune and make you feel that you were the only person in the world to whom he wished to talk. He could invite you to the cosy little parties in his house in Lord North Street and treat you like royalty. He could convince you that he was the only manager in London who really appreciated you and that only he could give you the plays you wanted, the parts you were bursting to play, the supporting cast you liked and the settings you deserved. To be treated like this is always delightful but how much more satisfying when it comes from a man who is elegantly slim and attractive, beautifully dressed and groomed, with exquisite manners, bursting with vitality and charm. His presence illuminated any gathering; with his radiant smile and his blue-grey eyes flashing with enthusiasm it was impossible to be either bored or boring. Some might think it unnecessary to attribute such importance to mere surface appeal, but there is hardly a branch of life in which an attractive appearance and personality are not considerable assets. If Binkie had been a fat, balding, ugly little man with a harsh provincial accent, thick spectacles and a truculent, taciturn manner, it is unthinkable that he could have enjoyed the same success, not with all his acumen, knowledge and energy. "It is the secret of his success that he speaks every man's language but his own," said Robert Morley. "Alone among the impresarios he understands actors. In his office it is always they who play the scene. Binkie is the friendly critic, the attentive audience, the committed fan. He never engages an actor, he makes sure the actor engages him and having done so becomes not his employee but his admiring client. It is Binkie who protects actors, congratulates and encourages them to greater efforts, to further flights. What actors admire most about him is his integrity."

In his autobiography, Michael Denison tells how he had been invited to join the Tennent repertory company, but not Dulcie Gray. "I asked to see the legendary Binkie. He must I suppose have looked younger than he did thirty years later but in manner and appearance he was to the end of his life one of the most unchanging human beings I have ever known. Always meticulously neat with office to match and speaking with hushed courtesy, he projected without apparent effort and even simultaneously the most conflicting impressions – relaxation and high tension, the wisdom of the ages and boyish enthusiasm, the hard-headed man of business and the idealist, the dangerous enemy and the most solicitous and loyal of friends."

Binkie could be all things to all men and all women. He could talk of Christian Science with Edith Evans, he could discuss the validity of the Roman Catholic faith as opposed to Anglicanism with Sybil Thorndike, cycling with Margaret Rutherford and fashion with Isabel Jeans. He was no less a chameleon with the men: he could talk cricket with Trevor Howard, music with Owen Nares, rugby with Clifford Evans, and gourmet food with Alfred Lunt who was himself an excellent cook.

The whole of the Tennent structure was based on the stars. A play without one was unthinkable, for they were the crown jewels of his empire and the centrepiece of his theatrical philosophy. He had them queuing up to work for him and keeping themselves available. Edith Evans said on many occasions that she would rather be out of work than do a play for any other management. "Binkie will look after me," she explained to the rejected managements, "he'll find me a play," and invariably Binkie did. Margaret Rutherford once turned down £300 a week to play Miss Marple in yet another Agatha Christie play and accepted Binkie's offer of £40 to play Lady Wishfort in *The Way of the World* at the Lyric Hammersmith. Binkie adored all his stars for what they were as well as what they could do for him and this wide-eyed adoration fastened itself particularly on the actresses.

Like many elegant, civilised homosexuals, he adored women which is not quite such a paradox as it may seem: since nature had endowed him with an extra layer of femininity he was able to understand them in ways which are not always open to heterosexual men. He could feel as they did, think as they did, see things and people from their point of view. He could, and did, advise them on their clothes, their make-up and hair-styles, their husbands, lovers and sex lives. He could take them out to parties, give them presents, fill their dressing-rooms with flowers, champagne, escort them to first nights, he in his neatly cut Savile Row dinner-jacket, she in a long gown, fur stole and jewels. What a joy to be with these goddesses whom he had worshipped from afar, to be not only an employer but also a valued and loving friend, to have them waiting in his outer office, to hear them calling him '*darling Binkie*', to feel the peck of their lips on his cheek and to know that they not only respected him as a successful man of the theatre but liked him as a person and valued his good opinion. In their company he could feel completely at ease.

Of course, he had his own way of dealing with them. When Jean Giraudoux's *Duel of Angels* was being prepared, Vivien Leigh wanted ten per cent of the gross and Binkie would only pay her five per cent. The way he worked on her filled those who were there with amazement. "Darling," he said, "if I pay you ten per cent I won't be able to afford to bring the play into town, I won't be able to afford the right clothes, it'll be Marks and Spencer's not Balmain. I won't be able to afford Cecil Beaton's designs and it will be a great shame if London can't see your splendid performance." Vivien finally agreed to his terms. Sometimes these goddesses would behave badly. Dulcie Gray remembers sitting in his office while he was talking to one of his star actresses on the telephone. She was obviously making unreasonable demands and being tiresome but Binkie did not betray his impatience until the conversation was over and the telephone receiver had been replaced. "They are such *nuisances*," he burst out. "They want this, they want that, they never remember what you do for them, they are ungrateful and sometimes quite impossible. Now, you're a good girl, Dulcie dear, you won't behave like that ever, will you?"

"If they're such nuisances," Dulcie asked naïvely, "will you want to work with them again?" He looked at her in surprise. "But of *course* I will," he said firmly.

There were, at different times in his life, three women for whom he had a special love which may have fallen just short of a *grande passion*, but not much. They all had much in common: they were elegant, beautiful, sympathetic and talented. Finding a truly kindred spirit, they loved him in return. All of them wanted to marry him being, as women have always been in this situation, confident that such a relationship would work. And why not, they argued. There is good historical precedent for the happy sexless marriage. When they had so much in common, what did sex matter? Companionship and a community of interests were surely enough for a very satisfactory relationship. Look at the Bernard Shaws. Look at the Lunts. One of these inestimable ladies succeeded in arousing him sexually, an astonishing achievement in the circumstances and one which she accomplished – if Broadway rumour can be believed – by the classical method discreetly referred to by its Latin name *fellatio*. It would seem that Binkie found the experience not altogether to his liking because when the lady proposed marriage he politely declined. She was greatly disappointed, but found some consolation in the fact that their friendship survived very happily even though he did not remember her in his will. They continued to correspond, writing a great many gossipy letters, for the rest of his life.

What was true of star actors also applied to star playwrights.

Terence Rattigan, Noël Coward, Emlyn Williams, Daphne du Maurier, Clemence Dane, Robert Bolt and many others, sent him their latest plays as a matter of course. Leading agents, Curtis Brown, Laurence Fitch, Jimmy Fraser and A. D. Peters, earmarked their choicest scripts for him. The pile of new plays on his desk was always high for however quickly he and the Tennent staff read them new ones arrived by every post. A popular joke of the time said that if a rival management wanted a good new play he had only to stand outside the front of the Globe Theatre and catch them as they fluttered out of the window of Binkie's office. Obviously, he had to reject ten times more than he could ever hope to produce for himself but this never bothered him for he knew what he wanted. As with the actors, it was good to have a wide margin of choice for this made it possible for him to keep up the highest standards. "He had a damn good nose for a play," was Bronson Albery's admiring comment.

Binkie knew by instinct what would work and what wouldn't: what would be a solid commercial success and what would be merely a *flop d'estime*; what he could cast satisfactorily and what he couldn't. He was, at all times, rather less concerned with making money than in doing plays which interested and excited him, plays which offered splendid opportunities to his favourite actors and stars, plays which would add lustre to the Firm's image. In short, it had to be a Tennent play, a category which it would be difficult to define, but was always easy to recognise. Anything which he felt did not qualify would be turned down instantly no matter how much money it was likely to make. Many of these were produced by rival managements with great success but Binkie was unresentful for he had little professional jealousy. He turned down an offer to do Agatha Christie's first play, *The Hollow*, and thus lost the chance of making history with *The Mousetrap*, a fact which Peter Saunders has related with some relish, and in considerable detail, in his book, *The Mousetrap Man*. Binkie didn't mind. It wasn't a Tennent play and thus he would have no interest in it.

With the peace, the Tennent staff was reassembled and re-organised. First to return to civilian life was John Perry. Their friendship was as close as ever, perhaps even closer, for the six-year absence had caused Binkie a lot of sorrow and pain. They shared the house in Lord North Street which Binkie had recently bought, and Dodie Smith's house in Finchingfield, on loan for the duration, but this was not enough. Binkie wanted to be with him every day, to keep an eye on him, to see he came to no harm and was happy and busy. So he gave him a job with the Firm; it was loosely defined but he was generally regarded as his personal assistant with his own office next to

Binkie's where he could interview actors and staff, talk to fellow-playwrights, hire and fire staff, discuss contracts with agents, take the stars and visiting American VIPs out to lunch at the Ivy or Savoy where Binkie had accounts, arrange charity matinées and pay regular visits to the productions to see that the standards were being maintained. Perry had no desire to pick up the threads of what he himself was the first to admit had been an undistinguished career as an actor but he renewed his writing partnership with M. J. Farrell to produce *Treasure Hunt* in which Sybil Thorndike played a dotty old aunt who spends her days in a sedan chair under the impression that it is the first-class compartment of the Orient Express. This opened at the Apollo in 1949 and ran for 358 performances. However, time would show if he had the talent for administration and management.

With the war safely over and the West End crowded with unemployed actors anxious to return to civilian life, Binkie now decided that the time had come to put into action a master plan he had contemplated as far back as 1939, only to see it aborted by the war. This was to assemble a company of young actors and put them under long-term contract to the firm. The great advantage was that instead of going into the open market for the supporting cast with the possibility that they would be working for somebody else when he wanted them, now they would be permanently available and could be moved from one play to another as the casting requirements dictated. And so it was. Prize-winning students from RADA and Central, particularly the gold and silver medallists, one female and one male per school term, would be offered ten pounds a week – the Equity minimum – to play as cast. The contract would be valid for one year with an option to renew on both sides. It did not matter that for the first year at least it was only walk-ons, small parts and understudies: the honour of working for Binkie and the limitless possibilities it opened up fully compensated for low money and humble beginnings. The Tennent contract became the most eagerly sought-after prize on the theatrical horizon.

Development meant diversification and this in turn meant extending the territorial limits of the empire. What the firm needed was a small suburban theatre where new plays could be discreetly and inexpensively tried out. "Playing safe" was the waspish comment Binkie had to suffer from his enemies so he took a lease on the Lyric Theatre, Hammersmith, where plays of doubtful commercial future, plays of the avant-garde could be given a month's run, transferred to the West End if they did well, and quietly forgotten without much financial loss if they did not. He handed the management of this to John Perry and installed Kitty Black in the offices above the Apollo

Theatre as casting director, a job she had always wanted and at which she excelled. As she was also translating and adapting plays from the French she quickly became a considerable power in the Tennent empire.

Binkie introduced the policy of having regular open auditions once a month not for a particular play, but for general casting and they would see anybody, literally *anybody*, who wrote in. Young hopefuls had to wait their turn but no request was refused and in the fullness of time a little blue card would slip through their letterbox inviting them to the Globe Theatre to learn a piece of their own choice not to exceed three minutes. Binkie attended most of these auditions with Daphne Rye, his casting director, a generous and much-loved lady who not only discovered actors from her indefatigable, talent-spotting tours of the reps, but frequently gave them accommodation in her spacious Earls Court flat, as Bryan Forbes has described in his memoirs, *Notes on a Life*.

H. M. TENNENT LTD.

GLOBE THEATRE, SHAFTESBURY AVENUE, LONDON, W.1.
Telephone No.: GERRARD 3647-8-9   20th Nov. 1953

Dear Mr. Huggett,

Would you care to come along to an audition for future productions. If so, would you kindly learn an excerpt from any play not exceeding three minutes and we will be pleased to hear you at 4.30 pm on Friday 11th December at the Apollo Theatre.

DAPHNE RYE
Casting Director

Binkie was a great believer in open auditions: you never knew what exciting talent might emerge from the avalanche of rubbish and mediocrity as sometimes it did with Dora Broadbent★ who achieved the minor miracle of making Binkie collapse with laughter and was immediately put into Noël Coward's first post-war play, *Peace in Our Time*. "Binkie liked naughty, camp, funny ladies," said Diane Hart who was discovered in the early fifties and was immediately starred in Rattigan's *Who is Sylvia?* "He liked them to have a wicked sense of humour and not to give a damn for anybody. Made a change from all those Dames and First Ladies, I expect."

Another actress who made Binkie collapse with laughter was Daphne Newton. She and Yvonne Mitchell, an old friend, auditioned on the same day. Daphne was wearing a very large, wide-brimmed summer hat with yards of flowing veil. The audition took place at the Globe in front of the *While the Sun Shines* set. She walked on to the stage through the prompt corner and all went well until the end of her second speech which, as she had rehearsed it, required her to walk backwards from the stage. Unhappily, the only exit was a door which was too narrow. The hat caught in the door and she found herself twisting and turning her head to get out, but even so it stayed there, hopelessly stuck, with the veil flying out in all directions while she disentangled her head and made a deeply embarrassed exit into the wings. She could hear loud laughter from the stalls. Horrified and confused, she ran upstairs to the stage door but before she could leave the theatre a man suddenly appeared as if from nowhere and blocked her exit. He was very young, slim and blond. She thought he must be an ASM though she hadn't seen him in the wings. "Miss Newton, please don't go." He smiled charmingly and shook hands with her. "Please come and talk to me." He led her upstairs to the top of the theatre, down a corridor and into a small, nicely furnished office with two small circular windows overlooking Shaftesbury Avenue. He sat her down, offered her a cigarette and then parked himself behind the desk. She had at that moment no idea who he was or why he wished to speak to her.

"Miss Newton, my name is Hugh Beaumont and I am the managing director of H. M. Tennent. I must begin by telling you that I greatly enjoyed your audition. Even if you didn't exactly intend it to be funny you nevertheless made me laugh and that's something I'm grateful for. I am assembling a company of actors and actresses to support the stars of my future productions and I would like you to join it. I can't offer you your name above the title or in lights but I can offer you permanent employment. To be quite honest, I don't think you'll

---

★Inexplicably, Noël Coward took a great hate to her name. "It is *most* unsuitable for the West End," he said firmly. At his insistence she changed it to Dora Bryan.

ever be a star but you will never be out of work as long as you want it. I need actresses who are capable, hard-working and above all, *reliable*. Do you like the idea?" She did and the following week she started work, with Yvonne Mitchell (who later did become a star of sorts and a novelist), in a rather sentimental play about a Spanish convent, called *The Cradle Song*. It had an all-female cast and they both played nuns.

There was no contract and there never would be, but Binkie was as good as his word, for she did work for him continuously for the next thirty years. And he was right about one thing: she never did become a star.

Binkie never gave contracts. A gentleman's agreement and a letter was considered sufficient. If he said £50 a week or £200 or seven and a half per cent of the gross, then that is what it would be and it arrived punctually every week. Stars as well as beginners, designers as well as technical staff, quickly learned that Binkie's word was his bond and they had no cause for alarm. "You wouldn't *believe* what it saves in terms of paper work and time and trouble," he would say happily. "I suppose that if anybody really wanted a contract and absolutely insisted on having it, then I would give it to him but so far nobody has. Some of my American colleagues are reluctant to trust anybody but when they come to see me they mysteriously lose their suspicions. It must be the relaxing effect of English life."

From the time of Harry Tennent's death to his own, Binkie went through a regular and unchanging routine for rehearsals and first nights. He always attended the first rehearsal, the read-through, with the director and author. Then he would disappear until the end of the second week at which point the company would have to give a complete run-through of the play without scripts. This was attended by all the senior Tennentry, consisting of Binkie, John Perry, the general manager, whoever he was (Bill Conway in the post-war years), Daphne Rye, Joe Davis, as well as the author, the designer and the director. It was an intimidating little judicial gathering, almost a Star Chamber, and you needed strong nerves to get through it without cracking. Equity allowed the management to dismiss actors at any time up to the end of the second week if they were found to be unsatisfactory, so actors had that period to work out an acceptable performance.★ Most of them could cope, though there were always a few who liked to work slowly and couldn't produce results in such a short time. They were the unlucky ones. But if they passed this Becher's Brook, they would receive a letter of agreement confirming

---

★ This was nothing to the Damocletian sword hanging over the heads of American actors who have to produce a satisfactory performance in *three days* or be dismissed.

the engagement for the run of the play. Now they could breathe a long sigh of relief and relax.

It was Binkie's strength that having employed only the best he then left them alone to get on with the job without interference. He was instantly available in a crisis and looked in on the rehearsals only if specially requested by the director. Otherwise his next appearance would be at the first dress-rehearsal, bringing to the production a fresh eye and thus able to see the faults and places for improvement unnoticed, perhaps, by the director who, having lived with the play for many weeks, would be suffering from blurred vision. The memories of his actors are full of admiring stories of how Binkie was able to put his finger in a flash on what was wrong and explain in the most practical terms how it could be put right.

He knew not only what to say but, equally important, just when to say it which sometimes involved keeping the director under control if he was working the actors too hard or being, in Binkie's opinion, unreasonably fussy. Keith Baxter remembers a good example of this at the dress-rehearsal of Peter Shaffer's first play *Five Finger Exercise* at the Comedy. Gielgud has always been known as a difficult and demanding director who suffered from an over-active brain and an over-creative theatrical intelligence and who changed his mind about everything every day. On this occasion he was at his most querulous and tiresome. "Oh, Michael, it's so *boring* just to come down a staircase," he said to Michael Bryant, who was playing the young Austrian tutor, "I think you ought to come in through the French windows."

"But, John, how can I come in through the French windows when the audience has just seen me go upstairs to the study?" he protested, not unreasonably. "Have I climbed down a drainpipe?"

"Oh, Michael, . . . you are so . . . so . . . *dreary* . . ."

It was a very good dress-rehearsal but Gielgud didn't think so. He moved quickly to the pass door only to be intercepted by Binkie who could move very fast indeed when he wished.

"Where are you going, John?"

"To give them some notes. It's terrible. I must talk to them."

"Not now. Go home."

"But, Binkie . . ."

"Go home. Go back to Lord North Street. Don't talk to them now."

"But . . . I have to . . ."

"Please, dear John," and there was an extra note of urgency in his voice, "go home and I'll talk to you later."

Reluctantly Gielgud did so. Binkie went backstage and spoke to the

assembled company relaxing complacently after what they all considered to be a very good run-through. "Darlings, that was absolutely
splendid. John is thrilled with it and all of you. He does have a few little
notes for you but he'll give them to you in the morning. In the
meantime, congratulations." Binkie knew what Gielgud, in spite of
his lifetime as an actor, had obviously forgotten, that after a long and
difficult dress-rehearsal the last thing actors want is to be torn to
pieces.

His routine for first nights was also fixed by years of custom. He
would hover in the crowded foyer near the box office, noting the size,
quality and celebrity rating of the audience, greeting his friends and
colleagues and listening eagerly to the advance comments on the play
from all within earshot. Nobody else recognised him, nobody knew
who this dapper but anonymous man was, so they could and did speak
their minds freely. Fifteen minutes before the start he would go
backstage through the pass door and visit every dressing-room in
turn, pop his head round the door and wish everybody good luck.
This included the small part actors and the walk-ons whose dressing-
rooms were at the top of the theatre. During the performance he
would watch the play, and even more important, the audience, from a
number of vantage points: an empty box, the back of the dress circle,
or the side of the stalls. When it finished he would quickly return
backstage and organise the curtain calls, giving instructions to the
stage manager in the prompt corner. Sometimes he would stand by
the open pass door listening to the applause and thus better able to
judge if the curtain should rise just once more. To measure the
intensity of the applause and judge when it is beginning to die away
and whether or not it justified another rise of the curtain is a highly
skilled affair, the result only of years of experience. Then round the
dressing-room, starting at the top of the theatre, for a brief word of
congratulation. He never gushed or flattered or made specific comment. Just a quiet "Good", or "Yes, nice", or, if he was particularly
pleased, "Yes, nice, *very* nice". Then down to the star dressing-room
where he would join the champagne-quaffing friends and enthuse
over his/her performance in rather greater detail.

His chosen life-style required a suitably elegant background and
base: a shared flat in Park Lane, however attractive, was not suitable,
so in the middle of the war he rented the house at 14 Lord North Street,
close to Westminster School, where John Gielgud had been educated,
and the Houses of Parliament. Early eighteenth-century houses face
each other across a picturesquely narrow street and are among the
most valuable properties in London. Because of the blitz which caused
something of a stampede out of London and reduced the value of these

houses, Binkie was able to get number fourteen very cheaply. He was taking a considerable risk. Nobody knew how long the war would last or whether the blitz would return. Big Ben, the Houses of Parliament, indeed the whole of Westminster, were high on the list of Nazi bombing targets, but the house survived without so much as a shattered window pane. Like so many of those period houses, it was larger than it looked. There was a basement, a dozen rooms spaced out over three floors, an attic and a back garden. The rooms were all rather small and although they were furnished and decorated more with an eye to comfort than beauty, the house had a charm and a cosiness which made it a great pleasure to visit. Binkie liked fitted carpets and easy, comfortable furniture. He liked bare walls where his paintings – a Dufy, a couple of Sickerts, a Max Beerbohm cartoon – could be seen to their greatest advantage. He loved blue china and the house was filled with little glass cabinets and enclosed shelves where these could be displayed, and, of course, he liked to have framed theatre posters covering every inch of the staircase walls.

Somebody once asked him what he wanted for his birthday and he said, "I love lions, give me a lion." So everybody did and soon the house was filled with lions in glass, porcelain, stitched on to cushion covers, paintings of lions, photographs of them. He even bought two massive stone lions which he placed in the back garden, guarding the back door. "When you move into a new house," he once said, "your friends will give you all the furniture and fittings you need, so don't spend too much money on them yourself. And the important thing is the windows. If they're pretty, don't curtain them but make sure they admit plenty of light." Binkie disliked central heating and always had open coal fires. As a result it tended to be very cold between November and March and was usually known amongst the Binkie circle as the Winter Palace.

A palace needs servants and here Binkie was lucky. He had three. Elvira was a middle-aged Italian, and Anna was her young niece. Jack Osborn was his chauffeur/valet and between them they kept Binkie and the house functioning smoothly. Elvira would mend his clothes, Jack would press his suits, Elvira and Anna between them did the cooking and would officiate at lunches, dinners and teas. Such a house was the perfect place for parties and Binkie gave a great many. Any excuse would serve. There were first-night parties, hundredth performance parties, end-of-run parties for plays which had been successful, musical parties at which guests were expected to sing, act, play or recite. Noël once sang from memory the entire score of *Our Miss Gibbs* a feat which, alas, was not recorded. There were parties for birthdays, Christmas, Easter and New Year. Sometimes there would be gala

parties to welcome a visiting star whom Binkie was presenting, Ingrid
Bergman, Katharine Hepburn, Mary Martin, or the Lunts. Then Lord
North Street would be *en fête* with long lines of Rolls-Royces and
Daimlers parked down the street and the guests in black ties, long
evening gowns and plenty of jewellery, all of which inspired another
nickname, Hotel Paradiso. On these occasions favoured guests and
close friends of Binkie would always make their way down to the
basement and talk to Elvira and Anna while they were cooking. This
was done on a range of antiquated gas ovens. Binkie had tried to
persuade them to allow him to modernise the kitchen with electricity
but they refused. Like Binkie, they were both traditionalists.

Binkie's behaviour at these parties where he was host was a little
unusual. He didn't circulate amongst the guests or indulge in silly,
trivial small-talk. Instead, he liked to take somebody and sit down
next to them on a sofa and talk of something solid and interesting. He
liked intelligent, serious conversation; he also enjoyed gossip as long
as it was about something. He didn't like scandal or anything unpleasant: he never said unkind, malicious things about people and
didn't like others to say them in his hearing. Later, when it became
available, he bought number fifteen, the house next door, for John
Perry. Although a connecting door was installed, it gave John the
required privacy and independence.

But a king needs more than a Buckingham Palace, he also needs a
Balmoral or a Sandringham. During and just after the war he had lived
in Dodie Smith's country retreat, Finchingfield in Essex, but when she
returned in 1951 to reclaim it, he found another one just on the Essex
border, and only ten miles from Cambridge. It was called Knotts
Fosse. Arthur Marshall was a frequent guest there: ". . . It had six
bedrooms and three bathrooms. It was a fairy tale thatched cottage and
at weekends it was always full. It had five acres of beautiful garden –
both Binkie and John were enthusiasts – and in time it sprouted a
tennis-court, a croquet lawn, a covered and heated pool and a sauna.
You never knew who were to be your fellow guests. A car would
crunch to a halt on the gravel and out would step the tall and elegant
Margaret Leighton. John Perry, after a lifetime in the theatre and no
respecter of persons, used to call her, affectionately, 'Lofty'. Or it
might be Diana Wynyard or Emlyn Williams or Adrianne Allen with
her daughter, Anna Massey. From time to time it would be the
Oliviers with Vivien, as real beauties sometimes do, looking a little
lovelier every day. One afternoon I found myself on the croquet lawn
and as a partner to Noël Coward who loved the game and wielded a
very keen mallet. Our opponents were Joyce Carey and Keith Baxter.
Noël kept up a constant rattle of encouragement and admonishment in

tones so characteristic that, if you turned your head away, it might have been one of his many imitators. If I managed to do a good shot the slightly adenoidal comment was, 'You are a complete and *utter* darling.' On the other hand, a bad shot was not very popular. 'You are a very, very silly COW!' John Perry and I were ardent tennis players and enjoyed single after single. On one occasion we had a doubles match and I partnered John Gielgud against John Perry and Ralph Richardson. At that time Gielgud, his mind elsewhere, was busy casting a play that he was to direct and it was disconcerting to hear a voice say loudly, and to nobody in particular, 'I *won't* have Martita Hunt,' or '*Why* won't Binkie let me have Pamela Brown?'"

Although Binkie did not play tennis, Emlyn Williams was known to be a dangerous player with the disconcerting habit of changing his racket from hand to hand so you never knew where to expect the ball, whereas Ralph Richardson's style was rather like that of Monsieur Hulot, serving you balls only when he was in the right position. Binkie played croquet very well, but was usually found gardening, of which he was particularly fond.

Clemence Dane was a regular visitor and very popular amongst Binkie's inner circle of friends. She could always be relied on to say something outrageous, some unintentionally lewd remark, in total ignorance of its true meaning. "Oh, the joy of waking up and seeing a row of tits outside your window," she once remarked. "My favourite meal is crabs, roast cock and Dick on toast," was another Winism, as Binkie called them, as was her famous and much-quoted comment when she descended to an open-air breakfast served on the lawn. The grass was carefully manicured, the flowers were in full bloom, the sky was blue and the garden drenched in early summer sunshine and sitting round the table were Binkie, John Perry, John Gielgud, Noël Coward, Terence Rattigan and Cecil Beaton. "Oh, it's simply too lovely," she proclaimed ecstatically, "it's just like fairyland." "No, she wasn't being funny or bitchy," Binkie would explain on the many occasions when he told the story, "she was totally innocent of any *double entendre*."

A local couple, Mr and Mrs Rogers, looked after the guests. The food would be sent down from London and unpacked from hampers and then supplemented by local shopping. Breakfast was always served and guests were encouraged to come down for it, though they didn't have to dress: pyjamas with or without a dressing-gown was acceptable. Lunch was served out of doors if the weather was fine and dinner at eight-thirty. People sunbathed, swam in the pool, lazed in the sauna – two horribly expensive additions to the sybaritic comforts of the house, installed in the fifties – went for walks into the countryside, read books and magazines or played cards. Binkie usually played bridge in the evenings with Zena Dare, Keith Baxter and Irene Browne and he was very good. But most of the time, the guests didn't do anything. They just talked and talked and always about the theatre, the one subject which everybody had in common and which never palled.

Casting was discussed, "No, I *won't* have Sonia Dreadful," which was Binkie's pet name for Sonia Dresdel, the *plus noires* of all his *bêtes*, deals were made with his occasional American visitors, "Alex, I can offer you twelve per cent and not a penny more," and plays would be read, bitched, praised and rewritten. Peter Shaffer spent a weekend after the spectacular success of his *Five Finger Exercise* and brought down his new play. On Sunday morning as he descended the staircase he heard Binkie and John Perry talking about it in the breakfast room. "You wouldn't believe it, Binkie darling, but it's set in the Andes mountains in South America and there's this Spanish army marching over them, and there's a big battle scene and they find this Inca king and all his Indians and there are blood sacrifices, and torture and mutilation and there's dozens of scene changes and a cast of hundreds . . ." There was a horrified pause and then Binkie whispered, "She's *mad.*" Needless to add, *The Royal Hunt of the Sun* (or *The Royal Cunt of the Hun*, as Binkie christened it) was politely rejected, "I'm sorry, Peter dear, but I really don't think it's *quite* right for us," and quickly passed it on to the National Theatre of whose board Binkie was a founder member.

Binkie always paid large and generous salaries to his stars and was prepared to spend the earth to get the services of a famous designer for the sets and costumes, for these were both essential expenses, but the actors in the lower ranks of the company were invariably paid the Equity minimum. He considered this a necessary and sensible economy for there is no point in spending good money where it can't be seen. He would swiftly counter any request for an increase, or any rumblings of complaint, by pointing out two unarguable truths: that they were lucky to be working at all, and they were *very* lucky, because it was such a privilege, to be working for Tennents.

There were other ways of making economies. He liked the conspiracies and scheming and politicking of the theatre above all else and his well-known deviousness was never seen to better advantage than when setting up a new production. He would approach the famous author, or his agent (or his estate if he was dead), thank him for his marvellous new play which he would be thrilled to present and then state that as it was going to be a very expensive production with all the stars which would be necessary, and because it needed to look wonderful with sets and costumes by somebody extra special, therefore he wouldn't be able to pay him his full royalty and would he settle for less? The author would usually say yes. Binkie would then speak to one of the stars he wanted: "Darling, I've got this marvellous new play with a terrific part for you but the author is being so obstinate and greedy and wants so much money that I don't think I'm going to be able to afford to pay you your usual salary." She too would settle for less. He would then phone the designer. "My dear, I'm crazy about your designs, they are just divine but I've got Isabel, Edith, Sybil, Flora, Peggy (whoever it might be) and you wouldn't believe what she wants. She's just pricing herself right out of the business, but what can you do? So I won't be able to pay you what your wonderful designs are worth . . ." By the time he'd worked this little deception on the author, designer and three or possibly four stars, he would get all of them for only a fraction of what it would cost anybody else.

It was Alexander Korda who initiated him into this game which he called 'Crying Poorhouse' and which he himself had used to great effect in the early days of London films. He was a supreme master of the game, for he had persuaded Charles Laughton to play Henry VIII in the film for nothing and only a tiny percentage of the profits. It soon became standard practice in the film world and still is, but Binkie was the first manager to use it in the theatre.

He economised too by the free gifts which firms made to the management in return for publicity. Cigarettes by Du Maurier or Abdullah, cigars by Ramon Allones, brandy by Courvoisier, whisky by Haig, chocolates by Fortnum and Mason, champagne by Bollinger, were all familiar items in the programmes and a regular supply of these would flow into the offices at the Globe. The big cupboard in Bernard Gordon's office became an Aladdin's cave of wine, spirits, cigarettes, cigars, chocolates and other items essential to the smooth running of the play. These all made useful Christmas presents for Binkie's friends and those actors in his employment whom he wished to honour and who all thought it extremely generous of him – which is just what he wanted them to think – and had no suspicion of their true origin.

Knowledge is power: like the original Eminence Grise Binkie needed to know everything and therefore employed an extensive intelligence service. He had, or contrived to plant, a friend not only in all of his own companies but in those of rival managements and every touring company of importance. It was the duty and pleasure of this friend to come to supper at regular intervals, drink lots of wine and become more and more indiscreet. The report would be made and thus by dawn Binkie would know everything which was happening in that company. Who had missed an entrance and how those on stage covered it up, who'd dried or fluffed and on which line, who had a row with whom, who was sleeping with whom, which relationships had broken up and which had been re-formed, who was queer and available and who wasn't, who had changed their agents and why, who had written a play and what had happened to it, who was looking for work from another management, who'd received an airmail letter from Los Angeles and from whom, what books the company was reading, what visitors they'd had backstage, what jokes they were telling and in which restaurants they were eating. This was in addition to the normal stage manager's report which officially gave them on a daily basis a brief and bald account of the play's progress, what time it started and what time it finished and any little incident which had occurred in the course of the evening.

"Binkie had a Mata Hari in every company," was Bobbie Andrews's description of the network. Binkie was particularly anxious to know if people had been talking about him and what they had said. When Helen Haye received a smaller sum of money in her weekly pay packet during the war she exclaimed angrily, "Oh, what can you expect from that horrible little Jewboy." This was overheard and faithfully reported back to Binkie who considered it not only racially inaccurate but deeply offensive. She never worked for him again. His appetite for apparently trivial detail was insatiable. He wanted to know what tailors or couturiers they frequented, what cigarettes they smoked, what films they'd seen on their Sunday night off. All this fascinating arcane information was securely lodged in Binkie's brain, to be drawn on when the occasion demanded.

Any misbehaviour or breach of professional regulations would elicit a short, sharp note from the office, usually signed by Bernard Gordon but always inspired by Binkie. "It has come to my attention that there is a great deal of noisy laughter in the corridors which can be heard on the stage . . . that backstage visitors before the play have stayed after the half has been called . . . that certain members of the company are arriving late at the theatre . . . that there has been whispering and laughter in the wings . . . etc. These must cease forthwith."

Constant vigilance was required to maintain the empire in a state of good repair so Binkie would make occasional and unannounced tours of inspection. Accompanied by either John Perry or John Gielgud and sometimes both he would spend an evening visiting all the theatres where his plays were being presented. Arriving unexpectedly, they would be shown by a suitably deferential theatre manager either to the back stalls if they were available or a standing place at the side if they were not. They would watch ten minutes of one, fifteen of another, sometimes more if he liked what he saw, sometimes less if he didn't. The next day little memos of approval, criticism or suggestion would be sent to the company manager.

One evening in the late fifties he looked in at the Strand Theatre where the comedy, *Sailor Beware*, was in its third year. He did not like what he saw. There was no time for a written memo so he went backstage in the interval and spoke to the company manager. His disapproval and anger were never more deadly than when he spoke quietly and without force or emphasis. The production had deteriorated badly, he said, the acting was tired and mechanical, the audience was bored and restless. Rehearsals for the whole company must be called in the morning and continue until he was satisfied. It was a *disgrace* to the West End and he was determined that no play of his should ever be seen in that condition.

"But, Mr Beaumont," exclaimed the astonished company manager, "I agree with every word you say but this is not your play."

"*Reeaallyyy?*" said Binkie thunderstruck. "Then whose is it?"

"Jack Waller's." This was a manager for whom Binkie had scant regard.

"Well . . . that explains *everything*."

Apart from his professional interest in people's lives, there was also the most devouring and passionate curiosity about everything and everybody. If you knew something which he didn't, then he wouldn't rest until he knew it also. He was always delighted to meet people from other worlds. If he was introduced to a famous jockey, a cabinet minister, a painter or a boxing champion, he would talk to them and somehow get them to talk to him. Keith Baxter remembers a young Cockney couple who, for some now forgotten reason, were brought to one of Binkie's parties. He sat with the girl on the sofa and talked to her for an hour. "That girl is *terribly* interesting and intelligent," was his verdict. "Do you know that her husband is a *house-painter*?" He then sat on the sofa with the husband for a further hour and had a long technical discussion on the subject of iron lead paints, supergloss, emulsions and undercoats. "How *charming*," said some. "How *devious*," said others, realising that Binkie probably wanted to have his house painted and saw a good way of getting it done cheaply.

Like the original Eminence Grise, he avoided publicity. His name never appeared on the playbills or in the programme, the presenting management being officially known simply as 'H. M. Tennent Ltd'.

On the letter heading his name appeared as required by law with the other directorial names but it was in the same, inconspicuous print and gave no indication of his status within the company. Until 1954 he never gave press interviews, never appeared on radio or television and while not actually forbidding people to take photographs he certainly gave no encouragement, making exceptions only in favour of old friends of tried and proven ability like Angus McBean. He was one of the lucky ones: his famous photograph carefully posed and fabricated in his studio, showed Binkie, exquisitely profiled standing above a toy theatre holding the strings of two little puppets of Emlyn Williams and Angela Baddeley in a scene from *The Winslow Boy*. The photograph was titled 'The Puppet Master'. Angus McBean remembers that permission had been sought and granted by the two actors but when he saw it Emlyn Williams did not like it. "It's not him that manipulates us but *we* who are manipulating *him*," he exclaimed. He was, of course, joking.

It was one of the first photographs of Binkie to be published (*Tatler* 1947). A few days later, Binkie received a curious letter.

Dear Mr. Beaumont,

In the excellent publicity picture of you as a Puppeteer (and so *handsome!*) the undersigned are the two puppets. We are both puzzled by two things: (a) the publicity has always been that you *avoid* publicity, and are *never* photographed. This must have been a real off day . . . but Angus can be very persuasive! (b) surely the point about puppets is that the public must not be reminded that they (the puppets) are being moved about by a Superior Person, but are acting of their own free will. Oh, you *have* let the cat out of the bag!

Would you mind if we both gave ourselves names? After much thought we have decided to be called

Emlyn and Angela.

Emlyn Williams recalled that Binkie laughed long and loud when he received it.

Eminence Grise was a description which might have been coined especially for Binkie. He liked to wear grey, dark in the winter, light in the summer. His laser-beam eyes were grey, dark or light according to his mood and temper, and the anonymity behind which he wielded his enormous power, had a grey tinge. And grey was the darkness of secrecy with which he surrounded himself. His dislike of publicity was partly due to a natural reticence which he was not able to shake off until the middle fifties, and partly the belief that he could play the Eminence Grise more effectively from behind the throne than sitting on it. Power is all the greater when its source is never seen and so low was the profile that for many years newcomers to the profession never laid eyes on him. It was little wonder that for many years his nickname within the profession was 'The Invisible Man'. There were, of course, plenty of other nicknames and most of them, curiously enough, were drawn from Russian history whose figureheads were generally thought to embody power and tyranny: Ivan the Terrible, Peter the Great and Diaghilev. Varying the pattern slightly, he was also known as a cross between Mary Rose and Shylock. The ecclesiastical similes abounded: Cardinal Richelieu was a popular one, and there were those who likened him to a Renaissance pope, all-powerful, unscrupulous and totally untrustworthy. "He's like Lucrezia and Cesare Borgia and all the other Borgias rolled into one," said one actor who crossed his path.

Even when he was at home dining with friends or visiting stars, he managed to be secretive about little unimportant things. If the telephone rang and the others were in earshot, he would never say anything which would reveal either the caller's identity or the subject of their conversation. All you would hear was Binkie's replies which were characteristically unrevealing and anonymous. "Ye-e-e-es . . . yes . . . perhaps . . . yes . . . how *interesting* . . . well, we'll have to see . . . mmmm . . . yes . . . no, I don't think so . . . well, goodbye." He would return to the table. He said nothing about the call and the others were not encouraged to enquire.

"People call me Emperor, and Czar," he said in a post-war interview, "but it's an absolute myth that I'm a Czar of the theatre. People want to believe it because one has been fairly successful over a number of years. It amuses me, of course, but it just isn't true. I don't have contact with stars. I don't control theatres. I *loathe* the word 'impresario'. I'm a theatre manager. That's much more modest. I love anonymity. I haven't the temperament to be a Cochran or a Diaghilev. If I'm standing near the box office on a first night people come and talk to you and say what you really want to hear and not what they think you ought to hear. Mind you, I enjoy arranging things. I'm not *that* retiring. I don't have any ideals and I don't want to change the theatre. I just want to delight the play-goers and to bring people together."

There were many who did not believe that he existed and that his name was a fiction behind which a large and unscrupulous team of power-hungry masterminds manipulated the Tennent empire. Vivienne Byerley, his publicity director, had the unusual task of keeping his name out of the papers and seeing that his privacy was respected which seemed, on the surface, to be a denial of all for which her office stood. She was affectionately known in the Firm as No-News-Is-Good-News-Byerley, a nickname generally attributed to Binkie's wise, witty, and waspish fellow-Welshman, Emlyn Williams, who also said, "Every Friday night Binkie pays Vivienne Byerley hush money." The press was very co-operative not, it seems, because they had any special respect for his, or anybody's, privacy but quite simply because they knew nothing about him and therefore were just not interested. That happy situation, though, was not to last long.

During the heyday he had first call on a number of the best West End theatres – Drury Lane, His Majesty's, Haymarket, Apollo, Lyric, Queen's and Globe, all these were Tennent strongholds. One play followed another without a break and it would be a very rare occurrence if another management could get in. If they did, then it would be a stopgap for a few weeks only while Binkie was waiting to bring in another play which was on tour. How did he do this? Theatre owners liked high-quality productions which made money and Binkie always delivered the goods. Also, two highly influential theatre owners, Prince Littler and Stuart Cruikshank, were on the Tennent board of directors.

If Binkie had a rival it was the Albery family. The dynasty had started in the 1860s with James Albery, the author, whose very successful play, *The Two Roses*, had not only given the young Henry Irving his first London success but had also provided the money to build three new theatres, Wyndham's, the New (now the Albery) and the Criterion. Bronson Albery, who had trained as a solicitor, served in the Royal Navy in 1914 and had been in active management since 1919, was generally regarded as a storehouse of ancient theatrical wisdom. By the time H. M. Tennent came into being Bronson was greatly respected as the Elder Statesman of the West End. He and Binkie enjoyed a very cordial and fruitful relationship. Like opposing Mafia gang bosses dividing the big city for their mutual convenience, they respected each other's boundaries and there were no territorial disputes. Albery acknowledged that Binkie had first call on his star performers and the star playwrights: there was no trespassing and no poaching. Their interests seldom clashed: both were anxious to find good commercial plays but the Albery taste was often more avant-garde.

Bronson's son Donald presented *Waiting for Godot* which Binkie would never have touched, and Graham Greene's first play, *The Living Room*, which Binkie didn't like and admitted he did not understand. Also, Donald was interested in musicals, which Binkie wasn't, and achieved a thunderous success with *Oliver*. Binkie enjoyed it but had no resentment. Once more it wasn't a Tennent show and it wasn't a Tennent cast which Albery had assembled, so he would have no interest in it.

Binkie, Bronson and Donald would meet for lunch once a month at Beoty's, an unpretentious little Greek restaurant, a few doors up from the New Theatre. Over olives, feta cheese, moussaka and Macedonian red wine they would discuss matters of mutual interest. Binkie could have any of the Albery theatres subject to availability. The Alberys knew that the plays would be good and successful. They also found reassurance in the simple fact that Binkie paid all his bills promptly. In business, he was not only honest but also punctilious.

During his heyday, he had first call on eighty of the best provincial theatres whose managers, or booking agents, were friends or colleagues, so a pre-London or post-London tour could be arranged without trouble. In the provinces as in London, they wanted good plays with stars, which would attract the public and fill the houses. Other London managers had to wait for good theatres or take second best. With ten, and sometimes as many as twelve, plays running in London simultaneously and perhaps half a dozen on tour waiting to come in, it was the closest London had experienced to a monopoly before or since.

Naturally, this aroused the fiercest feelings of jealousy from the rival managements who could not get good West End theatres or book good tours for their plays, but for two decades there was nothing they could do about it. They would admit, grumbling horribly and with great reluctance, that Binkie's plays were always superbly presented, acted, directed and designed, that they represented English theatre at its best, but this was no consolation if they were compelled to take the disaster theatres which nobody wanted, like the Playhouse (by Hungerford Bridge and rumbling with the noise of the passing trains), the Princes (now the Shaftesbury and at the wrong end of Shaftesbury Avenue), the St James's (a gem, but off the West End track), the Winter Garden (a huge echoing tomb at the wrong end of Drury Lane) and the worst of the lot, the Westminster (miles away from anywhere, tucked into a little side-street and scarcely visible from the main road which ran past Buckingham Palace).

At its peak Binkie's power and influence could only be described as frightening. It is no exaggeration to say, as was said in his lifetime, that he could make or break anybody's career if he chose. To work for Tennent's was every actor's dream. Not to work for Tennent's was social death. But to work for Tennents only once was slightly worse, for it was inevitably believed that somehow you must have blotted your copybook. Everybody stood in awe of him, many were actively frightened. "I was *terrified* of Binkie," said Stewart Granger. "Those cold grey fish-eyes bored right into yours and seemed to see through you, knowing what you were thinking and what you'd been saying. Even when he was being charming, which he always was to me, there was an air of tension. You could never really relax in his presence. It was like being a schoolboy in the presence of the headmaster."

Alexander Doré, a young actor, had reason to pay a visit to the top of the Globe. On his way out he found himself sharing the tiny lift with Binkie. Face to face, stomach to stomach, chin to chin, the proximity was a great strain for one who was already in a state of nerves. Binkie was smiling affably as his eyes flickered appreciatively up and down the young actor's neatly cut dark suit. Not a word was said as the lift creaked with crucifying slowness down to the ground. They stepped out and in silence crossed the foyer of the theatre, through the double doors and out into the street where Binkie's Rolls-Royce with uniformed chauffeur was waiting. "May I give you a lift?" asked Binkie courteously but Doré was in such a confused nervous state that he could only reply, "No, thank you, Mr Beaumont, but it's unkindly common of you." Binkie got into the car and Doré walked away and it was all of a minute before either of them realised just what had been said. Doré looked round at the departing car and Binkie sitting at the back turned round and looked through the rear window at the departing actor, both wondering . . .

With a young and passably good-looking South African actor, Art Gross, he was a little more specific. He was invited to Binkie's office and enjoyed a long and friendly discussion about the theatre and his part in Binkie's plans for the future. "In this profession if you wish to succeed you have to be *nice* to people," said Binkie in his silkiest voice. The actor asked him what he meant by being 'nice'. Binkie smiled patronisingly, "Well, if you don't know *that* you must be very naïve and innocent. You have to be *nice*. Very nice." The actor was then allowed to go, still uncertain what was meant by *nice*.

To illustrate the extraordinary power which Binkie had over the younger actors in the profession, there is a story which was frequently told in his lifetime and is securely part of the legend. A young actor auditions on the stage of the Globe and has a brief interview with Binkie in his office. Next day he receives a script of a new play which might be either Rattigan or Coward. The accompanying letter, signed by Binkie, suggests that he might be interested in playing a good supporting part which would propel into prominence the actor who was lucky enough to get it. The company would be led by a dame and a knight with designs by an artist of international renown. The actor reads the play in great excitement: it is superb and cannot fail to be a huge success. He returns to the theatre for another audition and is invited to meet the author, the dame and the knight, not in Binkie's office, but in his Lord North Street house where they make polite, enthusiastic conversation over the tinkling of exquisite teacups. It is pointed out that this invitation is a colossal honour and evidence that he is already high in Binkie's favour. The next day a letter of agreement is signed and he is asked to start rehearsals on the following Monday.

The young actor passes the week in a feverpitch of excitement and nervous tension. It all seems too good to be true but even at the last moment something might happen to prevent it. The weekend passes without incident and on the Monday morning, just as he is about to leave for the theatre, the postman arrives with a telegram. The actor almost faints with horror: obviously Binkie has had second thoughts and this is to break the news that he has been replaced by somebody better known. It would be the end of his career because nobody could live down the scandal. With trembling fingers he opens, reads it and then bursts into tears of happy relief. "What's the matter, darling?" asks his pretty young wife anxiously, and the young actor, managing to speak through his sobs, says, "It's quite all right, darling, perfectly all right, it's nothing at all, *nothing at all*, I promise you. It's just that Mother's dead."

The darker side of his nature was well known and there are plenty of hair-raising stories of his power-mania, his malice, and his ruthlessness circulated by old actors and actresses foolish or unlucky enough to cross his path. But what of the other side? What of the good things people said? "Binkie wasn't just a sinister, manipulating, Machiavellian sort of monster," says Judy Campbell, "that was just a pose. It amused him to pretend he was and it satisfied his sense of the dramatic because even though he couldn't act he had a profound sense of the theatre and this overlapped into his everyday life in all sorts of ways. Deep, deep down he was just a simple, innocent, wide-eyed boy, unsophisticated, hopelessly stage-struck, hopelessly in love with the theatre and everybody in it. He'd do anything for anybody if he really liked them." The truth, as it usually does, probably lies somewhere between these two extremes but there was no doubt of his loyalty and generosity to his employees.

Most of those who worked for him will have their own addition to the long list of unknown and unpublicised kindnesses they enjoyed from him. During the war, Anthony Quayle was engaged to Dorothy Hyson, then appearing in *Pink String and Sealing Wax*. Binkie liked her very much and went out of his way to encourage the love affair. When Quayle was on leave, he took Binkie to a little jeweller's in Duke Street, St James's, where there was on display the most beautiful diamond and ruby pendant which he wanted to buy for his fiancée, "But I can't possibly afford it," he said sadly. "How much can you afford?" enquired Binkie and Quayle told him. Binkie went inside and bought it, gave it to Quayle and refused to allow him to refund the money.

Michael Allinson, playing a waiter in *Quadrille*, was the victim of a rather tiresome practical joke. One of the actors told him that everybody in the company had received a Christmas bonus, except, apparently, Allinson. "Haven't you had yours yet?" they asked and he began to get worried. This went on for a whole day, matinée and evening performances, and it was Joyce Carey who said to the company, "You must tell him the truth before he goes home." So they did. Thus Allinson discovered that it was all a joke. Nobody knew who told Binkie or how he found out, but the next day Allinson found a letter from Binkie saying how sorry he was that by an oversight his Christmas bonus had been forgotten and enclosing two pounds. Ever-forgiving, Allinson bought a bottle of whisky and gave drinks to the whole company.

Binkie had a long list of old actors and actresses he had once employed and were now in retirement and would look after them in many unexpected ways – hampers at Christmas from Fortnum and Mason, birthday presents carefully selected by himself, discreet cheques to supplement their pensions when he heard that they were hard up and matinée tickets for all the Tennent productions. If it were at all possible in spite of age and infirmity, he would employ them, as with Nuna Davey whose speech had been rendered indistinct by a stroke. Nevertheless, he put her into the large cast of *The Visit* and arranged with Peter Brook to have her dialogue cut down to a few lines.

Brewster Mason worked for Binkie for a couple of years after the war as a contract player and then left to go to Stratford. He had bad trouble with his foot and the orthopaedic surgeon had recommended that he rest it for a year. "Of *course* you must take a year off," said Binkie, "don't worry, I'll look after you," and he did. He paid Mason a retainer of ten pounds a week for a year. Mason lived a life of total inactivity and the foot healed nicely.

"Binkie was endlessly kind," says Roger Stevens, the American producer. "If you were ill, he'd send for his doctor. If you needed to buy clothes or antiques or paintings he would personally take you to the best place. When my daughter Christobel wanted to go to

Cambridge, it was Binkie who put in a discreet word with the college authorities and got her in. When my wife and I needed a holiday in the sun he made a single phone call to Rex Harrison and the result of that was the exclusive use of his villa at Portofino for a whole month while they were away. Binkie was the master fixer of all time.''

Master Fixer was a good and accurate description of Binkie and it was one aspect of his legend which always aroused the liveliest curiosity. How did he do it? The answer was simple: he'd had plenty of experience, he was totally without shyness or inhibition when asking for favours and the fact that he was in a position to return them a hundredfold made it a lot easier.

During the war there had been an occasion when this particular skill was tested to the full. One night he received a phone call at about three in the morning. It came from an actor in his employment, an actor of great fame and distinction, a multi-faceted diamond in the Tennent crown, who was also a long-standing and close personal friend. The message was brief and alarming. The actor had been on tour with ENSA through the West Country and had been invited with some theatrical friends to a private party in the Bristol area. A party of Guardsmen from a local barracks had also been present and various forms of sexual misbehaviour had taken place, the sort which the judiciary still referred to with relish in that fine old biblical phrase as 'acts of gross and abominable indecency'. The police had raided the party, though it is not known to this day whether or not they were acting on information received. The others had managed to escape without being identified so only he and a couple of the Guardsmen were left to face the music, *allegro con fuoco fortissimo* by Tchaikovsky, Berlioz and Wagner in collaboration, he had said. It was entirely characteristic of this famous and distinguished actor that he was able to make a joke about it even at a time like that. The police had found them in circumstances that had left no possible doubt of what had occurred. Could anything be done? Binkie thought something could and leaped into immediate and effective action. A series of phone calls were made to exalted figures in Parliament, the Royal Household, the Home Office and finally the police. All these eminent men were surprised to be woken up so early in the morning but they accepted Binkie's urgent assurances that it was a crisis, a Grade A, Top Priority Emergency. If the matter were not suppressed it would be a truly horrible scandal and would do the most appalling damage: the actor's career would be ruined and the mud which the press would undoubtedly sling would hurt Binkie, hurt Tennents and affect the whole of the theatrical profession.

A deal was suggested. The actor of fame and distinction would be released at once, no charges would be preferred, his name would be erased from the charge book and other official documents and nothing would be said to the press or anybody. In exchange, Binkie offered two scapegoats who had been at the party; they could be arrested, charged and imprisoned. He pointed out that this was a form of justice very popular in the Middle and Far East where it is believed that if a crime has been committed then *somebody* must be punished but it doesn't have to be the guilty party. It doesn't matter who because justice will have been done and *seen* to be done.

Binkie's delicate and persuasive argument was convincing and the authorities agreed. One of the two scapegoats was a young actor named Tom Gill, well known for playing breezy service and Establishment types. He declared himself willing to go to prison for a year in exchange for £2,000 cash, £1,000 before and the other £1,000 afterwards, and the promise of permanent employment for the rest of his life. He wasn't news-worthy and with small newspapers as a result of wartime newsprint control, the matter was not reported. Binkie was as good as his word: the money was paid and the work flowed in whenever he wanted it. He had only to call at the office or telephone. "I took Binkie up on his promise and he always gave me a part: nothing very big or important but something," said Gill later. "But there was always such an air of embarrassment when I called on his office or met him in the street or at first nights that I eventually stopped. So I never again worked for Binkie after the war. But that was *my* decision, not his."

Gill had been sworn to secrecy but, like Binkie, he was a born gossip and chatterbox. He would tell the story to anybody in earshot while he propped up the bar at the Salisbury in St Martin's Lane, his favourite watering hole and second home. Inevitably, the news leaked out since a secret which is known to a dozen people has a limited lease of life, but it was common knowledge only within the narrow circle of the profession. It was never mentioned in the press and the identity of the famous actor (and the second scapegoat) has remained a secret.

Binkie had been not only resourceful but also fortunate in that he had the news sufficiently long in advance to give him a chance to make contingency plans, but when a similar situation cropped up in the next decade, he wasn't so lucky.

CHAPTER TWENTY-THREE

1945-7

Lady Windermere's Fan – Emlyn Williams – Richard Burton – *Oklahoma!*

1945 was the year in which a new star dropped into Binkie's lap to add richness to the Tennent empire but this time it wasn't an actor or a playwright but a designer. Cecil Beaton had never worked in the theatre but it had been his lifelong passion to do so and the chance came unexpectedly during a dinner party at Prunier's in the New Year. The hostess was Sybil, Lady Cholmondeley, formerly an actress who had managed to acquire two minor distinctions – she had created the part of Water in the original production of *The Blue Bird* and she had appeared in Peter Brook's first professional production, *The Infernal Machine*, by Cocteau at the tiny fringe theatre, the Chanticleer. The other guests included Binkie and John Gielgud. The conversation, naturally, dealt exclusively with the theatre and centred on the glories of *An Ideal Husband*, the last and arguably the finest of Rex Whistler's designs before a sniper's bullet stilled his hand and closed his eyes for ever. Even Beaton, who was prey to professional jealousy more than most of his calling, reserving a particularly spiteful malignancy for Oliver Messel, spoke with genuine enthusiasm. But then Whistler was safely dead and posed no further threat so it was not difficult to be generous.

An Ideal Husband, starring Roland Culver and Martita Hunt, had had a long run at the Westminster in 1943-4. Since Wilde's plays had been shown to be very much to the taste of the public, he toyed with the idea of reviving another. *A Woman of No Importance* was not the best Wilde, *Vera or the Nihilists* only intermittently amusing. This left *Lady Windermere's Fan*, Wilde's first big success and still a witty, well-constructed play with a powerfully dramatic last act. There were a number of good reasons why a revival would fit happily into Binkie's plans. It had not been done in the West End since the first time in 1893, it gave splendid opportunities for Binkie's production team to offer yet another example of English-Theatre-At-Its-Best, and since all the new plays of the last year had been modern and contemporary with little to please the eye, it seemed a good idea to return to a more colourful age of history and to bring back what Binkie believed to be the most elegant and beautiful of all periods – the 1890s.

Everything was decided quickly. Gielgud said he would like to direct it and when Binkie suggested Oliver Messel should be invited to design the sets and costumes, Beaton immediately volunteered his own services. "Yes," was Binkie's answer and it was as easy as that. An extended casting session took place. Beaton suggested Martita Hunt for Mrs Erlynne, the woman with a scandalous past who wishes to re-enter polite society, but Binkie shook his head. He was the first to admit that she was a superb actress and that her height, her commanding, imperious personality, her long, bony, sculpted face with its piercing eyes, made her the ideal Victorian *grande dame de scandale*, but she was notorious in the West End for being demanding and possessive, liable to make trouble by bullying the younger actresses and the stage management, to indulge in moods and displays of temperament, and to forget that there were other people on the stage with her. In short, she was *difficult*, a word which covered a multitude of sins and which, in Binkie's eyes, was a capital offence. Gielgud mentioned Isabel Jeans and Binkie was glad that he had made the suggestion because she was the ideal choice. She was the Koh-i-noor diamond in the Tennent crown and one of the three women whom Binkie loved as well as admired. She was an actress of superlative elegance and dignity: nobody could wear period costumes with such style and *chic*, looking as if she had been born in them and had never worn anything else. Her acting was a triumph of artifice over nature; watching her was like seeing a Fabergé jewelled clock working. As with Marie Tempest, you could observe the wheels moving, but they were the most beautiful wheels in the world, and to watch them in motion gave the keenest pleasure. Under the influence of Sarah Bernhardt, whom she had seen as a girl and never forgotten, she had cultivated that famous golden voice which gave a thrilling intensity to every line she uttered and lent a special glitter to the jewelled epigrams in the play of which, happily, she had the lioness's share.

Binkie wanted Rex Harrison to play Lord Darlington, who has a generous share of the epigrams – "A cynic is a man who knows the price of everything and the value of nothing". He puts the plot into motion by falling in love with Lady Windermere and persuading her to leave her philandering, unfaithful husband. But he was currently filming in *The Rake's Progress* in the Gainsborough Studios in Shepherd's Bush, playing one of those irresistibly charming scoundrels in which he specialised, and had almost committed himself to one of Binkie's ENSA tours in Germany of *French Without Tears*. Also, there was doubt if he would consider the part worthy of him now that he had achieved star status. Dennis Price was a good second choice but he was not accustomed to Gielgud's changeable and unpredictable method of directing and after a week he resigned. Finally, Binkie offered it to Griffith Jones. He was one of the most beautiful and elegant actors in the West End and Binkie admired him without reservation. He had been, and would continue to be, employed with some regularity but even though he was a fellow Welshman, he never became one of Binkie's friends, let alone part of the inner circle. "I wasn't that way inclined," was his brief explanation though a more complete one probably lay in his shyness, a reluctance to meet strangers and a distaste for social life. "Binkie did once invite me to a party in his London house," he said, "but I didn't go because I disliked parties. I still do."

Some of the casting was less easy. Lord and Lady Windermere are two exceptionally dull and lifeless characters who have nothing to do except keep the plot rolling with endless displays of outraged morality and turbulent emotion. To make them acceptable requires the handsomest performers available to ensure that the audience's eye is satisfied even if its brain is not. Geoffrey Toone and Dorothy Hyson qualified admirably. She was exquisitely pretty, he had a noble profile and sculpted features. Both could have stepped out of a Sargent painting.

Gielgud wanted Mabel Terry-Lewis to play the booming dowager, the Duchess of Berwick, and Binkie agreed. Another member of the Terry family would add lustre to an already lustrous cast: she was Gielgud's aunt, he was very fond of her and she had not worked for years, which added up to four very good reasons why she should play the part.

Cecil Beaton was a compulsive diarist who scribbled many thousands of words every day all his life, using the diary as a confessional and a friend. The diaries are factual, introspective and very revealing. Consequently, his biographer, Hugo Vickers, had the unique advantage over other historians in that he knew what his subject was doing, saying and thinking every minute of his waking life. Certainly, such an *embarras de richesse* can produce its own problems, but shortage of facts was not one of them. So posterity knows that after the party at Prunier's had finished, Beaton walked up the Haymarket with John Gielgud chattering compulsively, making a hundred suggestions about the designs; that having got permission to proceed he drove home to his country house, Ashcombe, and for three days worked without stopping, the ideas happily and easily falling into place. He remembered the gilded salons and terraces of Buckingham Palace, the corridors and reception rooms at Blenheim, the green silk walls of the Garrick Club, the fussy, overcharged upholstery of his grandparents' house, and the candy-striped silk of the first actress he ever saw at home. A week later the designs were complete and in Binkie's hands. They were superb and he accepted them without hesitation.

Only one thing tarnished the smooth development of the rehearsals. Old Mabel Terry-Lewis couldn't learn her lines and after a month of rehearsals neither Gielgud nor Binkie could turn a blind eye or a deaf ear to the fact that they had a crisis. It was old age, of course, plus the fact that she had not worked since her six months at the Globe in *They Came to a City* in 1943. Two years of unemployment can have a devastating effect on the nerves, and no less so than with an elderly actress in her seventies bearing a famous name. The Duchess is a very important part: for she has a long scene in act one full of plot-setting and comedy dialogue in act two, which could not be cut or trimmed so Gielgud had to break the news to her that she was going to be replaced, always an embarrassing matter and more so if it is your aunt you are dismissing. Her replacement was Athene Seyler, one of those delicious comediennes with a fat face, gurgling voice and slightly pop-eyes. Binkie had another reason for liking her and it was all due to an extraordinary conversation he had in his office when the engagement was confirmed and money was being discussed.

"How much do you want?" he asked.

"Oh, I don't know," she replied casually. "I'm not all that interested in money. Why don't you give me the same as last time?" Last time was during the run of *Candida* before the war, and the pound was not worth quite as much in 1945 as it had been in 1935. Binkie looked at her in amazement.

"You aren't interested in money and you aren't going to ask me for a rise?"

"No," she replied, "the money isn't that important. It's the work which matters."

Binkie smiled and blew smoke rings into the air. "This is quite amazing," he said. "You are *positively* the first actress who has declared that she isn't interested in the money and the first not to try and squeeze more out of me. Well, my dear Athene, I'm going to give you an extra ten pounds a week. How would that suit you?" It suited her very well, and she played the duchess at the Haymarket for two years at seventy pounds a week instead of sixty.

Lady Windermere's Fan started in Manchester and toured for five months before opening at the Haymarket in August. By that time not only the war in Germany had finished but also the war in Japan. Two days before they opened the atom bomb was dropped on Hiroshima, effectively putting an end to hostilities everywhere. So, for the record, *Lady Windermere's Fan* was positively the first of Binkie's post-war productions. The first-night audience included Sir George Alexander's eccentrically dressed, compulsively chattering widow, full of memories of the original production which her husband had presented at the St James's where he was actor-manager and in which he had played Lord Windermere. Also present was the author's son, Vyvyan Holland, happily drawing twelve and a half per cent of the gross receipts, for the play was still in copyright and would continue to be so for another five years.

The timing of this revival was perfect. After six years of war, Nissen huts, ARP, sandbags, gas masks, spam, fried eggs, clothes rationing, death, destruction, dreariness, discomfort and all the miseries of food shortages and the blackout, the London public was ripe and ready for a truly breathtaking visual experience. Cecil Beaton's sets and costumes were grand, extravagant and sumptuous in a manner which defies adequate description. Every set was applauded, starting with Lady Windermere's sun-drenched yellow silk boudoir and going on to the huge spacious ballroom with its chandeliers, gilded double doorways, moonlit balcony overlooking the garden, glimpses of the long carpeted corridors with the ancestral portraits and the shadows of the waltzing couples. The ball dresses of the guests whose separate entrances had been cunningly spaced out by Gielgud to give each the prominence they deserved, evoked gasps and moans of pleasure from an audience accustomed to the drab greyness of London life and mostly wearing the depressingly dull utility clothes of the war. All of which was merely a prelude to the production's visual climax when Isabel Jeans made a slow seductive entrance in act four which took her creeping stealthily from the doors upstage across miles of carpet to Lady Windermere down stage. She wore Cecil Beaton's most inspired creation, a purplish-reddish dress specially dyed to a colour he had invented which he called Flamingo Pink. It was received by the audience in the stunned, pin-dropping silence of true ecstasy. It was a moment of unique and unrepeatable theatrical magic and nobody who saw it will ever forget it.

But whatever genius is in the design it exists only as an adjunct of the play. The fourth act reveals Wilde's theatricality at its most ingenious and shows that the play-going of his early years over the previous three decades had not been wasted. He had learned two remarkably effective devices for sustaining the interest and keeping the audience in a state of nail-biting tension. One is to give the audience information which the characters in the play do not have, and the other is the use of anti-climax. In act three, the audience discovers that Mrs Erlynne is Lady Windermere's real mother, a fact unknown to Lady Windermere. In the fourth act when the two women are reconciled and Lady Windermere's preliminary hatred is turned to love and gratitude for this woman who has saved her from disgrace and scandal, the audience fully expects Mrs Erlynne to tell her and thus cement the new happy relationship. So when Mrs Erlynne makes that stately entrance it is not only the Flamingo Pink which catches the fascinated attention but also the anxiety of wondering if the long-held secret is now going to be revealed. As the two women chatter amiably like two sisters, the audience is sitting on the edge of its seats waiting for the moment of truth. They know that it will come, that it *must* come. But it doesn't. Mrs Erlynne finally leaves and the play is over with Lady Windermere condemned to spend the rest of her life in the innocent belief that her mother died when she was a baby. The plot is unresolved and the anti-climax is far more satisfying than any artificially induced strong ending.

That's how it was in 1892 and that's how it was in 1945, which clearly shows that certain basic theatrical responses do not change from one century to another. At any time in history this revival would have been acclaimed and applauded but coming after six years of war it caused a sensation. Nothing else that Binkie could have offered would have been half so worthy and suitable a tribute to the peace and the new world than this. His sense of occasion was triumphant.

Towards the end of the second year, Griffith Jones was offered the starring part in a film, *They Made Me a Fugitive*, in which he played a very sadistic gangster. Binkie was not happy about releasing him as he did not like actors to be working in the studios all day and arriving exhausted at the theatre in the evening, but Jones had a wife and two young children, Nicholas and Gemma, so he reluctantly gave his consent. Jones did his first day's film work and then arrived punctually at the theatre but as bad luck would have it the evening was disaster-prone. He made his first entrance, greeted Lady Windermere and immediately started talking about the fan which is supposedly lying on the table, "Goodness me, what a beautiful fan, where did you get it?" and as the fan is the subject of the whole opening pages of the play it is terribly important.

On that night the fan wasn't there: the stage management had forgotten to set it, so he had to improvise. "Er . . . er . . . Lady Windermere, where did you get that exquisite fan I saw outside on the hall table?" but Dorothy Hyson wasn't used to improvisation and didn't realise that the fan wasn't where it should be, so she went purple and murmured, "er . . . er . . . *What?*" Realising that he was on his own he went to the window hoping to attract the attention of the stage manager. He drew back the lace curtains but they had not been made to be moved so they just toppled down to the ground in a heap. He started to giggle. Outside the windows in the wings a brawny stage hand was standing. "Sorry, guv," he whispered, "we'll get the fan to you as soon as we've found it, honest we will, Mr Jones." So he went to the double doors of the boudoir: grasping the handles with both hands he opened them so hard and violently that one of the handles came off so he had to hide it in a nearby aspidistra bowl. Outside, he expected to see Stuart Bull, the elderly actor playing the butler, but he wasn't due to make his entrance for a couple of pages so he wasn't there. He shouted his name but forgetting it he shouted 'Protheroe' instead of 'Parker'. The only response was the backstage lavatory flushing and the sound of running footsteps.

Athene Seyler was there in the wings waiting to come on. She didn't know what was happening and she naturally assumed that Jones was either drunk or that the day's filming had exhausted him so much that he didn't know what was happening. Then the butler suddenly appeared and wheeled on the trolley containing the tea things, and there was the fan stuck right in the middle of the open tea-pot. So they were able to pick up the play, but they were all so hysterical that it wasn't easy. The following day they received a curt note from Binkie saying that he'd heard that they'd been giggling and asking them not to do it again.

It was half-way through the run of *Lady Windermere's Fan*, in 1946, that Binkie had a very rude shock. The Inland Revenue suddenly announced that Tennent Plays Ltd, previously exempt from paying Entertainment Tax and Income Tax, should now pay it. He appealed. As we have seen tax exemption had been granted four years earlier, the company having been established for charitable purposes only and to present plays of cultural and educational value, so why should he pay it? The explanation was very simple. Mr F. A. S. Gwatkin, chairman of both the Tennent companies and a greatly respected theatrical solicitor, had been responsible for drawing up the memorandum of Tennent Plays Ltd and carefully included every sort of entertainment which Binkie might want to present. One of those specified was dance halls. This turned out to be a rather unfortunate mistake and it was a curious oversight, for Gwatkin had had a great deal of experience in drawing up legal contracts. The Commissioners pounced on this and even Binkie couldn't claim that a dance hall had any cultural or educational value. He hadn't run any dance halls so far but the mere fact that he could if he chose effectively disqualified Tennent Plays Ltd from being regarded as a charity. Tennent Plays Ltd were thus forced to pay the Entertainment Tax retrospectively for the five years in which they had been in existence which meant for fifteen productions, a sum amounting to well over £15,000. Binkie was appalled. "We could go bankrupt," he suggested to Llewellyn Rees, newly appointed drama director of the Arts Council.* Rees was equally appalled at the suggestion. Binkie had to pay up. "I shall never be able to look at the Hammersmith Palais de Danse without shuddering," he said to Charles Landstone, who had been Drama Director for CEMA.

Keeping his house in order, he dissolved Tennent Plays Ltd in May 1947 and immediately formed another and entirely reputable tax-exemption company, Tennent Productions Ltd, which he took very good care to ensure had nothing to do with dance halls in its charter. This company undertook to pay off the tax liability which slightly exceeded its assets so for a time it was penniless. Binkie applied to the Arts Council for a loan to help out in this bleak period and was promised £5,000, but business started to pick up, the tax-exempt receipts started to roll in, and the £5,000 was ultimately not needed.

One of the Tennent regulars who had been unusually busy during the war was Emlyn Williams, starting in 1940 with *The Light of Heart*, the kind of play about actors and the theatre which every actor carries in his make-up box. This one was vintage: the theme was the old Shakespearean actor whose career has been ruined by drink and who now lives in squalid lodgings with his loving daughter and a small circle of camp followers. He is persuaded to make a come-back as King Lear. It is a deeply compassionate study of greatness in decline, of courage and hope under adversity and it gave to Godfrey Tearle the part of a lifetime. Angela Baddeley, one of the author's favourite actresses, played the daughter and Peter Glenville played her boy-friend. When Tearle left, Williams rewrote the part for himself but in view of the considerable age gulf between himself and Tearle, he made the part the girl's brother instead of father. It was a good idea and showed courage and enterprise but it didn't really work because although there is pathos and emotion in an elderly father being forced into retirement after a lifetime of success, there is noticeably less if it is a brother, a man of roughly her own age and with a correspondingly shorter career behind him. Emlyn Williams was the most sinister actor in England with a special talent for menace and evil but sentiment and pathos lay outside his range. It survived for 180 performances. He

---

* Following the dissolution of CEMA which had outgrown its usefulness once the war had ended, the Arts Council was formed to take its place.

enjoyed a greater success with *The Morning Star* which ran for over a year and a more modest one with *The Druid's Rest*, a charming light comedy set in a Welsh village at the turn of the century in which the seventeen-year-old Richard Burton made his London debut with the sixteen-year-old Stanley Baker, coincidentally a fellow-Welshman and also from the Valleys, as his understudy, drinking companion and life-long friend. He even found time in the midst of all this activity to adapt *A Month in the Country* which had a happy and successful run of nine months at the St James's with Michael Redgrave and Angela Baddeley who was a founder member of what could be loosely described as the Emlyn Williams Repertory Company.

Binkie was intrigued when Tyrone Guthrie breezed into his office with the script of a new play which he swore was Emlyn Williams' best. *Pen Don* was one of those plays which every author loves and cherishes as a mother does her mongol child: it was about an ancient Welsh tribe, the Lowri, attempting to find King Arthur's resting place. The title page was scattered with very Welsh names like Lowri Can Mlynedd, Bran Calon Lan, Clog, Niddle, Annwenn, Dydd a Nos Galan Mai, Mabinogion and Hengest. More suitable to an Eisteddfod than the commercial theatre, one would have thought, but Binkie was always loyal to his friend and fellow-Welshman even when his plays were not likely to have much commercial appeal, and he put it into production.

One day Guthrie whirlwinded yet again into his office bringing with him a thin, young Welsh actor with staring eyes and a rasping, astringent voice. His name was Kenneth Griffith. After forty years he retains a vivid memory of the occasion: "The two of us squashed into that famous lift and my instant impression of Binkie is that he was most beautifully tailored, very slim, handsome and good looking, and *enormously* charming. He told me that both Tony and Emlyn agreed that I should play the part because Emlyn considered that he was too old at thirty-nine, and he was thrilled to have me in his company. It was due to start rehearsals in six months. 'I wonder if I should put you under contract,' he said speculatively, 'we could use you to fill those six months.' I thought that he might ask me to be in a play I didn't like so I said, 'No, thank you. I'd much rather go back to my home in Stratford and spend the six months preparing for rehearsals, reading and studying the play and getting ready.' 'Well,' said Binkie, 'if you're absolutely sure . . .' I went home and waited for the call. After five months I had heard nothing so I phoned the office and was put through to Daphne Rye who moaned with alarm. '. . . Didn't we *tell* you? *Haven't* you heard? Surely *somebody* must have told you? . . . Well, we're not doing it.' I gathered that there had been some differences of opinion between Tony and Binkie and it had been cancelled. Daphne Rye took me out to lunch. I ordered a salad and it seemed to me that when a long pink worm crawled out of it that this was a highly appropriate piece of symbolism. A few months later I wrote a short, sharp angry letter to Binkie telling him that it was disgraceful that he should have let me down without even a letter of apology and that it was much worse that in these months of inactivity he had made no attempt to offer me work when he had already declared his unqualified admiration for my acting. I did receive a reply but I knew that this was the polite brush off. I never worked for him and I never even met him again."

Emlyn Williams finally decided that he wasn't too old to play the leading part and *Pen Don* started on a provincial tour, but even with the author starring it failed to make it to London and died a chilly death in Blackpool. "The production, just didn't work," he wrote years later, "so Binkie and I decided to shelve it and for me to rewrite it considerably. We both agreed that the play had been considerably harmed by the fact that the director simply had not understood the play. The director? Myself . . ."

Another return to his roots came with *The Wind of Heaven*, one of Williams' most striking and imaginative plays, a study of religion, mysticism and the supernatural, never far from the Welsh conscious-ness. A widely circulated joke of the time told how he walked into Binkie's office unannounced and unexpected – one of the few who had this privilege – and threw the typescript on to his desk. "I've written a play about the return of Jesus Christ," he said, "and I want twenty-five per cent of the gross." Needless to say he didn't get it: twenty-five per cent was something Binkie had never paid and never would, though he came dangerously close to it later in the decade.★ Com-pensation was found in its great success: it enjoyed a run of 268 performances and received the most gratifying attention from reps, tours and amateurs.

Then there was *Trespass*, a rather unexciting drama about a fake medium in a lonely Gothic castle, and finally *Accolade*, an intermit-tently interesting play about a famous novelist, recently knighted, whose career is threatened by a sexual scandal involving a young girl and blackmail. It was at this time that Kenneth Tynan, the *enfant plus terrible* of dramatic criticism who had just published his first book, a savage onslaught on the establishment theatre, *He Who Plays the King*,

---

★ It is only fair to state that Emlyn Williams had a different memory of this story. In his version Binkie had already read the play. When Williams entered his office he said, "I've read your new play, Emlyn, and I like it twice as much as your last," to which the author replied, "Does that mean you're going to pay twice my usual royalties?"

said, "The most startling feature of the current theatre is plays *by* Emlyn Williams, *for* Emlyn Williams and *about* Emlyn Williams." Since Williams' career had never been threatened by scandal, sexual or otherwise, and since there is no evidence that he had ever been blackmailed, this cannot refer to *Accolade* but to *The Corn is Green* which was openly and unashamedly autobiographical. He also found time to play Charles in *Blithe Spirit* on one of Binkie's ENSA tours round England and the Middle East with the beautiful and exotic Leueen McGrath as Elvira. Her part was short and funny: his part was much longer and not nearly so funny. "When people ask me what I did in the war," he later said, "I answer that I spent it fighting for laughs."

As his plays deteriorated so did the parts he wrote for himself, a not infrequent occurrence with busy actor/author/directors. Instead, he wrote superb supporting parts for others who usually contrived to steal the show with them: Gladys Henson in *Trespass*, Noel Willman as the seedy blackmailer in *Accolade* and Mervyn Johns as his twin brother in *Pen Don*.

In 1946 the chance came which every actor/author secretly wants: to play a big and important part in a play which he *hadn't* written. This was Terence Rattigan's latest, a court-room drama based on the Archer-Shee case of 1912 in which a fourteen-year-old cadet at Dartmouth Naval College was expelled for stealing a five shilling postal order. His father, convinced of the boy's innocence, hands the case to Sir Edward Carson, the leading KC of the day, who takes it to the House of Lords and finally to the High Courts where, after a delay of two years, the boy is eventually acquitted.

The Winslow Boy shows Rattigan's craftsmanship at its best: the long and complicated action is cleverly confined to a single room in the Winslow house. Emlyn Williams played the part of Sir Robert Morton, the KC, who is called in to take up the boy's case. It is not a large part, the Winslow father and daughter are much larger, but it is the sort of show-stealing part which any actor would give ten years of his life to play. He is talked about constantly throughout the first act, everything is done to stir up interest and excitement and finally, after an hour, he makes his first entrance just before the interval. Nobody who saw it will ever forget Emlyn Williams in black overcoat and white gloves walking slowly down the stage to come to rest on a chair by the footlights, a chilly, aloof, *frightening* little man slowly taking off his gloves. In the hands of a lesser actor this would be nothing, but Williams made it into a most riveting, hypnotic spectacle. He did it very slowly, finger by finger, and while he was doing it the audience was mesmerised by these fingers. Time came to a stop, nothing else in the world mattered or even existed while Sir Robert Morton was taking off his gloves. Then came the savage cross-examination of the boy.

Trial scenes are said never to fail, but they do not always succeed as enthrallingly as this. For ten pages he slowly destroys the boy and reduces him to hysteria and tears, the very picture of guilt, before the devastating curtain line said quietly and smoothly as he sweeps upstage and out, "Mr Winslow, the boy is plainly innocent. I accept the brief."

It was Binkie's favourite of all the Rattigan plays. Rattigan once said that *The Browning Version* was his passport to heaven but *The Winslow Boy* was the leather wallet which contained it. It ran for over a year at the Lyric, had a very successful season on Broadway, toured Britain and the United States, was filmed and has twice been televised. A great many talented actors have played Sir Robert but none has been able to approach the heights stormed by its creator, Emlyn Williams who, for the year in which he played it, achieved true greatness.

He and Binkie enjoyed a close, volatile and teasing friendship. They were constantly enjoying mutual hospitality and enjoyed scoring off each other. There was one occasion when he bumped into Richard Burton who was vibrating with excitement. "I've just come from Binkie Beaumont and he has asked me to play a nice little part in a new comedy. He's offering twelve pounds ten shillings a week."

"Twelve pounds ten shillings for a nice little part when you've just co-starred with Edith Evans in the film, *The Last Days of Dolwyn*. You're worth much more than that. Go back to him right away, tell him that you're getting married and that you want fifteen pounds a week." Slightly crestfallen, Burton did precisely that. "I want fifteen pounds a week, Mister Beaumont," he said in his thick Welsh accent, "I'm going to get married." Binkie looked long and hard at him, with only the faintest twinkle of amusement lightening the poker solemnity of his face. "We-e-e-ell," he said, "I see you've been talking to that Welsh pit pony." He got his fifteen pounds a week and he also got married, both events taking place within a month of each other.

Burton had been the subject of much interest and frustration at Tennents. It was in the summer of 1944 that Binkie received a summons from Nevill Coghill, now head of the OUDS, to pay a visit to Exeter College. He had been rehearsing a student production of *Measure for Measure*. The young man who was to play Angelo had been suddenly taken ill and his last-minute replacement was a student about whom Coghill was greatly excited for he showed the most splendid promise. Binkie must drop everything and come down without delay as there was to be only the one performance. Binkie did just that and his trouble and time were amply rewarded. The student turned out to be Richard Burton whom he hadn't seen since his brief appearance in *The Druid's Rest* six months earlier. He was still uncouth, surly, withdrawn, technically maladroit and vocally monotonous . . . *but*, and it was a very big 'but', there was something about him which riveted Binkie's attention and made it difficult for him to look at anybody else.

Afterwards Coghill gave a party for the company in his rooms and Binkie was invited. Binkie met Burton virtually for the first time, for on the opening night of *The Druid's Rest* it had been a quick good luck wish as he passed through the dressing-rooms. Binkie took in the unkempt student clothes with a practised eye. He realised that the boy did indeed show exceptional promise and if he privately thought that Coghill's assessment of him as a genius who would one day be a great actor, a successor to Laurence Olivier, was a trifle exaggerated, there was no doubt that there was an unusual talent on display. What was it, he was to ask himself endlessly in years to come? Sexual magnetism? Naked ambition? A profound inner fire which consumed everything it touched? Or was it that mystical quality which it seemed only Welsh actors possessed? Whatever it was Binkie knew that it couldn't be allowed to get away. Years later, Burton was to remember the conversation and to retell it with an uncommonly accurate imitation of Binkie's silken voice.

"What are your plans when you are demobbed from the RAF, Mr Burton?" he asked politely. "Do you wish to become a professional actor?"

"I really don't know, Mis-ter Beau-mont," Burton replied, turning on his thickest Welsh accent in the naïve hope that he might disconcert this smooth, elegant gentleman from London. "I might and again I might not. I'm not sure. It depends on how things turn out. I might go back to the mines. That's where I really belong."

Binkie was not disconcerted. "I would say that where you really belong is the theatre. However, it's your decision. But if you decide to turn professional, please contact me at the Globe Theatre. I might be able to help you."

Nevill Coghill had left Burton in no doubt of Binkie's exalted position in the theatre and had tried to impress on him the great honour which had been done. Others had tried to warn him of Binkie's reputation: devious, secretive, sexually ambiguous and dangerous to offend. But Burton was not impressed. He could take care of himself.

Three years later at the end of 1947 having made his first appearances on radio and television – no surprise that they were all in plays by Emlyn Williams – and having decided that there was more money in the theatre than in the coal mines, he took up Binkie's offer. He met him again in the office and was introduced to the Tennent triumvirate, John Perry, Bernard Gordon and Daphne Rye. All were impressed and Binkie offered him the standard Tennent agreement at ten pounds a week and valid for one year. Like all unusual talents he was difficult to cast. Binkie tried him out in an Irish country house play, *Castle Anna*, but his brief and undistinguished part of a local doctor attracted no attention. Binkie sent him on tour with *Dark Summer* but in the absence of its London star, Joan Miller, it had little attraction for the provincial public and soon died a chilly death. Once again, nobody noticed Burton. He walked on as an Arab in a revival of *Captain Brassbound's Conversion* with Flora Robson and Richard Leech at the Lyric, Hammersmith, but its author refused Binkie permission to transfer it to the West End. Shaw had become totally paranoic about money since he found himself in the super-tax class and was convinced that he would soon be penniless. Binkie made a special journey to Ayot St Lawrence to plead with him and try to knock a little bit of financial sense into him, but it was useless. Shaw was adamant. "Another success would ruin me," he said.

One day Binkie and Daphne had a serious talk about Burton's future. "What can we do with him, Daphne dear?" he asked plaintively. "There must be *something* which suits him." Binkie sent him to the St James's Theatre where Peter Glenville, now a full-time director, was casting Terence Rattigan's latest play, an epic about Alexander the Great, titled *Adventure Story*. It was to star the young and promising Paul Scofield. Glenville was impressed by Burton and cast him as Alexander's friend and supporter, Hephaestion, but after a couple of rehearsals the part was taken away. Glenville swore to Binkie that it was nothing to do with his acting but his height. The way Rattigan had written the play, it was necessary for Alexander to be shorter than Hephaestion and Scofield was several inches taller. But he later admitted that there was the matter of Burton's personality. Hephaestion had to be self-effacing and diffident, Horatio to Alexander's Hamlet, and there was nothing remotely self-effacing or diffident in Burton who contrived to bring an aura of danger and brooding authority even when he wasn't doing anything.

Being sacked from *Adventure Story* hurt him beyond all measure and it nearly happened a second time when Binkie sent him to the auditions for Christopher Fry's *The Lady's Not for Burning* which Gielgud was to direct. Burton's audition was so bad, inaudible, stumbling and confused, that he nearly lost the part but Binkie quietly suggested to Gielgud that it was nerves and that he should be given a second chance. Burton owed more than he realised to Binkie's perception: he got the part and on the first night started, at last, to live up to his promise. That audience witnessed an amazing phenomenon. Here was an unknown young actor who had no visible attraction or graces: his body thick and clumsy, his movement awkward, his voice monotonous, his face flat and round like a ploughboy with no distinguishing features except two large widely-spaced eyes. No acting skills were visible, he seemed to do nothing but yet he managed to make such a strong impression that there were those who said that he actually stole the play. If he did, then it was larceny on a grand scale for the others included John Gielgud, Pamela Brown, Harcourt Williams, Peter Bull, Esmé Percy, Eliot Makeham, Richard Leech and Claire Bloom. In one scene Gielgud and Pamela Brown had a face-to-face confrontation in the middle of the front stage. A long way behind, Burton was on his knees scrubbing the floor. His behaviour was scrupulously correct, he did not do anything which hadn't been directed, there was nothing to distract the attention, his occasional brief lines were expertly timed and quietly delivered. And yet the audience ignored the two stars and looked only at Burton, watching him carefully, wondering what he was going to do and say next. "It's sheer star magnetism," said Binkie excitedly at the party afterwards, "hypnosis at its crudest and fiercest." This assessment was fully borne out by the critics who were not slow to hail him as an outstanding newcomer to the West End and a future star.

Another Christopher Fry play seemed to be called for and one suddenly appeared. *The Boy with a Cart* about a young peasant who pushes his mother in a small cart across England, builds a church and becomes a saint. It had been performed only by amateur companies and this was its professional début. Burton played this for a month at the Lyric, Hammersmith and Binkie was pleased to note signs of improvement. Acting with Gielgud had rubbed off some of his rough edges. There was an added delicacy and refinement, some of his natural charm and humour was starting to surface.

Binkie had recently been invited to sit on the board of governors at the Stratford Memorial Theatre. The position was unpaid and gave him no official authority in choosing the plays and casting, such being the responsibility of the administration, but his influence could be felt in every department. His first gesture was to invite Anthony Quayle, the artistic director, to Hammersmith to see *The Boy with a Cart*. Quayle was planning something very special for the Festival of Britain, the 1951 season: a cycle of four history plays, including *Henry IV* parts 1 and 2 and *Henry V*. He was looking for a young actor with the authority to play Prince Hal in the first and Henry V in the second. When he saw Burton as St Cuthman, he knew he had found him. He engaged him without benefit of an audition. Burton accepted instantly and during the 1951 season proceeded to repay Binkie's faith by making himself the most exciting and talked-about actor in England.

Years later Binkie summed him up. "Dear Richard, he was such a dear *sweet* boy, really quite *gorgeous* but although nature had given him so much, she had also given him so little. He had this amazing magnetism and personality but very little acting ability to back it up and one is no use without the other. And he never learned. He didn't want to learn. I used to say to him, 'Richard, dear, you've got something absolutely unique and you must work on it, develop it,' and he used to say, 'Binkie, old love, if I work on it, whatever *it* is, I shall lose it.' He wanted Larry and John and Alec to admire him and he wanted their respect but he never did anything to earn it. So he never developed. And then he sold out to Hollywood and started all that drinking. I've tried to tempt him back to the West End but he turns down all my offers. Oh, it's so *sad*!"

Now that the war had finished, the traffic started up again, slowly at first and then increasing in momentum. Binkie's first ever trip to America took place in 1946 when he and Rattigan flew to New York to see the Lunts' triumphal opening in *Love in Idleness* (inexplicably and unnecessarily retitled *Oh Mistress Mine*) at the Empire Theatre. They were received by their ever-loving Broadway supporters as if they were conquering heroes who had won the war singlehanded and it was amazing, thought Binkie, that they were not also given a ticker-tape procession down Fifth Avenue like General MacArthur. The play ran for eighteen months on Broadway and three and a half years on tour, a lucrative five years which made a great deal of money for everybody, including H. M. Tennent.

He was in New York for only twelve days but he managed to see everything of importance, including Thornton Wilder's *Our Town*. He was deeply impressed by its charm and simplicity and made immediate arrangements to present it in London to be directed by its Broadway producer, Jed Harris. Here was a monster who made Basil Dean look and sound like a turtle dove; like Dean he was a genius who could make a bad play look good and a good play look like a masterpiece. All Binkie's Broadway friends told him the Harris atrocity stories and warned him most urgently to have nothing to do with him, but Binkie had had this experience many times before. "I never listen to gossip," he said firmly, "I always judge people as I find them. If what you say turns out to be true, I shall send Mr Harris home without pay, but let us not be *prejudiced*."

Harris lost no time in proving that all the stories were true. It turned out that he was a manic-depressive, a schizophrenic, a paranoic and an alcoholic. He took a great hate to London, to Binkie, to the New Theatre and to the cast, lovingly assembled by Binkie for the London run. He solved the problem by staying away from rehearsals, leaving the stage manager and the author's wife, Isobel Wilder, to take charge and see the play to its first night. Faced with a badly demoralised company, Binkie had no alternative but to bar him from the theatre and send him a polite note of dismissal, but by that time Harris was already on the *Queen Mary* sailing back to America, sulking horribly and vowing a hideous vengeance on Binkie and the English theatre. For the company there was an indescribable relief in his absence. No more would they have to endure those cold eyes, that rasping voice, that torrent of insults, sarcasm and abuse. But the black mark seemed to be on the play, or maybe Harris, calling on the gods of Jehovah, had put a curse on it. *Our Town* received tepid notices, respectful applause from the first-night audience and a run of only thirty-one performances.

In the meantime the Theatre Royal, Drury Lane, had been repaired and re-opened after its wartime hibernation and the extensive bomb damage which had taken it off the map for six years. The gala opening of England's oldest and most famous theatre needed something special and it was Binkie who suggested to Prince Littler, whose company owned the building, that Noël Coward should be invited to write a new musical for the occasion. This was partly a gesture of patriotism and partly good theatrical sense, for *Cavalcade* and *Bitter Sweet* had been two of the greatest successes of the thirties and there was no reason to suppose that Coward's extraordinary gifts for the musical theatre, inactive for fifteen years, should not surface and flourish. The result was *Pacific 1860*. It had charm, a handful of good tunes, a couple of witty patter songs, some ravishing crinolines designed by Gladys Calthrop – all that and Mary Martin too, making her London début. Unhappily, it failed lamentably to rise to the occasion. It seemed tepid, second-hand and derivative: it showed beyond doubt that Coward still belonged to the twenties and thirties and was completely out of touch with the contemporary theatre. It didn't die a quick death but lingered on for a disappointing four months. "They've come to see the theatre," said Binkie acidly, "not the show." Before the war it would have been a success but now after six years the public wanted stronger meat. They got it with *Oklahoma!*

The story of *Oklahoma!*'s passage from Broadway to Drury Lane turned out to be a chapter of bizarre and inexplicable accidents. "You'd think it was *Macbeth* the way things just piled up," said Binkie. "It was the most complicated thing I've ever had to do." The disasters

Seagulls Over Sorrento: with Nigel Stock, Ronald Shiner and Bernard Lee.

Edith Evans and Cecil Parker in *Robert's Wife.*

Celia Johnson and Margaret Rutherford in *Rebecca.*

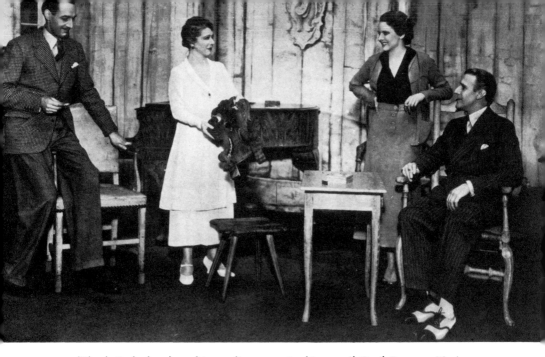

'Thank God, there's nothing to live up to in this room!' Cecil Ramage, Marie
Tempest, Ann Todd and Ivan Samson in *When Ladies Meet*.

Owen Nares and his son Geoffrey
in *Call It a Day*.

Gertrude Lawrence and Douglas Fairbanks Jr in *Moonlight is Silver*.

BELOW: Two productions of *A Streetcar Named Desire*. LEFT: Arletty and Jean Marais; RIGHT: Vivien Leigh and Bernard Braden.

Isabel Jeans in *Lady Windermere's Fan* with sumptuous sets by Cecil Beaton.

started with the ship due to carry both company and costumes catching fire in New York harbour. The two controllers of the Theatre Guild, Lawrence Langner and Jerome Whyte, with the costumes, transferred to the *Queen Elizabeth* which promptly ran into a sandbank. The company came by a number of different ships and planes at a time when any form of transport was exceedingly difficult to arrange. The six principals, including Howard Keel, the star, were travelling on a wartime freighter.

Every day, every hour, urgent phone calls and telegrams arrived at the Globe Theatre. The Customs had discovered that the dresses and costumes were unfinished and put them in bond, causing more delays. The Home Office stated that the company were all Unregistered Aliens because the Theatre Guild had neglected to arrange work permits. The Ministry of Food discovered that they did not have ration books. Binkie arranged for police, Customs and Food officials to travel to Manchester and deal with the necessary formalities on the spot while the company was in rehearsal. There was trouble over salaries which had been calculated in dollars and every week the equivalent in sterling had to be worked out afresh at a time of great financial fluctuation. Then it was Equity's turn to make trouble and threaten to cancel the show since none of the imported Americans were members, but Binkie, using all his charm and diplomacy, persuaded them to make special arrangements and give them temporary membership for the run of the show.

Binkie pointed out to the press that this was the first time in history that a Drury Lane musical had opened in Manchester and that everything was ready for the first night at the Opera House except for one little thing: Howard Keel and the five other principals were still somewhere in the Atlantic Ocean in their freighter. Nobody knew exactly where, but after keeping the telephone lines to the Admiralty open all day, the freighter was located just north of Dungeness. Binkie chartered a tug, lifted the principals off the ship, hired a fleet of fast cars with police escort – which thrilled the visiting Americans so much that the first night was something of an anti-climax – extracted some special petrol rations and rushed everybody up to Manchester. They arrived at the stage door with literally no more than forty-five minutes to spare, time enough to wash, make-up, change and get on to the stage for the performance. But since they had rehearsed in New York and on the freighter, they knew the play inside out.

After all that excitement, the official opening at Drury Lane on April 30th 1947 might have seemed just routine but of course it was not. The pulsating energy of the dancing, the musical splendour which seemed to guarantee that every number would be a smash-hit and nearly became so, the visual splendour of those sets and costumes dazzling in their colourful simplicity, all combined to make it a devastating experience. There had been such a strict clampdown on all performances and sales of the music that none of it had been heard in advance, so each glorious tune burst like a royal fireworks gala on a rapturous and unsuspecting public. At the end the audience, hysterical with delight, stayed to cheer and scream. The cast had to give endless encores, the audience simply would not let them go. The ecstasy lasted for forty-two minutes by Binkie's stop-watch. It was one of those evenings.

CHAPTER TWENTY-FOUR

1947

Peace in Our Time – Traveller's Joy

The Tennent empire used to be likened to the Royal Enclosure at Ascot: it was lovely if you had a member's ticket but it was a bit chilly if you didn't. Predictably, this situation aroused the strongest feelings of hatred and jealousy from those who were excluded and the most malicious reasons were put forward. "Of course, old boy, you had to be queer to work for Binkie, which is why I never did," disgruntled old actors used to say. "I wasn't going to put up with any nonsense like *that*. If Binkie didn't fancy you then you were bloody well out." At this very moment in time there are probably hundreds of disgruntled old actors propping up the bar in pub and club who will swear to the truth of this. Since this rumour was circulated widely in his lifetime and was generally believed, it is worth while considering.

Similar rumours about the private tastes and public preferences of famous theatrical managers abound. It was supposed that you had to be good at sports and especially play a good game of rugby and cricket if you wanted to work with Sir Frank Benson, and there is a true story of the young actor who received a telegram from Sir Frank, "CAN YOU PLAY RUGBY?" which just happens to be the name of the servant in *The Merry Wives of Windsor*. The young actor sent his reply instantly: "YES AND CRICKET TOO". Sir Gerald du Maurier, an ex-Harrovian, was supposed to employ only public schoolboys, with a special preference for ex-Harrovians (ex-Etonians were acceptable but only just). Cricket and a good war record with a show of medals were supposed to be important qualifications for Stratford in the early 1950s and to get in with Joan Littlewood in her years of glory you were advised not only to be working class but communist.

In no case were these rumours entirely true but actors would believe them and behaved accordingly. Potential Bensonians would talk of the tries they'd scored, not the parts they'd played, and would make sure they had rugby photos and trophies to show. Actors would wear an Harrovian tie when meeting Sir Gerald and they would put on filthy jeans, sweat shirt, gym shoes or boots, speak with a thick

Cockney accent and carry the *Morning Star* when auditioning for Joan Littlewood. Their efforts would not have been entirely wasted but it would have been foolish to have placed too much reliance on social, sporting or political qualifications. To be communist, middle-class, good at games or noticeably virile would certainly have been a help to employment, but never a substitute for talent.

So it was with Binkie. It is known that heterosexual actors sometimes camped it up a bit and said nothing about their wives and children in the hope of getting the job, and there is an ancient joke which has Binkie asking a young actor if he was queer. "No, Mr Beaumont," he replies in great embarrassment, "b-b-but I can assure you, I c-c-c-can faithfully promise you that it d-d-d-doesn't show from the f-f-f-front."

The idea that he employed only homosexuals is not only untrue but ludicrous as even the briefest glimpse at his programmes will show. He was a shrewd and intelligent man: he worshipped talent above all else and he had very high artistic standards. He would never have employed a bad actor merely because he fancied him: there was a lot of money and prestige at stake in every new production and it was unthinkable that he would knowingly have spoiled his beautiful ship for a pennyworth of pouffery. Of course, homosexual actors were employed but they had to be good, very good and right for the part. But the belief in a homosexual freemasonry dies hard and disgruntled actors gave and still give it as the reason for their exclusion from the Tennent enclosure. Alas, the truth is one which the old actor is unwilling to face and would be horrified to learn: that Binkie didn't think he was a good actor. Or he didn't like him. Or thought he was a bore. Or he had unwittingly offended Binkie in some mysterious way.

Binkie employed a great many heterosexual actors, but if they had conservative views on sexual deviation they had to keep them to themselves. Binkie wasn't happy if he heard that an actor had spoken against him or disapproved of him. He wasn't happy if he even *imagined* disapproval for this was one point on which he was very sensitive. This was perhaps why he was never on such easy, relaxed terms with the heterosexual male stars. It must be remembered that this was the forties and fifties when not only was homosexuality illegal, but the majority of public opinion condemned it without reservation. Admittedly, there was more friendly acceptance in the carefree and permissive world of the theatre than there would have been if he had been the manager of the Midland Bank or the chairman of Shell Oil, but many of the leading actors came from public schools, had served as officers in the war and brought the prejudices of their class with them into the profession.

The heterosexual actors may have been on outwardly friendly terms with him but Binkie, like so many members of a persecuted minority, was not slow to imagine hostility and to avoid it. Few of them figured in his social life outside the first-night parties and rehearsal lunches. Few were invited to Lord North Street or Knotts Fosse. "He was always exceedingly polite to me," said Barry Morse remembering the three years when he was in *There Shall Be No Night* at the Aldwych during the war. "He would enquire after my wife and three children with great enthusiasm, but there was always a slightly fulsome, over-eager note in his voice as he did it. I got the distinct feeling that he was rather nervous of me. But there was never any nonsense or hint of it. In a rather odd way he always kept his distance."

It was the heterosexual managers who unashamedly allowed sex to influence their artistic decisions. Charles Cochran was well known to be a voracious womaniser and any young girl who caught his eye would be invited to a special audition in his office where a large and very comfortable sofa had been installed behind his desk. This was the casting-couch and it is quite possible that the phrase started there. Coition preceded casting and contract and everybody was happy. Everybody knew about it and Cochran was not loved any the less because of it. Basil Dean always managed to sneak his current girlfriend or two into the cast of any play he was presenting: none of them appears to have had any talent, but in a large cast, as plays tended to have in the twenties and thirties, they could appear virtually unnoticed. In any case Dean had a special talent for getting performances out of unpromising material. All this was common knowledge and Dean was not disliked any the less because of it.

Respectability was of prime importance, for Binkie, like Caesar's wife, had to be above suspicion. This is why he liked to employ heterosexuals in the office to look after the administration, Bill Conway, Barney Gordon, Tony Chardet, and why he had heterosexual actors only under annual contract, Richard Leech, Brewster Mason, Bryan Forbes, Richard Burton, Richard Bebb Williams, John Bennett, to name only six. But not the good-looking, charming, talented young actors whose private lives, he suspected, were not entirely orthodox. Derek Aylward was a good example. Binkie had cast him in an ENSA production of *Blithe Spirit* which toured the army camps and garrison theatres and noted that both his performance and his behaviour were good. Three years later he remembered this likeable, handsome young actor when he was casting *Peace in Our Time*, Noël Coward's first post-war play. Derek was asked to audition for the part of Stevie, the Cockney son of the publican and his wife who jointly own the East End pub where the action takes place. His audition was excellent: he was short-listed, recalled once, twice and then told finally that he had got the part. He was called down into the stalls and there Binkie introduced him to Noël Coward. "Very good, Derek," said Binkie, warmly, "we thought you did the Cockney accent *terribly* well, and it's all the more creditable because you're so well-spoken in private life. I do like my actors to be versatile."

"You remind me a little of Bert," said Noël.

"Bert?"

"My manservant. Chauffeur. Butler. Valet. He came with me on my tour of South Africa during the war. He is as Cockney as a pork pie and a pint of bitter. A dear, *dear* boy."

He was to be paid fifteen pounds a week. Binkie apologised for this but he explained that the play had a very large cast, over twenty-five, and he couldn't afford to pay any more for what was only a small part. He further pointed out that this was good money for a young actor playing his first West End part and particularly when it is a new Noël Coward play, directed by the author and presented by H. M. Tennent in all its collective glory, thus guaranteeing the greatest possible prestige and public attention.

All went smoothly for the first week but at the beginning of the second the axe fell. Derek received a summons to Binkie's office. He and Noël Coward were there both looking like hanging judges. Binkie, who hated shilly-shallying, came straight to the point.

"Sorry, my dear, I hate doing this to an actor but I'm afraid, I'm *very* much afraid that it's not going to work. That's so, isn't it, Noël dear?"

"It's not quite what we want. All my fault, of course."

"You see, you've got the accent very well indeed. Very convincing," said Binkie smoothly.

". . . If it was a radio play," said Coward, "I'd be delighted . . ."

"But it's not quite enough. Everything about you is irretrievably middle-class."

"You're a gentleman, dear boy," said Coward. "A gentleman to your finger tips and that's something no actor can conceal. The way you walk, the way you talk, the way you stand, your face, all at odds with the accent."

"Which, we repeat, is very good," said Binkie.

"Is this the sack?" whispered Derek. There was a turmoil in his stomach, his knees felt faint and he had a strong desire to go somewhere and be sick. To be sacked by Binkie was theatrical death, for assuredly, once the news got out, he could never work in the West End again. He could already hear the loud voices and the false sympathy of his friends in the local pub, he could see the head-shaking of his agent and the tears of his parents. Perhaps he should emigrate to Australia,

South Africa, Canada, Brazil, anywhere in the world where he could lie low and be totally forgotten.

"Sack? Goodness no, don't be silly," laughed Binkie, "you're far too good an actor, we don't want to let you go. We want you to stay and play Mike. Of course, it's not such a good part, much smaller and not nearly so interesting but we'd also like you to understudy Stevie. Noël has found a young actor called Alan Badel, so *clever*, just out of the army like you. But he's a natural born Cockney.★ We'll pay you the same money, fifteen pounds, but please don't tell anybody about that or they'll get jealous and then their agents will start writing peevish, silly letters and that would be so *tiresome*, wouldn't it?"

Derek nodded and mopped his brow with a silk handkerchief, a recent acquisition from Turnbull and Asser bought to celebrate the job a week ago. Binkie, he had discovered, bought his shirts and ties there, and there was never any harm in a little diplomatic imitation. Binkie noticed this and smiled in genuine sympathy and friendliness. "Have a cigarette and a drink, my dear, you look as if you needed it." Derek did. He took one of Binkie's special Craven A, inhaled its delicious aroma, and sipped the glass of brandy which Noël placed in his trembling fingers. He felt a strong inclination to go away and cry. Cry with relief.

During the next two weeks he watched Badel's performance with interest not unmixed with envy. Badel caught the exact flavour of the accent and seemed to fit into the pub atmosphere without apparent effort. Badel, he was reluctantly forced to admit, was quite simply a much better actor. One day in the third week Coward took him aside during the lunch hour. "You've behaved very well over all this, dear boy. I'm grateful to you and so is Binkie. Always take your disappointments bravely. No tears, no fuss, no rows or sulks or bitterness. Take it cheerfully. Always be cheerful. That is true professionalism. Nothing kills a career more speedily than bitterness and self-pity. Better to be a bad actor than like that. Binkie will remember this in the future, I promise you."

They rehearsed in the Piccadilly Theatre. It had been badly bombed and had not yet been repaired. When the weather was wet, the rain fell through on to the floor. "Oh dear, oh dear," said Noël one day when it was particularly bad, "even God doesn't like us."

Peace in Our Time had a rapturous opening on July 22nd 1947 at the Lyric and a very mixed press ranging from unqualified praise from the *Daily Telegraph* to unqualified abuse from *The Times*. It was one of Noël Coward's darker plays, the first since *This Happy Breed*. No

★ Binkie was wrong. Badel was half-French and born in Manchester.

dressing-gowns, no champagne, no witticisms. It was a dramatic and intensely serious picture of London life as it would have been if Hitler had won the war. It was set in a West End pub which Coward considered to be a microcosm of London life, a centre point, the place where the classes could meet and mingle with something approaching equality. The mood was, for Coward, one of unusual savagery and violence, a story, painfully familiar all over Europe, of tyranny and treachery, of firing squads, moonlight arrests, torture and sudden death, of selfless heroism, of resistance, mortal danger and final victory.

Coward had been greatly irritated by the complacency of the country in accepting its victory as a matter of divine right and wished to show the public how very nearly the war had been lost. Only that narrow strip of water between Dover and Calais and the colossal good fortune of Winston Churchill's leadership had prevented his fiction from becoming a horrible reality. Coward did not wish to flatter the public by giving it a comfortable or reassuring play, but the truth as he saw it. His stage craft was superb. Nothing in the title or in the carefully controlled advance publicity prepared the public for what it was going to see and the entire company was bound to strict secrecy.

The play opened during the normal lunch-hour trade in the pub with Bernard Lee and Beatrice Varley as the publican and wife dispensing their usual good cheer to their regular customers who included Kenneth More. The radio is turned on and the one o'clock news is heard. The chimes of Big Ben strike a note of normality. "Funny you can still hear the chimes of Big Ben these days," says the wife and suddenly the audience is intrigued by this odd remark – why should it be funny? The news continues. "Herr Hitler, Field-Marshal Goering and Doctor Goebbels will attend a luncheon party at Buckingham Palace given by the King and Queen before driving with them to address the House of Commons . . ." and the lights slowly fade and that is the end of the first scene.

Binkie kept his reservations about the play to himself in the light of Coward's enthusiasm – "My best play yet, dear boy, the best I've ever written" – for who was he to question the Master's judgement? The houses were full for the first month but then business began to diminish and the receipts became alarmingly smaller. It seemed that Binkie was right. Maybe the timing was wrong. Maybe it was too soon after the war. Maybe the unpleasant terrors which Coward wanted to show were too painfully close to the truth. Maybe the Establishment felt under attack and that this was its devious way of hitting back. Royalty statements whose message became increasingly depressing were sent to America where Coward was supervising a revival of *Tonight at Eight Thirty* with his beloved Graham Payn and even more beloved Gertie Lawrence. Finally it was the notice. It had been six months. Not exactly a failure but certainly not the sort of success which Coward expected. Binkie shrugged his elegant shoulders and lit another Craven A. He'd given the play everything he could and if the public failed to respond that was not his fault. Perhaps Noël's next play would be a comedy. That's what Binkie liked, what the public wanted and what Noël did best. Unhappily, Coward was becoming rapidly disenchanted with the critics' habit of inflicting a routine savaging every time he wrote anything new. Revivals of his old successes were fine as long as he starred in them, as the recent revival of *Present Laughter* at the Haymarket had shown. Noël Coward as actor and personality had lost nothing of his magnetism and popularity. It had played to three months' capacity and Coward had left in obedience to his fixed rule never to play in anything for any longer to avoid the tedium of the long run. He had been replaced by Hugh Sinclair.

Binkie's enemies always pointed out that he never forgot an injury. His friends could say with equal truth that he never forgot a favour as Derek Aylward was to learn very much to his advantage. Noël Coward had been an accurate prophet. Binkie did remember his courteous and sensible behaviour over his demotion in *Peace in Our Time* and when *Traveller's Joy*, a delicious farce by Arthur Macrae about the problems of being literally penniless in an expensive foreign hotel when you have exhausted your travel allowance, was ready for casting in 1948, he offered Derek the part of Nicholas Rafferty, the heroine's young friend. It was not much of a part but it was a distinct improvement on the previous brief appearance in *Peace in Our Time* and it was in the company of nine others instead of twenty-one so he would get proportionately more attention and prominence. It was a mark of Binkie's increasing regard that he was sent a script and not required to audition. The part was his if he wanted it. He did want it and telephoned Binkie without delay to confirm the fact. Rather to his surprise, and yet another indication of his rising status in the Tennent empire, he was not kept waiting or asked to phone another time. He was put through without delay.

"I can only offer you twenty pounds a week," said Binkie firmly.

"Oh come on now, Binkie dear, is *that* the best you can manage?"

"It's very good money and it's certainly the most I would pay for a small part like that."

There was a pause from Derek. "Not pounds, Binkie dear, make it guineas and I'll say yes."

"Why guineas?"

"It's the difference between being treated as a gentleman and being treated like a tradesman. Sheridan said that to Charles James Fox after the first performance of *The School for Scandal*, and I've always thought it a neatly phrased sentence."

It was a further sign of Derek's increasing status that Binkie was more amused than offended by this delicate impertinence and the fact that it was a quotation from Sheridan made a further appeal. He conceded victory to the actor and paid him in guineas, the first and only time in his life he did this. From then on, he always referred to Derek Aylward as the Guinea Actor.

Traveller's Joy opened to a rapturously enthusiastic audience at the Criterion which did not surprise anybody as it was witty, charming and neatly constructed. It displayed Yvonne Arnaud at her most radiant and Charles Victor at his driest, as the stranded couple, Dora Bryan at her funniest as the humourless Swedish maid and Alexander Gauge at his heaviest as the Treasury official who threatens to bring the whole affair to an unhappy conclusion. It elicited unqualified praise from the press and once it was clear that it was going to run for ever, Derek embarked on a series of Binkie teases. He did not dislike him but on the other hand he did not particularly like him. "Binkie was cold, aloof and just a touch pompous. You hardly ever saw him. After it opened he never came backstage to see you unless you were the star, in which case he was in and out of your dressing-room all the time. If you passed him in the street and said 'Good morning' he would look at you vaguely as if to say, 'I seem to know this young actor, I suppose he's working for me somewhere,' but half the time he just wouldn't recognise you. I was never invited to his house in Lord North Street or any of his weekend parties. I wasn't part of the Inner Circle and we were never in any way lovers. I just wasn't his type. There was a sort of self-importance he carried around with him which I suppose comes from having too much power, and it slightly irritated me. I wanted to bring him down a peg or two if I could. Silly, but there you are."

Ways of doing this, of gently harassing Binkie, were varied and ingenious. Derek had a plaster cast made of his penis which was, he liked to think, unusually large, and put it in his dressing-room to *épater* such *bourgeois* as had the temerity to visit him after the performance. Everybody thought it was wildly funny except Binkie who was, it was regretfully noted, rather puritanical about certain things. One day it disappeared. Derek made enquiries but nobody knew what had happened to it, who had taken it or where it was now. Then came yet another summons to go to the office which could mean only one thing – a reprimand from Binkie. He informed Derek that it had been confiscated. "Not *quite* the sort of thing we want in a dressing-room in any theatre where I have a play, Derek dear. It could be offensive to some people. In fact I gather the cleaners were deeply shocked and we don't want a scandal, do we? This is a clean family play and Sir Bronson Albery who does, after all, own the theatre, is a Gentleman of the Old School. He hasn't complained *yet* but he might have done and then I would have to take action. Also, it might get into the gossip columns and that sort of publicity would do us no good. We have at all times to be very careful. So, Derek, my dear, let's forget all about it, shall we?" and with a bright dry smile and a dry bony handshake, Derek was dismissed.

Binkie was not amused. Or was he? Years later, Derek heard from a friend who had spent the weekend in Binkie's country house that the plaster penis was occupying a place of honour in the sitting-room, having been ingeniously converted into a table lamp.

There was more trouble. A heatwave hit London in 1949 and Derek got into the sensible habit of turning up at the theatre and walking round the West End wearing white shorts and an open-necked white shirt. All very clean and healthy and you would think he had just come from Wimbledon's centre court, but it was not the sort of thing which Binkie encouraged since he liked his actors to be smartly dressed at all times regardless of the weather. He was always, so why shouldn't they be? A message came from Binkie. "Mr Beaumont doesn't like his actors to wear short trousers in the West End. It must be a suit, collar and tie." Derek chose to ignore this.

Then there was the problem of his dressing-room partner, a German-Jewish refugee called Ernst Ulmann. He had greatly irritated Derek by constantly moaning and complaining about his sufferings under the Nazis. It was the only thing he could talk about and every night Derek had to sit and be drenched with a long boring stream of self-pity. Sympathy for the persecuted was certainly possible but, Derek felt, enough was enough. Ulmann made a late appearance in the third act. Permission to come in late would be given if requested but Ulmann liked to come in early and relax with Derek in the dressing-room and talk of pogroms, gas chambers, concentration camps, floggings, torture and sudden death. "Okay, so his family was wiped out by the Nazis and I'm very sorry but he doesn't have to keep on and *on* about it," said Derek to his friends in the company. One day he decided that he had had enough. He locked the dressing-room from inside and refused to let Ulmann in till the second interval, thus forcing him to spend the intervening time in somebody else's dressing-room. He sulked and complained and once again word got back to Binkie, who sent another message to Derek.

But nobody defied Binkie and lived to tell the tale. When *Traveller's Joy* finally came to an end after two glorious, lucrative years, Derek found himself on the black list. His agent submitted his name twice when Binkie was casting another play and received a very firm rejection. "Nice boy, good-looking, capable little actor, but I don't think . . . not *quite* the sort of actor I wish to employ . . . it's a *great* pity, but I think not." Derek never again worked for Binkie or in the West End.

CHAPTER TWENTY-FIVE

1947

Antony and Cleopatra – Macbeth – The Eagle has Two Heads – The Second Mrs Tanqueray – Lyric Hammersmith Repertory Season

As the post-war years of the heyday slowly passed, one of those simple but profound truths began to dawn on Binkie, that the secret of successful West End management could be summed up in four words: keep your stars happy. *Happy* meant *busy*, for the two states were virtually synonymous. If his stars loyally turned down work from other managements, then it was his duty to honour his promises and somehow find work for them. If a good new play with a suitable star part couldn't be found, then it must be a revival of either a past success or a classic. The problem was particularly urgent with Edith Evans. During 1943–4 she toured abroad for ENSA with *Heartbreak House* after its disappointing six months at the Cambridge with Robert Donat, too young and miscast as Captain Shotover, worked in Salisbury with Murray Macdonald where she not only appeared in fortnightly rep at the local garrison theatre but actually produced plays herself, and in early 1945 went to India for another ENSA tour of the ever-popular *The Late Christopher Bean*. But on her return he had to find something for her in London. The immediate answer was *The Rivals*, as she had never played Mrs Malaprop. Co-directing with William Armstrong and with Anthony Quayle in splendid support as Captain Absolute, it filled the Criterion for 166 performances. When she became Dame Edith in the New Year it was an occasion for real happiness and rejoicing for Binkie and a feather in his cap, for it was made clear in the citation that the award was not so much for her career as a whole but for her wartime tours, and Binkie could claim full credit for having organised those.

Edith, however, became increasingly difficult. Binkie made many suggestions, but nothing pleased her. Perhaps she felt her responsibilities more keenly now that she had a title and was thus officially acknowledged as one of the leaders of the profession. But it seemed to Binkie that she was being needlessly fussy in rejecting fine classical parts which would do her nothing but good. "How about a revival of *The Importance*?" he suggested. "It's five years since you first did it and there must be millions of people who were prevented from seeing it because they were all away in the war. It could be an even greater success." But she was tired of Lady Bracknell and had no wish for her career to consist only of revivals of her successes. "People will think I can do nothing else," she complained. "Never boil your cabbage twice.★ Noël said this to me and he was right." He suggested Lady Macbeth once more, opposite Godfrey Tearle at Stratford, but she refused for the same reasons as before. Tearle was deeply disappointed for he had boundless admiration for her, and accepted Diana Wynyard as a replacement with considerable reluctance. Binkie tried to persuade Edith to accompany him to Stratford to see the first night but if she had no interest in acting the part, she had even less in seeing it. The whole production was a disappointment: Tearle was past his prime, the fires were subdued, and it soon became clear that homicidal villainy and sexual fury lay outside Diana Wynyard's range: her pallid and dainty Lady Macbeth had never been nearer to Scotland than Tunbridge Wells.

Gertrude was another part for which Edith was ideally suited, and Stratford had plans to present Paul Scofield and Robert Helpmann playing Hamlet on alternate nights, but once again she took her cue from her Christian Science beliefs and refused. "Gertrude is a very wicked woman who has an adulterous affair with her brother-in-law and then connived at the cold-blooded murder of her husband," she explained to Binkie. "Surely you don't expect me to play somebody like *that*." "But surely you'd like to act with Paul Scofield," he said. "He's at a very critical stage in his career, he needs somebody like you to support him, and he's such a sweet, darling boy." Edith agreed with all this but the answer was still no thank you. Sometimes his suggestions were not so sensible. "How would you like to play Saint Joan?"

"Don't you think I'm a little old?"

"Sybil was in her forties when she played it."

"Sybil was forty-two and I'm sixty. There's quite a difference. Also, I doubt if Mr Shaw would give his permission."

"Just you leave him to me, Edith dear. He'd do anything for you. And anything for me."

"But it's Sybil's part. I can't play Saint Joan. It's *hers*. It would be wicked and sinful for me to do it."

But something good did turn up from an unexpected quarter.

★ The cabbage was to be boiled another four times, however. She played it on BBC Radio, recorded it for Decca, televised it in Canada and made the film in 1951.

Rodney Ackland had written another piece. Binkie had presented two of his early plays, but this talented and prolific author had never enjoyed the acclaim he deserved, always hovering on the fringe of success. He had written a new adaptation of *Crime and Punishment*, and although there were several in existence this was the one Binkie liked best, for Ackland had shown great skill in distilling the main events into three hours and confining the action into a single interior setting. The impoverished and consumptive Katerina Marmeladoff was a part which appealed to Edith; she accepted gladly and later was to score a notable success in it. But who was to direct? She wanted Gielgud but he had decided to play Raskolnikoff and did not wish to do both. Various names were suggested, Peter Glenville, Tyrone Guthrie, Olivier, Redgrave, Alec Guinness in partnership with Robert Helpmann but all were unavailable. Finally Anthony Quayle, who agreed to do it, was a good choice as he revealed an unexpected talent for direction. He was particularly good at handling crowds, dealing with multiple action, a cast of over forty and all the sound and lighting effects needed for this gloomy melodrama. It was real virtuoso stuff and he was generally hailed as a second Tyrone Guthrie. But even he couldn't get Gielgud to look like a penniless student or Peter Ustinov to give any hint of danger or menace as the elderly police chief, Porfiry Petrovitch. The former at forty-two was too old, the latter at twenty-four too young. Ustinov had already established himself as a brilliant character comedian, but he was not a good enough actor to play straight dramatic parts. When confronted by a part in which he was *not* required to be funny, his round, featureless face remained boringly impassive and his baritone voice droned monotonously. The production was a throwback to the palmy days of the Victorian theatre where the public flocked to see their stars without caring that they were too old or wildly miscast. After a run of 161 performances, first at the New, then at the Globe, the Theatre Guild bought it for New York on condition that Gielgud came too.

According to legend, Binkie was making a rather camp little joke when he offered Edith Evans a second chance to play Cleopatra and was truly astounded and not a little embarrassed when she accepted. In the light of her enthusiasm he could hardly withdraw the offer though he did his best to discourage her. But age and her title had made her obstinate and nothing would shake her resolve. It is difficult to understand why she was so anxious to repeat her Cleopatra after a gap of twenty years. Her first had been at the Old Vic in 1926 during the bleak, poverty-stricken Baylis years, and she failed lamentably to live up to the author's description of his heroine as simultaneously a 'triple-turned whore' and a 'most noble Empress'. Then she was thirty-eight and had enjoyed very little classical experience, but in the two decades that followed she had played a great many Shakespearean roles. Everybody is liable to miscast themselves given a chance, but there are few forces so powerful as the implacable determination of a middle-aged star actress to play a part which she and everybody else know to be grotesquely unsuitable.

Her Antony was Godfrey Tearle. They had worked together, briefly, once before: it was in 1928 when she invited him to play Mirabell in a revival of *The Way of the World* under her own management for a season at Wyndham's. Her reputation for being difficult and temperamental was enhanced when rumours started to circulate that she was at loggerheads with her co-star and not speaking to him. This was untrue. There was simply little rapport between them, there being marked differences of temperament which nothing could bridge. She was deeply religious with a strong vein of puritanism and disapproval; he was a hot-blooded sensualist with a cynically amused attitude towards conventional sexual morality.

He did sometimes make little jokes about her, calling her 'Damesy' and referring to her as 'the Dame'; "Did you hear that, Damesy?" during notes or "I don't think the Dame would like that" when the director suggested a move which would upstage her. There was no malice: Tearle had a wicked sense of humour which she did not, but she rather noticeably declined to respond to his gentle teasing. But there were never any rows or arguments. Whatever his private opinion of her he kept it to himself and was at all times thoughtful and courteous. After all, he was an actor of the old school and accustomed to treating his leading ladies with respect. His performance was magnificent and hailed as one of the finest in his long and distinguished career, whereas nothing could conceal the fact that the vulgarities of the Gipsy Queen had once again eluded her. His notices were superb, hers merely respectful. To be jealous was only human and Edith was always exceedingly human. There were other problems. The production by Glen Byam Shaw was uninspired, the multiple, skeletal set was an eyesore, but Anthony Quayle emerged with credit with his splendidly spoken and virile Enobarbus.

Binkie paid him a visit after the first night. "Well, Tony dear, that was splendid," he said eagerly, "just splendid. Now, what would you like to do next?" Quayle said he had always wanted to play Lopakhin in *The Cherry Orchard*. "Yes, of course, *what* a good idea. We must see to it." But when he presented the play at the Lyric Hammersmith, Quayle was at Stratford and there was never another chance.

The one star who was always busy and who never gave Binkie a moment's anxiety on that account – though he had good cause to be worried for other reasons – was Michael Redgrave. During the war he had divided his time between *Thunder Rock*, the Royal Navy, the film studios and a curiously gripping drama by Thomas Job called *Uncle Harry* about a lonely bachelor living with two monstrous sisters, whose plans for the perfect murder are too successful for comfort. It ran for the best part of nine months. But in Redgrave's case, busy did not mean happy. It was difficult to see just why, for he seemed to enjoy everything a man could possibly want. He was tall, very good-looking, he had a charming and sexually magnetic personality, a wide range of acting talents and a career spanning two continents which led eventually to a knighthood. He also had some literary talent, producing a novel, a play and his autobiography. And if all that wasn't enough he had a beautiful and talented actress-wife, Rachel Kempson, and three beautiful and talented theatrical children, Vanessa, Lynn and Corin. But the devil had taken possession, giving him a divided nature, a curious bisexuality which tortured him with guilt and anguish. All this made him difficult to work with.

Just after the war, in 1947, the urge to play Macbeth, which takes every classical actor in its clammy grip and will not let go, proved irresistible. This production was to live up most fully to its centuries-old reputation for bad luck and disaster and cause profound misery and frustration for a great many people. Redgrave was to make many mistakes and the first was his decision to invite his friend, Norris Houghton, to direct it. He was described by Douglas Wilmer, one of the actors in the company, as "a sweet little American college profes-sor who had done some designing but had never directed a play in his life". Redgrave had many revolutionary ideas about the play, some good, some terrible. In the latter category was his decision to have no fewer than six witches on the stage, the other three to be non-speaking and walk round the stage on stilts wearing devil-masks. Douglas Wilmer was offered one of these non-speaking witches, but declined.

"Think about it," said Redgrave.

"I don't need to think about it."

"Well, go home and sleep on it."

"I shall certainly go home but I won't sleep on it and the answer will still be no."

The following day Redgrave, admitting defeat, phoned to offer him Lennox. Wilmer accepted.

"Redgrave turned out to be the arch-shit of all time," remembered another member of the company. "He was a sado-masochist who loved making people miserable because it fed his sense of power. He was hated by just about everybody in the company. He started by contracting the whole company – apart from the principals – to play as cast and the first week was spent with the company reading all the parts in turn so he could decide. Can you imagine a better recipe for company jealousy, resentment and unhappiness? There we were, all of us, in open competition with each other, wondering who was going to get the best parts and hating them when they did. The rehearsals were a nightmare and the time quickly arrived when the company actually dreaded going to the theatre because nobody spoke to anybody and there was no sociability. Just tension, nerves and suspicion."

Redgrave, in his early address to the company, told them that this was going to be a production with plenty of supernatural production effects. The apparitions and the pageant of seven kings would have their faces painted with green and X-ray beams would light up their faces, making them hideous and ghastly. Nobody knew much about the effects of radiation, but fortunately it was one of those clever-clever ideas which died in the planning stage. Then there was the moving arm. Banquo's ghost would not appear but be left to the audience's imagination, contrary to Shakespeare's instructions. This caused the actor who plays Banquo, in this case the late Michael Goodliffe, a considerable frustration. The idea was that Banquo's chair should be specially angled by one of the servants, and that at a certain cue, a wooden arm should mysteriously fall from the back of the chair with a loud crash. The company were most impressed by this and spirits rose at this evidence that it was going to be an interesting and imaginative production. The play opened in Liverpool. Richard Bebb, cast as messenger, remembers that the stage director, Alison Colvil, pressed her button, there was a flash and a puff of smoke and no arm. The next night the arm did come down but owing to a malfunction in the electrical wiring, it went back up again, then down and up continuously throughout the banqueting scene. The company was in hysterics, nothing so funny had ever been seen or imagined. Redgrave had no sense of humour: he remained stern and unsmiling. The audience didn't make a sound. Presumably they thought it was part of the production.

It was not a happy company. One actor still recalls most clearly "Redgrave's appalling behaviour and manners to everybody. He was always very nice to me but he was horrid to everybody else, particularly to Ena Burrill, his Lady Macbeth. In rehearsal he shouted and savaged her most cruelly. Admittedly, she was badly miscast, but with Redgrave screaming and rampaging she didn't stand a chance. Nevertheless, she stole the notices in Liverpool which didn't please Redgrave at all. The next day he rehearsed her privately, upstaging her, forcing her to turn her back to the audience. Naturally, she never again got the acclaim or the notices."

With a company torn by dissent and tension, it was inevitable that there should be two actors who formed a particular dislike for each other, actor 'x' and actor 'y'. Throughout the run Redgrave had a habit of sending little notes to people. He even had a special memo sheet printed with the words 'A Note from Michael Redgrave' which was generally considered by the disrespectful and rebellious company to be the height of *folie de grandeur*. One of the company, Paul Hardwick, was a very good imitator of handwriting and produced two notes supposedly from Redgrave. The first was addressed to actor 'x'. "I've noticed that your performance is lacking in energy and has fallen off generally. Watch actor 'y' and note the vitality he exudes. I suggest you watch him from the wings whenever you can and do it as he does." He forged another addressed to actor 'y' telling him to watch actor 'x'. Copies of these notes were handed by Hardwick to both actors just as the second act started when it was too late for them to check their authenticity with Redgrave. Those in the company in the know watched the two actors as each took it in turn to watch his rival while standing in the wings. "It was the funniest thing in the world," said one of the watchers, "to see these two actors glaring at each other with eyes blazing with hatred and jealousy." After the performance both actors rushed to Redgrave's dressing-room but they were inter-cepted just in time and told the truth. Nobody knew how Binkie found out, but he did. He was said to have smiled tolerantly. A harmless practical joke didn't hurt anybody as long as it was not on the stage.

In February 1948, an incident took place which was to haunt and trouble Redgrave for the rest of his life and it was all due to Shakespeare's most difficult and tiresome stage direction, the cry of women offstage which is heard after Lady Macbeth's death. It had caused him a great deal of trouble; the production was now in its second month at the Aldwych, but this cry was still not right. One day he decided it must be many women and not just a single woman, so he called a rehearsal for all the girls in the company and worked them for hours until the right note of horror and anguish was achieved. At the next performance, a schools matinée, the cries of the women were greeted by a howl of uncontrollable laughter, as if it was the funniest thing since *Charley's Aunt*. Redgrave threw down his sceptre in fury, advanced quickly to the footlights and shouted, "QUIET!!!! THIS IS A VERY SERIOUS PLAY AND IF YOU DON'T KEEP QUIET I SHALL GO HOME." Deep shock and horrible embarrassment was the predictable result. Still shaking with fury, Redgrave gabbled his way through what was left of the play in order to get it over as quickly as possible. He refused to take a curtain call, rushed back to his dressing-room and found Binkie waiting for him.

It is not known who telephoned him. Officially it would have been Alison Colvil's job as stage director but she would normally have waited till the end of the day before making her routine report. It could have been one of the actors, disgusted by the incident, for every company had its Judas. Or it might have been one of the audience, possibly a member of the Tennent management who just happened to be watching the matinée. At the Globe, Binkie had leapt into action, rushed out to the street, grabbed a taxi, told the driver to get to the Aldwych Theatre stage door as quickly as possible and thus made the journey in a little over ten minutes, that being the time between Lady Macbeth's death and the end of the play.

When the two men confronted each other, Binkie was in a very great temper. The ensuing row lasted a long time and the noise, though not the words, could be heard as far as the stage and the stage-door lobby. The company, listening eagerly from the staircase at the end of the dressing-room corridor, heard the sound of the voices, Redgrave like a Wagnerian trombone and Binkie, cold, calm and deadly quiet, like an oboe. Just what they said to each other was not revealed at the time but twenty-five years later Redgrave threw some light on the incident.

"What I did was a terrible thing. An actor should never step out of character to abuse an audience for it kills the play far more effectively than the behaviour which provokes it. Binkie was white and shaking with fury. I've never seen him so angry. He said that he was astonished that an actor of my experience and status could be so unprofessional. I think he even used the word 'amateur' which really hurt. I remember shouting that I wasn't going to say the 'Tomorrow and tomorrow and tomorrow' speech to an audience of barbarians and drunken children and he countered that by saying that it was an actor's job to play to anybody, literally *anybody* who paid to see it, and that it was my responsibility to convert a bad audience into a good one. Eventually we both calmed down and he said that he did have sympathy with my obvious distress but that I must never *never* do it again. He added, rather menacingly, that if I did, he would replace me. He also advised me to rehearse a new cry of women because the one which had caused all the trouble sounded – so he'd been told – like a very loud collective fart. I think he may have been right. We did rehearse a new one and we never again had laughter or any trouble. I've always wondered if he was bluffing about replacing me."

As others were to discover in the future, when Binkie made threats of summary dismissal, he was never bluffing. In his eyes what Redgrave had done, *regardless of the provocation*, was a hanging offence, and if he had repeated it, he would have sacked him on the spot. He would have brought in the understudy, the excellent and saturnine Michael Goodliffe, and looked around for a suitable replacement. It might have been John Gielgud if the American management who was putting on *Crime and Punishment* in New York would release him, or Godfrey Tearle, temporarily resting before his forthcoming season at Stratford, or Robert Donat who had always wanted to play it, or Ralph Richardson, who fancied himself as a tragedian, or even the young Alec Guinness who, it seemed, could do everything. At a pinch, and it would have to be a horribly tight pinch, he might, just *might* – God help everybody at Tennent's – have brought in Donald Wolfit.

Happily for everybody, the situation did not arise. Redgrave never again harangued the audience and his offstage behaviour improved noticeably: the cry of the women no longer sounded like a collective fart, school audiences remained respectful, helped by Redgrave's appearance before the curtain at the beginning of the play, wrapped in a long black cloak. He would sternly inform the audience that *Macbeth* was tragedy and a supreme masterpiece of dramatic art, they must take it seriously and not laugh, and if they felt the urge to cough, they must wait until the interval, a request surely unique in theatrical history. The play continued to sell out, for *Macbeth*, regardless of its quality, is always relentlessly popular with the public and Binkie cut short the London run only because Redgrave (partnered this time by Flora Robson) was already committed to taking it to New York in March. For Binkie this was the end of *Macbeth*. It was the last time he was ever to present or have any association with it.

John Gielgud posed his own special problems because when he was out of work he became, like most actors, bored, restless and peevish. As Binkie was a close friend, fellow-director and near-neighbour he could not fail to be uncomfortably aware of the situation. 'When in doubt, *tour*' was another of Binkie's managerial principles. He assembled a company led by Gielgud and including Robert Flemyng, Margaret Rutherford, Pamela Brown and Jane Baxter, and a repertoire of two plays, *Love for Love* and *The Importance of Being Earnest*, both virtually unknown in North America. It gave theatre-goers in Canada and New York not only their first glimpse of these two popular classics but also of a company who all spoke with the same accent, something which astonished and delighted them and was ecstatically referred to by most of the critics as 'style'.

While he was in New York, Gielgud was approached by Robert Whitehead, one of Broadway's leading producers, and asked if he would be interested in directing Judith Anderson in a new translation of *Medea*. He was, but the casting of Jason, the hero, presented certain problems. Jason has to be young, athletic, virile and devastatingly handsome, like a Greek god. Many American actors were auditioned but none of them could speak the verse with sufficient musicality. Finally, at Judith Anderson's insistence, he agreed to play the part himself. He had the gravest possible doubts of his suitability, but he did his virile best to overcome nature's limitations. "Oh dear, it's so *boring* being butch," he was heard to moan, "but I do have nice legs." This led to a change in Binkie's Broadway connections. Until then, he had always had the first refusal of any of the plays presented by the Theatre Guild, and vice versa, but during the war this connection had begun to fade. Robert Whitehead took the Guild's place and thus became Binkie's principal Broadway contact.★ The new arrangement started with Whitehead suggesting *Medea* for the Edinburgh Festival but without Judith Anderson, who had been difficult and demanding. She had been upset when Gielgud left *Medea* after only three months to appear in *Crime and Punishment*, and when Binkie invited her to repeat her sensational performance in Edinburgh and London she refused. Not that Binkie was too concerned. He had created another star, one, he was convinced, who could take Judith Anderson's place.

It all started just after the war when Cocteau wrote a play, *The Angel of Death*, specially tailored to the talents and physique of his great friend, the actor, Jean Marais. Inside the handsome head was a shrewd theatrical intelligence. He knew what he wanted, what he could do best and he knew a good formula for success. "I want a play in three acts: in the first I say nothing at all and the audience must wonder who I am and what I am going to do. In the second I talk without stopping, and in the third I must have a really spectacular death scene. The death

★ Binkie's loyalties to his American colleagues were short-lived and constantly shifting: they tended to last only as long as it suited him. After years of mutually profitable business dealings with him, Robert Whitehead was in his office, negotiating the Broadway transfer of *Irma la Douce*. There was a little disagreement over the casting of Clive Revill whom Whitehead did not like. He wanted to replace him and Binkie did not. "Goodbye, and I'll see you tomorrow, Bob," said Binkie, with every sign of cordiality, as the meeting drew towards its end. Whitehead left but once in the street he remembered that he had left his overcoat behind. He returned, pushed open the door and, to his astonishment and displeasure, found David Merrick there. Binkie was very nervous. "Why h-h-hallo, B-B-Bob," he stuttered, "W-w-w-what do you want? . . . Oh, by the way, you do know David Merrick, don't you?" Whitehead nodded coldly and in an atmosphere of excruciating embarrassment, collected his overcoat and left. He neither spoke nor had any dealings with Binkie for many years.

scene of all time." With this formula in mind Cocteau turned out a fantasy about a queen in an unspecified part of Central Europe who is haunted by the fear of assassination at the hands of an unknown man. When the man appears she delivers a thirty-minute speech to him standing picturesquely at the top of a long curved staircase. She then takes him to her bed. In the last act he shoots her, takes poison and falls backwards down the staircase. This farrago of pseudo-poetic absurdities was first translated by Kitty Black, by now Tennent's in-house dramaturge, and then by Ronald Duncan, who produced a very acceptable slice of romantic theatre. Binkie had admired Eileen Herlie, a young Glaswegian, playing in Lillian Hellman's *The Little Foxes* at Liverpool, and had suggested to Murray Macdonald that she might suit the part of Andromache in the forthcoming revival of *The Trojan Women* at the Lyric, Hammersmith. She scored a distinct success in this part, the notices were excellent and she thus became a young actress whom Binkie wanted to watch. Building up a career was his speciality and he offered her the part of the Queen in *The Eagle has Two Heads* as it was retitled. She read it overnight and realised that it was the part of a lifetime. "I want to play it so much, I'll wait a year," she said eagerly. It was a little disillusioning for her to discover that Binkie had already offered it to Vivien Leigh, Edith Evans, Sybil Thorndike, Flora Robson, Peggy Ashcroft and Margaret Leighton to name only six and that they had all turned it down, not because they didn't like the play or the part, but because of that thirty-minute speech, a hurdle of intimidating difficulty, the theatre's answer to Becher's Brook. She mentioned this reproachfully to Binkie, but he was able to reassure her and give her confidence. "My dear, I wouldn't have offered it to you if I were not absolutely confident that you could do it. Now you have a chance to show that you can do better than they can, and once you've done it, then you will be a star and can join them." It was just as he predicted. The opening night in Hammersmith caused one of the great sensations of the post-war years: the thirty-minute speech was acclaimed as a *tour de force* and when the play transferred to the Haymarket and later to the Globe it ran for six months.

When that first-night audience responded with ever-greater intensity and enthusiasm with notices to match, he invited her to lunch at Lord North Street, just the two of them, and offered her a five-year contract. She refused. She did not wish to be tied to one management, she explained gently, but she gave him assurances that she would not work for anybody else while he had good quality plays for her. This impressed him. She knew her worth, she had a good business sense and she was certainly going to be loyal. As with all his stars there was never any contract for specific plays, just a verbal agreement. He paid her ten per cent of the gross and he also gave her something else, denied to the others: he gave her a guarantee of £300 a week.

One tragedy queen must surely follow another so when Judith Anderson declined *Medea*, he decided to present it at the Edinburgh Festival with Gielgud directing and Eileen Herlie in the title part. It aroused considerable interest and played to good houses in Edinburgh, but at the Globe, it died after only sixty-one performances. Tragedy queens from Ruritania were to London's taste, but not from Ancient Greece. The critics conceded that she had an awesome talent but didn't have the strength, the age or the experience to offer serious competition to Judith Anderson. The young Kenneth Tynan, though still at Oxford and within a year of starting his reign of terror as a full-time theatre critic, nevertheless made his views known in his brilliant first book, *He Who Plays the King*. He said that to make a success out of *Medea* you need three things: Judith Anderson, a director of genius and a translation which works. None of these, he added firmly, was now in evidence. Her reputation as an actress of rare tragic intensity was enhanced by this performance even if the public wasn't interested. All the right people came to see it and she enjoyed the great privilege of being the subject for wicked satire in one of Hermione Gingold's intimate revues. This, Binkie pointed out, was an accolade, and a *flop d'estime*, as he described *Medea*, would do her absolutely no harm at all. He proved this when he suggested her name to Laurence Olivier who was having some trouble in casting his new film *Hamlet*. A Gertrude who was old enough to be his mother and still young enough to make plausible the King's sexual fascination would be a novelty and a change from the usual hellcat of theatrical tradition. She got the part and thus made her film début.

No new play was suitable; tragedy queens are notoriously difficult to cast or create special vehicles for, so he decided to revive one of his favourite Victorian dramas, Pinero's *The Second Mrs Tanqueray*, which had not been seen in the West End since Gladys Cooper had played her in 1922. Eileen Herlie would not have to stand comparison with memories of Mrs Patrick Campbell, as Gladys Cooper had done, nor would she have Mrs Pat in the stalls watching her closely in her capacity of drama critic of the *Daily Mail*, which had also been Gladys' fate. But she would have Leslie Banks to play with her as the ideal Tanqueray, an actor who might have been born to play this epitome of a dignified English gentleman.

If things had worked out a little differently, it might have been more of a family affair. Leslie's youngest daughter, Evangeline, had just completed training at the Webber Douglas School. The part of Ellean, Tanqueray's young daughter, had yet to be cast. To have Leslie's

real-life daughter playing his daughter in the play would not only add
to the play's plausibility but would also inspire a lot of valuable
publicity. It was a charming idea and had it worked out, Binkie, with
his talent for career-building, might have added another embryo star
to the H. M. Tennent stable. But the idea was received by Leslie with
disapproval. He considered that the gesture would smack of privilege
and nepotism which would be embarrassing for both of them. He
considered that at twenty-one and fresh from drama school, Evangeline was too young and inexperienced to go straight into the West
End, to act an important and emotionally difficult part in a play which,
as with all Binkie's prestige productions, would command widespread attention. He further considered that she needed at least five
years' experience in provincial repertory before she even thought
about the West End. But nobody could be more persuasive than
Binkie when he had set his heart on something and Leslie just might
have been persuaded. Binkie would offer Evangeline one of his
famous contracts, she could get repertory experience in the Dolphin
Theatre in Brighton, and she could fill in small parts at the Lyric
Hammersmith.

A further obstacle to these plans lay in Evangeline herself. She had
plenty of talent and in time developed into a fine character comedienne
but she was nervous, timid and lacking in confidence. She loved her
father very dearly and had an enormous admiration for his talent, but
the idea of acting with him, and in a West End play, terrified her. She
had no hesitation in turning down Binkie's offer. It was her only
experience of the agonies a girl can suffer when she has a famous father
and chooses to follow the same profession.

The Second Mrs Tanqueray opened on August 29th 1950. Binkie sent
an invitation to Mrs Pat's daughter, Stella Patrick Campbell, who was
deeply unhappy and living in Weston-super-Mare, but she refused.
Her mother had treated her abominably, she hated her, had nothing
but bad, bitter memories and had no wish to be reminded of her. It had
been a good idea but Binkie had to admit defeat. The play was
established as a classic for a modern audience who had previously been
unacquainted with Pinero's skilful plotting, his witty, literate dialogue
and the solid romantic theatricality which only an ex-actor could
produce. Cecil Beaton's sets recaptured the grandeur of life in the
stately home of the nineties and the gowns he designed for Eileen
Herlie would have made Mrs Pat herself envious. But tragedy on the
stage was soon to be duplicated in real life. At sixty, Leslie Banks was
feeling his age. He was President of Equity with all the extra and
unpaid work which that involved, he was giving eight performances a
week and he was suffering badly from over-work. Something had to

give and something did. One evening he collapsed in his dressing-room and when he was found huddled on the floor by a distraught stage manager he could not move or speak. It was a stroke. His family lovingly nursed him back to health and after two years it seemed possible that he could return to work, at least on the radio. But he had a sudden heart attack and died very quickly. As for honours he was awarded a CBE but not a knighthood. So Gwen never became Lady Banks and Evangeline, sadly, never worked with her adored father. It was all very sad.

"*What* can we do with Eileen?" and "Is there life after *Tanqueray?*" were the two vital questions buzzing round the Tennent offices in the early fifties. "Yes, of course there is," was Binkie's immediate answer to the second, "we'll send her to Hammersmith." To the uninitiated who chanced to overhear this, it would seem to have an ominous ring. Everybody knows what happens when somebody is sent to Coventry, but what happens in Hammersmith? The opening of a second house turned out to be one of Binkie's brightest and most successful ideas. The money to start it and keep it going had been supplied by four production companies, Glyndebourne, the Arts, Cambridge, the New, Cardiff, and the Theatre Royal, Brighton. Each play would run for a month and then tour, playing a week at each of the four parent theatres. The presenting management was collectively known as the Company of Four and it was only a matter of time before Hermione Gingold started to refer to it in one of her satirical intimate revues as 'the Audience of Three'. Binkie did have his occasional failure but it was never quite as bad as that.

The first play, *The Shouting Dies*, by Ronda Keane, caused little comment. Inaugural plays are often disappointing. But *The Trojan Women* playing for seventy-five minutes, and *The Happy Journey to Trenton and Camden*, Thornton Wilder's enchanting evocation of rural American life performed on an empty stage without scenery, furniture or properties, brought trainloads of theatre-lovers to Hammersmith and the Lyric was on the map. One success followed another. *Spring 1600*, Emlyn Williams' picture of life at the Globe in Shakespearean times, Alec Guinness's adaptation of *The Brothers Karamazov* with himself, Ernest Milton and Frederick Valk and James Donald, *Pygmalion* with Alec Clunes and Brenda Bruce and *Captain Brassbound's Conversion* with Flora Robson, all made it clear that the success of the Lyric was evidence of a solid and lasting cornucopia of talent.

Within two years Binkie had succeeded in doing something which nobody thought possible: he made Hammersmith fashionable for the first time since its heyday under Nigel Playfair in the twenties. History now began to repeat itself. It was *The Way of the World* which caused the stampede in 1924 and another Restoration comedy which caused another stampede twenty-three years later. This time it was *The Relapse* in a splendidly vigorous and witty production by Anthony Quayle who, following so soon after *Crime and Punishment*, established himself as one of the finest directors in the country. The sets and costumes were pretty and colourful, and in the centre was Cyril Ritchard as Lord Foppington, queening, high-camping and low-camping it round the stage like some gorgeous pantomime dame but still very masculine withal. He made Foppington's catch-phrases, "Split me windpipe . . . strike me speechless . . . stap me vitals . . ." so unforgettably funny that they swept over the town just like those of ITMA. After playing to packed houses for the regulation four weeks with 'House Full' notice boards outside and long queues for returns, it transferred to the Phoenix and kept the post-war play-goers happy and glorious for eight months.

Thus it can be seen that the Lyric served as a very luxurious transit camp for Tennent actors, including the stars, who were temporarily unemployed. If Binkie didn't have anything for them, then 'darkest Hammersmith' was where they were sent to keep warm until something better turned up.

Binkie's dream of a permanent company led by John Gielgud in a repertoire of classics had not died as a result of the failure of the Haymarket season; it had merely lain dormant. So when Gielgud, Scofield, Herlie, Pamela Brown, Margaret Rutherford and Eric Porter were found to be simultaneously available and with nothing else on offer, to Hammersmith they went to do three plays and more if the season was a success. The preliminary announcements caused widespread interest and weeks of advance booking. Paul Scofield to play Richard II, directed by John Gielgud, seemed a perfect match: Scofield, London's most exciting young classical actor, and Gielgud, whose legendary performance of Richard II had been acclaimed as the greatest of his generation, was to pass on the accumulated wisdom and experience of his life to one increasingly described as his legitimate heir. But Binkie's highest artistic hopes were not achieved. Gielgud had never been good at directing other actors in parts in which he himself had triumphed, as Richard Burton was to discover in his New York Hamlet. Scofield had one other disadvantage: he had to stand comparison with Michael Redgrave who had just played the part at Stratford in a magnificent production by Anthony Quayle, which had vigour, virility, passion, colour and spectacle. In contrast, Gielgud's production was dainty, pallid, pastel-coloured and dull. Scofield's performance, though beautifully spoken and intelligent, was curiously lifeless. Nevertheless, the notices were good, public interest showed itself in full houses, sometimes fuller than full, and in one week takings were an unheard-of £2,000.

The Way of the World, with Gielgud as Mirabell and Pamela Brown bravely challenging all memories of Edith Evans in the part some twenty-nine years earlier and in the same theatre, was also a disappointment. Gielgud seemed nervous and restless: he couldn't find the character and seemed demoralised by the fact that Millamant has the better part and gets all the laughs. Pamela Brown, a fine dramatic actress, seemed oddly miscast in a part which required elegance, beauty, and comic radiance. Only Paul Scofield, as a superbly feline and mercurial Witwold and Margaret Rutherford, taking the stage like a battleship at a regatta as the definitive Lady Wishfort, emerged with credit.

To everybody's surprise, *Venice Preserved* was the real success of the season. Gielgud had long wished to revive it, a resolve doubtless fortified by the famous Zoffany painting of Garrick and Mrs Cibber in the dagger scene hanging in the Garrick Club Coffee Room which he saw every time he lunched or dined there. It offered the public a rare glimpse of Restoration tragedy, a genre neglected by the commercial theatre for over a century and it is not difficult to see why. Otway's plotting is cumbersome, a vortex of adultery, political conspiracy, insanity and murder; written in the blankest of blank verse, complex and confused and exceedingly difficult to learn. Gielgud, Scofield, Herbert Lomas, Eileen Herlie and a hand-picked Tennent inner-circle supporting cast put over the violent emotions with all the savagery and passion at their disposal. The designs by Peter Brook, who also directed, and Leslie Hurry created a Venice of subterranean darkness, murky horror and evil. But it was the occasional scenes of humour that made the greatest appeal and are best remembered, which suggests that Otway must have been a comic playwright *manqué*. Richard Wordsworth as a corrupt, masochistic senator crawling around the stage on all fours like a dog and begging Pamela Brown as a bored prostitute to whip him, squealing with joy at every stroke, gave the greatest possible pleasure to an audience already bored and bewildered by seventeenth-century Venetian politics. Belvidera was a part which gave the tragedienne everything she could want. She contracts a forbidden marriage in poverty and domestic tension, suffers her father's hostility, joins the plot against the Doge of Venice, is raped by a soldier, goes mad, and if all that isn't enough, she commits suicide with a goblet of poisoned wine and returns to haunt Venice as a ghost. Mrs Siddons had added immeasurably to her reputation with it, but Eileen Herlie was not happy. Binkie watched her closely and formed an opinion. He was the only person who realised that inside the tragedy queen was a brilliant comedienne bursting and struggling to get out. So when *The Matchmaker* came up for production, Thornton Wilder's farcical comedy whose provenance goes back to Germany in the mid-nineteenth century through a dozen different versions, now reborn in turn-of-the-century New York, Binkie asked her to play Mrs Molloy, the Irish dressmaker. "How did you know that I liked to make people laugh?" she asked eagerly when she read the script. "Instinct, my dear," he said, "just instinct. But I'm right, aren't I?"

On that first night at the Haymarket on November 4th 1954, the quintet of highly skilled players, Ruth Gordon, Eileen Herlie, Sam Levene, Alec McCowen and Arthur Hill, roared past the winning post in a colourful and well-paced production by Tyrone Guthrie who never let the fun flag for a moment. It is always a pleasure seeing somebody doing something really well but when it is unexpected, the pleasure is much greater. Seeing Eileen Herlie being funny with a strong Irish accent in a series of dazzling 1890 dresses was a delicious experience. Incredibly, the notices were mixed, the advance booking was not good, and the second-night house was only half full. Alec McCowen remembers that the company was rather gloomy and despondent, wondering how long they would be running. He shared a dressing-room with Peter Bayliss and that second evening Binkie came round before the performance with a message. He stood in front of the two actors and looked very sternly down at them.

"This play is going to be a success, isn't it?" he said, very fiercely.

"Yes, Mr Beaumont."

"It's going to be a great huge success and have a long and successful run, yes?"

"Yes, Mr Beaumont."

He extended his arm and pointed an accusing, hypnotic finger at each of them. "And we're all going to have a very long and successful run, aren't we?" he said, looking even more fiercely at them. Again they were overawed and replied, "Oh yes, Mr Beaumont, we certainly are." He went round to all the dressing-rooms doing exactly the same routine and as a result the company all believed that the play would be a success *and it was*. The morale of the company was very high and they were all very impressed by Binkie's managerial one-upmanship. It was another demonstration of the truth of a much-quoted saying by the late Dr Goebbels, that if you say something often enough and loudly enough it becomes true.

After the first performance of *Richard II*, a big company party took place on the stage of the Lyric, Hammersmith. Nicholas Amer who played Green and was endowed with strikingly poetic good looks, elegance and charm, assets which, it is greatly to be regretted, were shortly to become unfashionable, saw a little old lady standing by herself. Nobody was talking to her, she seemed to be not only alone but also rather lonely, so he generously went over to talk to her and put her at her ease. Making cheerfully polite conversation he asked her if she had enjoyed the play. Yes, she had and yes she did go a lot to the theatre because her son gave her tickets for everything she wanted to see. "He looks after me," she said, "he's very good like that." Amer naturally assumed that her son, whoever he may be, worked in one of the London box offices or for Keith Prowse or any of the big ticket agencies. Later in the evening, someone whom he had never seen before, approached and said, "Thank you for looking after my mother. She doesn't know anybody and has few friends so it's particularly nice when people are kind to her." "That's all right," said Amer, "she's a nice lady and I was glad to be able to talk to her. But who is she and who are you?" The young man gave him an amused smile. "I'm Binkie Beaumont, Nicholas dear, and I'm your employer. And I'm very glad to meet you after all this time."

This type of incident, which was to recur endlessly in Binkie's hey-day years, pinpoints two little-known aspects of his life: the policy of anonymity which he and Vivienne Byerley had pursued, had been a demonstrable success if he could mingle unrecognised with his company of actors and it also shows that he was not entirely devoid of family feeling. When he left Cardiff in the mid-twenties he arranged for his mother to sell the Cathedral Road house and follow him to London. He installed her in a suite at the Onslow Court Hotel and later arranged for her to buy a house nearby. With the money from the sale of the Cardiff house and contents and her income from the timber business she was a wealthy woman. She became a merry widow of South Kensington, living the life of a lady of leisure as it was between the wars. She converted her house into a bridge club, a game she played with enthusiasm and skill; she lunched at the Ritz, dined at the Savoy, attended the fashionable *thé-dansants* at the Waldorf, and became in the process a compulsive theatre-goer. Throughout her life, Binkie supplied her with theatre tickets for all his plays and any others, usually on first nights and usually in the stage-box.

The relationship was cool rather than close: he was a dutiful son rather than a loving one and although he was quite prepared to look after her, he had no desire to live with her. She could be very possessive and demanding at times and freedom from any sort of domestic aggravation was something he prized very highly. She had a tiresome habit of calling unannounced at the Globe offices, making endless telephone calls and getting in everybody's way. Binkie tried to dissuade her but it wasn't easy. "It's so terribly *boring* when she barges in at twelve-thirty and says, 'Take me out to lunch, Binkie,' and one is already committed . . . or when she wants to know who one's friends are or where one is going for a holiday." They had nothing in common but he was prepared to invite her to the occasional lunch at Lord North Street or the even more occasional weekend at Knotts Fosse. In the thirties he was greatly relieved when she married an elderly Jewish silversmith named Schwerzee. It was this which seemed to give extra confirmation that he was himself Jewish. For reasons which were never made clear, Binkie took a great hate against his second step-father.

With his brother, Jack, and his sister-in-law, Muriel, things were a lot more affectionate. Just as Binkie inherited his looks and style from his mother, so Jack inherited his from his father. He was short, strongly built with a big moustache and a mane of red hair: in spite of the obvious differences of temperament and life-style, the two brothers found when they grew up that they actually liked each other. To everybody's regret, Jack and Muriel did not succeed in having any children. "I would *love* to have been a wicked uncle," Binkie would say sadly, "we could have had so much fun." He was closest to his cousin Betty. She had entered the fashion world and worked as a couturier in Paris. When she paid visits to England, he always gave her theatre tickets, escorted her and took her out to dinner afterwards. He continued to love her dearly throughout his life.

CHAPTER TWENTY-SIX

1949

The Browning Version – Adventure Story – Ring Round the Moon

It was in the summer of 1948 that Binkie made one of the worst mistakes of his life. He turned down Rattigan's new play, *Playbill*. For Rattigan, it was a real break from the past for it consisted of two one-acters, a genre which had always fascinated him and which he regarded as a most intriguing challenge. The one-act play had been a mainstay of the theatre for a century and a half either as a curtain raiser or endpiece to a full theatrical bill, but since the end of the First World War it had fallen out of fashion and attempts to revive it had failed. Yet every author gets a good idea for a play which will simply not extend beyond an hour, or even less. But the public had been led to believe that with a one-acter they were not getting full value for money, and that two short plays are less in their total sum than one long play. This is, of course, nonsense. But how do you put this simple message over to the public and to the managers?

The first, *The Browning Version*, describes a crisis in the life of an elderly schoolmaster who finds out in one day that his wife doesn't love him and that a boy in his Greek classics class does. It is a deeply moving and profoundly compassionate study of old age, disillusionment, emotional instability and adolescent perception. Never had Rattigan's craftsmanship been more skilled and more subtle. It was a seventy-minute masterpiece. *The Browning Version* was accompanied by a much shorter comedy, *Harlequinade*, a backstage romp about a company of actors rehearsing *Romeo and Juliet* for a provincial tour. It was a very funny and imaginative satire on theatrical vanity, full of delicious in-jokes (including an oblique reference to Binkie himself) and biting comments on contemporary actors and institutions. Rattigan gave them to Binkie to read. He was to remember their subsequent conversation over lunch at the Ivy:

"I like them very much, Terry dear, *very* much. *The Browning Version*, particularly. I think it's your best. And the other one is great fun. But the public doesn't want one-act plays. I'd lose a fortune."

"But Noël made a lot of money with his *Tonight at Eight Thirty*."

"Yes, but he was a big, *big* star and so was Gertie. The public would flock to see them in literally anything."

"Well, Larry did *Oedipus* and *The Critic*. Packed houses every night. People queuing all night for the gallery and pit.

"They were both classics and that's different. I'm so sorry, Terry dear, but I think I shall have to say no. Of course . . . if you could get Johnnie to do both plays. Or Larry. Larry and Vivien would be fine. Could she play Mrs Crocker-Harris?"

"Well, I don't think so, Binkie dear. She's far too young and pretty."

"Couldn't you rewrite the part to make her young and pretty?"

"No. She's got to be old enough and sufficiently unattractive to be embittered and disillusioned, so she's really got to be fat and middle-aged."

"No? . . . We-e-e-e-ll, ask Johnnie and let me know what he says."

Rattigan and Gielgud met in New York. They went for a walk in Central Park while Rattigan waited in an agony of suspense for Gielgud's answer. Gielgud had previously rejected Sir Robert Morton in *The Winslow Boy* which was a happy decision because he would never have been so effective as Emlyn Williams but he compounded the error. "I have to be so very careful what I do now, Terry, my dear," he said, "the public have seen me in so much first-class stuff, do you think they would accept me in anything second-rate?"★ Second-rate?!! It was an inexplicably foolish judgement and one which caused the unhappy author the most unimaginable pain. Without Gielgud, the two plays had no further interest for Binkie though he took a friendly, compassionate interest in their future. Presented by a young manager, Stephen Mitchell, who had already picked up one of Binkie's rejects and would do so again before long, they opened at the Phoenix in September 1948 with Eric Portman and Mary Ellis. Opinions were divided about *Harlequinade*, as they usually are about light farcical comedies, but *The Browning Version* was unanimously hailed by press and public as a masterpiece. However, Binkie's lack of faith in its commercial appeal seemed to be justified when they ran for only six months, but if he had any temptation to rejoice in his theatrical perception, he had to think again. Stephen Mitchell made a sizeable sum out of his share of the film, television and radio rights and the subsequent productions all over the country and the world during the years to come. Binkie lived to see it become a modern classic and

---

★ Gielgud later revised his opinion, for he played Mr Crocker-Harris on BBC Radio and American TV.

experienced a little shudder every time he thought of it. "That was another one which got away," he would say casually whenever the subject came up, but only a few realised how deep the pain was.

This didn't stop him from repeating the same mistake some six years later when he rejected the two one-act plays which make up *Separate Tables*, Rattigan's superb picture of the anguish, boredom and misery which make up life in a provincial residential hotel. Once again, Stephen Mitchell was able to profit from Binkie's bad judgement and put it into production with the same team, Peter Glenville directing and Eric Portman starring, but now accompanied by Margaret Leighton who showed, in her persecuted, timid ugly-duckling daughter, what a superb character actress she had become. It ran for a year at the St James's and nearly a year at the Morosco Theatre on Broadway. A Hollywood film was made by Burt Lancaster, with David Niven, Wendy Hiller, Rita Hayworth, Deborah Kerr and Gladys Cooper. It enjoyed a long lease of life in the reps and on tour both at home and overseas. For all his theatrical intelligence there were some things which Binkie just could not and would not learn, and he paid a high price for his obstinacy.

Next, Rattigan gave himself the challenge with a genre he had never before attempted, the historical epic. History to a playwright is like blood to a tiger: once he had tasted it with *The Winslow Boy* he wanted more and more. More and bigger. Bigger meant an epic on Cecil B. de Mille lines. So far he had written only plays with one set and a small cast which dealt with small subjects. He felt restricted. He wanted to expand and allow his imagination to roam unfettered by the usual commercial considerations of the past. He wanted to write a heroic story with epic emotions and presented in epic style. He wanted to bring back the glories of the Victorian theatre, of Irving and Tree.

Adventure Story was about Alexander the Great. "He's a character which has always keenly interested me," he said to the press, "and I thought that after the war might not be a bad moment to write a play about a man who wanted to conquer the world, and what happened to him." He had retired to the country, to a little pub, The Stag and Hounds in Binfield, Berkshire, where a suite of rooms was permanently reserved for him. Here he was able to concentrate on the Ancient Greeks and produced a pageant play with ten scene changes, a cast of twenty-two and an action which covered eleven years of Alexander's life. It was superbly constructed and written, with splendid and highly actable characters and a fine sense of history. It wasn't a safe play or an easy play.

"It's the best thing I've ever done, Binkie old man," he said trying to speak casually as he handed the typescript over.

To his great relief Binkie agreed with him. "Your best yet, Terry dear," he said happily, noting that there were no battle scenes. He liked it very much but in addition he did feel a little guilty about his cavalier rejection of *The Browning Version*. He wanted to make amends and reassure Rattigan that he was still an honoured and welcome guest of the Firm. He put it into immediate production and it was a package only he could set up. Peter Glenville directing, sets and costumes by the brilliant Parisian designer, George Wahkevitch, music by Benjamin Frankel; and the up-and-coming Paul Scofield, aged twenty-six, as Alexander.

Scofield had already served a full and fruitful apprenticeship. There had been one memorable season at the Birmingham Rep under Peter Brook's direction where he played three classic parts: then three seasons at Stratford where he played a great many more, including Hamlet, alternating with Robert Helpmann. He had transferred twice to the West End, his Mercutio at His Majesty's and his Tom Fashion in *The Relapse* at the Phoenix were highly acclaimed. He had everything: he was tall, slim, good-looking, with a lean, leonine head and the sort of profile which had hitherto been Ivor Novello's monopoly. He also had that indispensable feature of a star actor's equipment, a voice of distinction, a voice one does not forget, a voice totally unlike anybody else's – its sharp, astringent, slightly nasal quality sang with its own special music. With looks, voice, personality and an assortment of acting skills, he was undoubtedly Binkie's most exciting prospect, poised on the very brink of a real, big success. It only needed one thunderingly good part in a modern play, full of good acting opportunities in a high-prestige production, for him to cross that Rubicon which lies between a much-admired leading actor and a true star.

The announcement that Rattigan's latest play was a complete break from the past caused enough excitement to guarantee that the opening night in Brighton should be attended by a galaxy of theatrical and social celebrities. But Chips Channon recorded in his diary that although the production was magnificent, the audience appeared puzzled by the play and that Scofield, understandably nervous, made little impression. Three weeks later when much the same audience assembled at the St James's Theatre on March 17th 1949, it was a different story. The audience understood the play, applauded the sets – the Hanging Gardens of Babylon caused great excitement★ – and gave Paul Scofield a standing ovation. It was an exciting evening and nobody who was there has ever forgotten it. There were eight curtain

★ Rattigan later admitted that writing the stage direction, 'The Hanging Gardens of Babylon', gave him as much pleasure as 'The river Rhine overflows its banks' gave to Wagner.

calls and it was clear that the audience had enjoyed itself immensely, considered that with a play lasting slightly more than three hours they had received good value for money, and had no reservations about its quality or its stature.

The party afterwards which Binkie gave at Lord North Street was one of the most nerve-racking of his life as he was to remember for years. As well as being the most ambitious play he had ever mounted it was also the most expensive, costing £8,000. "If only those critics would give you a chance, Terry dear," he said in the small hours when the party had thinned down to a few intimates, "if only they'd see what you're trying to do."

It was a forlorn hope and when the despatch rider on his motorbike from Fleet Street thundered up to the door, and handed over the precious pile of papers, it took only a minute for their message to sink in. They didn't like it. Not only did they think he had failed in his bid to escape from the tyranny of the modern play, they didn't even think he should have tried. Ambition, imagination, and initiative were qualities they sternly discouraged for author with such a record of success. Let him go back to writing light comedies and leave the epics to others. What others? the unhappy Rattigan might well ask, but answer came there none. Only a few kind words twinkled through the jungle of hostility. "A gallant failure worth a dozen so-called suc-cesses," from Ted Willis, a critic before his own playwriting days, but this was not likely to bring much consolation into Lord North Street.

Despite the critics, the second-night audience applauded to the echo. A week of full houses raised the company morale, Scofield's performance had acquired that extra strength and assurance which only success and applause can give to an actor, and the advance booking stretched into May. By the end of March it really looked as if Binkie had a success on his hands. But it was a false dawn. By the middle of May, after only two months, those ominous pockets of empty seats were appearing in the side of the stalls and circle, the advance had thinned down to a trickle, and at the beginning of June he was compelled to put up the notice. It was withdrawn in mid-June, the saddest moment in Binkie's life since the end of *Hervey House*, fourteen years earlier: worse, really, for that had been a Howard and Wyndham production, whereas *Adventure Story* was his.

Normally, Binkie was not one to waste time in post-mortems but this was a different case. With a superb play, a magnetic star perform-ance in the centre, and all those glorious sets, why did it fail? *Why?* He identified three sensible reasons: the disappointing notices; the choice of theatre, a fact he fully realised when he booked it, but he had no alternative as all the right-sized theatres in attractively central positions were full already: the St James's was a gem with a distinguished history, but off the beaten track, skulking in a side-street of mainly business premises and with no passing trade, unlike Shaftesbury Avenue or the Haymarket; and finally, there was the expense of a lavish production and a large cast. *Adventure Story* would have to run for at least six months to capacity houses to pay off the production costs and this was impossible in King Street, St James's.

In building up a star career, it was necessary to have not only continuity but variety. Binkie decided that Paul Scofield had done his fair share of tragic heroes, both classical and Shakespearean, and the time had now come for him to play something a little closer to the present day, by a contemporary author and, if possible, something lighthearted. For months Binkie looked at new plays and spoke to agents but the answer finally came from Paris. Word had reached him through Ginette Spanier that *tout Paris* was flocking to see a little bit of nonsense by Anouilh, described in the notoriously short-memoried press as a 'new author'. In fact he had been writing and producing plays since 1938 but this latest, *Ring Round the Moon*, was his first real success.

Binkie flew over to Paris and watched it glumly. Like so much in the French theatre at the time, the production was terrible: the French seemed to have no idea of costumes, settings or lighting and no idea what they could contribute to the whole. The acting was lively enough and his entrepreneurial eye was busy seeing its possibilities. The plot was thin to the point of emaciation: a shy young aristocrat, Frederick, living in a stately château is in love with a highly unsuitable girl and plans to marry her. His wicked brother, Hugo, an identical twin, imports a young dancer from the Opéra to distract him. A parade of colourful characters support this framework: a booming, bullying Countess *grande-dame* in a wheelchair with nervous companion, a butterfly collector unwittingly involved in the plot, a crumbling butler, a millionaire who renounces his wealth at the end and tears up many million-franc notes, and the dancer's mother, a chattering piano teacher.

The talents which Binkie assembled added up to a package that only he could produce. Oliver Messel to design the Edwardian costumes and the single set, a winter garden in a conservatory; Joe Davis to light it, which he did with such imagination and skill that each time the lights came up on a new scene (and there were six) it looked different and even more beautiful; Richard Addinsell to write the music which was so tuneful and charming that it had an independent existence outside the play; and a company which was a casting director's dream: Paul Scofield to play the twin brothers, Margaret Rutherford booming majestically from her wheelchair, Claire Bloom bringing her childlike innocence to the young dancing girl, Cecil Trouncer as the millionaire and Mona Washbourne as the piano-teaching mother. All that and Peter Brook too, bringing the full force of his technical virtuosity and imagination to the difficult task of merging all these disparate elements together and, in the process, creating a masterpiece of theatre, an evening of magic which, after thirty-eight years, is still regarded by many as the crest of Binkie's career.

Peter Brook's handling of the twins showed his particular director-ial talent. At the beginning Hugo appears wearing a very elegant light grey suit and playing with a wooden cup and ball. He is talking to the butler. When the short scene finishes he makes his exit on the right side of the stage. The butler calls him back and he reappears with his back to the audience, still playing with his cup and ball. The butler's little speech finished, Hugo dashes out of sight and at the same moment Frederick appears on the opposite side of the stage. Nobody who saw it will forget the gasp of astonishment from the audience who must surely have believed that the miracle of bi-location had at last been performed. It is now possible to reveal after nearly four decades that it was not Scofield who briefly reappeared, but his double, an actor of identical build and wearing an identical suit who stood there long enough for Scofield to make a race behind the set to reappear on the other side of the stage. The trick was played a second and then a third time and even though the audience was expecting it and kept a sharp lookout for the double, he was never identified and they were always taken by surprise. Scofield's doubling, without any change of make-up or costume, caused a sensation and there are many who think it was his finest performance. Unlike some, he did not fall into the easy and traditional trap of using his acting skills to make the twins as different as possible so that the audience would start to wonder how they could ever be mistaken for each other.* Instead, he showed their similarities and if there were occasional moments of genuine confusion for the audience, wondering which twin was now on the stage, the context of the play made it clear. It was only on a second or third visit that the actor's delicate skills were apparent when, with a slight change of vocal quality or the walk or the way he carried himself, you knew that these were two different young men.

The final accolade came from the author who watched it in delight

---

* According to the contemporary critics, this is exactly what Sir Henry Irving did when playing identical twins in *The Lyons Mail*.

and said, "I had no idea that my little play could look so marvellous. We in Paris have so much to learn from you in London," and if Binkie would like to have said, "Vous pouvez dire cela encore, Monsieur," he was too polite actually to do so.

CHAPTER TWENTY-SEVEN

1948–9

The Skin of Our Teeth – A Streetcar Named Desire

The cross-fertilisation between Broadway and Shaftesbury Avenue had virtually died during the war, for of the sixty plays which Binkie presented during those years only five were American. There was *Thunder Rock*, already mentioned. There was *No Time for Comedy*, by Sam Behrman, a witty comedy about a Broadway playwright's love affair with a Broadway actress which, suitably anglicised to make a vehicle for Diana Wynyard and Rex Harrison, filled the Haymarket for 348 performances before going on an extensive ENSA tour. *The Little Foxes* had been a huge success on Broadway with Tallulah Bankhead revealing that, under all that high-pressured showbiz nonsense and low camp, she was a fine dramatic actress. In 1942 Binkie cast Fay Compton, with the young Dulcie Gray and the even younger baby-faced Richard Attenborough in support and it should have lasted through the war and after but a piece of monstrous bad luck effectively killed it. London suffered a November fog so dense that all transport stopped, and audiences could not get into the West End. After three weeks of empty houses, Binkie had to withdraw it. The following day, the fog lifted and was replaced by brilliant winter sunshine. The Bette Davis film had been released and was playing in cinemas round the country and some attributed the failure to this competition but as Binkie had proved to himself and to others with *Rebecca* a film of a play, however good, never stops a theatre public from flocking to see the play.

The first American import which Binkie presented after the war was Thornton Wilder's very peculiar comedy *The Skin of Our Teeth*, which the author described as "a comic strip picture of mankind involving wars, the black pox, fire, flood and seven year locusts". Binkie had received the script from his old friends, the Theatre Guild. Strange, bizarre, surrealistic, he didn't understand it. But there was a central part of a comic maidservant, Sabina, which would keep an inspired comedienne on stage for the whole evening. Realising that it would suit Vivien Leigh, he sent it to the Oliviers. They both loved it so Binkie bought the English rights and set up an immediate production with Vivien starring and Olivier directing. Immediately, telegrams arrived from David O. Selznick reminding Vivien that she was still under contract to him and that she must withdraw from the play. She refused, and a battle between two legal heavyweights resulted: Sir Walter Monckton appearing for Selznick and Sir Valentine Holmes acting for Vivien. Neither Vivien nor Olivier appeared in court but Binkie and Elsie Beyer were both there to witness a *cause célèbre'* calculated to trigger much lighthearted publicity.

It was pointed out to Sir Walter that if Selznick refused Vivien permission to work in the theatre then she would be officially classified as unemployed and conscripted forthwith either into the services or to a munitions factory. Did he really wish to see her working at a lathe in oil-stained overalls and a headscarf for eight hours a day? Or crawling through a muddy shooting range carrying a rifle and bayonet? Quite apart from the fact that there were thousands of girls for that but only one Vivien Leigh whose war-work was keeping people happy with her beauty and her talent, there was her health to be considered, never strong at the best of times.

The case filled the popular press for days; it stopped being a quibble between two fine legal minds and became a simple matter of patriotism with a powerful American tycoon using his influence and wealth to demolish a delicate and vulnerable English rose. 'Hands Off Our Viv', screamed one headline. Binkie wrote private letters to the King and Queen, to Winston Churchill and to Anthony Eden. Clearly, it was unthinkable that Scarlett O'Hara should be degraded, and the picture of this exotic Bird of Paradise dying of hypothermia to the irrevocable theatrical loss of the entire civilised world caused great alarm. The judge gave his verdict in Vivien's favour.

In Edinburgh and throughout the provinces the public hated *The Skin of Our Teeth*, but they still flocked to see it. Irritation fought with bewilderment at the author's surrealist fancies; why did a brass band come on to the stage at certain key points to play the William Tell Overture? Why were chairs passed up from the stalls to the stage? What did it all mean? At the Phoenix during the first night, May 16th 1945, an incident occurred which caused great amusement throughout Fleet Street and Shaftesbury Avenue. Olivier was in his middle gangway stall watching the beginning of the second act. It was a very complex, difficult piece of production with an abundance of lighting and sound cues. His nerves were on edge. Suddenly, he saw James Agate creeping down to his aisle seat. Clearly, he had been in the bar and either did not know or did not care that the second act had started. Furious, Olivier rose, struck him on the shoulder and snarled, "Sit down, damn you." The elderly critic looked very startled as well he might. "Who's that?" he said tremulously. "You know bloody well who it is," snapped the actor. Both men sat down in their seats. On Sunday, Agate's notice bore no apparent ill-will for the assault. His notice was full of enthusiasm for the play and for Vivien, likening her to a dabchick and dragon fly sparkling and chattering and volatile as quicksilver. "That's the way we should treat critics," Olivier said to Binkie, "we should do it more often."

Vivien had been in excellent health, but after two months some alarming symptoms appeared. These included weight loss, headaches, dizziness, a persistent cough and periods of exhaustion alternating with periods of extreme exhilaration. One night Binkie saw the play and declared himself worried by her strained voice and by her thin face whose cheekbones were beginning to stand out with greater prominence than before. She was reluctant to admit that anything could be wrong and it took all his tact and persuasion to get her to a doctor. X-rays were taken, tests were made and the news was as bad as it could be, it was what she had been secretly dreading: TB. There was a tubercular patch on her lung.

Olivier was in Germany touring the ENSA camps with the Old Vic. She refused to tell him and swore Binkie to secrecy. Olivier must *not* be told. Binkie pleaded with her to be sensible but for once his celebrated diplomatic powers failed. Much against his better judgement he kept the secret, but as her appearance and voice continued to deteriorate and with them her performance, he managed to pass a discreet message to Olivier by means of a mutual RAF friend that he should return as soon as possible, though without giving any reason. When Olivier saw her he was appalled. Binkie closed the play after a run of only ten weeks while Olivier took her to hospital for further tests and observation. The specialist's verdict was a year's rest in a sanatorium, but, terrified that she might never come out, she flatly and passionately refused. Eventually Binkie managed to persuade her to take the year off, not in a cold, anonymous sanatorium surrounded by white coated nurses and doctors, but at Notley Abbey which Olivier had just bought. She agreed and spent the first four months in bed.

Olivier by then was working full blast at the New Theatre giving eight performances a week of a mixed repertoire of five plays. There were no Monday performances but the three matinée days meant being in the theatre without a break for nine hours at a time, crucifyingly hard work when it was the famous double-bill of *Oedipus* and *The Critic*. Outside the immediate family circle of Olivier, her daughter Suzanne and Olivier's son Tarquin, Binkie was the only visitor she had. She missed Olivier every minute of the day he wasn't there so Binkie had yet another opportunity to show what a generous and loving friend he was. He paid her regular visits when she was alone, bringing flowers, chocolates and books. He sat by the bed laughing and chatting: it was a silvery streak of gossip, anecdote and high-camp theatre talk. It was like the summer of 1940 all over again.

To a man like Binkie who loved gambling and racing and all games of chance, 1948 was always to be known as the Year of the Tennessee Williams Stakes, the year when *A Streetcar Named Desire* came on to the market. He had already written nine plays, including the greatly admired *The Glass Menagerie*, but it was *Streetcar* which made him into a star playwright. It also contrived to make another sort of legend out of the unknown Marlon Brando. Following its opening, no less than thirteen English managers, including Laurence Olivier who wanted it for the Old Vic, entered the race. Many of them made personal visits to New York to meet, dine with and flatter the producer, Mrs Irene Mayer Selznick, at that time Broadway's only female producer. Binkie didn't enter the race: it was evidence of his pride and confidence that he felt he didn't have to. A year earlier while on a ten-day play-spotting trip to New York, his great friend, the actress Margalo Gilmore, advised him with great urgency to take the train to New Haven to see this exciting new play which was destined to be a huge success and which he would certainly want for London. He decided against the trip. His return flight was booked and with all possible respect for Margalo's judgement, the play might turn out not to be worth the trouble. If the play was as good as she said, then he would certainly hear more about it. But he sensibly left his calling card by writing a short note to Mrs Selznick asking her to get in touch with him if she wished to present it in London. It was just a polite gesture: and after returning to London he thought no more about it.

Irene Selznick was by any standards, and would have been at any time in history, a most unusual and remarkable woman. She was born into the Hollywood royal family, the cinematic purple. Her father was Louis B. Mayer, one of the founding fathers of Hollywood, the second 'M' of MGM. Her husband was David O. Selznick, who single-handed produced and masterminded *Gone with the Wind*. In her position she had been a witness of the wheeling and dealing, the treacheries and loyalties, the horse-trading, the financial negotiations, the diplomacy, the creativity and destructiveness, the abysmal stupidities and the genius which go into making successful films. Nobody could have enjoyed a better apprenticeship for a career as a Broadway producer. The word 'dynamic' could have been coined especially for her. She was fast-thinking, quick-talking, aggressive, ambitious, and not slow to make decisions or enemies. But she was no fool, nor was she too proud to take advice when she needed it. However, she was not a feminist: she didn't think that any woman was worth ten men, but she knew that *she* was.

In the summer of 1948 she had decided to present *Streetcar* in London but with thirteen of the leading West End managers presenting their credentials, and with no knowledge of the London theatre, she had no idea which of these names to choose as co-producer. She showed the list to her agent, Harold Freedman, who unhesitatingly recommended Binkie.

"He's the best."

"Why?"

"Because he gets things done and he's very good at the job. He's cunning, shrewd, clever, he's got so much charm it's really not decent, he's absolutely the best in London but . . . well, he's entirely honest but you do have to read the small print. Take a long spoon when you eat with him. And don't be fooled by the charm for there is real, unique ability underneath."

All this may seem like an unqualified endorsement of Binkie but in her memoirs, *A Private View*, she said that she couldn't suppress a strong feeling of caution. If Freedman had said bluntly, "Beware of Binkie," she could not have been more alarmed and suspicious. They met at Waterloo Station surrounded by a mountain of luggage. What she saw was a thin, fair, apparently young man who might have been a university undergraduate, so self-effacing and anonymous that her first horrified thought was that Binkie had sent along some inexperienced, junior assistant. What he saw was a very striking and beautiful woman, tall and slim, with raven black hair, dark eyes, black eyebrows and an exquisitely sculpted profile.

"Mrs Selznick? My name is Beaumont. Welcome to England. Welcome doubly so to London. I've booked a suite at Claridge's. It's better than the Savoy. They're used to looking after royalty." He swept her into his Rolls-Royce and organised another car for her luggage and her travelling companion, Hildur. To be openly described as royalty was a very good beginning to their friendship. During the journey to the hotel she found herself being slowly seduced by his famous charm, so much so that in a moment of impulse she found herself confiding Harold Freedman's advice including the words 'Be very careful' and 'Read the Fine Print'. Binkie was vastly amused by this and laughed long and loudly. "He is absolutely right, my dear, what a clever man dear Harold is, bless him. Did he also tell you to take a long spoon when you dine with me? Yes? Well, we'll have dinner later and I'll get the restaurant to provide the longest they've got."

When they arrived at Claridge's, he joined her for drinks in her suite, they had dinner in the restaurant, and they stayed up late into the night in her suite chattering, planning, casting, praising their friends and bitching their enemies. Underneath that dynamic façade she was a great giggler and gossip and nobody could bring it to the surface better than Binkie. They spent twelve hours in each other's company before he finally excused himself and returned to Lord North Street, and out of that developed one of the closest friendships of his life. Not only did she put two of his greatest successes into his lap, she also became his financial adviser. Until then he hadn't been interested in money for himself, only for the Firm. She changed all that. She opened his eyes to the beauty of money as a thing in itself. On her advice he bought, developed and sold property, he made sensible investments, he bought stocks and shares. He even started to read the *Financial Times* and the *Wall Street Journal*. Irene became not only a loving friend but also a guru.

It may have started as a friendship but it quickly developed into a love affair. He gave her a cosy little lunch *à deux* at Lord North Street and with loving pride showed her his paintings and antiques. He took her round London to all the places she most wanted to see and became a tourist himself in the process. He took her to all the Tennent plays and those of other managements. He dined her at the Savoy, Caprice and Scott's. He gave her intimate candle-lit suppers at Lord North Street. He gave her expensive presents and took her to fashion displays. There were long sunny weekends at Finchingfield where they picnicked on the lawn and swam in the nearby river. He even invited her to sit in his office to read his letters, listen to his phone calls and witness his interviews and meetings. That was how she would learn not only about management but about the London theatre.

They even found time to talk about *Streetcar*. For hours they sat side by side each with copies of *Spotlight* on their laps: for hours they conducted one of those endless and repetitive casting sessions which producers and directors always enjoy far more than they are ever willing to admit. Irene suggested Vivien Leigh. Binkie agreed and told her that he'd sent the play to her, that she'd read it, considered it the greatest woman's part since Scarlett O'Hara and passionately wanted to play it. He warned Irene that if she really wanted Vivien to play Blanche she would have to wait for at least a year, but that Vivien was undoubtedly worth waiting for. She and Larry were leading an Old Vic company in Australia touring three plays, *Richard III*, *The School for Scandal* and *The Skin of Our Teeth*. This would take up six months.

Then there was to be a three-month season in London which might extend to a fourth and then they would have to go away for a much-needed holiday. Yes, at least a year. Did Irene have any ideas for a director? She wanted Elia Kazan – known to his friends as Gadge – who had directed it on Broadway but Binkie warned her that Vivien would not want to work with anybody except Larry and that Irene would have to have them both as part of a package or forget about it. In common with the rest of the world, Vivien had an enormous respect for Larry's directing skills as displayed in the *Henry V* and *Hamlet* films, and she did not want to be separated from him for a moment. They had been married only seven years and that was the measure of their love which was still, he was happy to report, enjoying its first golden flush.

Irene sailed back to New York, returning to London in May 1949. The fateful casting of Blanche Dubois had to be decided once for all. Vivien and Larry were at the height of their Old Vic season at the New Theatre. Few theatrical events had caused such excitement. The entire three-month season had been sold out within a week, every performance was crammed to bursting and a queue of hundreds of hopeful theatre-lovers waited for returns. For *Streetcar* the author's approval was needed for all major casting. As Tennessee Williams had never seen Vivien on the stage and had severe doubts if she could play the part, he flew in from a holiday in Rome prepared to spend a week theatre-going in London. Irene, too, had only seen Vivien in films. Binkie therefore took them both to see Vivien playing Lady Anne in *Richard III*, Lady Teazle in *The School for Scandal* and Antigone in a modern, updated version by Jean Anouilh. Tennessee Williams was not a theatre-goer, admitting, candidly, that it bored him. He enjoyed writing plays but he did not enjoy watching them. He further admitted that he had no interest in the classics and could not even understand them. But *Antigone*, being in modern speech, was more accessible and it was this which decided him. "Why do you force me to do these things?" he asked Irene wearily after the third night. "Because I don't have the courage to decide for myself," she replied.

Binkie had warned Vivien that Tennessee Williams and Irene were to be in the theatre and that the casting of Blanche depended on what they saw, so she was in effect giving three auditions. After *Antigone*, the matter was settled and a lively, triumphal party was given at Lord North Street where Binkie, Irene and Vivien giggled and gossiped into the small hours while Larry and Tennessee had a talk about possible cuts. Olivier liked the play, but considered it too long. The discussion was very brief, consisting of a courteous but firm refusal from the author to allow any cuts at all. "It's already been cut to the bone, Larry," he said apologetically. "And I just can't cut any more." But he was thrilled that Larry wanted to direct it. To have the prestige of an Olivier production meant more than all the plaudits of Broadway.

To cut or not to cut was the single cause of all the trouble which was to erupt and cloud the rehearsal period. In New York, the author's wishes are respected and nobody thinks of cutting without his consent. In London, the director enjoys greater freedom. Even though the author had a clause in the contract forbidding any cuts without his cabled permission, Olivier insisted that it was his prerogative as director to make cuts which in his judgement were essential. It was, he insisted, not just a matter of pride and authority, but also of theatrical good sense: *he* had to work with the actors and was ultimately responsible for everything the audience saw and heard. Irene tried hard to persuade him to leave the play as it was. It had already shown its power and quality on Broadway, so why change it? "It's repetitive and full of padding," said Olivier; "anyway, why should Tennessee mind? These cuts are actually improving it. Things are different in London." However, he did agree to use Jo Mielziner's set, a structure of different levels and a lot of gauze curtains which would allow the complex lighting plot required to set the mood and indicate the passage of time.

There were problems in casting the male lead, the savage Stanley Kowalski, salesman, drinker, compulsive all-night poker player for whom the word 'uncouth' could have been especially invented. He is a brutish moron with the charming habit of drinking ice-cold beer out of the bottle and allowing it to dribble on to his naked chest, of beating up his pregnant wife and of destroying the furniture of their tiny two-room apartment when out of temper. Curiously, the author had scattered his normally uncouth dialogue with traces of education: he uses phrases like "Let me enlighten you", and "I'll ask him to appraise it", and "Are you acquainted with the Napoleonic Code?" There was a distinct shortage of suitable American actors with British Equity membership and of course no American Equity actor would be allowed to fly over and play it, though everybody wanted to see Marlon Brando. Sam Wanamaker and Bonar Colleano were the only contenders and Colleano finally got it. Renée Asherson as the much persecuted sister and Bernard Braden as the gentle, kindly Mitch completed the principal casting. Rehearsals started in October but when Irene looked in to see how things were going, all ready and eager to give advice and help if it were needed – and confident that it would be – she was appalled to discover that Olivier had already made extensive cuts, that the cast had been given them and that she had not.

She appealed to Binkie. It was an awkward situation for him because he did not want to support Irene and Tennessee openly by showing himself hostile to the cuts, but on the other hand he did not wish to upset Olivier and Vivien by insisting that the author's contractual rights be respected and the cuts restored. Binkie knew when to keep quiet and when to protest. He advised Irene to wait and to be patient.

Then there was trouble over the production itself. Olivier bluntly refused to imitate Elia Kazan's original and insisted that he be given a free hand to do what he wanted. He had no desire to present London with a carbon copy; he had plenty of ideas of his own. Irene presented him with the Broadway prompt script with all the moves, lighting and sound clearly indicated but he refused to use it. After a couple of weeks he made the discovery that it just wasn't possible to go too far away from Kazan's production ideas since they were so closely wedded to the text and the designs, so he reluctantly decided to use some of them and to put a credit to that effect in the programme.

But there was more trouble over those wretched cuts, which Irene sent in a long cable to Tennessee then living in Florida. He in turn sent an anguished, furious cable to Binkie who returned a placatory answer. But it wasn't much use, for by then Irene had found further cause for discontent. It wasn't only the cuts which made her deeply unhappy, but also Vivien's interpretation which, she insisted, was all wrong and had nothing to do with the play, with Kazan's ideas or with Jessica Tandy's excellent and highly praised performance. The point at issue was simple: the play implies, without specifically stating, that Blanche is a prostitute. Vivien believed that she wasn't, that the play could be interpreted in different ways. Irene tried to convince her that the author and Jessica Tandy made it clear that Blanche *was* an immoral woman, but Vivien rightly insisted that she couldn't be expected to copy another actress however good or authorised her performance, and that she must be allowed to do it in her own way.

There were endless high-level meetings at Lord North Street, at Claridge's and at Notley Abbey. Discussion became arguments and arguments became heated exchanges of opinion. Nothing so vulgar as a row ever developed because the emotions were always carefully controlled and courteously spoken, but feelings ran high and sometimes came close to danger point. Telegrams now flew round the world; from Audrey Wood, Tennessee's agent; Harold Freedman, Irene's agent; from Tennessee himself, from the Writers' Guild and from American Equity. To all of these Binkie sent diplomatic replies, pouring as much oil as he could on the wounded pride, injured feelings and outraged professionalism. Privately, he urged Olivier to compromise and restore the cuts. The anti-cut lobby was strengthened by the arrival of Elia Kazan himself to direct Paul Muni in *Death of a Salesman*. He sent a cordial message to Olivier giving him full permission to use all his production ideas, but criticising the cuts which, he insisted, would spoil the play. Binkie's position was now very delicate. Irene and Tennessee were clearly going to be important and influential figures on the Broadway scene and he had no desire to antagonise them. Over a long weekend at Notley, Olivier found himself outnumbered with Irene, Kazan, Tennessee and Binkie all against him so he finally consented and restored the cuts. Irene was invited to see a run-through the following Monday and was able to cable Tennessee in jubilation that most of the important cuts had been restored and that peace now reigned at the Aldwych.

She was also able to tell him that the costumes were to be designed by Beatrice Dawson, known to her friends as 'Bumble'. In another gesture of independence, Olivier had decided not to use the Broadway designs which had apparently departed from the author's wishes but to follow the descriptions given in the text. Thus Blanche on her first appearance would wear, not the flowered flimsy chiffon, but a neatly waisted white suit with a fluffy bodice, white gloves and hat. This was one innovation welcomed by both Irene and the author.

But the Battle of the Cuts – as Binkie was later to describe it – was not quite over. There was just one more and it had nothing to do with Olivier. It was the Lord Chamberlain's office exercising its powers of censorship. The play had been given a clean bill of health except for one small point. In the sixth scene Blanche, having been out with Mitch, the gentleman escort whom she clearly wishes to marry, describes in a long speech her first marriage to a seventeen-year-old youth. It is implied that the reason why the boy committed suicide and why she had a nervous breakdown which drove her into the fantasy world of prostitution and ultimate madness was her appalled dis-covery that her young husband was a homosexual, though the word was never used in the play, the fashionable euphemism being 'degenerate'. It is further implied that she found him and his lover together.

> I came suddenly into a room which I thought was empty, which wasn't empty but had two people in it . . .
>> (A locomotive is heard approaching. She claps her hands to her ears and crouches over. As the noise recedes she straightens slowly and continues speaking.)
> Afterwards we pretended that nothing had been discovered. Yes, the three of us drove out to Mook Lake Casino very drunk and laughing all the way . . .

Most people would have thought this was quite harmless, but the puritan element was still very strong in 1949. Any reference to sexual perversion was considered an abomination, however vague or un-specific, and not all Binkie's influence at the court of St James's could save it. He received formal instructions that the words "but had two people in it" should be cut. This left those who hadn't read the newspapers, where this legal absurdity was described and condemned with relish, in total ignorance of just why Blanche's marriage had not been a success. They were able to find out when the *Daily Express* serialised the play and when John Lehmann published it in hardback. The official view meant that what was too disgusting to be heard was perfectly acceptable when read.★

With Olivier directing, Vivien starring and the advance publicity which inevitably emphasised the high sexual content of the play, public interest was at fever pitch. Advance booking started six months in advance and by the week of the opening over 10,000 applications for first-night tickets had been received for a theatre which held only 1,200. The queue for the 200 seats in the gallery started three days in advance. The all-night queue had become one of the most news-worthy and greatly loved features of wartime and post-war theatre-going when gallery seats were always unreserved. The press could be relied on to take eye-catching photos of these passionate theatre-lovers huddled in their blankets on the pavement outside the theatre, making proud, happy statements of their willingness to undergo considerable hardship to see the play of their choice at a price they could afford. Whoever was at the front – usually an unmarried woman of uncertain age working in the Civil Service – would have been there for at least twenty-four hours. There was an element of healthy competition in the all-night queue: comparisons would be lovingly made and some striking marathons had been achieved. For *Streetcar*, the head of the Aldwych queue was a Treasury clerk named Anne Day who had queued for a record-breaking thirty-five hours. On the morning of the first performance, there were over a hundred who had been there for one day, some for two. It was a cold and wet November day. Binkie arranged for a couple of canteen trolleys laden with coffee and toasted sandwiches to be sent out for their relief. His philanthropy did not extend to dispensing his largesse in person but he made sure that the press knew who was responsible.

★ The *Streetcar* triumvirate, Williams, Kazan and Irene, had even more trouble in Hollywood where the notorious Hays Office imposed a much stricter code of decency. Even the Lord Chamberlain's compromise was unacceptable. Instead, the whole speech had to be cut and rewritten with Blanche merely saying, weakly, "I guess he wasn't like other men . . ."

When the gallery doors opened at seven o'clock, there were over 500 waiting of whom only 200 could be admitted. The doors were closed for a numbers check and were re-opened with the announcement that there was room for five more. Predictably, this caused a stampede: women fainted, clothes were torn, faces scratched. The police were called, ambulances arrived, the wounded were carried to hospital. As the audience streamed in through the front a crowd estimated at 2,000 laid siege to see the white-tie and tiara celebrities arrive in their Daimlers and Rolls-Royces. It was a West End first night, as it used to be before the war.

The gallery's patience was finally rewarded by the sight of a Vivien Leigh they did not recognise. She was now blonde and her face was lined and haggard. She seemed old, despairing and tired. Her make-up as a disintegrating faded beauty, her voice with its nervous tension and the hoarseness of the habitual gin-drinker were triumphs of her skill as an actress of maturity. By the end of the evening it was clear why she yearned to play Blanche for it was the part of a lifetime. She never stops talking for three hours: even when she is off stage changing into yet another of her eight costumes she continues to talk from the wings. Blanche is one of the greatest of all women's roles in the theatre, requiring from the actress despair, grief, anger, happiness, yearning, sexuality and tears: she is flirtatious, coy, whimsical, teasing, violent, tipsy, kittenish, crumbling and authoritative. She gets raped by a big husky caveman with a hairy chest, ". . . We've had this date from the beginning, Blanche," and if all that was not enough, she goes mad. It had everything.

At the end there were fourteen curtains and when Vivien took her solo call she received a standing ovation. A large section of the gallery were heard to call "RENÉE, RENÉE, RENÉE . . ." Tennessee Williams knew how to write good supporting parts and the charming, pretty, unselfish sister, who gets beaten up by her man when pregnant and still loves him, struck a special chord of sympathy in the audience. It was given a most beautiful performance by Renée Asherson. Olivier refused to take a bow or make speeches. "They don't want to see me in white tie and tails," he said. "It would be a terrible anti-climax."

Binkie arranged for Anne Day to be escorted backstage to meet Vivien Leigh, her life's ambition. "You must be exhausted," Vivien said. "Not as exhausted as you must be," replied the Treasury clerk. Outside the theatre over 300 people were waiting and shouting for Vivien to appear. Binkie finally went in person to the stage door flanked by three policemen to announce through a megaphone that "Miss Leigh is so exhausted by the long evening that she will be unable to give any autographs. She is so sorry and hopes you will understand." Finally, at 11.45 p.m., the crowd's patience was rewarded. Vivien appeared flanked by Olivier, Elia Kazan, Irene Selznick and others of note, climbed into a Rolls-Royce and drove off to Lord North Street for one of Binkie's supper parties.

The notices, for the most part, showed an intelligent and articulate appreciation of the play's finer qualities and indicated that in purging the soul by pity and terror it was a tragedy according to Aristotle's definition. These would attract those discriminating play-goers who hadn't already bought their tickets. But there were a number of tabloids who took another point of view and denounced it hysterically. ". . . Obscene pornography . . . disgustingly squalid, vicious, degrading, a trip down a sewage tunnel, a running ulcerous sore in the bowels . . ." The queue outside the box office lengthened and the advance booking stretched forward to three months. The Sunday papers managed to improve on that. "A garbage heap, crude bellowings of sex, the reptile house at the Zoo, grunting like cesspools . . ." The queue continued to lengthen and the advance booking stretched to four months. "This revolting play will guarantee an enjoyable evening for those who like lust, vice and sadism." Clearly there were thousands who did like lust, vice and sadism for the queue at the box office now went down to the street and the advance booking extended to six months. "Don't worry, Irene dear," said Binkie consolingly when he took her out to lunch. "They said all that about *Ghosts* and *Pygmalion* and they haven't done too badly. These are just the sort of notices I want. We'll run a year at the very least, maybe two."

Streetcar was the sort of play which creates its own publicity. A vicar in Southwark preached a hard-hitting sermon on the Sunday after the first night. "A pathological obsession with sex is a mark of every dying civilisation from Sodom to Gomorrah, from Babylon to Rome," he said. "Let the United States of America keep its own sewage." Needless to say, the reverend gentleman had not seen it. Neither had the ladies and gentlemen of the Public Morality Council whose chairwoman, Lady Ravensdale, addressed a meeting of a hundred clergymen and their wives. "It is no excuse to say that this abominable play is well acted and directed. Our senses are being dragged down to the lowest possible denominator. The play is thoroughly indecent and we should be ashamed that children and servants are allowed to sit in the theatre and see it." On Broadway the play closed after 855 performances which allowed Binkie officially to publicise the fact that admirers of Tennessee Williams' masterpiece could now see it in London, and unofficially to indicate that they would see a far better production. The film rights were sold to Charles Feldman, a Hollywood producer of some eminence, who had, at

Binkie's invitation, flown in to London to see the first night at the Aldwych and had been dined and wined at Lord North Street. Vivien's performance finally decided him. No casting was announced or decided but as Irene, Kazan and Tennessee were all pushing for her, it was inevitable that Vivien would get the part. The price was a fee of £150,000, about three times the sum which had been paid for *Gone with the Wind* some fourteen years earlier.

Binkie spent a long weekend in Paris where he saw the French version, *Le Tramcar Nommé Désir* starring Arletty★ and directed by Jean Cocteau, who had cast Jean Marais, his good friend, as Stanley. Vivien was understandably curious. "Tatty as hell, darling," Binkie said when he saw her after his return. "Tatty like everything is in Paris. You wouldn't *believe* the sets and costumes. She's all right, I suppose, but far too old and she's completely the wrong type. But Jean Marais is just too *gorgeous* for words. Oh, if only his English was better, he might replace Bonar." At Binkie's invitation Arletty paid a visit to London when she had a short holiday, saw the play and met Vivien afterwards. The two Blanches toasted each other with champagne, chatted away in French which Vivien spoke fluently, and discussed with Binkie the possibility of an exchange, each company to play a week in each other's city. Never had the *entente* seemed so *cordiale*.

Binkie had decided to present *Streetcar* under the banner of his tax-exempt company, Tennent Productions Ltd. Tennessee Williams wasn't entirely unknown in London, but there was no reason to suppose that it would automatically be a big success even with Vivien's star appeal, and it might need some financial help such as could only be obtained from a sizeable tax exemption. This was not altogether a happy decision, for within a week of the opening questions were being asked and ominous paragraphs started to appear in the press. Why should *Streetcar* be exempt from Entertainment Tax? Can this play, which has an uncouth moron and an oversexed, unprincipled trollop for its central characters, *really* claim to have cultural and educational value? Thus snarled the *Sunday Express*. Other Sunday papers obsessed by Stanley Kowalski's table manners, pursued this theme. How could a play be called educational when its hero had such disgusting personal habits? These were described with relish: he picks his nose, eats his mucus, scratches his groin, gobbles

★ Her real name was Léonie Bathiat. She was always a greatly admired actress but it was her performance in *Les Enfants du Paradis* which made her into one of France's greatest stars. During the war she was accused of collaboration but was acquitted. Now she lives alone in Paris, blind and a total recluse.

his chicken with his fingers, licks the fingers and then wipes them on the table cloth and his wife's dress. All this in mixed company! What would happen to civilisation if the youth of England were to follow his example? It was with nonsense like this that the popular press filled its empty columns. Richard Clowes, speaking for H. M. Tennent and Binkie, replied calmly that the same hoggish table manners had been portrayed with equally repulsive detail in Korda's film *The Private Life of Henry VIII* made and released some thirteen years earlier, and there was no sign that civilisation had come to an end because of it.

Binkie heard that several West End managers, among them Emile Littler, Tom Arnold, Jack Hylton and Lee Ephraim, had formed a committee whose open and declared aims were implacably hostile to him and Tennent Productions Ltd. The trouble boiled down to one simple and disturbing emotion. Jealousy. The committee were complaining bitterly that because Binkie had accumulated such a large capital reserve by manipulating the tax laws, and other devious methods, he could now outbid all the other managers in securing the London rights of important and successful American plays. At that very moment, they pointed out with disapproval, he had no less than seven Broadway successes running in London: *Streetcar, Death of a Salesman, Summer and Smoke, The Heiress, Deep are the Roots, Dark of the Moon* and *The Glass Menagerie.* He had completely cornered the market and although they welcomed fair competition they considered that his tax exemption gave him an unfair advantage. They knew, as everybody did for it was no secret, that he was paying a royalty of seventeen and a half per cent for *Death of a Salesman,* currently drawing full houses at the Phoenix, and twenty per cent for *Streetcar* doing likewise at the Aldwych, and as well as substantial down payments, there were other inducements in the form of expensive presents and lavish hospitality. How could they hope to compete with all that?

Binkie and George Gwatkin, his financial adviser and lawyer, were invited to meet a Parliamentary sub-committee to answer some questions. Binkie made his appearance glowing with supreme assurance and confidence. He knew that jealousy and malignancy couldn't hurt him: he had a low opinion of these lesser mortals who were seeking to destroy him though he was far too shrewd and diplomatic to let this be seen. He knew that they found it impossible to forgive somebody who had been so successful so young and so quickly. But he was quite safe, there was nothing they could do to him. On being questioned about the customary royalty payments in the West End he admitted that ten per cent was usual, twelve and a half rather high and that seventeen and a half and twenty were exceptional and paid only because his rivals had matched it with an equal offer. If American producers accepted his bid it was only because they wanted him. It was not for him to argue with Mrs Irene Selznick, for example, if she preferred H. M. Tennent to other managements.

When he was asked just why she preferred him, he was able to answer with becoming modesty that the prestige of H. M. Tennent stood very high in America because of the artistic standards he had always set and always maintained. He had worked hard to achieve this and he believed that he deserved the rewards. "Everything you touch seems to turn to gold," said Sir Ernest Pooley, Chairman of the Arts Council. "Yes," replied Binkie, "one does seem to be on the crest of the wave but it hasn't always been like this. One's had a number of notable failures and neither the Shakespeare season at the Haymarket nor the revival of *Antony and Cleopatra* has made any money. And although *Streetcar* has been singled out for abuse by certain sections of the press, it has the highest reputation in America and has been awarded the Pulitzer Prize for the Best Play of the Year."

He further pointed out that theatrical history over the last century had shown that the great theatrical empires never lived for long. They started quietly, rose to their peak and crest and then slowly faded away. This happened to the Irving regime at the Lyceum, to Beerbohm Tree at His Majesty's, to the Abbey Theatre in Dublin, to the Mercury Theatre in New York and it would doubtless happen to him and H. M. Tennent. Now it was at its peak, but in the fullness of time, and he could only guess how long that was, it would eventually fade away and die.

Since he had seen to it that the financial administration of H. M. Tennent was meticulously correct nobody could find any fault in its business ethics. Binkie had broken no law. Although rival managers might complain, there was nothing they could do but wait patiently and bide their time until he made one fatal slip, which wasn't likely, or until the gathering storm of public opinion made it possible for further guerilla action to be taken.

CHAPTER TWENTY-EIGHT

1951–3

Festival of Britain – *Waters of the Moon* – *A Day by the Sea*

Few things caused more excitement than the government's announcement in 1950 of a gigantic, multi-million Festival of Industry and the Arts to be held exactly a hundred years after the Great Exhibition of 1851. The Festival of Britain, as it was officially known, made it clear to the London managements that they were expected to contribute their best stars and their best plays in order to make the West End the most startling and wonderful explosion of talent in the world – indeed, in the century. And this is exactly what it was. London in 1951 was where every theatre-lover wanted to be, and many millions were. There was Alec Guinness's second Hamlet, this time with a beard. John Clements and Kay Hammond presented themselves in *Man and Superman* and on Saturdays included the rarely-played third act with its Hell scene, and thus gave the world virtually its first glimpse of the entirety which, as it lasted well over four hours, was generally known as the Eternity version. Basil Dean revived *Hassan* with the young and handsome Laurence Harvey, the Oliviers revived *Antony and Cleopatra* and *Caesar and Cleopatra* running them on alternate nights with Vivien Leigh playing both Cleopatras, in yet another bid to show that her ambitions to be a classical actress and worthy to share the stage with her husband were to be taken seriously. There was all that and Danny Kaye too, attempting, and nearly succeeding, in recreating the glories of his first and legendary post-war appearance at the Palladium in 1947.

Binkie's contribution was no fewer than eight plays. *Relative Values*, Noël Coward's latest starring Gladys Cooper, Angela Baddeley and Judy Campbell, a charming comedy which dramatised the tensions in a country-house party when a visiting American film star turns out to be the sister of the lady's maid; a splendid *Three Sisters* with Margaret Leighton, Celia Johnson, Renée Asherson and Ralph Richardson; *The Winter's Tale* with Gielgud, Flora Robson and Diana

Wynyard, directed by Peter Brook; *The Lyric Revue* with Ian Car-
michael, Hermione Baddeley, Dora Bryan and Jeremy Hawk, generally regarded as the best of its sort since the wartime *Sweet and Low*
series; and *A Penny for a Song*, by John Whiting. This was an
enchanting farcical comedy about a local squire in 1814 who dresses up
as Napoleon to confuse the invading French army and is captured by
the English Home Guard who understandably think he is the real
Napoleon. With costumes and sets designed by the inventor and *Punch*
cartoonist, Rowland Emett, it starred Ronald Squire, Ronald
Howard, Marie Löhr and the young Virginia McKenna. There was
one of Arthur Macrae's translations from the French, *Figure of Fun*,
with John Mills (discovered at curtain rise standing on his head, an
unsuspected talent), and *Colombe*, another cynical Anouilh sneer with
Yvonne Arnaud playing a monstrous theatrical bitch clearly based on
Sarah Bernhardt.

These were like the crown jewels but the centre piece was a gentle
drama by a retired schoolmaster, N. C. Hunter, called *Waters of the
Moon*, about a group of lonely and unhappy people living out their
lives in a remote country hotel. They include Mrs Whyte, an elderly
widow whose husband and children have all died leaving her homeless
and penniless; Herr Winterhalter, a refugee from Hitler's Germany
who passionately loves opera; Colonel Selby, long since retired from
the army and living on his memories of the First World War; the hotel
manager's grown-up son, John Daly, whose dreams of Polar explora-
tion are effectively hampered by tuberculosis; Evelyn Daly, his sister,
loveless and frigid and clearly condemned to spinsterhood. Their lives
are suddenly disrupted by the arrival of the Lancaster family, whose
car has broken down and who are forced to stay the weekend in the
hotel. The Lancasters are very rich and very grand and very charming.
The play skilfully shows the impact of wealth on poverty, of success
on failure. It had wit, charm, pathos and perception. It was impossible
not to liken it to Chekhov whose echoes could be found on every page,
but it was none the worse for that. The part of Mrs Lancaster,
colourful, garrulous, charming, flamboyant could have been written
for Edith Evans and she accepted it with pleasure. Since the failure of
Bridie's *Daphne Laureola* in New York, she once again felt the urge to
glitter and sparkle.

Binkie used to say that successful play management was seventy per
cent good casting, and this meant casting that was not merely suitable
but imaginative, outrageous and daring. If your suggestions are
greeted by your colleagues with alarm then you know you are on the
right track. The elderly widow, Mrs Whyte, whose speeches are
seething with snobbery, self-pity and resentment was a small part and

not very interesting. She spends most of her time knitting quietly at the end of the sofa. Another of Binkie's maxims dealt directly with the casting of boring small parts. "Give it a star because you'll never know what she'll make of it." He decided to offer it to Sybil Thorndike. Everybody at Tennents expressed the most reassuring and satisfactory signs of panic. "You must be *mad*, Binkie dear . . . she'll never take it . . . she's quite wrong for it . . . it's ridiculous." Her son John Casson, in his memoirs, reported that her family tried to dissuade her. "Edith will swamp you. Don't do it," but Sybil was strangely attracted to the play and the part. "I think I can do something with it. She has to play the Chopin E minor prelude and I think it would be rather fun." It was not widely known outside her family circle, that she was an extremely good pianist – something she had in common with Yvonne Arnaud – and had once contemplated a musical career.

Others in the company included Wendy Hiller, Leo Bieber, Owen Holder, Kathleen Harrison, Nan Munro (who was also Edith's under-study for a further £10 a week, becoming in the process her good friend and part-time secretary/companion) and that-very-good-actor Cyril Raymond. Binkie didn't want him. "He's such a *boring* actor, Edith dear," he said over lunch one day, "I'm sure I can do better for you." She shook her head. "That's all to the good, the part is a boring part. Dear Cyril is so reliable. He'll do very nicely." Binkie surren-dered. The part wasn't important enough to justify any sort of fight and if it made Edith happy, that too was all to the good.

Like Topsy, the small part of Mrs Whyte just grew and grew and grew until it became the equal of Mrs Lancaster if not in size then certainly in importance. With Edith Evans, chattering endlessly and sweeping round the stage in her gorgeous Hardy Amies creations, being flirtatious with Herr Winterhalter, nostalgic with the Colonel, encouraging to John, generous to all the others and sparkling with that special radiance which reminded so many theatre-goers of her Milla-mant which, after only twenty-seven years, was well within living memory, and Sybil Thorndike, radiating icy, chilling disapproval and a lifetime of bitterness and resentment, it was indeed a battle of giants. The author had cleverly arranged that there should be a New Year's party at the end of the second act in which everybody gets gently drunk on the dry champagne provided by the Lancasters, and that the two ladies should have a scene of confrontation in which they start to argue and bicker about the poetry of Robert Browning, of all unlikely subjects.

Mrs Lancaster: I have always admired Browning.
Mrs Whyte: Pah! Tiresome old ranter!

Mrs Lancaster: At least he was vigorous, he was alive. He didn't mope and drool!

Mrs Whyte: Alive! I should think so! That heartiness! Poor Elizabeth – fancy being married to that rhyming rowing-blue!

Earlier, the arguments had been more personal with a lot more acid.

Mrs Lancaster: We must accept the conditions in which we are born and make the most of our abilities without self-pity. The rich man at his castle, the poor man at his gate, each has his place in the scheme of things.

Mrs Whyte: That's all very well for the rich man.

Mrs Lancaster: It's all very well for everybody.

Mrs Whyte: Supposing you had been born the daughter of a Neapolitan laundress.

Mrs Lancaster: I should have made just as good a washerwoman as anyone, just as good. And probably I should have contrived to have got myself kept by a wealthy spaghetti manufacturer.

Nobody was more skilled in the gentle art of scene stealing than Sybil when she was in one of her creative moods, and she did it by doing what appeared to be absolutely nothing. When she sat at the end of the sofa quietly knitting, those needles suddenly became objects of great beauty and importance, and you watched them closely. When she sat down in a darkened corner at the piano with her back to the audience and started to play the Chopin F major nocturne and E minor prelude, the world stopped and you could think only of the beautiful tragic music and the beautiful silhouette playing it.

Rumours started to circulate that she and Edith were not friendly, that they were at loggerheads, spoiling each other's performances by distracting business, upstaging, treading on laughs, the full catalogue of theatrical misbehaviour. All lies. They had always lived separate lives and had little sociability outside the theatre, but inside the Haymarket they enjoyed a totally professional and cordial relationship. But there was one occasion which came to mind at Sybil's memorial service. "She used to overact most terribly at matinées," said John Gielgud with a happy smile to a rustle of appreciative laughter from the congregation, "and would then apologise so charmingly afterwards saying that she had her grandchildren in front and wanted to give them something special to remember . . . which, of course, she always did." She once did this with such energy and enthusiasm that Edith felt obliged to complain to the director, Frith Banbury, who put the matter right with a short note to Sybil. She replied the following day with a heartfelt apology.

Edith's gowns, specially designed by Hardy Amies, were superb. Sybil, as befits the impoverished gentlewoman, wore old threadbare clothes. At the end of the first year Edith's were showing signs of wear. Binkie paid a visit to her dressing-room one evening and suggested that she should have a completely new set. How about a little weekend trip to Paris where the House of Balmain could supply what she needed? "That's fine, Binkie," she said, "as long as Sybil gets a new cardigan."

Waters of the Moon ran for a little more than two years and grossed a little more than three-quarters of a million pounds. Binkie paid ten per cent of the gross to both of the dames, about £800 a week each, and five per cent to the author, a special low royalty because he was unknown and this was his first play, though with £400 a week flowing in for two years he had no cause for complaint. But there was still a handsome profit for Binkie because he chose Tennent Productions Ltd to present it, a fact which was to cause no little embarrassment a few years later. Clearly, Norman Hunter was an author whom Binkie did not wish to lose. Binkie had sensibly taken out an option on his next play and he was wondering if dear Norman had anything else which might suit? Yes, he did. It was the mixture as before but none the worse for that. This time it was about a family living in a remote part of Dorset and close to the sea with a beach nearby. The characters include an ambitious but ultimately unsuccessful diplomat whose dreams of an ambassadorship are frustrated (John Gielgud), his feather-headed, bossy, nagging mother (Sybil Thorndike), his antique, endlessly grumbling uncle (Lewis Casson), an alcoholic doctor living with them on sufferance (Ralph Richardson), a childhood sweetheart now grown-up, divorced and with two young children (Irene Worth) and a lovelorn governess secretly in love with the doctor (Megs Jenkins). The plot was less than before, but the relationships between the characters were much more complex. It was Binkie's Law that when the dramatic content is thin, the casting must be especially thick. Gielgud had been knighted in the birthday honours' list to widespread rejoicing and in most people's opinion not a moment too soon. When the rehearsals started at the end of September the final countdown of stars was three knights and one dame, a cast which could be truthfully described as Cream of Tennent. Never again was Binkie to assemble a company with so many titles.

Getting Sybil wasn't easy. Initially she refused it: "I've had enough of those feather-headed, bird-brain women. People will think I can do nothing else. Haven't you something with a little more meat?" But Binkie knew how to get round her. "There's a very nice part for Lewis," he said. "It's not too long so he'll have no trouble remembering it. And he's sitting down most of the time." It was a trump card and a further indication of what John Casson has called his managerial genius. Binkie knew that with Lewis Casson in the company, it would not only keep Sybil happy but keep her under control. Her habit of over-acting, pulling funny faces and waving her arms around could be restrained only by her husband's vigilance and lovingly watchful eye. More than anybody else, Lewis could bring out the best in her.

Just as those who read *Pride and Prejudice* learn nothing of the Napoleonic Wars which took place at the same time, so those who today happen to read the script of *A Day by the Sea* and respond to its charm and delicacy, will probably not know that the play coincided with one of the biggest scandals to hit Binkie, H. M. Tennent and the whole of the West End. When stripped of all rumours, myths and legends, the facts are plain enough. On the evening of October 21st John Gielgud was arrested in Chelsea. He was taken back to Chelsea police station where Inspector Puckey charged him with a homosexual offence and ordered him to attend at the Chelsea magistrates' court at ten-thirty the following morning.

The question which was to be asked afterwards and endlessly in the future years was this: why did he not tell Binkie? Even at that late stage with barely twelve hours to go before the court hearing, Binkie might have been able to arrange something, perhaps for the case to be heard *in camera*. It would not be easy, for this was normally done only with cases involving government security, but with Binkie's energy and high-ranking contacts it was just possible. But Gielgud did not tell him, did not tell anybody. He later confided to Robert Whitehead that he did not wish to be a nuisance, that he felt so ashamed that he just could not speak about it, that he could not bear to see the look of disappointment in Binkie's eyes should he confess what he had done. But there was probably another and more important reason. Underneath the flab, there was strength and courage and sheer guts. He had made a bad mistake, he'd done something both foolish and criminal, but he was too proud to run away. It was not compatible with his dignity as a Knight Bachelor and an acknowledged star of the London theatre. He must face the music and take the consequences. He returned home and spent a sleepless night. It was the only time in his life that he seriously contemplated suicide. The next morning he stated that he was a clerk living at 16 Cowley Street, that he was self-employed and earned approximately £1,000 a year. He pleaded guilty and said: "I cannot imagine that I was so stupid. I was tired and had been drinking. I was not responsible for my actions." The magistrate, a Mr E. R. Guest, fined him ten pounds and suggested that he go and talk to his doctor. Gielgud bowed, thanked the magistrate and left the court. It had all been over in a few minutes. It had all been very quiet, very civilised, very English. The one possibility which really terrified him was the publicity. Journalists don't normally cover magistrates' court cases unless they have advance notice that something, or some-body, important is expected, and it so happened that there were no reporters in number one court that morning. But as bad luck would have it, a reporter from the *Evening Standard* just happened to be in the hall and through the open door leading into the court he saw a familiar face and heard a familiar voice. He went inside, attended the brief hearing and immediately telephoned the story to his news editor. By lunchtime the *Evening Standard* carrying the story in headlines hit the streets to be seen and bought by a deeply shocked and bewildered company. And this was how Binkie found out.

When the company assembled for the afternoon rehearsal they all knew and when Gielgud returned they were all there and waiting for him. A heavy silence fell and a terrible embarrassment gripped them, for nothing like this had ever happened to them and there were no guide-lines for the correct social behaviour. Should they ignore it as if it had never happened? Should they offer condolences? Or should they make light-hearted, perhaps jokey, references to it? It was Sybil Thorndike who knew just what to say. She punctured the balloon of tension and embarrassment with a carefully timed and chosen tactless remark. She rushed across the rehearsal room, embraced him, kissed him on both cheeks and said, loudly and laughingly, "Oh, John, darling, you have been a silly bugger." It was exactly the right thing to say in that context. Gielgud laughed loudly, everybody joined in and the rehearsal was able to proceed in a happy and relaxed atmosphere. With one exception. One woman in the cast thought the whole matter disgusting and horrible and she passed this opinion, for what it was worth, to Lily Taylor, the wardrobe mistress. From then on, her relationship with Gielgud, though outwardly polite, was distinctly cool.

That evening there was a meeting in Binkie's house with all the Tennent hierarchy and their legal advisers. What was to be done? Gielgud offered to give up the part and to retire from the theatre until the scandal had died down, but Binkie wouldn't let him. If he didn't face the public in this play then he would never be able to act again and he could retire permanently if that was what he wanted. In any case, who could replace him in a long and very difficult part at such short notice?

The three touring weeks, at Liverpool, Edinburgh and Manchester, passed without incident and all was ready for the grand opening at the Haymarket on October 26th. If it had been possible, Binkie would like to have closed the theatre to the public and filled it with Gielgud and Tennent supporters on invitation, but the box office had opened some weeks before the case and the house was already three-quarters sold. A disturbing rumour circulated round the West End that the gallery was planning a hostile demonstration so Binkie arranged for police and security men to be on duty to deal with any trouble-makers. In addition, he arranged for the stage managers from all the other Tennent plays to leave their theatres and mingle with the first-night audience to cope with any trouble and to lead the applause.

It is unlikely that there was ever a Tennent first night filled with such tension and gloomy foreboding. Gielgud's first entrance as Julian Anson, the diplomat, was a quarter of an hour into the first act, probably the longest and most crucifying fifteen minutes of his life. When the moment came he could not enter: he was paralysed and shaking with fear. Once again it was Sybil Thorndike who came to his rescue. She was on the stage having just completed a short scene with Irene Worth. When Gielgud didn't appear she could see him in the wings, knew what was the trouble and what had to be done. She walked off through the French windows, grabbed him and whispered fiercely, "Come on, John darling, *they won't boo me*," and led him firmly on to the stage. To everybody's astonishment and indescribable relief, the audience gave him a standing ovation. They cheered, they applauded, they shouted. The message was quite clear. The English public has always been loyal to its favourites and this was their chance to show that they didn't care tuppence what he had done in his private life, he was still their adored leading actor, still a star, still their own, their very own John Gielgud and that they loved and respected him dearly. It was a moment never to be forgotten by those who witnessed it, Sybil Thorndike hugging him and smiling with unmistakable defiance at the audience as if to say, "I don't think it matters, do any of you?" and Gielgud, the famous Terry tears visibly running down his cheeks, unable to speak. It was a long time before he could stammer out his first line, one of delicious triviality, "Oh dear, I'd forgotten we had all those azaleas . . ." which, at a moment of such cosmic significance, was greeted with a roar of laughter and renewed applause.

After all that, *A Day by the Sea* might have been an anti-climax but the quality of the play and the superb acting kept the audience riveted.

Singled out by the critics were Gielgud's two principal scenes of confrontation, being sacked from his Paris Embassy post by a senior Foreign Office official – played with excruciating complacency and smugness by Lockwood West – and proposing marriage to his childhood friend, played by Irene Worth, only to be rejected.

After the play the shouts, cheers, applause and endless curtain calls indicated beyond doubt or argument that the evening had been a huge success and that Gielgud had been fully restored to public favour. In the packed dressing-room, the relief was so intense that you could almost cut it with a knife: it was tears and kisses and unlimited glasses of dry champagne. At the height of this celebration, Binkie was called away and when he returned it was to bring some worrying news. A very large crowd had gathered outside the stage door filling Suffolk Street and numbering, according to press reports, some 300 people. There was no reason to suppose that they were all theatre supporters who had seen the play, there could well be a number of strangers anxious to make trouble, and there were further rumours of a gallery demonstration. In a courteous but misplaced attempt to avoid this and thus save Gielgud any further aggravation, Binkie had arranged for him to leave by the front of the theatre and for Jack Osborn to bring round the Rolls-Royce which would take them to Lord North Street for the party.

"No, Binkie, I'm an actor," he said firmly, "and I go out by the stage door whatever the consequences." And so he did. Binkie hastily assembled a Praetorian Guard of high-ranking Tennentry consisting of himself, John Perry, Bernard Gordon, Peter Glenville, Joe Davis, Charles La Trobe, the stage director, and Anthony Watson, the assistant house manager, with the stage-door keeper and the theatre's uniformed commissionaire in support. It was no more than thirty yards from the stage door to the car parked in Suffolk Place just round the corner but it took a long time for this phalanx to make its progression through the crowd. Once again, expectation had been confounded. They cheered loudly, applauded and shouted their praise and enthusiasm. Those who were close enough clapped him on the back and begged for autographs. It was a moment of emotion even greater than that of the first entrance in the play and once again the famous Terry tears were seen streaming down his face. "I've organised it very badly," said Binkie, "I really should have laid on a brass band and some fireworks."

It was even rumoured that his knighthood would be withdrawn. His election to the Garrick Club which might have been expected by this time, was only finally achieved in 1970. He was proposed by Laurence Olivier and seconded by Alec Guinness with twenty-five supporting signatures. Meanwhile in 1954 Robert Whitehead invited him to New York to play Prospero with the Stratford Memorial Company, but Gielgud was very reluctant to accept, fearing that the American press might indulge in an avalanche of scurrilous publicity which would be bad for the tour and the reputation of the company. Whitehead convinced him otherwise, and that he had nothing to fear. Plans for the tour progressed but then Whitehead had a message from the British Embassy in Washington who – it was intimated to him – had heard from the Foreign Office who in their turn had been advised by Buckingham Palace that the tour should be cancelled. It was feared that Gielgud's presence would be an embarrassment and the Palace would be grateful if plans could be quietly forgotten. This was the period when McCarthyism was in its unspeakable and venomous heyday and the popular hatred for Communism could well be whipped up against other minorities. It was four years before he appeared again on Broadway in his *Ages of Man* Shakespeare recital, by which time the scandal was ancient history and he enjoyed a very special triumph.

But it was Emlyn Williams who had the last word. "He should have put the whole affair into Vivienne Byerley's hands and asked her to handle the publicity. Then nobody would have heard a thing about it."

CHAPTER TWENTY-NINE

1950–4

Seagulls over Sorrento

Binkie's reputation for infallibility in the judging of new plays suffered some sharp knocks in the fifties. There were times when he had to be led, weeping and protesting, to his greatest successes. *Seagulls over Sorrento* was an example. It had been written by an immigrant Australian actor, Hugh Hastings, who had arrived in England just before the war and proceeded to turn his five years' experience in the Royal Navy to good use. The plot and characters can be simply summarised: five naval ratings volunteer for a special posting on a naval experimental base on a remote island off Scapa Flow. The work of the base is so secret that they themselves are not told what it is, but they are warned that it is highly dangerous. Inevitably with post-war service plays of this time, the five are of very different type and character. Badger is a loud-mouthed, fast-talking, quarrelsome Cockney spiv whose wife has eloped with a sailor called Cleland, permanently at war with the authorities though later incidents reveal a sensitive heart beneath his uncouth exterior. Haggis is a dour, morose Scot still devastated by the death of his baby boy and the insanity of his young wife. Lofty is the oldest of the bunch, but women and drink have kept him in trouble and effectively blocked his chances of promotion. He has friendly fatherly feelings for the youngest, Sprog, an orphan boy newly enlisted who, never having had a friend in his life, responds to the older man's kindness. There is Hudson, the boffin who is the scientist conducting the dangerous experiments in a nearby radar hut. He is the odd man out: he is well-mannered, well-spoken, educated and something of a man of mystery. Finally, there is the harsh, tyrannical Petty Officer Herbert, another indispensable feature of service drama, who bullies and victimises without any pity or scruple and who finally gets his come-uppance when the Commanding Officer learns the truth.

It was written with vivid and authentic service dialogue, a fine sense of character, all the comic and tragic incidents skilfully woven into a smoothly flowing whole. It promised to be first-class entertainment.

Unhappily, it didn't read well, something which is true of a great many good and successful plays. Hastings sent it to the agent, Eric Glass, who employed four outside readers and had a fixed rule that if all four gave a play a bad report then he wouldn't bother to read it himself. All four did. The play was then put on a pile awaiting return to the author and there it lay for several weeks. One evening his wife, Blanche, picked it up by mistake, thinking it was still under consideration and took it to bed, reading it through the night. "I can understand why they didn't like it," she said to Eric the following morning, "but there is *something* about it which I find very compelling. I think you'd better read it yourself." He did and he agreed with her and thus began the long anguished journey through two years of rejections.

The first submission was naturally to Binkie, with whom Eric Glass had enjoyed a fruitful professional relationship for some years. They were as friendly as any manager and agent can ever be. Binkie had a low opinion of agents whether they were representing authors or actors: they always tried to overcharge, always tried to sell you actors and plays you didn't want, always making trouble between him and the client, always nagging and whining for favours whether it be a first-night ticket or an invitation to a party, always bullying him to see plays and actors that meant interminable journeys to darkest Scotland or Wales. But Eric Glass was an exception. He was very selective and never sent a play to Binkie unless he knew it would be of interest to him and would fit the Tennent image. This offering wasn't a bit like the usual Tennent play but Eric felt that the power and quality of the writing would compensate. Alas, it didn't. Binkie paid Eric the compliment of always reading his plays first before sending them to outside readers. On this occasion he felt that Eric's judgement was badly at fault. He didn't like *Seagulls over Sorrento* at all. In fact, he *hated* it.

It was part of Binkie's snobbery that he disliked plays about the working classes and if it was about the armed forces as well that made it worse. Had it been a light comedy set in the ward room with a cast of officers, their wives and daughters with an occasional rating briefly appearing as a figure of fun, that would have been acceptable. But he assumed that if he wasn't interested in a *serious* play about the lower deck with the able seamen treated as real people then neither would the public. This attitude showed all too clearly how Binkie had been cut off from real life in his ivory tower above the Globe Theatre. Thanks to the war and National Service the dramas of the lower deck were now of interest and concern. But Binkie sent it straight back to Eric Glass who, for the next two years, submitted it to every management, every touring company, every rep. As the rejection slips mounted two reasons dominated: the all-male cast which women, who are the key figures of the theatre-going public, don't like; and its war theme – surely the public doesn't want to pay to be reminded? All of this was precisely what the West End managers had said about *Journey's End* in 1929 and it is sad and surprising that Binkie wasn't able to learn from history.

And it might have gathered dust in Eric Glass's office and never been heard of again were it not for a very lucky stroke of fate. Hugh Hastings was having a lunchtime drink with Cyril Pither, the company manager of the *Sweetest and Lowest* company at the Ambassadors where Hastings himself had worked as an understudy, and he just happened to mention this as yet unproduced play. "Let me see it," said Pither, "and if I like it I'll send it to the Repertory Players." He did like it and he did send it. It took longer than usual for the play to travel through the pipeline of readers and committees and voting: predictably, the women on the committee did not care for it, but the final vote was strongly in favour and it was finally presented for a single performance at the Comedy Theatre on April 10th 1949 which just happened to be a Bank Holiday Monday. Kitty Black, standing in for Binkie, remembers that the weather was foul and that heavy rain and sweeping winds all afternoon and evening effectively discouraged the attendance of other theatrical management representatives, except George and Alfred Black who had just started in management. The company, led by Basil Lord and Anthony Viccars, gave an excellent and spirited performance which roused Kitty Black to such enthusiasm that she telephoned Binkie at home in the country. "It's marvellous, you *must* do it." It was just like *George and Margaret* all over again.

The urgency of her recommendation can be measured by the fact that Binkie actually called on Eric Glass in person at his office to put in his bid. First, Binkie had to suffer the humiliation of being reminded that he had turned the play down two years earlier and that a very good offer had been made by the Blacks. Obviously, Binkie was the manager whom Eric Glass favoured but he wouldn't get it too easily. After a little haggling it was eventually agreed that the Blacks and Binkie should present it together, each to supply half the backing, though it was understood that the real work of casting and presenting the play should be done by Binkie, since he had a well-oiled administrative machine and the Blacks were as yet untried.

As usual, Binkie jettisoned virtually the entire Repertory Players company, preferring names which were either starry or at least familiar. Ronald Shiner who had completed five years' hard labour in the RAF evacuee comedy, *Worm's Eye View* and was now a star, was a good obvious choice for Badger. Bernard Lee whose recent film appearances, particularly in the immensely popular *The Third Man*, had given him a new public, was to play Lofty, and William Hartnell, hard-faced and cold-eyed, who had a virtual monopoly of bullying NCOs, was offered the part of Petty Officer Herbert. The only difficulty lay in the casting of Sprog, the shy, vulnerable, sensitive orphan boy who responds to the hand of friendship extended by the good and generous Lofty. "We can't let Terry Jackson play it, good though he was," Binkie said to Hugh Hastings in one of their long casting sessions. "He's far too beautiful. People will totally misunderstand the relationship. Do you have any ideas?" Various names were suggested but Hastings hadn't heard of any of them. "Well, run along to the New Theatre and have a look at Nigel Stock. He's playing Tony Lumpkin in that lovely revival of *She Stoops to Conquer* and I think he'll be fine." Hastings did as Binkie suggested and found that once again he was right. Nigel Stock wasn't beautiful by any stretch of the imagination, but his boyish good-looks were open and fresh. Most important of all, he was unarguably male. He got the part.

Nigel Stock was one of Binkie's earliest discoveries. Binkie had seen him in June 1936 when he was only fifteen doing an audition in a tent at the theatrical garden party which was open to amateurs of all ages. Nigel did impersonations and these included Charles Laughton as Macbeth (to whom Nigel had played Young Macduff in the previous year), Winston Churchill and Noël Coward. It was only when he had finished that he saw Coward in the audience sitting next to Binkie. Both men were laughing heartily and Coward even waved to him as he left the stage. A week later he received a letter from Binkie advising him to contact Cecil Madden at the BBC and the London office of MGM. The result of these introductions was his first radio engagement with Arthur Askey in *Bandstand* and his first film part in *Goodbye, Mr Chips* as one of the schoolboys eagerly enlisting in the army. Later in the year Binkie offered him the two parts of Hotel Bootboy and Theatre Callboy in the ill-fated *Farewell Performance*.

The *Seagulls over Sorrento* cast was completed by John Gregson as Haggis and David Langton making a late first act entrance as Cleland, the sailor who had eloped with Badger's wife. The confrontation between the two men provided the play with one of its comic highlights.

It opened in Portsmouth to an audience consisting of several hundred excited and excitable naval ratings. "I don't think any of them had ever seen a play before or set foot in a theatre and for the first twenty minutes it was sticky, they were sending it up with cat-calls, whistles and shouts at Bill Hartnell whose performance as the evil Petty Officer Herbert was horribly convincing," recalled Nigel Stock.

"But then the play grabbed them and there wasn't a peep out of them. They listened carefully and silently to all the sentimental and dramatic scenes and laughed uproariously at the comedy. At the end they tore the place to pieces and we had fifteen curtain calls. I never experienced anything quite like it. Of course, they were the perfect audience and their enthusiasm meant more to us than all the rave notices which we did eventually get."

The first performance at the Apollo on June 14th 1950 could not fail to be a slight anti-climax after the hysteria at Portsmouth even with an audience liberally sprinkled with high-ranking naval officers and their wives. The spectacle of so many Admirals of the Fleet, many of whom had titles and all glittering with decorations and gold braid on their sleeves and epaulettes, went far to reconciling Binkie to *Seagulls*. Any play which could bring such unaccustomed grandeur into the theatre couldn't be all bad. The King and young Prince Philip were both naval men and with a word in the right ear they too might be coaxed into paying the Apollo a visit. Only one small accident marred the evening: the sudden failure of all the spotlights at the rim of the dress circle which plunged the second act into semi-darkness. Binkie rushed backstage in the interval, sized up the situation, and sent immediately for Joe Davis. He was conveniently in the audience and did a quick and effective repair job taking up the whole of the second interval. The performance was smooth and otherwise without incident, the audience gave every appearance of having enjoyed itself hugely and the notices next day went still further in reconciling Binkie to the play. He couldn't continue to hate any play which sells out every night and secures three months of advance booking within a week of the opening.

A long run always imposes a strain on the company, but in an all-male cast with not a single woman around, not even in the stage-management team backstage, the strain is considerably greater. Some took it harder than others. Bernard Lee had a drink problem and as years at the Apollo followed each other, he became something of an alcoholic. He used to get through a bottle of gin in the course of the evening though it never had any visible effect on his excellent performance. For that reason nobody complained or thought to pass on the news to Binkie who would certainly have voiced a strong objection if he had known and would have banned all strong drink from his dressing-room. But one evening he did go too far. His great friend, the American actor, Sonny Tufts, was visiting England and he spent the weekend at Lee's home. Both men were drinking heavily. They thought up the most wildly funny joke which they put into effect on the Monday evening. Sonny Tufts, in his American army uniform, was smuggled into the theatre and walked on to the stage in the first act during one of the big scenes, smiling and waving, greatly to the confusion of the actors and the bewilderment of the audience. Later, Lee, in his able seaman's bellbottoms and tunic and cap walked out of the Apollo, through the stage door of the Globe and on to the stage during a performance of *The Lyric Revue* while Graham Payn was in the middle of one of his song-and-dance numbers. Once again, there was confusion and bewilderment. Later in the evening Binkie appeared backstage at the Apollo and demanded to speak to him, but Lee hustled him into the dressing-room. Nobody discovered what was said but Binkie took no further action. It was believed that Binkie was slightly afraid of him. He hated unpleasantness of any sort. Lee was a big, heavily-built man with an uncertain temper and although he was not known to be violent you could never tell with heavy drinkers. From then onwards, Lee kept his drinking under better control and nothing more was said about the incident.*

He and Shiner disliked each other intensely and were always complaining about each other's performance to the long-suffering stage manager, Anthony Peek, in Lee's case with some justification. Shiner had been a music-hall comedian and was used to standing alone on an empty stage and improvising his own jokes and patter. He had enjoyed little acting experience and even though this included five years in *Worm's Eye View*, he never understood that even if he was playing a star part he was still part of a team. The restrictive discipline of speaking somebody else's words and making moves which had been painstakingly worked out in rehearsal was still very irksome. Every performance, even within the limits of script and direction, was freely improvised and every night it grew broader. Peek had to pay regular visits to his dressing-room to ask him to keep it under control. Shiner would listen with barely concealed impatience and for a few nights would reluctantly do as he was asked. But at the end of the week when Peek took up his position in the prompt corner at the beginning of the play, Shiner would turn to him. "Oh no, you don't, Peek," he would say with a triumphant leer, "Saturday is Shiner's night," and

---

*Anthony Peek, the long-suffering and highly vigilant stage manager, has a rather different memory of this incident. "Sonny Tufts, wearing his American army uniform certainly did barge past the stage-door keeper and into the theatre. I met him on the staircase going down to the stage. I challenged him and he replied, very truculently because he was obviously drunk, 'Get out of my way, I'll knock your brains out,' and I said that this is exactly what he would have to do if he wished to go any further. Fortunately, the stage-door keeper with admirable initiative, ran down and said, 'I've got your taxi, sir, and it's waiting at the stage door,' and between us we managed to turn him round, steer him up the stairs and into the taxi which then drove off into the night."

off he would go on to the stage to make his usual mayhem to the disgust of the company and – it must be admitted – the delight of the audience. "He was the most selfish actor I ever met," complained Nigel Stock. "He hated anybody else to get a laugh and if anybody did he'd pester the director, Wallace Douglas, to give him the funny line. If this failed, he'd kill the laugh with some silly distracting piece of business. And when we complained he'd say with comparative inno-cence, 'But I'm the star, mate, it's me they're coming to see.' And he was mean. The only time in the entire run he ever bought me a drink was when he wanted to complain about Bernard Lee and knew that this was the only way to guarantee an audience."

Peek made his routine stage manager's report on Ronald Shiner's excesses and general misbehaviour to Bernard Gordon, Tennent's general manager, who would in his turn pass it on to Binkie. It was Binkie's strength that he knew when to crack the whip and when it was diplomatic not to. But sanctions come in slightly different shapes and sizes. Binkie waited. After two years, Shiner bored with the nightly routine, wanted to leave the play. He was on the standard run-of-the-play contract and Binkie's permission was required. Bink-ie refused. After six months, Shiner asked again. This time he agreed if Shiner would go with *Seagulls* on a tour of Germany which was, apparently, crying out for it. Reluctantly, Shiner agreed. Indeed, he had no choice.

"But no more Saturday nights, please."

Shiner looked bewildered. "Wot d'ja mean?"

"I think you know very well what I mean, Ronnie dear. No more Saturday Shiner nights. Do I make myself clear? And when you return we'll have another little chat. Y-e-e-s?" Binkie's voice was never silkier than when he was uttering delicately veiled threats. Shiner was no fool and he understood the situation very well. On the German tour he behaved himself and his performance gave no cause for alarm or discontent, not even on Saturday nights. Word got back to Binkie who nodded with satisfaction, but Shiner was still not off the hook. A tour of England, Scotland, Wales with *Seagulls* with the same company was scheduled. One Saturday evening Binkie went up to Manchester to see it, giving the company advance warning. Ronald Shiner's performance was, if such a word could ever be used about him, almost subdued. At the end of the tour he was given his release and his part at the Apollo taken over by Basil Lord. He had created the part in the original Sunday night try-out by the Repertory Players, but his agent had been unable to persuade Binkie to let him play the part in the West End.

"It's the first year that needs the star," explained Binkie smoothly, "but once the play has been firmly established in the public's mind as a success then it doesn't matter who plays the leading part as long as he is good. We can now safely allow dear Basil to play it and good luck to him," and so he did for the next two years, illustrating with his patience and gentle tenacity that everything will eventually come to him who waits.

The fatherly relationship which Bernard Lee (as Lofty) enjoyed with Nigel Stock (as Sprog) on stage found a curious duplication off it. Binkie suddenly started to become very friendly: from his office above the Globe, down in the lift, across Rupert Street and up to the first floor at the Apollo was a matter of only a few minutes and he used to drop into Nigel's dressing-room for long cosy chats usually in the second act when he had thirty minutes off between scenes. These chats became something of a regular feature, twice or three times a week and inevitably aroused some guarded speculation from the company and stage management. All fruitless, for although Nigel was young and attractive he was happily married to an actress, Sonia Williams. In any case, Binkie was far too much of a gentleman to make advances to somebody who was plainly not interested and far too sensible to do so to an actor who was in his employment. Business and pleasure should never be mixed. This friendship started and lasted so long, because Nigel was a good raconteur, an excellent mimic, could tell funny stories better than most and enjoyed sociability. He could make Binkie laugh and Binkie loved to laugh. Also, he wasn't frightened of him, as everybody else was, and in his company Binkie could relax and giggle and gossip as he could with very few others.

This friendship, pleasant though it was within the confines of Number Four dressing-room, did not extend beyond it. Nigel was never invited to Lord North Street or Knotts Fosse and when the film was being cast and Nigel was offered his part in it, Binkie refused to release him. "Sorry, Nigel dear, I can't do that," he said apologetically, "you're the linchpin of this play. We need you."

"But there are other linchpins, surely," he protested.

"Not as good as you. Without you, the whole play would collapse."

In the third year, Nigel was feeling the strain keenly and made another attempt to get his release. Once again Binkie refused. "You're the only member of the company we can't do without. We really do need you. Stick it out, Nigel dear, do stick it out till the end, it won't be long now. And I promise you something very good afterwards." *Seagulls over Sorrento* ran for over four years and in that time Nigel Stock had only one short holiday of two weeks and this was not by contractual right but as a favour from Binkie who was not slow to point out to the exhausted actor how lucky he was. The money was also a source of discontent: £25 a week was good money in 1950 but was worth noticeably less in 1954. Neither Nigel nor his agent, Derek Glynne, could persuade Binkie to pay more. "*Seagulls* ran for 1,551 nights," said the embittered actor years later, "and apart from that fortnight's holiday, I didn't miss a single performance."

But he did get his reward for sticking it out. Binkie never forgot a favour or a promise and turned out to be as good as his word. A few months after *Seagulls* finished, he put Nigel into a delightful light comedy translated from the French, *My Three Angels*. He wasn't altogether happy about being forced to act with Ronald Shiner yet again and many of the problems of *Seagulls* were to be repeated, but Devil's Island was a refreshing change from the mess deck at Scapa Flow, his part as the Third Angel was full of comedy – which Able Seaman Sims was not – and to complete his satisfaction, it ran only eleven months. "Just the right length for a West End play," he later said with satisfaction. "I wish all plays would run that long and no longer."

Another member of the cast feeling the strain of the long run was David Langton. This elegant, well-spoken actor was in his thirties and when *Seagulls* opened at the Apollo he played Cleland, who makes a comfortably late entrance in the first act. After the departure of Bernard Lee he was offered the longer, more difficult and infinitely more important part of Lofty. Binkie liked him and was happy to promote somebody in the company rather than bring in a stranger from outside. Langton's private and domestic life was deeply unhappy. His wife was ill, the marriage was foundering and his two sons at Haileybury and the baby son were heavy burdens of responsibility. In addition, the tedium and exhaustion of the twice-daily forty-mile journey from his house in Farnham to the West End by bus, train and tube added to the strain. The worry and anxiety was punishing as every evening at the theatre he thought about what might be happening at home in his absence. After three years of this it was clear that he was slowly reaching breaking point. And if all that wasn't enough, he was rehearsing a long and difficult leading part in a new play, *The Secret Tent*, for the Repertory Players, to be presented on the following Sunday, three days later. So for four weeks he was getting up at seven, rehearsing all day, acting all evening and getting home at midnight.

This punishing routine could not go on indefinitely. Something had to give and something did on the evening of Thursday, October 3rd 1953. After the performance he packed his personal possessions into a trunk and loaded it, with the stage-door keeper's help, into a taxi. At

London docks he booked a passage on an American cargo boat which left for New York the following day. Fortunately, he thought to leave behind a note for the company manager at the Apollo. "I have gone to Montreal to see my brother. Deepest apologies to you and for any upset I may have caused." He also thought to send an apologetic telegram to the Repertory Players who then had to find an actor who was capable of taking over the part in three days.

The wildest rumours circulated round the theatre and the Tennent office. By the evening, when it was clear that he wasn't going to come back the understudy was put on. Peter Wood, aged twenty-six, not long down from Cambridge, and much more interested in directing than in acting, now found himself facing every understudy's nightmare – to go on for a long and difficult part with only an hour's notice and with nothing behind him except for a bi-weekly understudy rehearsal. Under the circumstances he did as well as could be expected, but there was no question of his being asked to take over permanently so the vastly more experienced Brewster Mason, one of Binkie's contract actors, was brought in.

The news broke the following day. The papers were filled with photographs and stories about the English actor, Basil Langton-Dodds which, the company were surprised to learn, was his real name. Reporters clustered round the stage door pestering them for statements. "You only want something scurrilous about him and there isn't anything," protested Basil Lord, while William Hartnell who, in contrast to the sadistic and foul-mouthed parts he played on stage, was a quiet, gentle, civilised person off it, said sadly, "I've known Basil since we were youths together. He was very tired. We had noticed that he seemed to be behaving rather oddly, but I wouldn't say that he seemed unduly anxious about anything." The more energetic reporters travelled to Farnham to interview his wife: they found the house open but empty. Neighbours said that she had gone to visit her sister taking the baby boy with her. Meanwhile, his sister, a Miss D. Langton-Dodds, phoned the *Daily Mail* from her Kensington flat to say, "My brother is suffering from nervous strain. He has had a teensy-weensy nervous breakdown. He was on the point of collapse and is going away. No, he does not know what he wants to do or where he is going or when he intends to return."

Ten days later, on October 14th, he arrived in New York to find the British and much of the American press waiting for him. He later made a statement over the transatlantic telephone to the *Daily Mail*. "The whole business has been sudden and stupid. I've been suffering from a very great strain and as a result I'm very run-down. My father died a year ago and these things accumulate, you know. It was just one of those things which happened. When I left I had no idea that it would blow up into such a big thing. If I could get on to a plane tonight I'd go like a shot. My reason for leaving had nothing to do with the management and nothing to do with the play. My return depends on certain information I need and I shall be delighted to rejoin the cast when I get back. I have no intention of getting work here. I couldn't even if I wanted to because I am not a member of American Equity and have only a transit visa for the United States."

He returned on the *Queen Mary*, having been away for just three weeks. Without delay he went to see Binkie to apologise and explain. In fear and trembling he waited on the sofa in the outer office, fully expecting to be dismissed, expelled from Equity and never to work again, which would be the end of his career. But to his amazement none of these things happened. Binkie was all charm, courtesy and sweet reason. He understood very well that a nervous breakdown was just as much a failure of good health as TB or smallpox, and just as much an accident as being run over by a car or involved in a train crash. If a man is the victim of any of these unpleasant things he is in no way to blame. Langton was a fine actor: leading men of his style and quality were rapidly vanishing from the scene. He was also a gentleman and since the war and the Labour government had combined to reduce their numbers he was going to be very useful in Binkie's post-war plans. To destroy him and his career would be absurd: he must not be sacked, or even reprimanded, for something which quite clearly was not his fault. Binkie sat him down, gave him a cigarette and poured him out a stiff drink. "Now, David, I want you to do something. I want you to go to the theatre tonight and apologise to everybody. That is the least you can do. Alas, I can't put you back into the cast as the part is now being played by Brewster Mason who has a run-of-the-play contract, but I'm sending out a company to tour the Middle East which starts next month and I'd like you to play Lofty. And after that, we'll see."

Langton did pay individual visits to all the dressing-rooms to apologise and explain but he would have done this in any case without being prompted by Binkie. He was popular with the company and they were in the main cordial and sympathetic, though there were some actors who thought that a contract was sacred and that to walk out on it and let down your fellow actors, regardless of the cause and circumstances, was unforgivable.

So far from being cast into outer darkness, David Langton was reinstated with full honours and continued to work for Binkie for the next two decades. At intervals there would be an invitation to the office with warm handshakes, and then, "Well, David, what shall we do with you? What shall we offer you? I've got a nice little play with a *terribly* good part for you, it might amuse you. Here's the script. Do take it away and let me know." He was never required to audition. If he wanted it then it was his, and if he didn't qualify for the top star salary the money was always very good. The fifties and early sixties were filled with many highly prestigious plays: *The Devil's Disciple* with Tyrone Power, *A Touch of the Sun* with the Redgraves, Michael and Vanessa, and *The Pleasure of his Company* with Coral Browne. All these and many others filled his life before *Upstairs Downstairs* snatched him from the theatre and made him a star of international renown. Alas, Binkie did not live to see it.

CHAPTER THIRTY

1958

Irma la Douce – The Black-list – The Parliamentary Enquiry

How did you get on to Binkie's black-list? It wasn't difficult, alas, and by far the easiest way was to refuse when he offered you a job. He didn't like that. What Binkie liked to do, and this he always explained was the creative side of management, was to plan a career, to build it up play by play, part by part, not only to develop an actor's talents to the full but to bring him to the notice of the press and the public, and thus make him famous. By turning down offers of work an actor was breaking the pattern and all Binkie's efforts, and all his future plans, would be wasted. His attitude towards his actors was one of good, old-fashioned paternalism. In his eyes they were all children. Talented and delightful children, of course, but still children, capable of being foolish, headstrong and irresponsible who, if they were given half a chance, would spoil their careers with stupid decisions and faulty judgements. He loved his actors dearly but the love was possessive and jealous. If an actor wanted to have a successful career in the West End – or any career at all – he was strongly advised to go along with Binkie's plans. All this was particularly relevant if he was grooming an actor for stardom.

Elizabeth Seal was a good example. *Irma la Douce* was still playing very successfully in Paris in 1958 when Binkie bought the London rights and offered her the star part. She was exquisitely pretty with elfin looks, bursting with talent and personality and wholly delightful. Binkie took her to Paris for the weekend where they stayed with his old friend Ginette Spanier and her husband, Dr Emile Seidmann, in their huge and beautiful house in the Avenue Marceau. They saw the play and Liz had fittings at Balmain where Mme Spanier occupied a high administrative position, so high that she was able to arrange for Binkie to bring all his actresses for their gowns and clothes and to get a discount of fifty per cent.

Liz Seal remembers that he was always very particular about how his star actresses behaved and dressed off-stage. They had to look their best at all times and wear only the finest clothes. She had to be a credit to him and to H. M. Tennent, and to remember that the press and fashion photographers were always in pursuit and would take photos when you were least expecting them. Binkie and Ginette told her she must always wear long white gloves and soon she had a whole wardrobe full of them. Informal clothes, like jeans and a sloppy-joe pullover or a sweatshirt were strictly forbidden and if discovered would earn a reprimand in the form of a sharp note from Binkie's office. Naturally, all this was very expensive and a rather complicated series of negotiations occurred between Binkie and her agent, Eric Goodhead.

Binkie offered £120 a week which he insisted was very good money for an unknown even if it was the star part. Goodhead asked for a guarantee and Binkie said no.

"You want Liz to look and behave like a star, don't you?"

"Yes, of course."

"It'll be expensive. She'll have to have a star's salary. You get what you pay for. If you want her to dress according to her status and be seen in the best places she must have more money. That's why I want you to pay a percentage."

These were telling arguments and Binkie saw the strength of them. He agreed to pay five per cent of the gross and Liz ended up by earning £200 a week which in the late 1950s was very good money.

Her success in the part was enormous and her dressing-room was filled with celebrities from Princess Margaret to Groucho Marx, from Anthony Eden to Frank Sinatra. She repeated her success on Broadway and after four years in the play she had earned close on half a million pounds. She was now a Broadway and a West End star and all set for her career to go into orbit when she took a decision which Binkie thought very stupid. She married, had three children and retired. Binkie's plans for her had to be forgotten, and he left her in no doubt of his feelings of disappointment. Bad enough that she should marry a director called Zack Matalon of whom he disapproved, worse that she should show that she loved marriage more than her career. When she first returned to London in 1969 neither Binkie nor anybody at Tennent's would even speak to her. She had been silly and would be ignored until they decided that the silliness was over, that she would be cautiously allowed back in favour. It was ten years since she'd opened at the Lyric, her marriage was in ruins, she had three hungry children and no work. She phoned Binkie and consumed a large slice of humble pie.

"Hallo, Binkie darling."

"We-e-ell . . . Welcome back home. What's happening?"

"Binkie, my marriage is over and I want to return to work. Do you have something?"

"What about your children?"

"I can get an *au pair*."

"Leave it with me. I'll see what I can find."

What he found for her was *A Cat Among the Pigeons*, translated from Feydeau's farce, *Un Fil à la Patte*, by John Mortimer and directed by Jacques Charon, on loan from the Comédie Française of which he was one of the board of directors. Binkie looked after her most lovingly, having ravishing costumes made especially and arranging for Eleanor Fazan to help her with some private direction since Charon had little English. Fazan heard her lines and became a dresser, companion and baby-sitter. The play ran for a respectable 117 performances at the Prince of Wales, Liz had excellent notices and once more she was back in favour. Binkie had forgiven her.

She was lucky which is more than can be said about Isabel Dean. She had been in the 1944 Gielgud company at the Haymarket, played two good parts, Miss Prue in *Love for Love* and Hermia in *A Midsummer Night's Dream*, and understudied Peggy Ashcroft as Ophelia playing for several performances when Ashcroft was ill. Binkie let it be known that he was very pleased with her. Gielgud was to tour India with the *Hamlet* production and Isabel was once more offered Ophelia's understudy and the maid in *Blithe Spirit*. She felt that she should be getting rather better than that. She had played Ophelia several times and felt that she should be offered the part on the tour. The part went to Hazel Terry, a niece of Gielgud. It was clearly unashamed nepotism. She wrote a polite letter to Binkie refusing the offer. After walking on and understudying for two years she thought she was worthy of better things and for better money. She received an angry letter from Elsie Beyer, reminding her that Binkie had kept her in work throughout the war, that she had had all her early training and experience at his hands and that she owed it to Binkie to take this offer, failure to do so would seem to all at Tennent's as monstrous ingratitude. Isabel Dean wrote back an angry reply which was shown to Binkie. He was always very polite to her when they met but she never worked for him again. George Howe, who played Polonius in this same *Hamlet*, was asked to help Gielgud as assistant director. He agreed to do so on condition that he received a credit in the programme and publicity. Binkie was not prepared to give him this so Howe refused. His banishment lasted five years, when he returned to favour as Mr Pond, the headmaster in *The Happiest Days of Your Life*.

Ralph Michael had been a good friend of Binkie for years and even exchanged a series of witty and entertaining letters, but this did not do him any good when he was in *Relative Values*, Coward's play at the Savoy in 1951. "When the two-year run was coming to an end, Peter Glenville came to my dressing-room and asked me to go into *The Living Room* which the Alberys were doing at Wyndham's. This was Graham Greene's first play. I said no but he pressed and finally I agreed. I did the pre-London tour and at Brighton Donald Albery came to me and said, 'Ralph, I didn't want you in this play and I don't want you now, would you please leave the cast as I want to give the part to John Robinson.' Well, I had a contract for the run of the play but I didn't wish to stay in the face of such hostility so I left. I later gathered that it was Binkie who arranged for me to be sacked. Although he and the management were rivals they were very close and I think that Binkie was upset that I hadn't done the tour of *Relative Values*. In fact, I hadn't actually been offered it but I knew it was coming and Binkie expected his actors to keep themselves free as did the others and go out on it. So I was quietly black-listed and I never again worked for Binkie or properly in the West End. I saw him only once as we passed in the street. He would have passed without a word but I said 'Hallo, Binkie' and so he had to stop to say hallo which he did with a quick mirthless smile, 'Oh, Ralph, how are you?' and away he went without waiting for an answer. I never saw him again."

There was another way to get black-listed and that was to upset or annoy the stars. In Binkie's eyes, stars were like sacred cows: they must be treated with kid gloves, their every whim to be satisfied, they must be allowed to do exactly what they wanted without argument. In 1947 Peter Cotes was a much-talked-about young director whose work in the provinces and in his own theatre, the New Lindsey Theatre Club in Kensington, was arousing much interest and critical acclaim, particularly *Pick-Up Girl* which transferred to the West End, in spite of its controversial theme – child abuse and domestic harass-ment – attracting that indefatigable theatre-goer, Queen Mary. His wife, Joan Miller, was acknowledged as one of the finest dramatic actresses in the country.

Cotes was invited to have tea at Lord North Street – an accolade in itself and an indication of Binkie's high regard – to discuss possible plays to be directed by him. The final choice was *Deep are the Roots* by Arnaud D'Usseau and James Gow, a drama with a strongly racial theme which had been a success on Broadway under Elia Kazan's direction with the black actor, Gordon Heath, whom Binkie had invited to play the same part in London. After the second day's rehearsal Cotes received a message from Olive Harding of the Myron Selznick Agency and it was bad news. Binkie had phoned her to say that he wanted out – she was insistent that this uncharacteristic phrase was precisely the one he used – and that Cotes's services were no longer required. No reason had been given but it seemed that Heath was not entirely happy with his handling of the production and that what he wanted was a carbon copy of Elia Kazan's ideas. It was all very bewildering because there had been no rows, quarrels or even disagreements. Heath, in fact, had said very little but as soon as the rehearsal had finished he had telephoned Binkie to complain. Joan Miller who was also in the company, immediately resigned the part in protest. Cotes was paid off, but he complained forcibly to Binkie, through Olive Harding, that no amount of money could compensate for the cold-blooded and motiveless dismissal which in his opinion resembled the crueller techniques of the Star Chamber.

Whatever bad feeling simmered between the two men did not in any way affect Binkie's unqualified admiration for Joan Miller and he showed this by offering her a leading part in *Dark Summer* about a blind girl. After a month at Hammersmith it transferred to the St Martin's. Joan Miller scored a great success in the part, but because of bad health she had to leave the cast after only seventy-two performances. Without her the play had little chance of surviving and was withdrawn. The Cotes-Miller partnership was to achieve great things at the Boltons Theatre Club with *Mrs Basil Farrington*, *A Pin to See the Peepshow*, *Loaves and Fishes*, *Candida* and *The Children's Hour*. Binkie continued to be charming and cordial every time they met, but neither Cotes nor Miller ever worked for him again.

Harold Scott played the Colonel in *Waters of the Moon* for two years at the Haymarket. He was a genial, fun-loving hedonist whose flat in Chelsea contained a remarkable collection of pornography. One evening he was playing patience in his dressing-room, and being called to the stage for the second act, stuffed the cards into his pocket, but as bad luck would have it, they fell out on to the floor just as Edith Evans came out of her ground-floor dressing-room. She stooped to help him pick them up and saw that they were all photos of men and women engaged in various forms of explicit sexual activity. She screamed with shock, threw them at him and slapped his face hard. For the rest of the run she refused to address a single word to him offstage. Binkie paid him a visit the following evening. "Dear Harold, I gather you have some rather . . . *curious* . . . playing cards . . . rather *bizarre*?"

"That's right, Binkie."

"May I see them, please?"

Harold obediently produced them for inspection. Binkie looked closely at them. "W-e-e-ell . . . ye-e-e-s . . . mmmm . . . you seem to have upset the Dame, Harold dear," he said in his silkiest voice. "We don't really want to do that, do we? These cards are deeply interesting but I don't think they're the sort of thing I'd like one of *my* actors to have in one of *my* theatres. I think I'd better keep them until the run is over," and out he walked with the cards in his pocket. Needless to say, Harold never saw them again. He was black-listed, but only for six years, being finally restored to favour when he played Paul Scofield's father in *A Dead Secret* at the Piccadilly in 1957.

A journalist once asked Binkie about the notorious black-list. Predictably, Binkie denied all knowledge. "I do occasionally hear about it but you may take my word that it doesn't exist. It's just a figment of people's imagination. Naturally, there are some people whom I do not wish to employ for one reason or another, but that is every manager's privilege, just as every actor has the right not to work for me if he doesn't want to. But there is no list. Absolutely not."

True or false, actors believed in it and it was this fear of his displeasure which kept them under control when they had a legitimate grievance, as when an actor found himself understudying parts in two plays in two different theatres for one salary. This had happened just after the war: for a time the two principals enjoyed good health and the actor was not required to do the impossible and be in two places at the same time. But Binkie couldn't get away with this situation for long and one evening, as bad luck would have it, both principals were off with winter colds. The actor went on for one, but in the other theatre the only possible replacement was the stage manager who had to read the part from a script after he had made a deeply embarrassing apology. The audience complained, the press got wind of it and Binkie was sternly ordered by Equity never to do this again.

Binkie tended to take a rather cavalier attitude towards inconvenient Equity rulings and before long a young actor, David Evans – reputed to be a distant relation – found himself understudying in *Seagulls over Sorrento* at the Apollo and also appearing as the Monkey at the end of *The Little Hut* next door at the Lyric. He knew that this was illegal, but he kept quiet about it. If Binkie found out that he had complained to Equity he would never work in the West End again and in the early fifties that was the equivalent of the death sentence. If he had been paid a double salary that might have been acceptable but Binkie expected him to do the two jobs for a single salary of £16 a week.

Most of the discontent was due to Binkie's meanness and the low salaries he paid to all but the stars. Ray Witch was the stage manager for *Irma la Douce* and understudied no less than eight parts. "The whole run was a nightmare because I had only one rehearsal a week and I was paid £16 which seemed to be standard in those days. I later took over the part of Jo-Jo, the company went on tour and I asked for a raise, to £30. I was asked to go and see Bernard Gordon: he was sitting at his desk and the top was covered in money, piles of notes and bags of silver. He was counting out the various salaries. 'I gather that you want £30 a week, Mr Witch. This production is not making money so I'm afraid that the answer will have to be "no".' I then asked if I could see Binkie but I later received a letter from him offering me £25. I was advised by Frank Stevens our stage director, to accept it. There was no point in making waves, he said, and if I tried to put pressure on Binkie I'd be black-listed. There was one week when my throat was so bad that I could hardly speak. My doctor said I must not go on but Binkie wouldn't let me miss a performance. He wasn't going to take my or my doctor's word that I wasn't well enough and he brought his own doctor, a Harley Street specialist, who examined my throat and gave me a pain-killing drug which allowed me to speak without pain. I had these injections for the rest of the week and then I was allowed to go into hospital for two weeks. I was paid for those two weeks but when I was out and back at work I received a bill for £30 from the Harley Street specialist. Binkie called him but I had to pay him."

But Binkie had his own special way of compensating people, his own way of being nice and generous to them. There was a party given to celebrate the end of *Irma la Douce*'s first year. Everybody was dressed up and there was a splendid, impressive buffet with delicious pâtés, mousses and gâteaux from Fortnums and champagne. Ray saw a man in a light grey suit standing all by himself and thinking that he looked rather lonely, went over to chat to him and make him feel happy. After some desultory conversation, Ray Witch was bursting with curiosity about his identity. "By the way," he said, "who *are* you?"

"My name is Hughes Beaumont, Ray dear, and I'm your employer."

Ray had never seen him or seen a photograph and – as he neatly put it – "I nearly died of shock. I had no idea that the legendary Binkie would be so nice and charming and so *young*." They continued to chat and Ray asked him what he was planning to put on next.

"Well, Ray, there's a new musical which I'm interested in. Normally, it's considered bad luck to put your own money into a show but this time I'm going to do so because I think it's going to be a huge success. I could be wrong and if I lose it then I shall be the only person to blame but I don't think I will. And if it is the success I believe it will be, then I shall have enough money to keep me for the rest of my life." That show, it was later revealed, was *Hello, Dolly!* A little later, they discussed Ray's forthcoming holiday. He asked if he could have it in April rather than November and Binkie said no. But when November came, Binkie suggested that, instead of going away, he took his holiday in London and saw some of the plays which had previously been inaccessible because he had been working. So he gave Ray two tickets for *My Fair Lady*. "When I presented them, a liveried footman appeared, escorted me up the Grand Staircase and deposited us in the middle of the front row of the dress circle. These, I learned, were Binkie's private house seats. Throughout the evening the flunkey was in attendance: he brought coffee beforehand, drinks in the interval, and the manager was there at the end to see us off the premises. It was all very grand. Nobody knew who I was but it was enough that I was Mr Beaumont's guest. I thought it was very generous of him. I was impressed by his style."

Binkie was not always so generous. Even senior actors in the company had cause for complaint. Ralph Michael played a leading part in Noël Coward's comedy *Relative Values*, a part second only to Gladys Cooper's in importance. In the past, as with the *Private Lives* revival and *The Heiress* when he took over Morris Townsend from James Donald, he had always been paid £70 a week plus five per cent of the gross. But now Binkie was suddenly refusing to pay more than £60 and with no percentage. There was also a little dispute about the billing which Michael had insisted should be in large letters immediately below the title and alone on the line. When the play opened at Brighton he noticed with alarm and irritation that Binkie had not honoured his agreement: his name was in small letters and sharing the space with one other actor. Binkie paid him a dressing-room visit before the first night.

"Binkie," said the actor, "did you give me this part because you're sorry for me?"

"Ralph, my dear, would I cross the road if you were in trouble?"

"Yes."

"We-e-ell, I'll tell you what I'll do. I'll put you on a line by yourself. I can't increase the size of the letters but we'll spread it out a little. But I can't give you any more money." Michael threatened not to come into London but Binkie explained that the post-war boom years were over and he couldn't possibly afford to pay the same generous salaries. "Of course he could perfectly well afford to give me my usual. The post-war boom was *not* over. He was just being mean."

Another habit of Binkie's which caused great discontent was his insistence on entirely recasting plays which he had seen on a Sunday night try-out and wished to transfer. Not getting the part in a transfer, or not getting it in the film after a West End run is an occupational hazard, but some actors take it harder than others.

Brian Oulton was just such a victim. He discovered *The Happiest*

Days of Your Life, a wildly funny comedy about two schools, one for girls and one for boys. being evacuated to the same building. He played Mr Pond, the headmaster of the boys' school, in the original television production and afterwards had lunch with the author, John Dighton. "Like a fool I didn't buy an option on it or get him to sign an agreement that I should play the part if it transferred." He managed to persuade the Repertory Players to do it and enjoyed a huge success on his first and only stage performance in it. The following day he phoned the Repertory Players and was told by Betty Sumner, the secretary, that six managements wanted it and one of them was Tennent's. "They were so bemused by the magic name of Tennent's they let it go without any conditions." George Howe played it and with Margaret Rutherford as the headmistress of the girls' school it ran for over 600 performances.

"I was bitterly upset because it was my part and nobody else should have played it. That's why I had no time for Binkie. He wasn't a great manager, he was no more than an agent, looking after the stars, meeting them at the station, taking them to their hotel, filling the fridge with goodies and giving them expensive meals. He was like a butler in a stately home who is sycophantically obsequious to the second-rate aristocracy but will turn away anybody of real importance who doesn't happen to be wearing the right clothes. He was very good at doing straight plays but he never took any risks with new talent. Coward was a great man but Binkie was just a lackey."

1954 was the peak year of Binkie's heyday with sixteen West End productions. Those enjoying long runs included *Hippo Dancing*, Robert Morley's virtual one-man show about the problems of a market tradesman whose son decides to become a lady's dress designer, and Edith Evans just, but only just, keeping exquisite boredom at bay in Christopher Fry's latest poetic whimsy, *The Dark is Light Enough* ("Or *The Light is Dark Enough*," said Noël Coward, "it comes to the same thing"), *Someone Waiting*, in which Emlyn Williams and John Stratton try to commit the perfect murder, *The Sleeping Prince* by Terence Rattigan in which Laurence Olivier demonstrated that a modern light comedy exercises a great actor's talent just as much as a classic tragedy though the critics, ignorantly and snobbishly, showed marked reluctance to accept this, and *A Question of Fact* in which Paul Scofield, as a schoolmaster, discovers that Gladys Cooper is his long-lost mother and enjoys a dramatic reunion with her.

But while the money was tinkling into sixteen box offices, and the champagne corks were popping merrily at Scott's, the Savoy, the Ivy, the Caprice and Binkie's Lord North Street parties, while he and John

Perry were taking sun-baked holidays on the North African coast and playing croquet at Knotts Fosse with Noël Coward and Vivien Leigh, the storm clouds were gathering over the thorny problem of tax exemption and it was one which, however much Binkie disdained and ignored it, simply would not go away. It is impossible not to liken the situation to the final decade of Louis XVI's reign when the gilded, periwigged aristocrats danced their elegant, candle-lit gavottes and minuets at Versailles while the starved and tortured prisoners in the Bastille howled for freedom. Bill Linnit, a manager and by now no friend of Binkie, and a film star of the highest eminence living in California whose identity is still, alas, a carefully kept secret, had approached Woodrow Wyatt, the MP for Birmingham Aston, and asked him to investigate Binkie's empire and the methods whereby he received tax exemption on plays which were commercially so success-ful that they clearly did not need any financial assistance from the government. For five years he had been gathering information from the victims of Binkie's monopoly. Hundreds of actors, actresses, designers, authors, stage managers, even members of the Society of West End Theatre Managers, revealed their sad stories. Because they were not part of Binkie's inner circle, the actors could get no work, the authors failed to get their plays performed, and the managers could not get theatres either in London or in the provinces. It is evidence of Binkie's power, and the fear he continued to inspire, that all of them without exception begged Wyatt not to reveal their names for fear of reprisals. "I'd never work for him if he found out," they said nervously. So carefully were these dark secrets kept that even Binkie's intelligence service was unable to find out who they were. Wyatt was as good as his word. Their identities plus the nature of their complaints were never discovered in Binkie's lifetime and are still not known.

Armed with all this information Wyatt presented his bill at the House of Commons on March 10th 1954 to a packed House. 'To control non-profit-making theatrical companies' was the official title. Briefly, he described the situation, that Hugh Beaumont, of whom most of the honourable members had never heard, was a gentleman of the highest integrity and repute who had built up a great theatrical empire by skilful manipulation of the laws of tax exemption using concessions which were intended for other purposes. *A Day by the Sea* was currently making £3,000 a week of which £500 would normally be paid to the Treasury in tax except that it was being presented by Mr Beaumont's non-profit-making company, Tennent Productions Ltd. The purpose of a non-profit-making company was to present plays which were educational, but could *A Day by the Sea* be regarded as educational? He had seen it and didn't like it. Somebody from the Opposition benches then shouted, "It was tripe."

A lively debate followed which concentrated on the foolish and irrelevant question of education. Many had seen the play and had enjoyed it. But was *Waters of the Moon* or *A Streetcar Named Desire* or Daphne du Maurier's sentimental study of mother-love, *September Tide*, were any of these educational? When interviewed by the press on this last, Binkie replied, "The spectacle of Miss Gertrude Lawrence at the height of her talent is *always* an education," which everybody thought was a very good answer. The quality of the plays was not relevant. Shakespeare is generally considered educational but can one say that *Titus Andronicus* or *A Comedy of Errors* really adds to one's knowledge of life, or serves any useful purpose except that of passing exams? Wyatt was persistent and would not be side-tracked by red herrings. A monopoly such as Binkie enjoyed which resulted in only the favoured few getting work is in itself not healthy and should be broken.

The bill was given a second reading. It was hotly debated and widely reported. It finally failed, inevitably, because there was no evidence of dishonesty or irregularity in Binkie's dealings, and because Wyatt was unable to convince the House that a monopoly was a bad thing if it consistently produced so many splendid examples of English-Theatre-At-Its-Best.

This Parliamentary bill was a milestone in Binkie's life, because it was the first time he had ever been given publicity. His name was in the headlines: WHY SHOULD BINKIE BE SO POWERFUL? . . . ACTORS TIED BY NEAR-MONOPOLY . . . HUGH BEAUMONT: SHOULD ONE MAN TIE UP SO MUCH TALENT? . . . BINKIE IS THE MAN THEY DARE NOT OFFEND . . . THIRTY YEARS BINKIE HAS DOMINATED THE THEATRE. His photograph, sleek, elegant, smooth, non-committal, radiantly smiling, usually with a cigarette between his fingers or busily writing at his desk, was now reproduced. His face and his opinions were public property. People started to recognise him in the streets, they stared, sometimes they stopped to talk to him. He began to receive fan-mail . . . "Dear Mr Beaumont, I must tell you how much my wife and I enjoyed *A Day by the Sea* . . ." He was invited to talk on the radio, to appear on TV. This last was a brief appearance in Ginette Spanier's *This is Your Life*. Nothing before or since made him so nervous but he acquitted himself rather well. It was all very startling and he found that he was enjoying it. Publicity for a theatre man is like blood to a tiger: once you've tasted it you want more and more and more. Hitherto he had shunned the limelight. No longer. When photographers and newspaper reporters asked to see him, the door of his office at the Globe was always open, and Binkie was happy to talk and talk and talk. Up to 1954 his name and photograph had seldom appeared in the press. After that, it seldom stopped.

But the bill was also a turning point. His empire was safe – for a short time. He enjoyed three more years of tax exemption and then in 1957 it stopped. Wyatt continued to campaign, actors, authors and managers continued to whine about their exclusion from the world of privilege, rival managers continued to protest that they could never get the Theatre Royal, Haymarket, when they wanted it. The Conservative government decided that something should be done. Since all the trouble stemmed from the Entertainment Tax, the solution was to abolish it. This was bad news for Binkie. With Tennent Productions Ltd no longer needed, it was quietly dissolved. Now all the rival managers enjoyed financial equality of opportunity. Overnight, with a single stroke of the Chancellor of the Exchequer, Mr Peter Thorneycroft's pen, Binkie lost his advantage. Nothing was ever quite the same again. Binkie looked on the abolition of the Entertainment Tax rather as Al Capone viewed the end of Prohibition. Their two empires did not collapse overnight but their days were numbered.

CHAPTER THIRTY-ONE

1958–63

My Fair Lady

When *My Fair Lady* opened in New York in March 1956, every manager and producer in London was present. They had not flown in to enjoy themselves – after all, mere pleasure plays little part when important business decisions are to be made – but to buy the rights. They were all deeply disappointed, and in some cases furious, to learn that once again Binkie had beaten them to it, not by a head but by several lengths. He had been in possession of the English rights for eighteen months and had, characteristically, decided to keep it a secret.

A collective groan of anguish went through the assembled English theatrical hierarchy, Albery, Hylton, Grade, Delfont, Sherek, Clements, Saunders, Littler, Fox, Parnell. "How did Binkie do it? And *why* did he do it?" This second question was particularly relevant since it was well known that he wasn't interested in musicals. Or was he? It had once been true but no longer for Binkie was very interested in this one. As to *how* he got the rights, the truth did not emerge until 1978 when Alan Jay Lerner published his memoirs, *The Street Where I Live*, and revealed that it was just a good, old-fashioned piece of horse trading. An account of the background and birth-pangs of this legendary musical, the battle with MGM and the Chase Manhattan Bank for the rights, the agonised year of creation, the even more agonised months of rehearsals, touring and previews leading to its triumphant opening on Broadway, all this is not strictly relevant to the story of Binkie's life and in any case has already been described by Lerner in colourful and enthralling detail.

Contrary to popular belief, Rex Harrison was not their first choice for the part of Professor Higgins, nor was David Niven or Noël Coward though both these names have been included in the legend. The first choice was Michael Redgrave who had a number of distinct advantages over all competitors and successors. He was splendidly handsome in a fresh, open way: he had years of classical acting behind him, he had a charming and flexible singing voice supported by a good musical education and had actually sung the part of Captain Macheath in a wartime revival of *The Beggar's Opera*. In every way he was perfect casting. He himself was not entirely displeased at the prospect of starting a new and lucrative career in musical comedy. There was, after all, very little money to be made out of Shakespeare with top salaries at Stratford of £60 a week and a wife and three children to support. Ten per cent of the gross of the receipts of a successful large-scale musical would make him a rich man. But the job hinged on the length of the contract. The Americans wanted him to sign on for two years. The thought of a long run made him shudder: he offered six months. They compromised by offering him one year. He offered six months. Neither side would budge so the offer was withdrawn.

Binkie's involvement started in January 1955 when the *My Fair Lady* production team, consisting of Lerner, Frederick (Fritz) Loewe, the composer, Herman Levin, the Broadway producer, and Moss Hart, the director, arrived in London to offer the part to Rex Harrison. He and his second wife, Lilli Palmer, were then appearing for Binkie in *Bell, Book and Candle*, a charming light comedy about contemporary witchcraft by John van Druten in which they had already appeared on Broadway under Irene Selznick's management. In London it had opened at the Phoenix Theatre in October 1954 to excellent notices and to good, enthusiastic houses. But there was another comedy being played out behind the scenes and this one was not in the least bit amusing. The situation of a star actor at loggerheads with his star actress wife playing in a comedy which results in the two having furious rows offstage while being compelled to play tender love scenes on it, is traditionally regarded by the public as deliciously amusing. And so it is, inside the theatre, and over the centuries has inspired a number of delightful plays and films. But not in real life. It is, in fact, extremely distasteful and upsetting to be forced by your contract and your sense of professional responsibility to play love scenes involving a lot of hugging and kissing with somebody you dislike.

This was the unhappy situation in which Rex Harrison and Lilli Palmer found themselves. The Phoenix Theatre became a battle ground between two strong and determined personalities. Harrison's affair with Kay Kendall, his future wife, had already started. Lilli Palmer knew and, predictably, did not approve. Angry rows up and down the corridors and staircases, in and out of their dressing-rooms, alternated with long periods of angry silence when they refused to speak to each other and essential messages had to be passed through the long-suffering stage manager. Not that this had any noticeable effect on their performances. They were both accomplished professionals who took their work seriously and had a keen sense of responsibility to Binkie and to the public. They would never allow their private feelings, however anguished, to spoil the play. In fact, their scenes of love and tenderness were so convincing that when the *My Fair Lady* production team saw the play and paid a backstage visit to talk to Harrison, they were amazed to learn that the two stars were not speaking to each other.

They had little that was concrete to offer to Harrison: six numbers, a script, Oliver Smith's designs, all that and Cecil Beaton too. After five weeks of diplomatic and musical persuasion Harrison agreed to play Henry Higgins. Houses at the Phoenix were thin in that cold, miserable January: Binkie said he would certainly be withdrawing the play some time in the early spring. Rex Harrison could thus spend the summer in his Italian Riviera home at Portofino preparing for his musical début and rehearsals could start in September for a November opening on Broadway. That was the masterplan and had it worked out the history of Binkie and H. M. Tennent would have been markedly different. But the fates had other ideas.

The American tourist invasion started a little early that year, 1955, and business at the Phoenix suddenly started to improve. By the end of April it was once again playing to full houses. Alan Lerner and Moss Hart returned to London to play Harrison the remainder of the songs and found to their alarm that Binkie had cancelled his plans to withdraw *Bell, Book and Candle* and had decided to let it run through the summer. By the end of July it was still filling the Phoenix with long queues of hopeful customers waiting for returns, the advance was excellent, going up to Christmas, and there was no indication that business would decline. While this was good news for Binkie it was potential disaster for the Americans. Rex Harrison's eighteen months' contract with Binkie ran until April 1956 but in the meantime the company and crew for *My Fair Lady* had been engaged, theatres booked, postponement for a further year was impossible. Rex Harrison just had to be made available. What was to be done?

With this situation, which crops up not infrequently in theatrical and cinematic history, there is only one solution. The actor, whose services are so highly prized and so urgently needed, must be bought out of his contract at literally *any* price. Binkie was in a good strategic position and when Herman Levin flew over in August to discuss just how much he would want for releasing Rex from his contract, he was able to strike a very hard bargain. Yes, yes, he was delighted to make Rex available in December but in return he would require the English and continental rights for *My Fair Lady*, one and a half per cent of the Broadway and touring grosses, and £25,000 in cash to seal the bargain. It was just the sort of deal which Irene Selznick's father had made with David O. Selznick when he released Clark Gable, unique and irreplaceable, to play Rhett Butler in *Gone with the Wind*. Louis B. Mayer had been easily satisfied: all he wanted was fifty per cent of the American distribution rights.

Binkie and Herman Levin concluded their agreement swiftly and smoothly over lunch at Scott's. Levin accepted all Binkie's demands without hesitation and made no attempt to bargain. How could he? He had nothing left to bargain with. It was undoubtedly the most lucrative lunch Binkie had ever eaten and there was much gleeful hand-rubbing and rejoicing at the Globe when the contracts were signed and exchanged. There was also much rejoicing at the Phoenix Theatre. Business may have made a dramatic turn for the better, but relationships between its two stars had made a change for the worse no less dramatic. Life had become impossible for both of them and they couldn't wait to get away from the play, the theatre and each other. Both of them went separately to their doctors and tried to convince them that it would be very bad for their health if they were forced to act together any longer and succeeded in getting certificates of absence. Laurence Evans, the agent who handled both Rex and Lilli and spent a great deal of his time passing messages from one to the other when they weren't speaking, phoned Binkie one never-to-be-forgotten morning to say, "I've got two doctors' certificates in my desk, one for Rex and one for Lilli. What do you want me to do with them?"

"Keep them in your desk under lock and key," said Binkie firmly, "don't let them out of your possession. I don't intend to see them or have any part whatever in discussing them further." In December Rex flew to New York, getting there in time for Christmas and a January start to rehearsals. Robert Flemyng took over his part in *Bell, Book and Candle*, and once more peace reigned at the Phoenix.

The split-up with Lilli Palmer was complete and the love affair with Kay Kendall was now confirmed with a wedding planned as soon as he was free. The prospect of this happy union gave them great joy – and great sadness in view of the approaching months of separation while he was rehearsing *My Fair Lady*: there would be no time for her or anybody in what little was left of his private life during that tense, traumatic period. *Bell, Book and Candle* had no interest for the public in the absence of its two original stars so Binkie closed it and despatched a short provincial tour with Robert Flemyng and, irony of ironies, Kay Kendall. Everybody assumed that this was an act of kindness of Binkie's heart, because he didn't want her to be alone and unemployed during this difficult time and that's just what he wanted them to think. But a cynical view of this Mephistophelean act would be more realistic: "We don't want her in New York disturbing and distracting him at this difficult time, do we?" he confided to Robert Flemyng. "At all costs, she must be kept away from him." Binkie was characteristically protecting his investment and at the same time he was doing the Americans one more favour. This was always his sensible policy because he never knew when he might want one in return.

It is possible to see with hindsight that if Binkie hadn't given him his release from *Bell, Book and Candle*, Rex Harrison would never have appeared in *My Fair Lady*. The show was bigger by far than any of its stars, however distinguished, as the Americans were fond of saying in moments of crisis, and if Rex Harrison had been unavailable someone else would have been cast, Cary Grant, perhaps, who was later to be a strong contender for the part in the film. Binkie made possible the greatest triumph of Harrison's career and the twenty-year-old friendship between the two men was thus cemented and enhanced. But before long it was to be very sorely tested.

Rex Harrison stayed with *My Fair Lady* on Broadway for two years. He had originally been contracted for one, "But how can I possibly leave a success like this?" he said to Binkie. So it wasn't until early 1957 that plans could be completed for the London opening and the Theatre Royal, Drury Lane, booked for an indefinite period. Binkie launched a campaign to fill the newspapers with stories and photographs of the New York production, with the sensible idea of promoting interest in the show and whipping it to a fever pitch as the great day approached. He and W. Macqueen Pope, Drury Lane's publicity manager, reading the American papers every day, saw to it that something about the show was published every week. Even at that distance across the Atlantic, *My Fair Lady* was *news* and the English press gobbled it all up greedily and asked for more. No gossip, no tittle-tattle, no statistics were too trivial or too boring to appear. The campaign was master-minded by Vivienne Byerley. The old sneer of No-News-Is-Good-News-Byerley no longer applied: now her job was not to suppress but to publicise, and she did it with great efficiency and success.

Readers of the *Sunday Times* learned, for example, on October 1st 1957, that the show had given 647 performances, each with a capacity audience of 1,591, that top price for matinées was four dollars and at evening eight dollars, that the black market flourished with seats available from sinister little men in dark glasses at the unheard-of price of eighty-five dollars, that there were regular all-night queues for the forty standing places, that the production costs were an unheard-of half a million dollars which were entirely recouped in thirty weeks, that Rex Harrison was getting five thousand dollars a week, the sterling equivalent being close to two thousand pounds.

That October 1st Binkie announced that *My Fair Lady* would have its first London performance on April 30th 1958 and there was to be a Royal Gala in the presence of the Queen and Prince Philip on May 5th. *My Fair Lady* continued to make history: it was the first time that the theatre had been closed for three months to allow the installation of technical equipment and essential machinery including two enormous turntables for the revolving scenery; it was the first time that the box office opened for advance booking *six months* before the first night; the first time that ten mailbags containing many hundreds of letters and all with cheques were delivered *every day* to the theatre; the first time that Tommy Rees, the box-office manager, had been compelled to engage *twelve* extra staff to cope with the rush; the first time the agencies found themselves excluded from the game so that the public were compelled to get their tickets only from the theatre – a sensible device to stop that embarrassing and annoying double-booking which always seems to happen no matter how careful people are.

Binkie was not exaggerating when he said that this was to be the most expensive show in theatrical history: the pre-production costs were an unheard-of £85,000 but with a top price of £1-5s the advance booking totalled £132,000 within four months. By the beginning of March 1958 he was able to make the gleeful announcement that the costs had been fully paid off and that they were now well into profit. His press campaign was thus a proven and demonstrable success. Vivienne Byerley had every reason to be pleased with herself.

Binkie found other ingenious ways of protecting his investment. He persuaded the Society of Authors who looked after the Shaw Estate to allow him to impose a ban on all productions of *Pygmalion* in Britain for a ten-year period. The Society expressed polite surprise at such draconian methods until he pointed out that as they were getting ten per cent of the gross royalties they had a financial interest in the success of the show and it would not be a good idea if the public were distracted from seeing *My Fair Lady* because they had recently seen the play from which it sprang. The Society agreed that this made sense though they admitted to surprise when Binkie included a production announced for the Pitlochry Festival which took place annually in the Scottish Highlands. Binkie insisted that if the ban was to be effective it must be applied *everywhere* in the UK.

He also persuaded Lerner and Loewe to ban *My Fair Lady*'s songs and music from radio, television, the concert hall and the cabaret stage, but he was showing uncommon naïvety if he thought the music could be thus easily suppressed. A black market flourished and from the first week of the Broadway run urgent demands in England for the long-playing record and the published sheet music guaranteed that they would be smuggled into England by the crew and staff of airlines and passenger ships. Long before it opened at Drury Lane, many thousands of illegal copies were in circulation. Until the London cast recording was released, possession of the *My Fair Lady* original-cast LP was a great status symbol.

The first London rehearsal took place on Monday, March 15th. Rex Harrison, Julie Andrews, Stanley Holloway and Robert Coote, the principals from the Broadway production, had flown in from New York, the newcomers being Zena Dare as Mrs Higgins, grandly announcing that this was to be her official farewell to the theatre, Linda Gray as Mrs Eynsford-Hill, and Peter Gilmore as Freddy. In obedience to the old and sacred tradition of the American theatre they sat on a semi-circle of chairs while Alan Lerner, Moss Hart and Barney Gordon sat in an authoritative row at a production desk in the centre. Absentees included Binkie himself, who never came to first readings now, Robert Stanton, the stage manager currently directing the tour of *No Time for Sergeants* for Binkie, Herman Levin who did not plan to make an appearance until the opening night and Loewe who was ill with his recurring heart problem in a New York hospital.

The read-through took place smoothly and without incident in a relaxed atmosphere with no hint of the trouble which was shortly to come. When it finished, Moss Hart dismissed the company. "Thank you, ladies and gentlemen, I'll see you all tomorrow at ten o'clock." Rex Harrison strolled over to him and the conversation – as Alan Lerner was to remember some thirty years later with evident total recall – went as follows:

"Well, Moss, old man,★ you won't be needing me, will you, so I'll be seeing you in a fortnight or so."

"But I do need you, Rex," replied Moss Hart calmly, "so I'll see you tomorrow at ten."

"But dammit, I know every word and move of this show and so do Julie and Stanley and Bob, we've done it for two years. I don't need to rehearse all the bloody day."

"Sorry, Rex, but I do need you as I need Julie and Stanley and Bob. There are other principals who have not done it on Broadway for two years and they need to rehearse with you as you need to rehearse with them."

Harrison began to get irritated. "But this is *ridiculous*, old man. There's plenty of work you can do with the singers and dancers which doesn't concern me."

★ Laurence Evans is insistent that Rex Harrison never addressed people as 'old man', though he occasionally used the phrase 'old cock'. However, Alan Jay Lerner is equally insistent that he did. The reader must take his choice.

Leslie Banks as Claudius in the Gielgud *Hamlet* at the Haymarket in 1944. He looked convincingly evil, but the performance disappointed. BELOW: with his wife Gwen at home in Chelsea, 1939. The portrait on the wall is his first big success, *Clive of India*, which turned him from admired leading actor into a star. INSET: Evangeline, the Banks' youngest daughter, on her wedding day.

Paul Scofield in *Ring Round the Moon*, in which he had to run from one side of the stage to the other in order to re-appear as his twin. On a good night he could do it in five seconds.

Michael and Vanessa Redgrave, père et fille. She had no inhibitions acting with her father and in *A Touch of the Sun* they added one more to the very short list of fathers and daughters who have appeared as father and daughter in the same play.

Suite in Three Keys: at a photocall on stage at the Queen's Theatre Noël Coward, Lilli Palmer, Irene Worth and a young Italian actor Carlo Palmucci, with, INSET, his replacement, Sean Barrett.

John Perry and Arthur Cantor at the Globe Theatre after Binkie's death.

Mary Martin is cutting her mammoth cake on the night of her birthday during the first year of *Hello Dolly*. This is the only photograph of Binkie and David Merrick side by side smiling in carefully fabricated friendship.

Binkie's three passport photographs, including a page from his very first passport.

DESCRIPTION-SIGNALEMENT	★Wife-Femme
Profession / Profession: THEATRICAL MANAGER.	
Place and date of birth / Lieu et date de naissance: LONDON. 27. MARCH 1908.	
Residence / Résidence: ENGLAND.	
Height / Taille: 5 ft. 10 in.	ft. in.
Colour of eyes / Couleur des yeux: GREY.	
Colour of hair / Couleur des cheveux: BROWN.	
Special peculiarities / Signes particuliers:	

★CHILDREN-ENFANTS

Name-Nom   Date of birth-Date de naissance   Sex-Sexe

Signature of Bearer-Signature du Titulaire

"Sorry, Rex, but I do need you. There can be no exceptions. You will be here tomorrow at ten."

The argument continued. Harrison became increasingly petulant and tetchy while Moss Hart remained irritatingly cool. Finally, Harrison shouted, "Well, you *won't* be seeing me tomorrow and that's that," and out he walked.

Moss Hart immediately phoned Binkie to tell him that Rex Harrison had bluntly refused to rehearse and that a state of emergency was in existence. Always at his best and most decisive in a crisis, Binkie phoned Laurence Evans, Harrison's agent, to tell him that a most unhappy situation had suddenly blown up: a state of war between H. M. Tennent and Mr Harrison must now be declared and it was action stations for all hands. "I want you and your client to be at my house at eight o'clock tonight, Mr Evans."

"But why so formal?" asked Evans in bewilderment.

"Because we have a lot to discuss and it concerns both of you."

At eight, the summit meeting took place at 14 Lord North Street: those present consisted of Binkie, John Perry, Barney Gordon, Harrison, Laurence Evans, Moss Hart and Alan Lerner. Moss Hart coolly informed Harrison once again that he was required to rehearse like everybody else and the fact that he had already played the part for two years on Broadway was irrelevant. Harrison continued to refuse and Hart continued to insist. Binkie now played his trump card. "Rex, my dear, if you don't turn up for tomorrow morning's rehearsal you will be in serious breach of your contract since it says quite clearly that an artist must rehearse when called by the director. So I'm warning you that if you don't I will replace you. And I am not bluffing."

The argument continued and, like all passionate arguments, went round in circles with endless repetitions, increasingly loud voices and insults being thrown, some of them obscene, some merely scurrilous. "You Jewish cunt," screamed Harrison at Moss Hart, which – according to Alan Lerner who remembers this choice epithet rather clearly – was one of his favourite expressions, "if it hadn't been for me you would never have got this job directing the show in the first place." Soon everybody was screaming and raging at each other, except for Binkie who remained deadly cool throughout and merely repeated his threat, with increasing iciness, that if Rex refused to rehearse when called he would be replaced.

It must be stated at this point that Binkie was *not* bluffing: it would be a terrible loss, he freely admitted, but nobody was irreplaceable and there were others. John Gielgud and Michael Redgrave were two good contenders, particularly the latter who had, after all, been the first choice for Broadway; he had a charming singing voice, looked good and had the right commanding air. He was, admittedly, working for Binkie in *A Touch of the Sun* at the Shaftesbury, was promised to Stratford for the summer and had already turned it down, but he could be transferred and released from future obligations in the face of this greater need. Failing these two, Alec Guinness and Ralph Richardson were possibles. Ultimately, it did not matter who played Higgins as was later proved when a number of lesser actors took over the part for a year each and the houses continued to be filled to capacity. Binkie's resolve made thirty years earlier, that he would *never* be bullied or hustled by his stars, found new strength in this crisis.

The row continued for two hours and finally Rex Harrison capitulated. Everybody was against him, even his agent: Moss Hart and Lerner were both talking about replacements and although he didn't really believe that this would, *could*, happen, you could never be sure with Binkie. He had never expected to find such unity and he couldn't fight them all together. He agreed to rehearse in the morning and thereafter when called. But it was Moss Hart who had the last word. "Rex, please don't try any tricks, don't try to pull any fast ones with me. I'm older, wiser and much more experienced than you and I've been in the business years longer than you have. Please believe me when I say that I know all the tricks and a few that even you don't know," and with that the all-clear sounded.

Years later Binkie would recall that this was without doubt the worst evening of his life; "The situation had worsened horribly, there was a terrible state of enmity. I knew that unless everybody left the house good friends we would probably not open. It nearly killed me, but a little sanity did emerge and everybody started talking to each other once more."

But where there is high drama or tragedy, farce is only just round the corner except that in this case, paradoxical though it may seem, the farce wasn't in the least bit funny. Everybody had been invited to the party at Terence Rattigan's new penthouse flat in Eaton Square. The wives, Kitty Hart, Micheline Lerner, Kay Kendall and Mary Evans, had assembled in the house next door at number fifteen. Throughout the row they were closeted in the next room and listening to it through the connecting door. The consequences, if Binkie were forced to make good his threat, were truly appalling and when, at the end, they finally emerged they were white-faced and shaking.

All piled into the Daimlers, Rolls-Royces and taxis and drove off to Eaton Square arriving two hours late. Under the circumstances it was a very tense occasion. Binkie became very drunk. "He was the only person I ever met," said Laurence Evans, "who could get so drunk that he would quite literally fall down and then pick himself up again as if nothing had happened." In the course of the party Evans said to Moss Hart in a gallant attempt to pour a little diplomatic oil on his wounds, "Rex didn't mean any of those things." But Hart shook his head sadly. "I know Rex better than you, Laurie. He meant *everything* he said."

Casting the part of Freddie Eynsford-Hill, the foolish young man who falls in love with Eliza, turned out to be unusually tricky. It needs a good lyrical tenor voice to give full value to 'On the Street Where You Live', the only truly romantic number in the entire show: it needs good looks to explain Eliza's infatuation, a fine sense of period comedy for the two brief dialogue scenes, together with the appearance and personality of a gentleman. Finding an actor/singer who combined all four is like looking for the Holy Grail and after weeks of frustrating auditions Binkie was coming close to despair when Peter Gilmore suddenly turned up. He was young, only twenty-seven, and inexperienced – this was to be his West End début – but he had a splendid voice and strikingly blond, ruggedly masculine good looks. "He's like a Viking, a Nordic god," whispered Binkie excitedly, "he's *gorgeous*" and engaged him at the not inconsiderable salary of £75 a week. He rehearsed well but after a month it became clear that he was miscast. His toughness and undoubted virility were not compatible with Freddie's genteel foppishness and his voice was more baritone than tenor, too dark and not strong enough to rise effortlessly above the orchestra even though Cyril Ornadel, the musical director, gave him every help by reducing the dynamic level as well as thinning the actual orchestrations. Moss Hart wanted to get rid of him without delay but Binkie persuaded him to wait for a week or so. "Let's give him every chance, Moss dear," he urged. "I'm convinced that he'll be able to do it. Let's not do anything drastic."

Moss Hart agreed, but after another ten days he made the decision: Gilmore must go. On Wednesday evening, April 23rd, all unsuspecting, he walked on to the stage of Drury Lane for the final dress-rehearsal. He did not know that he was to be dismissed that evening, that his replacement had been secretly rehearsed and was at that very moment sitting in the stalls next to Binkie. The rehearsal went very smoothly, but at the end he received a message that he was to go to Honor Blair's office immediately. She held a post officially described as management representative which Binkie had created especially to cope with any crises and emergencies. He disliked embarrassing confrontations and all forms of unpleasantness: breaking the bad news to Gilmore was a task which he was happy to delegate. Consequently, it was Honor Blair who told the horrified actor that his services were no longer required and that he would be paid a fortnight's salary in lieu

467

of notice. The fact that his parents had travelled all the way down from Scotland to witness his triumph at the first preview on the next day was unfortunate, she readily admitted, but it could not influence the management's decision. All this was typical of American ruthlessness at its most cruel. There can be no room for sentiment, or even basic humanity, in business.

Binkie had hoped that the whole unhappy affair could be confined to the four walls of the theatre: H. M. Tennent was not in the habit of washing its dirty linen in public and it would be very bad publicity if the press got hold of the story. In this he was being inconceivably naïve, for a good story like this just could not be kept secret and all Vivienne Byerley's highly developed technique of evasion could not keep ELIZA'S BOY FRIEND SACKED from the front page of the *Daily Express*. Binkie now found himself in the humiliating position of having to make a public apology and to defend himself. "The management has made a bad mistake and we are deeply sorry. He should never have been engaged in the first place." So why was he? was the press's not unreasonable question. "Because he seemed right for the part at the time, but we soon discovered that his voice was unsuitable." But surely this must have been evident at the first audition, replied the press. "Maybe, but it doesn't always work like that," said Binkie, "you sometimes don't find out the truth until after the artist has rehearsed for a few weeks. That's what rehearsals are for."

A cheque for £150 was sent to Gilmore's agent representing the two weeks' salary as contracted. The agent swiftly sent a letter pointing out that sacking Gilmore was going to be a very expensive business, for the contract had been signed and therefore Binkie was liable to pay Gilmore for the entire run of the play. Nobody knew how long this would be, but if the success of the play in New York was anything to go by (it was now in its third year) it could be many years. Binkie replied by offering a month's salary. The agent refused and Equity wrote to Binkie confirming that Peter Gilmore must be paid for the run of the play whether he appeared on the stage or not.

Binkie had been expecting this and now he played his trump card. "I am quite prepared to pay Mr Gilmore £75 a week for the run of the play however long that may be," he said to the agent over the telephone, "but if I do he will have to turn up at the theatre every night at 6.55 p.m. for a 7.30 p.m. start, he will have to spend the evening in his dressing-room, which is quite liable to be on the top floor and not particularly comfortable, and he will not be able to leave until the show is over, which is approximately two and a half hours. During the run of the show he will, of course, not be able to do any other work without my express permission which, needless to say, I will not give:

no films, television, radio, no commercials, not even a Sunday night show in a theatre. Is this what you wish for your client?''

Clearly, five years of useless inactivity was not what anybody wanted, so he meekly accepted defeat and took the month's salary, £300. Game, set and match for Binkie. It was an old ruse which had been used regularly by Louis B. Mayer when dealing with mutinous contract players and he had learned about it from Irene Selznick.

This incident showed Binkie in a very bad light, but however appalling were the ethics, it must be firmly pointed out that he was well within his legal rights. A more kindly man would have offered a larger sum by way of compensation to the unhappy Gilmore who had, through no fault of his own, suffered the most dreadful professional humiliation, and before the war Binkie would undoubtedly have done so, but that sort of generosity had gone with the passing years. He had his American colleagues breathing down his neck and something of their hardness had clearly rubbed off on to him. It was this affair more than any other which Binkie's enemies had in mind when they spoke of his ruthlessness.

Within five months Gilmore was playing a leading part in Sandy Wilson's musical *Valmouth* and later he would star in *The Onedin Line*, a popular television series about a Victorian sea captain which, over a period of many years, gave him undreamed-of wealth and fame, a noticeably better fate than five and a half years of well-paid obscurity at Drury Lane. Being sacked from *My Fair Lady* did his career no harm at all: in fact, you could say it was a blessing in disguise.

His replacement was a young Australian named Leonard Weir who had recently come over to pursue a career in opera but found himself side-tracked into television. One day Lerner saw him singing duets on television with Rosalina Neri. He liked what he saw well enough to invite him to audition for Cyril Ornadel, his name being kept on file should it be needed. On Wednesday morning, April 23rd, he was invited to Drury Lane to sing 'On the Street Where You Live' on the stage with a rehearsal pianist. By now he had learned the number and was able to give a good account of it. ''That was very good, Mr Weir,'' said Binkie from the third row of the stalls. ''How do you feel about taking over the part tomorrow night, the first public preview?''

''Yes, okay,'' replied Weir.

''You can watch tonight's performance, the final dress-rehearsal, with me and Mr Hart.'' That night Leonard Weir sat in the middle-stalls with Binkie on one side and Moss Hart on the other, feeling rather guilty. ''It's very hard on him to sack him so suddenly, isn't it?'' he said to Binkie. ''Don't you worry about that, Mr Weir,'' said

Binkie smoothly, "that's my problem." On Thursday morning, he rehearsed the dialogue scenes in the dress circle bar with Moss Hart and the number on stage with the rehearsal pianist and that evening he sang it with the orchestra for the first time and met the other principals also for the first time. The preview took place in front of a packed theatre, smoothly and without any hitch. The essential difference between Binkie and Moss Hart can be seen by their behaviour to Leonard Weir in his dressing-room afterwards. Binkie thanked him politely, shook hands and left. It was all rather cool. But Moss Hart embraced him: "That was marvellous, Leonard, just fantastic," he gasped and offered him a drink.

London was now gripped by a special *My Fair Lady* hysteria, and as the press, television and radio were full of it, it seemed that nothing else was happening in the world. "I've never known anything like it," said W. Macqueen Pope in a daze: "can you guess how many telephone calls I've had in one day begging for first-night tickets?" Many thousands of public ticket applications for the first performance had flooded into the box office, enough to fill the theatre fifty times over, but in fact the general public received rather bleak treatment. Binkie allowed them unrestricted access to the upper circle, the unreserved gallery and the hundred standing places at the back of each – for which enthusiasts had queued up for two days and two nights, as the press were eager to announce – but the stalls and dress circle were VIP territory as exclusive, desired and privileged as the Royal Enclosure at Ascot.

Certain blocks of tickets were bespoke: the critics had their regular seats off the centre gangway, the regular first-nighters, whose good-will, word-of-mouth and support were essential to any play, had their seats in the front, the backers had theirs by right of contract. There was a large American contingent, friends of Herman Levin, Moss Hart, Lerner, Loewe and Columbia Broadcasting, but the rest of the stalls and circle were Binkie's to allocate as he liked. Sackloads of personal letters flooded into his office at the Globe begging for first-night tickets. It seemed that everybody he had known or worked with claimed intimate friendship and a place in the Royal Enclosure; small-part actors from his Cardiff days, publicans from Scotland in whose establishments he had once drunk a glass of wine, casual neighbours in Lord North Street to whom he might have said "Good morning", all these and Lady Docker too.

He spent many happy hours with Barney Gordon poring over the Theatre Royal seating plan and enjoying to the full the strange sense of power it gave him. No Belgravia hostess planning the seating for a grand dinner party could have enjoyed herself more. These tickets were as rare as fifty carat diamonds and their possession was a status symbol of such value that not only did Parliament cancel an all-night sitting to allow those lucky members who had them to attend, but several high-ranking members of the Diplomatic Corps turned down an invitation to dine with the Queen at Windsor Castle since they had a considerably more urgent engagement at Drury Lane. *The Times* agony column lived up to its name when it published a number of pathetic appeals, 'First-night tickets *My Fair Lady*, any price', while rumours that the ticket touts were charging £50 for a seat circulated and were eagerly believed. As if there wasn't already enough excitement, the *Daily Express* ran a large headline every day whipping it up even more: FIVE MORE DAYS . . . FOUR MORE DAYS . . . THREE MORE DAYS, etc., until April 30th when the headline simply said TONIGHT.

Everything was now in readiness for what the popular press insisted on calling 'The Opening of the Century' and on April 30th 1956 that's exactly what *My Fair Lady* was given. The streets from Drury Lane down to the Strand were lined with so many thousands of people waiting to see the audience that it seemed more like a coronation than a theatrical first night. Even by comparison with other grand first nights, this was something quite exceptional: on that fine, warm spring evening, success was crackling and sparkling in the air like static electricity, you could smell it, feel it, taste it. The King of the Touts managed to sell two black-market stall tickets for £200, not to a Texan oil millionaire and his wife, as might be supposed, but to a retired grocer from Bury St Edmunds who had realised his entire stock of War Bonds to provide himself with the necessary cash. At only one hundred times their face value, he considered that he had got a bargain.

Binkie had made his preparations well: the audience, which was finally, after some fifteen minutes' delay, persuaded to take its seats, cleverly mixed the cream of Equity, *Debrett*, *Burke*, the *Tatler*, even the *Almanach de Gotha*, an audience to drive social editors and gossip columnists wild with joy. He had always hoped that the music would burst on to an unsuspecting public like a firework display at Hampton Court, but it became speedily obvious that just about everybody in the audience knew the music intimately and were just waiting for their favourite numbers to come up: there were loud murmurs of delight as they started, for recognition of an old friend is one of the great joys of the theatre, and frenzied applause when they finished. So many people had flown in from America that they outnumbered the English: so many people had seen the show before that their reaction was more ritualistic than spontaneous, as Alan Lerner said wryly in his book, but this was probably the jaundiced view of somebody who knew the show too well. Binkie had no such reservations: in his view it was a unique and monumental triumph in every department.

The performance had only one small moment of discord. During the ballad number 'On the Street Where You Live', which Leonard Weir had been singing magnificently, there was a small croak, a slight roughness in his voice as he started on the chorus, followed by a brief, virtually unnoticeable pause. Binkie rose speedily from his seat and rushed to the back of the box which he was sharing with Irene Selznick and Arthur Marshall. There he was out of sight. He knelt down and put his fingers into his ears so if there was going to be a moment of chaos, he did not wish to see or hear it. Arthur Marshall said that it was the only time he had witnessed a crack in Binkie's steel-like control and poise. But the moment of disaster passed quickly, nothing happened and soon Binkie was able to return to his seat.

The curtain calls were truly operatic in length and splendour: the audience wouldn't let them go, the calls dragged for twenty-seven minutes with a cascade of flowers from the upper boxes, a record to be beaten only by the thirty minutes for *Oklahoma!* at the same address or by Callas in *Tosca* at the Opera House just round the corner. Binkie was immensely glad to see – as a further evidence of success – that the same crowds who had waited to see the audience go in were still there three hours later to see them leave. Two thousand happy people, humming the tunes, passed out and into Covent Garden where the market still flourished and where the descendants of Eliza and Alfred Doolittle kept the world safe for socially ambitious flower-girls and mendacious dustmen.

You can always judge a first night by the number of parties being given for the company. On this occasion there were literally dozens: every society hostess and every diplomatic attaché wanted to get in on the act. But there were four principal parties very much in competition with each other. Julie Andrews gave a small one in her suite at the Savoy: Mrs Whitney, the American Ambassador's wife, turned the whole of Winfield House in Regent's Park into a restaurant and dance-hall, this was the grandest. Then Herman Levin held court at the Dorchester with a fork supper, and finally Binkie gave his biggest and most lavish party at Lord North Street. This was the party which Rex Harrison attended, bringing Bob Coote and Zena Dare. But it was Stanley Holloway who gave the press their best quote on the subject: "I'm tired of this. I'm going home and will go quietly to bed."

The notices did, inevitably, contain a few petulant, fault-finding carpers for whom nothing is ever good enough, but otherwise they were all shrieks of joy and praise, "Like love letters," said Binkie happily. Within three days the entire first year had been sold out, bookings stretched well into the second and would extend even to the third as soon as Binkie could get the tickets printed.

But all this was merely a preliminary, an *aperitif*, for what Binkie always saw as the supreme climax of the show's success – the Royal Gala which took place five days later on May 5th. The Queen, Prince Philip and Princess Alexandra sat in the royal box which was gorgeously decorated with carnations and roses, presiding over an audience which, if possible, glittered and sparkled even more magnificently than that of the first night. "Let's have a good show tonight, lads," said Stanley Holloway, veteran of a thousand seaside concert parties, "the landlady's in front," a reference to the little-known fact that the theatre is Crown property. Alan Lerner, whose first Royal Gala it was, confessed himself a little worried that the Queen wasn't laughing or smiling and didn't seem to be enjoying herself. Binkie was able to reassure him. "Don't forget her Hanoverian ancestry," he said, "the Germans take their pleasures rather sadly and she is more German than English."

Afterwards, the royal party went backstage to meet the principals. Most uncharacteristically, the Queen made a special point of speaking to the stage manager, Robert Stanton, and managed to come out with one of those slangy, informal remarks which are guaranteed extensive quotation in royal memoirs and gossip columns. "I saw you quite clearly standing in the wings. I must confess that I don't like sitting in a box. You get such a *wonky* view of the stage." In the interval Binkie had been presented with Lerner, Loewe and Moss Hart, and thus enjoyed the rare pleasure of hearing Prince Philip describe how he learned French from an English nanny who spoke it with a very strong Cockney accent, something he proceeded to demonstrate with highly amusing results. What would his friends in Cardiff say if they could see him now? he thought; Hughie Morgan has done well for himself, who would have thought it? Whatever façade of acclaim and sophistication he had acquired over the decades, the small-town boy was never far below the surface.

Once the Queen had been to see it and had thus awarded the royal seal of approval, all her family followed. The Queen Mother, Princess Margaret, the Duchess of Kent, the Gloucesters, all paid their visits during the next weeks, followed by the foreign royals and the Commonwealth and Dominion leaders and foreign heads of state. At first Binkie dutifully made a managerial appearance, bowed, said the right things and took them backstage to meet Rex and Julie and Stanley, but the number of these special occasions became a nuisance and a bore and soon he stopped coming. "We all became very blasé about it all," said Robert Stanton. Because of its stunning visual and musical appeal, the Foreign Office decided it was ideal entertainment for distinguished visitors, which led to a marked increase in the number of yellow, brown and black faces visible in the royal box.

And so *My Fair Lady* passed into English theatrical history and started without delay to make its own legends. Hardly a day passed without some mention in the press, for the show was entirely self-promoting and stories filled the popular papers without any help from Binkie or Vivienne Byerley, as when the house manager noticed something so amazing that he couldn't believe his eyes: an empty seat in the stalls and this was in the first week of the run. Sitting next to it was a middle-aged woman. In the interval he approached her and asked if the empty seat belonged to her?

"Yes," she said sadly, "my husband was to have come with me, but he was killed in a car accident and so he couldn't make it."

"But it is a pity to waste a good seat and for this show," said the manager. "Couldn't you give it to another member of the family, or perhaps a friend?"

"Yes, I suppose I could do that," said the woman, "but you see they're all at the funeral."

Another incident which received publicity in newspapers all over the world told of a wealthy couple in a Mayfair flat who received a pair of complimentary front stalls in the post with a covering letter from some philanthropic church organisation telling them they had won them in a raffle. When they returned home after the performance, the flat had been burgled. A gang had known that tickets for Drury Lane was a good way of guaranteeing absence for the evening and having three clear hours at their disposal, they were able to do the job thoroughly.

The snob value of these was so great that those who were unable to get tickets would buy ticket stubs and programmes from those who had been luckier, and then leave them carelessly lying around their homes in order to impress their friends. Once again, the King of Touts did a thriving trade.

Some of these legends grew up backstage and many of them centred on the antique figure of Margaret Halstan, a character actress whose career had started with Irving, Tree and Mrs Pat. She had become a friend of Bernard Shaw and one of his favourite actresses, creating in the process a number of parts in his plays in the twenties and thirties. After the war she vanished from sight and it was with considerable concern and grief that Binkie discovered that she was living alone in a tiny Kensington flat. She was eighty years old, very frail, nearly blind, almost deaf, with no memory to speak of, and living on her old age pension just above subsistence level. She had been one of his most admired actresses and he had employed her regularly during and after the war.

Binkie did what few other managements would have done: he dragged her, feebly protesting, out of her retirement and cast her as the Queen of Transylvania. All she had to do was to walk on from stage left to the sound of trumpets and the Transylvanian national anthem, wearing the most gorgeous ballgown which Cecil Beaton could devise and glittering with diamonds, tiara and necklace. She stops stage centre, Eliza Doolittle is presented to her, she extends a white-gloved hand to lift the girl's chin, she says "Charming, perfectly *charming*", smiles radiantly all round and then leaves the stage to the final bars of the anthem.* She was on the stage for perhaps five minutes and it was the peak and crest of the first act finale, the show-stealing cameo for which everybody was hoping. It needed no great talent or strain on her energies and she did it superbly.

Everything was done to make it easier for her: if her voice failed as sometimes it did, then the orchestra would play a little louder: if her legs trembled or what was left of her sight began to fade, then she had been provided with a retinue of splendidly uniformed ambassadors who could act as guide dogs and lead her on and off. A less thoughtful employer would have put her on a third floor dressing-room to share with other ladies in the company and thus force her to climb up the stairs many times a night, but Binkie showed an intelligent compassion when he built a little dressing-room on stage level so that she had no stairs to climb and could thus enjoy her privacy. He arranged for her to have her own dresser, saw to it that she had a large photograph in the front of house and that she got her fair share of publicity. He paid her generously, double what the part was worth, and continued to pay her through her periods of winter illness even when they exceeded the limits laid down by Equity: if all that wasn't enough, he paid for a taxi to take her to and from the theatre every night. One evening when the taxi failed to arrive a member of the company gave her a lift in her car. "And what part do you play, my dear?" asked Margaret Halstan, and Julie Andrews replied, "I play Eliza Doolittle."

Binkie was, of course, showing shrewd managerial common sense in employing her, for *grandes dames* of her beauty and distinction are rare at any time in the theatre, but it was also an act of extraordinary generosity.

---

*Binkie invited her to tea at the Savoy to offer the part and introduce her to Moss Hart. "What exactly does the Queen say in this scene?" was her first, anxious enquiry. "Not much," said Binkie, "just *'charming, charming!'*" "Yes, I'm sure it's charming," said Margaret Halstan irritably, "but what exactly does she *say*?"

It was on the shoulders of Robert Stanton that the burden of responsibility fell the heaviest; to him Binkie delegated a task not normally given to a stage manager. "Keep Rex happy above all else," was Binkie's instruction and this became not only a way of life but a philosophy. The routine courtesies, "Good evening, Mr Harrison; Good night, Mr Harrison," and the customary visit to the dressing-room at the half-hour were clearly not enough. "What you need to do, Bob," said Binkie eagerly, "is to go to the dressing-room, slap him on the back and say, 'Hallo, Rex, old man, how *are* you?' etc., etc. . . ." "But that's simply not my style," protested Stanton, "I could never do that." Nevertheless, when he paid his next visit to Rex's dressing-room, he didn't content himself with merely saying "Good evening," he started to make conversation and found to his delight that Harrison responded with evident pleasure. He stayed twenty minutes and from then onwards this became a nightly custom. He'd look in at the half, chat till curtain time and thus a friendship was started. Soon, Harrison was inviting him to call at his house in the day and stay to lunch or tea or go back afterwards for a bite of supper. Stanton quickly discovered that Harrison was basically a very unhappy man, troubled by a profound shyness and insecurity who hated his own company and couldn't bear to be alone for a minute. It was a situation frequently found in the higher reaches of the profession: he had millions of fans, thousands of women were in love with him, but two of his three marriages had failed and he had very few real friends. He wanted them, but he didn't know how to make them and because of his fame and success few people were willing to make the first step.

Keeping him happy was a task which required endless patience and diplomacy, for he was always complaining about something. The revolving stages started to move either too late or too early, the orchestra failed to keep up with him, the offstage sound effects were either too loud or not loud enough, the dancers and chorus were making distracting noises and movements during his number in act one, the lighting was all wrong and not as had been rehearsed. Most of these complaints centred on the follow-spot which, he insisted, was always in the wrong place, leaving him to Give His All in the semi-darkness. The man operating the follow-spot was highly skilled, quick and resourceful but even he was liable to slip up when Rex made new, unrehearsed moves. One evening, Stanton thought of an excellent method for dealing with his unhappy star. Rex Harrison charged into Stanton's office in the interval seething with fury.

"Bob, I really must . . ."

"I know what it is, Rex. It's the follow-spot."

"That's right. It's just *terrible*. That man must be deaf, dumb *and* blind."

"Don't worry. I've sacked him."

Harrison looked deeply shocked. "You've *sacked* him?"

"Well, that's what you want, isn't it? So I've done it. You're quite right. We really can't have lazy, useless incompetents working on this show, can we?"

Harrison was now looking very disturbed. "Well, that's a bit harsh, isn't it? I certainly didn't expect you to *sack* him. A bit of a bollocking would do, I would have thought. But to sack him for a little thing like that – well, that's going too far."

"Well, it's done. Thought you'd be glad to know."

"No, I'm not. Couldn't you reinstate him and tell him it mustn't happen again?"

"We-e-ell . . ."

"Please, as a favour to me. Please."

"Well . . . er . . . okay, if that's what you want."

"Thanks," and he smiled with genuine relief. Of course, there had been no sacking nor would there be. This was just a Machiavellian ploy calculated to make Harrison feel guilty and apologetic, and one which Binkie would certainly have approved if he had ever got to hear of it. Stanton noticed that after that the complaints against the follow-spot man were dramatically reduced in number and finally stopped altogether.

As well as Rex, it was also important to keep the company happy and this was not easy. Disturbing reports had filtered from New York about Harrison's behaviour to the company. He was not popular: the chorus complained that he was aloof and distant and never spoke to them even if directly and politely addressed. His few friends insisted that it was mere shyness (as Stanton had discovered), but his detractors insisted that it was a terrible corrosive snobbery whereby a star shows he is a star by not speaking to anybody below his level. But Gertrude Lawrence and Yul Brynner were nice and friendly to the chorus and dancers and they were stars just as big as Harrison, said the complainers. Binkie was determined that there should be no trouble, that the company should be one big, happy family, that the world would discover that Harrison's reputation as an arrogant, quarrelsome, unsociable man was entirely unwarranted. So he arranged for a little drinks party for the company in the dress-circle bar shortly after the Royal Gala and urged Rex to put in a brief appearance. Sighing, he agreed. "Good evening, my dear, and what's your name?" he said to a handsome chorus girl. She told him, "and what's yours?" she replied promptly. She was joking, of course, but it seemed that Harrison had precious little sense of humour when it came to jokes against himself. He glared, left the party and, for the rest of his year in the show, never addressed a single word to anybody in the chorus.

As the stage manager, Robert Stanton had a job of intimidating, and sometimes crippling, responsibility. His power backstage was supreme, involving the entire running of the show and every decision relating to it. Understudies had to be rehearsed – after the first year – defaulters rebuked, replacements auditioned and hardly a day passed without somebody being ill or on holiday. Everything, however trivial, had to be reported to Binkie who was always available at the end of a telephone, day and night, weekday or weekend. *My Fair Lady* was like the most jealous and selfishly demanding wife who wouldn't let you out of her sight for a single minute.

On one horrible, traumatic, unforgettable evening his mother was lying seriously ill in St Mary Abbott's Hospital in Kensington. At 6 p.m. the hospital telephoned him at the theatre to say that his mother was dying, that she was not expected to survive the evening. If he wished to see her alive he must come immediately. By a monumental piece of bad luck, the deputy stage manager was away ill and there was quite literally nobody else to run the show. If he wasn't at the theatre the show would have to be cancelled. He phoned Binkie at Knotts Fosse and put the situation. "My dear Robert, I can't possibly give you orders or advice in a situation like this," said Binkie smoothly, "you must do as you think best. But I don't honestly see how you can possibly cancel a Saturday night performance in the West End, disappoint customers and force the management to refund £3,800. But I must emphasise that it is *your* decision."

It was unanswerable. Or rather there was only one thing to do and Stanton did it. He stayed in the prompt corner and theatre-goers happily got their money's worth, all unsuspecting of the human issues involved. A waiting taxi rushed him to Kensington and he arrived at eleven o'clock. But it was too late. She had died twenty minutes earlier.

But his devotion to duty and to Binkie's best interests did not ultimately do him any good. After stage managing the show for six and a half years and in addition directing the northern touring company for its two-year run in Manchester, he felt he had had enough. So when Binkie asked him to direct yet another company for a tour of the south and the west, he asked to be excused. "Binkie, I've lived with the show for nearly seven years and I'm going slowly out of my mind. I urgently need a change. I have to get away from it or I'll have a nervous breakdown. I need a long holiday and I need to get back to the outside world. I've never felt so cut off in my life. I'm hopelessly out of touch." But, as has already been explained, refusing work was a capital offence and the death sentence, without hope of reprieve, was automatic. The circumstances didn't matter, it was the one unforgivable sin. In spite of his superb record of hard work, efficiency and dedication, Robert Stanton was put on Binkie's black-list and never worked for him again.

But they did meet, some five years after *My Fair Lady* closed, when Binkie asked him to come to his office to discuss the forthcoming court case with Tonia Lee. She had been Julie Andrews' first understudy and had taken over the part in 1964. She was married to a Harley Street dentist, Dr Hepburn Miller, who by a curious coincidence treated some of Binkie's close friends, including the actor Richard Easton. One evening during a blackout after the Ascot scene, one of the male dancers trod on her foot, breaking the ankle and thus putting her out of action for a period of time exceeding that laid down by Equity and thereby giving Binkie the chance to sack her. In addition, he did not let her play the part on the northern tour in Manchester, as promised, on the grounds that her ankle hadn't sufficiently recovered and that its strength could not be relied on to carry her through a long and difficult performance. The truth was that Binkie didn't like her performance and was glad of a chance of getting rid of her.

Tonia Lee – whose real name was Beryl Foley – did something which nobody had ever done before: she sued Binkie for wrongful dismissal. Stanton attempted to talk some common sense to Binkie and advised him not to go ahead and to settle out of court, but Binkie was cocksure of winning and ignored this excellent advice. The fact that his defence lawyer was Quintin Hogg, QC, the future Lord Chancellor, probably gave him good cause for confidence. Stanton tried to tell Binkie that the case was not as easy or as clearcut as he imagined. The defence's case was that Tonia Lee had been guilty of negligence, that her exit during the fifteen-second blackout was not precisely as it had been directed and that therefore Binkie's dismissal was lawful.

It came to the Royal Courts of Justice on November 25th 1968 in front of Mr Justice Mocatta. Tonia Lee and her lawyers offered to settle out of court, but Binkie refused. The trial dragged on for ten days and for Binkie it was a dismal and humiliating experience. He went into the witness-box but was so grand and arrogant and sure of himself that the plaintiff's QC, Michael Eastham, had no trouble in making mincemeat out of him. Binkie was not a good witness and crawled out of the box "feeling terrified and horrible, it was a *degrading* experience . . ." as he commented to a friend. By contrast Tonia Lee was an excellent witness. She appeared, beautifully dressed and groomed, and proceeded to give what Binkie later described as "a magnificent performance which had the Judge eating out of her tiny hands". After eighteen witnesses had been called it was established that she had *not* been negligent and that Binkie's dismissal of her was therefore unlawful. She was awarded £4,125 damages and costs which amounted to £1,600.

His last words on *My Fair Lady* came in an interview. "I'm not very good at the job of presenting plays. I make the most terrible mistakes and I am always *plagued* by doubts. I could never imagine *Pygmalion* as a musical. I thought it was absolutely *insane*."

CHAPTER THIRTY-TWO

1960

Decline of the Heyday

The twentieth century enjoyed no fewer than two theatrical revolutions, and there are a number of interesting similarities. Both were assaults on the establishment theatre by the plays of ideas; both were outspokenly against the star system and the plays it inspired; both eagerly developed new authors but were less interested in new actors; both, by coincidence, started in Sloane Square, the fashionable district with the unfashionable theatre, at the Royal Court; and both had as their detonators plays by comparatively unknown authors, *Man and Superman* in 1905 and *Look Back in Anger* fifty-one years later. Both these plays were weak in plot and character but very strong in dialogue; both had a maniac rebel hero who talks interminably, attacking every belief and institution which his audiences hold most sacred, and in both plays was the tedium of propaganda made not only acceptable but immortal by its devastating wit.

The second of these revolutions started with the English Stage Company's season of new plays under the direction of George Devine, and if the opening play by Angus Wilson represented the first shots of the French Revolution in Paris, then *Look Back in Anger* was the fall of the Bastille, and John Osborne – to take this analogy a step further – was Robespierre to Binkie's Marie Antoinette. Osborne, like Shaw a self-proclaimed Messiah of the New Drama, was an actor whose career had flourished mainly in provincial tours and seaside reps. He made no secret of his hatred for the commercial theatre in general and Shaftesbury Avenue in particular, and it was his declared intention to destroy it, just as it had been Shaw's back in the nineties. But it took some time before the revolutionary mob reached Versailles: although the sensational success of Osborne's play was an ominous sign that the enemy was at the gate, H. M. Tennent had a few years to flourish before either Binkie or anybody realised that its days were numbered. In fact, the empire had never looked stronger, prouder, more confident than in May 1956, unquestionably a vintage month. Alec Guinness was in *Hotel Paradiso* at the Winter Garden,

481

Vivien Leigh was in Coward's *South Sea Bubble* at the Lyric, Edith Evans and Peggy Ashcroft were in *The Chalk Garden* and Sandy Wilson's new musical *The Buccaneer* had just opened at the Apollo and everybody hoped it would repeat the success of *The Boy Friend*. But the commercial theatre was much tougher than it looked as John Osborne discovered when he arrived at the Royal Court Theatre one day to find Vivien Leigh rehearsing Coward's farce, *Look After Lulu*, directed by Tony Richardson and with Binkie watching in the stalls. "We thought we were going to conquer Shaftesbury Avenue," he later said ruefully, "but it looked as if they were conquering us."

But revolutions in England have a strange habit of not quite succeeding in the way they were originally intended: Establishment has a crafty technique of welcoming the rebel forces and then slowly assimilating them to the point where they become part of the Establishment and fight to uphold its traditions. And thus it was at the Royal Court. Within a year Olivier had enjoyed a spectacular success in Osborne's masterpiece, *The Entertainer*, and was playing it to packed houses at the Palace Theatre: two years later his only musical, *The World of Paul Slickey*, played for only three controversial months at the same address. Far from destroying Shaftesbury Avenue, Osborne found himself one of its brightest jewels, so both the Establishment and the Revolution could claim success.

Binkie's heyday lasted for about twenty years – which is not a bad period for a heyday. It is difficult to pinpoint the exact date when the slow descent from the peak began, for history is seldom so tidy or thoughtful, but somewhere towards the end of the fifties, things began to go wrong. The first warning that the empire was beginning to crumble came when he planned to present *The Visit*. This was by the Swiss-German author, Friedrich Dürrenmatt, a grim affair about rape, murder, revenge, castration together with a number of interesting perversions such as cannibalism and bestialism which, if they were not actually shown, were strongly suggested. Not exactly a Tennent play, people thought, and it certainly indicated an unusual departure from Binkie's normal theatrical taste, but with a package which only he could arrange, the Lunts returning to London after eight years and Peter Brook directing, it could hardly fail to be a huge success.

It opened a pre-London tour in Dublin in 1958 and that was the time when Binkie discovered, to his horror and disbelief, that he couldn't get a London theatre. Prince Littler not only disliked the play intensely but he was also disgusted that Binkie should want to present it in one of his theatres. So, for positively the first time in his life, Binkie found himself in the humiliating position of having to go to the other theatre owners, cap in hand, begging for a home. All refused. It is possible that they too were shocked by the play and had no desire to see it desecrating their beautiful theatres. It is also possible that they refused out of malice, pleased at the situation where they were presented with a unique chance of bringing him down a peg or two. Characteristically, he did not waste time on futile battles or recriminations: he toured it around England, took it to New York where it opened the newly-built Lunt-Fontanne Theatre to enormous acclaim, and then toured it round America, coast to coast.

By this time a new theatre had been built in London, the Royalty in Kingsway on the site formerly occupied by that most monstrous of white elephants, the Stoll. Unhappily, the Royalty seemed determined to follow in the same grandiose tradition. It was huge and ugly, more suited to spectacular nude revues (which is what it eventually got), rather than intimate dramas of lust and retribution. It was also miles off the theatrical centre: everybody gloomily prophesied disaster and it was noted by the press with a pardonable touch of cynicism that there was no rush by the leading managers to present the first play there. But Bernard Delfont was willing to give a home to *The Visit* and it opened there in June 1960 after a Royal Gala Preview and a tidal wave of publicity.

The opening performance was a huge success, the notices were ecstatic but, alas, the Cassandras were proved to be right. Kingsway, being all offices, was dead after 6 p.m. and there was no passing trade: taxi-drivers didn't know where it was, and even if you looked for it and stood outside it, it was difficult to identify because by some extraordinary foolish regulation, the illuminated entrance had to be tucked away in a side-street virtually invisible from Kingsway. Nevertheless, dedicated theatre-lovers are not easily discouraged from seeing their idols and they kept the theatre full for three months, but after that audiences declined rapidly both in numbers and in quality. Such a production with all those names should have run for two years. It ran five months and lost a lot of money.

It had been a colossal disappointment and it was one of the first nails in Binkie's coffin. There were many others, for after *The Visit* nothing seemed to go right. He was fifty-three, the time when, according to the medical experts, a man goes through his menopause. Whether or not this was true, Binkie certainly began to behave in a strange and unpredictable way, to lose his good judgement and discretion and to do stupid, unnecessary things. One of these was to quarrel with Noël Coward who was not only one of the pillars supporting Tennent's but a close personal friend for thirty years. They had met in 1930 when Coward was in *Private Lives*: Coward had been extremely kind and generous to him and helped him to get started in management by introducing him to everybody he knew and subsequently giving him advice and assistance in many unexpected ways. From 1940 onwards, Binkie had presented all Coward's plays. The latest was *Waiting in the Wings*, a charmingly sentimental piece about old actresses in a retirement home. It was neatly constructed, full of pathos and humour with some of the Master's best wit sprinkled throughout. It was not quite up to Coward's best – how could anything be that? – but with the right cast it could be a big success. "He loved the play when I read it to him," wrote Coward, in his diaries, "but a week later, after he had been studying the script, he was a little too full of suggested alterations. The discussion between us went sour and finally he said that he wouldn't do it. I took this angrily at its face value and flounced out with all my lovelocks flowing. The next morning an anguished telegram arrived and everybody forgave everybody else. A further, calmer discussion then took place, I'm glad the scene took place. Binkie has changed a bit of late and this row brought us down to bedrock. Binkie at bedrock can be trusted entirely. On the other levels, he is liable to be devious and tricky."

This was the calm before the storm. Soon Binkie wanted more and more changes, leading inevitably to a request for a total rewrite which Coward refused to do. Finally, Binkie rejected it and Coward had to look for another management. He eventually found one in Michael Redgrave working in partnership with the American producer, Fred Sadoff. It was to be directed by Margaret Webster, actress daughter of Dame May Whitty, who had achieved a great New York success when she directed Maurice Evans in *Richard II* before the war and was now much in demand. Alas, Redgrave was inexperienced in the complexities and crises of theatrical management; rehearsals were endlessly marred by delays, technical troubles and administrative chaos. More than once Coward found himself missing Binkie's efficiency and powers of organisation, as when the company arrived at Dublin on a Sunday and found itself compelled to open on the Monday without having had a previous set-up of the scenery. "Oh, how I wish Binkie had done the play. This cheerful, optimistic, shoestring stuff terrifies me," he wrote in his diary.

It was just before the London opening that the full extent of Binkie's treachery came to light when Gladys Cooper asked him how did he *dare* write a play about retired actresses and not offer her a part in it. Astonished and indignant, Coward explained that he had written especially for her but that Binkie had told him that she had turned it down without comment. "Nonsense, he never even showed it to me," she replied with some asperity. Binkie had, it seemed, told

Coward that Edith Evans had actively loathed the play, but later he discovered that she hadn't even seen it or even knew that it had been written. Binkie's behaviour was much worse than telling black lies about who had seen it and what they had said: he had apparently gone round the West End telling everybody that the play was rubbish and that Coward was a spent force. Understandably, Coward was deeply hurt and refused to have anything to do with a man who could be so treacherous.

Binkie's behaviour is inexplicable. He must surely have known that any bad report would get back to Coward very quickly. What devil could have possessed him that he should have gone out of his way to antagonise and injure an old friend to whom he owed so much? It says much for Coward's extraordinary generosity that he eventually forgave him, but Binkie paid a high price for his disloyalty when he lost the chance of presenting Coward's last three musicals, *High Spirits*, *The Girl Who Came to Supper* and *Sail Away*. *Waiting in the Wings* finally opened at the Duke of York's in May 1960 with Sybil Thorndike supported by a team of splendid old actresses, many of whom had been coaxed out of their own retirement. It had mixed notices from a predominantly hostile anti-Coward press, but ran for a respectable six months.

Binkie was constantly being criticised for being too ruthless, and he frequently was, as his cavalier treatment of Coward shows, but he was never consistent. There were times when he was simply not ruthless enough. When Tennent authors who had written one very good and successful play followed it with one which was markedly inferior, Binkie would produce it. It was loyalty rather than good judgement which prompted him to present Robert Bolt's tiresomely coy little fantasy, *Gentle Jack*, and his very boring political diatribe *The Tiger and the Horse*, which not even the talents of Edith Evans and Kenneth Williams, of all unlikely combinations, in the first, or of the Redgraves, Michael and Vanessa, in the second could make acceptable. And surely it was a great mistake to present Enid Bagnold's two plays *The Chinese Prime Minister* and *The Last Joke*, the second being so extraordinarily bad that one watched it with total disbelief that so many famous and talented people could have had any faith in it. Obviously he was grateful to the author for *The Chalk Garden* which provided him with one of his greatest successes, but generosity can go too far. *The Chinese Prime Minister* starred Edith Evans and Brian Aherne and *The Last Joke* boasted John Gielgud and Ralph Richardson together for the first time since *A Day By the Sea*. Binkie's Law was that if you had a bad play you swamped it with stars in the hope that nobody would notice. But there is another law which operates with real ferocity: a big line-up of stars makes a good play better but a bad play much, *much* worse.

It opened at the end of August 1960 to a really dismal holocaust of abuse. "Much *much* worse than I got for *Waiting in the Wings*," wrote Noël Coward complacently in his diary, "and unanimous. As it is a very expensive production *and* at the Phoenix which is a big theatre to fill, this looks like a disaster for Binkie and, as far as I'm concerned, serve him bloody well right. He has really behaved badly to me of late and his treatment of *Wings* was bad and hurtful. Also very foolish. In the old days he used to love the theatre and allow himself to be gently advised by John G, me, Joycie, etc. Now his advisers are John Perry, Prince Littler and Irene Selznick and the change is *not* for the better. I am sad about the change in him because I thought he was really a friend. Too much power and too much concentration on money grubbing." When Coward saw *The Last Joke* later in the month he had, incredibly, some complimentary things to say about it which, in the light of Binkie's brutal treatment, indicates unusual generosity. "It was elegant, impeccably acted and, on the whole, enjoyable. A wonderful antidote to *Billy Liar*. First act excellent. Some lovely stylised language, lovely set and good acting." To his great satisfaction it played to empty houses, and closed after a month.

Like Noël Coward, Terence Rattigan was another of Binkie's prize authors who had outlived his heyday and was slowly becoming unfashionable. His 1958 offering *Variations on a Theme* was an ingenious updating of *The Lady of the Camellias* in which Marguerite is transformed into a former Birmingham typist now living with a millionaire in a suffocatingly wealthy style in a villa in the South of France and deeply in love with a young ballet dancer, also from Birmingham. It was written for Margaret Leighton, and it was a once-in-a-lifetime opportunity to go the gamut of emotions from A to Z and back to A again, never off the stage and changing into a succession of gorgeous clothes.

Binkie auditioned and interviewed a number of beautiful young actors for the part of the ballet-dancing lover and finally selected Tim Seely. He had been born into a wealthy landowning family in Nottinghamshire with many high political and royal connections. His mother, Vera, had been a close friend of the Prince of Wales in 1930 and there were persistent rumours that Tim was the Prince's illegitimate son. He had left RADA in a blaze of glory to go straight into a leading part in *Tea and Sympathy* at the Comedy under John Fernald's direction and was all set to be the golden boy of the fifties. To be offered a co-starring part with Margaret Leighton in Rattigan's latest play directed by John Gielgud and supported by H. M. Tennent in all its collective glory was a heaven-sent opportunity and should have opened the doors to stardom but unhappily it didn't work out like that.

Seely was talented and good-looking but he was inexperienced, entirely heterosexual and pitifully lacking in confidence. He found the whole experience terrifying. "I couldn't cope with all those famous people," he said, "they couldn't have been more courteous and kindly but it was all very unnerving. I remember being taken out to lunch by the entire hierarchy, Binkie, Terry, John Perry, Gielgud and Peter Glenville and feeling like a new boy at school meeting the headmaster and all the Board of Governors. I couldn't think of anything to say." Gielgud's trial-and-error method of directing was particularly difficult for a young actor who needed firm guidance and Seely goes down in history as the only actor who ever swore at Gielgud. "For Christ's sake," he shouted at the end of a particularly trying rehearsal in which everything had been changed a dozen times, "can't you make up your fucking mind. . . ?" At the end of the tour Binkie realised that he had been indulging in wishful thinking. Seely wasn't ready for this long and difficult part and was replaced by Jeremy Brett.

The play is one of Rattigan's most interesting and imaginative, with some of his wittiest and most perceptive writing but the critics had taken a great hate against star vehicles in lavish settings. Binkie made a great mistake in commissioning Norman Hartnell, the Queen's dressmaker, to design the costumes, for they received advance publicity well in excess of their importance in the play. It was greeted with devastating notices and lasted only four months, the shortest run of any Rattigan play.

The sixties was the decade when new managers began to make an impact on the West End. John Gale, Charles Ross, Peter Bridge, Michael Codron, Ray Cooney, Michael White, each with their own ideas and their pet authors and actors. No longer did agents send their best new plays to Binkie, and no longer did he have the virtual monopoly of the best theatres. Other managers were able to present new plays and revivals at the Haymarket, the Globe, Apollo and Lyric, all hitherto unassailable strongholds of the Tennent empire. The sixties was the decade when the Royal Shakespeare Company opened its London headquarters for new plays at the Aldwych, and the National Theatre under Sir Laurence Olivier had its preliminary seasons at the Old Vic: between them they started to offer very serious competition to the commercial managers. One by one his stars either faded away or deserted him. He quarrelled with Robert Morley and

H. M. TENNENT LTD.

CHAIRMAN: Prince Littler, C.B.E.   MANAGING DIRECTOR: Hugh Beaumont
DIRECTORS: Stewart Cruikshank, John Perry, J. D. C. Noble
SECRETARY: James Sharp

GLOBE THEATRE,
SHAFTESBURY AVENUE,
LONDON, W.I.

Telephone No.
GERRARD 3647-8-9.

Telegraphic Address:
TENMONT, LONDON, W.I

Cables:
TENMONT, LONDON.

26th October, 1965.

Richard Huggett, Esq.,
Arts Theatre,
London, W.C. 2.

Dear Richard Huggett,

Thank you for your letter, from which I am delighted to learn that "THE LUPIN-BLUE DRESS" has gone so well at Windsor.

Unfortunately, at the present moment, there is a complete lack of theatres available. We have Anouilh's play "THE CAVERN" on tour: this has been on the road for eight weeks and we are still unable to arrange a London house to bring it in; and we also have "THE GLASS MENAGERIE" on tour. This is because business in the London theatres is so good. Therefore, it looks very unlikely that until the New Year there is any chance of a house becoming available. I did, in fact, read the play myself and I am delighted to find that it has worked out so well.

I think, by the way, that Carl Toms' new 'Curtain-Up' is really delightful.

Yours sincerely,

The H. M. Tennent style. The attractive colophon was designed by Gladys Calthrop. The letter also shows Binkie's distinctive signature.

Alec Guinness, neither of whom worked for him again. Paul Scofield moved to the National Theatre. Edith Evans, Sybil Thorndike and Gladys Cooper were close to retirement. And Vivien Leigh died. He no longer put young actors under contract since there was little for them to do. The number of productions diminished year by year and eventually he was forced to say goodbye to June Collins who – following the retirement of Daphne Rye – had been his casting director, and shut down the department.

As the sixties progressed, the shortage of new plays became pressing and the empire began to feel the pinch. Binkie refused to have anything to do with the new drama which was taking possession of the theatre: he loathed *Look Back in Anger*, did not understand *The Caretaker* or any Pinter play, and was openly contemptuous of Joan Littlewood's Theatre Workshop whose brilliant, anarchical improvisations as shown in *The Hostage* (1959) and *Oh What a Lovely War!* (1963) were a total denial of everything theatrical which Binkie believed to be most sacred but which had, unaccountably, taken

London by storm. The Binkie of the heyday would have taken the sensible attitude that if you can't beat the rebels you must join them and would have shrewdly commissioned plays, but not the tired and disillusioned Binkie of the sixties. But without new plays, how could he keep and employ his stars?

He thus fell back on the old Tennent formula of lavish classical revivals, but again and again he showed that he had lost his judgement and taste. He decided to revive *Lady Windermere's Fan* and commissioned Cecil Beaton to design the sets and costumes, but they were a great disappointment to anybody who remembered the glories of the 1945 revival. The sets were cramped and fussy and the play seemed to be boring and trivial. Had Binkie lost his touch? people were asking, and it seemed that he had. He tried again with another *Ring Round the Moon*, but without the unique talents of Brook-Messel-Rutherford-Scofield, the magic had fled and it all seemed thin and dull. *The Rivals* with Sir Ralph Richardson was a little better, but Margaret Rutherford was feeling her age, had almost lost her memory and was so frail that she had trouble in holding her tea-cup, another example of Binkie's loyalty and affection overriding his good sense. *The Importance of Being Earnest* was sadly miscast in many of the leading parts and it was Miss Prism (Flora Robson) and Canon Chasuble (Robert Eddison) who stole the play and the notices, surely the first time in the play's history this had happened. But *The Merchant of Venice* was a dismal affair and it indicated beyond question that the evil and cruelty of Shylock was outside Ralph Richardson's reach as it had eluded that of John Gielgud before the war.

Binkie of the heyday, when setting up a farce by André Roussin, *Nina*, would not have cast Edith Evans who had never done farce before and accepted the assignment with many misgivings and much against her professional judgement. The heyday Binkie would certainly have cut his losses and cancelled it when he saw how deeply unhappy she was, or he would have agreed to Rex Harrison playing opposite her which she rather pathetically requested again and again, and would have postponed the play until Harrison was free to join her. The heyday Binkie would never have made the tragic mistake of forcing her to continue with the play until it became, at the Royal Court Theatre in Liverpool, the nightmare they had all been dreading and which all have agreed to forget.

And the heyday Binkie would never have put on the tired and second-hand *On the Avenue*, an intimate revue written to the old and now used-up formula. Nor would he have made a scene on the opening night which occurred in the foyer of the Globe Theatre. A group of people, two men and two women, were leaving to go for a drink in a nearby pub and talking rather loudly about the show and how bad it was. Binkie heard them, and on their way back he refused to admit them. "As you were not enjoying it there really isn't any point in seeing the second half, is there?" he said with steely razor-blade politeness. There was a scene; the party felt themselves aggrieved. They became abusive, the police were called and finally they left. The press were there with photographers. Pictures were taken and Binkie gave an interview. At next day's newspaper coverage heads were shaken. It was generally felt that the young Binkie would never have allowed it to happen, that it was all rather undignified and unnecessary, and that barring the public was like barring critics, something which was never justified and which was in the long run bad for the theatre.

CHAPTER THIRTY-THREE

1966

Suite in Three Keys

In his last years, Noël Coward was obsessed by his desire to make one final appearance on the London stage. But what should it be? There were no classic parts which he wanted to play and suitable vehicles for an actor caught in that twilight zone between middle-age and senility were difficult to find. Clearly, he would have to write it himself. That is how, after a lifetime of glorious achievement, his creative energies enjoyed one final spurt in the summer of 1965 with no less than three new and original plays. Doing one for three months would be a strain but doing three would give him no chance to get bored. They were all set in a hotel suite but they had different plots and three different sets of characters. They were collectively known as *Suite in Three Keys*. The first was a full-length play in two acts, *A Song at Twilight*, which has as its central character a world-famous novelist who receives an unexpected visit from his former mistress of long ago. She comes to blackmail him with a bundle of love letters written decades earlier to a young man, thus revealing that he is – surprise, surprise – a secret homosexual! Before the war the audiences would have been appalled by this reference to sexual deviation and it was a mark of how badly Coward had lost track of the times that the shock value of this had now vanished. This reservation apart, the play was witty, articulate, and very well constructed. Coward's contemporary awareness may have atrophied but not his skills. It was supposedly inspired by the last years of Somerset Maugham whom Coward had known but Coward always insisted that the real source of inspiration was Max Beerbohm whose final years, as told by his biographer, Lord David Cecil, were enlivened by just such a visitation. The second was a one-act play, *Come into the Garden, Maud*, about a hen-pecked, golfing American husband and his truly horrible, nagging American wife. It was a comedy and provided a good contrast to the sombre dramas of the first.

In the middle of May Binkie flew out to Les Avants, Coward's home in Switzerland, where a reading took place. "They're the best

I've ever written," said Coward crisply and Binkie could not suppress a sigh. Coward, indeed all playwrights, always said that. However, once the reading had finished – and Coward read them very well, an advantage he enjoyed over non-acting authors – Binkie had to admit that he was probably right. They were both very good. He made some intelligent comments and practical suggestions and flew back to London leaving Coward to rewrite *A Song at Twilight*, which he did extensively. Gone were the days when the complete play, unimprovable and ready to go, would fall straight on to the typewriter: now, second and sometimes third thoughts were best.

Coward returned to London for an orgy of theatre-going and read the revised version to Robin Maugham, himself a failed playwright and novelist. He had always adopted a curiously jealous and possessive attitude towards his Uncle Willie whom he clearly regarded as his own personal property. He didn't dislike the play, but he was alarmed that people might think it was a portrait of Somerset Maugham and upset that Coward had trespassed on what he firmly thought of as *his* territory. He tried to persuade Coward and Binkie to cancel the production but neither of them had the slightest interest in literary boundary disputes and Robin Maugham was mortified when both men turned a deaf ear to his complaints. He further warned them that Maugham might consider himself libelled since his homosexuality, though known to his family and close friends, had not been made public – a situation which was not to last long – and the dead male lover in the play, Perry Sheldon, obviously referred to Maugham's one-time boy-friend, Gerald Haxton. If Maugham was so advised he might take legal action to protect his good name and this could be embarrassing and expensive. Binkie was not impressed.

Coward dined with Binkie and they discussed possible directors and possible ladies for the cast. Binkie recommended Glen Byam Shaw and sent him the script of the first two plays. Shaw read them, liked them very much and eagerly offered his services. "I am very very glad that he is going to direct the plays," wrote Coward in his diary, "he is sensible, extremely experienced, and has a loving character. I *know* he will be of the utmost help to me."

As for the ladies, both Coward and Binkie wanted Irene Worth for the one and Margaret Leighton for the other. Binkie sent scripts for the first two to Margaret Leighton then married to Michael Wilding who had given up acting and was working as an actors' agent in New York. He had worked with her a number of times and they were old friends, so it was a source of considerable irritation when she started to behave like a prima donna. She took a long time to read them, ignoring Binkie's plea to hurry as time was short. Eventually she said she would do them, but then she said she wouldn't, then she said she wasn't sure and could she have more time? Then she wanted some rewriting with her parts enlarged, then she said she liked them as they were, but she couldn't leave Michael alone in New York for six months, could he come too if he obtained leave of absence from the agency? In short, it was the same *folie de grandeur* which so many star actresses had inflicted on him, from Marie Tempest to Gertrude Lawrence, and his original determination to stand no nonsense from his stars found extra confirmation from her neurotic and illogical behaviour.

Nor was the thought of an unemployed, ex-actor husband hanging round the rehearsal room and theatre at all reassuring. "Neither Binkie, nor Glen nor I want him to come," wrote Coward. "He'll only be an amiable nuisance and justify his idiotic existence by making imbecile suggestions and getting in my hair. Also, Maggie seems to have changed and become more scatty than ever: Hollywood values have obviously corrupted what there was of her mind. I am sad about her but I am not going to tolerate any more leading-lady airs and graces and tantrums for *anyone*. I have too much to do in creating my own performances." After a fortnight of vexing and expensive long-distance phone calls between Binkie's office and the Wilding/Leighton apartment in New York, it was finally decided to drop her and offer the parts to Lilli Palmer. She read the first two plays and accepted with enthusiasm. So did Irene Worth.

On August 20th Coward finished the third play of the trio, *Shadows of the Evening*, a return to the sombre theme of the first. This was about the last days in the life of a man who is told that he is shortly to die. How does he spend the evening? He goes to the casino and gambles a lot of money without caring in the least what happens to it, and with that indifference to support him it is implied that he will probably win a fortune. "I think it is one of the best plays I have ever written," he confided to his diary. "I may have to eat my words later on and consider myself a proper Charlie for having written it, but that is how I feel at the immediate moment. It is a sad theme but not entirely a sad play. It also has wonderful parts for all three of us, particularly me. I do think that to have written one full-length and two one-act plays in all the same set and with three characters and a waiter is a remarkable theatrical feat and I am mighty proud of myself."

Coward and Binkie made a special journey to Lilli Palmer's home and read the third play to her and Carlos Thompson, her husband. Lilli thought to warn him that in the eleven years since her last stage appearance she had forgotten everything: voice, timing, projection, because film technqiue called for the opposite of stage technique. Coward was not bothered by this: Lilli was an old and dearly beloved friend, a loved one, and he wanted her. "I can't stand listening to plays being read. I can't concentrate because I'm distracted and influenced by the reader," she wrote in her memoirs, "but here, as everywhere else, Noël was an exception. Carlos and I listened, fascinated, for the whole evening. And the fact that the London run was to be limited to three months was decisive for me." Coward was delighted by the evening and her decision. "I am enchanted by Lilli from every point of view," he wrote. "She is shrewd, sensible, untiresome and glamorous in addition to being a fine actress." These were words which before long he was to regret and retract with some venom.

All that remained was to find a young Italian actor to play Felix, the waiter. Coward went to Rome and sat in the luxurious office of Italy's leading theatrical agency interviewing a long succession of stunningly beautiful young men and enjoying himself hugely. None of them was suitable and none of them spoke English well enough, but after a week his patience was rewarded when Carlo Palmucci turned up with that supreme accolade, a signed letter of introduction from Franco Zef-firelli. Coward reported to Binkie that his English, though not perfect, was satisfactory, he had enjoyed considerable stage experience (which turned out to be a slight overstatement) and his looks were spectacular. "They'd better be," was Binkie's laconic comment.

In the meantime, there was another crisis. Glen Byam Shaw sent a letter to Binkie saying that he did not like the third play and wished to withdraw from the production. His suggestion that Coward should write another play in its place – perhaps a thriller? – naturally infuriated everybody. Binkie suggested that before allowing Glen to go, he should be given every chance to change his mind. A meeting was arranged for eight o'clock one evening at Binkie's house but for once the ever-reliable Jack Osborn had made a mistake and delivered him at seven. Binkie and Noël had hoped for an hour's private conference beforehand and now this was impossible. Glen was half-way drunk and this made him maudlin, lachrymose and self-pitying. Coward spent the time futilely trying to persuade him to change his mind, but it was useless.

"You're so brilliant, Noël dear," said the director weeping, "you're so clever and I'm so silly and stupid. I don't think I could direct you, you wouldn't listen to a thing I said, you'd put Irene and Lilli against me; you see, Noël dear, I'm *frightened* of you and I just couldn't cope."

Coward was deeply insulted by this cool assumption that he was so grand and arrogant that he wouldn't take direction even from somebody as experienced and capable as Glen Byam Shaw, "I'm a *professional*, Glen," he said repeatedly and firmly, "and I *do* take direction."

At this point Binkie, most uncharacteristically, lost his temper and flew at Glen as did Coward. All this took place over the dinner table and the screaming continued in front of Elvira and Anna who were cooking and serving, but they were both quite accustomed to being witnesses to Mr Beaumont's little dramas and they ignored it.

By the time they had reached the cheese and coffee, Coward had made his decision. Another director was needed. It was now half past ten and the car had been ordered for eleven so Glen was shunted into a little outer room until it arrived. As he was in earshot, there was a slightly Aldwych farce atmosphere with Coward and Binkie being forced to discuss the situation in whispers which quickly dissolved into giggles like schoolgirls in a dormitory after lights out – *silent* giggles of course. Finally, Jack Osborn and the Rolls arrived, Glen was taken away and Binkie was now free to make his phone call.

This is the point in the story where Vivian Matalon, aged forty-five, made a dramatic entrance. Like so many of Binkie's best directors, he had been an actor. He had first worked for Binkie during the previous year, 1964, directing a play by Arthur Marshall, *Season of Goodwill*, starring Sybil Thorndike. It had run for only three weeks at the Queen's Theatre, but it established his credentials as a good and hard-working director who could get on with actors and handle the stars with tact and diplomacy, this last being an important asset in Binkie's eyes. This assessment was confirmed when he directed *The Chinese Prime Minister* at the Globe in 1965. It was Enid Bagnold's last play and Edith Evans' last London appearance. Matalon did his best, but even he couldn't make a success of a play of such unravelled tedium and an ageing star who was rapidly losing her memory. It ran for only three months and proved to be a dismal experience for everybody.

He was currently directing Gwen Ffrangcon-Davies and Ian McShane in a revival of *The Glass Menagerie* and when Binkie's call came he had just returned from an extra evening rehearsal with McShane, whose performance was slow to take shape. He was to remember the telephone conversation with some clarity.

"Where have you been?" It was entirely typical of Binkie that he never announced his name or made any attempt to identify himself, but assumed that his voice would be instantly recognised. Matalon knew perfectly well who was speaking but something made him ask, "Who is this?"

"Binkie."

"Yes?"

"Get into your car and come over."

"Binkie, I can't. I have an early rehearsal tomorrow and I have to get some sleep."

"Come over at once."

"What's it all about?"

"Can't tell you over the telephone. Come over at once. There's somebody I want you to meet."

"Binkie, I'm very sorry, but I just can't."

At this point Binkie's smooth, silken, self-possession vanished and he snapped angrily, "If you know what's good for you, you'll come over *now*."

Matalon took the hint, got into his car and drove over to Lord North Street without delay. It was Binkie who opened the door and led him upstairs to the little sitting-room on the first floor. Sitting there was somebody whose face was very familiar but he couldn't for the life of him think of the man's name. Binkie performed a brief introduction. "I'd like you to meet an old friend of mine," he said. "This is No . . ." and at that very moment Matalon recognised Noël Coward. He was also introduced to Graham Payn, Coward's great friend and companion, and all four sat down. Briefly, Binkie explained the situation. Glen Byam Shaw had asked to withdraw from the production and a replacement was urgently needed.

"I saw your production of *Season of Goodwill*," said Coward, "and I liked it very much. Would you please do me the honour of directing these plays for me?" Any other young director would have been flattered into an immediate acceptance but Matalon, fortified by a couple of brandies, was nothing if not assured and confident. "Do you want a director or a stage manager?" he enquired. "I have always had a great respect and admiration for you. During your years of wilderness and exile I supported and defended your good name, and I don't want to work in any capacity which might lead to disillusionment." At this point Binkie, horrified by his brash outspokenness, started to make what Matalon later described as chicken noises of protest. But Coward only smiled. "You have just sneaked straight into my heart," he said smiling happily. "I want a director who has the courage to tell me what you have just told me. It's been eleven years since I last acted on the stage and I'm frightened. I need all the help I can get."

After Noël and Graham had left, Matalon was just about to go but Binkie insisted that he stay and talk. He poured out drinks for them both and they talked for five hours. "Binkie got absolutely *paralytic*," he remembered. "At one point he got so drunk that he filled a glass with whisky, took a water jug and tried to pour it in, but he missed and succeeded only in pouring it all over the carpet. Later he said, 'I want to tell you the story of my life,' and I replied, 'Please *don't*, Binkie, because if you do you'll later regret it and then you'll turn against me.' The trouble with Binkie was that you never felt entirely at ease with him because you were always wondering if he was telling the truth and how far you could trust him. John Perry was a much nicer person. If Binkie was angry with somebody for whatever reason or cherished a grudge, it was John who managed to sort things out and make the peace.

"When the contracts to direct the Coward plays had been signed and I was on the point of leaving for Switzerland to have early rehearsals and talks with Noël, I got the distinct impression that Binkie was angry with me. He became uncharacteristically cold, curt, snappy and remote. It was all very peculiar. I was getting a bit scared. What could I possibly have done? Then I got a phone call from John: 'Just to find out how you are, all set for the journey? Well, have a good time and I'm sure that it's going to be a big success.' He had taken the trouble to phone and put me at my ease and quieten any fears I might have had. But I never did discover what I had done, *if* I had done anything."

The master-plan was to rehearse for two weeks in Coward's home in January and move to Dublin for the remaining fortnight. They would open a short provincial tour there and then go to the Queen's Theatre, London, in March. As was his custom before starting work, and to satisfy his wanderlust, Coward went on his travels, taking in India, Kenya and the Seychelles. During these weeks he rewrote *Shadows of the Evening*. Binkie, Vivian Matalon, Irene Worth, Lilli Palmer and the American writer, Robert Ardrey, had all made the same suggestions and comments and he always welcomed intelligent, well-informed and constructive criticism. In fact, he had been so impressed by Vivian Matalon's comments on the play, which had been sent to him on a number of closely hand-written pages, that he had them bound in a leather folder and returned to him as a first-rehearsal present. Coward also put the spare time to good use by learning the three long and difficult parts he had written for himself. Then, on November 12th, there was bad trouble. The food he had eaten in the Seychelles hotel was appalling and the water in Government House was suspect: he was suddenly struck down with diarrhoea and vomiting, with a temperature of a hundred. He was in and out of hospital for weeks and hepatitis was suspected but happily this turned out not to be true. The holiday was cut short and he returned home to Switzerland and the tenderness and loving care of Cole Lesley for the Christmas holiday.

On December 16th, Somerset Maugham performed his last service for Binkie and Coward by dying in hospital at the age of ninety-one. It showed great thoughtfulness for the welfare and convenience of others as well as the most excellent timing. If there had ever been any serious possibility of legal action, this was now removed, for in law, mercifully, you cannot libel the dead. Coward had paid a short visit to the Villa Mauresque in September. "I'm glad I did because he was so wretchedly, pathetically grateful," he wrote. "He was living out his last days in a desperate nightmare, poor beast. He barely made sense and of course he knew his mind had gone. Poor, miserable old man. Not very sadly mourned, I fear." By an amazing coincidence, the day of Maugham's death was also Coward's sixty-sixth birthday. Amongst the avalanche of offerings which descended on him was a small but very useful item from Binkie which revealed his skill in giving sensible and unexpected presents. It was a pocket cassette tape-recorder. Coward immediately recorded all three parts, played them back whenever he was in the mood for study and was soon word perfect.

Christmas at Les Avants was always lively, filled with amusing people and 1965 was no exception. Binkie and John Perry flew out, Gladys Calthrop joined them and Joan Sutherland, a near neighbour, looked in. Vivian Matalon flew out for the New Year since Coward had asked him to spend a few extra days with him before the rehearsals started so they could get to know each other. "What about coming up with an umbrella title for the three plays?" murmured Binkie and Coward promptly did, suggesting *Suite in Three Keys*. They also discussed the poster design and whether or not it would be possible to omit the name of the actor who was to play the small part of the waiter, Felix. Matalon made himself useful in other ways. He generously brought out the three wigs which Coward was to wear to save time and Coward was very pleased with all of them. "Vivian is very bright and I like him more and more. All seems to be set fair for the play." These were dangerously rash words for within two days he collapsed with severe stomach pains and had to be rushed into a clinic where amoebic dysentery was diagnosed. The cure, which had been strongly recommended and which a lunatic doctor forced on him, was to eat large quantities of mashed potato *and nothing else* four times a day. It was a disaster and it was a debatable point as to which was worse, the disease or the treatment.

When he returned home, Coward was in a terrible state, bent double and in great pain. Obviously, the proposed opening in Dublin the following month was out of the question. Vivian telephoned Binkie to tell him that Coward was in no fit state to open and that the preliminary week in Dublin would have to be cancelled. Binkie said that this was nonsense. Vivian insisted that it wasn't. Binkie then accused him of being hysterical. "Binkie, you have a choice of two courses of action," said Vivian patiently. "You postpone now and get off cheaply, or you can wait a month and then postpone which will be much more expensive." He wasn't exaggerating. A last-minute cancellation would be disastrous. Binkie would lose his deposit on the Dublin theatre and be forced to refund all the tickets sold, and on Coward's name they would probably be sold out. Inexplicably, Binkie continued to refuse. He didn't believe, *couldn't* believe, that Coward was as ill as Vivian had said: it was the classic case of a man refusing to believe something he didn't *want* to believe. Coward struggled on for three more agonising days and then it was he who phoned Binkie to tell him the true state of health. He couldn't open at Dublin. He was very sorry but that was that. He would have to go into hospital and take things very easy, as the doctors ordered. In the meantime, the plays were re-scheduled for April.

Binkie flew out to visit Coward in hospital. He brought perfume, flowers and books, but best of all his own charming and sympathetic self. In this he was breaking the habit of a lifetime, for he hated disease and illness, disliked hospital visits and wanted nothing to do with those who were sick. But this was a crisis and rules had to be set aside. He was calm, cheerful and encouraging. He succeeded in calming Coward's legitimate fears that he would never get well and never act again. Slowly, he recovered and by mid-March he was well enough to fly to London and start rehearsals. The opening had been tentatively re-scheduled for the Queen's Theatre for May. Dublin was forgotten.

Anxious to get the maximum publicity for what Binkie privately knew would be Coward's last appearance on the London stage, and to contradict prevalent rumours that Coward was dying he arranged a massive photocall in the theatre. Edward Burrell, the stage manager, remembers that Coward sat on the sofa in the middle of the stage while all the Tennent staff, the staff from the Queen's, Apollo, Lyric and Globe, plus actors from other theatres who had heard he was there, all appeared in an orderly queue and filed past Coward to pay their respects. "I have never before seen such bowing and scraping, such unashamed sycophancy," he said, "most of them called him 'Master' and some actually kissed his hand. It was just like an exiled emperor returning home. I decided then and there that I would have nothing to do with that sort of thing. I always called him Mr Coward, nothing else, and we got on very well. He was always charming and friendly. I believe that deep down he despised anybody who was too fulsome." Edward Burrell had been Vivian Matalon's ASM at the Haymarket during *The Glass Menagerie* rehearsals and brief run. He had done well and when the three Coward plays came up Binkie asked him to be the deputy stage manager. He was strictly on probation and everybody thought he would be dismissed because of his inexperience, but he worked hard, did everything right and survived the first week. He was then promoted to stage and company manager.

Noël Coward's masterplan was to rehearse all three plays simultaneously for five weeks, the maximum time he would allow. Unlike some self-indulgent actors who love rehearsals and extend them as long as possible, Coward hated them and became horribly bored and impatient if they were unnecessarily prolonged. On consecutive nights in mid-April, *Twilight* and the double bill of *Evening* and *Maud* – as they were affectionately known – would have their openings to play on alternate evenings throughout the three-month season. But like so many of the best made plans, this one turned out badly.

As was his custom, Coward insisted that everybody learn their lines before the rehearsals started. "Can't work with a script in your hand," was his standard explanation. It was not a method which appealed to the majority of actors with whom he had worked and over the years he had had a good deal of trouble from those who either couldn't or wouldn't. He had learned his three parts well in advance and arrived at the first rehearsal with a good acquaintance with them, but he discovered, as all actors do, that you may know the lines in privacy but when you are on an open stage in a strange theatre with a large, empty auditorium in front of you and strange voices saying the lines you wrote months ago, these lines can sometimes mysteriously vanish. The services of Pauline Gaunt, the assistant stage manager and prompter, were in constant demand. Irene Worth knew hers best, but it was Lilli Palmer who knew hers the least. The rehearsals seemed to last for five years rather than five weeks and they were inconceivably dreadful. Lilli Palmer had been exaggerating when she claimed to have lost her technique and acting skills. She had not, but these skills were in a style totally alien to the subtleties of modern English acting and both Coward and Matalon disliked them. They were heavy and broad and tended to be over-emphatic. "Lilli, your acting reminds me of the German silent cinema of the twenties and thirties," said Coward crisply one day, "you provide a gesture for every word."

"But I wasn't in Germany in the twenties and thirties," she replied tartly which was not entirely true. She had great trouble with the lines and saying them without false emphasis. Her husband, Carlos Thompson, would frequently attend the rehearsals with a tape recorder so that she could play back her speeches at home for further study. But she just couldn't learn the lines and a great deal of time was wasted while she and Coward argued and bickered. Their happy relationship deteriorated quickly and soon it was all tensions and abuse. "You are selfish, irritating and a bloody awkward person to act with," he told her in front of the company one day. To his diary he spoke even more candidly, "Miss Palmer does NOT know her words for *Twilight* well enough and hasn't made any attempt to learn the other two plays . . . I have never, with the possible exception of Claudette Colbert, worked with such a stupid bitch."

Her professional behaviour declined in other ways. She argued interminably with Vivian Matalon about every little point, as when he tried to stop her from making endless little fluttering movements with her hands because they were silly and distracting. "Darling, I'm supposed to be an actress," she protested and ignored him. He was endlessly patient with her but she wouldn't take his direction and ended up by refusing to do anything he asked. She became increasingly difficult and soon became impossible. There was one rehearsal in which she was very melodramatic, throwing her arms around, filling the play with Teutonic exaggeration and emotionalism. Before Matalon gave notes he went to speak to Coward in his dressing-room to hear that Carlos Thompson had asked him to sack Matalon and give the task of directing to him. "I will give it music," he had said, "I will make it sing." Coward had been rightly appalled by this impertinence and it was clear to both men that Thompson had already been privately directing Lilli. "Vivian dear, I think you had better confront her and let her know who's in charge."

"What you did in the second act was interesting," said Matalon when he returned to the stage, "but it does rather throw the play off balance. If it's an experiment it's fine but if you intend to develop it then it's bad for the play."

"I've done exactly what I've always done."

"No, you have not."

"Yes, I have," she retorted. "Haven't I Noël?" she said turning to him.

"Noël Coward is *not* the director of this play," exploded Matalon, "*I* am, and the sooner you realise this the better for us all."

"How dare you speak to me like that."

"You're lucky that anybody speaks to you at all. You are *destroying* this play, you are playing it like a Nazi, all you need is a leather uniform, it was truly terrible . . ." He continued to abuse her. She was not popular with the company, who were not entirely displeased by the spectacle of her public humiliation. "I'm not going to stay here to listen to this," she shouted as she rose to leave, "I'm going."

"Do us all a favour and don't come back," he yelled at her departing figure. In the silence which followed Irene Worth said quietly, "Go after her, Vivian, make peace with her, she's suffering."

"*She's* suffering?" expostulated the hard-pressed director in-dignantly, "*I'm* suffering. *You're* suffering. *Noël* is suffering. The *play* is suffering." At this point Noël told the company about Carlos Thompson's treacherous behaviour in trying to get Vivian replaced. Even Irene Worth was shocked and silenced by this.

Later that evening he telephoned Binkie at home. Anna answered. "Meestair Matalon, plizz, Meestair Beaumont, he eez a leetel beet . . . drunk . . ."

"I must speak to him, it's really urgent." Binkie finally came on to the line but once again he was absolutely paralytic, mumbling and incoherent, unable to speak. Next day, tempers had cooled and the hostility was not so evident, but Matalon always had the feeling that Binkie had just pretended to be drunk so that he couldn't be forced to take action which might well have made matters worse. If this was the case, Matalon thought it was very astute of him: it was a good example of masterly inactivity.

In the meantime, there had been trouble with Carlo Palmucci who had been cast as Felix, the waiter in all the three plays. He had worked very hard on his English but it was just not good enough. But Coward did not want to lose him. "You're not working with him, Vivian, give him another chance." Matalon gave him extra coaching after re-hearsals but although he could speak the words, the pronunciation was all wrong. Matters came to a head one day when the following interchange of dialogue took place between Carlo and Irene Worth.

Hilde: Don't forget that little accident we had on Friday.
Felix: Friday is to be regretted, my lady, but if you remember, I
       was off duty. Giovanni is a most willing boy but he has not
       yet got accustomed to Sir Hugo's tastes.

Carlo chose to pronounce the last word as 'testes'. To the wretched boy's bewilderment, there was a huge explosion of laughter and when Coward had wiped away the tears of joy he said, "Well, I know this play is about homosexuality but that is going *too* far! . . . Also, it gives away the plot far too soon," he added when retelling this delicious story the following day. But even he had to admit that Carlo's English simply would not do, so a replacement had to be urgently found. Sean Barrett, a darkly good-looking young actor who could pass for Italian anywhere and who had played Audrey Hepburn's younger brother in the film of *War and Peace*, was engaged only ten days before the preview.

In act one of *Twilight* Felix has to serve a gourmet dinner for two while Coward and Lilli Palmer were exchanging some rather compli-

cated conversation. When it is considered how much cutlery, glassware, plates, serving dishes and linen is thus involved, everything to
be put down or taken up at precisely the right moment and all
synchronised with the dialogue, it can be seen that a great deal of
professional skill was involved. Binkie contacted the Savoy Hotel and
asked them to send along one of their staff. The massively dignified
Head Waiter who turned up was a splendidly military type with
pouter pigeon chest and posh Cockney accent. His name was Royton
E. Heath – "Sounds like a desirable bijou residence in Dorset" was
Binkie's crisp comment – the Coward influence was very catching –
and he was not only the head floor supervisor but the principal
instructor at the Savoy training school. He then proceeded to demonstrate to the fascinated young actor just how a professional in the
catering profession does his job and does it with style and panache.
Barrett enjoyed this scene and after his first rehearsal elicited a tribute
from Coward. "You did it very well, Sean dear: Carlo couldn't handle
the props without a lot of arm waving and body movement: it was just
like an under-water ballet."

Lilli Palmer continued to ignore Matalon's direction so he finally
gave up trying and let her get on with the play as she pleased.
Foolishly, she did not seem to realise that she was getting the cold
treatment. "Vivian, do you think I should put these cards on the table
before or after the line?"

"Whatever you like, Lilli."

"But which is better?"

"They're both fine."

They continued like this for a time. Suddenly she said, "Come up
here, please." He walked up to the stage. "You refuse to direct me,
Vivian?"

"That's absolutely true."

"Oh, you admit it?"

"Yes, I admit it."

"Why?"

"It's obvious why. You don't listen to a word I say so there's no
point in giving you directions." The row continued, ending with her
stormy exit from the stage. She and Matalon went up to the management office to see Binkie but he wasn't in so she spoke to John Perry
instead.

"I want somebody employed to sit in the theatre to watch my
performance."

"I think that's a very good idea," said Matalon. "Who would you
like?"

She was shocked. "You mean you don't want to direct me?"

"Lilli, it's no good. You don't listen to me, but if there is somebody you trust I will be happy for him to come in."

"It's not that I think Vivian is a bad director, I think he directed Irene and Noël very well, but he is not good for *me*." The row gradually simmered down, they shook hands and an armed truce prevailed as they returned to the rehearsal. But it didn't last long and soon the old hostilities were back with a vengeance.

Sean Barrett, together with the three understudies, Peter Hutton, Charmian Eyre and Kathleen Byron were to be enthralled spectators of the company rows, and there were two principal ones, increasing in volume and venom as the dreaded first preview came nearer. Lilli Palmer continued not to learn her lines. *Twilight* was okay, *Shadows* was satisfactory but *Maud* she didn't know at all. She insisted on reading it at a rehearsal – and this after ten days – but when Coward began to act rings round her and to demonstrate just what an experienced professional can do when he wants to, she put the script down and started to act. Vivian received phone calls from both Lilli and Irene one evening asking him to get Coward to agree that an extra week's rehearsal was urgently needed. Three weeks was just not enough, they weren't *nearly* ready to open. He refused.

Vivian phoned Binkie who promised that he would speak to Coward, and finally persuaded him, much against his will and better judgement, to change his mind. "I am bitterly angry and disgusted with them both," wrote Coward. "They are brilliant actresses and wonderful to work with but we could open all three plays by the end of this week if only they had co-operated and learned their words. If I could have opened the plays on consecutive nights, which is what I had originally planned, it would have been sensational. I have kept calm but I do not intend to repress too much. If I am provoked into a scene they will both buy it."

And provoked he was. The following day he and Lilli were squabbling over their dinner-party scene, he accusing her of vulgarity and gross exaggeration. Suddenly she peered out through the empty theatre, shading her eyes with her hand. "Is Binkie there?"

"Here I am, Lilli dear," he said quietly, suddenly slithering out of the darkness, "what can I do for you?"

"Could you come up, please?"

"Yes. But I don't want to interrupt the rehearsal."

"Come up, please."

He climbed on to the stage and went with her to the double-doors at the back where they were joined by Irene Worth. "Noël, would you join us, please? We have important things to discuss," said Lilli.

"Certainly not."

"Please, Noël. It's as important for you as it is for us."

"Oh, very well," he said snappishly. He rose and joined them.

"I'm keeping my temper, Noël darling," Lilli said, "but it's not easy."

"I don't intend to keep mine a minute longer than necessary. I'm fed up with both of you. You've been farting around like a pair of lunatics. You neither of you know your lines. You're lazy and totally unprofessional. And self-indulgent."

"That's not fair, Noël," interrupted Irene Worth angrily. "I do know *my* lines. In fact I know them better than you know yours." At this point Lilli stormed out through the double-doors and into her dressing-room followed by Coward, Irene and Binkie. In the dressing-room the row escalated into a screaming match for the whole theatre staff to hear, including Edward Burrell who was waiting in earshot in the next dressing-room in case he was wanted, as a good stage manager should.

"You great big German *cunt*," screamed Coward, "you should be on your knees in gratitude to me for having rescued you from all that B-picture shit."

"The person I blame for all this is Vivian," shouted Lilli. "I asked him to get Noël to agree to extra rehearsal and he didn't."

"Oh yes, I did," he replied firmly.

"Binkie says you didn't."

There was a long, long pause while the full significance of this sank in. "Then Binkie lied," said Vivian angrily. He turned to him. "*Did you lie, Binkie?*"

There was another long pause while Binkie looked him straight in the eyes. "Yes," he said calmly. "Yes, I did."

The row continued, with everybody shouting at each other, except Binkie who maintained his watchful silence. Eventually Coward stormed out and went to the props room where Pauline Gaunt had made coffee for the three understudies and Sean Barrett. "Would you like some coffee?" she enquired.

"Yes, please, and some opium too if you have it," replied Coward. "The row is . . ." dramatic pause . . . "*r-r-raging*," he added calmly, accepting the coffee. "I want nothing more to do with it. There was a time when I would tolerate other people's lack of professionalism but no longer. Now I don't care about the feelings of people who behave like fucking amateurs." A suspicion began to dawn in the company's mind that Coward was really rather enjoying these rows and had been actively provoking them. If this was true, it would have been an effective method of rising above the boredom and aggravation of these rehearsals.

The dreaded previews finally arrived all too quickly and on the first it was Lilli Palmer and Irene Worth who knew their lines and Coward who didn't. During the dinner-party scene in the first act of *Twilight* he stumbled and fluffed and dried to an extent which was highly embarrassing to the audience as well as to the company. There was, of course, every excuse: he hadn't acted on the stage for eleven years and 'ring rusty' is a phrase which can be applied just as accurately to an actor as to a boxer. Also he was suffering from that debilitating disease which was to cloud the remaining years of his life. No actor can be expected to give of his best when he has stomach pains, giddiness, fits of nausea, pains in the legs plus a general feeling of exhaustion and depression.

His adoring public would have been quite prepared to be sympathetic were it not for a most unfortunate interview he had given to the *Daily Express*. Binkie had raised the ticket prices since he considered that a new play by and starring Noël Coward was no ordinary event. There had been some rumblings of discontent in the press about this and Coward had said, rather pompously, it was thought, that if the public wanted to see first-class professional talents at work, then they must be prepared to pay extra for the privilege. In theory, this was perfectly true but it was generally regarded as a great shame that, for those early previews, the talent on view from the Master was noticeably less than first class. During the ten previews his acting and memory showed improvement. On the first night his nervous distress was obvious, but the applause and cheers which greeted his first entrance gave him the necessary confidence. His performance was excellent, the play was well received and the dressing-room afterwards was filled with all the people he wanted saying all those things which an actor wants to hear.

A rumour circulated around the company that Binkie was not inviting the understudies, stage management or Sean Barrett to his first-night party. This turned out to be true: Binkie had always been very snobbish about his party guest list and it was his custom to invite only the stars. Vivian complained to Coward who complained to Binkie: "You must invite *everybody*. The stage management work just as hard as the stars, the understudies carry just as big a load of responsibility without any of the compensations and rewards. You must invite them all. And Shornie-boy," which was his affectionate nickname for Sean Barrett to whom he had taken a great liking. Coward was a truly unsnobbish and democratic man with a genuine feeling for the theatrical underdog and Binkie did as he asked.

The house at Lord North Street was *en fête* and the guests, mingling freely round the buffet table, wandered in and out of all the rooms. For

Edward Burrell the pleasures of champagne and gourmet food by candlelight were offset by anxiety. He was the son of John Burrell who had been dismissed from directing *The Heiress* some eighteen years earlier and he was unhappily wondering if Binkie knew this and if so what he would do? Were the sins of the father to be passed on to the son? But he had no cause for alarm. At the end Binkie was full of charm.

"You're John Burrell's son, I believe?"

"Yes."

"We-e-ell . . . I have to tell you, Edward dear, that you have done a most *excellent* job on this play and I'm very pleased with you as is Noël. I know it hasn't been easy. And I think you should go far in your chosen profession."

When the double-bill of *Shadows* and *Maud* opened a fortnight later, the success was even greater. Irene Worth, undoubtedly the best of the three, scored a huge success as the nagging American wife screaming down the telephone in her hair curlers. Nobody could have looked and sounded less like a Mid-West golfing American than Coward even with a bag full of clubs, a crew-cut and an American accent, but it did not matter.★ Realism and plausibility was the work of lesser talents: Coward, the living legend, was back in the West End and there were many thousands of play-goers who were glad of it.

With a few predictable exceptions the notices for all three plays were excellent and *Suite in Three Keys* played to full houses for its scheduled three months. Coward's performances gained in strength and assurance though his memory still continued to plague him. Fortunately, the prompter, Pauline Gaunt, was an expert at this extraordinarily difficult and skilled job. She could anticipate a lapse of memory and give him the word at the beginning of that pause even before he realised that he needed it. The fact that these lapses invariably occurred in the same places made it a little easier. Coward depended on her to such an extent that one evening when she was absent from the theatre owing to her advanced state of pregnancy, he was in a state bordering on panic. Edward Burrell deputised for her, but Coward confounded expectation by sailing through the play without a tremor or a single lapse of memory. Once the crutches had been taken away, he was able to walk without trouble, but when she returned the following night, those same lapses and hesitations returned.

The three months finished in a blaze of glory with royal visits almost every night, standing ovations, strong hints from Mount-

---

★ "It is so *easy* to play Americans," said Coward to Sean Barrett one day. "All you have to do is to say 'Hi, folks' very loudly, and then do the rest in English."

batten that he should get a knighthood and, finally, election to the Garrick Club. But Binkie's plans to take the plays to New York in the New Year with Margaret Leighton replacing Lilli Palmer fell through. Coward's delicate health which deteriorated sharply during the autumn of 1966 finally forced him to face the fact that he was too weak and too bored to play a season in New York so, to his anguished disappointment, Binkie was forced to cancel it.

CHAPTER THIRTY-FOUR

1969–73

The Final Years

Binkie's decline, like that of the Holy Roman Empire, was so slow and gradual that it would be difficult for anybody to know at the time that it was actually happening. Certainly, at the start of the sixties the heyday seemed as strong as ever with Paul Scofield enjoying perhaps his greatest success as Sir Thomas More in *A Man for All Seasons* and Alec Guinness doing much the same as Lawrence of Arabia in *Ross*, Terence Rattigan's ingenious and imaginative chronicle/pageant play. They ran for nearly a year and two years respectively. But things started to go wrong in all departments. His health declined, he suffered the agonies of a slipped disc and was forced to spend an excruciating period on his back in the London Clinic where only close friends came to see him, notably Mary Evans who called almost every day to chat and gossip and make him laugh. The back was to plague him for the rest of his life and he was never to be totally free of pain or discomfort.

There was one occasion when he went down on his knees begging a certain actress to appear in a new play. As a romantic, Walter Raleigh gesture it fell flat, for his back suddenly cracked up, two spinal bones clicked out of position and he could not get up. Sweating with pain, he was trapped into a kneeling position until two burly stage hands lifted him bodily to a standing position, helped him into an ambulance and escorted him to the Middlesex Hospital where he was given some swift and effective treatment until his own osteopath was able to see him the next day.

Another and much deeper symptom of the decline lay in the speed with which he lost touch with the contemporary world. He found it difficult to accept that the world had changed since he was young, that manners and morals, fashion and deportment were very different from what they had been thirty years earlier. It wasn't just Binkie's problem, but that of any man in his mid-sixties. No longer did the young actors and actresses in his company respect him as once they did, no longer could they be disciplined by a verbal rebuke, a note from his office, the threat of dismissal from the production or exile from the West End. One young actress used to arrive at the theatre wearing sandals, jeans, sweatshirt and long untidy hair. "Don't you want to be beautiful and glamorous," he protested, "don't you want to be admired by other women and pursued by men? Don't you want to be a success and a credit to your employer? I just don't understand." But she laughed at him and it was not a kindly laugh. Another actress whom he rebuked in her dressing-room lost her temper and threw a bottle of make-up at him. She missed and hit the director instead causing a nasty mess on his face and suit. Nothing like that had ever happened to him before, and nothing rubbed home his diminishing powers more effectively than the fact that these girls could defy him, laugh at him, abuse him and get away with it. They were not dependent on him for work. If he refused to employ them, there were plenty of other managers. There were also the worlds of film and TV. They could do without him.

If all that wasn't bad enough, his emotional life was under stress.

He and John Perry had enjoyed a long and fulfilling relationship even though people outside the magic circle could be very unkind. Ann Fleming wrote to her brother, Hugo Charteris, in 1957 and described John as 'Binkie's paramour'.★ Then Perry found a new friend, a young theatre enthusiast who came to London to learn what he could about management and theatre administration. Binkie took him into the firm and taught him much of great value. He was drawn into Binkie and Perry's high-life, weekends at Knotts Fosse, dinners at Lord North Street, first nights, parties and lunches with all the stars. The friendship developed to the point where Binkie, watching it, as it were, from the front row of the stalls, suffered for the first time in his life the agonies of jealousy and neglect.

Perry may have been the junior in all business matters, but privately he was the dominant partner. It didn't help that Perry owed his career entirely to Binkie and that without him he might have remained just another actor/playwright. Binkie worked hard at making Perry feel important. "Do ask his advice from time to time," he said to Vivian Matalon, "it would make him feel so happy." Friends would some-times witness angry scenes between them with Perry making sarcastic remarks and leaving while Binkie slumped miserably in his chair. "You see how it is," he said unhappily, "I love him far more than he loves me." When his unhappiness reached its climax, Binkie was close

★ "Noël Coward appeared last night with a party of persons called 'Perry', 'Terry', 'Binkie', and 'Coalie', and seemed most annoyed that he was not received by the Edens." Ann Fleming, January 19th 1957.

to suicide. He got into the habit of phoning very special close friends – always women – like Rachel Kempson, asking them to come over to Lord North Street to keep him company. He would talk and talk, sobbing and weeping, all through the night, pouring out the agony which lay in his heart. Rachel Kempson was the ideal confidante, for it was a situation with which she was already painfully familiar in her own life.

Binkie finally solved the problem in a characteristically clever and devious way. He suggested to John Perry that their friendship was over, that he should leave Binkie, leave H. M. Tennent, leave Lord North Street and Knotts Fosse, go home to his beloved Ireland with his new friend and retire to the joys of racing, fishing, hunting and writing more charming light comedies about Irish rustic life. Binkie would, of course, miss him terribly, but he had no desire to stand in the way of what was quite clearly his true happiness with his new friend. It was something which Maugham himself might have devised and was not so unlike Clive Champion-Cheney's solution to a similar problem in the last scene of *The Circle*: it is quite possible that this provided him with the inspiration. There was one striking difference. In Binkie's case it worked. Perry's friend was not at all pleased at the prospect of being exiled from the wealthy high-life he had been enjoying and the rustic pleasures of Ireland were no substitute. He left Tennent's, left London and left the country. Perry accepted the situation and once more there was peace in Lord North Street.

His brightest discovery of the late sixties was Eileen Atkins and he had an enormous respect for her acting talents which were impressively on view in the Chichester Festival production of *The Cocktail Party* in which she co-starred with Alec Guinness. That voice, that profile, that face which her skills could make beautiful or plain, those flashing eyes, that personality alternately dominating and vulnerable, aggressive and winning, all combined to fascinate him. Relations between them were, however, volatile: storms alternated with peace, black clouds with blue sky and sunlight. *The Cocktail Party* finally transferred to Wyndham's under the Tennent management in November 1968 and ran for 150 performances which is as much as you can reasonably expect for any modern verse play.

Relations continued to be tense during the rehearsals and performances of *Vivat! Vivat Regina!*, a chronicle play about Elizabeth and Mary Queen of Scots by Robert Bolt who nearly became the Tennent house dramatist, the successor to Terence Rattigan. It is very surprising that this rich, robust, action-packed slice of Tudor history has not caught the imagination of more playwrights. Apart from Schiller's ineffably tedious verse epic with its entirely fictitious meeting between the two queens, it had been a blank until Robert Bolt filled it. His wife, Sarah Miles, did her best when cast as Mary making her plaintive, vulnerable, elfin and charming. It worked, though one suspected that the original Mary was a lot tougher and more determined. Elizabeth was the smaller of the two parts, but it might have been written specially for Atkins whose voice and appearance filled the theatre with drama.

Chronicle plays are always difficult to write and there were to be many disagreements about the structure and contents. Should Elizabeth have extra scenes in which she is speaking about Mary the better to build up the suspense before her first entrance? Should Mary have extra scenes to build it up into a big star part? And what about the ending? Bolt had originally written it with a long and thrilling dramatic speech for Elizabeth but Binkie managed to convince Bolt that it would be better to end it with Mary's execution. The play was such a success that it ran for over a year and Binkie made plans with David Merrick to present it in New York. Atkins however was not keen on repeating on Broadway the tiring role which meant wearing heavy Elizabethan costumes eight performances weekly.

And that might have been the end of the matter, but for *Suzanna Andler*, a play by Marguerite Duras, which Atkins had done at Wimbledon. Binkie did not consider it promising West End material, but eventually it was agreed that Atkins would do *Vivat! Vivat Regina!* on Broadway and H. M. Tennent would present *Suzanna Andler* on a short tour and in the West End. Initially Binkie could not find a West End theatre available to take it, but eventually, after an eighteen months' lull, the Aldwych (London home of the Royal Shakespeare Company) became vacant for three weeks. After the first night, on March 5th 1973, Binkie declared that it was a superb play and that he had enjoyed every minute of it. Harold Hobson gave it a splendid notice in the *Sunday Times* and stated it was entirely due to Binkie and the provincial tour that it had ever come into the West End. This was of course only half true.

It was the last play Binkie saw.

Money had been running short and Binkie found it difficult to get new backers since the old ones were most annoyingly placing their funds in the hands of rival managers. The empire had been shrinking fast. Even as early as May 1964, normally a peak period in the Tennent year, there were just four plays and all survived just a month. Only Jean Kerr's empty little comedy, *Mary, Mary*, had survived from the previous year (helped by Maggie Smith's performance). 1965, but for Noël Coward's *Present Laughter* (364 performances) and *Hello, Dolly!*

(794 performances) would have been a disaster. However, *Hello, Dolly!* meant facing the tiresome necessity of working with David Merrick, a situation which was to recur once more at the end of the decade. The 1966 Tennent schedule shows just six London productions and only three of these were new plays (by Arthur Miller, Neil Simon and Noël Coward – *Suite in Three Keys*). 1967 and 1968 were little better, with Peter Ustinov's *Halfway Up a Tree* the one new play, to have any real success.

By 1969 Binkie was getting backing from a film company, Commonwealth United, to fund three new productions, *Play it Again, Sam*, Woody Allen's fantasy comedy about the actor who believes he is Humphrey Bogart, starring Dudley Moore, *Promises, Promises*, fresh from its Broadway triumph and *The Battle of Shrivings*, Peter Shaffer's only commercial failure. The head of drama production for Commonwealth was a young actor/playwright who had briefly left the boards to work in administration. His name was Leo Maguire, born and bred in Glasgow: "The first thing which struck me about Binkie was that on our first meeting he kept me waiting for around ten minutes in the foyer of the Globe Theatre, despite the fact that I represented the Big Bucks to be invested in the forthcoming shows. When he did appear, all silken, apologetic murmurs, our initial business was conducted quietly on the banquette seat in that same foyer while customers and staff wandered to and fro around us. I was both amused and bemused by this ploy, for it seemed to me a rather old-fashioned psychological trick, calculated to establish that he was very much the Emperor receiving an emissary – and conducting the encounter on his own terms. Ninety per cent of me was a hundred per cent charmed by him, and ten per cent, perhaps the watchful, Gorbals survivor portion, found something a little chilling in him. There was an element which was hard to define, but was almost palpable, which suggested that every word – and he had a voice like buttered silk – was buffed and polished and monitored before it was allowed to emerge. He could have charmed alligators out of the swamps – and then made them into handbags before they knew what hit them. I think the best trick in his bag was to suggest that it was You and He against the rest of the world. A kind of benign conspiracy of two which would triumph for good over the small crimes or follies of those flawed people with whom we had to work.

"When I next met him it was in his office at the Globe. I was *bouleversé*. A man who had been the leading impresario of the London theatre for decades might have sported an office out of *Dallas* or *Dynasty*. Rather, his inner sanctum reminded me of nothing more than the back room of a second-hand bookseller. Only the posters and portraits dispelled this illusion but there was a paper-strewn desk, a dusty clutter of scripts and documents. I learned something new about him. He didn't give a damn for ostentation."

When David Merrick – co-presenting with Binkie – arrived, already there was bad trouble. The row was over the sum of £80,000 which David Weinstein, the head of Commonwealth United, was going to release to set up *Promises, Promises*, but at the last moment he decided to release half now and half later. Maguire had the task of telling this to David Merrick. He fully lived up to his reputation for being uncouth and foul-mouthed.

"What's all this shit? Your boss promised me £80,000."

"He's changed his mind. You can have £45,000 now and the rest later."

"He's a fink, a schmuck."

"Don't say that about my boss. He's totally honest."

"Now look here, Maguire . . ."

"Don't call me that. Either Leo or Mr Maguire and don't call my boss a schmuck."

"And who's going to stop me?"

They advanced on each other like rival gunmen in a Western and Maguire would have been prepared – indeed, perfectly happy – to hit him, but Binkie slithered between them "like Lytton Strachey insinuating himself between his sister and the raping German soldier", as Maguire described it. "Now then, my dears, this conversation is getting rather *louche*," said Binkie smoothly, "shouldn't we repair to the Ivy and fight over some oysters?" and proceeded to pour a Sheik's ransom of oil on the troubled waters. Incredibly, he got an apology out of Merrick who was not accustomed to making them. "Waaaal, I guess I shouldn't have said that." As they all turned to leave, Merrick said, "Leo, what you said about Weinstein, I didn't know loyalty like that could be bought." "Well, you ken noo," replied Maguire and so they all went to the Ivy where a reasonably cordial lunch took place.

Rehearsals were not smooth. Binkie and Maguire had a chat in his office. "We've got to be brave," said Maguire, "we've got to put our shoulder to the wheel. We've got to be united. If this show is to open and succeed we need an act of faith." At the first-night party which was held in Bernie Cornfeld's huge mansion in West Halkin Street, Maguire saw Binkie standing alone and drinking. He went over to join him. "We-e-e-ell, Leo, you were quite right," he murmured. "Quite right about that act of faith." Maguire noticed a tiny speck of mucus coming out of his nostril: he took Binkie's pocket handkerchief, speedily wiped it away and then replaced the handkerchief in his breast pocket. "The one thing which gave me any cause for pause [said Leo

Maguire] was his over-indulgence in the bottle, most noticeable after 6 p.m. I never saw him the worse for wear but there was often in his manner that ultra-care in speech which circumspect people resort to if they wish to give the impression of stone cold sobriety. There was also a smell of strong peppermint on the breath which was never before 6 p.m. but always present later. My general impression was that he was a spent force, not so much due to diminished ability as to a loss of his life-long passionate care for the theatre."

Binkie no longer attended first rehearsals and seldom looked in at the dress-rehearsal. When he did, his comments to the company were often stupid, unnecessary, pointless and indicated that he no longer had any real understanding of the actors' problems. He cut down on his first-night dressing-room visits, putting his head round the door only with the stars.

The drinking grew steadily worse. He was not an alcoholic though in the opinion of some he came dangerously near to it. He managed to keep away from it during the day but at six o'clock he would come home from a hard day at the office, take a couple of whiskies and continue drinking until he collapsed and had to be put to bed. And then in the morning he would wake up at six and soon be on to the telephone to Mary Evans, Maggie Leighton, Ingrid Bergman or Irene Selznick and chat as bright as a button. His friends noticed all this with dismay. "My dear friend Binkie got as pissed as a newt . . . Binkie was absolutely paralytic . . ." were two items which started to recur with increasing frequency in Noël Coward's diaries. "He was a sweet man and we liked him a lot," said Joss Ackland, the Brassbound in the Ingrid Bergman revival of the play, "but he was obviously very lonely and unhappy. He used to get drunk a lot and it wasn't funny." Anthony Quayle remembers dining at Lord North Street in the last year. "He was looking very vulpine. He drank far too much, waved his hands in the air and talked a lot of nonsense. We didn't enjoy that at all."

At many of his own parties, he would have two strong young men in dinner-jackets standing in attendance as minders. When he could no longer stand, they would help him upstairs and put him to bed. It was evident to those watching that this was a frequent occurrence. "It was very odd that a man who was so strong, so self-controlled, self-reliant and so much the master of his own destiny should be unable to control his own fleshly appetites," said Robert Flemyng. "If he had, he would be alive now." One evening Flemyng was driving him home to supper and offered him a glass of whisky. "No, thanks, Bobby dear," said Binkie, "I'm drinking white wine now. If you haven't got any at home, would you mind if I brought some in myself?" It wasn't only the drinking. The excessive smoking was also a serious problem. "I can't give it up," he would say lighting up yet another in the daily chain. "I've been smoking forty a day all my life and if I've already got lung cancer then I've got it and I can't unget it." There were occasions when his mind seemed to be affected by his excessive drinking. There was an evening, a hotel banquet, which one actress will never forget. She was at one table and Binkie was close by at another. He was horribly drunk, fighting drunk, worse than ever, and suddenly in a loud voice he started to scream abuse. "There's that stupid bitch" – he indicated the actress – "she's going to ruin her life just as Maggie Leighton did by getting involved with the wrong man." The actress lost her temper and understandably started to hurl abuse back at him. Those present were deeply shocked, for raising his voice was some- thing Binkie *never* did, whatever the provocation. Everybody round fell into a deeply embarrassed silence until Robert Stephens and Maggie Smith took control and led him from the room.

His personal appearance deteriorated. He who was always so beautifully dressed, so well-groomed, so meticulous about his cleanli- ness, now appeared in public in scruffy, unpressed suits with dandruff, cigarette ash and drink stains. His skin began to get blotchy and his hair began to thin. There were nicotine stains on the fingers and bad breath which even the peppermint lozenges couldn't altogether dis- guise. "He looked tired and grey and ill," said Peter Gale rehearsing for *No, No, Nanette*, "and it was clear that he had lost his grip on things." Rehearsals were fraught with every sort of trouble. He had engaged Wendy Toye to direct it and Anna Neagle to appear as the heroine's mother. Wendy Toye was not convinced that at her age, all of sixty-nine and touching seventy, she could do all those high kicks and complicated dancing. "Oh yes, she can," said Binkie. "I saw the New York production with Ruby Keeler and she assures me that she will be able to do everything." Wendy was not sure. "She's very assured, she moves gracefully, but it's very energetic stuff, she's not a tap dancer and what about the trenches?" Binkie now became very agitated. "But she assured me she could," he burst out. "She *told* me, so obviously she *must*." And she did. On that first night Dame Anna danced and tapped and high-kicked as if she was seventeen not seventy. The audience at Drury Lane rose to her, something they hadn't done for decades. But Binkie wasn't there to see it.

He had to keep busy. If he stopped then he would never start again. There must be conferences, auditions, interviews, production meet- ings, agent-lunches, and long cosy chats over the Atlantic telephone. *The Constant Wife* had to be set up and cast. He invited John McCallum to meet him at the office and offered him a part in it. "I was shocked by

Binkie's appearance," he wrote in his memoirs, "he had always taken good care of his health, and had always looked well and trim. But now he looked grey and old, his cheeks were sunken, his teeth were badly discoloured and his clothes were creased and rumpled." That was the last time they met. Robert Flemyng's last glimpse was during the weekend at Knotts Fosse. He was touring *Sleuth* and on the Sunday night he had gone to say good night before moving back to his Cambridge hotel. Binkie was lying in a deck-chair by the swimming pool, huddled up in an overcoat and he looked terrible. Pale, grey, lined and like death. They said goodbye affectionately. "See you next week, Bobby dear," murmured Binkie and then quietly fell asleep.

It was Anna who discovered him on the morning of March 23rd when she brought up his breakfast tray of coffee and toast. He was lying on his back, his eyes and mouth wide open and a pile of scripts on top of the bed. He was obviously dead. Sobbing, she telephoned James Janvrine, Binkie's personal doctor for many years and medical adviser to H. M. Tennent. He rushed round from his house in Hans Crescent, swiftly diagnosed cardiac arrest brought on by atheroma, and signed the death certificate to that effect. It was he who telephoned the news, first to John Perry at his flat in John Islip Street, then to James Noble, Binkie's legal adviser, at his house in Cambridge. This was the moment when Mary Evans phoned from her bath for her usual early morning chat to be greeted to her alarm by a loudly sobbing Anna. Dr Janvrine took the call. "I have some terrible news for you," he said quietly. "Binkie is dead. He died in the night." She burst into tears, scrambled hastily out of the bath, and rushed to Lord North Street, arriving at the same time as Brian Bedford, then appearing with Peter Ustinov in *The Unknown Soldier and His Wife*. He was staying in the house, but had spent the previous night with friends. But now there was trouble, arising from the inexplicable behaviour of James Noble. It was a great pity that the anguish suffered by Binkie's friends should be made worse by the resurgence of old hostilities.

When Mary Evans rang the bell, it was opened by Anna and Elvira who had the embarrassing task of telling her that they had been forbidden to allow anybody into the house through the front door. This compelled them to go down the area steps and enter through the basement kitchen. Still in a state of shock and weeping copiously, Anna and Elvira told them that Mr Noble had expressly forbidden them to allow anybody upstairs into the bedroom, an instruction which, Mary Evans was astonished to learn, he was within his legal rights as executor to give. Why he chose to do this was, and still is, a mystery. Predictably, they decided to ignore this order. They went upstairs and paid their last respects to the dead man, lying peacefully in the bed and wearing his famous black pyjamas.

As well as being Binkie's legal adviser, James Noble was a director of the company, one of three Executors, and also a long-standing friend. Not all Binkie's other friends could understand the trust and affection which Binkie bestowed on him. But there was worse to come, as Mary Evans relates. "He refused to invite Laurie and me to the funeral, nor would he tell us the place or the date. I had to telephone John Gielgud. 'Have you ever heard anything like it?' I asked. 'Never,' he replied, 'I think you had both better come with me as my guest.'"

The shock waves travelled rapidly. Binkie's death had this one thing in common with President Kennedy's assassination and the outbreak of the Second World War – everybody in the theatre remembers what they were doing and where they were when they heard the news. Dora Bryan was flying back from India and saw the news in a headline at the airport. Alexander Cohen was at a producers' conference at the St Regis Hotel in New York when he was called to the telephone to hear Mary Evans weeping loudly. He was so upset that he couldn't return to the conference so he just wandered off back home in a daze.

Cole Lesley writes movingly in his biography of Noël Coward about the dreadful moment when he and Graham Payn had to break the news to the Master. ". . . It should be stressed that apart from their business rifts and aside from his 'family', Binkie was for the last twenty-five years the friend with whom Noël had been in closest touch by telephone, or letter, and to whom he always hurried on arrival in London for another of their suppers at Lord North Street. Noël never completely recovered from the blow of Binkie's death: it seemed hauntingly unbelievable that his vitality should have been snuffed out for ever, that never again should we see the attractive smiling face, listen to the wickedly funny gossip, or hear him laugh." He continued to be obsessed about Binkie's death, he couldn't get it out of his mind and both Graham and Lesley had to be supremely tactful to steer the conversation away to subjects where Noël could laugh. He worried about the servants, Anna, Elvira and Jack Osborn who were also old friends of Coward. "What will they do? Binkie *will* have looked after them, won't he?" Again, they would have to reassure him. Binkie loved his servants and would assuredly have made generous provision for them in his will.

They were in no position to learn the truth. He hadn't made one. All his life he had firmly resisted all attempts by Lawrence Harbottle, his lawyer, to get him to make a will. Binkie was superstitious about these things: he believed, as do many sensible, civilised people, that if you make a will, you will die shortly. Finally, in the autumn of 1972, only six months before he died, Binkie did consent to write out a few provisions on paper. It wasn't a proper and complete will, but it was better than nothing. He left everything to John Perry, the house at Lord North Street with contents, the house at Knotts Fosse and the money in his bank. Nobody else was mentioned except for Roger Stock, a young man who had become Binkie's principal friend in the last years. Binkie left him a flat near Victoria Station and his entire estate after the death of John Perry. And that was all. Nobody else is mentioned, nothing was left to the servants, Anna, Elvira and Jack Osborn, nor to his closest friends like John Gielgud, Ginette Spanier, Irene Selznick, Joyce Carey, Coral Browne, Bernard and Mary Gordon. It was James Noble, as Executor, who made good Binkie's neglect by selecting various treasured objects and sending them to a list of close, long-standing friends: a silver box, a vase, a water-colour, a plate or a wine-glass. It wasn't much, but it was better than nothing and it did take away a little of the grief and resentment at not being remembered properly in the will.

The empire had shrunk to three productions at the end. On the night he died there were *Suzanna Andler*, *Private Lives* and *A Private Matter*. Noël Coward, more dead than alive, had just managed to attend the first performance of *Private Lives* at the Queen's, though he had to be virtually carried by his attendants into the stage box. He received the greatest ovation of his life from an audience who knew by a dreadful instinct that this would be the last time they would ever see him. It had been a triumphant evening. It is not every actor's gruesome fate to be compelled to play Elyot in the presence of the Master sitting only a few yards away but Robert Stephens coped manfully and elicited a "Very good, dear boy," later. Afterwards at the party in Lord North Street, Coward praised Maggie Smith in no uncertain terms. "Much better than Gertie. She always wanted to be the perfect lady but Amanda is common and that's what Maggie captured so well." *A Private Matter* was by James Bridie's son, Ronald Mavor, and it was about an elderly author who is writing the biography of a famous, now-deceased general and runs into bad trouble with the family who wish to suppress the truth. It had all the good old-fashioned virtues but in one respect it was very modern and up-to-date. There was nudity. Derek Fowlds, a talented and handsome young actor, had to strip off and reveal all. This was the first and last time that such a thing had happened in a Tennent play and it was Binkie's only gesture towards the 1970s. It shocked the elderly author – Alastair Sim, dithering exquisitely as ever – far more than the audience but it was a richly entertaining piece and was playing to capacity business on the night of Binkie's death.

Binkie died five days before his sixty-fifth birthday. Had he lived just a few days more he would have become an old-age pensioner. He would therefore have qualified for a number of privileges. He could visit the Chelsea Classic Cinema without charge together with the Chelsea Pensioners in their splendid scarlet and gold uniforms. He could get a free bus pass and be able to travel all over London. He could visit the Wimbledon Tennis Museum and he could get into matinées in the West End theatres (sometimes) at half price. To be able to sit in the stalls of a half-full theatre and watch Robert Stephens and Maggie Smith demonstrate that there are many ways of performing Noël Coward plays without actually imitating him and for only five pounds instead of ten, was a situation whose irony would have made a great appeal. How Binkie would have liked that. How he would have laughed.

Noël Coward died five days later in his Jamaican house at the not inconsiderable age of seventy-three. Like Binkie, he died of a heart attack and for the same reasons: he had been advised to give up smoking and drinking and he had firmly refused. Like him, he followed this course of self-destruction in spite of the pleading of his friends and associates and, like him, he paid a high price for his obstinacy. Binkie died in harness but Coward died after some years of retirement, watching the royalties flow in and exulting in the knighthood which was belatedly but happily bestowed by an ever-affectionate and admiring royal family.

Binkie's memorial service was held at St Paul's Church, Covent Garden, on April 17th 1973. He would have been flattered to see that it was crammed to capacity and it is not difficult to imagine Binkie and Noël Coward chuckling gleefully in their stage box in heaven as they looked down. "Standing room only, Noël dear, do you think it'll run, and what *will* the critics say?" He would have been flattered to note the number of stars in the audience and in the cast: Ralph Richardson read John Donne's 1624 Sermon on Mercy, John Gielgud recited the inevitable 'Fear no more the heat of the sun', from *Cymbeline*, Paul Scofield read an obituary piece by Enid Bagnold, and the vicar of St Paul's recited the still-more inevitable Twenty-third Psalm, 'The Lord is my Shepherd'. All very worthy but hardly appropriate, many thought, for a man who didn't believe in God, in whose life religion played absolutely no part and who had never set foot in a church from one year to another except to attend the occasional wedding. "I think the script needs a lot of work," one can imagine him saying, "but what

I'd really like is a Royal Gala, All-Star Midnight Matinée of *My Fair Lady* at Drury Lane with a champagne reception afterwards provided by Fortnum's."

With Noël Coward, 1973. Cartoon by Glan Williams.

Five days after his death, the *Spectator* published a two-page article written under the pseudonym Will Waspe, whose true identity was, and still is, a carefully guarded secret. It described Binkie as a vindictive, vengeful, power-crazy tyrant, grinding his boots in the faces of real talent and using his homosexuality to build up his essentially second-rate empire. The scurrilous innuendo and unashamed malignancy were all the more damaging because it was well written and the facts on which it was based were all true. Binkie would have been flattered by the outcry of anger: the West End combined their forces to defend his good name, to denounce the piece and attack its author. And he would have been most flattered by *A Day's Loving* (Bachman and Turner, London), a novel by the actor, Hubert Gregg, who had been briefly in Binkie's employment during the wartime run of *While the Sun Shines*. Not published until a year after Binkie's death, it was about a homosexual theatrical manager who has the whole of the West End tied up in his devious little hands. He is in the habit of manipulating the lives of beautiful young actors and playwrights by inviting them down for the weekend to his house in the country where he attempts to seduce them. It was widely assumed to be inspired by Binkie and his circle and if this is true then Binkie would have been delighted that his personality, life-style and achievements had been sufficiently interesting to stimulate a writer's imagination and produce such a remarkably well written and engrossing novel. The author firmly insists to this day that it was *not* about Binkie and that any resemblance is a conincidence. The readers must decide for themselves.

By the end of April, the house at 14 Lord North Street, with all the paintings and *objets d'art*, had been sold at a public auction realising, with the rest of his estate, nearly half a million pounds. John Perry retired to a wealthy but lonely seclusion at Knotts Fosse. Roger Stock opened a small residential hotel outside Cambridge. Elvira and Anna found employment with the Sainsbury family, friends of Binkie and near neighbours at 5 Smith Square. Jack Osborn retired to Wimbledon. James Noble started to write his autobiography. And the firm of H. M. Tennent Ltd, moving into another chapter of its life story, passed into other hands, leaving the London Theatre wondering if there was life after Binkie.

And a great blanket of dullness and depression fell upon the West End.

EPILOGUE

I met him on a number of occasions, one of the last being in Eileen Atkins' dressing-room at the Piccadilly Theatre after an evening performance of *Vivat! Vivat Regina!* We were old friends and I invited her to have supper with me. She accepted. Suddenly Binkie was in the room. I knew that he had totally forgotten all about our previous meetings. His handshake was cold and dry and the tight little mirthless smile which accompanied it was distinctly unfriendly. Time was when Binkie would have gone out of his way to be nice and polite to a young actor found in a star dressing-room, but now he was beyond all that. He was bored and impatient and he showed it. He turned his back and ignored me rather pointedly as he spoke about that evening's performance to Eileen. "*Very* good, my dear, very good . . . that final scene has never gone better . . . I'm very pleased." Making general conversation, Eileen happened to mention that I had just finished in a big American musical, *1776*.

"Oh yes," he said disdainfully, "not a bad little show. I might have enjoyed it more if I could have understood it, but all those American jokes and names and historical references . . . I mean, what was I supposed to make of 'we do things rather differently in Boston' . . . what is *that* supposed to mean?"

"It's quite simple," I said, "it means that in Boston . . ."

"Thank you, you don't have to explain," he said, interrupting me rather rudely, I thought, "I *know* what it means now. I spoke to Alex Cohen and he told me . . ."

There was a long pause while he gazed coldly at me. I realised that I wasn't going to get that supper, so I took my leave.

It was all very different from my first meetings with him during the rehearsals and run of *The Visit* in 1960. Of course, he had been present at the auditions but I hadn't actually seen him. He was merely a shadow in the stalls, a disembodied voice asking me my age and politely enquiring about my recent experiences of theatre work and not in the least interested in what I'd done in the cinema or on television. I was told afterwards that he and Peter Brook, the director, had disagreed with each other about me. Peter wanted somebody much younger and Binkie urged him to take me because he felt the part needed somebody of my age and weight: I was thirty-one and starting to get fat. As usual, it was Binkie who got his own way: he arranged for me to be short-listed, auditioned again and again and finally to be engaged. I was particularly interested in this remote contact because not only had I never met him, I'd never even seen him, or seen a photograph of him, and I didn't include anybody in my wide circle of theatrical friends and acquaintances who had. As a result of this I had fashioned a weird little fantasy in my mind that he didn't exist and that Binkie Beaumont was a fiction behind which a team of resourceful and powerful masterminds manipulated the empire. I didn't actually set eyes on him until after our two weeks' rehearsal had finished. We had just gone through a long and exhausting dress-rehearsal and we had all been called on to the stage for notes. A slim, elegant young man appeared on the side of the stage in a beautifully cut light grey suit and stood for a moment watching the note-giving. George Rose, who played the Burgomaster, pointed him out to me. So *that's* what he looks like, I thought. Smooth, thin, astringent, a bit camp but not outrageously so. Who was it who said that the Voice is the Man? Not always true but it was true for Binkie.

My first meeting with him was a few days later after the first performance when the audience had finally gone away and the theatre was empty. It had taken Binkie two years of scheming and planning to get the play into the West End and the event had confirmed all his highest hopes. Alfred Lunt and Lynn Fontanne had given their greatest-ever performances – and, alas, their last in London – breath-taking in their power and savagery, Teo Otto's sets had never looked so darkly splendid and Peter Brook had directed a forty-strong cast with stunning virtuosity. A packed and celebrity-studded audience had roared and screamed its love and approval and everybody had said that it was like a pre-war first night, the way it used to be, the way it *should* be. I was one of the last out of the theatre and I ran into Binkie in the passage leading to the stage door. He was on a high cloud of ecstasy and who shall blame him? He stopped as he saw me. "Hasn't it been *wonderful?*" he burst out. "Hasn't it been the *greatest* evening of your life?" and he clutched me round the shoulders with both hands in a fever of passionate enthusiasm. "I will never forget it, *never*. We will remember it *all* our lives." I noticed that his eyes were beginning to moisten and that his hands were trembling. I realised that some sort of answer was required, but what could I possibly say except "Yes, Mr Beaumont, it has been wonderful and I will never forget it either," which was a totally true and sincere comment on the situation.

I have never before seen a man so happy, so radiant, so *glowing*. This was the Binkie I should like to remember: not the bored, tired, disillusioned elderly man who was feeling his age and didn't seem to like people any more, but the stage-struck boy who, on the night of one of his greatest triumphs, glowed like a furnace and bubbled with irrepressible joy like a magnum of the dry Bollinger he loved to drink. He adored the theatre above all else and served it with fanatical loyalty and industry. The theatre was the only true reality. All the rest of life outside it was nothing.

POSTSCRIPT

The King is dead. Long live the King. Or rather, long live the two Crown princes who, passing without delay into the succession as if by divine right, joined forces to reign together on more or less equal terms. Arthur Cantor, who had managed to acquire a majority of the company shares, invited John Perry to emerge from his retirement and join him. As twin managing directors Cantor would bring the much-needed American money and his own experience as a Broadway producer while Perry would bring his artistic talents and extensive knowledge of the London theatre. Between them they would revive the glories of the Tennent heyday. This was the master plan and for the first year it looked encouraging. *No, No, Nanette* was steered into Drury Lane and ran for a respectable nine months while *The Constant Wife* opened finally at the New Theatre (now the Albery) and ran for 264 performances. Both these were part of Binkie's heritage. After that, they were on their own. *Billy*, a musical version of *Billy Liar*, the Keith Waterhouse comedy, starred Michael Crawford and was directed by Patrick Garland. This was a success but *Thomas and the King* and *Lenny*, a tribute to the late Lenny Bruce, were not.

John Perry had not been happy. It had been with some reluctance that he had moved back into the Globe Theatre and into Binkie's old office. But in 1974 he retired. It had been a difficult year. He missed Binkie most horribly and the memories of those halcyon years rose to haunt him every day. In spite of the support and co-operation of everybody in the firm, it became clear to him and to everybody else that he did not possess the impresario's gift, so it was with some relief that he finally shook the dust of Shaftesbury Avenue from his feet and retired permanently to Knotts Fosse.

His replacement was Helen Montagu, formerly the general manager of the Royal Court Theatre. She brought a number of bright ideas of which the best were a system of installing a repertory company in the Lyric Theatre, Shaftesbury Avenue, and presenting a series of plays for short rather than long runs, the foundation of an annual Hugh Beaumont Award for young fringe directors and grants for talented new authors. The first produced a superb farce by Ben Travers starring Joan Plowright and John Moffat, *The Bed Before Yesterday*, the third produced *The Family Dance*, commissioned from

531

Felicity Browne, which had a respectable run at the Criterion. In addition she persuaded Alastair Sim to transfer his unique and splendid performance of Lord Ogleby in *The Clandestine Marriage* from Chichester to London. It was the final flowering of his comic genius and it is fitting that it should be his last appearance in London. All three were events which would have pleased Binkie very much. Successful management, as Binkie showed over 400 times, requires an individual with entrepreneurial flair and skills, and as Helen Montagu had these qualities she might have galvanised Tennent's back into something resembling its former vitality, but there was a dispute over the cost of presenting Zeffirelli's production of *Filumena* and she resigned to form her own company, Backstage Productions.

Her place was taken by a young ex-agent, Nicholas Salmon, who came to the Globe Theatre from the Old Vic's revival of *The Ghost Train*. At about this time there was an exodus of former Tennent executives. Vivienne Byerley was told that her services were no longer required; Bernard Gordon, who had always secretly hoped to succeed Binkie as managing director, retired to Brighton for reasons of health and finally died a disappointed man. James Noble and Kenneth Gillespie, another director, both left the firm and with their departure all links with the glorious past were severed. There was nothing left of Binkie's heritage, not even the monies from the touring, repertory and TV revivals of the plays which Binkie had successfully presented. Now, when plays by Coward or Rattigan are presented anywhere in the world, the royalties all go to the authors' estate. H. M. Tennent Ltd doesn't get a single penny.

In 1980 Harry Saltzman, former co-producer of the James Bond films, was invited to become the chairman. He brought with him much-needed film money. He also brought his son, Stephen, to whom he sublet the suite of offices on the top floor for the promotion of pop music and records. Today, Tennent's are still presenting the occasional play and have enjoyed some success. Maggie Smith in *Virginia Woolf*, a transfer from Stratford, Canada, *Number One*, by Anouilh starring Leo McKern and *A Month of Sundays* starring George Cole which won the Best Comedy of the Year Award, are all plays which Binkie would have liked.

Superficially Tennent's seems unchanged. The smallest lift in the world still creaks slowly up to the back of the balcony though the passage leading to it from the foyer of the theatre has been walled up and entry can be made now only from the street entrance to the upper circle. The partition which once enclosed the little telephone exchange has been taken away and is replaced by a comfortable open-plan reception desk. Binkie's office has been redecorated, though his desk and the settee are still there. His carved wooden chair, together with the framed photographs of Gertrude Lawrence, are now in the room occupied by Anne Rawsthorne, a director of the company. The floor to ceiling cupboard in the little ante-room leading to the loo is still stacked with playscripts and programmes and the walls are everywhere still covered with framed playbills. Upstairs, in what used to be Harry Tennent's office the press-cutting albums, photographs and correspondence files are neatly preserved. Whatever the future holds, the present staff at H. M. Tennent make sure that the past is not forgotten.

SOURCES

PROLOGUE, pp. 19–29

For years I had heard that Binkie spent the last day of his life in conference with a high-ranking American producer to discuss co-productions for the next two years. I could never discover who he was. In December 1986 I was in America for research and meetings and was invited by Roger Stevens, Administrator of the Kennedy Centre in Washington, to have lunch with him in its palatial top-floor restaurant. As usual with American food it looked marvellous and tasted of nothing. But it was here that Stevens revealed that it was he who spent the final day with Binkie.

Anna Tuberti, Binkie's faithful housemaid, was another elusive person. I had been told that she had gone without delay into the service of another family but nobody could remember which one. Finally, while writing the last chapter, I discovered that she had moved next door into the house occupied by the Sainsbury family known not as 12 Lord North Street, as it should be, but as 5 Smith Square. When I contacted her she refused to talk. She said that there was nothing she could tell me which could be of the slightest interest to me, one of those remarks which make a biographer want to scream. In the end, after much persuasion, she consented to answer my questions by letter.

Terence Rattigan was a man who was always friendly and helpful to young actors and young playwrights. When I met him I was both. Over the years on many occasions he spoke to me about Binkie. A few months after Binkie's death, he told me of the conversation he'd had with him on the night he died. "Wasn't it bizarre that your play [*The First Night of Pygmalion*] should have been one of the last he read and that you turned down his offer to put Johnny G. and Peggy into it? You were quite right, of course. They would both have been totally miscast."

Ingrid Bergman wrote in her memoirs of her final meeting with Binkie and also added some telling details when we lunched during the run of *The Constant Wife*. At the time there was a chance that she might play Mrs Patrick Campbell in my play – there is never any lack of actresses who see themselves in the part – but my pleasure at the prospect was slightly offset by alarm at the thought of how those exquisitely jewelled epigrams would fare when mispronounced in a Swedish accent . . . "marradge is da peace of da double bed after da hulry-bulry of the sofa . . ."

Vivienne Byerley, Binkie's hard-working and greatly maligned publicity chief, initially refused to help me because her great friend, Kitty Black, was writing her memoirs of the years with Tennent's and although it was not in any way a biography of Binkie, there would be a lot about him. Divided

537

loyalties can be embarrassing and it wasn't until years later, by which time *Upper Circle* had been published and successfully, that she agreed to meet me.

CHAPTER ONE, pp. 33–42

The richness of the London theatres in 1908 is drawn from the theatre columns of *The Times*. Information about Binkie's parentage, background and upbringing was provided partly by his elder brother, Jack, a wealthy timber merchant with business interests in London, and partly by his cousin, Betty Gunn, who shrieked with laughter when I asked her if Binkie was Jewish. "There isn't a drop of Jewish blood in the entire family," she said, "we are all solidly Welsh and solidly Baptist." Further information was supplied by Myfanwy Williams who might have become Mrs Hugh Beaumont if Nature had not had other ideas. She surfaced in Australia in 1983 in response to an appeal I had published in a local newspaper. She had been living there since her family had emigrated in the early twenties; she had been married and widowed and married again, and happily gave me relevant details of her childhood friendship at the nursery school. A miraculous stroke of luck which enriches every biography and goes a long way to compensating for the failures and frustrations. Iowerth Howells was one of those who saw my appeal in the *South Wales Echo* and wrote a letter to the correspondence column giving colourful details of Binkie's life and behaviour at his school.

CHAPTER TWO, pp. 43–53

Information about Harry Woodcock in this and the following chapter comes partly from Bobbie Andrews who knew him well, partly from Mrs Beaumont as quoted by Tony Chardet (one of the Tennent company managers) who knew her in the early fifties and later passed on what she had said about those early years in Cardiff, and partly from Binkie himself in private conversation. The account of Binkie's tea-time meeting with Sir Gerald du Maurier at the Royal Hotel was given to me late one night at the Garrick Club over the inevitable potted shrimps and sherry by Ronald Squire who was enjoying a nostalgic conversation with Nicholas Hannen. The back numbers of the *South Wales Echo* and the *Western Daily Mail* in the Cardiff reference library have been a cornucopia of fascinating information about Cardiff's theatrical life in the mid-twenties.

CHAPTER THREE, pp. 54–64

A week in Cardiff in 1983 enabled me to retrace Binkie's steps and see for myself the key points of his life. As the city has changed remarkably little in sixty years, I was able to walk from Cathedral Road – still much as it was though, to my intense disappointment, the family home had long been demolished – to the town centre, noting all the landmarks which Binkie and Harry Woodcock would have passed on the daily journey. The Playhouse changed its name to the Prince of Wales in the late thirties but structurally the inside and outside remain as they were. I was able to sit in the gallery where Binkie spent his Saturday afternoons, and explore the suite of offices in the dressing-room wing. The theatre was horribly neglected, smelled of damp and dry-rot and, although still open to the public, was showing crude sex films, the ultimate degradation of a once proud and prestigious theatre.

The offices and dressing-rooms had been unused for decades. They were a maelstrom of broken furniture, wicker baskets filled with papers, old filing cabinets stuffed with files, and everywhere dust, dirt and rubbish of every description. But once again my luck was in. Asking permission from the elderly custodian to examine the contents of some of the files, I found a folder of carbon copies of letters sent by Binkie to Harry Tennent. I was not allowed to take them but I was able to make notes. Since I am by law unable to quote them direct, I have contented myself by summarising their contents.

Information about Binkie's first job comes partly from Binkie himself speaking in various press interviews, partly from the newspaper files and partly from Bobbie Andrews who knew him well in those prehistoric Cardiff days. Dai Jones, the chef at the Royal Hotel, was still alive in 1983 though long since retired. He gave me a full and colourful account of his weekly conference with Binkie over the Saturday night supper menu. The hotel manager gave me a tour showing me the famous Captain Scott room where Binkie's suppers took place and ended by presenting me with a copy of the signed menu which is still available to diners, though at a price. Binkie's inspired public-relations gesture still lives on.

CHAPTER FOUR, pp. 65–83

On my first visit to New York in 1967, Alfred White who had been Tallulah Bankhead's company manager and close personal friend all the time she was in England, gave me a detailed account of her arrival at Cardiff and the increasingly hectic week she spent there. Like so many of those I met, he seemed to enjoy total recall even after forty years and was able not only to tell me what she said but gave me an hilariously accurate imitation of her saying it. I have to thank Mrs Bunny Bruce, Nigel's widow, for an account of Binkie's hospitality to the four senior actors in *The Creaking Chair* company and his attempts to organise cricket matches for them to keep boredom at bay while they were in Cardiff.

The Fifty-Fifty Club, as with the more famous Gargoyle Club, figures in both Noël Coward's memoirs, *Present Indicative*, and that of Henry Kendall, *I Remember Romano's*. To Nancy Mitford I owe my knowledge of Syrie Maugham and her special high-camp slang which she invented and which was copied by everybody in fashionable London: this was over lunch in her little house in Versailles. She had memories of Binkie over *The Little Hut* production, but I got the distinct feeling that she did not really care for him or for anybody to do with the theatre. That she had no play-writing skills of her own was the theatre's great loss, but her translation of *La Petite Hutte* was superb and it was typical of Binkie's inspired management that he should have thought to commission her to make it. John Gielgud in his book, *Early*

Stages, has much of interest to say about Philip Ridgeway and the theatre at Barnes and was able to amplify it during one of those glorious conversational monologues at the Garrick Club. It was there one evening that he told me of the 'all spots and puberty' comment made by Robert Farquharson. Philip Ridgeway's son, Philip junior, was able to pass on some interesting memories of his father.

CHAPTER FIVE, pp. 84–96

The history of Verrey's restaurant comes from Verrey's own publicity department who give away to all customers an elaborate and beautifully illustrated souvenir menu. But once again I enjoyed miraculous good luck when the waiter who attended Binkie and Harry Tennent, phoned me in Australia where he was living and still working, to tell me about that – for him – unforgettable occasion. I asked him how he could after fifty-four years remember it in such detail. "By a coincidence, it was my twenty-first birthday also and it was also my first day at Verrey's. I had always been interested in the theatre. I was totally fascinated by everything I saw and heard on that day and lapped it all up. Anyhow, I kept a diary and I rushed home to write it all down while it was still fresh in the memory. I stayed on at Verrey's for some years and always attended Mr Beaumont and Mr Tennent when they lunched or dined there."

Harry Tennent was always a shadowy figure but there is enough information about him in the newspaper files to fill in the gaps. *The Times* obituary is a model of precise and accurate information. His influence on Binkie's clothes and worldly behaviour was observed with cynical amusement by a number of people, most notably Hannen Swaffer whom I occasionally met in the company of his friend and sparring partner, Philip Hope-Wallace. Swaffer was an expert at the noble art of decayed dandyism. His black stock was always flecked with dandruff and cigar ash, and his neatly tailored suits were usually rumpled, baggy and covered with food stains.

Binkie's first appearance in London society at Cannon Hall was recalled to me with amused sympathy by Joan Morley, Gladys Cooper's daughter. Details of Marie Tempest's house and life-style can be found in Hector Bolitho's boringly sycophantic biography. Binkie used to talk about this first meeting with her.

Having promised a mutual friend that she would talk to me, Ginette Spanier changed her mind and telephoned me to say that she wouldn't. She explained that she was loyal to her great friend's memory, that she considered it in the worst possible taste to talk about anybody after they had died, that she abhorred gossip. No, she *wouldn't* tell me where she had first met him; no, she *wouldn't* give me an account of his visits to her in Paris and on no account would she speak of the arrangement whereby he was able to buy Balmain gowns at reduced prices for his star actresses. Within five minutes she had succeeded in working herself up into a fine old temper over this request which she saw as an outrageous intrusion on her privacy and an appalling act of desecration of Binkie's grave. This moving picture of a vulnerable and persecuted old woman bravely fighting off the attacks of the philistine hordes was slightly spoiled when she regained her composure to tell me that she would be very interested to read my book and would I please send her a complimentary copy when it was published, the insolence of which request virtually deprived me of breath. The following week I discovered in the Westminster Library three volumes of autobiography which she had published. They were well written, for she did not lack literary talent, and filled with revealing and gossipy anecdotes about Binkie and his circle. From this only one conclusion was possible: it was bad to talk about your friends but permissible to write about them. Such, it seems, is the logic of women.

The portrait of Binkie in 1930, complete with colourful sartorial details, was painted for me by Peter Cotes over tea and crumpets in the lounge of the Lansdowne Club. Details of the court case in which Binkie had to give evidence against the girl who had stolen his shirts and cuff-links were given to me by Bobbie Andrews who was present at the time.

CHAPTER SIX, pp. 97–125

J. B. Priestley telephoned me from his house at Stratford-upon-Avon to tell me of his lunch-time meeting with Binkie.

It is lucky for his biographer that Binkie decided early on in his career that it was important to keep a complete record of his activities: from 1933 he lovingly collected all the press-cuttings, photographs and programmes, most of which are preserved in the H. M. Tennent offices above the Globe Theatre. Those cuttings dealing with his first production, *When Ladies Meet*, are conveniently gathered together in three albums. Further details about the play, its background, rehearsals and run, were supplied by Mary Newcombe with whom I spent a long and satisfying weekend in her house at Stinchcombe, Dorset. The dinner plates and the silver ornaments all portrayed stags being torn to bloody pieces by the hounds in horrific detail and when she wished the butler to clear the plates and bring in fresh ones, she did not ring a bell: instead, she grasped a silver hunting horn and blew a short blast. I was disappointed to see him walking in instead of galloping. I gathered from the many hours of delightful reminiscence that Marie Tempest did not normally like other women but she made an exception of Miss Newcombe, for she was beautiful, charming, talented and, if all that wasn't enough, had married into the higher reaches of English society. Thus the two Marys became friends.

It was a chance meeting in 1962 with Vincent Korda at the MGM Studios at Elstree during the filming of *The Yellow Rolls-Royce*, in which I briefly appeared, which provided me with the news of Binkie's first meeting and continued association with Alexander Korda. Vincent had designed the superb sets and still occasionally put money into H. M. Tennent productions. Details of Robert Donat's involvement with Binkie and the circumstances of his departure from *When Ladies Meet* are in J. C. Trewin's well-researched biography of Donat.

CHAPTER SEVEN, pp. 126–34

There are a number of biographies of Ivor Novello – that by James Harding is irrefutably the best – but the massive tome by W. Macqueen Pope, so boring and bland as to be virtually unreadable, does give the facts, as well it might, because the author was Press Officer at Drury Lane and knew Novello well from the mid-thirties to his death in 1950. This makes his book very useful as a reference and I have found it most helpful where the financial background and running costs of *Proscenium* are concerned.

CHAPTER EIGHT, pp. 135–45

Sheridan Morley's biography of Gertrude Lawrence is the best of the three but the full story of *The Winding Journey* and *Moonlight is Silver* can be found in the press-cuttings and the memories of Tyrone Guthrie and Cecil Parker. I met the first in Dublin during the 1962 Festival and the second at the film studios where we were both working. Clemence Dane passes briefly through a number of theatrical memoirs but I have to thank Val Gielgud who lunched with me on a number of occasions for his colourful description of the Clemence Dane circle at work and play, which included Binkie's remark about Madame de Sevigné. Details of Clemence Dane's Hollywood assignment are to be found in Alexander Walker's beautifully illustrated biography of Greta Garbo.

CHAPTER NINE, pp. 146–62

I have drawn much of the material on *Sweet Aloes* and *Hervey House* from Tyrone Guthrie's *A Life in the Theatre* and from the many conversations I had had with him in Dublin. He had seen the musical, *Fursey*, in which I played a leading part, and invited me to lunch at the Shelbourne Hotel in whose spacious and peaceful dining-room he was able to chat about the glorious past with a fine memory for dialogue and detail. On a later occasion I returned the compliment with a late supper in the Bailey Tavern, the only pub where Brendan Behan had not been banned.

Further information about *Sweet Aloes* was provided by the author herself, Joyce Carey, living in peaceful retirement in a tiny Eaton Place flat covered from floor to ceiling with hundreds of photos of the great love of her life, Noël Coward. Jack Allen, a fellow-member of the Green Room Club, told me of Diana Wynyard's unsympathetic behaviour and of Marie Tempest's carefully organised malice at the Ivy. Laurier Lister who came out to South Africa to direct me in *The First Night of Pygmalion*, told me of the *Hervey House* billing and poster crisis, of the near-disaster attending Desmond Tester's late entrance and of Gertrude Lawrence's financial drama when she had to pay her hotel bill in Manchester.

Sources

CHAPTER TEN, pp. 163–70

Robert Morley's *Reluctant Autobiography* has supplied the colourful details about *Short Story* and Marie Tempest's life-style in rehearsal. Rex Harrison has also written revealingly about her in his book, *Rex Harrison: An Autobiography*. Further details can be found in John Casson's life of his parents, *Lewis and Sybil*.

CHAPTER ELEVEN, pp. 171–9

In 1959 I had tea with Basil Dean in his house in St John's Wood. Contrary to what I expected – having heard all the horror stories – he was charming, genial and generous. We sat down at a large table loaded with cakes, sandwiches, muffins, crumpets and several varieties of jam. It was like the headmaster entertaining a new boy. The purpose of the meeting was to talk about Leslie Banks but Binkie could not be kept out of the conversation for long and soon Dean was giving me a colourful and detailed account of the traumas and crises of the *Call it a Day* rehearsals which later found splendid confirmation when Dodie Smith published her memories of the same events in her book, *Look Back with Astonishment*. Bryan Coleman was able to tell me about Binkie's friendship with Geoffrey Nares and the crisis over his one scene which might have been cut but mercifully was not. Peter Osborn, an Anglican priest in Adelaide, Australia, told me, amongst many other things, of Owen Nares' decision to take off his toupée and of Fay Compton's horrified reaction, and finally I have to thank Timothy West, *Trainophilius Maximus* (if the coinage doesn't exist then it should) for information about the Flying Scotsman in the mid-thirties, its time of arrival, conditions of travel and its catering.

CHAPTER TWELVE, pp. 183–98

Clifford Mollison, actor and light comedian who specialised in musical comedy, who died at the age of ninety, was in his final years president of the Green Room Club but had long established himself as a theatrical encyclopaedia. He knew everything and everybody and could quote conversations verbatim after a gap of seventy years. It soon became evident that he disliked and despised Binkie and made no secret of it, but he knew a great deal about him. This book owes much to his good memory. I have to thank Lillian Gish and Sebastian Shaw, sole survivors of that unhappy company, for information about *The Old Maid* and Michael Redgrave and Rachel Kempson for filling in so many of the background details of *The Ante-Room*. Marius Goring in the Garrick Club told me what he remembered of *The Ante-Room* and Joe Davis, also of the Green Room Club, told me of Binkie's devious handling of Guthrie McClintic's offer of employment, but bore him no ill will. Nigel Stock, Griffith Jones and Vincent Korda remembered the curious episode of *Farewell Performance*; details of the sequence of unsuccessful plays presented by Binkie in the early years of his management can be found in the Tennent files.

CHAPTER THIRTEEN, pp. 199–207

Happily, Gerald Savory gave me a full and enthralling account of the *George and Margaret* genesis. I met Harry Stoker in the late fifties and learned of the amazing circumstances which led him from being a retired Commander of the Royal Navy to a very busy and successful character actor. Irene Handl told me about her brief involvement in the play.

CHAPTER FOURTEEN, pp. 208–16

It was with great excitement that I learned one afternoon that thirty-six letters from Bernard Shaw to Binkie were to be auctioned at Sotheby's. I rushed there and found that I was too late. The auction had taken place only an hour earlier (fetching the not inconsiderable sum of seven thousand pounds) but the letters had not yet been collected by the purchaser. My request for xerox copies was sternly refused; this could only be done with permission from the purchaser, Richard Macnutt, a dealer of Tunbridge Wells, who told me that he was acting as an agent for Harvard University and it was their permission I needed. However, the head of Sotheby's manuscript department allowed me to see the letters which were all passed up in a large bound album. I was allowed to make notes under close supervision.

But who was the vendor? Alas, an impenetrable blanket of secrecy surrounded the name. Binkie had clearly stuck them into an album and taken them home, which he was fully entitled to do. When I spoke to John Perry, beneficiary of Binkie's estate, on the telephone he denied all knowledge of the letters or the auction.

Athene Seyler and another actor (who wishes to be anonymous), the only survivors of that distinguished company, have told me what they remember. Miss Seyler was particularly amusing when she came to recounting Shaw's objections to her drunken scene and her own objections to Shaw's idea of what a gentlewoman is like when she has had too much to drink.

CHAPTER FIFTEEN, pp. 217–27

The stage and company manager in a play occupies a position of great importance since very little happens in or outside the theatre which he does not know. This is the point in Binkie's history when Bernard Gordon joined the firm and worked continuously first as stage manager and then, after the war, as general manager for the whole of H. M. Tennent. In the sixties and seventies I got to know him quite well and much of the material in this chapter comes from him. Kitty Black also joined the firm in the late thirties and her book *Upper Circle* has been valuable as a work of reference for, amongst other things, she lists all of the 500 productions together with dates, length of run and names of theatres. John Gielgud has written and spoken of his involvement with Marie Tempest, and John Justin has laughingly described his dyslexic meeting with Binkie at the Dorchester.

Sources

Henry Kendall wrote of Marie Tempest's last and sadly aborted engagement in his book *I Remember Romano's*, and later told me more about it.

CHAPTER SIXTEEN, pp. 228–41

The passing years, starting roughly in the late thirties, increase the number of those still alive who have been able to talk to me. Binkie's epigram about the mixing of guests at Lady Castlerosse's luncheon party was quoted in my hearing by Sir Thomas Beecham at the Savage Club shortly after the war. Lady Castlerosse's offensive comment on Binkie was quoted in Cole Lesley's excellent biography of Noël Coward. Lady Castlerosse's remark about 'the baby-faced butcher' is quoted by Cole Lesley in his biography of Noël Coward and was mentioned in a speech he made at the Phoenix Theatre when the Noël Coward bar was ceremoniously opened. I have to thank Sir Alec Guinness for information about Binkie's friendship with Anthony Eden and the curious story that he had influenced Eden in making one of his most important political decisions. This last he heard from Terence Rattigan and Richard Clowes, Binkie's press officer and friend.

I have to thank Judy Campbell who told me of the tour of Noël Coward's two plays and the rehearsals one evening at a Christmas party at Denville Hall.

CHAPTER SEVENTEEN, pp. 242–51

Rex Harrison's *Autobiography* casts an interesting light on the London production of *Design for Living*. I wish I had shares in the Noël Coward industry. There are dozens of books about him and more arriving every year. The facts are easily obtained from any of them though Cole Lesley's is easily the best since he lived with the Master, had access to all the correspondence, and was strategically in a good position to know who did what, where, when and to whom.

The story of Edith Evans and her dates comes from Bryan Coleman himself. Binkie's comment on Edith Evans as Lady Bracknell was passed to me by Bernard Gordon though Binkie himself repeated it in my hearing while chatting to Alfred Lunt at the end of a rehearsal for *The Visit*. It is a source of great grief for everybody in the theatre that Emlyn Williams refused to write the story of his remarkable life beyond 1935 to which the first two volumes, *George* and *Emlyn*, have brought it. But there is enough in the various prefaces, introductions and casual writings to provide some information about *The Corn is Green* and the wartime years. Judy Campbell was in the original company assembled for *This Happy Breed* and *Present Laughter* which toured England in the war and enjoyed a brief season at the Haymarket.

With the war, documentary evidence gets thicker with each year. Irving Wardle, in his excellent biography of George Devine, Peter Ustinov in his disappointingly unfunny memoirs, *Dear Me*, Alec Guinness in his vastly entertaining autobiographical fragments, *Blessings in Disguise*, and Kitty

Black have all written about the traumatic experiences of that first day when war was declared. Glen Byam Shaw, Bernard Gordon, Stephen Mitchell and the actor, Llewellyn Rees, have all provided extra details. The conversation between Binkie and Basil Dean at the ENSA meeting was recounted to me by Dean himself with extra comments on Binkie. It was Margaret Rutherford who passed on to me Binkie's remark about drums and was later quoted by Kenneth Tynan in an interview. Vincent Korda was able to tell me of the political machinations which led to the opening of the *Rebecca* film being postponed for three months and I can draw on my own childhood memories for the display boards in the Leicester Square cinema.

I found Stewart Granger, now in partial retirement in Hollywood, living in a beautiful flat overlooking the Pacific Ocean. The bathroom was filled with huge film posters and the main room was lined with hunting trophies and animal pictures. He admitted that he did not enjoy his wartime appearance in *Rebecca*, but was happy to tell me about it.

CHAPTER EIGHTEEN, pp. 252–69

Harry Tennent's will and death certificate are available to the public in the archives at Somerset House. I knew nothing about Captain George Astley nor did any of my other contacts in the theatrical or military worlds, and I spent a lot of time going through old army lists, writing fruitlessly to the War Office (made useless by the heavy blanket of official secrecy) and to various regimental depots until Terry Plunket Greene, my Deep Throat in this investigation, told me that he was currently working for the Society of Authors. To my joy, he was willing to talk and gave me much of the relevant information about Harry's will.

Much of the information about *Blithe Spirit* comes from Mary Gordon who was the stage manager on the tour and West End run, with extra details supplied by Margaret Rutherford and Joyce Carey.

CHAPTER NINETEEN, pp. 270–96

I had the great pleasure and privilege of talking to Vivien Leigh on a number of occasions: sometimes in her dressing-room at the Apollo during the run of *Duel of Angels*, twice in her flat at Eaton Square, and once when she took me to lunch at the Ritz. I can confirm the legend in all its glory, her charm, her well-stocked mind, her lively wit and her essential kindness. Much of the information in the chapter was supplied by her.

It was little short of a diplomatic triumph to persuade Cyril Cusack to break the silence of a lifetime and tell me about the unhappy circumstances which led to his dismissal from *The Doctor's Dilemma* company, which he did first over dinner at the Garrick and then later in my flat. Supporting testimony comes from Leslie Phillips and one other member of the company who was even more reluctant than Cusack to talk but eventually did so at great and fascinating length. He has asked that his name shall not be mentioned. Tiresome though this condition always is, I must respect his wishes. Peter Glenville, on a brief visit to London for his mother's funeral, spoke to me over the telephone and filled in some extra details about his taking over the part of Dubedat and in the process killed the curious legend that he was actually in the audience of that St Patrick's Day evening and thus saw everything. Felix Barker's superbly written biography of the Oliviers is the principal and most reliable source for the wartime concert party *Spring Meeting* of which no programme has survived. Alec Guinness and Michael Wilding have both written about it. And it was Anthony Quayle in person who told me of his friendship with Binkie and how it became especially close in Gibraltar. Vivien Leigh told me about the King's comment on the entertainment and gave me a very clever and accurate imitation of his famous stutter: mimicry was evidently one of her lesser-known gifts. The joke about the two-minute silence in the Ivy has been variously attributed, notably to Beatrice Lillie, but Vivien was emphatic that it was said by Binkie.

The complexities of the Entertainment Tax have been clarified in Charles Landstone's excellent book *Onstage* and also in *The Actor's Right to Act* by Joseph MacLeod. It was Tyrone Guthrie who told me of Lilian Baylis's appearance at Number 10 Downing Street.

John Gielgud has written and spoken most eloquently of his wartime *Macbeth*. Frank Thornton filled in the gaps with some fascinating and amusing detail and Gwen Ffrangcon-Davies gave me her opinion of it all one day when we were both on location for the film *The Devil Rides Out*.

CHAPTER TWENTY, pp. 297–306

My proposed biography of Leslie Banks which occupied my spare time between 1958 and 1962 was never completed but the extensive material I gathered has been very useful, particularly when his life and Binkie's overlapped as they do in this chapter. Mrs Gwen Banks was very co-operative at the beginning and told me about the *Love for Love* crisis and her efforts to dissuade Leslie from playing Mr Tattle. Later, with admirable honesty, she did admit that her opposition was a mistake. It was over lunch at Gerry's Club that John Gielgud told me of the dinner party at Leslie's house and of Gwen's relentless hostility to the project. Leslie's love affair with Mary Newcombe was common knowledge in the West End: Bronson Albery and the actors John Boxer and Austin Trevor were amongst those who told me about it as well as Mary Newcombe herself. It was Michael Redgrave who passed on Leslie's embittered comments on his wife's lack of sympathy, confirming that Gwen's influence on her husband's career had not been a good one.

Lewis Casson's part in Binkie's life has been described by his son, John, by his grand-daughter Diana Devlin in her biography, *A Speaking Part*, and by Charles Landstone. A full account of the famous season at the Haymarket can be found in Ronald Hayman's *John Gielgud*. Peggy Ashcroft, Rosalie Crutchley and Isabel Dean have all made some revealing comments.

CHAPTER TWENTY-ONE, pp. 307–19

Terence Rattigan's life has been well documented in no less than two biographies, *Terence Rattigan* by Michael Darlow and Gillian Hodson and *The Rattigan Version* by B. A. Young. Information about Alfred Lunt and Lynn Fontanne has been found in the definitive biography by Jared Brown. I have also drawn on my own memories of them in the 1960 production of *The Visit*. Binkie's voluntary hospital work at St George's with Alfred Lunt during the war was the subject of a hilarious conversation which took place in my hearing in Alfred's dressing-room at the Royalty Theatre which Binkie was in the habit of visiting. It was there that I heard about the rather alcoholic party given by the King of Greece at Brown's Hotel.

CHAPTER TWENTY-TWO, pp. 323–51

Edith Evans' tribute to Binkie was part of a speech she made at the Arts Theatre Club in a dinner given in her honour. The famous actress who preferred Congreve to Christie was first mentioned in Peter Saunders' book, *The Mousetrap Man*, and who later in private conversation revealed that it was Margaret Rutherford. The amusing account of Daphne Newton's disastrous audition with its happy and unexpected results was given to me by the actress herself during the run of *The Visit* in which we both played. The furnishing and decoration of the house at 14 Lord North Street and the life-style which took place inside it has been described by a number of people, notably Keith Baxter in a long discourse in his dressing-room during the run of *Corpse*. Thanks to the present occupier, Mrs Teresa Gorman, MP for Billericay, I was able to see the house, still unchanged structurally, and the tiny back garden, still much as it was. The only item which survived the auction and which is still in Mrs Gorman's possession, is a magnificent set of heavy brocade curtains which hung by the first-floor sitting-room windows. The 'Sonia Dreadful' joke was quoted by John Gielgud over supper at the Garrick Club and John Perry's summary of the plot of Peter Shaffer's new play, and Binkie's horrified comment, were passed on to me with enormous glee by Brook Williams. Anthony Chardet, one of the Tennent company managers and a good friend of Binkie, passed on the information about the special functions of the Tennent stage and company managers. Donald Albery has spoken of the cordial relations between the two managements and his monthly lunches with Binkie at Beoty's restaurant. The account of his sexual misdemeanours and his willingness to act as a scapegoat was told to me by Tom Gill at the MGM studios at Elstree when we were both appearing in *The Yellow Rolls-Royce*. The name of the second scapegoat cannot yet be revealed as he is still alive and I do not wish to cause him any distress.

CHAPTER TWENTY-THREE, pp. 352–70

Cecil Beaton's published diaries have revealed some interesting and gossipy information about the *Lady Windermere's Fan* production, the genesis, rehearsals and performances, but not nearly as much as I would wish. The unpublished diaries *in toto* are preserved at St John's College, Cambridge, in the Cecil Beaton Library and are available for inspection but the handwriting is discouragingly difficult to read, in some passages impossible. I can only hope that one day somebody will do for them what was once done for Pepys, transcribe and publish. Athene Seyler, aged ninety-five, bedridden and crippled but still with her memory unimpaired, spoke to me from her first-floor flat in Chiswick of her part in *Candida*. Griffith Jones spoke to me at the Barbican Theatre canteen, remembering the fan in the teapot as if it were yesterday.

I have to thank Kenneth Griffith for his memories of his aborted engagement to play in *Pen Don*. Emlyn Williams provided a number of good anecdotes for this chapter either in letters to me or in the various articles he has written for *Plays and Players*. When I met Richard Burton at Elstree Studios during the filming of *The V.I.P.s* he kept us all greatly amused by his imitation of Binkie offering him a Tennent contract.

CHAPTER TWENTY-FOUR, pp. 371–80

Derek Aylward was happy to describe his brief acquaintance with Binkie and his involvement with *Peace in Our Time*, and *Traveller's Joy*. Noël Coward's comment was quoted to me by Anthony Peek, actor in the company and later manager of the Haymarket Theatre.

CHAPTER TWENTY-FIVE, pp. 381–99

Bryan Forbes's biography of Edith Evans, *Ned's Girl*, provides extensive information about her and quotes her refusal to play St Joan. Anthony Quayle has spoken eloquently about the *Antony and Cleopatra* production with further intriguing details provided by other actors in the company, Alan Brown and Philip Guard. I have drawn on Michael Redgrave's autobiography, *In My Mind's Eye*, Richard Findlater's biography, *Michael Redgrave*, and Rachel Kempson's memoirs but the more colourful aspects of the unhappy and controversial production of *Macbeth* were supplied by the surviving members of the company, Richard Bebb, Douglas Wilmer, Wilfrid Carter and the late, alas, Paul Hardwick, who spoke to me for a delightful hour only the day before he died of a heart attack in Leicester Square while in the comedy *Little Lies*. I was lucky to be in Johannesburg at the same time as Michael Redgrave in 1974. We were both being presented in our respective plays by the same local producer, the dynamic and fast-talking Shirley Firth. It was her sensible custom to give Sunday brunch parties for her companies and during one of these Redgrave gave me his memories of those painful *Macbeth* weeks. He was suffering from Parkinson's Disease but he could still act and his memory of those distant post-war events was unimpaired. It was Robert Whitehead, speaking from his deliciously cluttered office overlooking Times Square, who told me of Gielgud's appearance in *Crime and Punishment* on Broadway and who quoted Gielgud's comments on his legs.

Eileen Herlie, now a resident in New York and the star of a very popular mid-afternoon TV serial, gave me the background to her sensational début in *The Eagle has Two Heads* and her later involvement in *The Matchmaker*.

I met Evangeline Banks in Northampton in whose repertory company we were both working. In those early days of our regrettably short-lived friendship we used to frequent the Subway, a local snack-bar much used by the company and it was there, over a convivial cup of coffee, that she told me of Binkie's offer to her to play in *The Second Mrs Tanqueray* with her father and what a cruel agony it was to be forced to make the decision which I strongly suspect she has always regretted. Binkie's leadership on the second night of *The Matchmaker* was not so much described as re-enacted by Alec McCowen with production effects and in stereophonic three-dimensional sound. It was in the shower room of the YMCA in Tottenham Court Road, of which we were both members, that Nicholas Amer described his meeting with Binkie's mother. Further information about her possessive behaviour came from John Gielgud who also wrote to me about her third marriage. The discussion between Binkie and Terence Rattigan about *The Browning Version* was retold by Rattigan over lunch.

CHAPTER TWENTY-SIX, pp. 400–7

John Gielgud's unkind remark to Rattigan in refusing *The Browning Version* has been well attested in both Rattigan biographies and many newspaper articles.

Surviving members of the *Adventure Story* company had told me what they remember, Anthony Peek, Noel Willman, Peter Glenville and Gwen Ffrangcon-Davies. To my great disappointment Paul Scofield, having for two years promised to talk to me, finally changed his mind and told me that he was going to keep his memories for the book he would one day write himself.

CHAPTER TWENTY-SEVEN, pp. 408–23

There is plenty of material about the London production of *A Streetcar Named Desire* to be found in any of the dozen or so books about the Oliviers and in Irene Selznick's autobiography, *A Private View*, where she implies that it was not to her liking, though when I spoke to her in the Hotel Pierre in New York, where she is a permanent resident, she spoke rather more forcefully on the subject. But there is a curious gap in the *Streetcar* literature: there is nothing about it in Tennessee Williams' own memoirs, not a single word, and only one reference to Vivien Leigh in the whole book and that is in connection with the film, *The Roman Spring of Mrs Stone*. The author's silence on the subject in view of his deep involvement is inexplicable. The complexities of the Entertainment Tax and the enquiry into Binkie's involvement have been nicely clarified by Charles Landstone in *Offstage*.

Sources

CHAPTER TWENTY-EIGHT, pp. 424–33

Edith Evans' little joke about Sybil Thorndike's cardigan has been endlessly told and retold but I felt it should be included because there will always be somebody who hasn't heard it. The press-cuttings in the Tennent office include a small selection of those relating to *A Day by the Sea*, and Vivienne Byerley, Geoffrey Toone, Peter Glenville and Anthony Peek have added some more telling details. I have to thank Robert Whitehead for further information about Gielgud's proposed American appearance in *The Tempest* and his later triumph in *Ages of Man*.

CHAPTER TWENTY-NINE, pp. 434–45

Eric Glass, Hugh Hastings' agent, had a lot to tell me about the background to *Seagulls over Sorrento* in a series of meetings in his script-filled office overlooking Berkeley Square. Nigel Stock talked to me in his sun-drenched patio overlooking Hampstead Heath and allowed me to see copies of letters he had received from Binkie which, regrettably, I am not allowed to use. David Langton spoke to me with commendable honesty of his nervous breakdown which took him away from the play and from England for ten days, and of his eventual reinstatement.

CHAPTER THIRTY, pp. 446–57

Elizabeth Seal and Ray Witch have given me detailed accounts of their involvement with Binkie in *Irma la Douce*. Isabel Dean, George Howe, Ralph Michael, Peter Cotes and Harold Scott have all, at different times, talked candidly about the circumstances which led them to the notorious black-list. The parliamentary enquiry into the Entertainment Tax Exemption was reported verbatim in *Hansard*.

CHAPTER THIRTY-ONE, pp. 458–80

Laurence Evans told me of the doctor's certificate which Binkie urgently asked him to keep hidden. He also told me of the dramatic act one finale confrontation between Binkie and Rex Harrison over his possible replacement. This was confirmed in all its colourful detail by Alan Jay Lerner who also told me of Rex Harrison's initial reluctance to rehearse. "Did he *really* call Moss Hart a Jewish cunt?" I asked curiously. "Indeed he did," he replied. "I've often heard him use the phrase." Binkie's comment on the crisis is quoted by Peter Saunders in his book, *The Mousetrap Man*. To get material, Saunders persuaded Binkie to make a long interview which is probably the only surviving record of Binkie's voice. Peter Gilmore wrote to me to confirm the circumstances of his dismissal and Leonard Weir gave me a detailed account of how he was asked to take the part of Freddie at such short notice. Alan Lerner reported Binkie's remarks about the Queen's ancestry as well as his reflections that he had come a long way since Cardiff. It would seem that Lerner was one of the very few people who knew that Binkie's real name was Morgan. I owe to Robert Stanton the fascinating account of the show's background and politics. Not only did he speak to me on many occasions in his little office at LAMDA, he also lent me his entire correspondence files together with the souvenir programme and other memorabilia. The proceedings of the lawsuit, H. M. Tennent *v*. Beryl Foley for wrongful dismissal are available in transcript from the Law Society.

CHAPTER THIRTY-TWO, pp. 481–90

Information about *The Visit* comes from Myles Eason, George Rose, Alfred Lunt and Lynn Fontanne. It also comes from my own personal involvement in it. Noël Coward has a lot to say about *Waiting in the Wings* in his diary and Margaret Webster has virtually a whole chapter in her book, *Don't Put Your Daughter on the Stage*.

CHAPTER THIRTY-THREE, pp. 491–508

Most of the pre-production traumas and rehearsal confrontations were told to me by Vivian Matalon in his New York apartment and were later confirmed by Sean Barrett, Edward Burrell, Pauline Gaunt and Kathleen Byron plus Noël Coward's enormously entertaining diary. The Savoy Hotel Press Office was able to supply biographical detail of Royton Heath, their head floor supervisor.

CHAPTER THIRTY-FOUR, pp. 509–22

The unhappy relationship which clouded Binkie's life in the sixties has been described by Geoffrey Toone, Vivian Matalon, Peter Glenville and Rachel Kempson. Ann Fleming's letter appears in *The Letters of Ann Fleming*, edited by Mark Amory (London, Harvill Press, 1985).

Leo Maguire, Robert Flemyng, Anthony Quayle and Joss Ackland have all spoken with great sadness about Binkie's drinking in the final years.

ACKNOWLEDGMENTS

A great many people all over the world have given me valuable help in one form or another. They are here listed and I offer my grateful thanks.

Rodney Ackland, Sir Bronson Albery, Donald Albery, Jack Allen, David Rayvern Allen, Michael Allinson, Hardy Amies, Mark Amory, Robert Andrews, John Arnatt, Miss Ashbee, Peggy Ashcroft, George Astley, Eileen Atkins, Maxine Audley.

Angela Baddeley, Tallulah Bankhead, Evangeline Banks, Mrs Gwen Banks, Sean Barrett, Kenneth Barrow, Jane Baxter, Keith Baxter, Pamela Benson, Kitty Black, Roger Braban, Dirk Bogarde, Edward Burrell, Sally Brown, John Byron, Dora Bryan, Tony Britton, Mrs Bunny Bruce, Ballard Berkeley, Richard Briers, Hal Burton, Walter Brown, Angus McBean, Jeremy Brett, Michael Bryant, John Boxer, Coral Browne, Mary Bruton, Lucy Barker.

Peter Cotes, Tony Chardet, Terry Charman, Shelley-Anne Claircourt, Rosalie Crutchley, Lydia Cullen, Alexander Cohen, Joyce Carey, Judy Campbell, Bryan Coleman, Noël Coward, Alec Clunes, Wilfrid Carter, Cyril Cusack, John Clements, Anne Casson, John Casson, George Cooper, Peter Crouch, Patience Collier.

Isabel Dean, Michael Denison, Bruan Derbyshire, Michael Dow, Basil Dean, Nigel Davenport, John Donat, Joe Davis, Alexander Doré, Haydon Davies, Bryan Drew.

Baroness Elliott of Harewood, Nicholas Eden (Earl of Avon), Mrs Edwards (Cardiff), Edith Evans, Gwen Evans, George Eisel.

James Frasher, Bryan Forbes, Laurence Fitch, Sheila Fermoy, Michael Franklin, Robert Flemyng, Lynn Fontanne, Gwen Ffrangcon-Davies.

Alec Guinness, Dulcie Gray, Howard Golliet, Pauline Gaunt, Peter Glenville, Peter Gilmore, Reginald and Peggy Gosse, Kenneth Griffith, John Gielgud, Val Gielgud, Tyrone Guthrie, Peter Gale, Eric Glass, Betty Gunn, Stewart Granger, Tom Gill, John Gale, Teresa Gorman, Marius Goring.

George Hoare, Peter Hall, Lord Hailsham, Iowerth Howells, Peter Hepple, Jon Holliday, George Howe, Tony Howell, Jeremy Hawke, Joan Heal, Diane Hart, Robert Harris, Helen Haye, Nicholas Hannen, Paul Hardwick, Laurence Harbottle, Patricia Hastings, Michael Henderson, Michael Hoover, Eileen Herlie, Dorothy Hyson, Patricia Hayes, Stanley Hall, Walter Hall.

Griffith Jones, Dai Jones, Isabel Jeans, Ursula Jeans, John Justin.

Vincent Korda, Paul Kemp, Rachel Kempson, Joan Kemp-Welch, Henry Kendall.

Herman Levin, Alan Jay Lerner, Victor Langley, David Langton, Laurier Lister, Dan Laurence, Vivien Leigh, Michael Logan, Marie Löhr, Alfred Lunt, Charles Laughton.

Joan Miller, Arthur Marshall, Joan Morley, Robert Morley, Sheridan Morley, Vivian Matalon, Daniel Massey, John Moffat, Ralph Michael, Nan Munro, Penry Morgan, Cecil Maddern, John Mills, Stephen Mitchell, Alan Melville, Helen Montagu, Leo Maguire, Tom McDonald, W. Macqueen Pope, Clifford Mollison, Murray Macdonald, Brewster Mason, Ted Matthews, Bernadette McCarron.

Jeanne Newlin, Joan Newell, Anna Neagle, Mary Newcombe, George Nestor.

Laurence Olivier, Peter Orton, Brian Oulton.

John Perry, Veronica Padwick, Peter Plouviez, Terry Plunket Greene, Leslie Phillips, Anthony Peek, Cecil Parker, Nigel Patrick.

Anthony Quayle.

Craig Raymond, Michael Redgrave, Llewellyn Rees, Philip Ridgeway, Cyril Raymond, Terence Rattigan, Margaret Rutherford, Hilary Roberts, George Rose, Peter Roberts, Beryl Reid.

Athene Seyler, Dorothy Swordlove, Nigel Stock, Dodie Smith, Lewis Shaw, Ronald Squire, Glen Byam Shaw, Harry Saltzman, Elizabeth Seal, Irene Selznick, Diane Stiles, Jeffrey Simmons, Donald Sinden, Gerald Savory, Abner Stein, Peter Saunders, Robert Stanton, H. G. Stoker, Frank Shelley, Roger Stevens, Sebastian Shaw, James Sharkey, Robert Stevens, Irene Sutcliffe, Marie St Juste, Joyce and Stephen Simpson

Frank Thornton, Ann Todd, Austin Trevor, Sybil Thorndike.

Robert Urquhart.

Roma Woodnutt, Bernard Walsh, Tony Wells, Ronald Wilkinson, Stewart Williams, Myfanwy Williams, Sarah Woodcock, Arthur White, Alan Webb, Robert Whitehead, Noel Willman, Brook Williams, Emlyn Williams, Leonard Weir, Timothy West.

Books Consulted

Mark Amory (ed.)	The Letters of Ann Fleming	Harvill Press
Felix Barker	The Oliviers	Hamish Hamilton
Kenneth Barrow	Mr Chips	Methuen
Kitty Black	Upper Circle	Methuen
Jared Brown	The Fabulous Lunts	Atheneum, New York
John Casson	Lewis and Sybil	Collins
Noël Coward	Autobiography	Weidenfeld & Nicolson
Noël Coward	Diaries	Weidenfeld & Nicolson
Michael Darlow and Gillian Hodson	Terence Rattigan	Quartet
Michael Denison	Overture and Beginners	Gollancz
Paul Ferris	Richard Burton	Weidenfeld & Nicolson
Richard Findlater	Michael Redgrave	Heinemann
Bryan Forbes	Ned's Girl	Elm Tree
Brendan Gill	Tallulah	Michael Joseph
Martin Gottfried	Jed Harris	Little, Brown, Boston
Stewart Granger	Sparks Fly Upwards	Granada
Alec Guinness	Blessings in Disguise	Hamish Hamilton
Tyrone Guthrie	Life in the Theatre	Hamish Hamilton
James Harding	James Agate	Methuen
James Harding	Ivor Novello	W. H. Allen
William Douglas Home	Home Pronounced Hume	W. H. Allen
Penny Junor	Richard Burton	Sidgwick & Jackson
Henry Kendall	I Remember Romano's	Macdonald
Karel Kulik	Alexander Korda	W. H. Allen
Alan Jay Lerner	The Street Where I Live	Hodder & Stoughton
Cole Lesley	Noël Coward	Weidenfeld & Nicolson
John McCallum	Googie	Heinemann
Joseph MacLeod	The Actor's Right to Act	Laurence & Wishart
Arthur Marshall	Life's Rich Pageant	Hamish Hamilton
John Mills	Up in the Clouds, Gentlemen Please	Weidenfeld & Nicolson
Robert Morley and Sewell Stokes	Reluctant Autobiography	Simon & Schuster, New York
Sheridan Morley	Gladys Cooper	Heinemann
Sheridan Morley	Gertrude Lawrence	Weidenfeld & Nicolson
Garry O'Connor	Darlings of the Gods	Hodder & Stoughton
Laurence Olivier	Confessions of an Actor	Weidenfeld & Nicolson
Margot Peters	Mrs Pat	Bodley Head
W. Macqueen Pope	Ivor Novello	W. H. Allen
Michael Redgrave	In the Mind's Eye	Weidenfeld & Nicolson
Michael Sanderson	From Irving to Olivier	Athlone

559

Peter Saunders	*The Mousetrap Man*	Gollancz
Irene Mayer Selznick	*A Private View*	Weidenfeld & Nicolson
Dodie Smith	*Look Back with Gratitude*	Muller, Blond & White
Dodie Smith	*Look Back with Astonishment*	W. H. Allen
Bob Thomas	*Marlon Brando*	W. H. Allen
J. C. Trewin	*Robert Donat*	Heinemann
Wendy Trewin	*All On Stage*	Harrap
Hugo Vickers	*Cecil Beaton*	Weidenfeld & Nicolson
Alexander Walker	*Greta Garbo*	Weidenfeld & Nicolson
Alexander Walker	*Vivien Leigh*	Weidenfeld & Nicolson
Kenneth Williams	*Just Williams*	Dent
Tennessee Williams	*Memoirs*	W. H. Allen
B. A. Young	*The Rattigan Version*	Hamish Hamilton

Index

Index

Index

Index

Index

Index

573

Index

FOR 30 YEARS
THIS FACE
HAS DOMINATED
THE THEATRE

LOUNGE SUIT

E " MANAGER'S
HIRTS STOLEN

aditions were shattered
d last night when Mr.
t, the manager of the
mpany at the Prince
e, appeared in the foyer
t instead of in the cus-
dress.

ntional costume, all the
le on the second night
production, had a simple

's flat in Pitt's Head-
ark-Jane, W., had been
before the evening per-

o called to see me found
smashed open, and a
me at the theatre. I
and found that all my
waistcoat buttons, and
ry, and all my dress
tcoats had been taken.
and some of my letters
d in Hyde Park.

telephone call on Tues-
nown woman who told

s 52, a bachelor,
d has been on
one of the com-
theatre for
30 years.

the managing
of H. M. Tennent,

Theatre Note

Tennents' Nine Productions

Coward, Rattigan & Emlyn Williams

By GEORGE W. BISHOP

HUGH BEAUMONT is a
remarkable man. He is in
charge of one of the biggest—if
not the biggest — theatrical
organisations in the world,
H. M. Tennent Ltd., Tennent
Productions and the Company of
Four, and he looks almost as
young as when I first knew him
25 years ago in those memorable
Komisarjevsky seasons at the
Barnes theatre. He and his
associates are connected with
some six or seven of the current
productions in the West End, and
there are plans for nine more
plays this year.

Despite the immense amount of
work he gets through, Mr. Beaumont
never appears to be hurried or flurried Anyhow, he had time last week
to talk to me for an hour about his
forthcoming plans. One of the most
interesting productions will be a
revival of Pinero's " The Second Mrs.
Tanqueray," with Eileen Herlie in
the leading part and scenery and
costumes by Cecil Beaton. It is to
e directed by Murray Macdonald,
and a long tour, before the West End,
begins in May.

BEAUMON
WILL HEL
TO RUN
NATIONAL
THEATRE

Express Parliamentary Repo

MR. HUGH
BEAUMONT, the W
End theatre chief,
named yesterday as one
10 people who will cre
and run the Nation
Theatre Company.

Others on the board (ch
man Lord Chandos) will be
Sir Kenneth Clark, form
chairman of the Arts Coun
Sir Ashley Clarke, retir
Ambassador to Italy:
William Keswick, a director
the Bank of England ;
Douglas Logan, principal of
University of London ; He
Moore, the sculptor ; Mr. De
Salberg, Midlands thea
impresario, Lord Wilmot, a
Mrs. Freda Corbet, M.P.

The theatre and an ope
house are to be built
London's South Bank at a c
of about £2,300,000.

Appointments to a separa
board that will organise t
actual building were al
announced yesterday. The
include Mr. Prince Little
another West End theatre chie
and Sir Isaac Hayward, lead